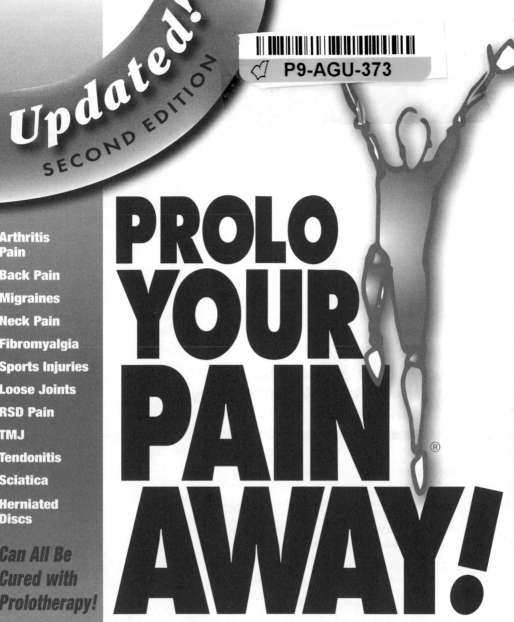

Updated!
SECOND EDITION

Arthritis Pain
Back Pain
Migraines
Neck Pain
Fibromyalgia
Sports Injuries
Loose Joints
RSD Pain
TMJ
Tendonitis
Sciatica
Herniated Discs

Can All Be Cured with Prolotherapy!

PROLO YOUR PAIN® AWAY!

Curing Chronic Pain with Prolotherapy

Ross A. Hauser, M.D.,
Physical Medicine and Rehabilitation Specialist

and

Marion A. Hauser, M.S., R.D.
Executive Director and Registered Dietitian

Prolo Your Pain Away!
Curing Chronic Pain with Prolotherapy
Updated, Second Edition

ISBN 0-9661010-9-X

Illustrations and Charts by Thomas Penna, M. Hurley, and Joe Faraci
Photography and illustrations by Doug Skinkis

Published by Beulah Land Press
715 Lake Street, Suite 600, Oak Park, Illinois 60301

Printed in the United States of America

Design by Teknigrammaton Graphics
773-973-1614 • Teknigram@ATTGlobal.net
7312 N. Hamilton • Chicago, IL 60645

Table of Contents

DISCLAIMER

The information presented in this book is based on the experiences of the authors, publishers, and editors, and is intended for informational and educational purposes only. In no way should this book be used as a substitute for your own physician's advice.

Because medicine is an ever-changing science, readers are encouraged to confirm the information contained herein with other sources. The authors, publishers, and editors of this work have used sources they believe to be reliable to substantiate the information provided. However, in view of the possibility of human error or changes in medical sciences, neither the authors, publishers, or editors, nor any other party who has been involved in the preparation or publication of this work warrants that the information contained herein is in every respect accurate or complete, and they are not responsible for any errors or omissions or for the results obtained from the use of such information. This is especially true, in particular, when an athlete or person in pain receives Prolotherapy and a bad result occurs. The authors, publishers, and editors of this book do not warrant that Prolotherapy is going to be effective in any medical condition and cannot guarantee or endorse any certain type of Prolotherapy, solution used, or practitioner. It is the responsibility of the individual athlete or person who receives Prolotherapy to thoroughly research the topic and pick a particular practitioner that they feel is qualified to perform the procedure. As of this writing there is no certification available in Prolotherapy training. Any licensed medical or osteopathic doctor in the United States can perform Prolotherapy according to the laws.

Physicians should use and apply the technique of Prolotherapy **only** after they have received extensive training and demonstrated the ability to safely administer the treatment. The author, publisher, editors, or any other person involved in this work, is not responsible if physicians who are unqualified in the use of Prolotherapy administer the treatment based solely on the contents of this book, or if they receive training but do not administer it safely and a bad result occurs.

If Prolotherapy or any other treatment regime described in this book appears to apply to your condition, the authors, publisher, and editors recommend that a formal evaluation be performed by a physician who is competent in treating pain and athletic injuries with Prolotherapy. Those desiring treatment should make medical decisions with the aid of a personal physician. No medical decisions should be made solely on the contents or recommendations made in this book. ■

DEDICATION

This book is dedicated to God, who created the marvelous wonder we call the human body. Thank You, God, for giving us pain so we would know when something is wrong with the body You gave us. Thank You for allowing us to help the body heal. We acknowledge that all true healing comes from You.

"Jesus replied, 'Go back and report to John what you hear and see: The blind receive sight, the lame walk, those who have leprosy are cured, the deaf hear, the dead are raised, and the good news is preached to the poor.'" [1]

This book is also dedicated to two of God's faithful servants: Gustav and Helen Hemwall. They have traveled across the United States and to many countries helping orphans, the poor, and the destitute.

Many could testify that the "you" Jesus referred to in the following passage could be substituted with Gustav and Helen Hemwall. "Then the King will say to those on his right, 'Come, you who are blessed by my Father; take your inheritance, the kingdom prepared for you since the creation of the world. For I was hungry and you gave me something to eat, I was thirsty and you gave me something to drink, I was a stranger and you invited me in, I needed clothes and you clothed me, I was sick and you looked after me, I was in prison and you came to visit me.' Then the righteous will answer him, 'Lord, when did we see you hungry and feed you, or thirsty and give you something to drink? When did we see you a stranger and invite you in, or needing clothes and clothe you? When did we see you sick or in prison and go to visit you?' The King will reply, 'I tell you the truth, whatever you did for one of the least of these brothers of mine, you did for me.'" [2]

On November 22, 1998, the world lost one of the pioneers of Prolotherapy and one of its truest "gentle-men," Gustav A. Hemwall, M.D. When he died, we lost not only our mentor, our friend, confidant, advisor, and role model. This book is especially dedicated to him, as he would like nothing more than for Prolotherapy to flourish across the globe. He hoped to live to see the day that this occurred. He died at a ripe old age of 90, but despite his fortitude, Prolotherapy was never accepted by mainstream medicine. Perhaps it will be this book that finally turns the tide. We know one thing for sure—the message that he taught us is now being loudly and boldly proclaimed across the country: There *is* a cure for chronic pain and that cure is Prolotherapy. ■

Gustav and Helen Hemwall

Acknowledgements

Life has been good to us. We have enjoyed the support of parents who always told us to "just do your best," and the love of a wonderful family, especially that of Mom and Dad Boomer, Mom and Dad Hauser, Staci, Kyle, Alex, Torin, Ellen, Sara, Tommy, and Liz. Grandma and Grandpa, we cannot thank you enough for all you have taught us. We love you and miss you every day.

A pupil is only as wise as his teachers. We have had wonderful teachers along the way. Of course, none of the work in Prolotherapy would have been possible without Gustav A. Hemwall, M.D. Thank you Dr. Hemwall, for sharing your vast knowledge, and more importantly, what it means to be an "old fashioned" doctor. We miss you.

We would like to thank some of our colleagues who have shared their knowledge with us to help us learn more things to help people: Doug Kaufmann, Jean Liu, Gail Gelsinger, R.N., William Mauer, M.D., and Su Auberle, R.N., and her husband, Mike. We owe a great debt to Steven Elsasser, M.D., who mentored us and started us on the vast search of finding ways to heal the body naturally, without pharmaceuticals. We are who we are, in part, because of the influence of our late pastor and his wife, Peter and Marla Blakemore, in our lives. We cannot begin to thank you for all of the things you have taught us. Pastor Peter, we look forward to seeing you in heaven. We still miss you every day. Marla, you are a great friend and confidant. Thank you for being there when we need you.

We have lost many loved ones along our journey through life. A day does not go by that we do not think of you: Grandma, Grandpa, Pastor Peter, Pastor John, Dr. Steve, Dr. Dave, Dr. Hemwall, Aunt Karen, and Larry. We look forward to the day when we will see you again in heaven.

Thank you to our new pastor, Ray Pritchard, and his wife, Marlene. You have helped us to "keep believing," even through the tough times. Thank you to Calvary Memorial Church for making the message of Jesus Christ come alive!

What would we do without friends? We have been blessed with great friends: Don and Kristy; Marla and the kids; Tim, Sheila, and the kids; Steve and Candace; Larry and Mary; and the whole clan at Calvary Memorial Church.

We have the greatest staff in the world at Caring Medical and Rehabilitation Services. Thank you for making work so enjoyable. We can tell that you love Prolotherapy as much as Ross does! Look out world! Thank you all for working so hard and going the extra mile. Thanks for giving so willingly of yourselves with hugs, listening ears, and tears to those who have walked through our doors with their many hurts and sorrows.

We also have great consultants who help us keep everything together. Tim, Dennis, Matt, Polly, Paul, Sharon, JoAnne, Hazel and the rest at Kenny & Kenny—you have been a godsend, special friends. To our computer wizards and internet gurus Randy, Seth, Dave, Jake, Daniel, Corey, Alex, and the whole team at Birkey/MIS—thanks for your expertise and many hours of development and dedication to making our systems work. Thanks to Tim, Jack, and Mike for making Caring Medical the facility it is today.

Thank you to Thomas Penna, for coming through in the clutches with your wonderful illustrations. Thank you to Joe Faraci for providing all of the initial illustrations.

Thank you to the many volunteers who give of their time to Beulah Land Natural Medicine Clinic, especially Daphene and Steve Huffman; Mary Ellen Schlamer; Pastor Carl and Linda Fisher; Kim and Rodney Van Pelt, M.D.; Dick Boomer; Mark Wheaton, M.D.; Marge Cain; Brodie Hackney; Rita Gaus; Kurt Ehling, D.C.; Bill Hambach, D.C.; Peter, Andrew, Gracelyn, Elizabeth, and Marla Blakemore; Michelle Henry, N.D.; Tim, Sheila, Heidi, and Heather Phillips; Eddie Bennett; and the rest of the wonderful volunteers from the First Baptist Church in Thebes, the folks from southern Illinois and southeast Missouri, and all of the other doctors and volunteers who help us when they can.

Thank you to Kurt Pottinger for your many hours spent putting *Prolo Your Pain Away!* together. You helped make it a best-seller!

Thank you to Barry Weiner from Media for Doctors for your undying support, your humor, your invaluable advice, your many, many hours of work, and most of all, your friendship. What would we do without you?

Of course, where would we be without M. Hurley, who we have kept busy for five years putting all these books together? Thanks for your hard work and dedication.

Ross especially wants to thank Marion, his wife and best friend, for the many hours spent editing and writing this book: thanks for getting us out of all of the fiascos I get us into and sticking by me no matter what. Thanks for changing your career and running our clinic together.

Marion to Ross: Thanks for the ideas behind the books. I know I will never be out of a job! Thanks for the opportunity to work on these projects with you. Your diligence is amazing!

Finally, we want to thank the One who makes everything possible. Thank you God for the gift of grace and salvation. King David wrote several thousand years ago: "But as for me, I will always have hope; I will praise You more and more. My mouth will tell of Your righteousness, of Your salvation although I know not its measure. I will proclaim Your righteousness, Yours alone."[1] ■

FOREWORD

By Mark Wheaton, M.D.

My first experience with Prolotherapy was a personal one. Among the many sports I enjoyed, tennis was my main focus and where I had my most success. In my college days, when I first injured my low back playing tennis for the University of Minnesota, I was told that surgery was my only option. Then, someone suggested to my family that I explore an alternative treatment for low back pain. That treatment was Prolotherapy and the doctor was Gustav Hemwall, M.D., of Oak Park, IL. I drove from Minnesota to Chicago without knowing exactly what this treatment was. I had one Prolotherapy treatment and returned to Minnesota. I did not return for further treatment because my final year of college had started and I was also too young to realize that several Prolotherapy treatments were necessary to achieve maximum benefit.

My memory of Prolotherapy soon faded as I went through eight long years of medical school, internship, and residency training. Then, in 1992, Prolotherapy and Dr. Hemwall's name came up in a conversation with a physician colleague in California. At that moment, I realized that this was the treatment that I received while in college twelve years earlier. I decided that I would like to learn how to do Prolotherapy to help people with their pain. Soon thereafter, I found a course that taught doctors how to perform Prolotherapy and learned from Dr. Hemwall and his pupils. It was at this conference that I met Dr. Ross Hauser, who had worked closely under Dr. Hemwall before he retired.

Dr. Hemwall, I learned, had used Prolotherapy to cure C. Everett Koop, M.D. of his back pain. Dr. Koop was the United States Surgeon General during the 1980's. Ironically, Dr. Koop had been instrumental in my acceptance to the George Washington University Medical School. We had met only briefly when he was in Minneapolis giving a lecture while I was a pre-medical student in college. So, upon applying for medical school, I wrote to him hoping he would put in a good word for me with the admissions office. Although he probably did not even remember our previous meeting, he responded to my letter by calling me and promising he would contact the George Washington University Medical School Dean of Admissions to recommend me. During my medical school years in Washington, D.C., I would visit him every year at the Office of the Surgeon General to just talk and to thank him for his kindness.

It is obvious to me that the chain of events—my treatment in college with Prolotherapy by Dr. Hemwall; Dr. Hemwall curing Dr. Koop's back pain with Prolotherapy; meeting Dr. Koop who helped me get into medical school; learning about Prolotherapy twelve years after I was first treated by Dr. Hemwall; taking a Prolotherapy course taught by Dr. Hemwall and his pupils; meeting Dr. Hauser, who had worked closely under Dr. Hemwall before his retirement—was divinely orchestrated in order for me to learn Prolotherapy.

The Hausers (Ross and his wife, Marion) and I became good friends and, desiring to add to my rapidly expanding Prolotherapy skills, I went to spend a few days at their clinic in Chicago to observe Dr. Hauser's technique. I then applied my Prolotherapy skills to my patients with pain in Minnesota, successfully treating every joint for a multitude of conditions. I was absolutely astounded with the results. I cleared my shelves of anti-inflammatory drugs and narcotic painkillers. Patients were no longer succumbing to unnecessary surgeries. When a person gets their life back and becomes active again, something else happens. They express their gratitude verbally, in a card or even just a look in their eyes. Prolotherapy can lift the veil of suffering and the stressful burden of pain from those in chronic pain.

I decided it was my turn to be on the receiving end of the Prolotherapy needle. Injuries were not a part of my life until I was a junior at Minnetonka High School, when I severely tore ankle ligaments playing volleyball in a physical education class. Since that time, I have experienced a veritable catalog of athletic injuries (and some non-sport injuries as well for good measure) of nearly every joint one could possibly find in a sports medicine book. Here is a listing as best I can recall:

- Seven severe ankle sprains (tennis, basketball)
- Front right tooth knocked out, twice, and a root canal (hockey)
- Right shoulder rotator cuff strain and tendinitis (tennis)
- Left shoulder benign bone tumor with surgical grafting from the left pelvic bone causing chronic instability
- Low back herniated and degenerative discs, twice, with a pinched nerve in the leg (tennis, running)
- Stress fractures of both feet (tennis)
- Sprained neck/whiplash and slipped rib (fainting episode at home, car accident)
- Severely torn ligaments in both knees and chronic instability (hockey)
- Tennis elbow (tennis)
- Golfer's elbow (golf)
- Injured jaw, TMJ syndrome, from chin hitting cement (roller-blading)
- Severely torn hamstring muscle (water skiing)
- Chronic hip pain (wear and tear) and numerous strains, contusions, and gashes

While these injuries were not enough to permanently "put me out to pasture", they did take a toll on my body and my ability to engage in sports and other everyday activities. Many of my injuries have been substantially improved or eliminated since being treated by Prolotherapy. Nothing brings out a doctor's compassion and empathy for his patients quite like being a patient himself and a patient's pain seems to be somewhat lessened by the knowledge that his or her doctor has had to be the pincushion. It also demonstrates the doctor's belief in the treatment. An unspoken bond between doctor and patient from shared experiences may be at work but I also can't help but think patients relish that their doctor is getting a "taste" of his own medicine.

My younger brother, David, is a professional tennis player on the Association of Tennis Professionals (ATP) Tour. He has achieved a world ranking of 12, has beaten the likes of Andre Agassi, Pete Sampras and Michael Chang, and was a semi-finalist at Wimbledon in 1991, the same year he won the world's richest event, the Grand Slam Cup. But hip trouble, and later elbow pain, threatened to end his career. In 1997, after I had started to see many patients cured by Prolotherapy, David was playing a professional tennis tournament in the Chicago area, still struggling with his hip arthritis. I told him that since he was so close to the Hauser's office, he should be treated at the tournament's conclusion. He was seen and evaluated by Dr. Hauser, who then performed Prolotherapy on David's hips. When David returned to Minnesota, I continued to treat him with Prolotherapy for the next several months. Remarkably, he was able to discontinue the use of all anti-inflammatory drugs and instead began taking natural supplements recommended to him by Dr. Hauser to encourage soft tissue healing. He returned to a full schedule with no stiffness or restriction in his hips!

David, unfortunately, has a body like mine, and training and tournaments put great stress on his joints. He soon developed elbow pain, which once again jeopardized his career. The primary treatment was Prolotherapy which he received at my office with great results in four to five treatments. He returned to the pro tennis tour in 1999 with no discomfort in his elbow. David now has a renewed confidence that he can finish his career without being restricted by chronic injuries.

Why don't more people, or at least physicians, know about Prolotherapy since it works so well? First, doctors are not taught Prolotherapy in medical schools, though I have no doubt that this will change in the future. Second, physicians are taught that inflammation is bad, when, in fact, this is the first step of the healing process and Prolotherapy is able to stimulate this step. Third, the substances used in Prolotherapy are natural, and are relatively common and inexpensive. There is no marketing potential of these substances for drug companies looking to make profit. Fourth, using Prolotherapy could prevent many surgeries and this would not be a good thing for those who make their living doing surgery. Fifth, "it's too simple". This is the answer that Dr. Hemwall gave to me when I asked him why it had not become a commonplace procedure.

It would be hard to find a soft tissue injury or joint pain that could not be successfully treated by Prolotherapy. The following conditions respond beautifully to Prolotherapy:

WHIPLASH
TEMPOROMANDIBULAR JOINT (TMJ) DYSFUNCTION
ROTATOR CUFF TENDINITIS
LOW BACK PAIN
FIBROMYALGIA
TENDINITIS
SPRAINS AND STRAINS
BURSITIS
DAMAGED LIGAMENTS AND TENDONS IN ANY JOINT
MIGRAINE AND TENSION HEADACHES
SHOULDER INSTABILITY
PLANTAR FASCIITIS
SCIATICA
DISC INJURIES
TENNIS ELBOW
CARPAL TUNNEL SYNDROME
ARTHRITIS
AND MANY OTHER INJURIES AND CONDITIONS.

Once a physician skilled in the use of Prolotherapy makes a proper diagnosis, the applications of Prolotherapy to treat pain and connective tissue weakness are almost limitless. When people discover Prolotherapy, they respond with a renewed hope that they can be rid of constant pain and enjoy their lives as they have always wanted but didn't think was possible. In my practice, I have personally seen and have read in letters and testimonials how Prolotherapy has changed lives for the better, where other treatments have failed and where unnecessary surgery or a lifetime of drugs are associated with so many potential complications. Wouldn't it be smarter to keep your original parts and avoid disfiguring scars that can disrupt or interfere with movement and internal organ function? Wouldn't it make more sense to treat the cause rather than put on a "Band-Aid" to cover the symptoms the way drugs do which then wreak havoc on your mind and body? Prolotherapy is safe, simple, well-tolerated, treats a multitude of problems, treats the cause permanently, not just the symptoms temporarily, utilizes common, naturally-occurring substances to stimulate the healing process and doesn't disrupt daily life. Also, it avoids wasted time and money spent on other treatments and the inherent dangers of drugs and surgery. What value do you place on your health?

With the breakthrough books written by Dr. Ross and Marion Hauser, *Prolo Your Sports Injuries Away, Prolo Your Pain Away,* with subtitles, *Prolo Your Neck and Headache Pain Away, Prolo Your Back Pain Away, Prolo Your Fibromyalgia Pain Away, and Prolo Your Arthritis Pain Away,* the public and health professionals alike have easy-to-understand, well-written books now available to them. Besides describing every sports injury, overuse injury and chronic pain of any joint or region of the body which can be successfully treated by prolotherapy, these books provide in-depth information on testing and supplements that assist Prolotherapy and overall healing, while pointing out the dangers of drugs and surgery as well as other things that should be avoided.

The Hausers have the vision of bringing Prolotherapy to as many people as possible, even if they cannot afford it. The Beulah Land Natural Medicine Clinic in southern Illinois was set up by Ross and Marion Hauser in 1991 to treat anyone with chronic pain, using Prolotherapy and other natural medicine methods.

In 1997, they invited me to participate as a volunteer at Beulah Land to provide Prolotherapy to the many people who needed treatment for their pain. As many as 500 patients sign up for each two-day clinic, four times a year, all free of charge, demonstrating a great need for this type of clinic. There are thousands of people from all across the country who have benefitted from Beulah Land Clinic since it opened. No other clinic exists that gives free Prolotherapy and nutritional care to anyone who needs it.

Prolotherapy is, without doubt, the most effective treatment for chronic pain and injuries. With books like *Prolo Your Sports Injuries Away!, Prolo Your Pain Away!* and now the updated, Second Edition of *Prolo Your Pain Away!*, available to the public and health care providers alike, it will only be a matter of time before it will become a routine part of injury care. Prolotherapy...The *Natural Solution* for Pain. ■

Mark Wheaton, MD

Mark Wheaton, M.D.

Preface

In the spring of 1995, I trotted down to Southern Illinois with my friend Peter Blakemore and immediately upon arriving in Beulah Land, I feverishly started writing. During that week, I slept, then wrote. Slept some more and wrote some more. In a week, *Prolo Your Pain Away!* was born. It was brought to life by the tremendous editing job of Kurt Pottinger and my wife, Marion, and was released in late 1997. Well, it is now seven years later and, praise God, all three printings of the book have sold out!

We have sacrificed a lot to put into print our six Prolotherapy books, including the mammoth 900 page monster, *Prolo Your Sports Injuries Away!* Believe it or not, we have one more Prolotherapy book in us—the soon-to-be-released *A Woman's Guide to Curing Chronic Pain.* We have noticed with each book written, there are additional facts and illustrations that would be helpful to the reader to clarify certain points—thus, the necessity to update *Prolo Your Pain Away!*

In this new book, there are several new chapters that were not in the first book, including: the original research done by George S. Hackett, M.D., on Prolotherapy, two chapters dealing with chronic diffuse body pains and their etiologies and treatments, as well as new chapters on healing and connective tissue deficiency, which is the primary reason many people do not heal after an injury. Besides the new chapters, many of the old chapters have been expanded to include updated information with more vivid illustrations and graphics.

Of course, this new book would not have occurred unless Prolotherapy was gaining widespread popularity for curing chronic pain and sports injuries. We are grateful to the many patients, physicians, and media personnel who spread the word. For those who have not heard the message, it is quite simple...Remember that no matter what happens in life, no matter how bad the pain gets, you can always "Prolo Your Pain Away!" and there is a way to be pain-free and that is by "Curing **Your** Chronic Pain with Prolotherapy!" ■

Sincerely with warm regards,

Marion A. Hauser, MS, RD
Ross A. Hauser M.D.

INTRODUCTION

by Lloyd R. Saberski, M.D.

An open mind is an important asset in medicine. There is far more we do not understand about the body than is written in all the collective libraries of the world.

Prolotherapy has achieved in its 50 years of practice many staunch supporters both as providers and recipients, but has not become a part of mainstream medical care. Why is this so? First of all, one has to look at how medical research is processed in the United States. Industry, government, hospitals and universities produce the vast majority of good scientific research. In order to maintain appropriate statistical significance, achieve the highest ethical standard, and respect the quality of human and animal life, the studies become extraordinarily expensive to operate. Thus to launch research at any of these institutions there must be appropriate funding. In the case of government, it takes an executive decision or act of Congress. Universities need grants. Industry sponsors research at institutions, government, and their own facilities, if there is potential profit. Unfortunately, Prolotherapy, which uses simple and readily available compounds, has never attracted pharmaceutical interest. Thus nationally organized research has not been initiated. On the other hand, a fair amount of study into the field has been provided by individual clinicians with interest in and commitment to Prolotherapy. Their research is underfunded and criticized for study design, lack of controls, and openness of data collection (not blinded). To me this is very understandable, since Prolotherapy in this context is provided as part of clinical practices. *In the trenches of reality, the doctor's office, the physician is thrust daily into situations where patients with intractable symptoms beg for help. In such situations it is difficult for clinicians to perform research with placebo controls and blindness, the standards of allopathic medicine.*

Prolotherapy has not made it into mainstream Western medicine not just because of lack of funding, but also because few students are exposed to it during their formative years of career choice: medical school. Allopathic medical schools pride themselves on adherence to scientific methodology and tend to emphasize the science of medicine, not its clinical delivery. Prolotherapy, and other nonscientific but clinically useful pursuits, i.e., chiropractic, osteopathic, etc., are not even touched upon. Also problematic for the development of Prolotherapy is the traditional breakup of medicine into body parts and systems, such as orthopedics, pulmonary medicine, and oncology. There is no one left with the responsibility of teaching or ministering to the soft tissues. *Allopathic medicine's omission has allowed for many non-traditional fields to flourish.*

Allopathic medicine, the cornerstone of modern medicine, is predicated on the scientific method. Knowledge is gained in a stepladder fashion. Each new piece of the research puzzle defines one element of a question. Thus there is an organized pattern to the world's enigmas. Alternative medicine, referred to as complementary medicine, accumulates its wisdom through empiricism—information gathered via trial and error. (Prolotherapy falls under the umbrella of complementary medicine because of its empirical methodology of data collection.) The data collected has variability dependent on the skill and focus of the clinician. This lack of consistently reliable data has biased Western medicine to avoid alternative/complementary medicine for the more predictable allopathic medicine. Unfortunately, potentially effective treatments go unrecognized, buried deep within alternative/complementary medicine.

A rebirth of interest in alternative/complementary medicine, kindled in part from Western medicine's poor track record with preventative medicine, combined with general interest in healthy lifestyles, nutrition, and exercise, has stimulated many allopathic physicians to visit the teachings of alternative/complementary medicine and to seek information they believe useful in their practice of medicine. In addition, some researchers have taken paradigms of alternative/complementary medicine and have begun challenging them with the scientific method. This melding of alternative/complementary medicine with the scientific method provides a yield of predictable information that is far more beneficial than either perspective operating alone. This marriage has already led to treatments now widely accepted in Western medicine (some antibiotics and chemotherapy).

Prolotherapy has become increasingly popular over the past few years. Its popularity stems from success achieved in specific types of injury—most particularly ligament injury. It is theorized that injury to ligaments not only causes pain but also abnormal mechanical performance of a joint. Ligaments are the supportive rubber bands that hold joints in place and allow them to maintain optimal mechanical advantage for muscular driven activities. When ligaments are torn or stretched, the mechanics of the joint are altered. This leads to direct and referred pain. Injections of irritants, such as dextrose, cause a localized inflammatory response that stimulates deposition of collagen which strengthens ligaments. This, in a sense, tightens the rubber band holding the motion segment (joint) together, improves joint performance, and both directly and indirectly decreases pain. Conditions reported to respond well to Prolotherapy include: Achilles tendon tears, tennis elbow, sacroiliac joint dysfunction, facet joint arthropathy, as well as others.

Ten years ago I was skeptical regarding Prolotherapy—I had heard the testimonials and I had spoken to senior physicians. I thought it was professional mass confusion until I developed my own experience. I was surprised about positive and lasting results on selected patients. **In my practice today, I routinely uti-**

lize Prolotherapy for management of mechanical low back pain discomfort and various sports-related injuries. The mechanical back pain patients typically present with long-standing pain, refractory to interventions, including multiple surgeries. Often mechanical components develop because disc disease with leg pain causes a limp, which leads to a pelvic shift, pulling on muscles, and results in pain. Physical examination reveals pain palpable along the sacrum at midline and where sacrum joins the pelvis (SI joint). If I can touch the pain in the sacral region, the pain is unlikely coming from lumbar discs which are deeper and further up the spine. If the patient fails to get better with osteopathic manipulation and shoe orthotics, which compensate for pelvic shift, we provide proliferative injections.

Prolotherapy is the only methodology I have ever utilized that demonstrates potential for significant benefit, yet has limited risk. This technique has been reserved for refractory patients that manage to find a proficient provider, but is most effective on sub-acute injuries. As a practitioner of Prolotherapy, I encourage athletes and chronic pain patients with chronic soft tissue injuries to consider Prolotherapy. ***Prolotherapy is a secret that needs to be discovered.*** ■

Remember—keep an open mind!

Lloyd Saberski

Lloyd R. Saberski, M.D.
Former Medical Director,
Yale University School of Medicine
Center for Pain Management
New Haven, Connecticut

Chapter 1

My Story: What Is a "Physiatrist?"

I was born on September 14, 1962...Just joking! You have to learn to relax! Did you know that when we were children we laughed 80 times per day, but as adults we chuckle a measly 15 times per day?! This is especially significant because we do so many funny things.

While attending the University of Illinois Medical School, I had a difficult time deciding on an area of specialization. Family medicine seemed appealing, but working in the intensive care unit was not for me. Then a friend of mine, Steve Primack, now an attending radiologist at the University of Oregon, gave me a book that contained a comprehensive list of medical specialties. After reviewing it and praying with my wife about our future, I decided to look into the field of Physical Medicine and Rehabilitation.

Physical Medicine and Rehabilitation is a medical discipline approved by the American Board of Medical Specialties. After World War II, many soldiers returned home with disabilities, including amputations and spinal cord injuries. Previously, these veterans would have died from infection, but due to the discovery of penicillin they survived their injuries. Unfortunately, physicians had not been trained to care for those suffering from such disabilities. Out of this need eventually came the field of Physical Medicine and Rehabilitation, or Physiatry.

Physiatry

A doctor who specializes in Physical Medicine and Rehabilitation is called a Physiatrist (pronounced *fizz-ee-at-trist*). No, I'm not a Psychiatrist. Look again. Physiatrist. Currently, there are approximately 6,000 board-certified Physiatrists in the United States. Physiatry requires four years of residency training after medical school. Rotations in stroke, multiple sclerosis, traumatic brain injury, amputations, cardiac rehabilitation, electromyography (EMG), spinal cord injury, neurology, sports medicine, orthopedic rehabilitation, and, of course, both acute and chronic pain management are all part of the residency program.

Physiatrists care for patients who suffer from a chronic or acute disease that has affected their ability to enjoy life and perform daily functions. A stroke victim, for example, requires medical attention as well as rehabilitation. Difficulties in blood pressure control, urination, speech, and swallowing are common problems that result from a stroke. Rehabilitation helps the patient relearn how to walk, talk, and live life.

Unfortunately, most people do not consult a Physiatrist because they do not know the profession exists. Even many Family Practice Physicians and Internists are unaware of Physiatry, which is probably due to the fact that a rotation in Physical Medicine and Rehabilitation is not mandatory in medical schools.

Physiatry is one medical field where a shortage of doctors exists. As a human's lifespan increases and more people survive disabling diseases, more Physiatrists will be needed.

Where It All Started

I became fascinated with pain during my Physical Medicine residency. I began accumulating articles on bizarre pain syndromes and obtained quite a collection. (Everyone needs a hobby, right?) What struck me most was the magnitude of the pain problem. It seemed as though everyone either had pain themselves or knew someone who was suffering from chronic pain. I also saw the lack of significant pain relief by modern treatments such as surgery, physical therapy, and anti-inflammatory drugs.

It appeared that the longer people had pain, the less likely such treatments were going to help cure their chronic pain. Pain clinics and pain programs do help some people, but have a poor cure rate. Pain programs teach people to live with their pain. The psychological aspect of the pain is addressed, but in many cases the cause is not determined.

When I began seeing pain patients during my residency training program in Physical Medicine and Rehabilitation, I thought they were a very difficult group of people to treat. They often appeared depressed, and traditional approaches to pain management did not seem to help. Then I said to myself, "How would I feel if I had pain day after day and no one could find a cure?" The families of many who suffer from pain often begin doubting the reality of their loved ones' pain. Many chronic pain patients who frequent pain clinics experience broken homes and lose their jobs because of the pain. It became evident to me that these patients' pain was indeed real and that pain pills and support groups did not cure the pain.

Natural Medicine

Then came Natural Medicine. I began learning about Natural Medicine the day I married Marion, a dietitian, on December 20, 1986. I watched as my life and surroundings slowly changed. Not long after we moved her things into our condominium (after we were married—we're old fashioned, what can I say?), Marion axed fast food from my diet. I have not eaten a can of Spaghetti-Os since our wedding. What sacrifices I have made! Marion introduced me to good-tasting spinach and drastically altered my diet. The chronic fatigue that I thought was from the intensity of medical training began to subside. I guess the rest is history!

Natural Medicine employs natural substances such as organic foods, herbs, vitamins, and minerals, as well as rest, exercise, and attention to faith in God to maintain and restore health. I began to see that modern medicine was not a cure-all for chronic diseases. Its lack of healing ability was especially evident as it pertained to chronic disabling conditions caused by pain, multiple sclerosis, rheumatoid arthritis, and cancer. I knew there had to be something to help all these suffering people.

One of my instructors, Oleh Paly, M.D., gave me a book by Linus Pauling, M.D., on the use of vitamin C in disease. He also directed me to various resources and organizations that specialize in natural healing techniques. This was my first real taste of Natural Medicine.

Soon after, I found myself taking acupuncture lessons and reading up on natural healing techniques. I tried the techniques on my wife. (After I have learned a technique, she always wants to be the first patient.) Since she survived, I tried them out on a few friends. (Most of them are still friends.) A friend from church, Mrs. Wright, was experiencing terrible pain. I tried all the treatment modalities and gizmos I knew of, but without success. Mrs. Wright eventually received treatment from Gustav A. Hemwall, M.D., the world's most experienced Prolotherapist. The Prolotherapy she received in her shoulder gave her a significant amount of relief. Mrs. Wright then encouraged me to learn about Dr. Hemwall's treatment.

Prolotherapy

In April 1992, I contacted Dr. Hemwall and he allowed me to observe him in his clinic. I was astonished to see him perform 30, 50, or 100 injections on a patient at one time! He called his treatment Prolotherapy. The only other time I had come across the term was when a fellow resident showed me a book on the treatment. I later discovered that Dr. Hemwall was one of the authors of that book!

During the next few months, I spent a considerable amount of time in Dr. Hemwall's office. People traveled from all over the world to be treated by this 84-year-old man. I have nothing against age, but to think that someone would travel from places like England, Mexico, Florida, and California to receive pain management was incredible. I learned that if someone suffers from pain and someone else has a technique that will help alleviate the pain, time and expense are minor considerations.

It was clear that Dr. Hemwall was helping those whom traditional medicine had not helped. His average patient had been in pain for years and had tried it all: surgery, pain pills, anti-inflammatory medication, exercise, therapy, acupuncture, and hypnotism. Most patients had seen more than five physicians before consulting Dr. Hemwall. Almost all the patients I observed improved after one or two Prolotherapy treatments. People found relief from pain that had plagued them for years. Many said they wished they had known about Prolotherapy years ago.

Three months later, I began utilizing Prolotherapy in my medical practice as a treatment for chronic pain. I have effectively used Prolotherapy in nearly every joint of the body. In January 1993, I began working alongside Dr. Hemwall in his Prolotherapy practice. Since then, my wife and I have opened Caring Medical and

Rehabilitation Services, S.C., a Natural Medicine clinic that cares for people with chronic diseases using natural methods, including Prolotherapy.

Caring Medical and Rehabilitation Services (CMRS) seeks to provide the most comprehensive, effective treatments from both traditional and non-traditional medicine. The following are some of the Natural Medicine services we provide:

- **Prolotherapy:** An injection technique to stimulate the growth of healthy, strong connective tissue to help eliminate many chronic painful conditions.
- **Insulin Potentiation Therapy for Cancer:** A cancer-killing treatment with minimal negative side effects.
- **Metabolic Typing:** A testing protocol to determine your individual body chemistry for a personal diet regimen.
- **Chelation Therapy:** An IV treatment to improve circulation and remove heavy metals.
- **Oxygen Therapies:** Treatments to increase your immunity, detoxify chemicals, and destroy various bacteria.
- **Intravenous Vitamins and Minerals:** Treatments for various immune dysfunctions, cancer, and other chronic conditions.
- **Photoluminescence:** Ultraviolet blood irradiation used to boost the immune system.
- **Natural Gynecology:** Natural approach to menopause, post-pregnancy, and premenstrual syndromes.
- **Neural Therapy:** An injection technique of local anesthetics to scars and trigger points to eliminate "interference fields."
- **Natural Hormone Replacement:** Restoring and renewing the body for both men and women.
- **Therapeutic Skin Care Analysis:** Skin care analysis and natural treatment of conditions such as acne, rosacea, psoriasis, aging, and sun damage.
- **NeuroCranial Restructuring:** Manipulation of the sphenoid bone, through the nose, that successfully treats such conditions as sinus problems, headaches, and vision problems.
- **Whole Body Hyperthermia:** Using heat and elevated body temperature to increase blood flow and oxygen to the tissues. This technique is used with Insulin Potentiation Therapy in the treatment of cancer.
- **Mesotherapy:** An injection technique to help heal the mesoderm, or connective tissues of the body. It safely and effectively helps remove cellulite and wrinkles as well as some chronic pain.

CMRS treats virtually every human disease utilizing some of the best natural treatments from around the world. CMRS is particularly well known for Prolotherapy and cancer therapies such as **Insulin Potentiation Therapy (IPT).**

IPT is a treatment that involves administration of a small dose of insulin given to the patient that induces a state of low blood sugar (hypoglycemia). When the patient begins to have symptoms, such as a feeling of lightheadedness and weakness (hypoglycemia symptoms), low doses of traditional chemotherapy are given by intravenous push. When insulin is given, the cancer cells are fooled into thinking they are going to be fed food, when in reality they are going to be destroyed by chemotherapy. The doses of chemotherapy used during IPT are one tenth to one fourth of the traditional doses given during high-dose chemotherapy, therefore the side effects are minimal. Patients are given immune-stimulating treatments along with the IPT, thereby allowing the patients with cancer to receive many of the cancer-killing effects of traditional chemotherapy without as many negative side effects.

Since learning Prolotherapy and Natural Medicine, the practice of medicine has become more enjoyable. Prolotherapy has enabled us to offer a treatment that eliminates long-standing pain. Chronic pain, like cancer, sucks the lifeblood out of a person. It can disrupt families and lead them into bankruptcy if the pain prohibits the patient from holding a job. What a joy it will be when you or your loved ones find pain relief. We believe this book will lead you, or someone you know, down the path to healing chronic pain naturally with Prolotherapy. ■

The Caring Medical and Rehabilitation Services Team

Chapter 2

Prolotherapy: The Technique and Its History

"Nothing was worse than a chronic low back pain patient walking into my office," said Gustav A. Hemwall, M.D., the world's most experienced Prolotherapist. "I would try exercise, corsets, and surgery, but nothing really helped."

In 1955, when Dr. Hemwall visited a scientific exhibit at the national meeting of the American Medical Association, that all changed. Recalling the meeting, Dr. Hemwall said, "At one particular exhibit I noticed a crowd of doctors listening to a doctor say he had a cure for low back pain. This fellow had written a book on it as well." That fellow was George S. Hackett, M.D., the father of Prolotherapy. **(See Appendix C, The Prolotherapy Crusade.)**

Once the crowd diminished, Dr. Hemwall asked Dr. Hackett how he could learn the treatment described in his book. Dr. Hackett responded by inviting Dr. Hemwall to observe him administering Prolotherapy. Dr. Hemwall became so proficient at administering the technique that Dr. Hackett would later refer patients to him. **(See Figure 2-1.)**

Dr. Hemwall remembers, "When I returned from that meeting, I quickly read Dr. Hackett's book describing Prolotherapy and treated my first patient. After a few sessions of Prolotherapy, this patient, instead of coming into the office in a wheelchair, ran to catch four buses. From that point on, instead of dreading patients with low back pain, I began to look for them." That was 40 years ago. Since that time, some 10,000 patients have received Prolotherapy from Dr. Hemwall.

Prolotherapy Case Reports

Chronic low back pain management has taken a drastic turn from when the American Medical Association presented Dr. Hackett's Prolotherapy work at their national meetings in 1955. Now Prolotherapy is not covered in its journal and is rarely mentioned at national meetings. Unfortunately, for the millions of Americans suffering from chronic back and body pain, several events have led to the reduction in the number of physicians using Prolotherapy.

On August 8, 1959, the *Journal of the American Medical Association* reported a fatality after a Prolotherapy injection series. In the case report, Richard Schneider, M.D., wrote, "...in the instance reported here, it must be emphasized that the sclerosing solution [Prolotherapy solution] was not the usual sodium salt of fatty acids and vegetable oil as described in the original monograph [by Dr. Hackett], but instead a solution of zinc sulfate in 2.5 percent phenol." [1]

This physician also apparently injected this solution into the spinal canal, not at the fibro-osseous junction where ligaments and tendons attach to bone. Dr. Schneider ended the case report with, "...this technique of precipitating fibro-

GEORGE S. HACKETT, M. D.
616 FIRST NATIONAL BANK BUILDING
CANTON 2, OHIO

Jan. 25, 1957

Mrs. Lloyd D. Anderson
315 South 12th Street
Albia, Iowa

Dear Mrs. Anderson:

In reply to your letter of the 21st, I would suggest that you consult: -

Gustav A. Hemwall, M.D.
839 North Central Avenue
Chicago, Illinois.

Dr. Hemwall is the only man that I know of in your part of the country who is experienced with this technic of treatment. He was out here on several occasions and was instructed in the technic by me, and I can recommend him highly.

As to whether your condition could be benefitted by this procedure, it is impossible to give you any answer without first having examined you to determine your disability.

If I can be of further service, please feel free to call on me.

Sincerely,

George S. Hackett, M.D.

Figure 2-1

osseous proliferation appears to be neither sound nor without extreme danger." It should be noted that the article was written by several physicians from the neurosurgery department at the University of Michigan Hospital.

This tragic case occurred because the physician used too strong a proliferant and did not follow a cardinal rule of Prolotherapy: Prolotherapy injections are given only when the needle is touching the bone at the fibro-osseous junction, with the only exception being joint injections. Unfortunately, early Prolotherapy physicians did not follow Dr. Hackett's technique. The flawed method these physicians utilized caused some harmful effects and discouraged other physicians from administering Prolotherapy. When properly administered, and the body possesses the ability to heal, Prolotherapy has few side effects and is effective in eliminating chronic pain.

PROLOTHERAPY SOLUTIONS

In his 19 years of using Sylnasol, a sodium salt of vegetable oil fatty acids, Dr. Hackett observed no side effects. Dr. Hemwall noted that a number of years after Dr. Hackett's original work was published, Sylnasol was taken off the market due to a lack of demand. After several years of using various solutions, Dr. Hemwall found that a simple dextrose and Lidocaine solution was the ideal proliferant. It produced only a small amount of pain following the procedure, yet resulted in complete pain relief after only a few treatments. More dextrose solution could also be injected at one time than with the sylnasol, allowing more areas of the body to be treated per visit.

Only recently has modern medicine figured out what Dr. Hemwall knew some 35 years ago: that a simple dextrose solution is all that is needed to eliminate pain. Min-Young Kim, M.D., and associates from Yonsei University Medical College in Seoul, South Korea, studied 64 patients with chronic pain. Dr. Kim compared using a five percent dextrose solution with the current standard trigger point injection solution of 0.5 percent Lidocaine and placebo. The study found that not only did the dextrose solution prove to give statistically significant pain relief ($P<.01$) against placebo, it was that much better when compared to the Lidocaine solution. The study also found that in follow-up, the pain relief with the dextrose solution remained. [2, 3]

The Prolotherapy solution used at Caring Medical and Rehabilitation Services is 15.0 percent dextrose, 10.0 percent Sarapin, and 0.2 percent lidocaine. Dr. Hemwall used the same solution without the Sarapin. The dextrose is a corn extract and makes the solution more concentrated than blood (hypertonic), acting as a strong proliferant. Sarapin is used to treat nerve irritation and, in our experience, acts as a proliferant. Sarapin is an extract of the pitcher plant and is one of the few materials listed in the *Physicians' Desk Reference* that has no known side effects. Lidocaine is an anesthetic that helps reinforce the diagnosis because the patient will experience immediate pain relief after the Prolotherapy injections.

The current Prolotherapy technique described in this book, using these solutions, has been administered by Dr. Hemwall and our clinic to more than 18,000 patients in more than 50,000 treatment sessions, with more than five million injections given. Not one case of permanent nerve injury, paralysis, or death has been documented. The main side effect has been one to two days of soreness and stiffness after the procedure. This is not only from inflammation caused by the Prolotherapy injections, but occurs because the needle pierces the muscle to reach the fibro-osseous junction of the ligaments and tendons being treated.

The dextrose solution, is safe, and will not affect a diabetic's blood sugar level. If a patient is corn-intolerant, other proliferant agents can be used. Such agents include sodium morrhuate (an extract of cod liver oil), preservative-free zinc sulfate, manganese, pumice, or a dextrose-glycerine-phenol solution known as P2G. Incidentally, P2G was the proliferant used in the two double-blind studies that will be described in Chapter 4.*[4,5]

MYOFASCIAL PAIN THEORY

In the early 1960s, after the damaging report in the *Journal of the American Medical Association,* Janet Travell, M.D., Internist, developed a treatment program for what she termed "Myofascial Pain Syndrome." She noted that patients with chronic pain had tight muscles. After the muscles were stretched or relaxed the pain would diminish. She also described trigger points, areas where muscle is tender to palpation. These trigger points refer pain to other areas of the body. She described these referral pain patterns in detail.[6]

Dr. Travell was an outstanding physician and gave successful care to then Senator John F. Kennedy, five years prior to his presidential election. This led to her promotion to White House physician under President Kennedy and President Lyndon B. Johnson. Needless to say, her myofascial pain theory received a great deal of publicity and is embraced today as the main theory for chronic pain management.

Upon examination, the referral pain patterns laid out by Dr. Hackett in 1956 for ligament laxity are strikingly similar to the referral pain patterns described for muscles by Dr. Travell many years later. **(See Figures 2-2 to 2-5.)** The similarity exists because of the relationship between ligament laxity and muscle tenseness. Ligament weakness causes laxity, or looseness, in a joint. To stabilize the joint, the muscles tighten up. The overlying muscle is then overworked in an attempt to stabilize the loosened joint. This tense muscle produces trigger points, or "knots."

Clinicians who use myofascial stretching techniques for tight muscles often find that the chronic pain is relieved temporarily but returns with the same intensity at some point after treatment. Myofascial therapy often only treats a symptom of the ligament weakness and, because the underlying ligament weakness is not dealt with, pain returns. Prolotherapy, by causing the growth of ligament tissue,

* *Caring Medical does not necessarily use all of these proliferants.*

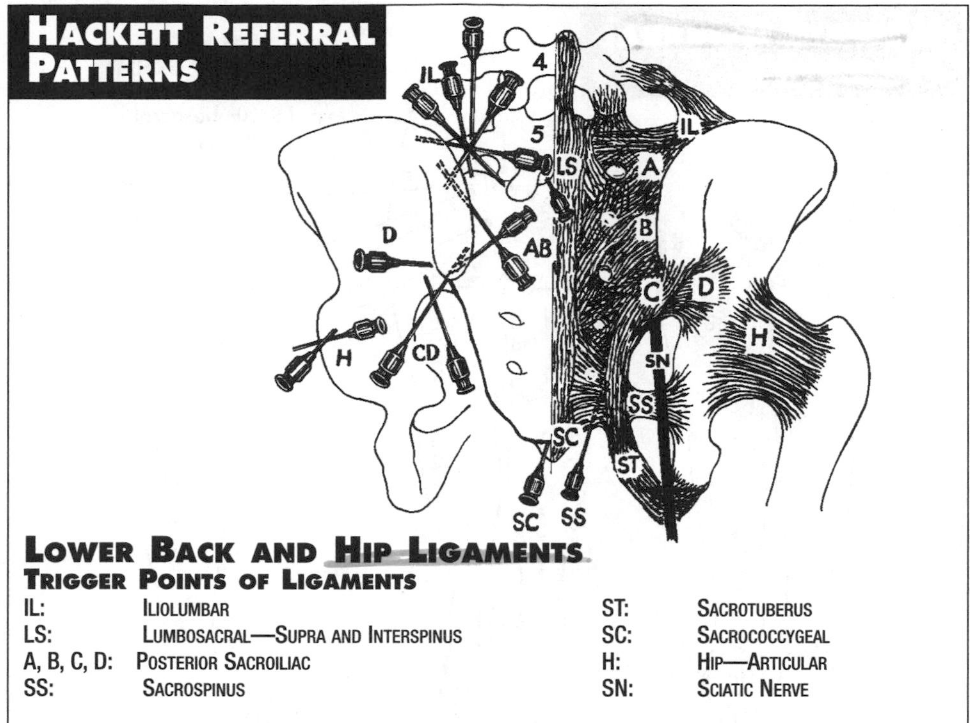

Figure 2-2: Ligamentous Structures of the Lower Back and Hip that Refer Pain Down the Lower Leg

The illustration shows the trigger points of pain and the needles in position for confirmation of the diagnosis and for treatment of ligament relaxation of the lumbosacral and pelvic joints.

treats the root cause of myofascial pain. By strengthening the ligaments, the joint stabilizes, so the muscles have no need to tighten. It is only then that trigger points and muscle tenderness are permanently eliminated.

CAT Scans, MRI Scans, and X-Rays

The next reason for the diminished use of Prolotherapy was the invention of the computerized axial tomography (CAT) scan. The CAT scan became widely available in the early 1970s and was used, among other things, to view the intervertebral discs. Chronic pain physicians in the early 1970s found abnormalities in this area and concluded that the disc problems caused chronic pain. Millions of people underwent surgical procedures to correct some "abnormality" of the disc, as seen on the CAT scan, only to experience minimal pain relief.

Not until the early 1980s were the CAT scans of people without pain examined.[7] A study published in 1984 by Sam W. Wiesel, M.D., found that 35 percent of the population, irrespective of age, had abnormal findings on CAT scans of their lower backs even though they had no pain complaints. In CAT scans of people over 40 years of age, 50 percent had abnormal findings. Twenty-nine percent

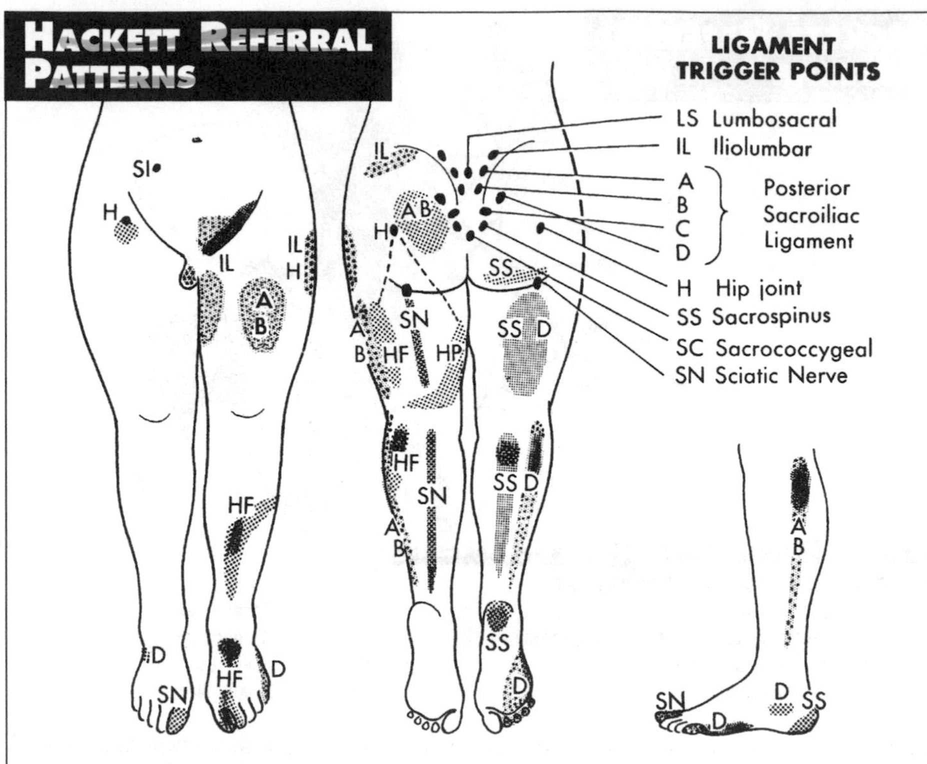

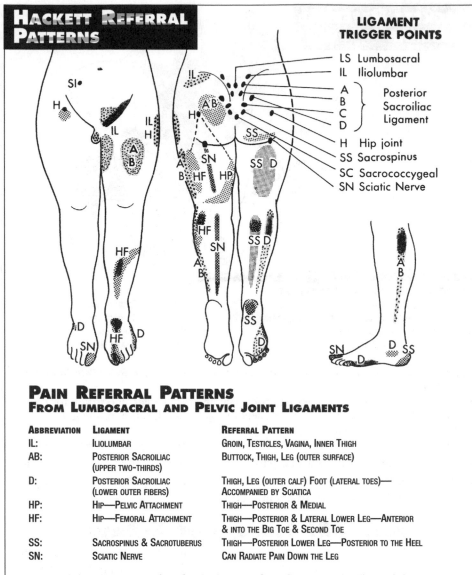

Pain Referral Patterns
From Lumbosacral and Pelvic Joint Ligaments

Abbreviation	Ligament	Referral Pattern
IL:	Iliolumbar	Groin, Testicles, Vagina, Inner Thigh
AB:	Posterior Sacroiliac (upper two-thirds)	Buttock, Thigh, Leg (outer surface)
D:	Posterior Sacroiliac (lower outer fibers)	Thigh, Leg (outer calf) Foot (lateral toes)—Accompanied by Sciatica
HP:	Hip—Pelvic Attachment	Thigh—Posterior & Medial
HF:	Hip—Femoral Attachment	Thigh—Posterior & Lateral Lower Leg—Anterior & into the Big Toe & Second Toe
SS:	Sacrospinus & Sacrotuberus	Thigh—Posterior Lower Leg—Posterior to the Heel
SN:	Sciatic Nerve	Can Radiate Pain Down the Leg

Figure 2-3: Ligament Referral Pain Patterns from Structures in Figure 2-2

showed evidence of herniated discs, 81 percent facet degeneration (arthritis), and 48 percent lumbar stenosis (another form of arthritis). In other words, for people over 40 years of age who do not have symptoms of pain, a 50 percent chance of abnormality on their CAT scans exists, including a herniated disc.

In regard to pain management, diagnostic tests, such as x-rays, magnetic resonance imaging (MRI) scans, or CAT scans, should never take the place of a listening ear and a strong thumb to diagnose the cause of chronic pain. It is necessary for the clinician to understand where the pain originates and radiates. In other

Hackett Referral Patterns

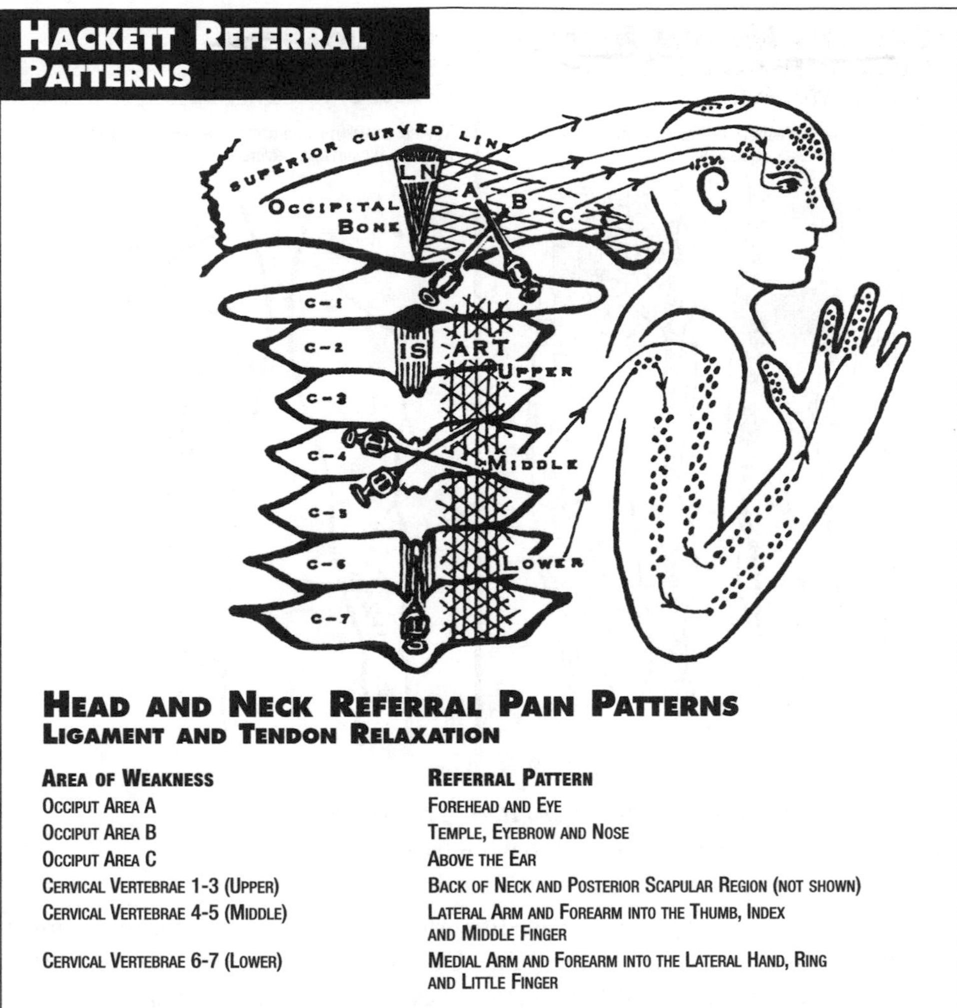

Head and Neck Referral Pain Patterns
Ligament and Tendon Relaxation

Area of Weakness	Referral Pattern
Occiput Area A	Forehead and Eye
Occiput Area B	Temple, Eyebrow and Nose
Occiput Area C	Above the Ear
Cervical Vertebrae 1-3 (Upper)	Back of Neck and Posterior Scapular Region (not shown)
Cervical Vertebrae 4-5 (Middle)	Lateral Arm and Forearm into the Thumb, Index and Middle Finger
Cervical Vertebrae 6-7 (Lower)	Medial Arm and Forearm into the Lateral Hand, Ring and Little Finger

Figure 2-4: Head and Neck Ligament Referral Pain Patterns

words, what is the referral pattern? Unfortunately, most physicians do not know the referral patterns of the ligaments, as seen in **Figures 2-2, 2-3, 2-4,** and **2-5.** In summary, it should be obvious that an x-ray should not be used solely as the criterion for determining the cause of a person's pain.

To properly diagnose the cause of a person's pain it is important for the physician to touch the patient. Medical doctors are too quick to prescribe an anti-inflammatory medication or order an MRI. The best **MRI** scan is a physician's thumb, which we call **M**y **R**eproducibility **I**nstrument, used to palpate the ligament or tendon suspected to be the problem. If the diagnosis is correct, a positive "jump sign" will occur because the weakened ligament or tendon will be very tender to palpation. If the physician does not reproduce a person's pain during an examination, the

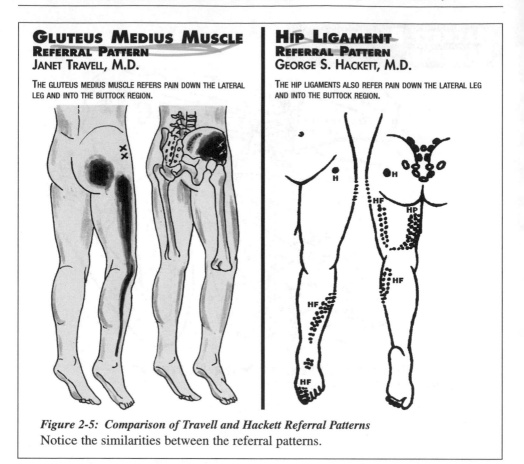

GLUTEUS MEDIUS MUSCLE
REFERRAL PATTERN
JANET TRAVELL, M.D.

THE GLUTEUS MEDIUS MUSCLE REFERS PAIN DOWN THE LATERAL LEG AND INTO THE BUTTOCK REGION.

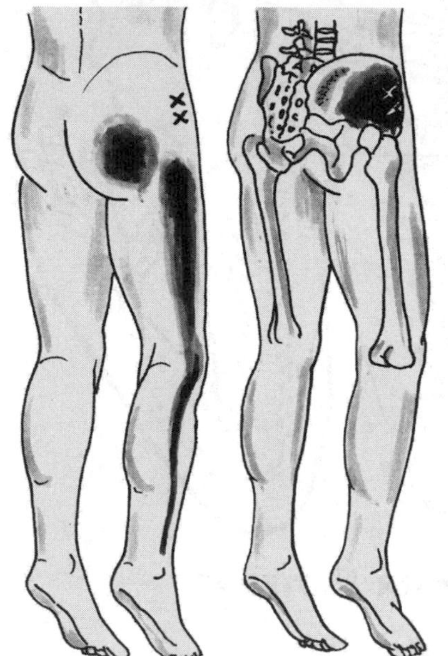

HIP LIGAMENT
REFERRAL PATTERN
GEORGE S. HACKETT, M.D.

THE HIP LIGAMENTS ALSO REFER PAIN DOWN THE LATERAL LEG AND INTO THE BUTTOCK REGION.

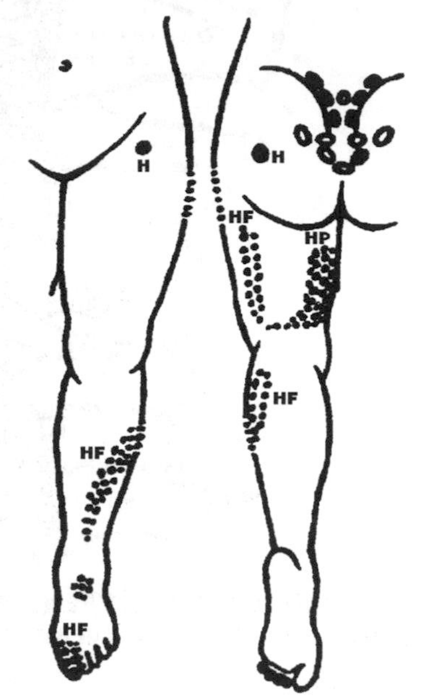

Figure 2-5: Comparison of Travell and Hackett Referral Patterns
Notice the similarities between the referral patterns.

likelihood of eliminating the pain is slim. How can a physician make a correct diagnosis without reproducing the pain? Our patients often say that this initial examination was the first real examination they have had for their pain.

It is not uncommon for a patient to leave our office after the initial consultation, before beginning Prolotherapy treatments, keenly aware of their pain source area. When patients confront Dr. Hauser with this, he always smiles and says, "What did you expect? You came to a pain doctor!" The point is, a physician must reproduce the pain in order to document the exact pain-producing structure. Once this is located, Prolotherapy injections to strengthen the area will likely eliminate the pain.

THE INSPIRATION FOR THIS BOOK

The inspiration to fulfill our dream of writing these books about Prolotherapy came in the summer of 1995 when we visited Cornerstone to Health, a Natural Medicine clinic operated by Gail Gelsinger, R.N. Dr. Hauser examined 18 of the clinic's patients who, despite being on good nutrition programs, continued to suffer from chronic pain. Each was successfully treated with Prolotherapy. When we returned a few months later, twice as many patients desired Prolotherapy treatments. Unfortunately, our schedule prevents us from returning. As a result, a myriad of people needlessly suffer from chronic pain because the treatment of Prolotherapy is unavailable. We then realized how people could benefit from books about treating chronic pain with Prolotherapy.

Another reason for writing this book is to carry on where Dr. Hemwall has left off. In June 1996, Dr. Hemwall, at the age of 88, retired after 60 years of practicing medicine and 40 years of administering Prolotherapy. Because Dr. Hemwall had the privilege of learning Prolotherapy from its originator, the more books that share his knowledge, the better.

During the 40 years that Dr. Hemwall administered Prolotherapy, he treated more than 10,000 chronic pain patients. One of those 10,000 patients said his pain "originated in my spine, went down across my inguinal ligament, down the inside of my thigh, skipped my knee, went down the inside of my calves, skipped my ankle, and came out the dorsum of my foot like a burn." The patient was describing a sacroiliac referral pattern, and Prolotherapy to the sacroiliac joint very effectively eliminated the pain. This patient would later become the surgeon general of the United States, C. Everett Koop, M.D.

Dr. Koop says, "I personally know the benefits of Prolotherapy. I had intractable back pain which traveled down my leg. I received Prolotherapy to my back by Dr. Hemwall. After a few treatments, it [the pain] was gone. Seeing the benefits of Prolotherapy on myself, I used the technique on the parents of my patients. I was a pediatric surgeon. When I saw the parents of my patients limping or having trouble taking off their coats, I would offer to treat them with Prolotherapy. I did it all *pro bono*. Prolotherapy does remarkably well at eliminating the pain caused by ligament relaxation or weakness. For someone experienced in the technique, it is extremely safe and effective. I utilized the technique of Prolotherapy from 1960 to 1980 and found it extremely effective in eliminating the chronic pain that comes from ligament relaxation." [8]

For the past 25 years, Dr. Hemwall had been the main proponent and teacher of Prolotherapy in the United States. He was responsible for training more physicians and treating more people with Prolotherapy than anyone else. Without his perseverance, the Hackett technique of Prolotherapy may have vanished. We have been blessed to have worked under Dr. Hemwall as students, with him as partners, and beside him as colleagues. In this book, we hope to disseminate what we have gleaned from a man we very much admire.

The Weakness of Modern Medicine

While a wonderful and effective procedure known as Prolotherapy has been achieving pain relief for more than 50 years, modern medicine continues to search for drugs, devices, and surgical procedures to eliminate chronic pain. Anti-inflammatory drugs have become a multi-billion dollar business. While these drugs provide temporary relief, they do not correct the underlying condition causing the pain. Migraine headaches are not caused by an ibuprofen deficiency. When these drugs do not give permanent relief, the next step is typically exercise or physical therapy. As with the drugs, physical therapy and exercise provide temporary relief for the pain during the therapy, but the pain often returns once the therapy concludes.

The next step down the wrong path for the chronic pain patient is a referral to a surgeon. Unfortunately for many, surgery has not been the promised end to their pain and often makes the problem worse. Surgeons often use x-ray technology as a diagnostic tool. This is often not appropriate to properly diagnose the pain source. It is not uncommon for an x-ray to reveal terrible arthritis in someone who experiences no symptoms, whereas an x-ray of someone who has terrible pain symptoms may reveal nothing.

After examining these x-rays, a surgeon may decide to remove a disc or cartilage tissue in an attempt to alleviate pain. The two questions to ask are: Who put that tissue there? For what purpose? God placed disc tissue there to stabilize and cushion the lower back, and cartilage tissue in the joints so that bones glide smoothly over one another. What happens when the disc and cartilage tissue are removed? If the disc is removed, the vertebral levels above and below the surgerized segment develop proliferative arthritis. This happens because these segments have to carry more of the force than they were designed to carry in the lower back. If the cartilage is removed, the bones no longer glide smoothly over one another. Soon after this, a person notices a crunching of the joint where the cartilage was removed. This crunching sound is arthritis. The end result of surgical procedures that remove cartilage, ligaments, and bone from knees, backs, and necks is often arthritis.

Unfortunately, medicine has lost the art of clinical diagnosis without the aid of fancy tests and machines. Prolotherapists (physicians who practice Prolotherapy) are trained to reproduce and effectively treat a painful area without the need for x-rays or expensive tests.

PROLOTHERAPY AS PAIN MANAGEMENT

Other unnatural, ineffective, and/or destructive means to relieve pain include the implantation of a spinal cord stimulator, botulism toxin injections into muscles, and radiofrequency thermocoagulation of nerves and other bodily structures. These treatments sound impressive but end up changing or destroying God-given anatomy or other bodily processes often without a long-term cure of the painful condition. Chronic pain is not due to a spinal cord stimulator or botulism toxin deficiency. A more sensible, natural approach to pain management would be to repair the damaged and weakened tissue. Chronic pain is almost always due to weakened, damaged tissue. A herniated disc, for example, is better treated by allowing the regrowth of ligament tissue through which the disc herniated, than by removing the disc.

Nathaniel W. Boyd's book, *Stay Out of the Hospital*, describes ligament relaxation. "Once forcibly stretched by trauma, ligamentous tissue is unable to snap back to its original length. This being the case, it should not be very difficult to understand how the ligaments of any joint, once over-stretched, will leave the joint wobbly, loose, and unstable. Along with this instability very often comes chronic pain. The object of 'needle surgery' in treating unstable joints is to inject a sclerosing agent into the ligaments, causing the contraction and thickening of the ligament, thus strengthening its supporting effect on that joint." Boyd is describing Prolotherapy.[9]

Boyd continues by saying that the cause of back pain in a so-called ruptured disc is not pressure of the disc on nerve roots, as orthopedic surgeons would have you believe, because the disc is absorbed by the body in a few weeks. The back hurts in such cases because once the disc has disappeared, the spinal column loses vertical height and the ligaments become too long and loose to keep the structure stable. This instability and unwanted motion create core irritation, congestion, and inflammation.[10]

Surgery and other invasive treatments are directed at relieving pain but not relieving the underlying condition that caused the pain in the first place. What happens when you cover up a problem and do not solve it? Can you imagine "solving" your financial problems by paying your bills with your credit card? By doing so, your financial problems actually worsen. When treatments cover up the pain without correcting the underlying problem, the initial condition that caused the pain may actually worsen. The person may require more and more pain medicine or other treatments in order to alleviate the pain. It is our hope that by educating more patients and physicians about Prolotherapy we can end the onslaught of these procedures and correct the "true" underlying cause of the pain. ■

Chapter 3

The Prolotherapy Pioneer: George S. Hackett, M.D.

It is hard to believe as we enter into the 21ST century that pain is still treated with immune-suppressing substances such as steroid shots, NSAIDs, and narcotic medications. This is especially difficult to accept when one considers the work of just one man, George S. Hackett, M.D., "The Prolotherapy Pioneer." **(See Figure 3-1.)**

George S. Hackett, M.D., was a graduate of Cornell Medical School, class of 1916.[1] He was a busy consulting trauma surgeon at Mercy Hospital in Canton, Ohio. He describes it best. "During a period of over 20 years while engaged in a tremendous traumatic practice, I was also regularly called upon for special examinations by approximately 70 accident insurance companies to report accurate diagnoses and prognoses. I became aware of the indefinite and variable conclusions of our best diagnosticians in dealing with low back disability. Finally, in 1939, I arrived at the conclusion that relaxation of the articular ligaments was responsible for a considerable number of low back disabilities.

Figure 3-1: George S. Hackett, M.D., coined the term Prolotherapy as well as pioneered the treatment.

"I decided to attempt strengthening the ligaments by the injection of a proliferating solution within the fibrous bands to stimulate the production of fibrous tissue. The treatment proved to be satisfactory almost from the beginning, and it was cautiously extended until now, articular ligaments of the entire spine and pelvis and some other joints are treated with great satisfaction both to the patient and to me."[2]

From Surgery to Success... The Switch to Prolotherapy

Dr. Hackett, in his role as a trauma surgeon and consultant to insurance companies, was often asked his opinion of whether surgery would help people with their back pain and, if they had already had a back operation, could anything still be done for their pain that remained. Here are some of his observations that led to his belief that ligament laxity, especially around the sacroiliac joint, was where the answer lay.

"Over two decades ago, three ideas appeared which definitely changed the course of events in low back treatment. One was the description of the ruptured

Minneapolis Morn

MINNEAPOLIS, MINN., WEDNESDAY, SE

MINNEAPOLIS TRIBUNE PHOTO BY POWELL KRUEGER

It Hurts Here Dr. G. A. Hemwall, Chicago (left), got a lesson in back pain Tuesday from Dr. George S. Hackett, Canton, Ohio. The American Academy of Physical Medicine and Rehabilitation ended two days of meetings at the Leamington hotel, and the American Congress of Physical Medicine and Rehabilitation got ready for three days of meetings starting today. Hackett injects what he calls "an irritating solution" into weak backs to strengthen the ligaments—or, as he puts it, "stimulate production of new bone and fibrous tissue cells to strengthen the weld of ligament to bone." The method is not generally accepted, but Hackett claimed good results over 20 years.

Figure 3-2: Prolotherapy in history.

nucleus pulposus in 1934 as described by Mixter and Barr. It is a definite scientific entity and will endure. However, **it has gotten out of control because of the confusion in diagnosis and has resulted in too many *unsatisfactory* operations.** Barr pointed out in 1951 that, 'Too many backs are being irretrievably damaged by ill-advised and ill-considered operations.' The mass production of unnecessary, unsatisfactory spinal operations that were turned out in the post-war decade by inexperienced surgeons, whose training was overemphasized on the mechanical side, helps to confuse the public and make them wary. I am frequently consulted by patients who have had disc and spinal fusion operations by surgeons who do not consider the sacroiliac joint and its ligaments as causing any trouble. These patients continue to have the same pain, referred pain and sciatica from relaxation of the ligaments that support the lumbosacral and sacroiliac articulations that they had previous to the operations.

"I have successfully treated them in cases that have not been too extensively **mutilated** by operations which sacrifice important ligaments and bone prominences that have been developed to give leverage for attached ligaments and tendons. The belief that the pain and disability of lumbosacral instability from ligament relaxation can be eliminated by lumbosacral fusion is **erroneous**. Even if the fifth lumbar vertebra was solidly fused by operation to the sacrum, there would remain the forward rotation of the upper sacrum at the sacroiliac joint. This would continue to place tension on the relaxed fibers of the iliolumbar and upper portion of the posterior sacroiliac ligaments, and frequently to a greater degree than before the fusion was performed."[2]

Dr. Hackett in the 1930s could see that spinal operations were not the answer to the chronic pain problem, and this was the impetus for him to look elsewhere for the answer. As he puts it, "No spinal fusion operation in the past has survived its originator, nor will probably any now in vogue, nor any in the future, for **most fusion operations impair function and usually result in limited activity and continued discomfort**. Eighteen years ago, I decided that much of the low back pain and disability was due to relaxation of the articular ligaments and considered methods of strengthening them. Having had some experience in operation on cases of hernia, which had previously been injected with a proliferating solution, I was impressed with the increased density and strength of the tissues which were encountered. I applied the proliferating injection treatment to the relaxed ligaments by injecting the solution within the fibrous bands, and within a short time I was impressed with the clinical results obtained and the patients were most enthusiastic."[2]

Prolotherapy: The Treatment

George S. Hackett, M.D., coined the term Prolotherapy, fine-tuned the technique, and taught it to other physicians. **(See Figure 3-2.)** As he describes it,

> "The treatment consists of the injection of a solution within the relaxed ligament and tendon which will stimulate the production of new fibrous tissue and bone cells that will strengthen the 'weld' of fibrous tissue and bone to stabilize the articulation and permanently eliminate the disability.
>
> To the treatment of proliferating new cells, I have applied the name *Prolotherapy* from the word *proli* (Latin), meaning offspring; *proliferate*—to produce new cells in rapid succession (Webster's Dictionary). My definition of Prolotherapy as applied medically in the treatment of skeletal disability is 'the rehabilitation of an incompetent structure by the generation of new cellular tissue'...I have developed special techniques, particularly for lumbosacral and sacroiliac joint stabilization, that make possible the injection of a small portion of the solution at from 10 to 15 places against bone from one insertion of the sharp needle through the skin . . .

I am so confident of my diagnosis, the depth of the ligament, and my tactile sensation that I usually only use the proliferant combined with the anesthetic solution and no anesthetic solution alone before entering the ligament or tendon. Usually the needle is inserted at the trigger point of either ligament or tendon until the point of the needle contacts bone. The local pain is reproduced, confirming the diagnosis. The proliferating solution is injected while the point of the needle is held against the bone." [2]

PROLOTHERAPY: THE HISTOLOGY

Histology might also be called microscopic anatomy. When put under a microscope, does Prolotherapy do everything that Dr. Hackett claims? He didn't wait to find out—he did most of the research on it himself! As he explains, "There was a need for this investigation because, although both the patients and I were satisfied that the clinical results of proliferation of ligaments in the stabilization of relaxed joints were entirely satisfactory, it became increasingly evident that **some physicians were skeptical of the method**. Also, no previous scientific work had been done which demonstrated the volume of strong fibrous tissue which could be generated by the introduction of a proliferant within the articular ligaments."[2]

Much of the research that Dr. Hackett performed was done in the 1950s on rabbit tendons. The first investigation was done using Sylnasol, a fatty acid proliferant, on the gastrocnemius and superficial flexor tendons, analogous to the Achilles tendon in man.[3] Microscopic slides were made through sections from the rabbit tendons following the Prolotherapy injection at various time intervals. The injections of proliferating solution were distributed throughout the tendon from its origin in the muscle to its insertion into the bone. The second injection was given six weeks after the first, and the third or last injection was given five months after

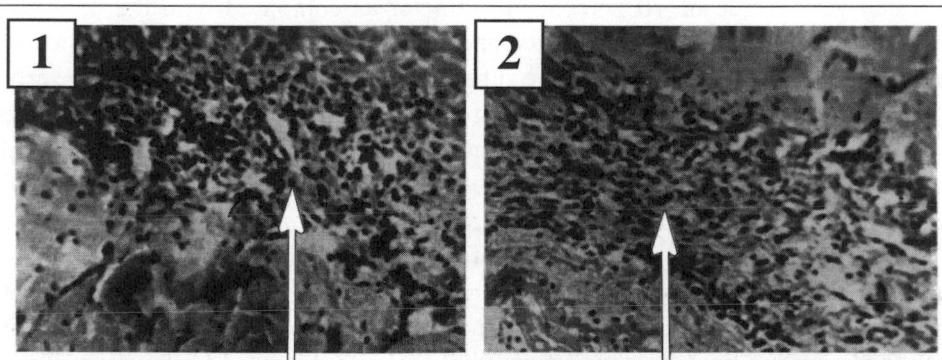

Figure 3-3: Microphotographs of sections from rabbit Achilles tendons following the injection of the proliferant, Sylnasol. The same technique was done as that which is used clinically.

1. Arrow points to moderate infiltration of lymphocytes 48 hours after injection of proliferating solution. Note absence of cell-death in surrounding tissues.
2. Beginning fibroblastic organization present in adjacent tissues. Arrow points to capillary proliferation with moderate infiltration of lymphocytes. *Two weeks after injection, this microphotograph shows new tissue growth.*

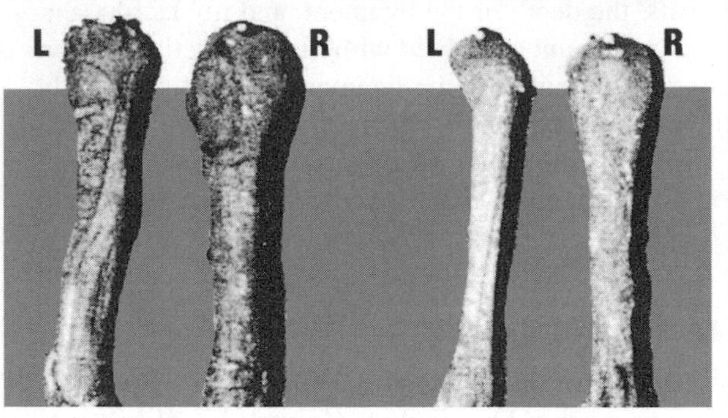

Figure 3-4: Photograph of Rabbit Tendons at Nine and 12 Months after Three Injections of Proliferating Solution into the Right Tendons

Left, controls; *right,* proliferated. The tendons on the right reveal an increase in diameter of 40 percent, which is estimated to double the strength of the tendon. The upper portion reveals the attachment of the ligament to the bone, which has increased 30 percent in diameter. The proliferating solution stimulates the production of new fibrous connective tissue cells, which become organized into permanent non-elastic fibrous tissue.

the first, so that animals in all cases under two months' duration received only one injection, those under five months received two injections, and the longer cases received a total of three injections. The results of the experiments showed that there was **no** necrosis of any of the specimens and **no** destruction of any nerves, blood vessels or tendinous bands. It became evident from the histology that Prolotherapy stimulated the **normal inflammatory reaction. (See Figure 3-3.)**

Figure 3-4 shows the right and left tendons of two rabbits after nine and 12 months of proliferating treatment. In both cases, the left tendon was not injected and was used as a control. The right tendon in each case received three injections. At the end of nine and 12 months, the injected right tendons in each case revealed an increase of 40 percent in diameter as compared with the controls, while the end of the bone with the attached tendon disclosed a 30 percent increase in diameter. **Figure 3-5** shows the proximal end of the tibial tarsal bone of the rabbit with the attached gastrocnemius and superficial flexor tendons. The films were made at one and three months after a single injection of proliferant solution had been distributed. It reveals that soft tissue increase at one month is pronounced due to the presence of inflammatory reaction, while at three months the increase is due to the production of permanent fibrous tissue. It also reveals a marked increase of bone at one month, as compared with the control, and a further increase of bone at three months. The increase of bone is significant because it results in a strong fibro-osseous union where sprains, tears, and relaxation of the ligament take place during proliferation.[3] Prolotherapy, besides inducing tendon growth and bone growth, was indeed causing fibro-osseous proliferation, just as Dr. Hackett said. **(See Figure 3-6.)**

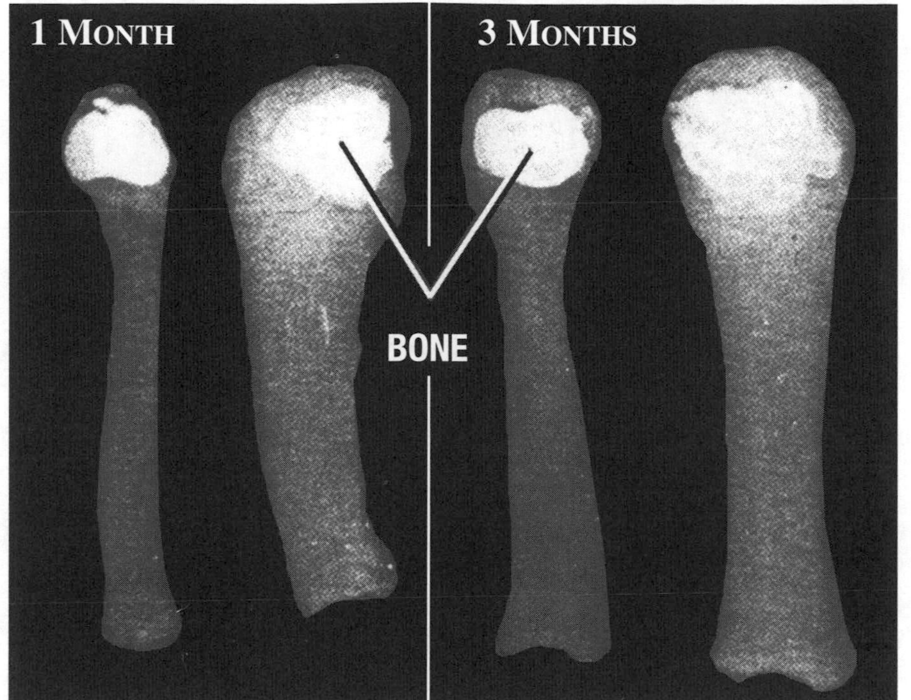

Figure 3-5: Roentgenograms of the Proximal End of the Tibial Tarsal Bone of the Rabbit with the Attached Gastrocnemius and Superficial Flexor Tendons

The films were made one and three months after a single injection of proliferant solution had been distributed throughout the tendon.

They reveal a marked increase of bone at one month, as compared with the control, and a further increase of bone at three months.

The increase in soft tissue at one month was pronounced, due to the presence of new fibrous tissue cells, while at three months the increase was due to the production of permanent fibrous tissue.

The increase of bone was significant because it resulted in a strong fibro-osseous union ("weld") where sprains, tears, and relaxation of the ligament chiefly take place and where the sensory nerves are abundant.

Prolotherapy: The Solutions

After 21 years of clinical experience and eight years of doing animal experiments, Dr. Hackett published a study on the use of various solutions to induce fibro-osseous proliferation.[4] In regard to the technique of fibro-osseous proliferation he says, "The technic [technique] consists of injecting a combined proliferating and local anesthetic solution within the weak fibro-osseous attachment. A few drops are distributed in proximate positions while the point of the needle contacts bone. The new bone and fibrous tissue cells become strong in four to six weeks. The patient returns for re-evaluation in eight weeks and additional injec-

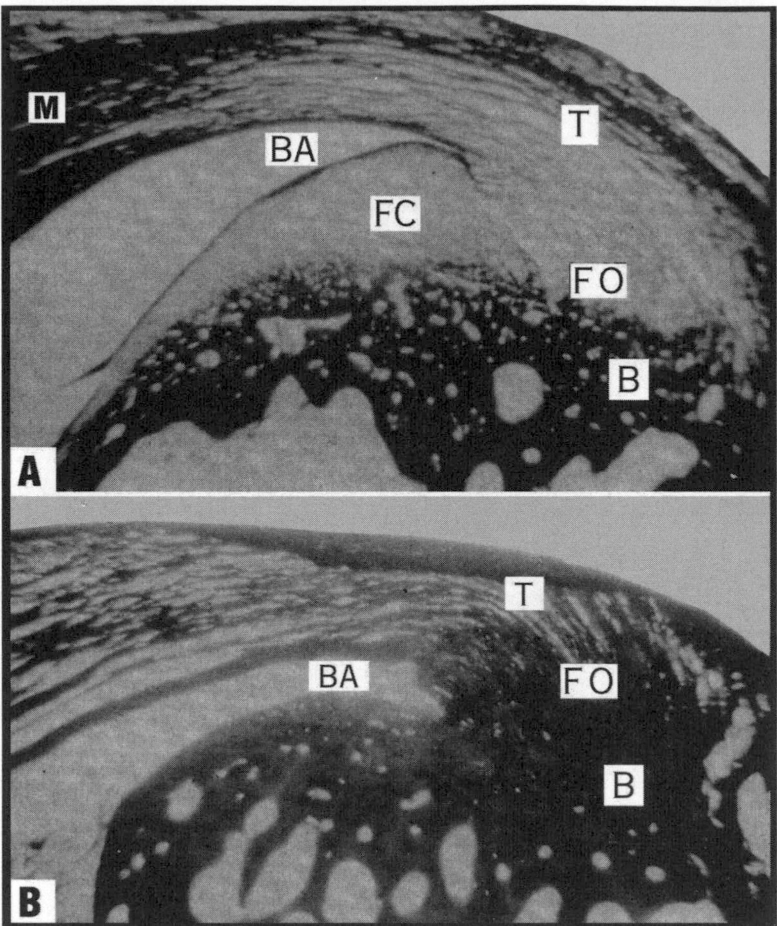

Figure 3-6: Microphotographs of Induced Fibro-Osseous Proliferation Bone—B, Tendon—T, Muscle—M, Fibro-Osseous Junction—FO, Fibrocartilage—FC, Bursal Area—BA

Microphotographs of decalcified Achilles tendon attachments to the tibio-tarsal bones of a rabbit, two months after one injection of 0.5 cc of a proliferating solution (Sylnasol 25 percent in Pontocaine) was made into the right leg [B]. The injection was made against bone within the fibro-osseous attachment of the tendon. The control left leg [A] was not injected.

A. Control leg (above)—The tendon fibers (T) blend with the periosteum and continue into bone (B). They are firmly attached by calcification which extends outward into the fibro-osseous junction (FO).

B. Injected leg (below)—Proliferated new bone cells increase bone density (B), extend outward, and increase the area and density of the fibro-osseous junction (FO), and encroach on the fibrocartilage (FC) and bursal area (BA), without penetrating the tendon capsular sheath. The weld of tendon to bone is strengthened.

tions are given when indicated."[4] The study consisted of injections of proliferant within joints, at the site of fractures, at fibro-osseous junctions, and intrathecally (to monitor safety) in rabbits. Dr. Hackett noted that even when the Prolotherapy solution was injected into the spinal canal that no noticeable effect was seen. When purposely increasing the dose into the spinal canal, again no long-term consequences were found. In regard to healing fractures, he showed that Prolotherapy could hasten healing with the zinc sulfate and Sylnasol solutions. He found that cortisone had an inhibitory effect.

RATING SCALE:

0 = control or no growth, 1 = slight growth,
2-4 = moderate growth,
5 = maximum growth or proliferation

SOLUTION USED:	FIBRO-OSSEOUS PROLIFERATION
Controls	0
Sylnasol 33 % in Saline	5
Sylnasol 25 % in Pontocaine	4
Sylnasol 25 % in Pontocaine w/Cortisone	1
Zinc Sulfate (stock solution)	5
Calcium Gluconate	1
Cortisone	0
Silica Crystals	5
Silica Oxidate	3
Whole Blood	1
Effect of Daily Exercise	1

Figure 3-7: Dr. George S. Hackett's Animal Research

Dr. George Hackett showed that Prolotherapy caused ligament and tendon growth, whereas cortisone did not.

Dr. Hackett was mainly concerned with documenting fibro-osseous proliferation. He, therefore, used 192 rabbit Achilles tendons to determine the amount of new bone and fibrous tissue that was induced over variable periods from a few days to one year, following one or more injections of various solutions into the fibro-osseous junction of tendon to bone. **Figure 3-6** shows the comparative fibro-osseous proliferation that resulted over a period of eight weeks following a single injection of 0.5 cc of various solutions. Again, various solutions were found successful in inducing fibro-osseous proliferation. **(See Figure 3-7.)** In regards to the strength of the proliferation, he found Sylnasol, silica, and zinc sulfate to work the best. The proliferants Sotradegol, Varisol, Q.U., and whole blood were modest in their proliferative effect. Calcium gluconate and daily exercise had minimal proliferating capabilities. Cortisone and estrogen had none. Cortisone, however, is not neutral but inhibitory. This can best be seen in the x-ray studies shown in **Figure 3-8**.

PROLOTHERAPY: THE REFERRAL PATTERNS

Besides doing the animal research which showed that fibro-osseous proliferation was possible, Dr. Hackett discovered a technique by which ligament and tendon relaxation could be documented. He describes it this way, "Ligament and tendon relaxation is diagnosed when trigger point tenderness is demonstrated by pressing the **thumb** over the attachment to bone. The diagnosis is invariably confirmed by intraligamentous injection of a local anesthetic solution. The anesthetic produces intense pain, which disappears within two minutes as the anesthetic takes effect. Knowledge of areas in which individual ligaments may produce referred pain is extremely valuable in diagnosis, as attention may be directed to the specific ligaments from which the pain originates. Dermatomes of referred pain have been determined from observations that were made while giving approximately **20,000** intraligamentous injections in diagnosis and treating ligament and tendon relaxation in 1,816 patients over a 20-year period."[5] **(See Figures 2-2, 2-3, 2-4.)**

For the Prolotherapist and the person in chronic pain, knowing the ligament referral patterns helps in determining the pain-producing structure. Then, by reproducing the pain during Prolotherapy and/or relieving the pain immediately after Prolotherapy (because of the anesthetic in the solution), the diagnosis is confirmed. This gives the patient and the doctor confidence that the correct structures were treated and a positive outcome will occur.

PROLOTHERAPY: THE RESULTS

In regards to a medical therapeutic intervention, perhaps the most important factor is the benefit to side-effect ratio. Is there an excellent chance of benefit with very little risk of harm? It is clear from Dr. Hackett's research that the answer is a

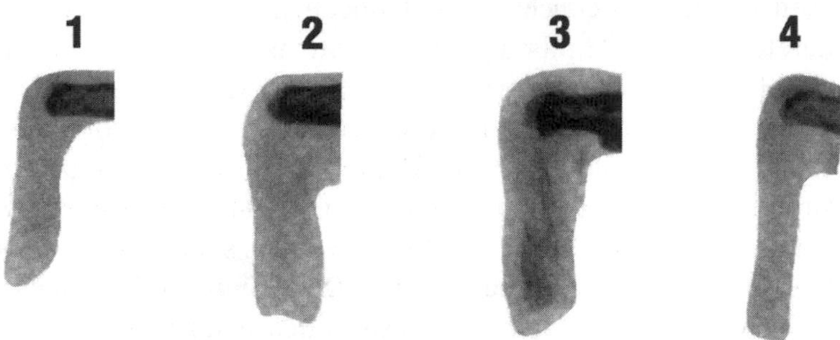

Figure 3-8: X-Rays of Induced Fibro-Osseous Proliferation

1. CONTROL 2. SYLNASOL 3. ZINC SULFATE 4. ZINC SULFATE + CORTISONE

X-rays of the Achilles tendon attachment to the tibio-tarsal bone of a rabbit, one month after one intraligamentous injection of 0.5 cc of fibro-osseous proliferants.

1. CONTROL. A faint shadow reveals bone extending into the tendons at the fibro-osseous junction where the tendon fibers enter the end of the bone and are firmly attached by ossification.

2. and 3. INJECTIONS OF SYLNASOL AND ZINC SULFATE solutions have stimulated the proliferation of new bone as revealed by bone enlargement and increased density, which also extends further within the tendon where ossification of the fibers strengthens the weld of tendon to bone.

4. INJECTION OF ZINC SULFATE AND CORTISONE SOLUTIONS combined (3 to 1) reveal that cortisone inhibited the proliferative action of the zinc sulfate solution.

TELEPHONE (708) 848-7773

G. A. HEMWALL, M.D.
715 LAKE STREET
OAK PARK, ILL. 60302

TO WHOM IT MAY CONCERN:

In 1955, I attended the annual AMA meeting in Atlantic City and in the Scientific Exhibits, Dr. George Hackett had an exhibit on Prolotherapy. I purchased his book and started to use the procedure with great success. In December, 1955 at the mid-year meeting of the AMA, I met Dr. Hackett again and he invited me to come and study with him in Canton, Ohio, which I did. We became friends, and I travelled with him to help in his exhibits. Later, with a few other doctors, we founded the Prolotherapy Association to further the teaching of the procedure.

Since that time, I have treated about 8000 patients in the U.S.A. and around the world with a 90% rate of cure or marked improvement of cases of head, neck, shoulder, low back, temporo-mandibular and joint pain of the extremities. Teaching seminars are held in various parts of the country each year.

G. A. Hemwall

G.A.Hemwall, M.D.
Associate Professor
Rush University
College of Medicine

Figure 3-9: Letter from Dr. Hemwall Describing His Training and Long-Term Results

resounding yes. In his words, "In approximately 5,000 injections, no unfavourable incident has occurred."[6] "During a 21-year period, 1,857 patients with ligament/tendon disability were treated by Prolotherapy in our clinic and hospital. The technic of diagnosis and treatment was improved and extended from the low back to the occiput and into the extremities in collaboration with our colleagues to include several thousand patients in which a high degree of success continues. **Good to excellent results were reported by 90 percent**—82 consecutive patients with occipito-cervical disability treated by Prolotherapy during the past four years. There were no unfavorable sequelae."[7]

In a study of 206 traumatic headache patients done by Dr. Hackett and colleagues, 79 percent were completely relieved of their headaches and 89 percent of the participants in total had some decline in their headaches with the use of Prolotherapy.[8]

In regards to low back pain, Dr. Hackett found that about 90 percent of the patients had evidence of some type of ligament laxity, typically of the sacroiliac joint.[9,10] In one of his analyses, of the 1,857 patients treated for ligament laxity in the lower back, 1,583 experienced sacroiliac ligament relaxation.[11] In his experience, 82 percent of people with this condition are cured with Prolotherapy.[12] As he states it, "At the end of 14 years, a survey revealed that 82 percent of 1,178 patients treated with Prolotherapy considered themselves cured. I believe that I am now curing about 90 percent of the patients with instability of joints due to ligamentous relaxation to their satisfaction."[10] Guess where that last statement was published? Believe it or not, it was published in the *Journal of the American Medical Association* in 1957. A physician explained that in 82 percent of **chronic low back cases** the pain was cured by a simple, safe, office procedure, yet almost nobody in the medical profession paid attention. Nobody except a young Christian physician by the name of Gustav A. Hemwall, M.D.

Fortunately for us, Dr. Hackett taught Dr. Hemwall the technique in the mid-1950s. **(See Figure 3-9.)** After Dr. Hackett died in 1969 at the age of 81, it was Dr. Hemwall who, until his death at the age of 90 in 1998, taught the majority of physicians the technique of Prolotherapy. **(See Figure 3-10.)** This is why the technique of Prolotherapy utilized at Caring Medical is called the "Hackett-Hemwall Technique of Prolotherapy." Ross wonders if Dr. Hemwall taught him the technique of Prolotherapy and turned his practice over to Ross because his last name started with "H"—so eventually it would be known as the "Hackett-Hemwall-Hauser Technique of Prolotherapy."

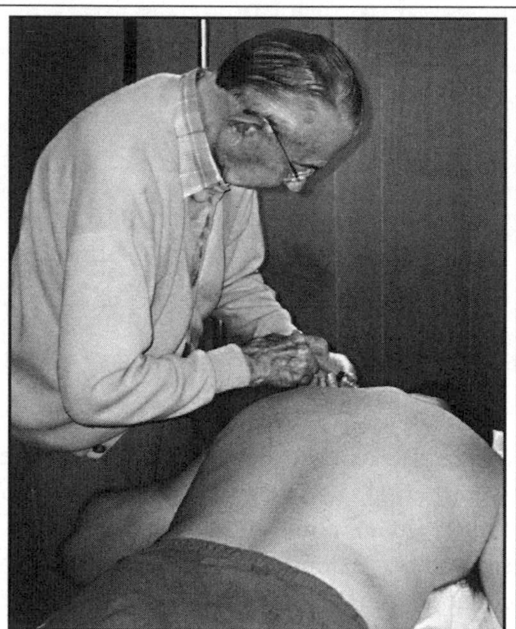

Figure 3-10: Dr. Hemwall doing what he did best—injecting and teaching Prolotherapy. *(Taken at Prolotherapy Course, Beulah Land Natural Medicine Clinic, 1998)*

SUMMARY: THE PROLOTHERAPY PIONEER

Those suffering from chronic pain owe George S. Hackett, M.D., a great debt, as do all practitioners of Prolotherapy. His contribution to the field of pain management and Prolotherapy are monumental. Included in his achievements and discoveries are the following:

- coined the term Prolotherapy
- showed through microscopic examination that Prolotherapy caused tendon growth
- documented histologically and via x-ray that Prolotherapy induced fibro-osseous proliferation
- quantified the amounts of tendon and fibro-osseous growth with various solutions
- proved cortisone inhibited fibro-osseous proliferation
- showed the safety through microscopic examination of the various proliferating solutions that he used
- discovered the referral pain patterns of the ligaments of the neck and lower back
- published his research in peer-reviewed journals
- presented his research at American Medical Association conventions
- documented the response of his patients over many years
- wrote a book on Prolotherapy and printed three editions
- taught the technique of Prolotherapy to other physicians
- presented Prolotherapy at various medical meetings across the country
- helped start The Prolotherapy Association
- over many decades followed his patients to prove that Prolotherapy does indeed cure chronic pain

The story of George S. Hackett, M.D., has not been made into a Hollywood movie, because his technique of fibro-osseous proliferation is, in large part, ignored. One does wonder what the world would be like without headaches, back aches, or chronic pain. For that matter, what would your life be like without suffering from daily chronic pain? The powers that be may not shout out his name, but for the person who has seen Prolotherapy work or felt its benefits, to you, Dr. George S. Hackett, we say a most heart-felt "thank you." ■

CHAPTER 4

Why Prolotherapy Works

"A joint is only as strong as its weakest ligament."
—George S. Hackett, M.D.

Simply put, pain is due to weakness. If Ross and our buddy Joe were to pick up a piano, we can guarantee they wouldn't be holding it long. After a few seconds, Joe's back would be hurting and about everything on Ross would be aching. We would be in pain because, unlike Hercules, we are too weak to lift a piano. Likewise, most neck, back, and other musculoskeletal pains are due to weakness, specifically weakness in the ligaments and tendons.

"Ligament relaxation is a condition in which the strength of the ligament fibers has become impaired so that a stretching of the fibrous strands occurs when the ligament is submitted to normal or less than normal tension."[1] This statement was made 40 years ago by George S. Hackett, M.D., who believed chronic pain was simply due to ligament weakness in and around the joint. Dr. Hackett coined the phrase "ligament and tendon relaxation," which is synonymous with ligament and tendon weakness, and subsequently developed the treatment known as Prolotherapy.

PROLOTHERAPY DEFINED

Webster's Third New International Dictionary defines Prolotherapy as "the rehabilitation of an incompetent structure, such as a ligament or tendon, by the induced proliferation of new cells."[2] Prolotherapy is the injection of substances at the site where ligaments and tendons attach to the bone, thus stimulating the ligaments and tendons to proliferate or grow at the injection site. This area is called the fibro-osseous junction. "Fibro" means fibrous tissue, which forms the ligament or tendon, and "osseous" refers to the bone.

Prolotherapy works because it addresses and corrects the root cause of chronic pain: ligament and tendon relaxation.

LIGAMENTS AND TENDONS

A strain is defined as a stretched or injured tendon. A sprain is a stretched or injured ligament. Blood flow is vital to the body's healing process and, because ligaments and tendons have naturally poor blood supply, incomplete healing may result after an injury to that structure.[3, 4] This incomplete healing results in decreased strength of the area. The ligaments and tendons, normally taut and thus strong bands of fibrous or connective tissue, become relaxed and weak. The weakened ligament or tendon then becomes the source of the chronic pain.

Ligaments and tendons are bands of tissue consisting of various amino acids in a matrix called collagen. Tendons attach the muscles to the surface of the bone,

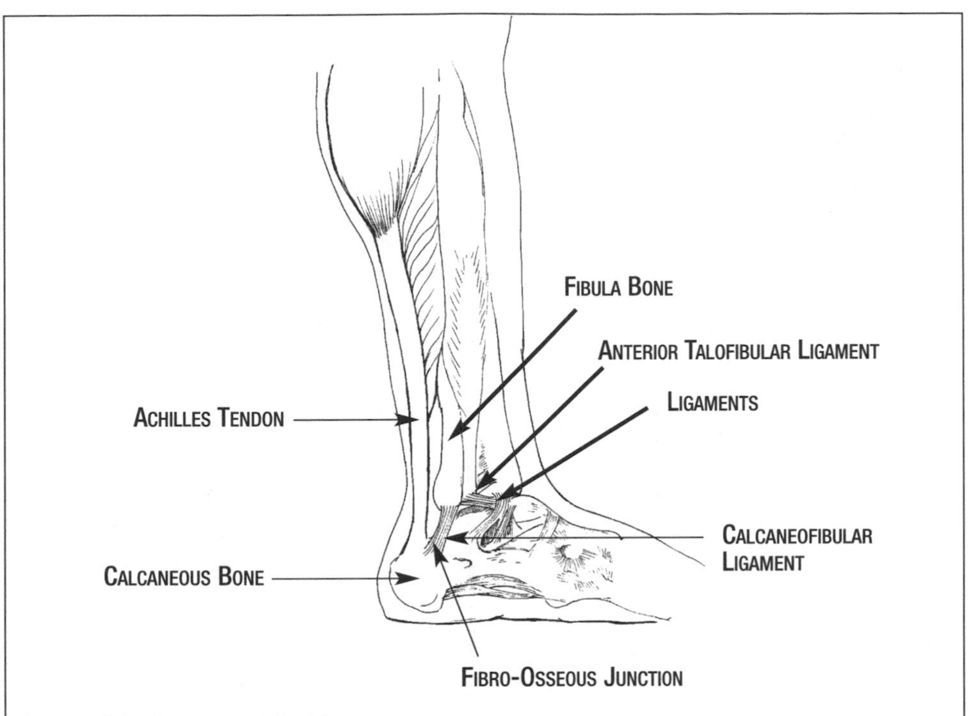

Figure 4-1: Anatomy of the Foot
The fibro-osseous junction is the area where ligaments and tendons attach to the bone.

enabling movement of the joints and bones. Ligaments attach one bone to another, thus preventing over-extension of bones and joints. **(See Figure 4-1.)**

Damage to ligaments and tendons will cause excessive movement of the joints, resulting in chronic pain. Damage to ligaments causes joints to become loose or weak and often manifests itself with a cracking sensation during movement. Tendon weakness produces painful and weak joints.

For example, there are many causes of chronic elbow pain, including tennis elbow (extensor tendonitis), annular ligament sprain, and biceps muscle strain. Since muscle, ligament, or tendon injury can all cause pain, a proper diagnosis is needed to permanently alleviate the pain. Tennis elbow is diagnosed when the physician notices weakness and pain with wrist extension and tenderness at the elbow where the extensor tendons attach. Annular ligament sprain is diagnosed by the physician palpating this ligament in the elbow and eliciting a positive "jump sign." **(See Figure 4-2.)**

Another source of elbow pain is biceps muscle strain. When the biceps tendon is weak, resisted flexion (resisting the upward movement of the forearm) of the elbow is painful. Since the bicep muscle flexes at the elbow, carrying a box or turning a screwdriver may produce the painful symptoms associated with strain or weakness of this muscle. Since the extensor tendons, bicep muscle, and annular lig-

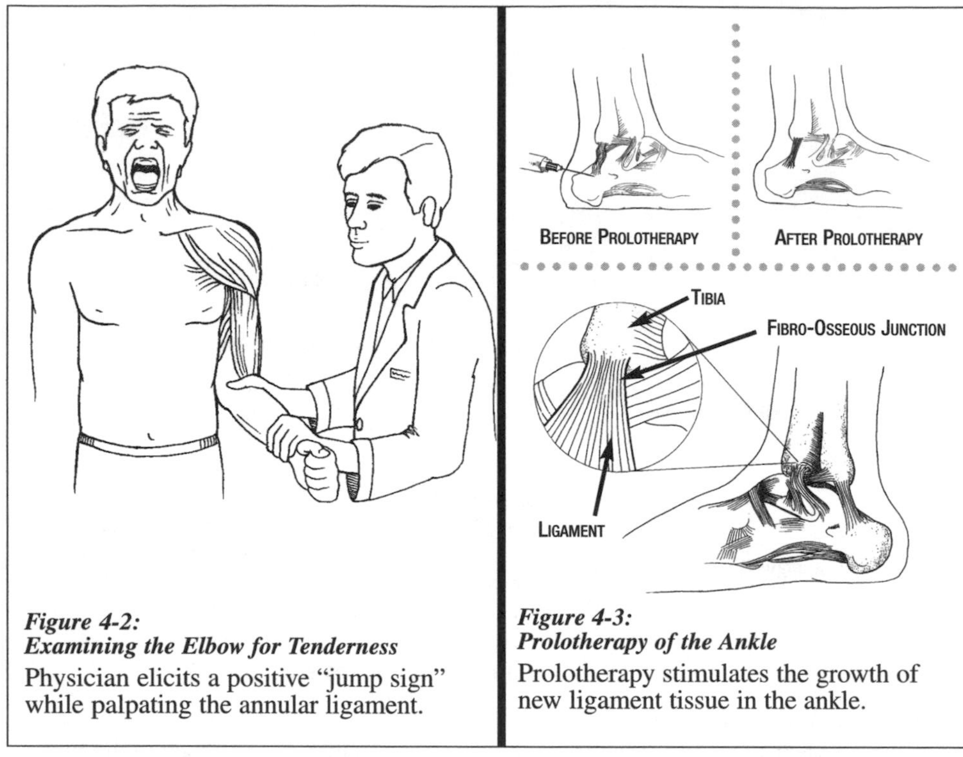

Figure 4-2:
Examining the Elbow for Tenderness
Physician elicits a positive "jump sign" while palpating the annular ligament.

Figure 4-3:
Prolotherapy of the Ankle
Prolotherapy stimulates the growth of new ligament tissue in the ankle.

ament all attach to the bone in the elbow, good palpatory skills are necessary for proper diagnosis. Prolotherapy is given at the fibro-osseous junction where the positive "jump sign" is elicited. Prolotherapy causes proliferation, or growth of tissue at this point. **(See Figure 4-3.)** Prolotherapy will strengthen the muscle, tendon, or ligament tissue at the fibro-osseous junction, which is needed to alleviate pain.

WHAT ARE LIGAMENTS AND TENDONS?

The most sensitive structures that produce pain according to Daniel Kayfetz, M.D., are the periosteum and the ligaments. It is important to note that in the scale of pain sensitivity (which part of the body hurts more when injured), Dr. Kayfetz notes that the periosteum (outer layer of bone) ranks first, followed by ligaments, tendons, fascia (the connective tissue that surrounds muscle), and finally muscle. Articular (joint) cartilage contains no sensory nerve endings. The area where the ligaments attach to the bone is the fibro-osseous junction. This is why injury to this area is so significant. It causes massive amounts of pain. This is where the Prolotherapy injections occur and thus the strengthening of these areas and subsequent relief of pain.[5]

Ligaments provide stability of the joints. If joints move too much, the bones may compress or pinch nerves or blood vessels, resulting in permanent nerve damage. Weakened structures are strengthened by the growth of new, strong ligament and tendon tissue induced by the Prolotherapy injections. This is illustrated in a relatively common back condition called spondylolisthesis. A weak area of bone, in conjunction with stretched ligaments, allow vertebrae to slip and pinch a nerve, resulting in terrible back pain and radiating pain down the leg. Prolotherapy strengthens the weakened areas and realigns the vertebrae, relieving the pinched nerve and eliminating the chronic pain. **(See Figures 4-4A and 4-4B.)**

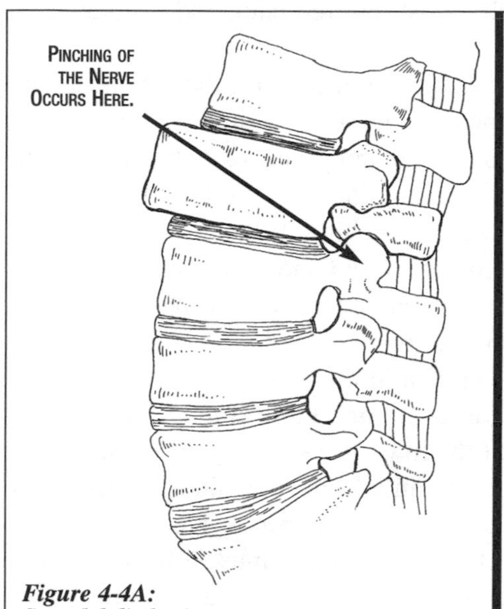
PINCHING OF
THE NERVE
OCCURS HERE.

Figure 4-4A: Spondylolisthesis— Slippage of the Vertebrae

Weakened ligaments lead to spondylolisthesis and pinching of the nerves.

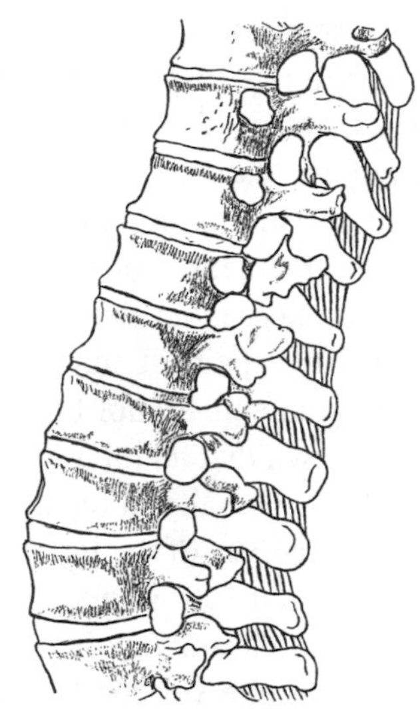

Figure 4-4B: Proper Vertebral Alignment After Prolotherapy

Prolotherapy strengthens the ligaments and joints that support the vertebrae to move into proper alignment and relieves nerve pinching.

The Role of Prolotherapy

Prolotherapy permanently strengthens tissue. Strengthening weakened structures produces permanent pain relief. Prolotherapy effectively eliminates pain because it attacks the source of the pain: the fibro-osseous junction, an area rich in sensory nerves.[6, 7] When a weakened ligament or tendon is stretched, the sensory nerves become irritated, causing local and referred pain throughout the body. These referred pain patterns of ligaments were outlined in Dr. Hackett's observations after he performed more than 18,000 intraligamentous injections to 1,656 patients over a period of 19 years.[8]

A referred pain occurs when a local ligament injury sends pain to another area of the body. Dr. Hackett described the referral patterns of the ligaments involving the hip, pelvis, lower back, and neck. **(See Figures 2-2, 2-3, 2-4.)** Physical therapists, chiropractors, family physicians, and orthopedists are usually unaware of ligament referral pain patterns. From the illustration, note that the hip ligaments refer pain to the big toe. The sacroiliac ligaments refer pain to the lateral foot, which causes the symptoms resulting in a common misdiagnosis of "sciatica." Pain traveling down the back into the leg and foot is usually from ligament weakness in the sacroiliac joint, not pinching of the sciatic nerve. Patients who are misdiagnosed with "sciatica" are often subjected to numerous tests, anti-inflammatory medicines, and surgical procedures with unsatisfactory results. Prolotherapy eliminates the local ligament pain, as well as the referred pain, and is curative in most cases of sciatica.

Ligament injuries may cause crushing severe pain because the ligaments are full of nerves, some of the nerve tissue being free nerve endings.[9, 10] Movement may aggravate the damaged nerve in the ligament and produces a shock-like sensation, giving the impression that a nerve is being pinched. It is a nerve-type pain that is due to a ligament stretching, not a nerve pinching. When a weak ligament is stretched, the nerves inside the ligament often send shock-like pain to distant sites, as in sciatica pain. If the ligament is strengthened with Prolotherapy, the nerves in the ligaments do not fire, thereby relieving the pain.

It is well known that an injury in one segment of the body can affect other distant body parts, especially in regard to ligament injury. For example, when dye is injected into the nerves of the ligaments of the lower neck, the dye will travel four segments above and four segments below the initial injection site. The dye may be seen in the autonomic (sympathetic) nerves in these areas.[11] This implies that ligament laxity at one vertebral level could manifest pain, muscle tension, adrenal, or automatic dysfunction four segments above or below the actual injury site. This is one of the explanations as to why ligament pain is often diffuse and can take on a burning quality.

Knowledge of referral pain patterns, along with a complete patient medical history, allows physicians who practice Prolotherapy to make accurate diagnoses of specific weak ligaments, even before performing an examination. A Prolotherapist, for example, may examine a back pain patient with pain radiating down the leg to the knee. This reveals that the source of the pain is likely the "A" and "B" areas of the sacroiliac ligaments. **(See Figures 2-3 and 2-4.)** Pain continuing to the lateral foot indicates weak "D" area sacroiliac ligaments. Pain radiating to the big toe reveals the source is in the hip area.

The physician examines the appropriate area utilizing his most important diagnostic tool—the thumb. We call it our personal **MRI** scanner: **M**y **R**eproducibility **I**nstrument. A diagnosis is made when a positive "jump sign" is observed. This occurs when the injured ligament is palpated, causing the patient to jump off the examination table due to the severe tenderness of the ligament. The pain is caused by something between the pressing thumb and the bone. The something between these two areas is the ligament. **(See Figure 4-5.)** The positive "jump sign" gives both patient and physician confidence that the pain-producing structure has been identified. Ligament injuries are often not detected with CAT or MRI scans

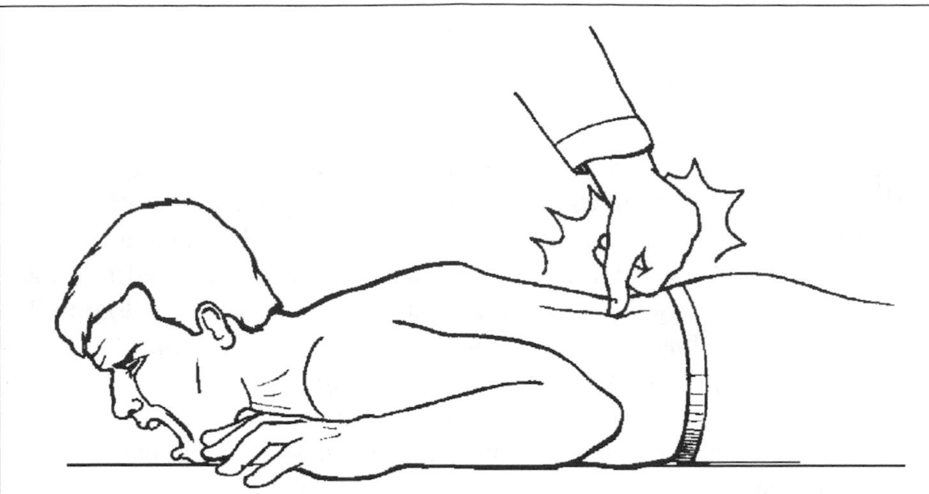

Figure 4-5: Physician Eliciting a Positive "Jump Sign"
The best **MRI** scanner is **M**y **R**eproducibility **I**nstrument—which is the thumb.

because ligaments are such small structures. If a positive "jump sign" can be elicited, then permanent pain relief with Prolotherapy is likely.

Prolotherapy is so successful because it attacks the root cause of chronic pain, which is most commonly ligament laxity (weakness). Signs of ligament laxity or injury are the following:

- chronic pain
- referral pain patterns
- tender areas
- positive "jump signs"
- pain aggravated by movement
- cracking sensation in the joint when moved
- chronic subluxation
- temporary help from physical therapy, massage, or chiropractic manipulation

Prolotherapy helps strengthen chronically weak ligaments and relieves all of the above. In summary, Prolotherapy works by permanently strengthening the ligament, muscle, and tendon attachments to the bone—the fibro-osseous junction. Because the cause of pain is addressed, Prolotherapy is often curative. ■

CHAPTER 5

Prolotherapy Provides Results

Prolotherapy is effective because it attacks and eliminates the root cause of chronic pain: ligament and tendon relaxation. Ligament relaxation causes joints to loosen. A weak ligament will have difficulty holding a joint in place. The nerve fibers within the weakened ligament are activated and cause local pain. They may also cause a referred pain pattern as shown in **Figure 2-4.** The muscles surrounding the loose ligament contract to help stabilize the joint—the reason why people with loose ligaments and chronic pain have tight, painful muscles. Only when the weakened ligaments are strengthened will the local and referred pain patterns, as well as the muscle pain, subside. The same is true for tendon weakness.

Research has been conducted exhibiting the effectiveness of Prolotherapy. The following studies are just a sample of the research that has been done during the past 40 years.

GEORGE S. HACKETT, M.D.

Although chronic pain has many causes, the vast majority of chronic pain sufferers have loose joints caused by ligament weakness. This is evidenced by Dr. Hackett's research study described in the third edition of his book, *Ligament and Tendon Relaxation Treated by Prolotherapy*, published in 1958.[1] The study consisted of the following:

- sample size: 656 patients
- patient age range: 15 to 88 years old
- duration of pain prior to treatment: three months to 65 years
- average duration of pain prior to treatment: four-and-a-half years
- duration of study: 19 years
- number of injections given: 18,000

Twelve years after the Prolotherapy treatment was completed, 82 percent of the patients considered themselves cured. Dr. Hackett believed that the cure rate with Prolotherapy was over 90 percent due to improvements in the technique over the years.

In 1955, Dr. Hackett analyzed 146 consecutive cases of undiagnosed low back disability during a two-month period. He found that 94 percent of the patients experienced joint ligament relaxation. In 1956, a similar survey of 124 consecutive cases of undiagnosed low back disability revealed that 97 percent of patients possessed joint instability from ligament weakness. The sacroiliac ligaments were involved in 75 percent of the low back ligament laxity cases. The lumbosacral ligaments were involved in 54 percent. He also noted that approximately 50 percent had already undergone back surgery for a previous diagnosis of a disc problem.[2]

At this time, Prolotherapy produced an 80 percent cure rate even though 50 percent of the people treated had undergone back surgery. Obviously, the surgical procedures did not relieve the patients' back pain. Rarely does a disc problem cause disabling back pain. Chronic pain in the lower back is most commonly due to ligament weakness—the reason Prolotherapy is so effective.

Dr. Hackett attributed ineffective response to Prolotherapy to the following:

- inability to clearly confirm the diagnosis by the injection of a local anesthetic solution
- failure of the patient to return for completion of the treatment
- treatment in the presence of another disability
- a less refined technique and less experience in the earlier studies
- lowered morale from years of suffering and disappointment from unsuccessful treatments and dependence on prescription pain medications
- non-responsiveness to the stimulation of proliferation.

Prolotherapy works because it causes ligament and tendon growth. Dr. Hackett used Sylnasol, a sodium salt fatty acid, as a proliferant in his original work. Animals were given between one and three injections of the proliferating solution into the tendon and the fibro-osseous junction. There was no necrosis (dead tissue) noted in any of the specimens. No destruction of nerves, blood vessels, or tendinous bands was noted. Compared to non-injected tendons, tendons treated with Prolotherapy showed a 40 percent increase in diameter. The fibro-osseous junction, where the tendon attaches to bone, increased by 30 percent, forming permanent tendon tissue. Dr. Hackett believed the 40-percent increase in diameter of the tendon represented a doubling of the tendon strength.[3]

GUSTAV A. HEMWALL, M.D.

Gustav A. Hemwall, M.D., learned the technique of Prolotherapy from Dr. Hackett and then proceeded to treat more than 10,000 patients worldwide. He collected data on 8,000 of those patients. In 1974, Dr. Hemwall presented his largest survey of 2,007 Prolotherapy patients to The Prolotherapy Association. The survey related the following:

- 1,871 patients completed treatment
- 6,000 Prolotherapy treatments were administered
- 1,399 patients (75.5 percent) reported complete recovery and cure
- 413 patients (24.3 percent) reported general improvement
- 25 patients (0.2 percent) showed no improvement
- 170 patients were lost to follow-up

More than 99 percent of the patients who completed treatment with Prolotherapy found relief from their chronic pain. These results are similar to those published by Dr. Hackett, showing that Prolotherapy is completely curative in many cases and provides some pain relief in nearly all.[4]

Y. KING LIU, PH.D.

In 1983, Y. King Liu performed a study using the knee ligament in rabbits.[5] This study was done to confirm Dr. Hackett's earlier work and better quantify the strength of the tissue formed by Prolotherapy. In this study, a five percent sodium morrhuate solution (an extract of cod liver oil) was injected into the femoral and tibial attachments of the medial collateral ligament (the inside knee ligament).

The ligaments were injected five times and then compared to non-injected ligaments. **(See Figure 5-1.)** The results showed that in every case Prolotherapy significantly increased ligamentous mass, thickness, and cross-sectional area as well as the ligament strength. In a six-week period, ligament mass increased by 44 percent, ligament thickness by 27 percent, and the ligament-bone junction strength by 28 percent. This research was yet another attestation to the effectiveness of Prolotherapy, showing that Prolotherapy actually causes new tissue to grow.

THE EFFECTS OF FIVE PROLOTHERAPY TREATMENTS TO THE MEDIAL COLLATERAL LIGAMENT

	Prolotherapy-Injected Ligaments	Saline-Injected Ligaments (Control)	% Change
Ligament Mass (mg)	132.2	89.7	44
Ligament Thickness (mm)	1.01	0.79	27
Ligament Mass Length (mg/mm)	6.45	4.39	47
Junction Strength (N)	119.1	93.5	28

Figure 5-1: The Effects of Five Prolotherapy Treatments to the Medial Collateral Ligament
Prolotherapy causes a statistically significant increase in ligament mass and strength as well as bone-ligament junction strength.

J.A. MAYNARD, M.D.

To confirm the work of Dr. Liu and describe how the proliferants in Prolotherapy grow tissue, J.A. Maynard, M.D., and associates, treated rabbit tendons with proliferant solutions. After the proliferant injections, the actual tendon circumferences increased an average of 20 to 25 percent after six weeks.

They found that "the increase in circumference appeared to be due to an increase in cell population (immune cells), water content, and ground substance (glue that holds the collagen together)...Consequently, not only is there an increase in the number of cells but also a wider variety of cell types, fibroblasts, neutrophils, lymphocytes, plasma cells, and unidentifiable cells in the injected tissues." [6]

The findings were similar to what normally occurs when injured tissue is repairing itself. Prolotherapy induces the normal healing mechanisms of the body. After Prolotherapy, there is increased circulation bringing with it not only nutrients, but cells. These immune cells then begin the growth of collagen tissue to rebuild the injured tissue. Eventually, new collagen tissue forms, creating stronger ligaments and tendons.[7]

ROBERT KLEIN, M.D.

In human studies, Robert Klein, M.D., and associates, administered a series of six weekly injections in the lower back ligamentous supporting structures with a proliferant solution containing dextrose, glycerin, and phenol. Biopsies performed three months after completion of injections showed statistically significant increases in collagen fiber and ligament diameter of 60 percent. Statistically significant improvements in pain relief and back motion were also observed.[8]

THOMAS DORMAN, M.D.

In a 1989 study, Thomas Dorman, M.D., noted, "I biopsied individuals before and after treatment with Prolotherapy and submitted the biopsy specimens to pathologists. Using modern analytic techniques, they showed that Prolotherapy caused regrowth of tissue, an increased number of fibroblast nuclei (the major cell type in ligaments and other connective tissue), an increased amount of collagen, and an absence of inflammatory changes or other types of tissue damage." [9]

Dr. Dorman performed a retrospective survey of 80 patients treated with Prolotherapy for cervical, thoracic, and lumbar spine pain, or a combination of these. Thirty-one percent of the patients had litigation or workers' compensation cases. The patients were evaluated up to five years after their Prolotherapy treatment. Analysis of the 80 patients showed a statistical significance of $P < .001$ for improvements in: **1.** severity of pain, **2.** daily living activities, and **3.** influence of sleep pattern. Prolotherapy was shown to eliminate pain, improve activity level, and help the patients get a good night's sleep.[10]

MILNE ONGLEY, M.D.

Using the same solution as Dr. Klein, Milne Ongley, M.D., and associates, demonstrated a stabilization of the collateral and cruciate ligaments of the knee joint with Prolotherapy. All subjects treated showed an increase in activity and reduction in pain.[11] Two double-blind studies where patients received either an injected proliferant solution or a solution without proliferant concluded that Prolotherapy was effective in eliminating pain.[12, 13]

A problem with controlled studies using Prolotherapy injections is that the control group still receives an injection, though without any proliferant. An injection into a tender area is a treatment utilized in pain management. The result is that the control group actually receives a therapeutic intervention. Despite these concerns, Prolotherapy in the above two studies was shown to be an effective treatment for chronic low back pain.

K. Dean Reeves, M.D., Modern-Day Prolotherapy Pioneer

Perhaps nobody has put more effort to get Prolotherapy accepted by modern-day allopathic medicine than K. Dean Reeves, M.D. Dr. Reeves is a Physical Medicine and Rehabiliation Specialist, in private practice, in Shawnee Mission, Kansas. He was fortunate to learn Prolotherapy from Dr. Gustav Hemwall and went on several missionary trips with him. He is one of the premiere lecturers, teachers, and researchers of the Hackett-Hemwall technique of Prolotherapy.

Dr. Reeves has helped Prolotherapy penetrate allopathic medicine by writing whole chapters on Prolotherapy that were published in mainstream medical journals and books including *Physical Medicine and Rehabilitation Clinics of North America*, *Physiatric Procedures*, and *Pain Procedures in Clinical Practice*.[14-16] Anyone desiring a clear, concise, scientifically sound explanation of Prolotherapy is encouraged to read Dr. Reeves' writings.

He was also the primary researcher performing two randomized, prospective, placebo-controlled, double-blind clinical trials of dextrose Prolotherapy injections on osteoarthritic joints.[17, 18] The first was on 77 patients (111 knees) who had radiographically confirmed evidence of symptomatic knee osteoarthritis.[17] These patients had an average weight of 193 pounds and pain for more than 10 years in the qualifying knees. This study included 38 knees with **no cartilage** remaining in at least one compartment.

Analysis revealed a statistically significant benefit from the Prolotherapy injections, over the control group. At six months, patients experienced less pain and swelling, fewer episodes of knee buckling, and an increase of knee flexion range of motion. Data from one year (after six bimonthly injections of Prolotherapy) revealed pain improvement of 44 percent, swelling improvement of 63 percent, knee buckling improvement of 85 percent, and a range-of-motion improvement in flexion of 14 degrees. X-rays at one year showed no progression of osteoarthritis and have been followed for three years to further confirm this. In the study, 62 percent of the people with ACL (anterior cruciate ligament) laxity were no longer lax at the conclusion of one year. The people with ACL laxity treated with Prolotherapy showed statistically significant improvements in rest pain, walking pain, stair-use pain, and swelling complaints.

Summary of Dr. Reeves' Studies

	Improvement from Prolotherapy
Knee Pain	44 %
Knee Swelling	63 %
Knee Buckling	85 %
Knee Motion (Degrees)	14 %
Finger Pain	53 %
Finger Motion (Degrees)	8 %

Figure 5-2: Summary of Prolotherapy Studies on Osteoarthritic Fingers and Knees

Dr. Reeves found that dextrose Prolotherapy significantly improved pain and function in osteoarthritic fingers and knees.

The second study was on 27 patients with finger osteoarthritis and an average age of 64 years.[18] One hundred fifty joints met the radiographic criteria and the symptom-duration criteria of more than six months of pain (average pain duration was more than four years). After three injections of 0.5 ml of dextrose Prolotherapy on either side of each symptomatic joint, pain with movement of fingers and flexion range of motion improved significantly in the Prolotherapy group compared to the control group. After six injections of dextrose Prolotherapy, pain improvement averaged 53 percent, and there was a range-of-motion gain of eight degrees. X-rays at one year showed a statistically significant improvement in joint narrowing score in the dextrose Prolotherapy group. **Figure 5-2** summarizes some of the findings of Dr. Reeves' Prolotherapy studies for osteoarthritis of the fingers and knees.

Robert Schwartz, M.D.

In another study by Robert Schwartz, M.D., on the effects of Prolotherapy on 43 patients with chronic low back pain who had been unresponsive to other treatments including surgery, Prolotherapy treatments were given over a six-week period into and around the sacroiliac joint. At two weeks, 20 of 43 patients reported 95 percent improvement, 31 of 43 patients reported 75 percent or better improvement, and 35 of 43 reported 66 percent or better improvement. Only three of 43 reported no improvement. The result of this study of chronic resistant low back pain revealed that 93 percent of the patients experienced pain relief with Prolotherapy after the six weeks.[19]

Harold Wilkinson, M.D.

Between 1979 and 1995, Harold Wilkinson, M.D., a professor and former chairman of the Division of Neurosurgery at the University of Massachusetts Medical Center, who has been practicing Prolotherapy for 30 years, gave 349 posterior iliac Prolotherapy injections for chronic low back pain. Generally, the patients had undergone prior spinal operations and had been referred to him because they were "failed back patients." In other words, no one could help them. Of the 349 injections, one injection totally relieved 29 percent of the patients, and a total of 76 percent of the patients received significant pain relief with one injection. A full 93 percent of the people received pain relief with only one Prolotherapy injection in the lower back.[20]

In regard to other areas of the body, besides the lower back, Dr. Wilkinson reported on results of 115 Prolotherapy injections. Forty-three percent of these completely eliminated the person's pain and 89 percent of the patients, with only one Prolotherapy injection, received some pain relief. Dr. Wilkinson, in compiling the data, stated that it was noteworthy that "a sizeable portion of people with unresolved chronic pain had more than a year's pain relief with only one Prolotherapy injection."

Dr. Wilkinson explained that exercise and massage help trigger points (tender points) originating from muscles by increasing blood circulation, but these treatments do not help ligamentous or periosteal (fibro-osseous) trigger points. This is because just increasing blood circulation is not enough to grow the new ligament tissue. Prolotherapy must be done to stimulate the growth of ligamentous tissue at the periosteal junction.

CONFIRMING DIAGNOSIS

There are two aspects by which the correct diagnosis can be completely and reliably confirmed without extensive tests. The first method involves palpating the area involved until a positive "jump sign" is elicited. If a patient's pain can be reproduced by manual palpation, the prognosis for complete relief with Prolotherapy is excellent.

The second method of confirming the diagnosis is by the Prolotherapy treatment itself. The Prolotherapy solution contains various proliferants along with an anesthetic. Prolotherapy is one of the few treatments that actually treats the condition while confirming the diagnosis. Since Prolotherapy injections are given where the ligaments and tendons attach to the bone (fibro-osseous junction) the patient will feel immediate pain relief after the treatment, if the diagnosis is correct. This is due to the effect of the local anesthetic blocking the pain coming from the injured ligaments and tendons. Immediate pain relief after Prolotherapy treatments, along with the reproducibility of the pain when the ligament or tendon is palpated, gives both the patient and the physician confidence that the diagnosis of ligament and tendon relaxation is correct.

SUMMARY

Prolotherapy works because an accurate diagnosis of ligament and tendon weakness can be confirmed by an appropriate patient history and a reproduction of the pain by direct palpation of the injured structure. The pain is immediately alleviated due to the effect of the anesthetic from the Prolotherapy solution. This provides further confirmation that the diagnosis of ligament and tendon relaxation is correct.

Prolotherapy causes a thickening of ligament and tendon tissue. This increases the strength of the ligament and tendon and causes the chronic pain to subside. According to Dr. Hackett and Dr. Hemwall, Prolotherapy is more than 90 percent effective in either eliminating chronic pain or significantly decreasing pain complaints. It is for these reasons that many people are *Curing their Chronic Pain with Prolotherapy!* ■

Chapter 6

Answers to Common Questions About Prolotherapy

After years of suffering from chronic pain, many people find it hard to believe that there is a treatment they haven't heard about, that it has the potential to cure them and, on top of it, has been around for 50 years. As hard as it is to believe, there is a treatment that can cure chronic pain and, yes, Prolotherapy has been around for 50 years.

We enjoy questions. Ross once asked Marion if she thought he was the greatest. She replied, "You're the greatest person I know to get us into a fiasco." That was not the answer he was looking for! Anyone contemplating any procedure, including Prolotherapy, should have all of their questions answered. They should also understand why they are getting the procedure and what it is supposed to accomplish.

1. Do Prolotherapy Injections Hurt?

As the saying goes with bodybuilders, it also goes with Prolotherapy, "No pain, no gain." Shots are shots. "Do they hurt?" every new patient asks, as sweat begins to form on the patient's forehead and palms as the needle approaches its target. Let us put it to you this way—our patients begin to sweat when they see us in the grocery store. We don't know why—we're nice people! All doctors were taught the appropriate answer to this question in medical school: "It hurts a little." Does anything the doctor sticks you with really hurt just a little? Some people have many Prolotherapy injections and do not flinch, while others receive a few shots and have a rough time.

A good friend and an expert in orthopedic medicine, Rodney Van Pelt, M.D., told us the following story about his first Prolotherapy experience. He once attended a conference where Gustav A. Hemwall, M.D., the world's most experienced Prolotherapist, discussed the technique and asked for a volunteer to help illustrate an actual Prolotherapy procedure. So, Dr. Van Pelt, being the adventuresome Californian that he is, jumped out of his seat and volunteered.

For many years, Dr. Van Pelt had suffered from back pain without finding a curative treatment. Due to the deteriorated state of his back, he required quite a number of Prolotherapy injections. Before Dr. Hemwall had finished the treatment, the pain from the injections caused Dr. Van Pelt to pass out. Dr. Hemwall just went on injecting and instructing the physicians on the use of Prolotherapy for chronic low back pain. He then informed the audience that he would rather treat 100 women than one man.

Let's face it. God made women able to deliver babies. It has been said that if men were to deliver babies, the human race would become extinct. The amount of pain experienced during the Prolotherapy treatment is insignificant compared to the pain the chronic pain patient experiences every day. Many say after the

Prolotherapy treatment, "It wasn't that bad." There are a few people, however, like Dr. Van Pelt, who need a little pampering.

Pampering to lessen the pain may consist of the physician giving the patient anesthesia or a prescription for Tylenol with codeine or Vicodin to be taken prior to Prolotherapy treatments. Other physicians, including Dr. Hemwall and Dr. Hauser, may use a device called Madajet which sprays an anesthetic such as Lidocaine into the skin to deaden the pain when the needle pierces the skin. The needle piercing through the skin is the most painful part of the procedure.

For those requiring injections in many areas at one time or in very delicate areas like the neck, intravenous anesthesia such as Demerol, which is a narcotic, may be used. The intravenous anesthesia is the most dangerous part of the procedure. Occasional nausea and a few "upchucks" were the only side effects that Dr. Hemwall witnessed after administering thousands of intravenous anesthetics. The anesthesia does make a person "woozy" but some people prefer it because it eliminates the pain of the procedure. Most of our patients receive Prolotherapy without any anesthesia and do quite well.

2. How Safe Is Prolotherapy?

In his study published in 1961, Abraham Myers, M.D., states that in treating 267 patients with low back pain, with and without sciatica, from May 1956 to October 1960, "Over 4,500 [Prolotherapy] injections have been given without the occurrence of any complication."[1]

Prolotherapy is much safer than taking aspirin day after day. Prolotherapy is also much safer for the body than living with pain. The most dangerous part of receiving Prolotherapy treatments at our office is fighting Chicago traffic!

Pain not only decreases one's enjoyment of life, it creates stress in the body. Stress is the worst detriment to good health. A body under stress triggers the "fight or flight" response, which means the adrenal gland begins excreting hormones such as cortisol and adrenaline. The same thing occurs when a gun is pointed at you during a robbery, but for a shorter period of time.

The adrenal gland, also known as the stress gland, secretes cortisol to increase the amount of white blood cells that are activated, as in cases of allergic or infectious stress. It puts the body "on alert." The adrenal gland is one of the reasons a person wakes up in the morning. Chronic pain causes the adrenal gland to be in a continual "alert mode," secreting cortisol as would occur with an infection or when a person is being robbed. As the chronic pain lingers, cortisol is continually produced. Cortisol levels are supposed to be low at nighttime, putting the body in the sleep mode. With chronic pain, high cortisol levels put the body in the alert mode and insomnia results. The increased cortisol production eventually wears the body down, resulting in increased fatigue. This explains why many chronic pain patients have difficulty sleeping and complain of non-restful sleep.

The adrenal gland also secretes adrenaline, more properly named epinephrine, which is the hormone that stimulates the sympathetic nervous system. When the sympathetic nervous system is activated, blood vessels constrict and blood pressure rises—an unhealthy situation long-term. This produces free radicals, causing oxidative damage to the body. Long-term stress from chronic pain results in long-term oxidative damage. This is one reason that people who suffer from chronic pain are ill more frequently and age prematurely. This can also explain why they seem "stressed-out." Physiologically, they are! For chronic pain patients, the only way to turn off the adrenaline system is to eliminate the pain. If the chronic pain is due to ligament or tendon laxity, Prolotherapy is required.

Pain causes enormous stress on the body which further enhances the need to rid the body of the pain. Prolotherapy is recommended for every patient with structural chronic pain. Structural pain from a loose joint, cartilage, muscle, tendon, or ligament weakness can be eliminated with Prolotherapy.

Dr. Hemwall, who treated more than 10,000 patients with more than four million injections, had not one episode of paralysis, death, permanent nerve injury, or infection. In the words of Dr. Hemwall, "not even a pimple" has formed at the site of the injections. It is common, however, to experience muscle stiffness after the injections for a few days.

3. WHAT ABOUT PRESCRIPTION NARCOTICS?

Dr. Hemwall prescribed analgesics, like Tylenol with codeine, to ease stiffness and pain after Prolotherapy treatments. We occasionally use codeine, but we more commonly use Tylenol or Ultram (which do not decrease inflammation), or natural analgesics, like bromelain, or natural muscle relaxers, such as magnesium. We **do not** recommend chronic use of narcotic medications like codeine, Vicodin, or Darvocet. These are wonderful painkillers, but chronic pain is never due to a Tylenol with codeine deficiency. Chronic pain always has a cause. If that cause is eliminated, the pain will disappear.

Most people understand the addictive quality of narcotics. This is a good reason not to use narcotics for more than a few days. Another reason to avoid narcotics is that narcotic medications suppress the immune system.

Chronic use of narcotics has been shown to decrease both B-cell and T-cell function, reduce the effectiveness of phagocytes to kill organisms like Candida and cause atrophy of such important immune organs as the spleen and thymus.[2, 3] The spleen and thymus glands are two structures in the body that are vital to helping the immune system fight off infections. Another study on the use of narcotics concluded that people with the potential for bacterial or viral infections should be cautioned against the use of narcotic medication.[4]

Narcotic medications, because of their potential immune-suppressing effect as well as their addictive properties, should be used as little as possible. Narcotic medications, as indicated above, can cause the shrinking of such important glands as the thymus and spleen.

A much more viable option than suppressing the pain with narcotic medications is to determine the root cause of the pain and correct it. Prolotherapy accomplishes this. If pain medicine is needed, Tylenol or Ultram can be used because they do not suppress inflammation. Anti-inflammatory medications, such as Motrin, Advil, or Voltaren, cannot be used because they suppress inflammation and block the beneficial effects of the Prolotherapy. Most people with chronic pain admit that they want to stop using pain medications. Often they say, "I just don't feel right being on those." Of course not. Would you feel "right" if your spleen and thymus were shrinking?

4. How Many Treatments are Necessary and How Often?

The anesthetic in the solution used during Prolotherapy sessions often provides immediate pain relief. The pain relief may continue after the effect of the anesthetic subsides, due to the stabilizing of the treated joints because of the inflammation caused by the Prolotherapy injections. This pain relief normally continues for a few weeks after the first treatment.

Between the second and fourth weeks, the initial stabilization induced by the Prolotherapy subsides and, because the initial growth of ligament tissue is not complete, some of the original pain may return during this "window period" of healing. Follow-up is recommended six weeks after each treatment to ensure an accurate assessment of results, avoiding an evaluation of a patient during the "window period." Prolotherapy is performed every four to six weeks because most ligaments heal over a four to six-week period.[5] **(See Figure 6-1.)**

As healing progresses, the quantity of injections required per treatment usually decreases. The pain generally continues to diminish with each treatment until it is

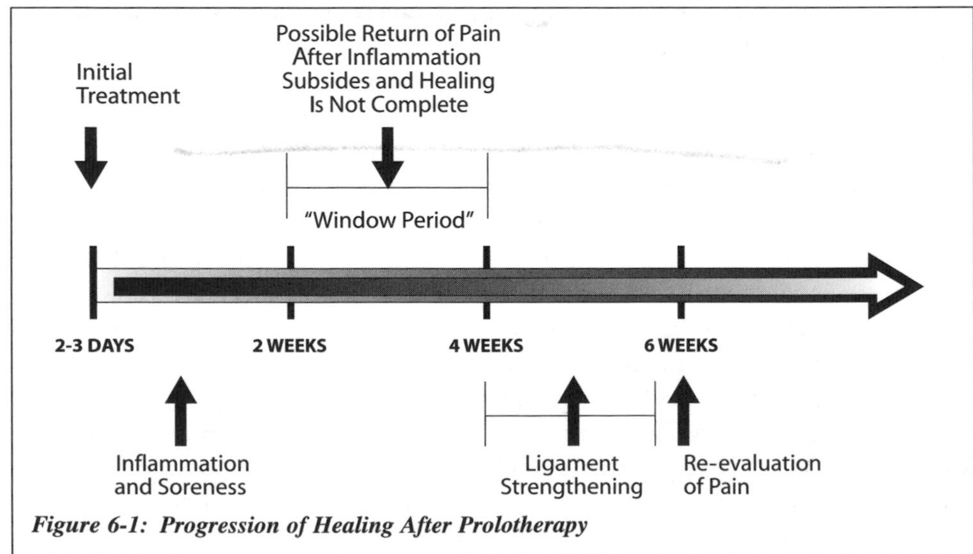

Figure 6-1: Progression of Healing After Prolotherapy

completely eliminated. Four to six treatments are normally required to eliminate pain. Because everyone is unique, some people may only require one treatment while others will require as many as eight treatments. Rarely are more needed.

In some cases, patients will experience no pain relief after their first or second Prolotherapy treatment. This does not mean the therapy is not working, rather it is an indication that the ligaments and tendons are not yet strong enough to stabilize the joints. The amount of collagen growth required for stabilization of the joint is different for each person. A patient who experiences pain relief at rest but not during activity, requires further treatment to strengthen the area. If Prolotherapy treatments are continued, there is an excellent chance of achieving total pain relief with the resumption of all previous activities.

All prospective patients who receive disability insurance or workers' compensation, who are involved in a legal matter, or are on a leave of absence from work, are told that the ultimate goal of Prolotherapy treatments is to help them return to normal function, including returning to work. In individuals who do not have a real desire to return to work or discontinue receiving disability insurance, Prolotherapy is not indicated. In such cases, the individuals do not possess a "real" desire to heal and Prolotherapy will not ease the pain, as pain relief would be an admission that disability checks are no longer needed.

The above situation is a rarity in our office. The overwhelming majority of people suffering from chronic pain desire to find pain relief and return to work. A few patients have a phobia of needles. For those individuals, other Natural Medicine treatments are prescribed, but the results are significantly less dramatic than what is expected with Prolotherapy. Herbs and vitamins will not stabilize a chronically loose joint. Exercise will not stabilize a chronically loose joint. Prolotherapy is the one treatment that will. There is no substitute for Prolotherapy with regard to curing pain.

Patients who do not attain pain relief because of a phobia of needles, or give up on Prolotherapy after one or two sessions because of slower than expected pain relief are needlessly living with chronic pain, especially when a conservative, curative treatment is available. The number one reason for partial pain relief with Prolotherapy is not completing the full course of Prolotherapy sessions. It is important that the patient does not become disappointed if the pain is not relieved after one or two sessions, especially a patient who has been in pain for decades. We have seen severe pain cases that require only one treatment and relatively simple cases that require six sessions.

Overcoming phobias and fears is difficult but worthwhile, and it often produces the most happiness. Ross' phobia was girls. In high school, he was often too scared to ask a girl for a date. There was one particular girl's picture he fell in love with when he was 12 years of age while looking through his yearbook at Jack Benny Junior High School in Waukegan, Illinois. It wasn't until after high school graduation that he was brave enough to call her. We talked and laughed for hours at Bevier Park in Waukegan, Illinois, on July 19, 1980. Twenty-plus years later, we are still talking and laughing. We're sure glad that he had the courage to call Marion that day. Our lives would be pretty empty without each other! We must often overcome our fears to enjoy the true happiness that life offers.

5. Is Prolotherapy Covered By Insurance?

Some insurance companies cover Prolotherapy while others do not. The usual reason for denying coverage is that Prolotherapy is not a "usual and customary treatment." **(See Figure 6-2.)**

ThePrudential

Jan Behm
Claim Consultant
Illinois Group Claim Division

The Prudential Insurance Company of America
P.O. Box 567
Matteson, IL 60443-0567
(708) 503-7360

April 2, 1993

G.A. Hemwall, M.D.
715 Lake St.
Oak Park, IL 60302

Re:
SS#:

Dear Dr. Hemwall:

We have completed our review of claim file as it pertains to the prolotherapy rendered to her on 4/11/92, 5/30/92 & 8/15/92.

Her claim file, along with the additional information you submitted, has been reviewed by our local Medical Department and our Corporate Office. As a result, we find that prolotherapy or proliferant therapy is considered an acceptable form of treatment for pain relief and for breaking down calcification around ligaments. Accordingly, benefits will be released for the services rendered 5/30/92 & 8/15/92. (Payment was already made for the treatment on 4/11/92.)

Please accept our apologies for the delay in replying to your last appeal. Should you have any questions, please feel free to contact our office.

Sincerely,

Jan Behm

Jan Behm
Claim Consultant
Illinois Group Claim Division

Figure 6-2: Typical Letter Approving Insurance Reimbursement for Prolotherapy
Patients must educate insurance companies about Prolotherapy in order to obtain reimbursements.

The Chicago Medical Society, the largest local medical society in the Chicagoland area, reviewed a case for Aetna Life & Casualty Company and submitted the following on April 20, 1976 to Dr. Hemwall regarding their decision: "In response to the insurance carrier's request of whether your treatment [Prolotherapy] is an approved and appropriate method, the Subcommittee on Insurance Mediation has made a decision on the above entitled matter. On the basis of the information presented, it is the Committee's opinion that this procedure is an accepted procedure." [6]

A few years later, the procedure was again reviewed by the Chicago Medical Society. In a letter dated November 1, 1979 to the Life Investors Insurance Company of America, the chairman of the Medical Practice Committee wrote, "It is the opinion of the Committee that, while the treatment does not enjoy widespread acceptance in medical circles, it is a well recognized procedure in veterinary medicine: animal models of disease and treatment form the basis for a great deal of medical knowledge and progress. It is significant to this Committee that Dr. Hemwall has performed this procedure on a great many people over an 18-year period of time and our Society has never received a patient complaint on the procedure. It appears to us that this record speaks for successful treatment. We do not feel that either we, or an insurance carrier, are in a position to declare an uncommon, but apparently successful, procedure as an improper one. Because the method is not widely used does not mean that it is not compensable. A search of our records reveals that another Committee of our Society was presented with a similar question regarding 'Prolotherapy' (the previous reference) and they found it an accepted procedure and recommended payment of the physicians fees. We agree."[7]

The third time the Chicago Medical Society reviewed Prolotherapy was on November 5, 1987. Peter C. Pulos, M.D., the Chairman of the Medical Practice Committee wrote this concerning Prolotherapy, "We understand that this procedure has been used by many medical and osteopathic physicians both in this country and in Europe. It is significant that Dr. Hemwall has performed this procedure on many people for almost 30 years and our Society has never received a complaint on the use of the procedure. It appears to the committee that this record speaks for successful treatment, and it is long past the stage where it is considered experimental.

"...In light of our current review, it is the opinion of the Medical Practice Committee that the procedure of ligament injection, known as Prolotherapy, is a clinically accepted procedure and we recommend payment of the physicians' fees by the insurance company."[8]

As the above verifies, the Chicago Medical Society (one of the largest medical societies in the country) gave its stamp of approval for Prolotherapy on three separate occasions—over 20 years ago. So in some circles, Prolotherapy has been an accepted procedure for decades.

6. If Prolotherapy Is So Effective, Why Is My Doctor Not Aware of It?

Prolotherapy has been presented and taught for years by the American Association of Orthopedic Medicine, the American Board of Sclerotherapy, and The George S. Hackett Foundation. **(See Appendix C, The Prolotherapy Crusade.)** Presentations on Prolotherapy have been given at numerous medical conferences including the first and second Interdisciplinary World Congress on Low Back Pain, sponsored by the University of California at San Diego, "Practical Approaches to Low Back Pain," sponsored by the University of Wisconsin Medical

School, and the New Frontiers in Pain 1996 meeting. In October 1996, at the national meeting of the American Academy of Physical Medicine and Rehabilitation, K. Dean Reeves, M.D., Ed Magaziner, M.D., and Ross A. Hauser, M.D., presented a symposium on the treatment of chronic pain with Prolotherapy. There are many other conferences given every year on Prolotherapy for the physician desiring to learn about the treatment.

In addition to medical conferences, abundant references and research regarding Prolotherapy is available. The latest book on the different procedures used in Physical Medicine and Rehabilitation, *Physiatric Procedures in Clinical Practice,* contains a chapter devoted exclusively to Prolotherapy.[9] In addition to writing that chapter, Dr. Reeves contributed an article on Prolotherapy in a recent issue of *Physical Medicine and Rehabilitation Clinics of North America.*[10] William Faber, D.O., and Thomas Dorman, M.D., have written numerous articles and have published several books devoted to the treatment of chronic pain with Prolotherapy.[11-13] Physicians such as these have done their best to spread the word about Prolotherapy, but it is still relatively unknown.

Instead of asking why your doctor is not aware of Prolotherapy, give your doctor this book and ask him or her that question. Anyone involved in chronic pain management has the opportunity to learn about Prolotherapy.

7. Why May Physical Therapy, Massage, and Chiropractic Manipulation Provide Only Temporary Relief?

For the chronic pain patient, the source of the pain is most commonly due to ligament laxity. These therapies usually treat the symptoms and not the underlying cause. Physical therapy modalities, such as TENS units, electrical stimulation units, massage, and ultrasound, will decrease muscle spasm and permanently relieve pain if muscles are the source of the problem. The chronic pain patients' muscles are in spasm or are tense usually because the underlying joint is hypermobile, or loose, and the muscles contract in order to stabilize the joint. Chronic muscle tension and spasm is a sign that the underlying joints have ligament injury.

Manual manipulation is a very effective treatment for eliminating acute pain by realigning vertebral and bony structures. Temporary benefit after years of manipulation treatment is an indication that vertebral segments are weak because of lax ligaments. Continued manipulation will not strengthen vertebral segments. Weak vertebral ligaments are the cause of the malaligned vertebrae, known as subluxation.

The common source of chronic pain is loose joints, which is not resolved by manipulative treatment. However, any treatment that improves blood flow while undergoing Prolotherapy, such as massage, myofascial release, body work, ultrasound, and heat will enhance the body's response to Prolotherapy.

8. What Enhances or Limits Ligament and Tendon Tissue Healing?

There are many factors that are involved in a person's ability to heal after Prolotherapy. Age, obesity, hormones, nutrition, sleep, physical activity, medications, concurrent treatment regimes used, and infections are some of these factors. All of these have an effect on a person's immune function. Good immune function is needed for a person to adequately heal soft tissue injuries and respond well to Prolotherapy.

Prolotherapy initiates the growth of ligament and tendon tissue, but the body actually grows the tissue. If the body is deprived of the necessary building blocks to grow strong new tissue, the response to Prolotherapy will be reduced. Therefore all factors that decrease tendon and ligament growth should be increased before and during Prolotherapy to ensure complete healing. Prolotherapy's effectiveness and the body's ability to complete the healing process is different for each individual. [14-18]

9. What Is the Effect of Age on Healing?

We are frequently asked to speak to retirement groups and are always amazed how few people truly enjoy retirement. Marion's father retired about 15 years ago. He currently exercises three times a week, enjoys wonderful health, visits his children and grandchildren, and travels with his wife around the country. At our charity clinic in southern Illinois, he uses his work experience as a chemist to perform all of the REAMS testing. He has far more energy than most younger folks at the clinic. This is how retirement should be for everyone!

What we have seen is usually the opposite. People's faces grimacing in pain when getting up from a chair, and a body that is bent over a walker when ambulating is more typical. Unfortunately, people are forced to use canes, walkers, or wheelchairs for transportation. Some reside in nursing homes because of their ill health. We would prefer our dad's type of retirement.

It is also amazing how few people seek out Prolotherapy treatments after learning that relief from their pain is possible. It appears that the feeling among the aged is that pain is just a normal part of the aging process. There is no honor in suffering needlessly from pain.

Losing the ability to be mobile and active is possibly the worst thing that can happen to people as they age. Activity truly keeps the blood flowing. Joints, like the hips and knees, depend on walking and weight-bearing activities to provide nourishment to the joint cartilage. No walking, no nourishment. No nourishment, no cartilage. No cartilage, no movement. Walking keeps people alive and keeps the body functioning. If stiffness sets in, the grave may follow. **(See Figure 6-3.)**

Because most bodily functions decline with age, the ability to heal an injury and the immune system response are slower. With age, the ligament and tendon tissue contain less water, noncollagenous protein, and proteoglycans.

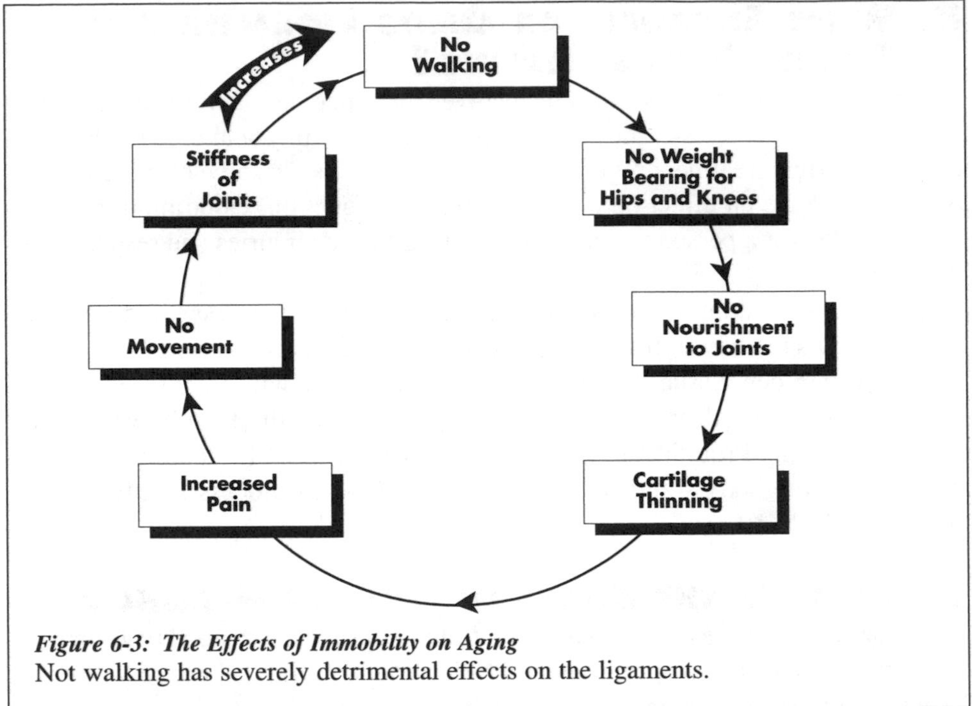

Figure 6-3: The Effects of Immobility on Aging
Not walking has severely detrimental effects on the ligaments.

Proteoglycans are a proteinaceous material containing a large quantity of water. The proteoglycans and subcomponents, such as glucosamine and chondroitin sulfate, allow structures like ligaments, intervertebral discs, and articular cartilage to withstand intense pressure.[19-21] The collagen matrix becomes disorganized and prone to injury. Chronic ligament and tendon laxity is a reason for chronic pain in the aging population. For these reasons, older people may respond slower and, because of this slower healing, more Prolotherapy sessions may be needed. Teenagers, because they are in the growing phase of life, rarely need more than one Prolotherapy treatment to eliminate chronic pain. People in their 90s will heal slower because of their age and often require more than the typical four Prolotherapy sessions to cure their chronic pain.

Pain is not a normal part of the aging process. Chronic pain always has a cause and that cause is not "old age syndrome." Chronic pain is almost always due to ligament weakness. Prolotherapy can help strengthen ligaments at any age and is the treatment of choice for chronic pain, regardless of age.

10. What Is the Effect of Obesity on Healing?

Ligaments, which provide stability to the joints, resist stretching (good tensile strength). Tensile strength of ligaments is much less than the tensile strength of bone. Thus, when a joint is stressed, the ligament will be injured prior to the bone because it is the weak link of the bone-ligament complex.[22] The ligament will stretch and sprain before the bone will fracture. The area where the ligament is injured is the fibro-osseous junction.

The strength of the ligament required to maintain the stability of the joint depends directly on the pressure applied. The heavier the force applied to the joint, the stronger the ligament must be to hold the joint in place. A tackle by Dick Butkus, former middle linebacker of the Chicago Bears, requires ligaments to withstand more pressure in order to maintain knee stability than being tackled by us. This explains why overweight people, exhibiting a positive "basketball-belly sign," are prone to chronic pain and impaired healing. The excess weight places increased pressure on the ligaments, especially in the lower back, hip, and knee areas. These ligaments stretch and weaken and begin the process known as osteoarthritis.

Weight loss is effective for decreasing the pain of osteoarthritis and chronic ligament and tendon weakness because it diminishes the stress on the joints. Stabilization and movement of the joint requires less work by the ligaments and tendons, resulting in reduced pain.

11. Do Hormones Play a Role In Healing?

The endocrine system produces and secretes hormones for the body, including adrenal hormones such as cortisol, thyroid hormones, Growth Hormone, melatonin, prostaglandins, and insulin. Hormones such as testosterone, cortisol, and thyroxine regulate the growth of tissue. An inadequate endocrine system will propagate ligament and tendon weakness. Soft tissue healing of ligaments and tendons will be compromised if any of these hormones are deficient.[23-25] Hormone levels also naturally decrease with age. Therefore, these hormones may need to be supplemented in order to ensure complete healing.

To be evaluated for hormone deficiencies and the use of natural hormones, an evaluation by a Natural Medicine physician should be considered.

12. What Is the Role of Nutrition In Healing?

Nutritional deficiencies are epidemic in modern society affecting both overall health and the healing of ligaments and tendons. Ligaments and tendons consist of water, proteoglycans, and collagen. Collagen represents 70 to 90 percent of the weight of connective tissues and is the most abundant protein in the human body, approximately 30 percent of total proteins and six percent of human body weight.

Collagen synthesis requires specific nutrients including iron, copper, manganese, calcium, zinc, vitamin C, and various amino acids.[26] Proteoglycan synthesis requires the coordination of protein, carbohydrate polymer, and collagen synthesis, along with trace minerals such as manganese, copper, and zinc. Proper nutrition is an essential factor in soft tissue healing. A diet lacking in adequate nutrients such as vitamin A, vitamin C, zinc, and protein will hinder the healing process and the formation of collagen tissue. For these reasons, everyone should take a good multivitamin and mineral supplement.

It is also important that we eat an appropriate diet for our metabolism and take vitamins according to our metabolic type. To assist healing after Prolotherapy, we recommend nutritional supplements which contain specific nutrients that are needed in soft tissue healing. Some of the supplements we use are Prolo Max, Skin and Nails, and Pro-Collagen, manufactured by Ortho-Molecular Products. **(See Appendix F, Nutriceuticals: Helping the Body to Heal, for information.)**

Water is the most necessary nutrient in the body. The human body is composed of 25 percent solid matter and 75 percent water. Many of the supporting structures of the body, including the articular cartilage surfaces of joints and the intervertebral discs, contain a significant amount of water. Seventy-five percent of the weight of the upper part of the body is supported by the water volume stored in the disc core.[27] Inadequate intake of water may lead to inadequate fluid support to these areas, resulting in weakened structures that may produce chronic pain. In order to determine the amount of water you should drink daily, divide your body weight in pounds by two. This equals the amount of water you should drink in ounces per day. For example, a 150-pound man should drink 75 ounces of purified, filtered water per day.

13. What Is the Role of Sleep In Healing?

Chronic pain patients are often prescribed antidepressant medications, like Elavil, to aid sleep. These medicines provide some temporary pain relief and aid sleep. However, chronic pain is not due to an Elavil or other pharmaceutical drug deficiency. Chronic pain has a cause. Until the etiology is determined and treated, all therapeutic modalities will provide only temporary relief. Prolotherapy injections to strengthen the ligament and tendon attachments to bone cause permanent healing.

Chronic pain and chronic insomnia go hand in hand. The adrenal gland secretion of the hormone cortisol normally decreases at night, and the pineal gland secretion of melatonin increases, thereby enabling sleep. Unfortunately, the chronic pain patient's secretion of cortisol does not decline because chronic pain is seen by the body as stress, thereby stimulating the adrenal gland, which reacts to stress, to produce cortisol. This results in chronic insomnia. **(See Figure 6-4.)** The secretion of cortisol will stop only when the chronic pain is relieved. Chronic insomnia increases chronic pain. Prolotherapy breaks this cycle. Pain relief leads to a good night's sleep.

Effect of Chronic Pain on Cortisol Levels & Sleep

Chronic pain leads to high cortisol levels at bedtime which results in an awake state of mind and chronic insomnia.

	Pain-Free	Chronic-Pain
Night Cortisol Levels	Low	High
State of Mind at Bedtime	Restful	Restless
End Result	Sleep	Insomnia

Figure 6-4

Sleep is vital to health maintenance. Sleep stimulates the anterior pituitary to produce Growth Hormone. Growth Hormone is one of the main anabolic, meaning to grow or repair, hormones in the body whose job is to repair the damage done to the body during the day. Every day, soft tissues including ligaments and tendons are damaged. It is vital to obtain deep stages of sleep, as during this time Growth Hormone is secreted.

Without deep stages of sleep, inadequate Growth Hormone is secreted and soft tissue healing is inadequate. **(See Figure 6-5.)** Growth Hormone levels also appear to be increased with exercise and amino acid supplementation with ornithine, arginine, or glutamine.[28, 29]

A natural way to increase sleep and improve deep sleep is aerobic exercise, like cycling, walking, or running. Melatonin, L-tryptophan (an amino acid), valerian root, and gamma hydroxybutyrate are also beneficial natural sleep aids.

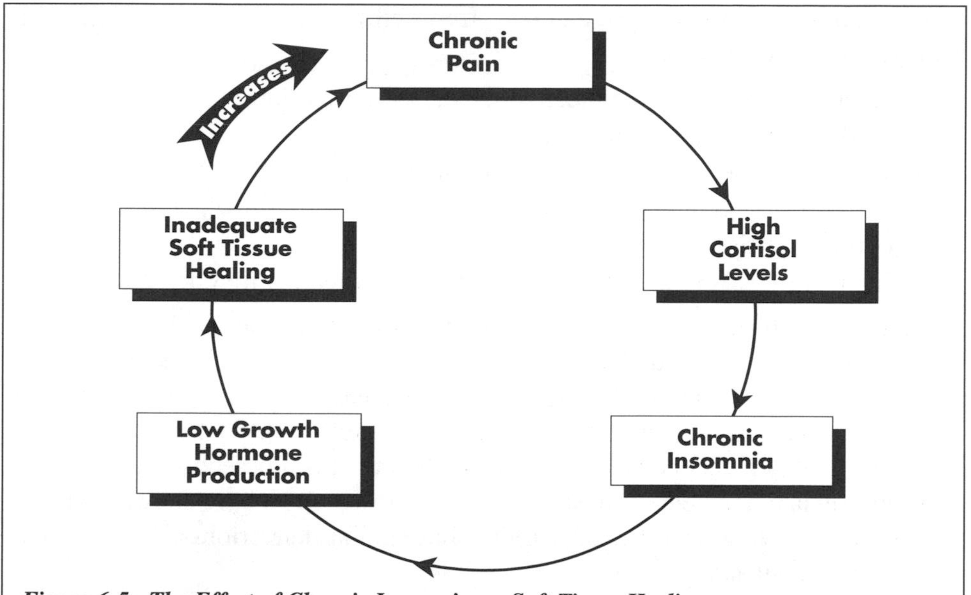

Figure 6-5: The Effect of Chronic Insomnia on Soft Tissue Healing
Chronic insomnia causes low Growth Hormone production which leads to inadequate soft tissue production.

14. WHAT IS THE ROLE OF PHYSICAL ACTIVITY IN HEALING?

Exercise is currently the traditional treatment of choice for chronic pain. Chronic pain patients often experience an exacerbation of their pain when exercising. This is an indication that ligament laxity is the cause of the pain. Ligament laxity generally causes pain when the joint is stressed, which occurs with activity. The proper treatment is not to "work through the pain," but to correct the source of the pain. The main function of exercise is to strengthen muscle, not to grow ligament tissue.

Aggressive exercise may worsen ligament injury and is not recommended until Prolotherapy has strengthened the joint sufficiently to provide pain relief. A good rule-of-thumb is: if doing something hurts, don't do it. Doctors are smart aren't they? Once healing begins and the pain has decreased, dynamic range-of-motion exercises, like walking, cycling, and swimming, are more helpful than static-resistive exercises like weight lifting.[30] A more formal exercise program is necessary after the ligaments strengthen and the joint stabilizes. This exercise program will strengthen the muscles around the joint and increase the flexibility of the muscles which protect the joint from reinjury.

15. Should I Immobilize the Injured Area?

Immobilization, also known as stress deprivation, is extremely detrimental to the body's joints and ligaments. Immobilization causes the following changes to occur inside joints:

- proliferation of fatty connective tissue within the joint
- cartilage damage and necrosis
- scar tissue formation and articular cartilage tears
- increased randomness of the collagen fibers within the ligaments and connective tissues
- ligament weakening with a decreased resistance to stretch.[31-33]

A study performed on animals revealed that after several weeks of immobilization, the strength of the ligament tissue was reduced to about one-third of normal.[34-37] Immobilization also significantly decreases the strength of the fibro-osseous junction, the bone-ligament interface.[38] Eight weeks of immobilization produced a 39-percent decrease in the strength of the fibro-osseous junction of the anterior cruciate ligament of the knee.[39, 40] Other researchers have shown that even partial immobilization (restricted activity) has similar deleterious effects on ligament insertion sites.[41]

Immobility causes decreased water content, decreased proteoglycans, increased collagen turnover, and a dramatic alteration in the type of collagen cross-linking of the ligaments, producing a weak ligament.[42, 43] Immobility is one of the primary reasons ligaments heal inadequately after an injury.

Unfortunately, the standard treatment for a tendon strain or ligament sprain is **R**est, **I**ce, **C**ompression, and **E**levation, also known as **RICE**. Any emergency room physician or sports medicine book will recommend this same course of treatment. A newsletter from a local hospital recently came in the mail. It recommended the **RICE** treatment for an acute soft tissue injury of a ligament or tendon. This treatment is provided because the pain is relieved in the short-term. However, research reveals that the **RICE** treatment actually impairs healing and contributes to chronic ligament and tendon relaxation. Any treatment that impairs

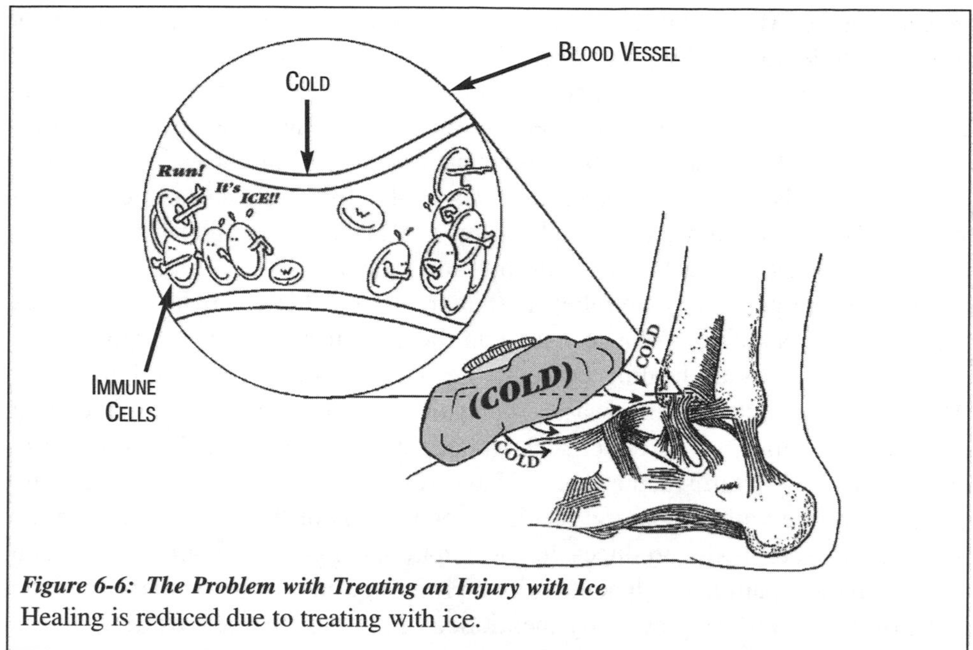

Figure 6-6: The Problem with Treating an Injury with Ice
Healing is reduced due to treating with ice.

soft tissue healing increases the risk of incomplete ligament and tendon repair and predisposes the structure to future injury and becoming a source of chronic pain.

16. Should I Put Ice on My Injury?

As a result of immobilization (rest), ice, compression, and elevation, blood flow is decreased, resulting in reduced immune cell production necessary to remove the debris from the injury site. This produces formation of weak ligament and tendon tissue. **(See Figure 6-6.)** Swelling is the physical manifestation of inflammation. Swelling is evidence that the body is working to heal itself. Use of ice will obviously prevent the body from doing its work. Ice treatment has many harmful effects. It has been shown that as little as five minutes of icing a knee can decrease both blood flow to the soft tissues and skeletal metabolism.[44] Icing an area for 25 minutes decreases blood flow and skeletal metabolism another 400 percent. Healing is hindered by a decrease in blood flow and metabolism to the area. Icing increases the chance of incomplete healing by decreasing blood flow to the injured ligaments and tendons. This increases the chance of re-injury or the development of chronic pain.

17. Is Prolotherapy Useful for Acute Injuries?

If inflammation is so beneficial, why not use Prolotherapy for the treatment of an acute injury? Prolotherapy is beneficial and will speed the recovery process of an acute injury. However, the first treatment course should always be the most conservative one. A more conservative approach to treating acute injuries to ligaments and tendons is **M**ovement, **E**xercise, **A**nalgesics, and **T**reatment, also known as **MEAT**. While immobility is detrimental to soft tissue healing, movement is beneficial.[45] Movement and gentle range-of-motion exercises improve blood flow to the area, removing debris. Heat also increases blood flow so this is recommended after an acute injury. If movement of the joint is painful, then isometric exercises should be performed. Isometric exercising involves contracting a muscle without movement of the affected joint. An example of this is a handshake. Both parties squeeze, creating a muscle contraction without joint movement.

Natural analgesics or pain relievers that are not synthetic anti-inflammatories may be used. Natural substances, such as the enzymes bromelain, trypsin, and papain, aid soft tissue healing by reducing the viscosity of extracellular fluid. This increases nutrient and waste transport from the injured site, reducing swelling or edema.[46] A narcotic, such as codeine, may be prescribed short-term for an extremely painful acute injury. Narcotics are wonderful pain relievers and do not interfere with the natural healing mechanisms of the body, if used in the short-term. Your body produces its own narcotics, called endorphins, which work to reduce pain from an acute injury. Other options for pain control include Tylenol or Ultram. As previously mentioned, these can be used, as they relieve pain but do not decrease inflammation.

The "**T**" in **MEAT** stands for specific Treatments that increase blood flow and immune cell migration to the damaged area, which will aid in ligament and tendon healing. Treatments such as physical therapy, massage, chiropractic care, ultrasound, myofascial release, and electrical stimulation all improve blood flow and assist soft tissue healing. **(See Figure 6-7.)**

If circumstances are such that time is a factor, some Prolotherapy physicians will use Prolotherapy as an initial treatment for acute pain. Rodney Van Pelt,

RICE VS MEAT

The RICE protocol hampers soft tissue healing whereas MEAT encourages healing.

	RICE	MEAT
Immune System Response	Decreased	Increased
Blood Flow to Injured Area	Decreased	Increased
Collagen Formation	Hindered	Encouraged
Speed of Recovery	Delayed (lengthened)	Hastened (shortened)
Range of Motion of Joint	Decreased	Increased
Complete Healing	Decreased	Increased

Figure 6-7

M.D., is one Prolotherapist who utilizes Prolotherapy in the management of acute injury. An individual who would normally wait two to three months for an acute injury to heal, may heal in only two to three weeks if given Prolotherapy. Dr. Van Pelt has seen this increased speed of recovery in a multitude of injuries, including ACL (anterior cruciate ligament) sprains of the knee. We have seen the same results in our office. The late David Brewer, M.D., who was an obstetrician and gynecologist, used Prolotherapy in the treatment of low back pain of pregnancy. This safe and effective treatment is extremely helpful in relieving the low back pain experienced during and after pregnancy.

18. Can I Take Anti-Inflammatory Agents?

Anti-inflammatory medicines, like Motrin, Advil, aspirin, Clinoril, Voltaren, prednisone, and cortisone, all inhibit the healing process of soft tissues. The long-term detrimental effects far outweigh the temporary positive effect of decreased pain. Aspirin does have a beneficial effect on the heart, but a detrimental effect on soft tissue healing. When a ligament or tendon is injured, prostaglandins are released which initiate vasodilation in noninjured blood vessels. This enables healthy blood vessels to increase blood flow and immune cell flow to the injured area to begin the repair process. The use of anti-inflammatories inhibits the release of prostaglandins, thus ultimately decreasing the blood flow to the injured area.[47]

As previously stated, nonsteroidal anti-inflammatory drugs (NSAIDs) have been shown to produce short-term pain benefit but leave long-term loss of function.[48] NSAIDs also inhibit proteoglycan synthesis, a component of ligament and cartilage tissue. Proteoglycans are essential for the elasticity and compressive stiffness of articular cartilage. Suppression of their synthesis has significant adverse effects on the joint.[49-51]

NSAID prescription for acute soft tissue injury is considered standard practice. The administration of NSAIDs, in combination with the **RICE** treatment, nearly eliminates the body's ability to heal. Is it any wonder so many people live with chronic pain? In our opinion, the current medical treatment for acute soft tissue injuries is contributing to this epidemic.

NSAIDs are the mainstay treatment for acute ligament and tendon injuries, yet efficacy in their usefulness is lacking.[52] Worse yet is the long-term use by people with chronic pain. Studies in the use of NSAIDs for chronic hip pain revealed an acceleration of arthritis in the people taking NSAIDs.[53-55]

In one study, NSAID use was associated with progressive formation of multiple small acetabular and femoral subcortical cysts and subchondral bone-thinning. In this study, 84 percent of the people who had progressive arthritis were long-term NSAID users. The conclusion of the study was, "This highly significant association between NSAID use and acetabular destruction gives cause for concern."[56] As it should, acetabular destruction, femoral subcortical cysts, and subchondral bone-thinning are all signs that the NSAIDs were causing arthritis to

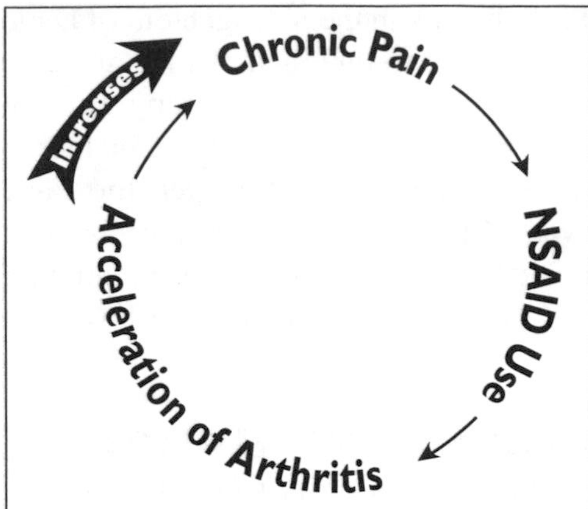

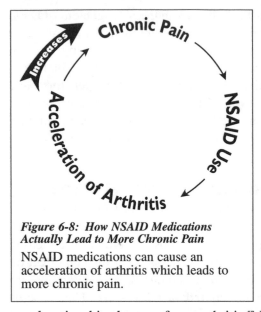

Figure 6-8: How NSAID Medications Actually Lead to More Chronic Pain
NSAID medications can cause an acceleration of arthritis which leads to more chronic pain.

form more quickly. This is one explanation why people taking Motrin, Advil, Voltaren, or any other NSAID will likely require more medicine to decrease their pain. Eventually the medicine does not stop the pain because the arthritis process is actually accelerating while taking the medicine. **(See Figure 6-8.)**

The end result of taking NSAIDs for pain relief is an arthritic joint. How many times has Motrin or any other NSAID cured a person of his or her pain? Prolotherapy eliminates the cause of chronic pain and often cures the person's pain. Even long-term aspirin use has been associated with accelerating hip damage from arthritis.[57] When comparing the long-term use of Indomethacin in the treatment of osteoarthritis of the hip, it was clearly shown that the disease progressed more frequently and the destruction within the hip joint was more severe with drug use than without.[58]

For women of childbearing age who want to have children but have pain, Prolotherapy is a better choice for another reason. NSAIDs have caused concern that they may be associated with an increased rate of infertility in females because they delay the egg from being released.[59] NSAIDs are truly anti-inflammatory in their mechanism of action. Since all tissues heal by inflammation, one can see why long-term use of these medications will have harmful effects. Osteoarthritis and other chronic pain disorders are not an Indomethacin or other NSAID deficiency. This is why the use of these drugs will never cure any disease. Their chronic long-term use will not cure; it will hamper soft tissue healing and accelerate the arthritic process.

Prolotherapy, because it stimulates inflammation, helps the body heal itself. Prolotherapy stops the arthritic process and helps eliminate the person's chronic pain, often permanently. NSAIDs should not be taken while undergoing Prolotherapy because they inhibit the inflammation caused by the treatment. For that matter, anyone with chronic pain should seriously consider stopping NSAIDs and starting Prolotherapy.

19. WHAT ABOUT STEROID INJECTIONS?

The next assault to the already weakened ligament and tendon tissue, after **RICE** and NSAID treatments, is the steroid injection. The unfortunate person who has been subjected to **RICE** and NSAID treatments will likely be offered a

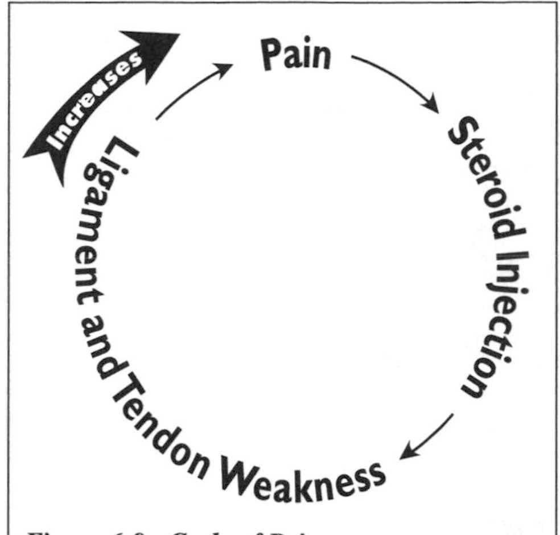

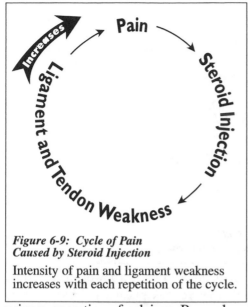

Figure 6-9: Cycle of Pain Caused by Steroid Injection

Intensity of pain and ligament weakness increases with each repetition of the cycle.

steroid injection for the pain which has now become chronic. The **RICE**- and NSAID-weakened ligament and tendon will be further attacked by each subsequent steroid injection. A cyclical pattern of injury, improper treatment, further injury, and ultimately, chronic pain, emerges. This leads to further weakness in the tissue, and the cycle repeats itself. **(See Figure 6-9.)**

Corticosteroids, such as cortisone and prednisone, have an adverse effect on bone and soft tissue healing. Corticosteroids inactivate vitamin D, limiting calcium absorption by the gastrointestinal tract and increasing urinary excretion of calcium. Bone also shows a decrease in calcium uptake, ultimately leading to weakness at the fibro-osseous junction. Corticosteroids also inhibit the release of Growth Hormone which further decreases soft tissue and bone repair. Ultimately, corticosteroids lead to a decrease in bone, ligament, and tendon strength.[60-65]

Corticosteroids inhibit the synthesis of proteins, collagen, and proteoglycans in articular cartilage by inhibiting chondrocyte production—the cells that comprise the articular cartilage. The net catabolic effect (weakening) of corticosteroids is inhibition of fibroblast production of collagen, ground substance, and angiogenesis (new blood vessel formation). The result is weakened synovial joints, supporting structures, and ligaments and tendons. This weakness increases pain and the increased pain leads to more steroid injections. Corticosteroids should not be used as a treatment for chronic pain due to ligament and tendon weakness. The treatment of choice for such conditions is Prolotherapy.

20. What Is pH and How Does It Affect Healing?

We utilize a simple diagnostic testing procedure known as Metabolic Typing to determine a person's underlying physiology.[66, 67] The test consists of, among other things, determining blood, urine, and saliva pH. The tests consistently reveal that chronic pain patients suffer from chronic dehydration. Chronic dehydration produces a reduction in the shock-absorbing capabilities of the intervertebral discs and articular cartilage, placing additional stress on the ligaments to stabilize the joints. The end result is ligament laxity, injury, and resultant chronic pain. **(See Figure 6-10.)** It is very important for the person in chronic pain to drink six to eight glasses of purified water per day.

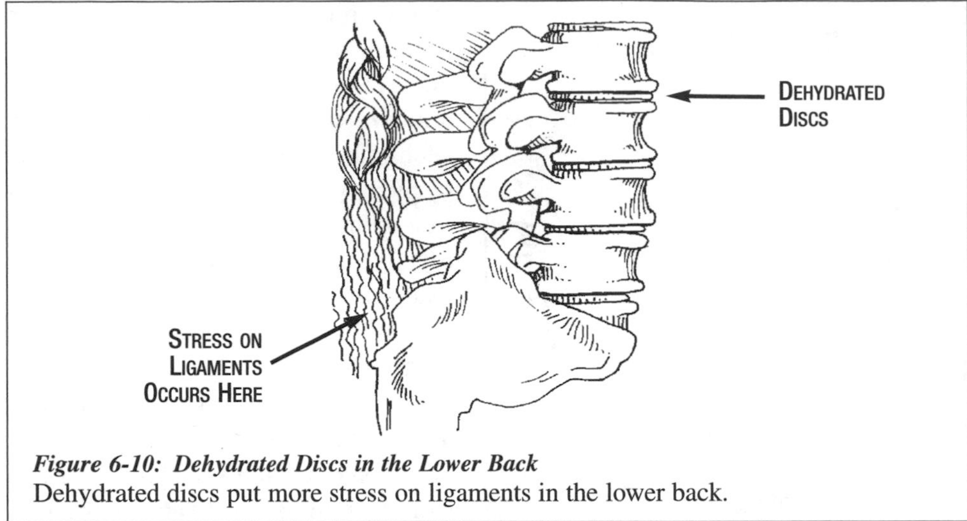

Figure 6-10: Dehydrated Discs in the Lower Back
Dehydrated discs put more stress on ligaments in the lower back.

A significant number of chronic pain patients also have a lower than normal venous blood plasma pH.[68] A person with low venous plasma pH has what is termed acid blood. Acid blood is typically dark in color due to low oxygen content. Oxygen is the food that allows the body to extract and store energy from the blood. A low oxygen content in the blood compromises healing capabilities.

The treatment for acid blood is to consume foods and supplements which neutralize the blood pH. This is accomplished by consuming items which are alkaline, and by reducing the intake of acidic items. Caffeine, sugar, wheat, citrus fruits, soda pop, and potatoes should be avoided, whereas protein and vegetables should be the majority of the meal. Supplements such as green algae or alfalfa also help neutralize acidic blood. A diet similar to that discussed by Barry Sears, Ph.D., in the book *The Zone* works very well.[69] Nuts, seeds, brown rice, or soy products are good sources of protein if a vegetarian diet is preferred. People with acid blood are typically carbohydrate addicts and consume very little protein. Protein is needed in the diet because collagen, which makes up ligaments and tendons, is the most abundant protein in the body. Collagen is the building block for ligament and tendon tissue. A healthy diet with adequate amounts of protein for soft tissue growth is essential for healing ligament and tendon injuries.

21. Does Chronic Infection Affect Healing?

Chronic pain patients commonly possess a myriad of other conditions, including diabetes, allergies, and fungal and sinus infections. The immune system's primary function is to sustain life. If chronic sinus or fungal infection exists, the immune system will preferentially fight these conditions versus healing a ligament or tendon injury. Controlling all infections, allergies, or other chronic health problems is essential to healing chronic ligament or tendon injury. We prefer to use natural treatments, like garlic, echinacea, tea tree oil, and goldenseal, to fight infections. Facial dipping which cleanses the nose is helpful for allergies. The nose is a filter and should be cleansed periodically. Facial dipping involves dipping the face in an iodine-salt-water mixture and breathing it up into the nostrils. It works great! Natural botanicals such as stinging nettles, curcumin, and quercetin also decrease allergic symptoms. **(See Appendix F, Nutriceuticals: Helping the Body to Heal.)** This is one of the reasons that anyone with chronic pain should see a Prolotherapist, who also practices Natural Medicine.

22. WHAT IS THE ROLE OF IMMUNE FUNCTION IN HEALING?

All of the above reasons for inadequate soft tissue healing have one thing in common, they all lead to suboptimal immune function. Immune function declines with age, and endocrine or nutritional inadequacies. Immobility, **RICE**, NSAIDs, infections, allergies, acid blood, and poor tissue oxygenation all cause a decline in the immune response. This poor immune response causes poor ligament and tissue healing, resulting in chronic pain. Chronic pain may lead to immobility and subsequent use of NSAIDs, which leads to insomnia and depression, which causes some people to eat "lousy" (or at least gives them an excuse), which can lead to acid blood and poor tissue oxygenation, producing further tissue and tendon weakness. There is only one thing that can break this cycle: Prolotherapy.

If these above issues are addressed, a person who has chronic pain as a result of ligament or tendon injury has an excellent prognosis for complete healing with Prolotherapy. ■

Chapter 7

Prolotherapy, Inflammation, and Healing: What's the Connection?

During Ross' fourth year of medical school, while on a dermatology rotation with four other medical students, he had the opportunity to train under Gary Solomon, M.D., one of the most respected dermatologists in the country. Dr. Solomon told the class he was going to provide the secret to understanding human disease. If we knew the secret we would be leaps and bounds ahead of our colleagues and be masterful clinicians. Ross couldn't wait to hear it!

When that day finally arrived, Dr. Solomon explained that *inflammation* was the most important concept to understanding health and healing, especially in regard to the etiology and treatment of human ailments. Most clinicians do not understand inflammation, he said.

Inflammation?! Egads! Everyone knows about inflammation. At that time, Ross dismissed his comments and left disappointed. Years later when he learned about Prolotherapy, he realized Dr. Solomon had been right. Inflammation is the mechanism by which the body heals, regardless of the illness.

An Olympic-Size Example

Kerri Strug became the heroine of the 1996 Summer Olympics by "sticking" her final vault to secure a gold medal for the American team in womens' gymnastics. The most dramatic aspect of this vault was that she flew through the air and landed on a badly sprained ankle. As she lay wincing in pain after her heroic vault, she was mauled by medical personnel.

Unfortunately, she was observed throughout the rest of the Olympics with her ankle wrapped and her foot elevated. "What will happen to Kerri Strug? Will she finish the competition?" viewers wondered. "Will she be left with a weak ankle? Will she have chronic pain?" If the medical treatment she received at the Olympics is any indication, she will be anti-inflaming her pain to stay.

Kerri Strug suffered a ligament sprain. Ligaments are the supporting structures of the musculoskeletal system that connect the bones to each other. A stretched and weakened ligament is defined as a sprain.

Immediately after her ligament injury, Kerri Strug was given the currently accepted mode of treatment known as **RICE**. This treatment is prescribed by most physicians, athletic trainers, physical therapists, and chiropractors for an acute injury of a ligament or tendon. The treatment consists of **R**est, **I**ce, **C**ompression, and **E**levation in order to immobilize the joint and decrease the swelling. The short-term result of this treatment is a reduction in pain. For the treatment of soft tissue injury, however, the **RICE** treatment decreases blood flow, preventing immune cells from getting to the injured area. This impairs the healing process, causes greater pain long-term, and increases the chance of incomplete healing of the injured ligament. **(See Figure 7-1.)**

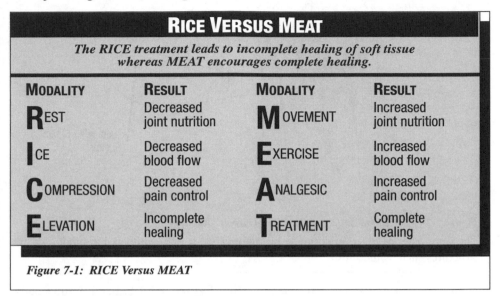

RICE VERSUS MEAT

The RICE treatment leads to incomplete healing of soft tissue whereas MEAT encourages complete healing.

MODALITY	RESULT	MODALITY	RESULT
REST	Decreased joint nutrition	MOVEMENT	Increased joint nutrition
ICE	Decreased blood flow	EXERCISE	Increased blood flow
COMPRESSION	Decreased pain control	ANALGESIC	Increased pain control
ELEVATION	Incomplete healing	TREATMENT	Complete healing

Figure 7-1: RICE Versus MEAT

WHERE COMPLETE HEALING BEGINS

All human ailments, including ligament and tendon injury, involve inflammation. Inflammation is defined as the reaction of vascularized, living tissue to local injury.[1] The first stage of inflammation is the actual injury. Inflammation is the body's reaction to a local injury. Healing an injured area is dependent on the blood supplying inflammatory cells to repair the damaged tissue, which explains why vascularized, living tissue is crucial to the repair of any injured area. Vascularization refers to the blood supply to an area. Poor blood flow proportionately reduces healing.

Chronically weak ligaments and tendons are a result of inadequate repair following an injury and occur because of poor blood supply to the area where ligaments and tendons attach to the bone, the fibro-osseous junction.[2-4] **(See Figure 7-2.)** Due to the poor blood supply, the immune cells necessary to repair the affected area cannot reach the injury. Inadequate healing is the result. Nonsteroidal anti-inflammatory drugs (NSAIDs) and ice treatments decrease the blood flow even further, thus hampering the body's capability to heal the injured tissue.

Healing of an injured tissue, such as a ligament, progresses through a series of stages: inflammatory, fibroblastic, and maturation.[5-7] The inflammatory stage is characterized by an increase in blood flow, transporting healing immune cells to the area, often resulting in painful swelling. Swelling tells the body, especially the brain, that an area of the body has been injured. The immune system is activated to send immune cells, called polymorphonuclear cells, also known as "polys," to

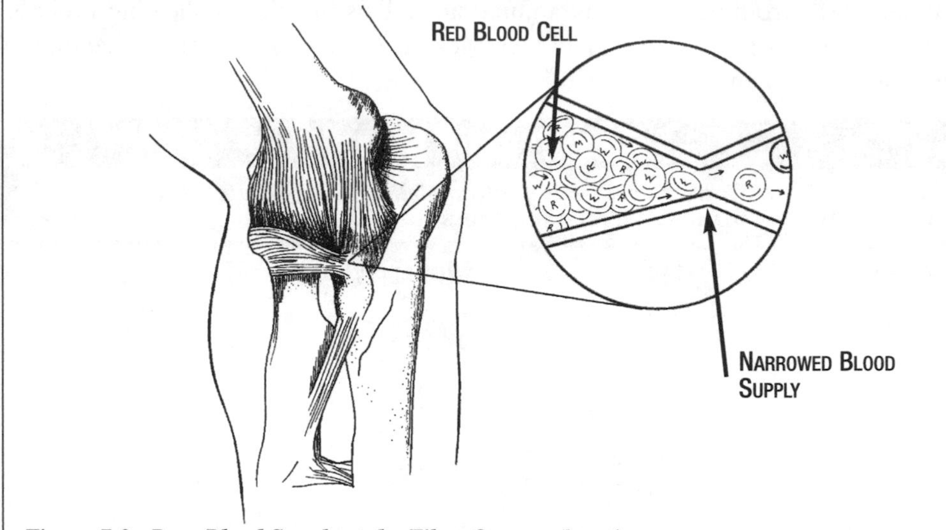

Figure 7-2: Poor Blood Supply at the Fibro-Osseous Junction
The fibro-osseous junction normally has poor blood supply compared to other structures such as muscles.

the injured area and remove the debris. **(See Figure 7-3.)** Other immune cells, including the monocytes, histocytes, and macrophage cells, assist in the cleanup. The macrophages and polys begin the process of phagocytosis, also called dinner, whereby they engulf and subsequently destroy debris and any other foreign matter in the body.

A day or two after the initial injury, the fibroblastic stage of healing begins. The body forms new blood vessels, a process called angiogenesis, because of fac-

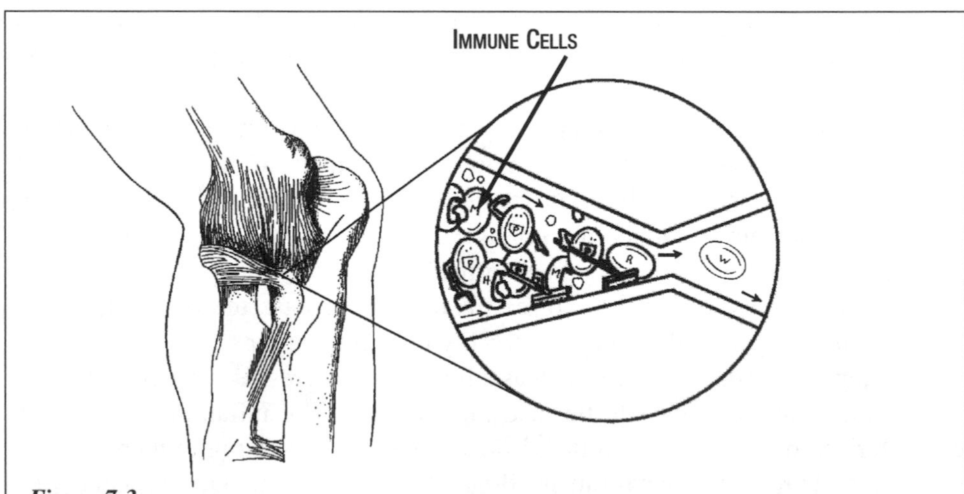

Figure 7-3:
Immune System Activity at the Fibro-Osseous Junction Immediately After an Injury
Responding to an injury, the immune system activates to remove debris.

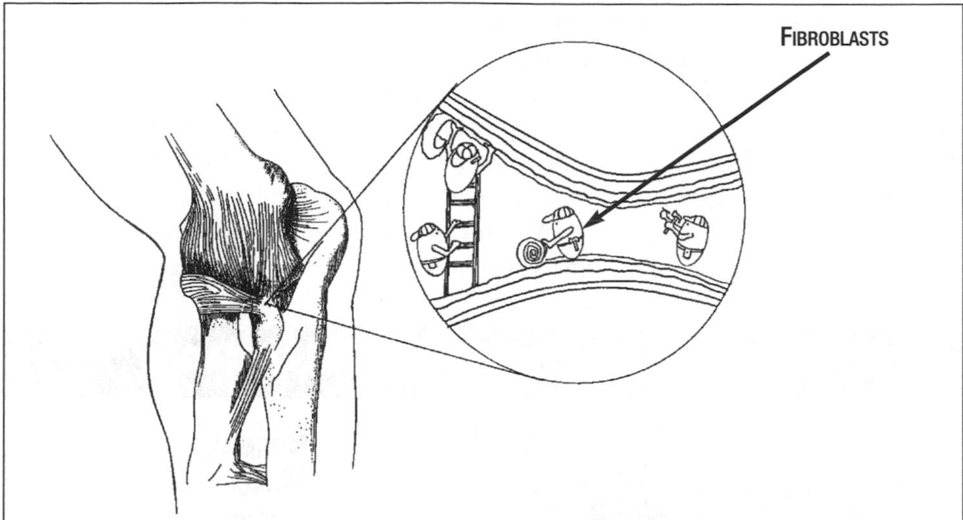

Figure 7-4: Immune System Growing Tissue at the Fibro-Osseous Junction
Fibroblasts forming new collagen tissue which makes the ligament and tendon strong.

tors released by the macrophage cells. Fibroblasts are formed from local cells or other immune cells in the blood. They are the carpenters of the body that form new collagen tissue, the building blocks of ligaments and tendons. **(See Figure 7-4.)** Collagen is responsible for the strength of the ligament and tendon. The fibroblastic stage continues for approximately four to six weeks after the injury. Consequently, Prolotherapy treatments are typically administered every four to six weeks, allowing maximal time for ligament and tendon growth.[8]

The maturation phase of healing begins after the fibroblastic stage and may continue for 18 months after an injury. During this time the collagen fibers increase in density and diameter, resulting in increased strength. **(See Figure 7-5.)**

THREE STAGES OF HEALING

	INFLAMMATORY	**PROLIFERATIVE**	**REMODELING**
Effect on blood	Increased blood flow	Formation of new blood vessels	New blood vessels mature
Symptoms	Swelling and pain increase	Swelling and pain subside	If tissue is strong, pain subsides
Physiology	Immune cells, called macrophages, remove damaged tissue	Immune cells, called fibroblasts, form new collagen	Increased density and diameter of collagen fibers occur if healing is not hindered
Length of time	Immediate response occurs for a week	Begins at day 2 or 3 after injury and continues for 6 weeks	Continues from day 42 until 18 months after injury

Figure 7-5: Three Stages of Healing After Soft Tissue Injury

Anything that decreases inflammation is detrimental to the healing process of soft tissue injury. NSAIDs, for example, should only be prescribed when inflammation is the cause of the problem. In the case of soft tissue injury, inflammation is the cure for the problem. Prolotherapy injections stimulate ligament and tendon tissue growth, which only occurs through the process of inflammation. **(See Figure 7-6.)** Dr. Solomon was indeed right. Inflammation is the key to the treatment of human ailments. Those who suffer from chronic pain have a choice: Anti-inflame the pain to stay or inflame your pain away with Prolotherapy. ■

Prolotherapy Stimulates Inflammation

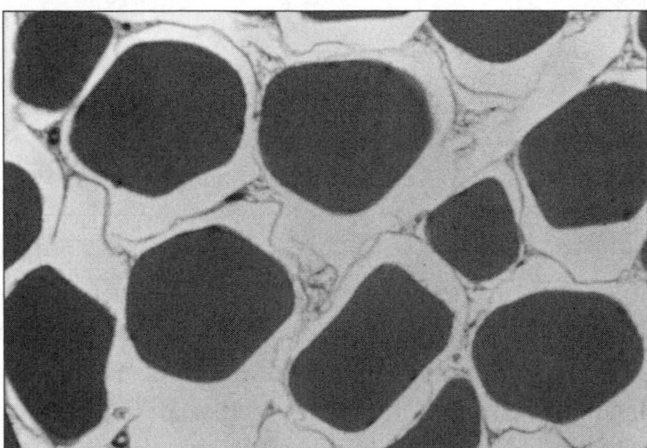

Normal Muscle Tissue

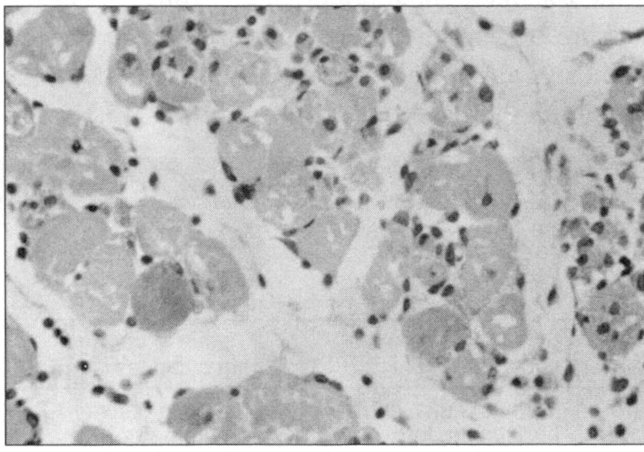

Muscle Tissue 48 Hours after Prolotherapy:

Injections with 12.5 percent Dextrose in 0.5 percent Xylocaine

Notice the massive inflammatory reaction—the basis of Prolotherapy.

Slides prepared by Gale Bordon, M.D., from K. Dean Reeves, M.D. Used with permission.

Figure 7-6: Prolotherapy Stimulates Inflammation
Prolotherapy stimulates the natural healing mechanisms of the body via inflammation.

Chapter 8

Prolo Your Back Pain Away!

Baseball has its original iron man, Lou Gehrig, and more recently Cal Ripken, but hockey's iron man will always be Stan Mikita of the Chicago Blackhawks. For 22 seasons, Stan dazzled hockey fans. His hockey career extended over four decades, from 1958 to 1980, during which time he amassed 1,467 total points, played in 18 playoff series, and was a member of the 1961 Stanley Cup championship team. Stan Mikita is truly an iron man.

But Stan did not feel like an iron man six weeks before the 1971-72 training camp. He had such excruciating back pain that he could not even get out of bed. Stan had learned to deal with constant back pain since injuring his back during a game in the 1960s. He had sought treatment from the Mayo Clinic and some of the best sports clinics and rehabilitation specialists, without success.

"I knew something had to be done. I couldn't get out of bed," Stan said. "I had heard about Dr. Hemwall's Prolotherapy treatments and decided to give it a try." Gustav A. Hemwall, M.D., the world's most experienced Prolotherapist, treated Stan's lower back twice in three weeks. Aggressive treatment was given because Stan had to report to training camp.

"The results were unbelievable!" Stan exclaimed. "For the last eight years of my career I was completely pain free. I'd say Prolotherapy definitely helped prolong my career." In 1983, Stan was elected to the National Hockey League Hall of Fame.

Limitations of MRI and CAT Scans

Most medical physicians rely too heavily on diagnostic tests, especially for low back problems. Consequently, many who suffer from low back pain do not find relief. The typical scenario is as follows: A person complains to a physician about low back pain that radiates down the leg. The physician orders x-rays and a CAT or MRI scan. The scan reveals an abnormality in the disc—such as a herniated, bulging, or degenerated disc. Unfortunately for the patient, this finding usually has nothing to do with the pain. As discussed in Chapter 2, 50 percent of people over age 40 who are asymptomatic have such findings on a CAT scan.

In the 1980s, modern medicine developed another high-tech diagnostic tool to look at vertebrae, nerves, and discs on film—the MRI scan. Again, the same types of abnormalities were found in the vertebral discs and bones. People were subjected to various treatments and surgeries for these "abnormalities" in the hopes of curing their pain. Very few people were cured. But all received hefty bills for the tests and surgeries.

Ten years of using MRI technology passed before research was conducted on the MRI findings of the lower back of people who had no pain symptoms.[1,2] Scott Boden, M.D., found that nearly 100 percent of the people he tested who were over

60 years of age with no symptoms had abnormal findings in their lumbar spines (lower backs) on MRI scans. Thirty-six percent had herniated discs, and all but one had degeneration or bulging of a disc in at least one lumbar level. In the age group of 20 to 39, 35 percent had degeneration or bulging of a disc in at least one lumbar level.[3]

In a study published in *The New England Journal of Medicine* in 1994, Maureen Jensen, M.D., and associates, studied MRI scans of the lumbar spine in 98 asymptomatic people. Only 36 percent had a normal scan, 64 percent had abnormal findings overall, and 38 percent had abnormal findings in more than one lumbar vertebral level. The conclusion was, "Because bulges and protrusions on MRI scans in people with low back pain or even radiculopathy may be coincidental, a patient's clinical situation must be carefully evaluated in conjunction with the results of MRI studies."[4] In other words, physicians should begin listening with their ears and poking with their thumbs! X-ray studies should never take the place of a good history and physical examination. Unfortunately for many, x-ray findings have nothing to do with their pain.

DIAGNOSIS OF LOW BACK PAIN

Low back pain is one of the easiest conditions to treat with Prolotherapy. Ninety-five percent of low back pain is located in a six-by-four inch area, the weakest link in the vertebral-pelvis complex. At the end of the spine, four structures connect in a very small space, which happens to be the six-by-four inch area. The fifth lumbar vertebra connects with the base of the sacrum. This is held together by the lumbosacral ligaments. The sacrum is connected on its sides to the ilium and iliac crest. This is held together by the sacroiliac ligaments. The lumbar vertebrae is held to the iliac crest and ilium by the iliolumbar ligaments. This is typically the area treated with Prolotherapy for chronic low back pain. **(See Figure 8-1.)**

The diagnosis of ligament laxity in the lower back can be made relatively easily. Typical referral pain patterns are elicited, as previously described in **Figures 2-2 to 2-5.** The sacroiliac ligaments refer pain down the posterior thigh and the lateral foot.[5, 6] The sacrotuberous and sacrospinous ligaments refer pain to the heel. The iliolumbar ligament refers pain into the groin or vagina. Iliolumbar ligament sprain should be considered for any unexplained vaginal, testicular, or groin pain.

The first step in determining ligament laxity or instability is by physical examination.[7] The examination involves maneuvering the patient into various stretched positions. If weak ligaments exist, the stressor maneuver will cause pain. Do this simple test at home: Lie flat on your back and lift your legs together as straight and as high as you can, then lower your legs. If it is more painful to lower your legs than to raise them, laxity in the lumbosacral ligaments is likely. The next step is palpating various ligaments with the thumb to elicit tenderness. A positive "jump sign" indicates ligament laxity. **(Refer to Figure 4-5.)**

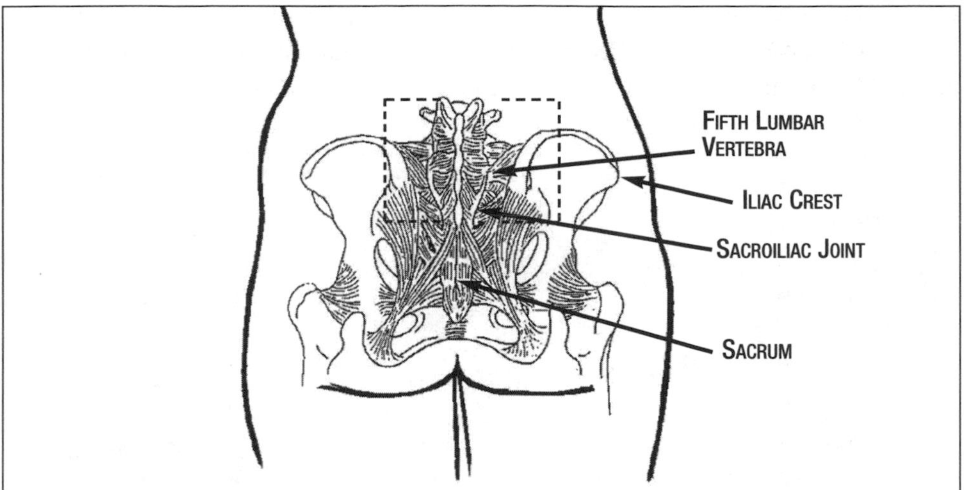

Figure 8-1: Almost All Chronic Pain in the Lower Back Occurs in a Six-by-Four Inch Area
Pain in the lower back occurs in the area where the lumbar vertebrae join the sacrum and iliac crest.

TREATMENT OF LOW BACK PAIN

The most common cause of unresolved chronic low back pain is injury to the sacroiliac ligaments, which typically occurs from bending over and twisting with the knees in a locked, extended position. This maneuver stretches the sacroiliac ligaments, placing them in a vulnerable position.

How effective is Prolotherapy in relieving chronic low back pain? In one of his original papers, George S. Hackett, M.D., noted 82 percent of people treated for posterior sacroiliac ligament relaxation considered themselves cured and remained so 12 years later.[8]

HERNIATED AND DEGENERATED DISC

A herniated disc is a common diagnosis given to patients by their doctors. A person with a degenerated, bulging, or herniated disc must realize that this may be a coincidental finding and unrelated to the actual pain he or she is experiencing. A degenerated disc is one that is losing water and flattening. This is a usual phenomenon that occurs with age. It is also normal for a disc to bulge with bending. A herniated disc occurs when the annulus fibrosus no longer holds the gelatinous solution in the disc. The result is a weakened disc. The annulus fibrosus is basically a ring of ligament tissue. What is the best treatment to strengthen ligament tissue? That's right...Prolotherapy.

Why did the disc degenerate in the first place? Degeneration of a disc begins as soon as the lumbar ligaments become loose. Once they loosen and weaken, the vertebral segments move excessively and cause pain. The body attempts to correct this by tensing the back muscles. Visits to a chiropractor or medical doctor typically begin at this time. The hypermobile vertebral segments add strain to the vertebral discs. Eventually these discs cannot sustain the added pressure and begin to flatten and/or herniate. **(See Figure 8-2.)** The lumbar ligaments then work harder because the discs no longer cushion the back. A dismal, downward path of pain is the end result.

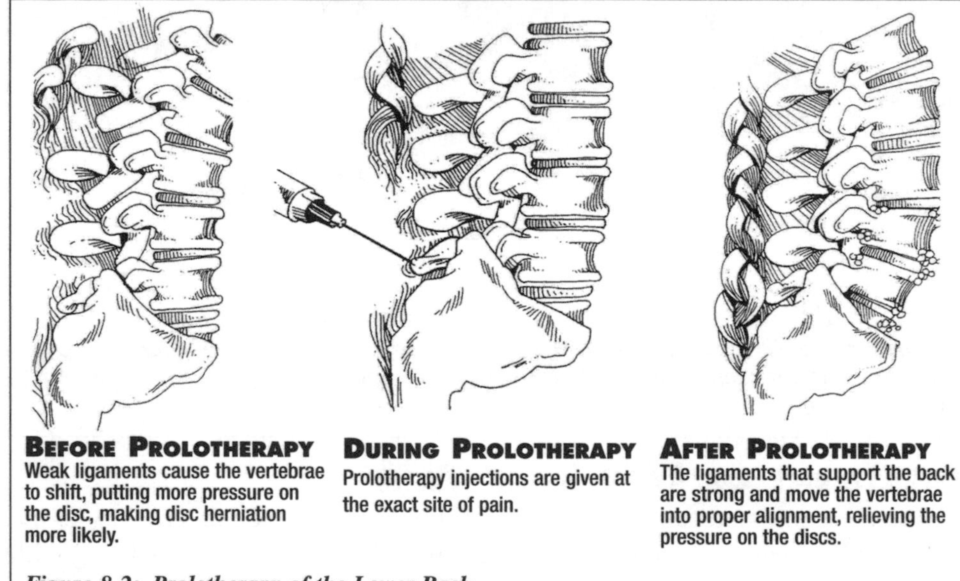

Before Prolotherapy
Weak ligaments cause the vertebrae to shift, putting more pressure on the disc, making disc herniation more likely.

During Prolotherapy
Prolotherapy injections are given at the exact site of pain.

After Prolotherapy
The ligaments that support the back are strong and move the vertebrae into proper alignment, relieving the pressure on the discs.

Figure 8-2: Prolotherapy of the Lower Back
Prolotherapy stimulates the growth of soft tissues, such as ligaments and tendons, relieving chronic back pain.

Prolotherapy is the treatment of choice to strengthen the lumbar vertebral ligaments and prevent the progressive degeneration that occurs with age to the intervertebral discs. Prolotherapy will cause ligament and tendon growth regardless of age. Prolotherapy patients in our office range from four to 94 years of age. Children and adolescents usually require only one Prolotherapy treatment to resolve a ligament or tendon injury. The young body is already primed to grow new tissue, making Prolotherapy treatments extremely effective.

Adults and the elderly may require more treatments because they are not in the growth mode of life. An adult being treated for chronic pain will receive an average of four to six sessions of Prolotherapy per area. Those with excellent immune systems will grow more ligament and tendon tissue per session and will, therefore, require fewer sessions. Those with poor immune systems, especially smokers, require more than the average four sessions. The Prolotherapy treatments are generally given every six weeks to allow the treated area ample time to grow strong ligaments and tendons.

A patient with chronic low back pain is typically treated with Prolotherapy injections into the insertions of the lumbosacral, iliolumbar, and sacroiliac ligaments. The initial assessment may reveal that the chronic low back pain and referred leg pain may be caused by a referred pain from other areas such as the pubic symphysis, hip joint, ischial tuberosity, sacrospinous, and sacrotuberous ligaments. Therefore, these areas are also examined.

Off-centered low back pain is often caused by a posterior hip sprain or osteoarthritis of the hip. The hip joint often refers pain to the groin and down the leg to the big toe. Prolotherapy is very effective in this area, often alleviating the necessity for hip replacement surgery.

The Role of Surgery

Except in a life-threatening situation or impending neurologic injury, surgery should always be a last resort and done only after all conservative treatments have been exhausted. Pain is not a life-threatening situation, although it can be very anxiety-provoking, life-demeaning, and aggravating. Pain should not be an automatic indication that surgery is necessary. Conservative treatments such as vitamins, herbs, massage, physical therapy, chiropractic/osteopathic care, medications, and, of course, Prolotherapy should precede any surgical intervention. Conservative care for back pain is complete only after treatment with Prolotherapy.

It is not uncommon for patients to say that surgery has been recommended to resolve their painful back conditions. Reasons for surgery may be herniated discs, compressed nerves, spinal stenosis, severe arthritis, and intractable pain. Such conditions may have nothing to do with the problem causing the pain. As previously discussed abnormalities noted on an MRI scan, such as a pinched nerve or herniated disc, rarely are the reasons we find for someone's chronic back pain. We find at Caring Medical that ligament weakness is the number one reason for chronic low back pain, and this diagnosis is not made by an x-ray. It must be made by taking a thorough history and poking the loose ligaments and looking for a positive "jump sign."

Trying conservative treatments before undergoing surgery is only common sense. Surgery is fraught with many potential risks, one being the required anesthesia. General anesthesia greatly stresses the body and complications may occur while under, including kidney and liver failure or a heart attack. A significant percentage of anesthesia-related deaths result from the aspiration (swallowing) of food particles, foreign bodies like dentures, blood, gastric acid, oropharyngeal secretions, or bile during induction of general anesthesia.[9] Other possible complications include damage to the mouth, throat, vocal cords, or lungs from the insertion of the anesthesia tube. If you have ever seen anyone after anesthesia, you know it's no Sunday picnic!

In more than 95 percent of our patients, the true diagnosis causing the pain is different than the diagnosis the patients had been previously given. Rarely will a physician describe a ligament or tendon injury as a cause of chronic pain. Remember, ligaments and tendons often do not appear on x-rays. The diagnosis of ligament or tendon weakness cannot be made by a blood test, electrical test, or x-ray. It must be made using a listening ear and a strong thumb.

Even back in early 1981, as new and more effective methods of conservative treatments were being used (including Prolotherapy), the need for surgery was decreasing. Bernard E. Finneson, M.D., pointed out in a survey of surgical cases that "80 percent that should not...have been brought to surgery." It is quite possible that with the widespread use of Prolotherapy this percentage would be even higher.[10]

In more than 95 percent of pain cases, surgery can be avoided by utilizing Prolotherapy. Dr. Hemwall, having treated more than 10,000 pain patients, resorted to surgery for resolving a chronic pain complaint in only one percent of the patients. Our experience has been similar. In the event that surgery is necessary, the previous Prolotherapy treatment will not hinder the subsequent surgical procedure. Prolotherapy causes normal ligament and tendon tissue to form. The surgeon will observe an area treated with Prolotherapy containing strengthened ligament and tendon tissue.

PINCHED OR COMPRESSED NERVES

Another cause of back pain, although rare, may be a pinched or compressed nerve. A wonderful conservative treatment for this condition is chiropractic/osteopathic manipulation. These therapies have a high success rate for acutely compressed nerve cases because bony malalignment (subluxation) of the vertebrae is often the reason the nerve is pinched.

Why did the vertebral bones slip out of alignment? The answer is ligament laxity, which causes the vertebrae to slip out of place and pinch the nerve. Nerve blocks utilizing a 70.0 percent Sarapin and 0.6 percent Lidocaine solution are often given, in addition to Prolotherapy, for this condition. This solution will relax the nerve, providing pain relief, while Prolotherapy grows ligament tissue. Upon nerve relaxation, the vertebrae will realign and the nerve compression will cease. A series of Prolotherapy treatments along with nerve blocks will usually resolve the pain. **(See Figures 8-3A and 8-3B.)**

People considering surgery should exhaust all conservative treatments, including Prolotherapy, before succumbing to surgical intervention. Surgery removes tissue. Prolotherapy repairs tissue. The discs, the bones, and the joints are there for a reason. Surgical procedures removing tissue in an attempt to alleviate lower back pain will almost always leave a long-term detrimental effect on the body. Surgery ultimately makes the body weaker by removing tissue, whereas Prolotherapy makes the body stronger by growing tissue.

PROLOTHERAPY VERSUS SURGERY: A STUDY

In 1964, John R. Merriman, M.D., compared Prolotherapy versus operative fusion in the treatment of instability of the spine and pelvis and wrote, "The pur-

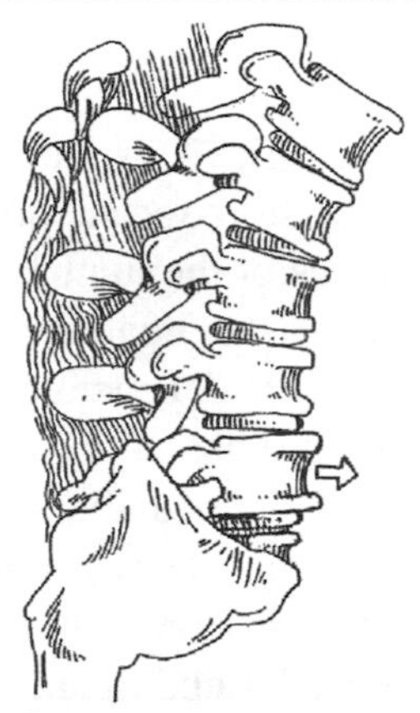

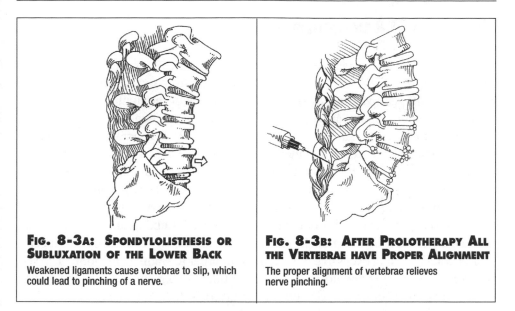

FIG. 8-3A: SPONDYLOLISTHESIS OR SUBLUXATION OF THE LOWER BACK

Weakened ligaments cause vertebrae to slip, which could lead to pinching of a nerve.

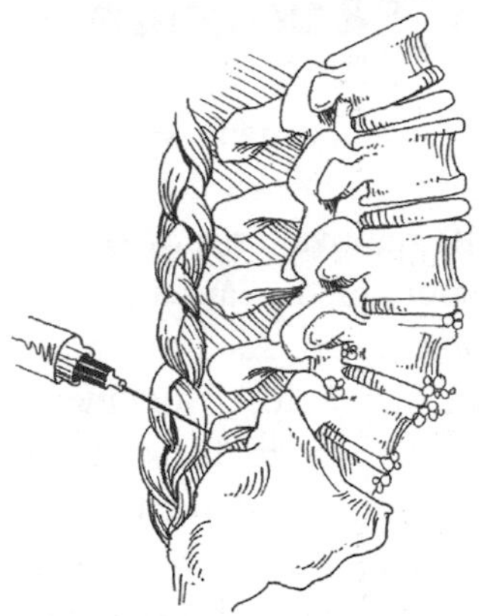

FIG. 8-3B: AFTER PROLOTHERAPY ALL THE VERTEBRAE HAVE PROPER ALIGNMENT

The proper alignment of vertebrae relieves nerve pinching.

pose of this article is to evaluate the merit of two methods of treating instability of the spine and pelvis, with which I have been concerned during 40 years as a general and industrial surgeon...The success of either method depends on regeneration of bone cells to provide joint stabilization, elimination of pain and resumption of activity...Ligament and tendon relaxation occurs when the fibro-osseous attachments to bone do not regain their normal tensile strength after sprain and lacerations, and when the attachments are weakened by decalcification from disease, menopause and aging." [11]

The figure below describes Dr. Merriman's results:[12]

AREAS AFFECTED	RESPONSE TO PROLOTHERAPY (PHYSIOLOGIC TREATMENT)	RESPONSE TO FUSION OPERATION (MECHANICAL TREATMENT)
NEW BONE	PROMPT	RETARDED
LIGAMENTS	STRENGTHENED	EXCISED (REMOVED)
TENDONS	STRENGTHENED	INCISED (CUT)
SPINOUS PROCESS	STRENGTHENED	SACRIFICED
JOINT MOTION	PRESERVED	ABOLISHED
PAIN	ELIMINATED	MAY CONTINUE
LOSS OF TIME	NEGLIGIBLE	CONSIDERABLE
RESULTS	80-90 PERCENT CURES	VARIABLE

Dr. Merriman summarized that conservative physiologic treatment by Prolotherapy after a confirmed diagnosis of ligamental and tendinous relaxation was successful in 80 to 90 percent of more than 15,000 patients treated.

TYPES OF BACK SURGERY

LAMINECTOMY

The most common back surgery is a laminectomy. This surgical procedure involves removing some of the bone, called lamina, from the supporting structure of the back. Its removal creates stress on other areas of the lumbar spine.

Because some of the lamina are removed, the discs, ligaments, and muscles have to do more work. As a result, the vertebral discs degenerate. The vertebral segments then move closer together and eventually become hypermobile. Back muscles tense to stabilize the segment. When they cannot stabilize the segments, the vertebral ligaments are then forced to do this alone. They eventually become lax and subsequently cause pain. This is probably why back pain so commonly occurs several years after this operation. If the muscles and ligaments cannot stabilize the joints in the lower back, the vertebrae loosen and eventually rub together and crack, causing excessive bone growth in order to stabilize the joint. The stabilization results in spondylosis, or arthritis of the lumbar spine. Often the person then succumbs to another operation for the arthritis that formed as a result of the first operation. Unfortunately for the patient, the second operation is not a panacea of pain relief either. A simpler approach is for Prolotherapy to correct the underlying ligament laxity that was causing the pain in the first place. This sequence of events is also applicable to other areas of the body. **(See Figure 8-4.)**

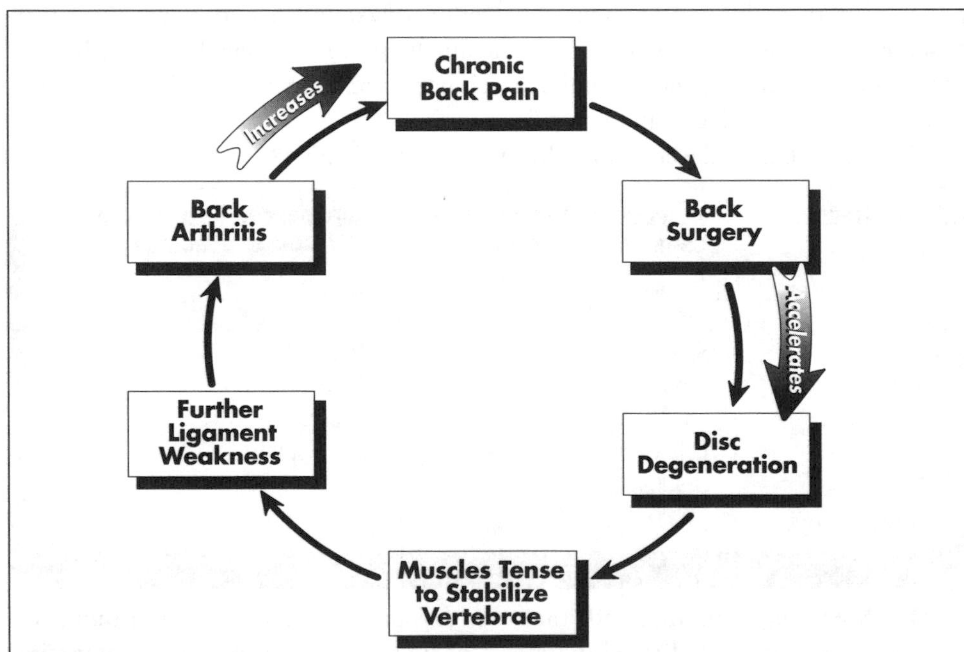

Figure 8-4: How Back Surgery Leads to the Perpetuation of Chronic Pain
Back surgery, by removing important tissue, puts greater strain on remaining tissues, which eventually weaken and become a source of chronic pain.

Discectomy

Discectomy, another common back surgery, follows the same degenerative sequence as a laminectomy. Once the disc material is surgically removed, stress is added to the segments above and below the removed disc segment. These segments may eventually degenerate and become a cause of chronic pain. In a study by John Maynard, M.D., 10 percent of people after disc operation re-herniated the same disc at a later date. Four years after surgery, 38 percent of the patients still had persistent pain in the back and 23 percent had persistent pain in the lower limbs.[13]

Lumbar Spinal Fusion

Lumbar spinal fusion operations fuse together several segments of the vertebrae. Such an operation is commonly performed for spondylolisthesis, a condition where one vertebral segment slips forward on another. **(See Figures 8-3A and 8-3B.)** This causes back pain, especially when bending. By definition, spinal fusion causes permanent bonding or fusing of several vertebral segments. Mobility is decreased, causing increased stress on the areas above and below the fused segment. Over time, this stress may create weakened ligaments. The weakened ligaments lead to a degenerated disc, which eventually leads to a degenerated spine resulting in a painfully stiff back.

Prolotherapy is a much safer and effective alternative to a laminectomy, a discectomy, or a lumbar spinal fusion. Prolotherapy initiates the repair process of the loose ligaments in spondylolisthesis and degenerated and herniated discs. For these reasons, Prolotherapy should be performed before a patient considers a surgical procedure to alleviate pain.

In her article, published in the *Journal of the American Medical Association* in 1992, entitled "Patient outcomes after lumbar spinal fusions," Judith A. Turner, Ph.D., noted that there has never been a randomized or double-blind study comparing lumbar spinal fusion with any other technique. In some cases, only 16 percent of the people experienced satisfactory results after the operation. On average, 14 percent of the people experience incomplete healing of the surgical site. The most frequent symptom persisting after the operation is low back pain, which is often the reason for the operation in the first place. Turner concluded her article by saying that the wide variability in reported success rates is bothersome and should be carefully considered by patients and their physicians when contemplating this procedure.[14]

Prolotherapy After Back Surgery

Many people only become aware of Prolotherapy after they have undergone a surgical procedure for back pain. Although the pain may not be as severe as it was before the surgery, most people continue to experience significant back pain after surgery. Why? Because the back surgery involved removing supporting structures, such as a lamina, facet, or disc, thus weakening surrounding segments.

Prolotherapy injections to the weakened segments in the lumbar vertebrae often result in definitive pain relief in post-surgery pain syndromes. Back pain is

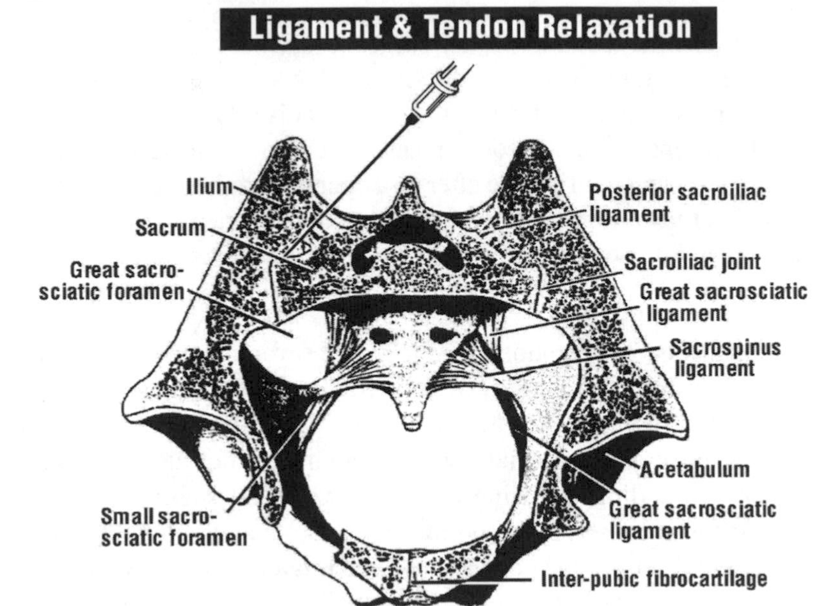

Figure 8-5: Prolotherapy of the Sacroiliac Joint
Above is a transverse section through sacroiliac joints, with needles in position of full insertion to the joint margin of the posterior sacroiliac ligament.

commonly due to several factors and surgery may have eliminated only one. It is possible, for example, to have back pain from a lumbar herniated disc and a sacroiliac joint problem. Surgery may address the herniated disc problem but not the sacroiliac problem. In this example, Prolotherapy injections to the sacroiliac joint would cure the chronic pain problem. **(See Figure 8-5.)**

Unfortunately, it is common for a person to have lumbar spine surgery for a "sciatica" complaint diagnosed from an "abnormality" on an MRI scan. The "sciatica" complaint was a simple ligament problem in the sacroiliac joint and the MRI scan finding was not clinically relevant—it had nothing to do with the pain problem. For the majority of people who experience pain radiating down the leg, even in cases where numbness is present, the cause of the problem is not a pinched nerve but sacroiliac ligament weakness.

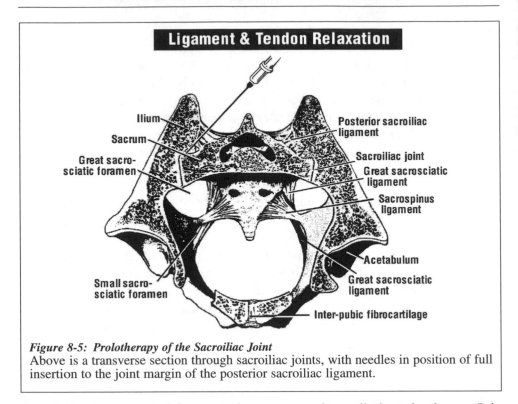

Ligament laxity in the sacroiliac joint is the number one reason for "sciatica," or pain radiating down the side of the leg, and is one of the most common reasons for chronic low back pain.[15] This can easily be confirmed by stretching these ligaments and producing a positive "jump sign." Ligament weakness can cause leg numbness. Most people sense pain when they have ligament weakness, but some people experience a sensation of numbness. Doctors typically believe nerve injury is the only reason for numbness, a reason so many people believe they have a sciatic nerve problem. In reality, it is a sacroiliac ligament problem. The referral patterns of the sciatic nerve and the sacroiliac ligaments are similar. **(See Figures 2-**

2 to 2-5.) In this scenario, it is unfortunate that thousands of dollars were spent on surgery and post-operative care. Had Prolotherapy treatments been performed on the pain-producing structure, this could have been avoided.

Diagnosis of Arachnoiditis

Arachnoiditis is typically diagnosed in someone who has undergone back surgery and still suffers severe back pain that radiates down the legs and often to the feet. The pain has a persistent burning, stinging, or aching quality.[16] The diagnosis is occasionally made when similar symptoms are felt in the neck, arms, or the mid back with radiation into the chest. This pain is typically unresponsive to pain medications and muscle relaxants.

The term arachnoiditis signifies an inflammation of the arachnoid membrane which covers the spinal cord. The diagnosis of arachnoiditis is generally inaccurate because no signs of inflammation, such as redness, fever, or an elevated sed rate (blood test that identifies inflammation), are seen in these patients. All that is seen is scar tissue on the MRI.

Arachnoiditis is another condition that is typically diagnosed by the large metal box with a magnet in it. For the patient who succumbed to surgery, only to be left with continued or worsened leg pains, repeated MRI and CAT scans are done. Eventually, one of these scans will show some scar tissue. The physician will then inform the patient that the mysterious cause of the pain has been found, "You have arachnoiditis. Scar tissue is pinching the nerves."

It is common for someone with severe burning pains in the legs to receive a diagnostic study, such as an MRI or CAT scan of the lower back. These tests are performed because they are supposed to reveal the source of the problem to the physician. The problem with this logic is that the MRI or CAT scan is designed to reveal density and configuration of structures, not diagnose conditions. Physicians are supposed to diagnose but, unfortunately for many people with chronic pain, physicians have left the diagnosing to a large metal box with a magnet in it.

The patient in the above scenario is, at first, ecstatic because "the cause" of the pain has been found. The patient's jubilation is short-lived when the physician tells the patient that arachnoiditis is not curable, but the pain can be "controlled." Imagine having surgery for back and leg pain and coming out of the surgery with the same back and leg pain. The doctor then says the pain is due to scar tissue pinching on the nerves. How did the scar tissue get there? The answer is from the surgery, of course.

The problem with this diagnosis is that the scar tissue was not present before the surgery, but the back and leg pains were. So what explains the back and leg pain that occurred before surgery? Answer that one and you will have the answer to why the person suffers from back and leg pain after surgery.

A more logical conclusion is that the surgery did not address the cause of the back and leg pain. Furthermore, the scar tissue seen on x-ray most likely has nothing to do with the current pain complaints of the patient. The number one cause of low back pain radiating into the legs is sacroiliac ligament laxity. Shooting pain down the leg is commonly due to ligament weakness in the lower back, including the sacroiliac, iliolumbar, sacrospinous, sacrotuberous, and hip joint ligaments. **(See Figures 2-2 and 2-5.)**

The person in the above scenario needed a Prolotherapist to relieve the pain, not a surgeon. Anyone carrying the diagnosis of arachnoiditis needs the immediate attention of a Prolotherapist before succumbing to epidural steroid injections, more surgeries, spinal cord stimulator implantation, or other invasive treatments that are only marginally helpful.[17, 18]

Arachnoiditis has been described as occurring after invasive treatments in and around the spinal column such as neck or back surgery, cortisone injections, spinal anesthetics, or myelography (a technique whereby dye is injected around the spinal cord to visualize the nerves).[19] The question is: What percentage of people will develop a scar as evidenced on x-ray after back surgery? If you said 100 percent, you are correct. Each time a person undergoes surgery, a scar will develop. It is that simple.

Many people with the diagnosis of arachnoiditis have a repeat surgery to remove the scar tissue that is pinching on the nerves. Unfortunately, the results after a second surgery are dismal when it comes to permanent pain relief.

RESEARCH STUDY

A study consisting of 36 patients with arachnoiditis noted that each patient averaged three previous myelograms and three back surgeries.[21] They endured three pokes in the back for the myelogram and three knife treatments. Don't you think *your* x-ray would show scar tissue after all of that?! In this study, 88 percent of the patients were diagnosed with arachnoiditis by x-ray and the other 12 percent by surgery. Do you see a problem? What about a patient history? What about the thumb? A few pokes on the sacroiliac joint, eliciting a positive "jump sign," and the cause of the pain would have been accurately identified.

Often people with the diagnosis of "arachnoiditis" experience significant difficulties in walking or holding down a job. The most startling result observed from the study was that the average life span was shortened by 12 years. Anyone who has had back surgery with recurrent pain should be evaluated for another cause of the pain besides arachnoiditis. Since scar tissue occurs 100 percent of the time after surgery, an MRI showing scar tissue should not be used to make a diagnosis. People who carry this diagnosis usually have the history of repeated tests and invasive procedures, with the end result being a life expectancy shortened by 12 years.[21]

Prolotherapy to the weakened structures, such as the sacroiliac ligaments causing the pain, will cure the condition and alleviate the pain. Once the weakened structure in the back becomes strong, the pain stops. Once the pain stops, the CAT and MRI scans and subsequent surgeries also stop. Consequently, many people with arachnoiditis are choosing to Prolo their pain away!

MID-UPPER BACK PAIN

James Cade, M.D., in Hattiesburg, Mississippi, described the following case: "W.M., a 34-year-old with severe mid-upper back pain between the shoulder blades, found no relief despite chronic use of Vicodin pain pills. The MRI, regular x-ray, and bone scan of W.M.'s thoracic spine showed no abnormalities. W.M. was offered surgery, costing $28,000, with little hope of success. I palpated the costovertebral ligaments and reproduced his pain. He agreed to the Prolotherapy injections and was on the way to healing his chronic pain."

This case illustrates many important points concerning routine chronic pain management. It is common for people to be offered surgery because nothing else has helped. Surgery should never be considered as routine—like slicing a ham sandwich. Surgery involves someone cutting, slicing, grinding, tearing, and pulling out your body parts while you're asleep. We contend that if people were shown a video of the surgery prior to the operation, few would consent. No one should have surgery "just to try it." Surgery should only be performed for chronic pain management in the most extreme circumstances and only if all other conservative treatments have not been successful.

Most of the body's ligaments are not revealed on x-ray. The diagnosis of ligament injury is made by history and physical examination, not by x-ray. Dr. Cade was familiar with ligament injuries and their referral patterns and prevented W.M. from an unnecessary operation that, in all likelihood, would not have solved the problem. W.M. had ligament weakness at the rib-vertebrae junction, allowing his ribs to move too much, which further stretched his costovertebral ligaments leading to more pain. Costovertebral ligament laxity often refers pain from the mid-upper back to the chest. **(See Figures 8-6A-D.)** This is one of the causes for chronic chest discomfort.

Costovertebral ligament injuries are very slow to heal, or heal incompletely, because they are constantly under stress from the movement of the rib cage during breathing. The costovertebral junctions are prone to being injured any time the rib cage is jarred. This may occur from being hit in the chest, after receiving CPR, or from the effects of heart or thoracic surgery. During these types of surgeries, the sternum is opened and the ribs are spread apart, commonly causing injury to the costovertebral junctions. Chronic chest or upper-back discomfort after heart or lung surgery is almost always due to injury to the ligament support at the rib attachments in the thoracic spine or on the sternum. Prolotherapy is extremely effective at eliminating discomfort of the chest and upper back following surgical procedures such as cardiac-bypass.

Prolotherapy, as in the case illustrated, is extremely effective at stabilizing vertebral segments and vertebral-rib segments. Costovertebral ligament laxity is a common cause of chronic mid-upper back or chest pain. This is why many people are choosing to Prolo their chronic mid-upper back and chest pain away!

Figure 8-6A: Physician Reproduces Pain at the Rib-Vertebrae Junction

Weakness at the rib-vertebrae (costovertebral) junction ligaments is a common source of mid-back pain.

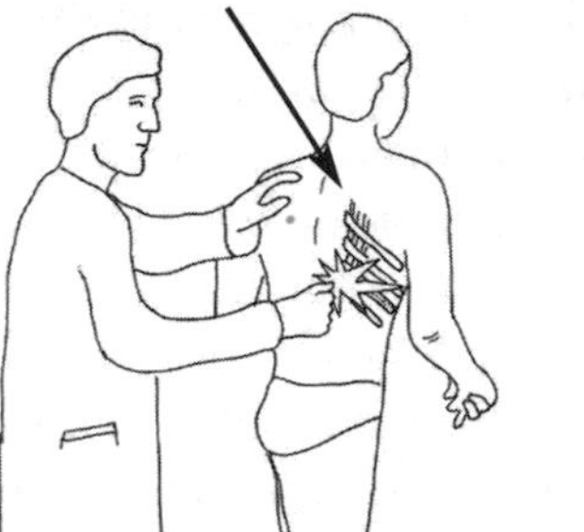

Figure 8-6B: Referral Pain Pattern of the Rib-Sternal Junction

Rib-vertebrae (costovertebral) ligament weakness can cause pain to occur in the chest.

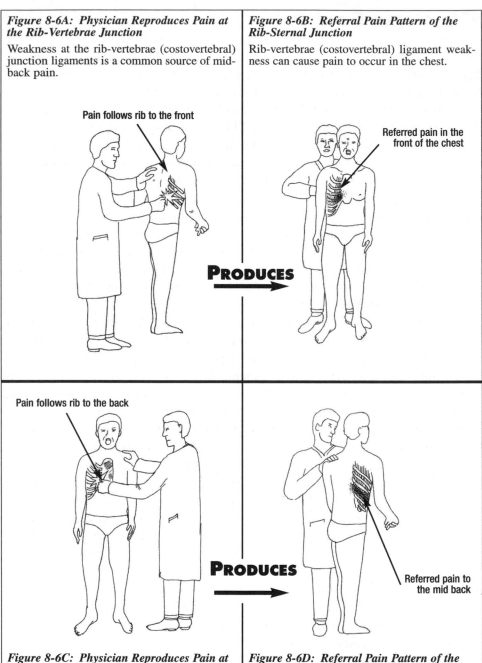

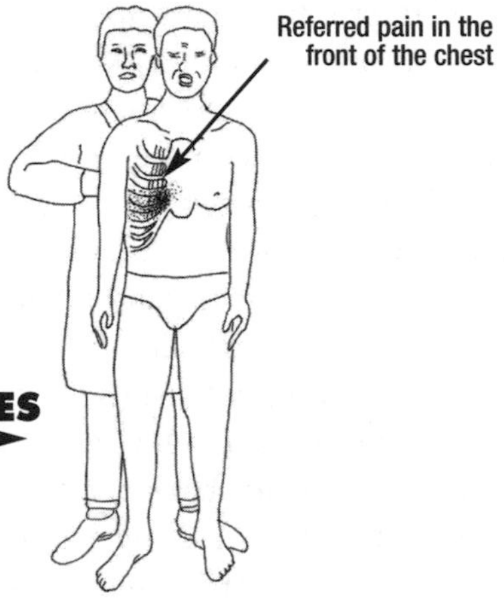

Referred pain in the front of the chest

PRODUCES

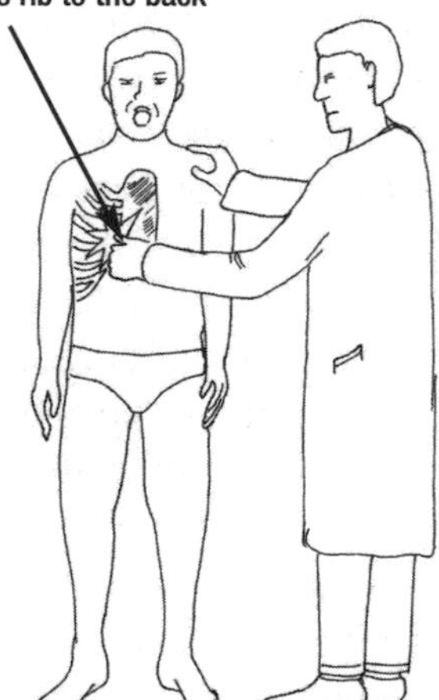

Figure 8-6C: Physician Reproduces Pain at the Rib-Sternal Junction

Weakness at the rib-sternal (costochondral or sternocostal) ligament junction is a common source of chest pain.

PRODUCES

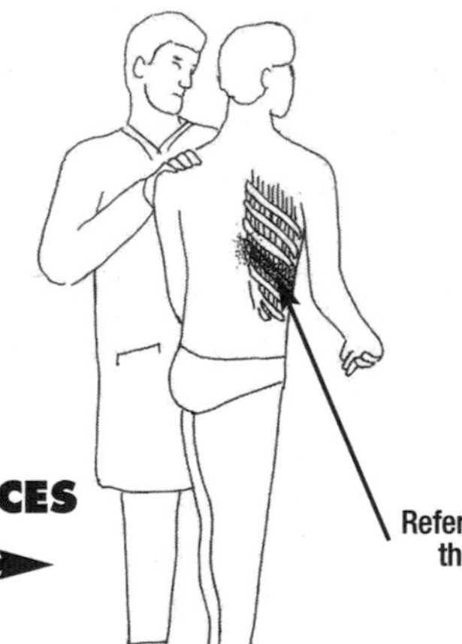

Figure 8-6D: Referral Pain Pattern of the Rib-Vertebrae Junction

Rib-sternal (costochondral or sternocostal) ligament weakness can cause pain to occur in the side or mid-back region.

PAIN FROM SCOLIOSIS

Scoliosis is a lateral curvature of the spine of 11 degrees or more. An estimated 500,000 adults in the United States have symptomatic scoliosis.[22] Scoliosis is usually discovered during adolescence and is called idiopathic scoliosis, a fancy term meaning the doctor has no idea what caused the scoliosis.

In common language, scoliosis means that the spine is crooked. The spine is held together by the same thing that holds all the bones together, ligaments. The patient often experiences pain at the site where the spine curves. At the apex of this curve, the ligaments are being stretched with the scoliosis, and localized ligament weakness is one of the etiological bases for it.

Traditional treatments for scoliosis, especially during adolescence, include observation, bracing, and surgery.[23-25] Observation of a crooked spine does not sound very helpful, bracing has been shown to decrease the progression of mild scoliosis, and surgery involves placing big rods in the back to stabilize the spine. Surgery is generally utilized for severe scoliosis when bracing has failed to stop the progression.

Again, every disease has a cause. Since scoliosis involves the spine moving in the wrong direction, treatment should be aimed at why this is occurring and at correcting the problem. Ligament laxity is probably the main plausible explanation for the development of scoliosis and its pain. Prolotherapy treatments to strengthen the weakened ligaments can have potentially stabilizing and curative effects in scoliosis. If the scoliosis is progressing quickly, then bracing would be necessary in addition to Prolotherapy.

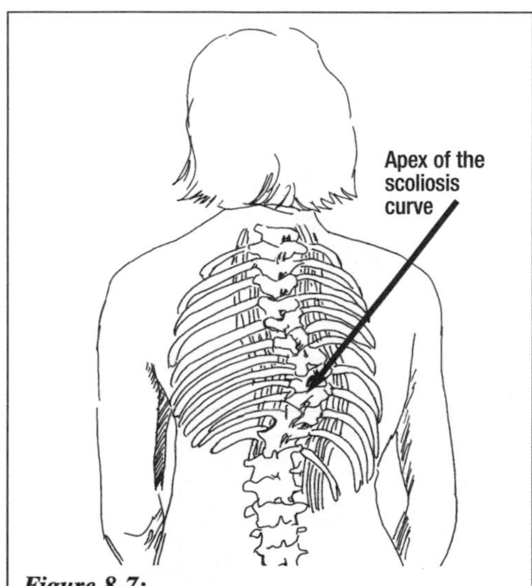

Figure 8-7:
Scoliosis of the Thoracic Vertebrae
Weakened ligaments at the apex of the curve cause pain in scoliosis.

Scoliosis pain has common patterns depending on where the scoliosis is located. These pain patterns are easily reproduced by palpating the ligaments over the scoliotic segments of the spine. A positive "jump sign" will be elicited, ensuring the diagnosis. The most common reason for pain with scoliosis is ligament weakness at the apex of the scoliotic curve. **(See Figure 8-7.)** Prolotherapy treatments over the entire scoliotic segment are effective at eliminating the pain of scoliosis. It has the added benefit of causing the ligaments to strengthen, which will help stabilize the segment. For these reasons, Prolotherapy should be a part of comprehensive scoliosis management.

Summary

In summary, the treatment that should be utilized in resistant cases of back pain is Prolotherapy. Prolotherapy eliminates chronic back pain in conditions such as degenerated discs, herniated discs, spondylolisthesis, post-surgery pain syndromes, arachnoiditis, and scoliosis. The most common cause of chronic low back pain and "sciatica" is laxity of the sacroiliac ligaments. Prolotherapy should be tried before any surgical procedure is performed for chronic back pain. Prolotherapy is an extremely effective treatment for chronic low back pain, because it permanently strengthens the structures that are causing the pain. It is for this reason that many people are choosing to Prolo their chronic back pain away! ■

CHAPTER 9

Prolo Your Headache, Neck, TMJ, Ear, and Mouth Pain Away!

Most chronic pain commonly occurs in either the neck region or the lower back. This is most likely due, in part, to the stresses of life which seem to accumulate in these two areas. Unfortunately for many people who have chronic neck pain, the diagnosis of muscle tension pain is given. Doctors "pooh-pooh" the complaint and tell the person that the condition is all stress-related. This may be partly true, but does nothing to help cure the problem.

As with pain in all other body parts, neck, headache, and facial pain are almost always caused by weakness in a soft tissue structure. Ligament weakness in the neck accounts for the majority of chronic headaches, neck, ear, and mouth pain. Because Prolotherapy stimulates the growth of the weakened ligament causing the pain, many people obtain permanent pain relief with this treatment. No matter if you have migraine, cluster, or tension headaches, Prolotherapy can help decrease or even eliminate the pain associated with these conditions.

HEADACHE PAIN

MIGRAINES

Another Saturday night was about to be ruined when a migraine headache began taking away Marion's cheery disposition. She claims her migraine headaches started the day we were married. I, of course, know this was purely coincidental, as Marion has the most giving and wonderful husband.

Migraine headaches tend to take over a family. If one member is "out" with a migraine headache, another member is helping them cope. Anyone who has experienced a migraine headache or has seen a loved one suffer through a migraine attack knows it is a most unpleasant experience.

Typical medical management of migraine headaches involves the avoidance of various foods like chocolate, tyramine-containing cheese, and alcoholic beverages.[1] Various medications are used in an attempt to abort the migraine once it has started. Prophylactic medications, such as Propranolol, are used in an attempt to prevent the dreaded migraine. Unfortunately, a migraine headache is not due to a Propranolol deficiency. Neither is it an aspirin, Motrin, Tylenol, Imitrex, or Elavil deficiency. Migraine headaches have a cause and that cause can be determined by a careful examination. The cause of migraine headaches can nearly always be found by a good listening ear and a strong thumb.

CAUSES OF MIGRAINES

If the migraine headaches occur at a particular part of a woman's menstrual cycle, a hormonal abnormality is likely involved. The hormonal abnormality is usually due to a low progesterone level during the second half of the menstrual cycle. Giving natural progesterone during this part of the menstrual cycle will often relieve the problem.

If the migraine headaches occur when eating particular foods, during particular times of the year, or when exposed to certain scents, an allergic component to the migraines should be investigated. Migraine headaches are a common symptom of food allergies. Eliminating the suspect food from the diet will likely solve the migraine problem. At Caring Medical in Oak Park, Illinois, we use Metabolic Typing to test the pH of the blood, urine, and saliva of patients experiencing migraine headaches. Balancing a patient's pH is generally very helpful in eliminating migraine headaches.

TREATMENTS OF MIGRAINES

Current traditional drugs for migraine headaches, such as Ergotamine, Fiorinal, codeine, and other medications, provide only temporary relief. The patient dependent on these drugs for headache relief lives in fear of the next migraine attack. Patients describe their migraine headaches as similar to having one half of their head hit repeatedly with a baseball bat.

On the particular Saturday night described above, Marion finally agreed to let Ross administer Prolotherapy injections to the back of her head and neck. At the time, he had been using Prolotherapy for about a year. Our living room couch was transformed into an examining table. In 10 minutes, Marion had completed her first Prolotherapy session. Her migraine headache immediately vanished. Two additional treatments were necessary to make the formerly weekly migraine headaches a rarity.

Prolotherapy is the best curative treatment for migraine headaches. Often the migraine sufferer will say that neck pain or tightness is associated with the migraine and will signal the start of the headache. This is a sign that the source of the migraine is in the neck. Having personally treated hundreds of patients with migraine headaches, only a few did not have a positive response to Prolotherapy. The success rate of Prolotherapy in the total elimination of migraine headaches is at least 90 percent. Such a high percentage will seem unrealistic to some people, but this claim is dependent upon an accurate diagnosis. If the primary cause of the migraine headache stems from ligament or tendon injury in the neck, a high success rate with Prolotherapy is expected.

Sometimes a person has other factors, in addition to ligament weakness in the neck, associated with initiating the migraines, including food sensitivities, hormone deficiencies, and yeast infections. In these instances, Prolotherapy must be combined with Natural Medicine techniques, such as elimination of allergic foods from the diet, natural hormone supplementation, or yeast infection treatment, to obtain completely curative results.

People who have suffered for years can still find relief with Prolotherapy. Prolotherapy has helped thousands of people with tension, migraine, cluster, and other nagging headaches.

"I had cluster migraine headaches off and on for about 16 years," said Kendall Gill, a guard for the Chicago Bulls professional basketball team. "The headaches would last for one to two months. It did not matter how many pain pills or pain shots I took. They would only return with a vengeance. They would hamper my daily activities to the point where all I could do was stand still and hope the pain would go away." After receiving one Prolotherapy treatment by Gustav A. Hemwall, M.D., the world's most experienced Prolotherapist, Kendall Gill was headache-free for two years.

After a flare-up of his headache pain, Kendall Gill knew where to turn, and it was not to the local pharmacist. He learned that headaches are not due to a pain pill deficiency. Headaches, even cluster and migraine headaches, have a definitive cause. The most common cause of headache pain is ligament laxity in the neck. The best treatment option for long-term curative results is Prolotherapy, because it addresses the underlying cause of the problem, ligament weakness.

Kendall Gill had one more Prolotherapy session on his neck and head region and has been headache-free since. "I wish I had known about it [Prolotherapy] 16 years ago," he says. "I recommend it for anyone suffering with headaches." Kendall recently came in for a tune-up on his head and neck areas with Prolotherapy. Due to his career, he is constantly getting banged and jostled, and, therefore, prone to re-injury.

Barré-Lieou Syndrome (Headache with Chronic Sinusitis/Allergies)

Early in his Prolotherapy practice, Dr. Hemwall noted some interesting phenomena occurring after Prolotherapy injections. His patients' neck pain was relieved with Prolotherapy and to his surprise their dizziness, headaches, nausea, blurred vision, and tinnitus (ringing in the ears) were also alleviated. A few patients even had improvements in their vision after receiving Prolotherapy injections to their neck. People who suffer from chronic sinus congestion may find immediate relief from Prolotherapy treatment in the neck. Other serendipitous findings included improvement in paresthesias (pin-pricking sensations in the arms), generalized weakness, and ear, face, and tongue pain. The reason for this was puzzling until Dr. Hemwall learned about Barré-Lieou Syndrome.[2]

In 1925, Jean Alexandre Barré, M.D., a French neurologist, and in 1928, Yong-Choen Lieou, a Chinese physician, each independently described a syndrome with a variety of symptoms thought to be due to a dysfunction in the posterior cervical sympathetic nervous system. The posterior cervical sympathetic syndrome became known as Barré-Lieou Syndrome. The posterior cervical sympathetic nervous system is a group of nerves located near the vertebrae in the neck.

Symptoms that characterize Barré-Lieou Syndrome are listed below.[3,4]

- Headache
- Vertigo
- Hoarseness
- Sinus Congestion
- Facial Pain
- Tinnitus
- Neck Pain
- Chest Pain
- Ear Pain
- Loss of Voice
- Severe Fatigue
- Sense of the Eyeball Being Pulled Out

Other symptoms may include dysesthesias of the hands and forearms (painful pins-and-needles sensation), corneal sensitivity, dental pain, lacrimation (tearing of the eyes), blurred vision, facial numbness, shoulder pain, swelling of one side of the face, nausea, vomiting, and localized cyanosis of the face (bluish color).

A reasonable question to ask is: How can one disorder cause all of these problems? The answer lies in understanding the function of the sympathetic nervous system, which is part of the autonomic nervous system. The autonomic nervous system operates automatically. That is why it is called the autonomic nervous system. It keeps your heart pumping, your blood flowing through your blood vessels, your lungs breathing, and a myriad of other activities that occur in your body all the time, every day of your life. The sympathetic nervous system is part of the autonomic nervous system. It is activated when the body is "on alert." For instance, if you are being robbed your body shifts into "fight-or-flight mode." Your heart rate, blood pressure, and breathing rate dramatically increase. The blood vessels shift blood away from the intestines into the muscles, enabling you to run or fight the offender.

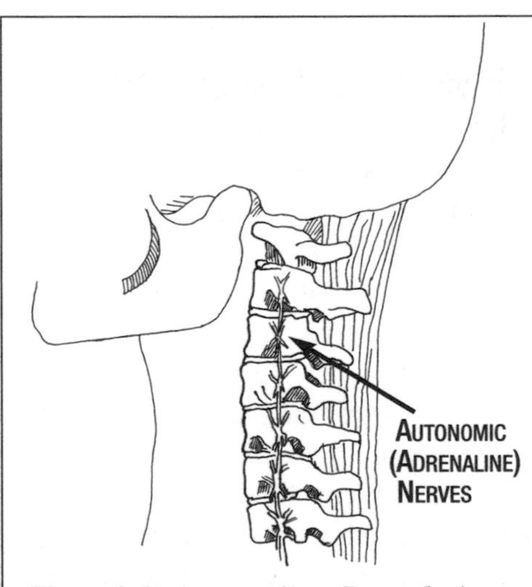

Figure 9-1: Autonomic or Sympathetic Nerves in the Neck

These small nerves are easily "pinched" by subluxations (excessive movement) of the vertebrae.

The posterior-cervical sympathetic nervous system signals the sympathetic part of the autonomic nervous system that controls the head, neck, and face area. In Barré-Lieou Syndrome, the posterior cervical sympathetic system is underactive because the vertebrae in the neck are pinching the sympathetic nerves. **(See Figure 9-1.)**

What symptoms are produced in the face, head, and neck when the sympathetic nervous system is not working well in these areas? The primary symptom is a headache, since headaches are caused by dilation of blood vessels, as in Barré-Lieou Syndrome. The main medicines used to abort severe headache pain, as in migraines, are Cafergot, Ergotamine, and Sumatriptin, all of which constrict the blood vessels. These medicines work, but only temporarily. The medicines act on the symptom of the dysfunction, but not the cause. Thus, the benefit is only temporary. Prolotherapy to the vertebrae in the neck is the treatment of choice to permanently eliminate Barré-Lieou Syndrome. This occurs because Prolotherapy causes the vertebrae in the neck to move posteriorly (back) and no longer pinch the sympathetic nerves. **(See Figure 9-2.)**

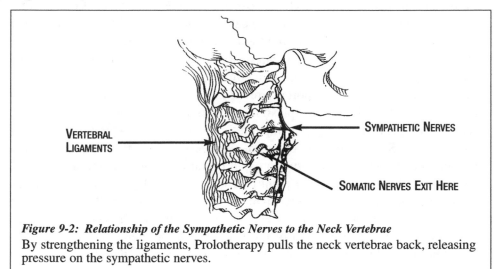

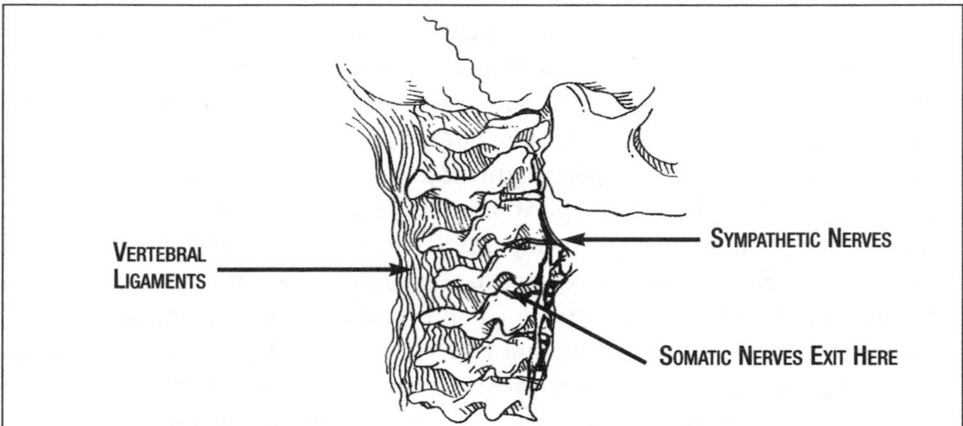

Figure 9-2: Relationship of the Sympathetic Nerves to the Neck Vertebrae
By strengthening the ligaments, Prolotherapy pulls the neck vertebrae back, releasing pressure on the sympathetic nerves.

Another symptom of Barré-Lieou Syndrome is tinnitus (ringing in the ears). A decrease in sympathetic output to the inner ear will cause an accumulation of fluid in the inner ear. When fluid accumulates in the inner ear, as is often the case with an upper respiratory infection, the ear feels full and the body feels off balance. A ringing in the ear can occur, along with vertigo (dizziness). When Prolotherapy is performed on the head and neck, the posterior sympathetic nervous system begins to function correctly. Conditions such as dizziness, tinnitus, and vertigo (Ménière's Disease) can all be eliminated with Prolotherapy, if the symptoms are due to Barré-Lieou Syndrome.

If sympathetic output to the sinus area is low, fluid will also accumulate in this area. Often, immediately after Prolotherapy injections to the posterior head and neck areas, patients with Barré-Lieou Syndrome who have had sinus trouble for years experience clear breathing, which they have not had in years. People using decongestants for years for "chronic allergies" and "chronic sinus infections" are often immediately helped by Prolotherapy injections into the head and neck region.

The other symptoms, such as blurred vision, severe fatigue, dysesthesias (pins-and-needles sensation down the arm), low blood pressure, and low heart rate, are easily understood by a decrease in the output of the sympathetic system of the head, neck, and face areas. Prolotherapy injections to the head and neck region cause the vertebrae to realign, which decreases the compression of the nerves. Upon realignment, Barré-Lieou Syndrome and its symptomatology are abated.

Causes and Diagnosis

Barré-Lieou Syndrome occurs because of ligament weakness in the neck. Signs of ligament weakness in the neck are chronic neck pain, decreased range of motion of the neck, a head-forward posture, and difficulty in keeping the head supported on its own during a lecture, "Boring Lecture Syndrome." Look around a classroom and notice the people with weak neck ligaments. They are the people with head-forward posture supporting their heads with their hands.

Ligament weakness in the neck can occur suddenly, such as after a whiplash injury during a car accident, but it more commonly occurs slowly over time.

Daniel Kayfetz, M.D., reported treating 189 patients, from March 1956 through May 1961, who had whiplash injuries to their necks, with Prolotherapy. Fifty-two percent had associated sympathetic nervous system symptoms (as seen in Barré-Lieou Syndrome), 55 percent of the people had symptoms longer than three months, 81 percent had symptoms and injuries in other parts of the body, in addition to the neck, and 49 percent had some kind of legal action because of an auto accident (79 percent were involved in auto accidents). By all practical purposes these were not simple cases of neck strain, yet Prolotherapy totally eliminated the pain in 60 percent of the patients, and 86 percent of the patients considered the end result to be satisfactory (in other words, they had pain relief with the Prolotherapy).[5]

Barré-Lieou Syndrome can also be a late sequela of whiplash injury. C.F. Claussen noted that in Germany in 1992 they had 197,731 cases of whiplash injuries due to traffic accidents. About 80 percent recovered within a few months. However, about "15 to 20 percent developed the so-called late whiplash injury syndrome, with many complaints of the cervico-encephalic syndrome, including headache, vertigo, instability, nausea, tinnitus, hearing loss, etc." It is evident that these symptoms are compatible with Barré-Lieou Syndrome, and this explains why Prolotherapy is so effective in treating whiplash injury and its sequelae.[6]

Barré-Lieou Syndrome more commonly occurs because most people spend a good portion of their day hunched over while working. Their work may consist of typing on a computer, punching buttons on a cash register, or balancing a check book. All of these activities precipitate the head-forward position and put the cervical vertebral ligaments in a stretched position. **(See Figure 9-3.)** Over time, these ligaments weaken and cause pain. The ligament laxity causes an even more head-forward position, as the ligaments can no longer keep the cervical vertebrae in their proper posterior alignment. The paracervical muscles (the neck muscles) tighten to stabilize the joints and head. As the muscles tighten, they create more pain. Eventually, the muscles can no longer stabilize the vertebrae and the ligaments are stretched even more. Neck pain increases and the cycle continues to

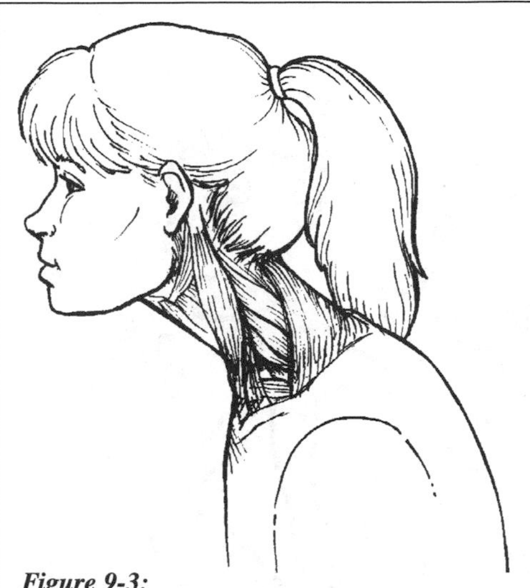

Figure 9-3: Incorrect Head-Forward Posture
Head-forward posture causes strain on the neck muscles and ligaments, resulting in pain.

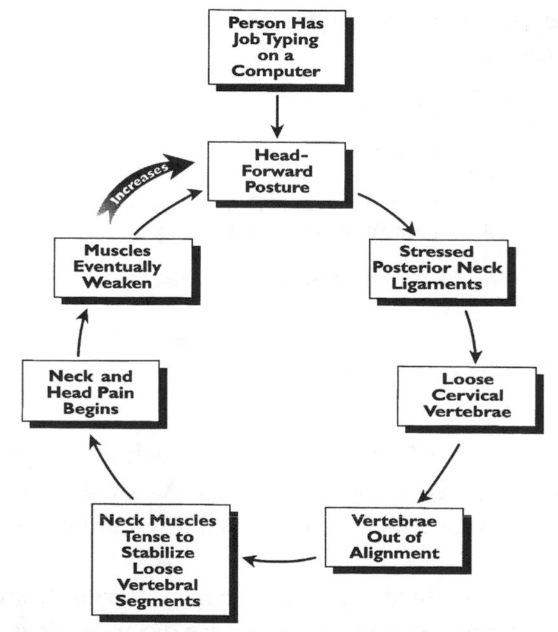

Figure 9-4: How Head-Forward Posture Perpetuates Chronic Neck and Head Pain
Head-forward posture, by straining neck ligaments, can be the cause of chronic neck pain and headaches.

repeat itself. **(See Figure 9-4.)** Massage therapy, physical therapy, chiropractic/osteopathic manipulation, and pain medicines all help to temporarily relieve the pain. They do not, however, correct the underlying problem of ligament laxity. Prolotherapy addresses the root cause of neck pain, ligament laxity, and is consequently effective at eliminating the problem.

Neck and Headache Treatments

Most people say a headache starts at the base of the neck, moves up the neck, behind the eyes, in the temples, and into the head. Migraine sufferers know that pain on one side in the base of the neck may be the beginning of a migraine headache. This is an important clue that the etiology of the headache is in the neck and is producing referred pain. George S. Hackett, M.D., the father of Prolotherapy, described the referral patterns of the ligaments of the neck in detail. **(See Figure 9-5.)** These patterns are important to know because the most common cause for pain radiating from the neck to the arm is not a pinched nerve in the neck, but actually a weak ligament in the neck. The most common reason for a pins-and-needles sensation or numbness in the arm is not a pinched nerve, but ligament laxity in the neck.

To accurately diagnose the cause of neck or head pain, a listening ear and a

Hackett Referral Patterns

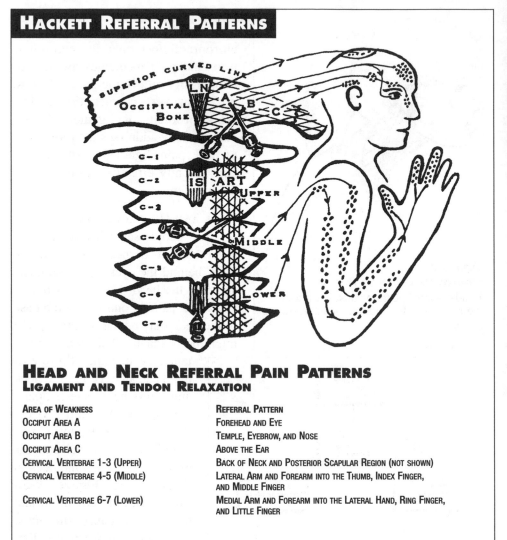

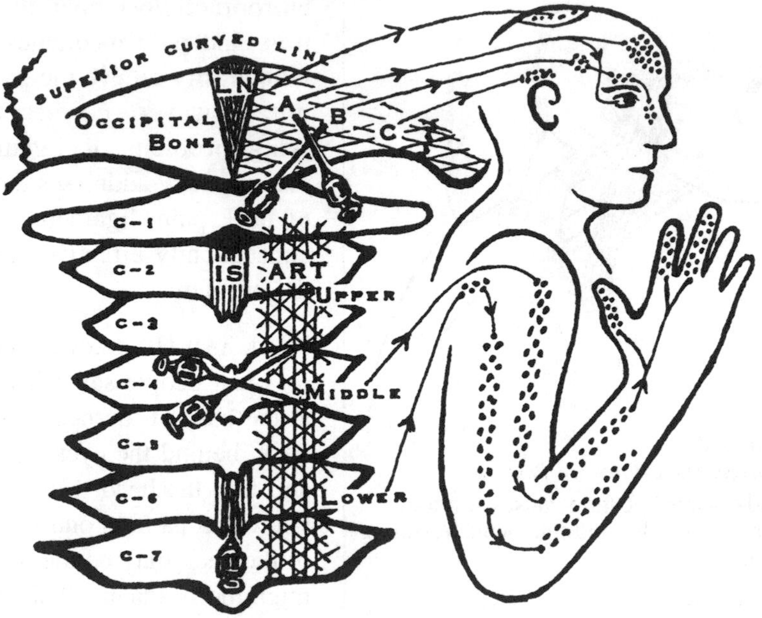

Head and Neck Referral Pain Patterns
Ligament and Tendon Relaxation

Area of Weakness	Referral Pattern
Occiput Area A	Forehead and Eye
Occiput Area B	Temple, Eyebrow, and Nose
Occiput Area C	Above the Ear
Cervical Vertebrae 1-3 (Upper)	Back of Neck and Posterior Scapular Region (not shown)
Cervical Vertebrae 4-5 (Middle)	Lateral Arm and Forearm into the Thumb, Index Finger, and Middle Finger
Cervical Vertebrae 6-7 (Lower)	Medial Arm and Forearm into the Lateral Hand, Ring Finger, and Little Finger

Figure 9-5: Head and Neck Ligament Referral Pain Patterns

strong thumb are generally all that is needed. Diagnostic tests, such as x-rays, CAT scans, and MRI scans, cannot diagnose the source of pain. As already discussed, CAT and MRI scans routinely show abnormalities that are unrelated to the person's pain complaints.

Once a thorough medical history is obtained from the patient suffering from chronic neck and/or head pain, and other associated symptoms are discussed (e.g., Barré-Lieou Syndrome), a palpatory examination of the posterior head and neck is performed and tender areas are noted. Again, the accuracy in diagnosing the actual pain-producing area is excellent, because the physician recreates the patient's pain by palpating the neck and posterior head carefully until a positive "jump sign" is elicited. This gives the patient and the physician confidence that the pain-producing structure is between the physician's thumb and the underlying bone. The structure that is typically involved is the cervical vertebral ligaments. These tender areas are treated with Prolotherapy injections. Typical areas treated during a Prolotherapy session for chronic headaches and neck pain are the base of the skull, cervical vertebral ligaments, posterior-lateral clavicle, where the trapezius muscle attaches, as well as the attachment of the levator scapulae muscle. **(See Figure 9-6.)** Because there is an anesthetic in the solution, generally the neck or headache pain is immediately relieved. This, again, confirms the diagnosis both for the patient and the physician.

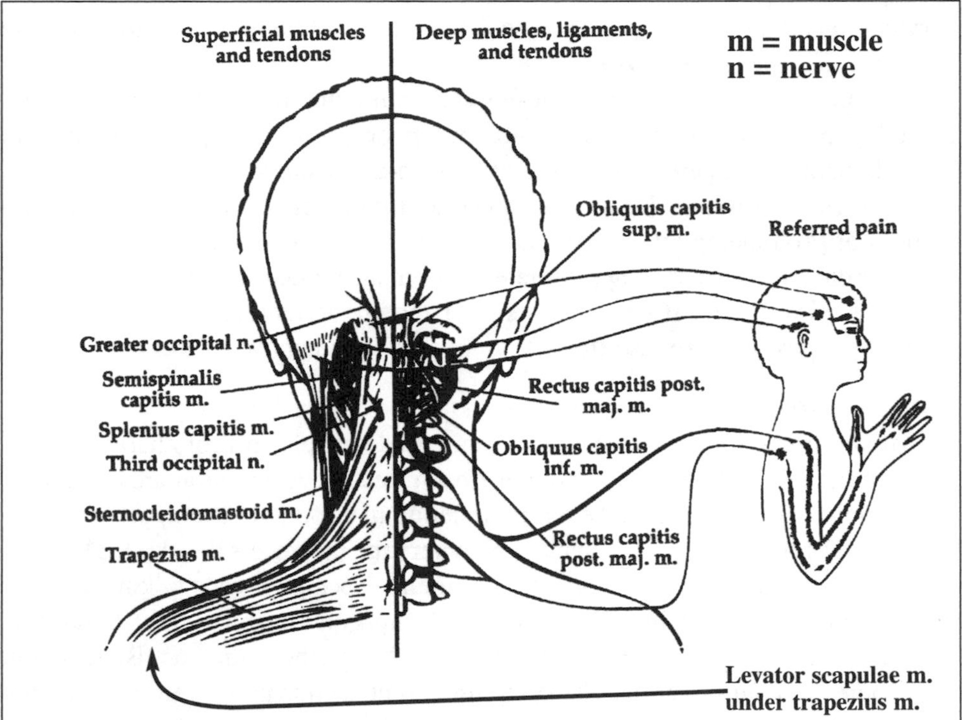

Figure 9-6: Anatomy of the Neck Showing Muscle and Ligament Referral Pain Patterns
Prolotherapy injections strengthen all of the above structures.

Dr. Hackett reported good to excellent results in 90 percent of 82 consecutive patients he treated with neck and/or headache pain.[7, 8] Dr. Kayfetz and associates treated 206 patients who had headaches caused from trauma. They found that Prolotherapy was effective in completely relieving the headaches in 79 percent of patients.[9] John Merriman, M.D., of Tulsa, Oklahoma, reported at the 1995 Hackett Foundation Prolotherapy Conference that in treating the necks of 225 patients with Prolotherapy, 80 percent had good to excellent results.[10] These studies did not differentiate between the different types of headaches. Prolotherapy is effective against migraine, cluster, and tension headaches, if ligament laxity is present.

There are several possible reasons why the cure rate is not even higher. Tension headache, also called muscle-contraction headache, affects at least 80 percent of the world's population.[11] It is a problem principally of adult life, with women affected three times as often as men. Aching or squeezing discomfort is typically bilateral in the occiput (base of the skull) or the frontotemporal muscle mass (temple area). There is often also an aching in the base of the neck. This typically occurs because of the head position we all subject ourselves to every day. Whether as a computer operator typing at the terminal, a cook cutting up carrots, or a surgeon performing an operation, the head-forward neck-bent posture stretches the cervical ligaments and the posterior neck muscles, including the levator scapulae and trapezeii. **(See Figure 9-3.)**

Prolotherapy controls the pain of muscle-contraction headache and neck pain. Prolotherapy, however, will not overcome poor posture or poor dietary and lifestyle habits. If a person is continually sleep-deprived, stressed-out, nutritionally starved (a coffee and doughnut diet), and types on a computer all day, no amount of Prolotherapy will cure that person's neck aches. The cure begins with a proper diet, adequate rest, appropriate stress management, and proper ergonomics at the workstation. If pain persists after the above measures are taken, most assuredly a positive response from Prolotherapy treatment will be experienced.

TMJ Syndrome

Another reason a person may not respond adequately to Prolotherapy is that some of the affected areas may not have been treated. A common area forgotten in headache and neck pain is the temporomandibular joint. The temporomandibular joint (TMJ) is the physical connection where the jaw meets the skull. The TMJ is necessary to keep the jaw in proper alignment, especially when talking and eating. A painful and clicking TMJ is called Temporomandibular Joint Syndrome (TMJS). The symptoms of TMJS are essentially the same as Barré-Leiou Syndrome. It is our belief that the symptoms, such as dizziness, vertigo, etc., that physicians ascribe to TMJS, are actually due to Barré-Lieou Syndrome.

Causes of TMJ Syndrome

It is well known that there is a relationship between head posture and jaw position. This can easily be shown by a person putting the head in proper alignment. This position will be comfortable if the lower jaw is back. If the lower jaw is forced forward while the neck and head are in the position, tension is felt in the back of the neck.

Typically in TMJS the lower jaw (mandible) is extended forward. A head-forward posture exaggerates the problem.[12, 13] This forward mandible aggravates the cervical ligament laxity, which increases the neck pain. Again, an endless cycle of pain and disability is created in the neck, head, and face region.

Prolotherapy injections to strengthen both the cervical vertebrae and the temporomandibular joint will solve this problem. **(See Figure 9-7.)**

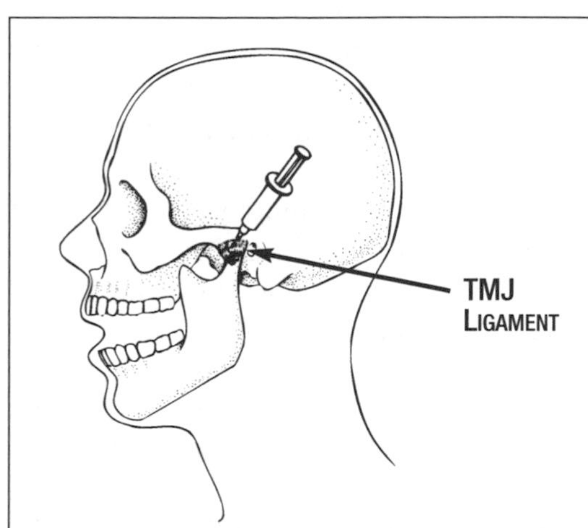

Figure 9-7: Prolotherapy of the TMJ
Prolotherapy is very effective at eliminating the pain and clicking of TMJ Syndrome.

Eventually, the mandible moves forward to the extent that it will stretch the lateral TMJ ligament and produce pain. Once the lateral TMJ ligament becomes lax, the joint will click. It is important to note that clicking in any joint is an indication of ligament laxity of that joint. Joint clicking is never normal or a good sign. Joint clicking, whether it is in the TMJ, knee, neck, or lower back is always abnormal. It is a sign that the bones are beginning to rub against each other. The body's compensatory mechanism for such a situation is to tighten muscles and to grow more bone. The end result will be degeneration, arthritis, and stiffness in that joint. Prolotherapy can stop this process. Prolotherapy will stop a joint from clicking and stop the arthritic process from continuing.

Another reason why patients may have a lax TMJ ligament is their sleeping position. For example, if a patient sleeps with his or her head turned to the right, the TMJ on the left side will be continually stretched throughout the night. Over many decades, continually sleeping in this manner, puts the left TMJ at risk for TMJ ligament laxity. The person with a TMJ problem is advised to sleep with the head turned to the side of the problematic TMJ.

The worst case of TMJS to come into the office was a man called T.W.. T.W.'s jaw popped so loud that the action of opening his mouth could be heard in the other room. The first Prolotherapy session to his TMJ caused a 60-percent reduction in the clicking of his jaw. After the second treatment, the clicking was eliminated completely. T.W. told us that his dentist was amazed. Most dentists and oral surgeons believe TMJ Syndrome is permanent and the best hope is for temporary symptom relief. We can verify in our own practice that TMJ Syndrome can be cured with Prolotherapy. By the way, did the dentist call us to find out what we did? No, they never do.

TREATMENT OF TMJ SYNDROME

Louis Schultz, M.D., an oral surgeon, reported in 1956 that after 20 years of experience in treating hypermobile temporomandibular joints with Prolotherapy, the clicking, grating, or popping was controlled in all of the several thousand patients that had been under his care, without any reported complications or deleterious effects.[14, 15] Dr. Schultz wrote, "Various types of treatment used in the past [for TMJ Syndrome] and still employed by some operators appear to be unsatisfactory. Surgery is one." One problem with surgery is the resultant scars. Anywhere surgery is done, scar tissue will form. Again, as in all chronic painful conditions, there are a myriad of treatment options. A treatment that includes a surgeon's knife should be reserved until all conservative treatment options have been exhausted.

Prolotherapy in the TMJ is very simple. One to two milliliters of a mixture of 25 percent dextrose, 20 percent Sarapin, and 0.4 percent Lidocaine is injected into and around the temporomandibular joint(s). The patient is placed on a soft diet until the mouth is able to fully open. The TMJ Prolotherapy injections cause an awkward bite and a tight jaw for a couple of days. The patient should not force the mouth open during this time period. Generally, this is an excellent time to start a diet, since most people with chronic pain have a positive "basketball-belly sign" due to inactivity because of the pain.

Modern medical practitioners will pressure sick people to utilize their services. Options now available for people with head and neck pain are TMJ arthroscopic surgery, TMJ implants, cervical spine surgery (many varieties), botulism toxin injections into muscles,[16] and the latest gizmo, surgical cauterization, which zaps the bones with a radiofrequency wave, destroying the treated area.[17] This last technique may eliminate a patient's pain because it destroys the fibro-osseous junction, where the pain originates. Why destroy or remove a structure when there is a treatment that will help strengthen and repair it? Prolotherapy causes a permanent strengthening of ligaments and tendons and eliminates the root cause of the pain.

EAR AND MOUTH PAIN

EAGLE SYNDROME AND ERNEST SYNDROME

One of our patients, J.M., told us, "I have been to a hundred doctors and all I get is a hundred different creams. I am drowning in creams, drops, and pills." Some doctors tell him that the problem is in his ear, others say the ear is fine.

J.M., like many others, suffers from terrible ear and mouth pain. Various diagnoses are typically given for such complaints, including *otitis media, otitis externa* (ear infections), trigeminal neuralgia, atypical facial pain, or TMJ Syndrome. These diagnoses may be accurate for some; however, chronic unresolved ear, mouth, face, temple, or head pain generally has a ligament laxity etiology. Instead of creams, drops, or pills, J.M. needed a physician to press on his stylomandibular ligament. Most likely he would jump off the table in pain. Chronic pain must be reproduced in the doctor's office to properly diagnose the source of the problem, and thereby provide appropriate treatment.

The stylomandibular ligament originates at the styloid process underneath the ear and inserts on the medial side of the mandible (the lower jaw). **(See Figure**

9-8.) Pain from the styloid portion of the ligament is called Eagle Syndrome.[18, 19] Pain from the mandibular portion is called Ernest Syndrome.[20, 21]

The following symptoms have been described with both Eagle and Ernest Syndromes.[22, 23]

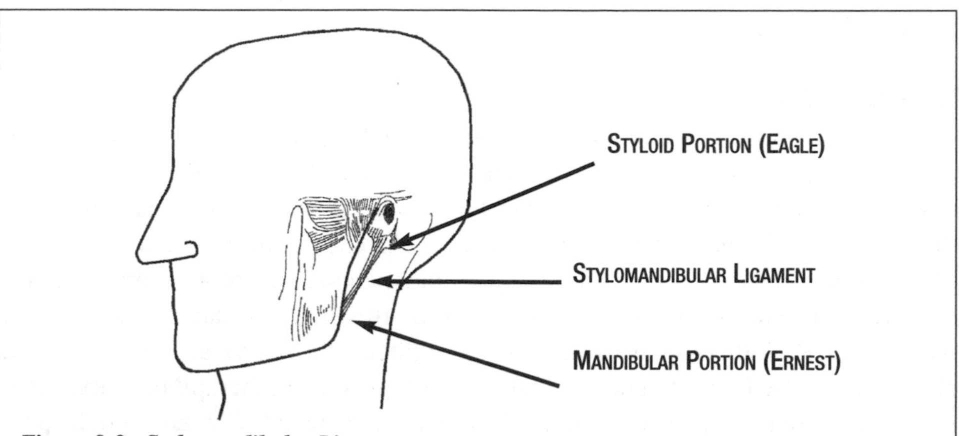

Figure 9-8: Stylomandibular Ligament
Weakness of the Stylomandibular Ligament is responsible for the symptoms of Ernest and Eagle Syndromes.

- Facial pain
- Ear pain
- Dizziness
- Vertigo
- TMJ pain
- Tooth pain
- Eye pain
- Excessive lacrimation (tearing)
- Pain on swallowing
- Cough
- Neck pain
- Difficult jaw opening
- Mouth pain
- Throat pain
- Shoulder pain
- Pain upon opening the mouth
- Voice alteration
- Forehead pain
- Jaw pain
- Sinusitis
- Tinnitus
- Stuffy nose
- Bloodshot eyes
- Pain upon turning the head

Most physicians have not heard of these syndromes and do not know where the stylomandibular ligament is located. For this reason, many people with the above complaints do not obtain relief from their pain. If the diagnosis is wrong, obviously the treatments the physician prescribes will be ineffective.

The stylomandibular and lateral TMJ ligaments attach the jaw to the head. Abnormal motion, excessive movement, or trauma to the jaw may weaken these ligaments. For example, those of us who talk a mile a minute may be prone to TMJ, Eagle, or Ernest Syndromes.

If someone chronically experiences any one of the above symptoms, the stylomandibular ligament must be palpated. If a positive "jump sign" can be elicited, the culprit for the chronic ear-mouth pain has most likely been located. Prolotherapy injections at the stylomandibular ligament bony attachments will start the repair process. Once the stylomandibular ligament is strengthened, the chronic ear-mouth pain, tinnitus, dizziness, vertigo, and other pain complaints subside. This is why many people with chronic facial complaints are choosing to Prolo their pain away.

SUMMARY

Chronic headaches, including migraines, neck, TMJ, ear, and mouth pain, originate from ligament laxity in the head, neck, and TMJ. Prolotherapy strengthens the weakened ligaments to relieve the pain. Research has demonstrated that Prolotherapy eliminates 80 to 90 percent of chronic headaches and neck pain. Migraine headaches, as well as other symptoms, including chronic sinus congestion, vertigo, tinnitus, and dysesthesias in the arms, may be due to Barré-Lieou Syndrome. Prolotherapy permanently strengthens the cervical ligaments and eliminates Barré-Lieou Syndrome and its symptoms. Prolotherapy is an extremely effective treatment for chronic neck, head, TMJ, facial, ear, and mouth pain because it strengthens the structures that are causing the pain. This is why many people are choosing to Prolo their pain away! ■

Chapter 10

Prolo Your Shoulder Pain Away!

The shoulder was uniquely designed by God to have tremendous mobility. The shoulder enables a person to scratch the head, between the shoulder blades, and even the back without pivoting anything but the shoulder. The lack of big ligamentous structures supporting this joint allow its mobility. The shoulder, when abducted and externally rotated, is more vulnerable to injury due to a lack of bony and ligamentous stability in this position. The primary support for the shoulder involves the rotator cuff muscles, which also move the shoulder. People who frequently abduct and externally rotate their shoulders, especially athletes such as pitchers, gymnasts, tennis players, quarterbacks, swimmers, and volleyball players, are prone to chronic shoulder problems. Any activity done with the hand away from the body involves some sort of shoulder abduction and external rotation.[1] **(See Figures 10-1A and 10-1B.)**

A shoulder that crunches and "pops out of joint" is unstable, and is always a sign of weakness in the joint. People who suffer from this condition will feel their shoulder coming out of the socket when they abduct and externally rotate it, because the ligamentous and bony support of the joint is minimal in this position. When this occurs, a person is said to have shoulder subluxation or instability. This diagnosis can be confirmed by abducting and externally rotating the shoulder and pushing the arm forward from the back. In the case of anterior shoulder instability, a positive "frighten sign" (the cousin of the infamous positive "jump sign") will be displayed on the patient's face; the patient is afraid his or her shoulder is going to dislocate.

Cause and Treatment of Shoulder Instability

Traditional treatment for shoulder instability is rotator cuff strengthening exercises, specifically of the supraspinatus muscle, the primary muscle responsible for the external rotation of the shoulder. The rotator cuff is a group of four muscles: the supraspinatus, infraspinatus, subscapularis, and teres minor. **(See Figure 10-2.)** The rotator cuff muscles help stabilize the shoulder and assist with movement. Rotator cuff strengthening exercises help strengthen shoulder muscles but often do not cure the underlying problem of shoulder instability: joint laxity.

To cure shoulder joint instability, the ligamentous and shoulder capsular structures must be strengthened. The main capsular structure involved in the stability of the shoulder is the glenoid labrum, which holds the humerus bone to the glenoid cavity of the scapula. **(See Figure 10-3.)** A shoulder is usually unstable because the structures are torn or stretched. Another important structure to note in **Figure 10-3** is the glenohumeral ligament. Once these structures are stretched or

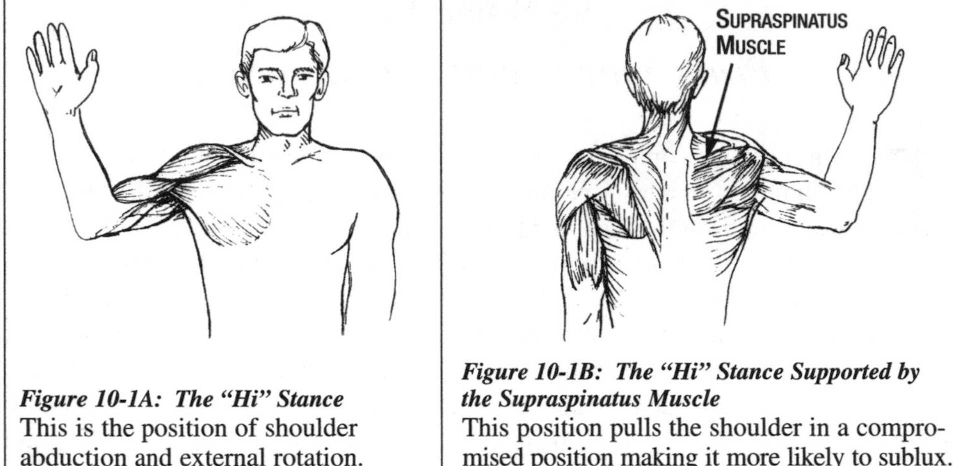

Figure 10-1A: The "Hi" Stance
This is the position of shoulder abduction and external rotation.

Figure 10-1B: The "Hi" Stance Supported by the Supraspinatus Muscle
This position pulls the shoulder in a compromised position making it more likely to sublux.

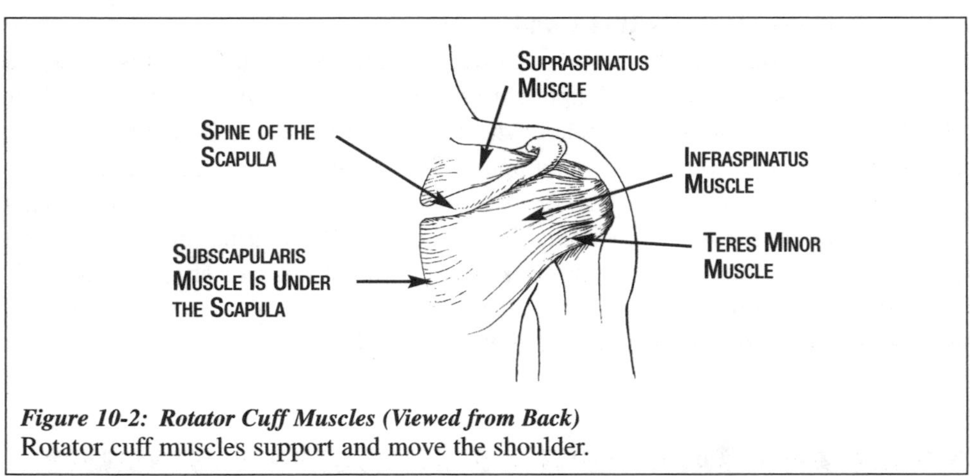

Figure 10-2: Rotator Cuff Muscles (Viewed from Back)
Rotator cuff muscles support and move the shoulder.

loosened, no amount of exercise will strengthen the shoulder joint enough to permanently hold it in place.

Shoulder instability is one of the easiest conditions to treat with Prolotherapy. Gustav A. Hemwall, M.D., the world's most experienced Prolotherapist, who treated thousands of such cases with Prolotherapy, never had a pain patient with chronic shoulder instability who required surgery. All cases treated with Prolotherapy have recovered without any shoulder limitations, as long as the condition was due to ligament laxity. We have had a similar experience. We have found that even patients with complete shoulder dislocations have fully recovered after being treated with Prolotherapy and have returned to normal activities, including competitive sports such as tennis, football, baseball, and volleyball.

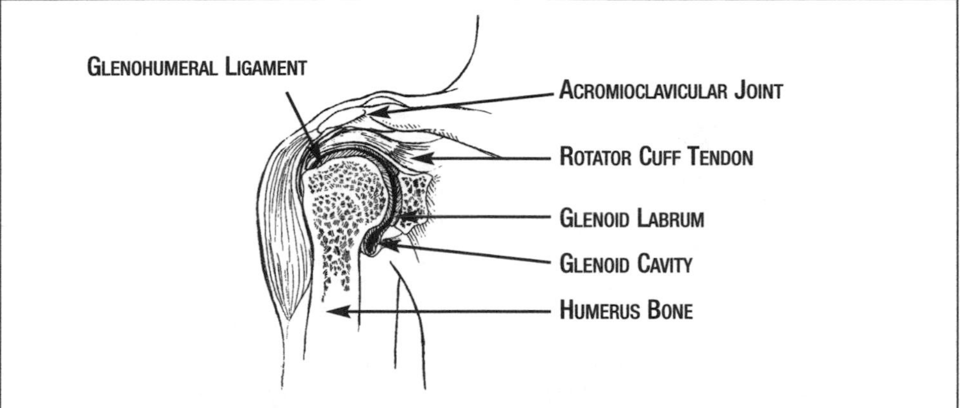

Figure 10-3: Anatomy of the Shoulder (Viewed from Front)
The glenoid labrum and rotator cuff tendons help support the shoulder.

Rotator Cuff Tendonitis

The most common cause of chronic shoulder pain, however, is not shoulder instability, but supraspinatus tendon weakness, also known as rotator cuff tendonitis.[2,3] As noted, the ligamentous, capsular, and bony support of the shoulder in the abducted and externally rotated position is minimal, so the supraspinatus tendon works harder to provide support. The supraspinatus tendon eventually weakens and laxity develops. A supraspinatus tendon problem is manifested by pain with abduction and external rotation of the shoulder, especially when reaching for things above shoulder level, or pain in the shoulder after sleeping due to compression of the supraspinatus tendon. The supraspinatus tendon often refers pain to the back of the shoulder. **(See Figures 10-4A and 10-4B.)** The supraspinatus tendon is the main abductor and external rotator of the shoulder. Sleeping on the shoulder causes a pinching of the rotator cuff muscles and can lead to rotator cuff weakness. There are cases where the cause of the rotator cuff tendon laxity was due to years of sleeping on the shoulder.

In most cases, traditional therapies such as exercise and physical therapy will resolve rotator cuff tendonitis. It is not uncommon, however, for rotator cuff injuries to linger because blood supply to the rotator cuff tendons is poor.[4] Poor blood supply is a reason the rotator cuff is so commonly injured. In chronic cases of shoulder pain due to rotator cuff weakness, Prolotherapy is the treatment of choice. Prolotherapy will cause the rotator cuff to strengthen and eliminate shoulder pain. If rotator cuff weakness is not corrected, the shoulder's range of motion will deteriorate. Rapid deterioration can occur, especially in people over 60 years of age.

As previously stated, the supraspinatus muscle causes shoulder abduction and external rotation. When this muscle weakens, movement becomes painful. Those who have supraspinatus tendon laxity causing pain will stop moving their arms

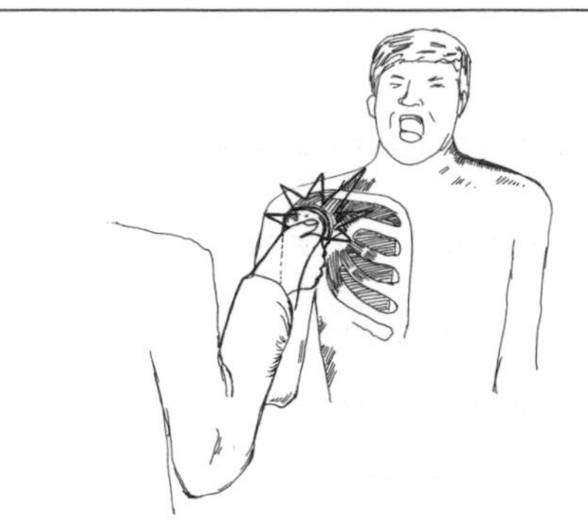

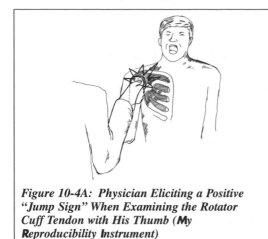

Figure 10-4A: Physician Eliciting a Positive "Jump Sign" When Examining the Rotator Cuff Tendon with His Thumb (My Reproducibility Instrument)

Often times the patient feels pain in the back of the shoulder from rotator cuff weakness.

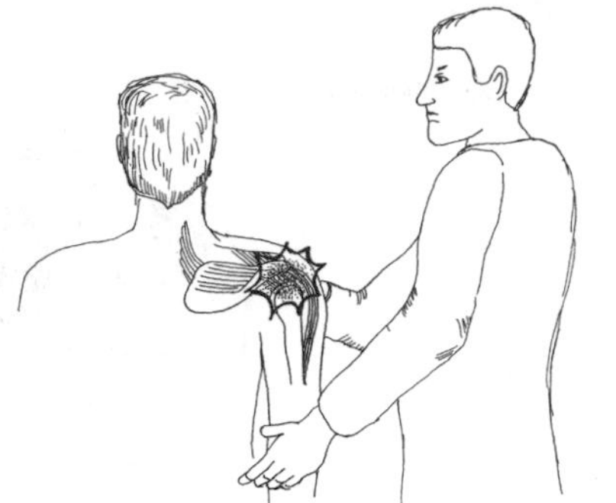

Figure 10-4B: Referral Pattern of the Rotator Cuff Tendons

Pain from the rotator cuff is often referred to the back of the shoulder.

into the painful position. Although they may not realize it, they are slowly but surely losing shoulder movement. What begins as a simple rotator cuff muscle weakness, easily treated with Prolotherapy, has the potential to become a frozen shoulder because of scar tissue formation inside the shoulder that was left untreated. The scar tissue formation, which causes a decrease in the ability to move the shoulder, is called adhesive capsulitis. Pain means something is wrong. Prolotherapy, because it eliminates the cause of most chronic pain, should be tried before a complication of the pain occurs, as seen in the above example.

FROZEN SHOULDER (ADHESIVE CAPSULITIS)

A frozen shoulder is also treatable with Prolotherapy, but healing occurs over a longer period of time. The term adhesive capsulitis refers to scar tissue that forms inside the joint due to lack of movement. If a joint is not moved through its full range of motion every day, scar tissue will form inside the joint. Adhesive capsulitis is especially common in stroke victims who are paralyzed on one side, because they are unable to move their shoulders through a full range of motion.[5]

The first line of treatment for a frozen shoulder is physiotherapy. Physical therapy modalities, such as myofascial release, massage, range-of-motion exercises, and ultrasound, can often release scar tissue. If these do not relieve the problem, then the scar tissue can be broken up within the joint by the physician injecting the shoulder full of a solution made up of sterile water mixed with an anesthetic. The numb shoulder can then be gently manipulated. Often several sessions of this treatment regime are needed to achieve the shoulder's original full range of motion.

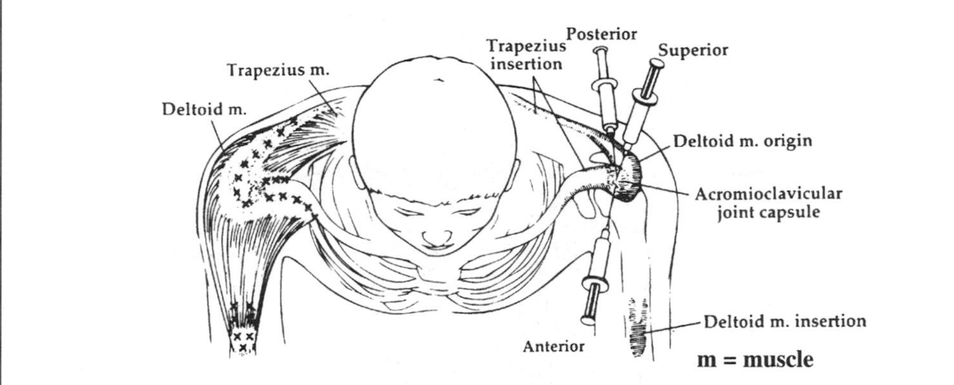

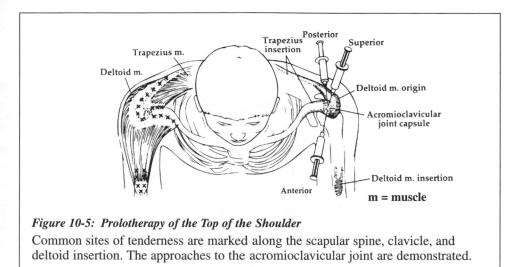

Figure 10-5: Prolotherapy of the Top of the Shoulder
Common sites of tenderness are marked along the scapular spine, clavicle, and deltoid insertion. The approaches to the acromioclavicular joint are demonstrated.

Since the initial cause of the adhesive capsulitis was supraspinatus (rotator cuff) weakness, Prolotherapy injections to strengthen the rotator cuff are done in conjunction with the above technique. Complete to near-complete resolution can be accomplished using this combined approach.

A misunderstanding of the supraspinatus tendon's referral pattern keeps clinicians from diagnosing the rotator cuff problem. This tendon refers pain to the back and side of the shoulder, leading clinicians to believe their patients have a muscle problem, when in fact they have a tendon problem. A complaint of shoulder pain is almost always a rotator cuff weakness problem. Prolotherapy is extremely effective at strengthening the rotator cuff tendons.

ACROMIOCLAVICULAR JOINT/CORACOID PROCESS

Another common cause of chronic shoulder pain is a weak attachment of the clavicle to the acromion. This joint is called the acromioclavicular joint and is noted on the surface of the skin at the apex (top) of the shoulder. **(See Figure 10-5.)** This joint is usually injured in a fall or by a hyperextension of the shoulder.[6] When this occurs, the weight of the body is transmitted to the acromioclavicular joint. This joint, like all joints, is held together by ligaments. When these ligaments are injured and become lax, the joint grinds and grates and causes pain. Acromioclavicular ligament laxity causes pain upon lifting or activity involving the hands in front of or across the body. Prolotherapy is extremely effective at strengthening the acromioclavicular ligaments, eliminating the shoulder grinding and chronic shoulder pain from this area.

A lesser-known cause of shoulder pain emanates from the coracoid process. From this little nub of bone, stem some very important structures, including the pectoralis minor muscle, coracobrachialis muscle, biceps muscle, coracoacromial

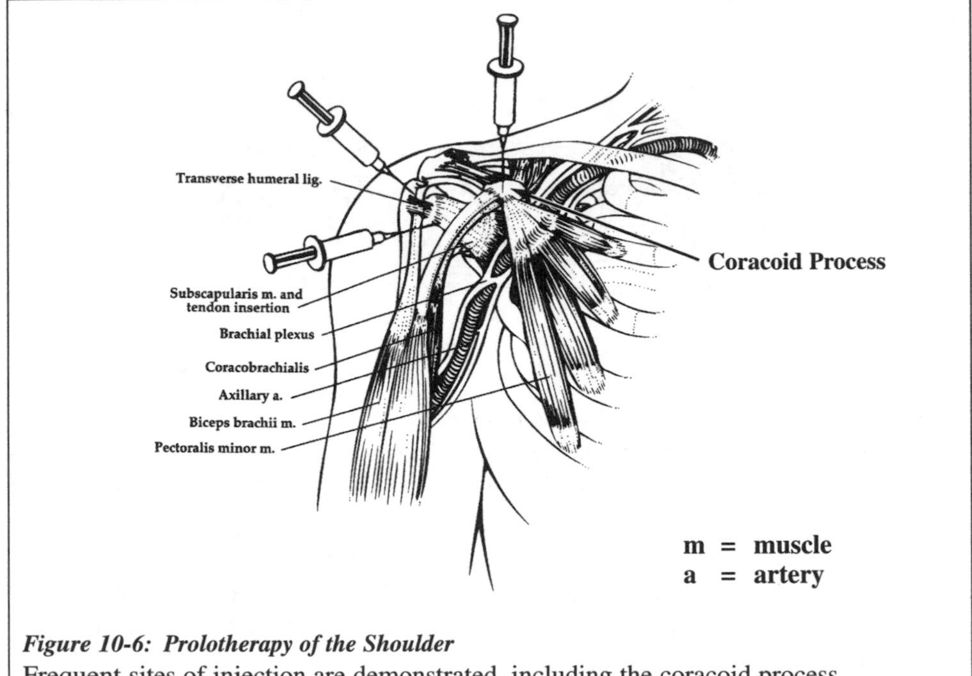

Figure 10-6: Prolotherapy of the Shoulder
Frequent sites of injection are demonstrated, including the coracoid process, subscapularis tendon, and the greater tuberosity.

ligament, coracoclavicular ligament, coracohumeral ligament, and parts of the articular capsule. All attach on a nub of bone no bigger than the tip of the little finger. Although small, this area is "mighty" in regards to importance. This area of the shoulder is palpated during a routine Prolotherapy shoulder examination. Chronic shoulder pain patients are typically very tender in this area and a positive "jump sign" can be elicited upon palpation. Prolotherapy injections are given to strengthen the fibro-osseous junctions of all the above structures at the coracoid process. **(See Figure 10-6.)** This area is routinely treated to relieve chronic shoulder pain.

Impingement Syndrome

Approximately five percent of patients with chronic shoulder pain do not find relief from Prolotherapy injections. These people usually have Impingement Syndrome. This is caused by the supraspinatus tendon being pinched between the coracohumeral ligament—from the clavicle above and the humerus below. People often have a bony spur on the clavicle that decreases the space through which the supraspinatus tendon must travel.[7]

Occasionally, surgery is needed to give the supraspinatus tendon more room to move. (Like us, it needs its own space.) The diagnosis can be easily confirmed in the office by observing a grimaced and painful face upon abducting and internal-

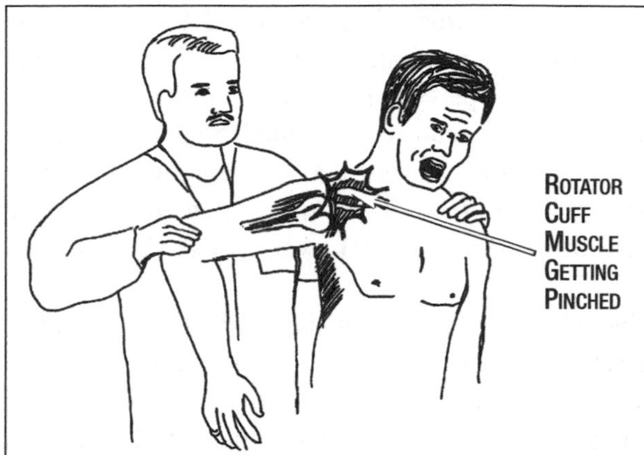

Figure 10-7: Physician Eliciting a Positive "Impingement Sign"

The rotator cuff muscles get "pinched" when the arm is abducted and turned in, if a person has arthritis in the shoulder.

ly rotating the shoulder, producing a positive "impingement sign." **(See Figure 10-7.)** It should be noted that even with an initial diagnosis of Impingement Syndrome, the majority of people obtain complete or satisfactory relief of their pain with Prolotherapy alone. For the few patients who have needed surgery for Impingement Syndrome after Prolotherapy, the response rate of the combined approach has been excellent. The Prolotherapy has strengthened the rotator cuff tendons and surgery has eliminated the impingement of those tendons, leading to complete relief of the chronic shoulder pain.

PROLOTHERAPY FOR SHOULDER PAIN

Prolotherapy will cause the growth of the rotator cuff tendons whether or not they are torn, stretched, or pinched as described above. Prolotherapy causes the growth of any ligament, tendon, capsule, or muscle tissue at the fibro-osseous junction. Prolotherapy is ineffective only if there has been a complete tear of the ligament or tendon. In such cases, surgery must be performed. However, 98 percent of all chronic pain cases do not involve complete ligament and tendon tears, and Prolotherapy is the treatment of choice.

It is always worthwhile to have an evaluation by a physician skilled in Prolotherapy prior to any surgical procedure for pain. Physicians who utilize Prolotherapy in their practice understand ligament referral patterns and are skilled in diagnosing ligament and tendon relaxation. In more than 95 percent of cases, surgery performed simply on the basis of chronic pain can be avoided by using Prolotherapy.

UNRELIABILITY OF MRI FOR DIAGNOSIS OF LIGAMENT INJURY

Many researchers have shown that x-ray studies of the shoulder often do not reveal the source of the problem, as abnormal MRI results are often seen in patients with no shoulder pain symptoms.[8-10] Vijay Chandnani, M.D., and associates, presented results of a study involving people 25 to 55 years of age who were asymptomatic. The following were the findings from their MRI scans of the shoulder: 35 percent had bone spurs of the acromioclavicular joint; 35 percent had evidence of rotator cuff pathology; and 50 percent had abnormalities in the glenoid labrum. C. Neumann, M.D., and associates, examined 55 asymptomatic shoulders with T1-weighted MRI scans and showed that 89 percent had abnormalities in the supraspinatus tendon.[11] It is incredible that 89 percent of people have abnormalities in their rotator cuff tendons on MRI, even though they have no symptoms whatsoever!

The most recent study conducted by Jerry Sher, M.D., and associates, published in 1995, examined MRI scans of 96 people who had no symptoms of shoulder pain. This study revealed that 34 percent of the individuals showed a partial tear of the rotator cuff and 15 percent had evidence of complete full-thickness tears. This is obviously an erroneous reading because people with complete tears of the rotator cuff would not be asymptomatic: They would not be able to move their shoulders much at all. People over 60 years of age had MRI scans showing 54 percent with rotator cuff tears and 28 percent with full-thickness tears. This means that people over 60 years of age, without any shoulder problems whatsoever, have a 54-percent chance of the MRI scan showing a tear of the rotator cuff. They also have a 28 percent chance of the MRI scan showing a complete full-thickness tear of the rotator cuff.[12]

Remember, these studies were conducted on people who did not have any symptoms of shoulder pain. If someone goes to an orthopedic surgeon for chronic shoulder pain, guess what treatment is going to be recommended based on the MRI scan? You guessed it! Sliced shoulder! It is imperative that an evaluation be done by a Prolotherapist because diagnostic tests can often lead a clinician astray.

A patient once came to our office with an MRI scan showing a complete tear of the rotator cuff. Upon physical examination of this patient, it was evident that the tear was not complete. After several sessions of Prolotherapy, the patient's shoulder was symptom-free. There is no substitute for a listening ear and a strong thumb. If physicians cannot reproduce their patient's pain in the office, they probably cannot get rid of it either. A Prolotherapist can reproduce a patient's pain using his or her own **MRI** (**M**y **R**eproducibility **I**nstrument, the thumb) and can eliminate the pain. Reproduction of pain by a good physical examination, combined with elimination of the pain by Prolotherapy, is far more effective in diagnosing the cause of chronic shoulder pain than any CAT or MRI scan. **(See Figures 10-4A and 10-4B.)**

SUMMARY

Chronic shoulder pain is usually due to a weakness in the rotator cuff, specifically in the supraspinatus tendon, because the tendon has poor blood supply. If left untreated, this supraspinatus tendon laxity leads to adhesive capsulitis, or frozen shoulder. Other common reasons for chronic shoulder pain are acromioclavicular ligament laxity, shoulder instability due to a weakened glenohumeral ligament or glenoid labrum tear, and weakness of the structures that attach to the coracoid process.

MRI scans of the shoulder are often abnormal in individuals without any shoulder symptoms whatsoever. The best diagnostic procedure for chronic shoulder pain is palpation of the structure, causing a positive "jump sign," and relief of the pain immediately after the structure is treated with Prolotherapy. Prolotherapy is the treatment of choice for chronic shoulder pain because it corrects the underlying weakness causing the pain. This is why many people are choosing to Prolo their shoulder pain away! ■

Chapter 11

Prolo Your Elbow, Wrist, and Hand Pain Away!

Because of our modern high-tech society, many people sit all day looking at a computer screen, typing on a keyboard. Some children in first and second grades are required to do their schoolwork on computers. Because of this technological surge, more injuries to the elbows, wrists and hands are emerging.

Typically, people who perform repetitive tasks with their hands are the patients with chronic elbow, wrist, and hand pain.[1] This includes mail handlers, assembly line workers, carpenters, computer operators, secretaries, and the thousands of other jobs that keep people in one space doing the same thing day after day. Is it any wonder that after repeating a movement 10 billion times that a part of the body breaks down?

After a long hard day of work or strenuous exercise, it is quite normal for muscles to hurt for a short period of time. This is often a "good hurt." You worked hard and deserve to have your spouse rub your feet. (But how many of them do?) The muscles ache after a good workout because muscle cells were actually injured during exercise. Yes, you read that correctly. Exercise and repetitive work does cause injury to muscle cells. But such injury is good for the muscles because they have a tremendous blood supply, and this "temporary injury" stimulates muscle cells to multiply and grow. If you exercise daily, new blood vessels form and soon you may be as "studly" as Arnold Schwarzenegger.

God made muscles with the ability to be ready for a fight. It is a necessary defense mechanism that, at a moment's notice, the blood supply to our muscles can increase tenfold. If you wake up to find that your house is on fire, the blood supply to the muscles can increase to give them the strength to rescue you. Exercise is necessary for good health and keeps the muscles strong.

This "good hurt" with exercise should not last more than an hour or two. If the muscles hurt longer than this time period, you are either exercising too much or need to take more breaks during work.

An extreme case of overexertion occurred when Ross ran the Chicago Marathon in 1988. He knew he would be a little stiff after the race, so he planned to take the following week as vacation. Prior to the race, 16 miles was his longest practice run. He ran the race with his buddy, Glenn, who had already finished several marathons.

Unfortunately, the day of the race was too cold for anyone other than polar bears. Four hours and eight minutes after he started, he crossed the finish line a winner. Yes, a winner. At the end of the race, everyone is told, "To run is to win." However, for the next five days Ross felt like a loser. He was nauseated, stiff, achy, extremely hot, and totally drained. No amount of massage, ice, heat, or tender loving care (this almost always works) could make him feel well after that amount of "exercise." Fortunately, he was eventually able to walk again!

Many people attempt similar feats of stardom on the weekends. They are known as weekend warriors. A good example of a weekend warrior is our friend, Kurt. At least once a month, he injures himself doing some sporting event. Kurt somehow thinks that sitting at a desk all day is training enough to become Karch Karaly on the volleyball court during the weekend. The main point is to exercise at a level consistent with your lifestyle. If your main exercise during the week is getting up from the couch, putting down the remote, and going to the kitchen to get ice cream from the freezer, it is not wise to play in a basketball league on weekends.

Muscle injuries usually heal with plain and simple rest. To speed up recovery from muscle injuries, it is beneficial to stretch the muscles after exercising.[2] Nutritional supplements also help muscle injuries heal.[3]

Chronic pain that is not relieved by rest is likely due to a ligament injury. Pain with repetitive motion may be an indication of tendon injury. Ligaments attach bone to bone. While the ligaments stabilize the bones, the tendons and muscles enable the bones to move. This is why ligaments often hurt when the body is at rest and tendons often hurt from activity.

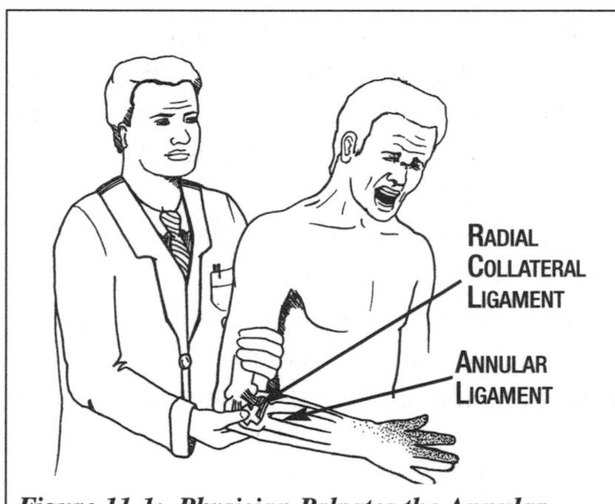

Figure 11-1: Physician Palpates the Annular Ligament, Eliciting the Referral Pain Pattern Down the Arm

Weakness in the annular ligament refers pain to the thumb and the index and middle fingers.

ELBOW PAIN

ANNULAR LIGAMENT WEAKNESS

Eighty percent of chronic elbow pain is due to a sprain of the annular ligament. **(See Figure 11-1.)** This ligament is rarely examined by a family physician or an orthopedic surgeon. Nearly all of our patients with chronic elbow pain tell us their doctors told them they have tennis elbow. Tennis elbow is also known as lateral epicondylitis. The latest treatment for this condition is the dreaded cortisone shot! Cortisone weakens tissue, whereas Prolotherapy strengthens tissue. Cortisone has temporary effects in regard to pain control whereas Prolotherapy has permanent effects. However, cortisone does have one permanent effect: Continual use will permanently weaken tissue. Anyone receiving long-term prednisone or cortisone shots will confirm this fact.

The annular ligament is located approximately three quarters of an inch distal to the lateral epicondyle. Its job is to attach the radius bone to the ulnar bone. It is this ligament that enables the hand to rotate, as in turning a key or a screwdriver.

Because of the tremendous demands placed on the fingers and hands to perform repetitive tasks, the annular ligament is stressed every day (like a lot of people we know). Eventually, this ligament becomes lax and a source of chronic pain.

The lateral epicondyle of the humerus bone is very superficial, so it is much more inviting to the dreaded cortisone-filled needle of an orthopedist than the deeper annular ligament. Typically, people with chronic elbow pain are tender over the lateral epicondyle but do not elicit a positive "jump sign" in that area. Only palpation over the annular ligament elicits the positive "jump sign." The annular ligament also has a distinct referral pain pattern. It refers pain to the thumb, index, and middle fingers. This is the same referral pain pattern as is exhibited in Carpal Tunnel Syndrome.

Unfortunately, many patients with elbow and hand pain have been misdiagnosed with Carpal Tunnel Syndrome. Carpal Tunnel Syndrome refers to the entrapment of the median nerve as it travels through the wrist into the hand. The nerve supplies sensation to the skin over the thumb, index, and middle fingers. A typical Carpal Tunnel Syndrome patient will experience pain and numbness in this distribution in the hand. Because most physicians do not know the referral pain patterns of ligaments, they do not realize that the fourth and fifth cervical vertebrae and the annular ligament can refer pain to the thumb, index, and middle fingers. Ligament laxity can also cause numbness, as already discussed. Cervical and annular ligament laxity should always be evaluated prior to making the diagnosis of Carpal Tunnel Syndrome. Surgery for Carpal Tunnel Syndrome should not be done until an evaluation is performed by a physician who understands the referral patterns of ligaments and is experienced in Prolotherapy.

Seldom do patients find relief from the "Carpal Tunnel" complaints of pain in the hand and elbow with physical therapy and surgery because the diagnosis is wrong. The most common reason for pain in the elbow that refers pain to the hand is weakness in the annular ligament, not Carpal Tunnel Syndrome. Several sessions of Prolotherapy will easily strengthen the annular ligament and relieve chronic elbow pain.

ULNAR COLLATERAL LIGAMENT WEAKNESS

Another common cause of chronic elbow pain is an ulnar collateral ligament sprain. **(See Figure 11-2.)** This ligament supports the inside of the elbow. It is responsible for holding the ulnar bone to the distal end of the humerus. This enables the arm to flex, pivoting at the elbow. A patient's complaint of pain on the inside of the elbow will cause a physician to examine the lateral epicondyle's "sister," the medial epicondyle. For example, the diagnosis of golfer's elbow is often made without examining the ulnar collateral ligament.

The ulnar collateral ligament is approximately three-quarters of an inch distal to the medial epicondyle. The ulnar collateral ligament refers pain to the little finger and ring finger. This same pain and numbness distribution is seen with aggravating the ulnar nerve. The ulnar nerve lies behind the elbow and is the reason

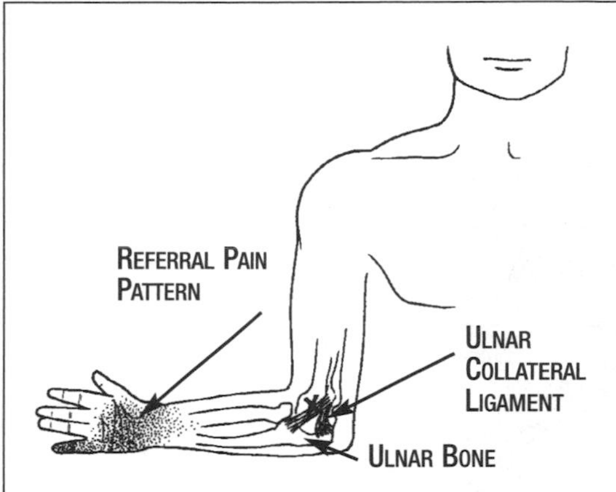

Figure 11-2: Ulnar Collateral Ligament Referral Pain Pattern
Weakness in the ulnar collateral ligament refers pain to the third and fourth fingers.

why hitting your funny bone causes pain. Because most physicians are not familiar with the referral pattern of ligaments, patients with elbow pain and/or numbness into the little finger and ring finger are diagnosed with an ulnar nerve problem, Cubital Tunnel Syndrome. A more common reason is ligament laxity in the sixth and seventh cervical vertebrae or in the ulnar collateral ligament—not a pinched ulnar nerve.

As stated, a patient given the opinion that surgery on the ulnar nerve is needed for a pain complaint should obtain a second opinion from a doctor who is competent in the treatment of Prolotherapy. Surgery should be performed only after all conservative options, including Prolotherapy, have been attempted. Prolotherapy to the ulnar collateral ligament is the most successful way to eliminate medial elbow pain.

If medial epicondylitis (golfer's elbow) or lateral epicondylitis (tennis elbow) is causing elbow pain, the muscles that attach to these areas are attempting to repair themselves, causing inflammation. The treatment should not be to "anti-inflame," as is the case with cortisone or with anti-inflammatories like ibuprofen. The correct treatment is to strengthen the muscle attachments that are inflamed due to the body's attempt to strengthen the area. The muscles that extend the wrist attach at the lateral epicondyle and the muscles that flex the wrist attach at the medial epicondyle. Prolotherapy to strengthen these muscle attachments is very effective in eliminating chronic elbow pain.

WRIST PAIN

Weakened ligaments commonly cause chronic wrist pain. The weakened ligaments allow one of the eight wrist bones to become unstable and shift positions. This condition is called carpal instability. The wrist is actually eight oddly shaped bones in a sea of ligaments.[4] **(See Figure 11-3.)** The most common wrist bones that become unstable because of loose ligaments are the capitate, scaphoid, and lunate.[5, 6] Thus, the most common ligaments treated with Prolotherapy for chronic wrist pain are the dorsal capitate-trapezoid, hamate-capitate, scaphoid-triquetral, and scapholunate ligaments. Again, the diagnosis is easily made by direct palpation of these ligaments, as the wrist bones are very superficial to the skin.

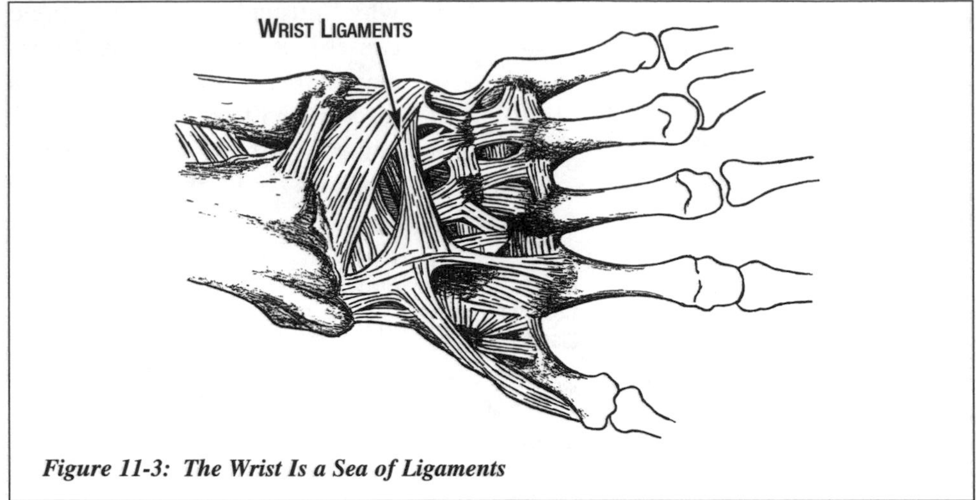

Figure 11-3: The Wrist Is a Sea of Ligaments

The weakened ligament can be palpated and a positive "jump sign" elicited. Several Prolotherapy sessions in this area resolves the problem.

A few points need to be made about bony alignment and the role of Prolotherapy. Prolotherapy injections strengthen the ligaments, which attach to the bones. The ligaments, after returning to normal strength, will produce proper bone alignment. Patients who are under the care of a chiropractor, in addition to a Prolotherapy physician, often comment that their chiropractor is amazed by how well the spine has moved into alignment.

Remember, Prolotherapy is an effective treatment for any structural pain problem that involves a weak ligament or tendon. Regardless of the area of the body involved, four Prolotherapy sessions are usually all that is needed to resolve the chronic pain problem in a healthy individual.

HAND PAIN

When it comes to hand pain, the most common problem involves the thumb because of its unique role in the hand's function. Whenever a doorknob is turned, a screwdriver is used, or something is held, the thumb is part of the action. When typing, what part of the hand must continually hit the space bar? The thumb. Because thumbs have to work so much harder than fingers, it is usually the first to elicit pain. The thumb ligament that joins the wrist to the base of the thumb is called the radial collateral ligament, the same name as the ligament inside the elbow. The thumb ligament that joins the base of the thumb (the first metacarpal) to the succeeding joint (proximal phalanx) is the collateral ligament. **(See Figure 11-4.)**

These two joints of the thumb, called the carpometacarpal (CMC) and metacarpophalangeal (MCP), are usually the first areas where pain is experienced. If the ligaments in these joints are not strengthened, arthritis will eventually occur. Arthritis starts the day a joint becomes loose. The looser the joint, the greater the

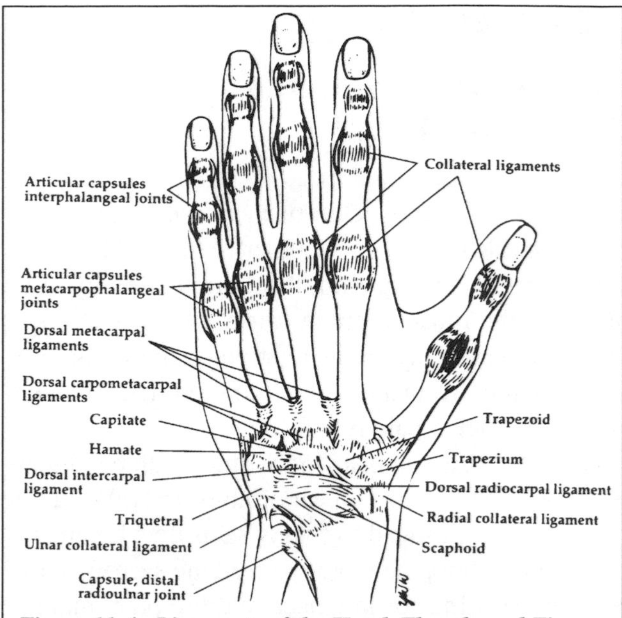

Figure 11-4: Ligaments of the Hand, Thumb, and Fingers
Note that all the joints of the hand, thumb, and fingers are primarily supported by ligaments.

chance it has of becoming arthritic. Arthritis in the thumb, as well as other phalangeal joints in the hand, are a major cause of disability, especially among the elderly.[7, 8] The progression of osteo-arthritis stops the day the ligaments become strong and are able to stabilize the joint. **(See Chapter 15, Prolo Your Arthritis Pain Away!)**

Prolotherapy is the treatment of choice for patients suffering from stiff, sore hands or thumbs. Once the ligaments are strengthened, the pain and stiffness in the thumbs and fingers subside. Again, four Prolotherapy treatment sessions are usually all that is needed.

SUMMARY

Chronic pain in the arms, elbows, wrists, and hands is primarily due to the type of work people perform in a modern high-tech society. The repetitive motions of the upper extremities eventually wear out the ligamentous support of the elbows, wrists, and thumbs. The end result is loose joints that cause pain and stiffness. Prolotherapy injections start the healing process to cause the growth of ligaments that stabilize these joints. Once the ligaments return to normal strength, the chronic pain is eliminated. Because of this, many people with chronic elbow, wrist, and hand pain are choosing to Prolo their pain away! ■

CHAPTER 12

Prolo Your Groin, Hip, and Knee Pain Away!

The old saying that "the foot bone is connected to the knee bone is connected to the hip bone" sure holds true when it comes to leg and hip pain. To adequately eliminate hip, knee, and leg pain, the entire extremity must be evaluated. As stated in Chapter 8, the most common cause for low back pain is laxity in the sacroiliac joint. Prolotherapy injections to strengthen the sacroiliac joint eliminates the pain. As usual, the original cause of the sacroiliac ligament laxity must be addressed to ensure long-term pain relief.

In 1911, Ronald Meisenbach, M.D., observed that "individuals with pendulous abdomens are frequently in a state of lipomatosis with very flabby and relaxed ligaments."[1] In common language, flabby bellies lead to flabby sacroiliac ligaments. The more weight that hangs over the belt line, the more stressed the sacroiliac ligaments become. To ensure long-term healing for low back and hip pain, maintenance of a proper weight is encouraged. Dr. Meisenbach also wrote that "it is now beginning to be recognized that almost all of the sciaticas are due to sacroiliac relaxation."[2] This is exactly what Gustav A. Hemwall, M.D., the world's most experienced Prolotherapist, taught.

GROIN PAIN

Another common cause of chronic hip pain is the Iliolumbar Syndrome.[3] This syndrome is caused by ligament laxity of the iliolumbar ligaments. The common symptoms are not only hip pain, but also pain referred to the groin. **(See Figures 2-2 and 2-3.)** Iliolumbar ligament laxity should be explored as a diagnosis for any patient with unresolved groin pain.

Several years ago, the late David Brewer, M.D., a personal friend and a respected obstetrician/gynecologist, examined a young woman with unresolved lower abdominal/groin pain. The young woman was scheduled for an exploratory laparoscopic surgery to the pelvic region. The possible diagnosis was endometriosis or an ovarian cyst. Interestingly, the surgery had to be postponed until Dr. Brewer returned from a conference. At that conference, Dr. Brewer learned about Prolotherapy and the ligament referral patterns.

When this young woman returned for her pre-surgery physical examination, Dr. Brewer proceeded to examine the iliolumbar ligament. You can guess what happened—a positive "jump sign." He treated the area with Prolotherapy and immediately the chronic lower abdominal and groin pain were gone. Whew! Another surgery prevented! Needless to say, Dr. Brewer became a quick believer in Prolotherapy.

This case illustrates a point that has been made over and over again. Prior to any surgical procedure for pain, it is important to have an evaluation by a physician familiar with Prolotherapy. The main cause of unresolved chronic pain is weakness in a ligament. Surgery does not cause ligaments to regrow but can cause harm and will surely empty your pocketbook.

Chronic groin pain is easily treated with Prolotherapy because there are multiple ligament laxities that cause groin pain. This diagnosis is accomplished by the physician having a listening ear and a strong thumb. An interesting case will illustrate this point.

A young woman came to see Ross. She had been suffering for more than 10 years with terrible groin pain. She had stepped into an animal trap, which wrapped around her leg. This caused the trap to engage and, before she knew it, she found herself hanging upside down from a tree limb with the rope lassoed around her ankle. Alone in the forest, she hung there for what seemed like eternity until she was finally rescued. As a result of this incident, she was left with chronic groin and back pain. As a health food store owner, she turned to numerous healing techniques. She also sought relief from many doctors who diagnosed her as having, among other things, a groin sprain, a disc problem, and a tendon strain. Nothing permanently relieved her pain.

Her medical history clearly indicated one thing that could have caused the problem. Ross compressed the pubic symphysis (the pubic joint ligament) with his thumb on the side of the leg that had been caught in the rope. Wow! That caused a whole-body "jump sign." He treated that area with Prolotherapy. For the first time in a decade, she walked without pain.

Only once has a patient said that a physician had examined the pubic symphysis. The pubic symphysis is the front joint of the pelvic bone. **(See Figure 12-1.)** The back joint of the pelvic bone is the sacroiliac joint. If the sacroiliac joint is lax, there is a good chance that the pubic symphysis will also be lax. Regarding the treatment of chronic pain with Prolotherapy, it is advisable to treat both sides of a joint to ensure its strength. Someone suffering from low back pain should not only have the sacroiliac joints examined, but the pubic symphysis as well. Likewise, patients with groin pain should have the sacroiliac joints palpated. Sacroiliac ligament laxity can also refer pain to the groin.[4]

The pubic symphysis is actually a disc. It is a fibrocartilaginous disc that, like any other disc in the body, can be disrupted. It is supported on top by the superior pubic ligaments. Typically, people with groin pain are assumed to have a groin strain. This refers to a strain of the adductor muscles that attach to the pubic bone. **(See Figure 12-1.)** Chronic pain that does not respond to exercise, massage, or manipulation is most likely a ligament problem. In the case of pain reproduced by palpating the pubic symphysis, the cause of the pain is pubic symphysis diathesis. This means a loose pubic symphysis area. Unfortunately, mild laxity in the joints can only be diagnosed by palpation. There is no x-ray study

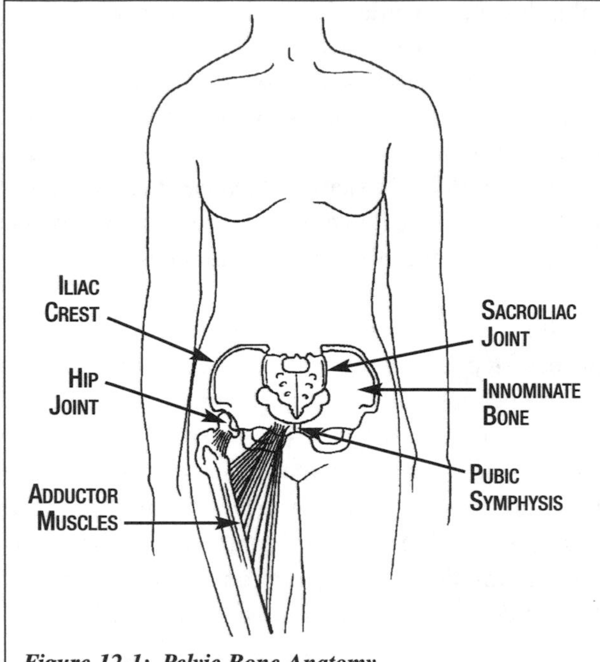

Figure 12-1: Pelvic Bone Anatomy
The pelvic bones connect in the front at the pubic symphysis and in the back at the sacroiliac joint.

that can be done to confirm it. This is also why many physicians do not diagnose it. The diagnosis of ligament laxity can generally only be made by a listening ear and a strong thumb.

The pubic symphysis joint is stressed when the leg is pulled out from underneath, as in the case of the lassoed lady. This can also be caused by falling, tripping, or slipping. In sports, pubic symphysis injuries are relatively frequent. Swimmers who do the breast stroke often suffer groin pain from a pubic symphysis injury. Prolotherapy for pubic symphysis diathesis entails injections into the fibro-osseous junction of the superior pubic symphysis ligament and injections in the pubic symphysis itself. Prolotherapy is extremely effective in strengthening the pubic symphysis and relieving chronic groin pain in this area.

Hip Pain

The hip joint joins the leg to the pelvis. Unfortunately for most people, both legs are not exactly the same. They may look the same, but from a biomechanical standpoint, they are not the same. One leg may be rotated either in or out, or one leg may be shorter than the other. The latter is especially common if one leg was broken during childhood. Because the hip joint connects the leg to the pelvis, the hip joint will sustain the brunt of any biomechanical abnormality that may occur. If one leg is shorter than the other, the hip joints will be stressed because the leg-length discrepancy causes an abnormal gait (manner of walking). The gait cycle is most efficient when the iliac crests (pelvis) are level. Unequal leg lengths cause the pelvis to move abnormally. This is evidenced by the waddling gait of someone with a hip problem. This waddling gait helps remove pressure on the painful hip.

With leg-length discrepancy, either hip joint can cause pain and usually both hip joints hurt to some degree.[5] To propel the leg forward, the hip joint must be raised which strains the gluteus medius muscle and the posterior hip ligaments.

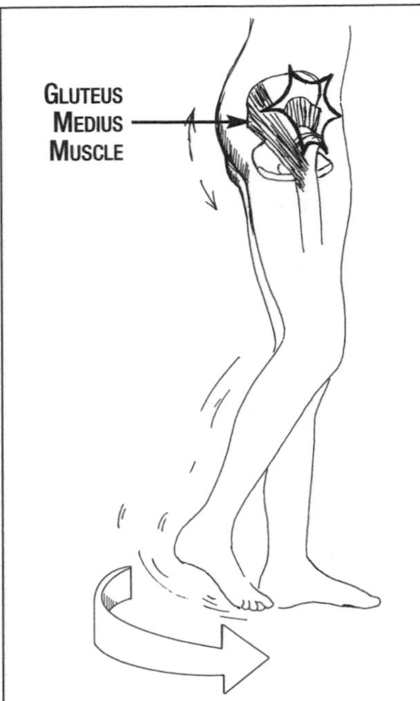

Figure 12-2: One Leg Longer Than the Other Causes Hip Pain
Weakness of the hip ligaments eventually occurs in the longer leg.

(See Figure 12-2.) Leg-length problems are also associated with recurrent lower back problems because they cause the pelvis to be asymmetric.[6] Prolotherapy to the sacroiliac and hip joints will correct the asymmetries in the majority of cases. The leg-length discrepancy disappears as a result of the leveling of the pelvis. If asymmetry remains after treatment, a shoe insert or heel lift will generally correct the problem.

A problem in the hip may commonly manifest itself as groin or inguinal pain. Someone suffering from groin pain should be examined at the pubic symphysis, sacroiliac joint, iliolumbar ligaments, and hip joint. Pain from the hip joint may also be felt locally, directly above the hip joint in the back. When the hip joint becomes lax, the muscles over the joint compensate for the laxity by tensing. As is the case with any joint of the body, lax ligaments initiate muscle tension in an attempt to stabilize the joint. This compensatory mechanism to stabilize the hip joint eventually causes the gluteus medius, pyriformis muscle, and iliotibial band/tensor fascia lata muscles to tighten because of chronic contraction in an attempt to compensate for a loose hip joint. The contracted gluteus medius can eventually irritate the trochanteric bursa, causing a trochanteric bursitis. A bursa is a fluid-filled sac which helps muscles glide over bony prominences. Patients with chronic hip problems often have had cortisone injected into this bursa, which generally brings temporary relief. But this treatment does not provide permanent relief because the underlying ligament laxity is not being corrected. Prolotherapy injections to strengthen the hip joint and iliocapsular ligaments will provide definitive relief in such a case.

It is interesting to note that trochanteric bursitis, Pyriformis Syndrome, and weakness in the iliotibial band also cause "sciatica."[7,8] Someone suffering from "sciatica" should request the physician to examine the following structures: sacroiliac joint, hip joint, sacrotuberous and sacrospinous ligaments, trochanteric bursa, and iliotibial band/tensor fascia lata. The sciatic nerve runs between the two heads of the pyriformis muscle. When the pyriformis muscle is spastic, the sciatic nerve may be pinched. Lumbosacral and hip joint weaknesses are two main causes of pyriformis muscle spasm. Stretches and physical therapy directed at the pyriformis muscle to reduce spasm help temporarily, but do not alleviate the real

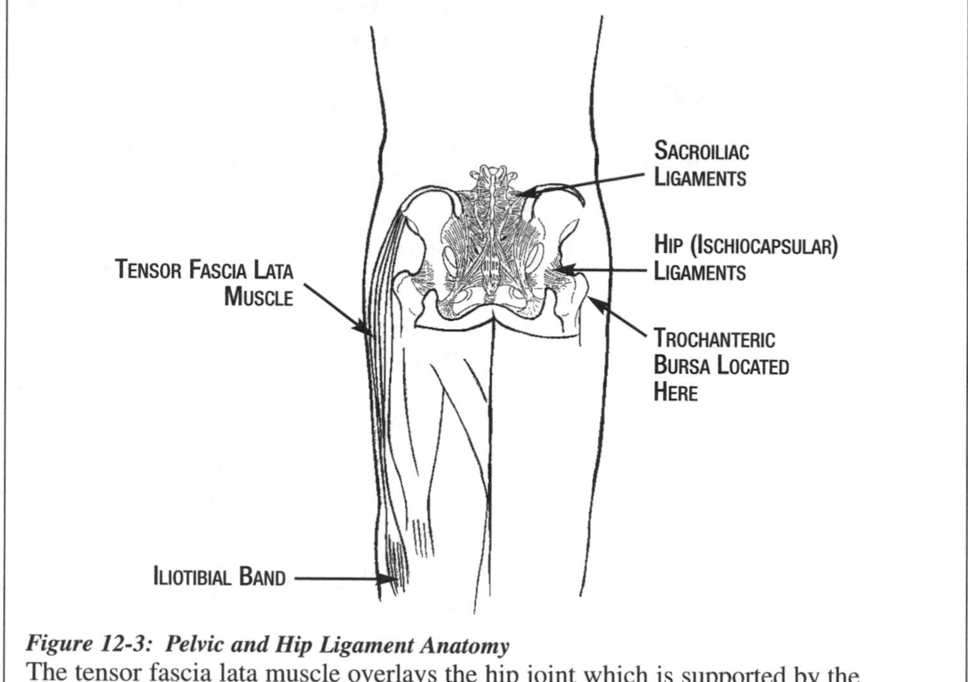

Figure 12-3: Pelvic and Hip Ligament Anatomy
The tensor fascia lata muscle overlays the hip joint which is supported by the hip ligaments.

problem. Prolotherapy of the hip and lower back strengthens those joints, thus eliminating the pyriformi muscle spasms.

The iliotibial band/tensor fascia lata extends from the pelvis over the hip joint to the lateral knee. **(See Figure 12-3.)** Its job is to help abduct the leg, especially during walking so the legs do not cross when walking. When this band/muscle is tight, it puts a great strain on the sacroiliac and lumbosacral ligaments.[9] Stretching this muscle is very beneficial to many people with chronic hip/back problems.

Hip Replacement Surgery

In 1994, the National Institutes of Health gathered 27 experts in hip replacement and component parts to evaluate hip replacement. In their report, they noted that 120,000 artificial hip joints are implanted annually in the United States. They further stated, "Candidates for elective total hip replacement should have radiographic evidence of joint damage and moderate to severe persistent pain or disability, or both, that is not substantially relieved by an extended course of nonsurgical management."[10] The National Institutes of Health is clearly recommending conservative treatment modalities prior to surgical intervention.

A concern with hip and knee replacements is that the replacement part becomes loose and requires replacement. A loose hip replacement can be treated successfully with Prolotherapy.[11]

Knee Pain

It is dangerous to have knee pain and walk into an orthopedic surgeon's office. Apparently, because of the ease of sticking probes into the knee joint, arthroscopic surgery is the favorite pastime of orthopedic surgeons. When patients are asked the reasons for their surgery, the typical response is "to shave cartilage" or "I don't know." The best treatment, as long as it is a partial tear, is to help the body repair the injured area. Remember, removing any tissue that God has put in the body will have a consequence. The tissues most commonly removed during arthroscopic surgery in the knee are parts of the meniscus and the articular cartilage. Both of these structures are needed by the body to help the femur bone glide smoothly over the tibia. **(See Figures 12-4A and 12-4B.)** When either of these structures is removed, the bones do not glide properly. Eventually, whatever meniscus or articular cartilage is left after the arthroscopic surgery is worn away. Once this occurs, bone begins rubbing against bone and proliferative arthritis begins. After a course of cortisone shots, nonsteroidal anti-inflammatory drugs, and several trials of physical therapy, the patient is again under the knife, this time for a knee replacement. Once an arthroscope touches the knee, the chance of having arthritis in the knee tremendously increases.

Before letting an arthroscope touch you, it is imperative to have an evaluation by a physician familiar with Prolotherapy. Prolotherapy will begin collagen formation both outside and inside the knee joint depending on the structure(s) that are injected.[12] Prolotherapy stimulates the body to repair itself. Surgery in the knee is appropriate when a ligament is completely torn, such as would occur from a high-velocity injury. Prolotherapy is only helpful to regrow ligaments if both ends

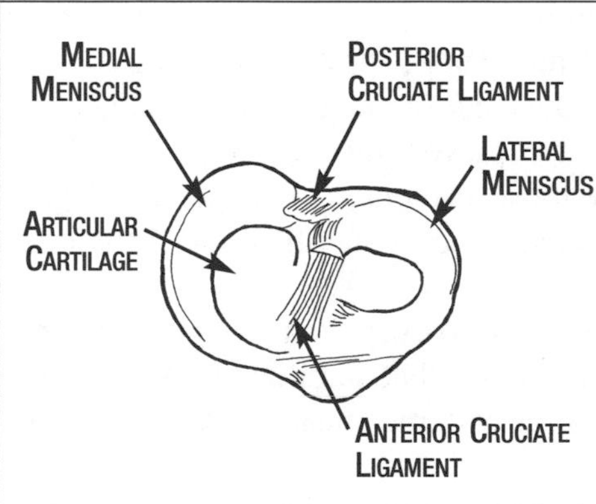

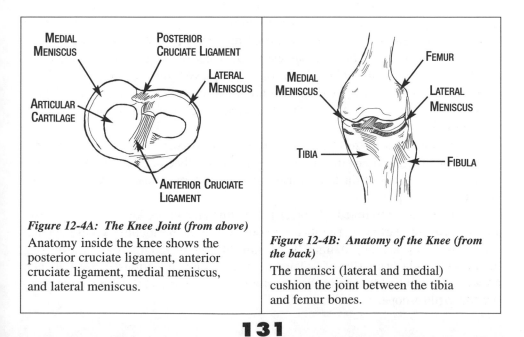

Figure 12-4A: The Knee Joint (from above)
Anatomy inside the knee shows the posterior cruciate ligament, anterior cruciate ligament, medial meniscus, and lateral meniscus.

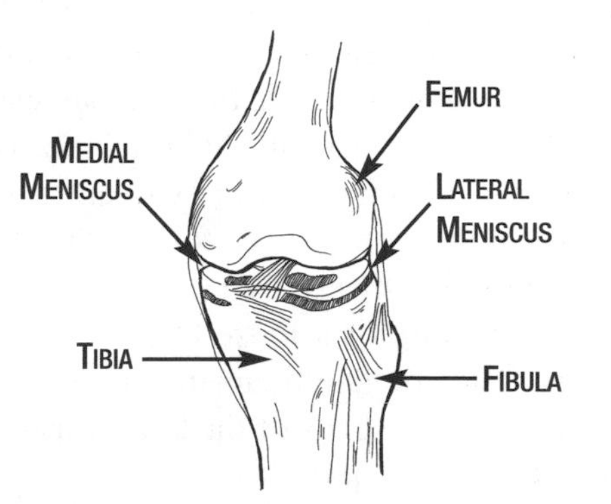

Figure 12-4B: Anatomy of the Knee (from the back)
The menisci (lateral and medial) cushion the joint between the tibia and femur bones.

of the ligament remain attached to bone. Remember, 98 percent of ligament injuries are partial tears for which Prolotherapy would be helpful.

Instability of the knee is effectively treated with Prolotherapy. The following case will illustrate the point. We received a call from a frantic young woman who was unable to get out of bed because of severe knee pain. We went to her house and found her lying in bed writhing in pain. She explained that as a child she would entertain other children by popping her knees backwards. She had recently seen an orthopedic surgeon to have her knees scraped. He told her that the ligaments in her knees were shot and her only option was knee replacement.

We administered Prolotherapy to her unstable knees. Later that day she was out of bed. In a week, she was back to work. After three sessions she was nearly pain-free. Due to the severity of her case, she received nine Prolotherapy sessions to her knees. That was more than eight years ago and she remains pain-free. Prolotherapy strengthens joints. Even in severe cases like this one, as long as the two ends of the ligaments are attached to the bone, Prolotherapy has a good chance of relieving knee joint instability.

DIAGNOSIS OF KNEE CONDITIONS

In diagnosing the cause of knee pain, it is important to carefully examine the knees. A patient whose knees cave inward has a condition known as knock-knees. **(See Figure 12-5.)** This stresses and weakens the medial collateral ligament on the inside of the knee. Prolotherapy will strengthen this ligament. Alternately, knees with an outward curvature is a condition known as bow legs. This position applies additional strain on the outside knee ligament, the lateral collateral ligament. **(See Figure 12-6.)**

It is important to understand the referral patterns of these two ligaments. The medial collateral ligament refers pain down the leg to the big toe and the lateral collateral ligament refers pain to the lateral foot. **(See Figures 2-2 and 2-3.)**

The ligaments inside the knee are called the anterior and posterior cruciate ligaments. These ligaments help stabilize the knee, preventing excessive forward and backward movement. If these ligaments are loose, even in a young person, degenerative arthritis begins to form.[13] Prolotherapy causes a stabilization of the knee after these ligaments are treated.[14]

The feeling of a loose knee is reason enough to suspect a cruciate ligament injury. The cruciate ligaments are the power horses that stabilize the knee. They refer pain to the back of the knee. Posterior knee pain may be an indication of cruciate ligament injury.

As previously mentioned, the other main structures in the knee are the menisci and the articular cartilage. The menisci consist of a lateral meniscus and a medial meniscus. They are approximately 11 millimeters in length, four millimeters thick, and made primarily of collagen. Prolotherapy injections cause collagen growth. A patient with a meniscus tear should try Prolotherapy before agreeing to see Mr. Arthroscope.

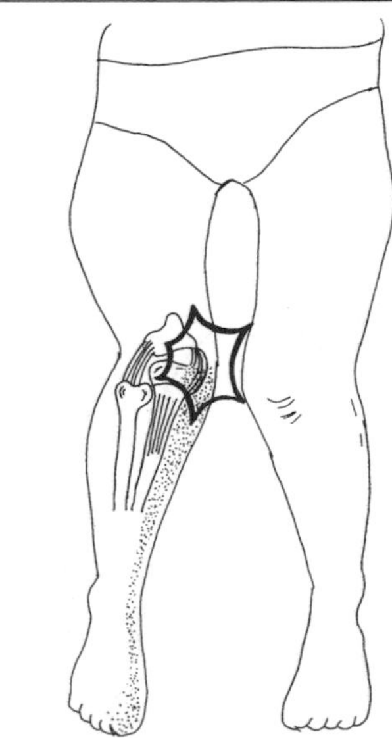

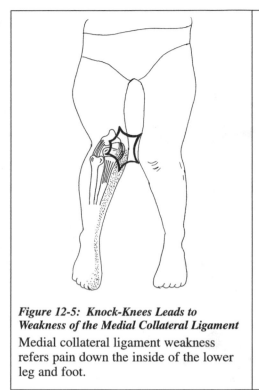

Figure 12-5: Knock-Knees Leads to Weakness of the Medial Collateral Ligament
Medial collateral ligament weakness refers pain down the inside of the lower leg and foot.

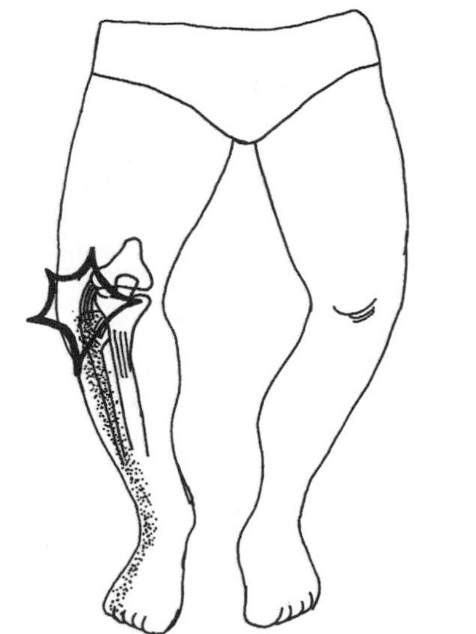

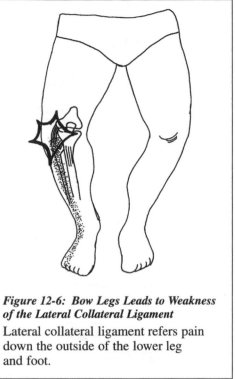

Figure 12-6: Bow Legs Leads to Weakness of the Lateral Collateral Ligament
Lateral collateral ligament refers pain down the outside of the lower leg and foot.

Meniscal injuries are suspected if the patient reports a "catching sensation" in the knee or if the knee must be "jiggled" to produce full range of motion. Articular cartilage injuries exhibit similar symptoms making it difficult to clinically differentiate them. However, they can be differentiated using x-rays.

Prolotherapy is indicated regardless of whether the injury causing the knee pain is due to a meniscal or articular cartilage injury. Prolotherapy injected into a joint requires a more concentrated solution because the joint fluid has a diluting effect. The typical solution for joint injections is 25 percent dextrose, 20 percent Sarapin, and 0.04 percent lidocaine.

Physicians will traditionally prescribe a nonsteroidal anti-inflammatory medicine, like ibuprofen, in an attempt to treat an arthritic knee. Arthritis, however, is not the result of an ibuprofen deficiency. The condition producing the arthritis is laxity in some structure of the joint. **(See Figure 12-7.)** In the knee, the laxity is typically from one of the cruciate or collateral ligaments. When articular cartilage or meniscal tissue is removed from the knee, additional stress is placed on the rest of the knee's supporting structures. Arthroscopic knee surgery results from this type of stress.

A patient with knee pain will often see Mr. Arthroscope instead of Mr. Prolotherapist, and the result is the articular cartilage on the inside of the knee is removed, as well as some of the medial meniscus, leaving the patient with a

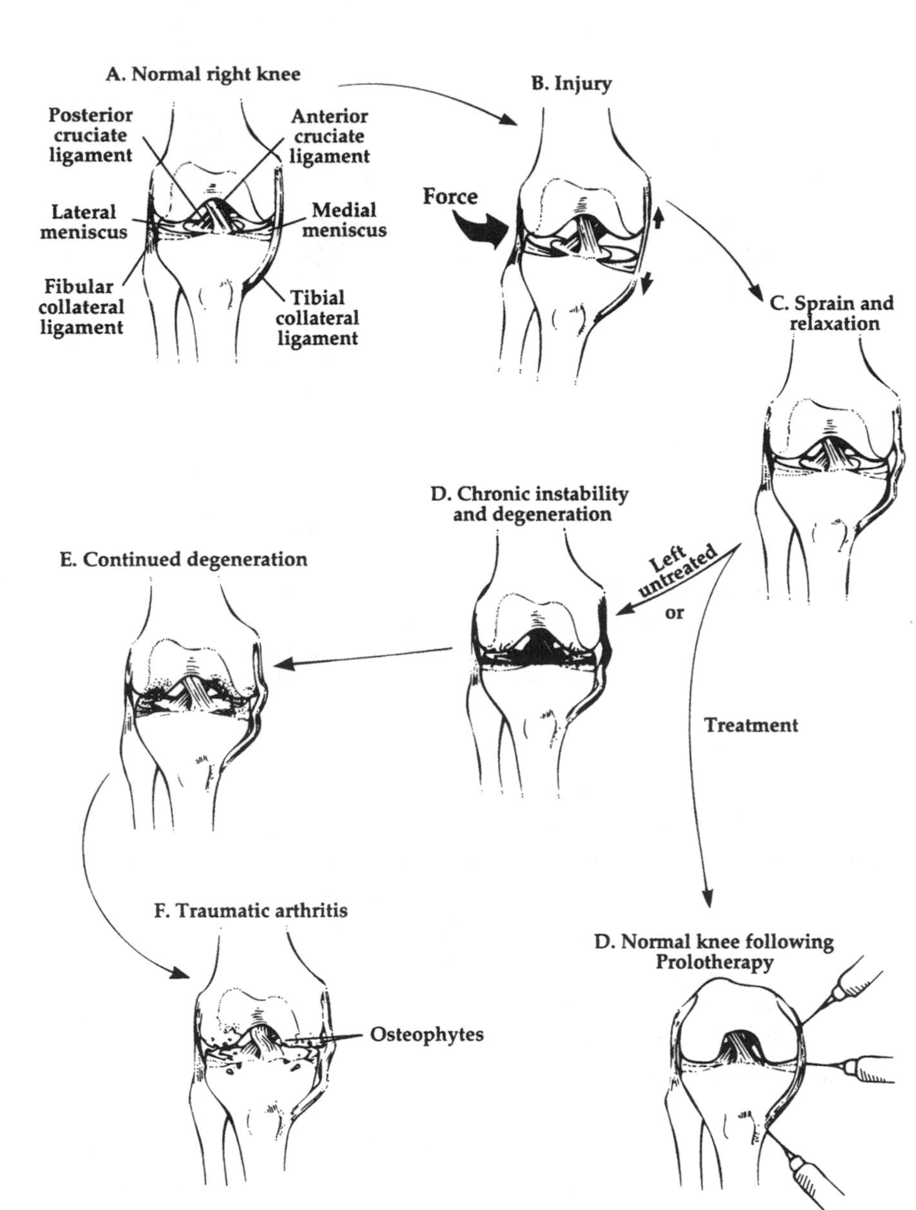

Figure 12-7: How Soft Tissue Injury Leads to Degenerative Arthritis

Following trauma, ligaments become sprained. When healing does not occur, the ligaments become relaxed, resulting in chronic instability and degeneration. When left untreated, post-traumatic "arthritis" or degenerative osteoarthritis follows. This degenerative process can be prevented with appropriate intervention through Prolotherapy.

reduced amount of cushion on the inside of the knee. Walking now necessitates increased ligamentous support of the knee to maintain stability, eventually causing ligament laxity and pain. This ligament laxity causes the muscles of the pes anserinus and tensor fascia lata to tighten in an attempt to stabilize the knee. The muscles will inevitably break down, resulting in increased pain. The tissue on the inside of the knee deteriorates, causing additional stress on the ligaments and exacerbating the pain. The body, in an attempt to stabilize the joint, grows more bone. This additional growth of bone is called arthritis. Arthritis is the body's attempt to stabilize a joint. The end result is another trip to the orthopedist's office, this time for knee reconstruction.

A much more beneficial approach is to repair the meniscal tissue or any weakened ligament with Prolotherapy. This will prevent the downward spiral of events that lands you in the orthopedist's office.

The most common cause of knee pain is not ligament injury. (We realize that this is shocking, since we have been explaining that ligaments are normally the cause of chronic pain.) The most common cause of chronic knee pain is weakness in the pes anserinus tendons. Below the knee cap, on the inside of the knee, are the attachments of three tendons: semimembranous, semitendinosus, and gracilis. Together, these tendons create the pes anserinus area. **(See Figure 12-8.)**

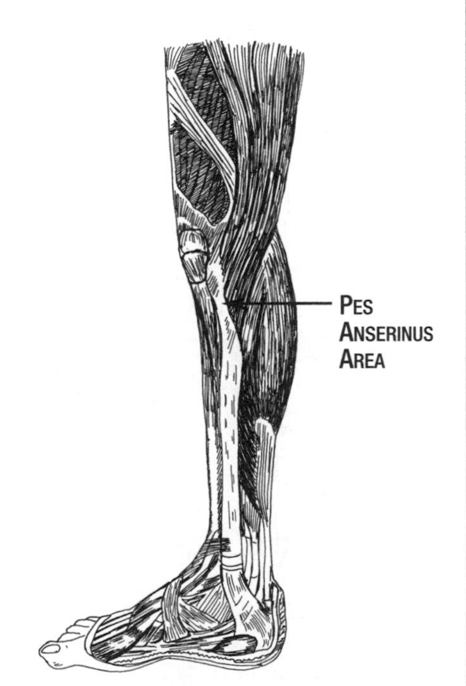

Figure 12-8: Muscles and Tendons of the Inside Leg
The pes anserinus area is a common site of chronic pain.

Ross came across a classic pes anserinus case while on rounds as a new doctor in the hospital. A 35-year-old nurse told him that her rheumatologist diagnosed her with arthritis and had prescribed anti-inflammatory medicine. Ross examined her knee and found that she had full range of motion. Full range of motion of the knee makes it likely that arthritis is not the cause of the knee pain. He pressed his thumb into her pes anserinus area and hoopla-bingo! A positive "jump-off-her-chair sign" was elicited. She had pes anserinus tendonitis. Ross told her about Prolotherapy but she never chose to have treatment. She probably still suffers from the pain, because "arthritis" was not the cause. Even in cases where arthritis is the cause, it is never caused by an anti-inflammatory medication deficiency. Interestingly enough, if someone takes anti-inflammatory medication long enough they will probably get arthritis. Maybe her rheumatologist was talking about the future?

During presentations, Ross enjoys asking the audience, "What is the number one reason for severe knee pain in the elderly?" The overwhelming response is arthritis, which is incorrect. The number one reason for severe knee pain in the elderly is pes anserinus tendonitis which, when left untreated, may contribute to developing arthritis. Even in cases of significant arthritis, crippling knee pain is most often due to pes anserinus tendonitis or bursitis. This condition is easily treated with Prolotherapy, eliminating the chronic knee pain.

The pes anserinus tendons are also known as the inside hamstring muscles. Most of us have very, very, very weak hamstring muscles that are very short because we sit for a large portion of our day. The pes anserinus tendons flex the knee and stabilize the inside of the knee. Patients with fallen arches are prone to strains in these muscles. The tibia tends to rotate outward to compensate for the fallen arch. **(See Figure 12-9.)** This outward rotation of the tibia places additional stress on the pes anserinus tendons. Eventually, these tendons become lax and are no longer able to control the tibial movement, adding to the chronic knee pain. An arch support may be prescribed to re-establish the arch. Prolotherapy injections along the arch of the foot will also prove beneficial. Prolotherapy injections into the pes anserinus attachments to the bone strengthen the tendon attachments of the pes anserinus, resolving the chronic knee pain. The next chapter will provide more information on ankle and foot pain.

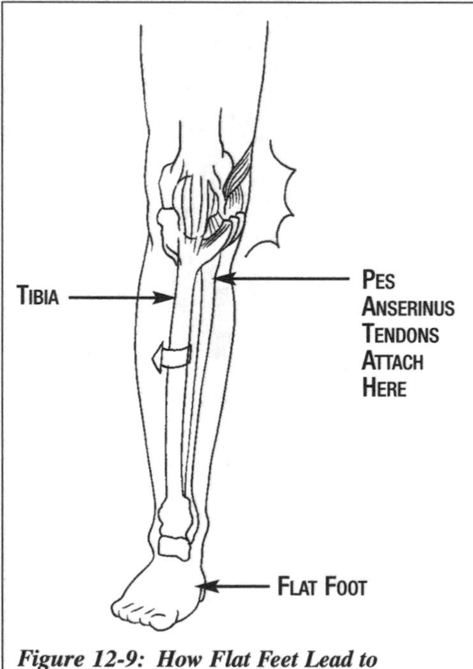

Figure 12-9: How Flat Feet Lead to Knee Pain
Flat feet cause tibial bone rotation leading to pain in the pes anserinus tendons.

Osgood-Schlatter Disease

Chronic knee pain may develop in young people, especially teenage athletes, and is often due to Osgood-Schlatter Disease, a condition whereby the tibial tubercle becomes painful where the patellar tendon attaches to the tibia. **(See Figure 12-10.)** Pain occurs because the tendon attaches to the same area of the tibia that is growing. The pain is exacerbated by physical activity, especially running and jumping, and often limits participation in sports, resulting in the young athlete's physician recommending cessation of playing sports. Needless to say, this advice is not popular. A better treatment is to strengthen the fibro-osseous junction of the patellar tendon onto the tibial tubercle, eliminating the problem.

In a small study published in 1993, Prolotherapy was 83 percent effective in eliminating the pain of Osgood-Schlatter Disease.[15] In this study only one to two treatments were needed to resolve the problem.

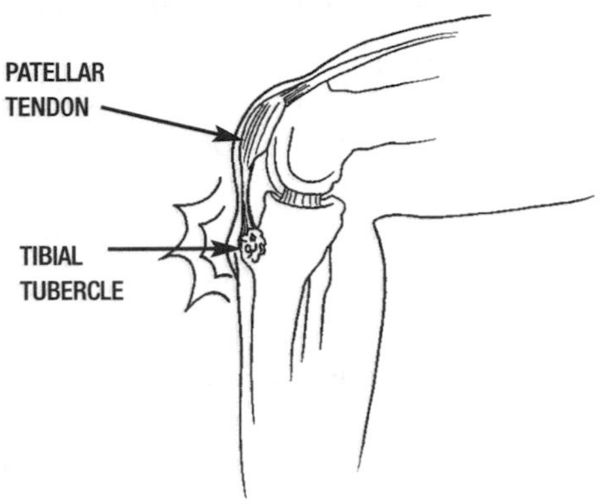

Figure 12-10: Osgood-Schlatter Disease
Patellar tendon weakness leads to tibial tubercle swelling that is characteristic of Osgood-Schlatter Disease.

Chondromalacia Patella

Another common source of knee pain is known as chondromalacia patella. (*Chondro* means cartilage, *malacia* means breakdown, and *patella* means knee cap.) Thus chondromalacia patella refers to cartilage breakdown underneath the patella. This condition is also called patellofemoral dysfunction or patellar-tracking dysfunction.[16] A more accurate description is that chondromalacia patella begins as a patellar-tracking problem. This means that the knee cap scrapes the bones underneath when the knee is moved. Typical conventional treatments for this condition include taping the knee, exercising to strengthen the thigh muscles, and stretching exercises. These treatments may be effective but are usually not curative.

Prolotherapy should be considered as a treatment option, especially for resistant cases. If the patella does not track properly in the femoral groove, it may be due to a weakened vastus medialis muscle. The problem would be solved if this muscle could be strengthened independently of the other muscles of the knee. Unfortunately, this is impossible. There is a treatment, however, that can preferentially strengthen one tissue at a time. Do you know what it is? Prolotherapy injections at the site of the weakened muscle attachments onto the knee cap will help alleviate the problem. Prolotherapy injections for chondromalacia patella are also given intra-articularly (inside the knee joint). Generally, after four sessions of Prolotherapy the anterior knee pain is resolved.

Summary

In summary, "the ankle bone is connected to the knee bone is connected to the hip bone." Due to the tremendous weight placed on the structures of the lower back and leg during walking, it is important to evaluate the leg and back as a unit. There are many overlooked causes for "sciatica" and chronic groin pain. These include pubic symphysis diathesis, ischiocapsular hip sprain, iliolumbar ligament laxity, sacroiliac laxity, Pyriformis Syndrome, trochanteric bursitis, and iliotibial/tensor fascia lata weakness. Prolotherapy to strengthen the weakness in these tissues helps resolve chronic low back pain, "sciatica," and chronic groin pain.

The most common cause of chronic knee pain is weakness in the pes anserinus tendons, even in the elderly. This is often because a fallen arch in the foot causes rotation of the tibia and stresses the pes anserinus tendons which help support the inside of the knee. Prolotherapy injections to strengthen the tendons help resolve the chronic knee pain. An arch support is also recommended to enhance the chances of permanent healing.

Arthritis of the knee is precipitated by the removal of tissue, such as the articular cartilage and menisci, during arthroscopic surgery. Prolotherapy to help heal tears in the damaged tissue should be attempted before any arthroscopic procedure.

Anterior knee pain due to chondromalacia patella is primarily due to abnormal tracking of the knee cap on the femur bone during movement. This condition is improved by Prolotherapy injections given intra-articularly and at the fibro-osseous junction. This will strengthen the weakened muscles that cause the tracking problem. Anterior knee pain in young athletes is often due to Osgood-Schlatter Disease. Prolotherapy is extremely effective in eliminating this condition. Because of these facts, many people are choosing to Prolo their chronic groin, hip, and knee pain away! ■

Chapter 13

Prolo Your Ankle and Foot Pain Away!

When we watch a boxing match, we are amazed to see the pounding those guys take! What's even more remarkable is that they choose to do it. Even that pounding is minor compared to the pounding feet take every day. The average person takes 3,000 to 10,000 steps per day. The foot's job during the process of walking is to traject the body weight up one inch with each step. If, for example, a woman weighing 125 pounds takes 5,000 steps in a day, her feet have lifted 625,000 pounds during that day. If a 150-pound person walks one mile, 60 tons of force is exerted through the small area that encompasses the ankle and feet. Is it any wonder feet are sore by the end of the day?[1]

Foot Biomechanics

Poor foot biomechanics may be responsible for a myriad of chronic complaints, including pain in the feet, knees, lower back, and neck.[2] The feet act as a spring, propelling the body forward with each step. If the spring is not working, the propelling force must come from the knees, hip, or lower back. Because these areas are not designed to function in this manner, they eventually deteriorate and the chronic pain cycle begins.

The most important factor in evaluating a person's gait (walking cycle) is to observe the stability of the arch and the ability of the foot to spring the body forward. The most important arch in the foot is the medial arch. **(See Figure 13-1.)** It is abnormal for the arch to collapse during the gait cycle or while at rest. This collapsing of the arch is known as flat feet, or pes planus. A collapsed arch indicates tissue breakdown. Supporting tissue is no longer able to elevate the inside of the foot. The plantar fascia is the first tissue to be affected. Pain resulting from this weakened tissue is called plantar fasciitis. If the condition continues, a terrible thing will occur. The person will pay a visit to a podiatrist and receive a cortisone shot for the inflamed fascia. Cortisone will eventually weaken the fascia. If the fascia is not strengthened, a painful heel spur will result. Prolotherapy to strengthen the fascia is a superior treatment option.

The next affected structures are the ligaments that support the inside of the foot, especially the calcaneonavicular ligament. **(See Figure 13-3.)** When this ligament is weakened, the arch pain will increase. Eventually, the posterior tibialis tendon in the knee must help support the arch. This tendon eventually weakens, resulting in knee pain added to the original foot pain, as the arch continues to collapse. Because the arch and the knee can no longer elevate the foot, the entire limb must be raised during a step, putting additional strain on the hip. **(See Figure 13-2.)** The spring in the foot and the efficiency of the gait are drastically reduced due

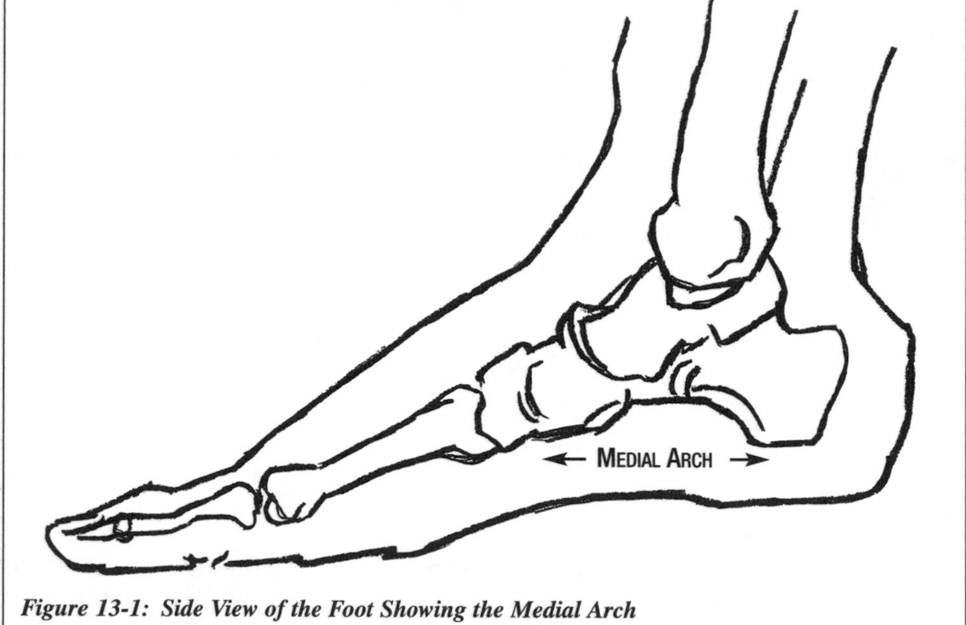

Figure 13-1: Side View of the Foot Showing the Medial Arch
Collapsing of the medial arch is known as pes planus (flat feet).

to the collapsed arch. This requires more energy from the foot, resulting in further deterioration of the medial arch. The more severe the collapse of the arch, the greater the likelihood of pain. The deterioration cycle will continue until something is done to support the arch. Contrary to popular belief, cortisone shots will not accomplish this! Arch pain in the foot is not a cortisone deficiency! **(See Figure 13-2.)**

FALLEN ARCHES

The medial arch is supported by fascia and ligaments. As previously explained, ligaments maintain proper bone alignment. Loose ligaments allow the bones to shift, resulting in chronic pain. The main supporting structure is the plantar fascia, also known as the plantar aponeurosis. **(Refer to Figure 13-4.)** The plantar fascia is essentially a strong, superficially placed ligament that extends in the middle part of the foot from the calcaneus to the toes. Another important structure is the plantar calcaneonavicular ligament which passes from the lower surface of the calcaneus to the lower surface of the navicular bone. This ligament resists the downward movement of the head of the talus, supporting the highest part of the arch, and is responsible for some of the elasticity of the arch. This ligament is also known as the spring ligament.

An arch support insert is the typical treatment for a fallen arch. Many people experience dramatic pain relief, while others continue to suffer from chronic achy feet. (The only thing worse than chronic achy feet is chronic stinky feet!)

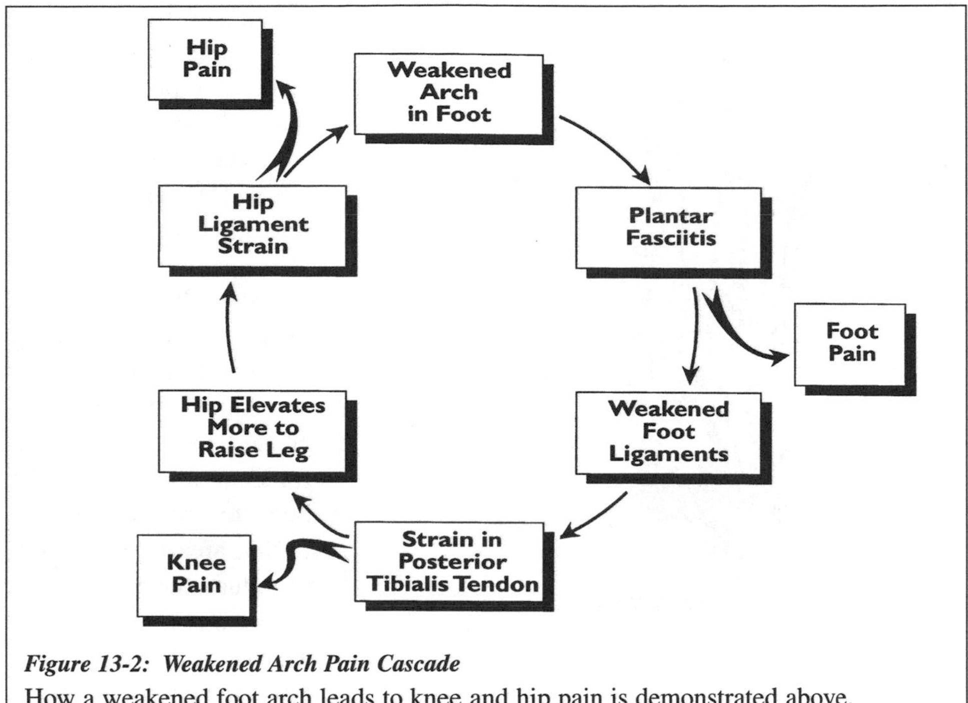

Figure 13-2: Weakened Arch Pain Cascade
How a weakened foot arch leads to knee and hip pain is demonstrated above.

Prolotherapy is the treatment that makes the most sense for a fallen arch due to weak ligaments. Prolotherapy injections into the fibro-osseous junctions of the plantar fascia and calcaneonavicular ligament, which supports the arch, will strengthen this area. If the condition is diagnosed early on, the ligaments can be strengthened to support the arch. If the process has gone on for years, an arch support may be needed in addition to Prolotherapy. But even in the latter case, Prolotherapy can eliminate the chronic arch pain.

HEEL SPURS

Many patients with foot pain come to Caring Medical saying they have been diagnosed with "heel spurs." Others were told they had "plantar fasciitis." Patients have anxiety night and day because they have "heel spurs" and "plantar fasciitis." (It does sound kind of scary, doesn't it?) Such a diagnosis resulted from an x-ray that revealed some extra bone where the plantar fascia attaches to the calcaneus.[3] This extra bone is called a "spur." **(See Figure 13-4.)** Because it involves the heel, it is ingeniously named a "heel spur." It is located where the plantar fascia attaches to the heel, hence plantar fasciitis.

Treatments such as the dreaded cortisone shot or, even worse, surgery to remove the spur, have claimed many victims. These treatments do not correct the underlying defect. The plantar fascia supports the navicular, talus, and medial

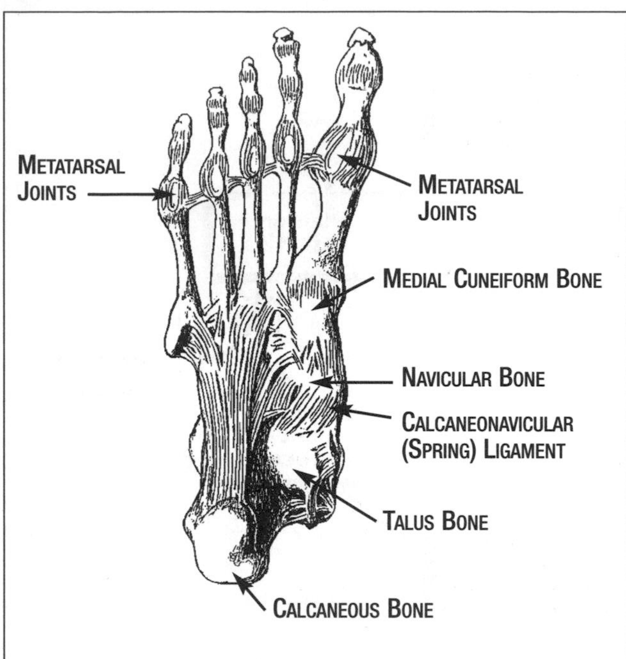

Figure 13-3: Bone and Ligament Anatomy of the Bottom of the Foot
The plantar fascia has been removed to show the spring ligament and other bones of the foot.

cuneiform bones. When the plantar fascia must also attempt to support the arch, excess pressure is placed on the calcaneus bone. The calcaneal spur forms because the plantar fascia cannot adequately support the arch. The plantar fascia is "holding on for dear life" to its attachment at the calcaneus. This "holding on for dear life" causes the body to grow more bone in that area in an attempt to reduce the pressure on the ligament, resulting in a heel spur. The same kind of pressure would occur if you were hanging from a ledge of a tall building by the tips of your fingers. You can bet when you were finally rescued that the ledge might have some marks in it where your fingers were located.

Cortisone may temporarily relieve the pain in some cases, but it will always weaken tissue long-term. Prolotherapy to the fibro-osseous junction of the plantar fascia will cause a permanent strengthening of that structure. Once the plantar fascia returns to normal strength, the chronic heel pain will be eliminated. "But what about the heel spur?" people complain. Remember, the heel spur is just an x-ray finding. Many people have heel spurs without any pain. Prolotherapy will not remove the heel spur, but it will eliminate the chronic pain by eliminating the cause. So relax and enjoy a foot without pain.

Bunions

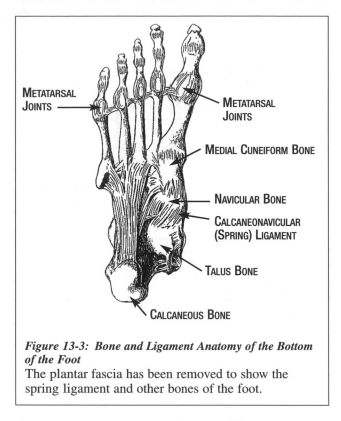

Bunions are another problem that excite the surgeons. Nothing makes a foot surgeon happier than an elderly patient with bunions. Bunions are an overgrowth of bone at the first metatarsophalangeal joint. **(See Figure 13-5.)** What causes an overgrowth of bone? You're learning...ligament weakness. When ligaments weaken, the bones move. This is visually evident because bunions are a result of a gross displacement of the bone. Bone movement due to ligament laxity causes the bones to hit each other. This hitting causes an overgrowth of bone, as an attempt to sta-

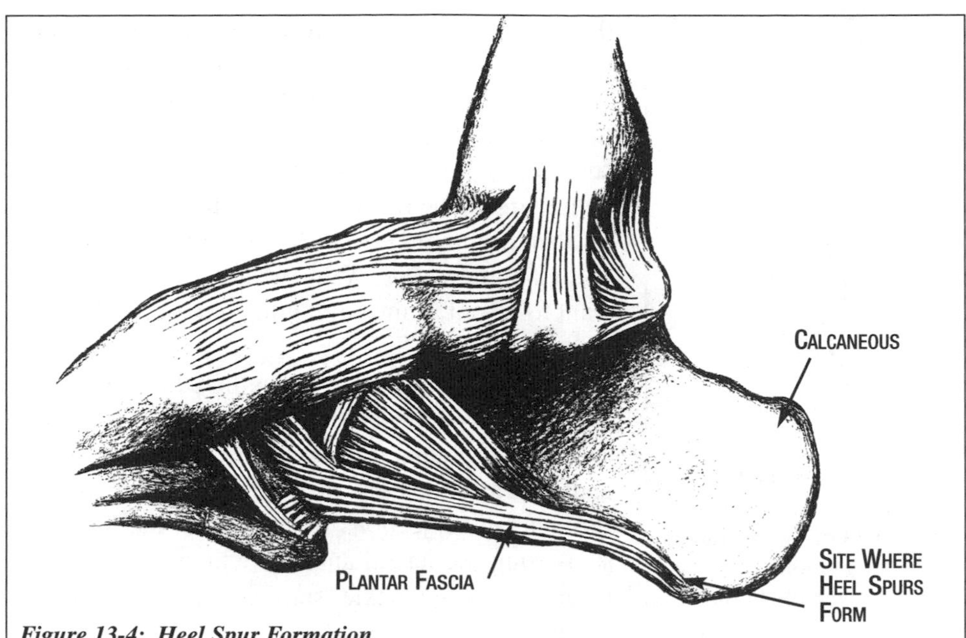

Figure 13-4: Heel Spur Formation

Weakness in the plantar fascia (called plantar fasciitis) causes inflammation to occur at the calcaneal attachment, causing a heel spur.

bilize the joint. Thus, a bunion is the body's response at the great toe to compensate for a weak ligament.

Prolotherapy eliminates bunion pain. It will not eliminate the toe deformity, but it will eliminate the pain. Many people are satisfied with that because don't we all have weird looking toes? You should see Marion's toes—they look like fingers. If she wanted to, she could eat a meal with her toes. (Please don't try it, honey!)

The foot is similar to the wrist. It consists of several bones in a sea of ligaments. Stretching of any of these ligaments can be a source of chronic pain. John Merriman, M.D., in a 1995 study, obtained good to excellent results in 79 percent of the 204 patients with foot pain who were treated utilizing Prolotherapy as the only modality.[4]

ANKLE PAIN

Ankle sprain is likely the most frequent ligament injury in the body. It is estimated that 26,000 people sprain their ankles every day. Unfortunately, ankle sprains are not always simple injuries and can result in residual symptoms in 30 to 40 percent of patients.[5]

The most common ankle sprain is an inversion injury, turning the ankle inward, injuring the ligaments on the lateral side of the ankle, usually the anterior talofibular and the tibiofibular ligaments. **(See Figure 13-6.)** The most common symptom of this type of injury, besides lateral ankle pain, is a propensity for

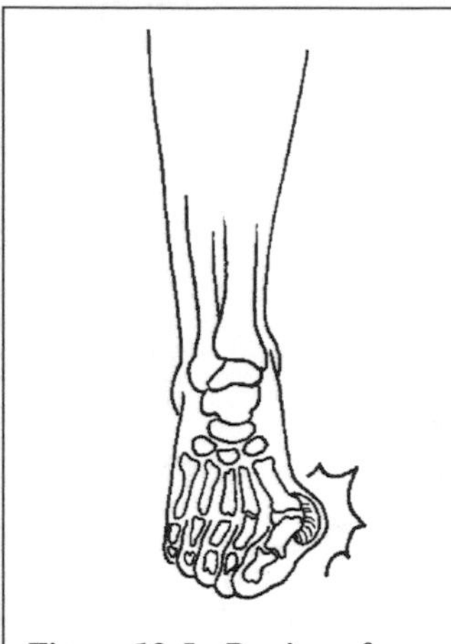

Figure 13-5: Bunion of the Big Toe
Weakness of the ligaments leads to a crooked big toe and subsequent bunion.

the ankle to continually turn inward. Ross suffered from this as a child and it prevented him from ice and roller skating. His ankles would continually turn inward. They were so weak, he did not have the strength to hold himself on skates. The Prolotherapy treatments he received as an adult have eliminated that problem. Ross still doesn't ice skate, but that's another issue. Why would any sane person want to be out in the cold, going around and around on a piece of ice?

Exercises designed to strengthen the muscles that support the lateral ankle are beneficial, but rarely solve the problem. Taping ankles, as many trainers and athletes do, only provides temporary benefit. Prolotherapy injections to strengthen the ligaments supporting the lateral ankle provide more definitive results. Chronic ankle sprains are eliminated by Prolotherapy treatments.

The inside of the ankle is held together by the deltoid ligament. This ligament is injured from turning the foot outward, as can happen when falling down stairs or mis-stepping. Again, Prolotherapy injections at the fibro-osseous junction of the deltoid ligament eliminate the chronic ankle pain in this area.

Morton's Neuroma and Tarsal Tunnel Syndrome

Chronic foot pain and/or numbness

It is quite common for people with the diagnosis of a neuroma, or nerve entrapment, to undergo multiple surgeries attempting to alleviate the entrapment. One individual came to us with a history of 15 surgeries! This occurs primarily because most physicians incorrectly believe numbness is equated with a pinched nerve. Ligament and tendon weakness in the limb also cause chronic numbness in an extremity.

Morton's Neuroma is often diagnosed from the symptom of burning pain in a toe or toes. This is a neuroma involving the nerves located between the toes. These nerves allow sensation to be felt on the skin of the toes. A neuroma is a nervous tissue tumor. Despite years of experimental research and clinical investigation, the painful neuroma has remained difficult to prevent or to treat successfully when it occurs. More than 150 physical and chemical methods for treating neuromas have been utilized, including suturing, covering with silicone caps, injecting muscle or bone with chemicals such as alcohol, and many others.[6]

Surgical treatment has been problematic with poor results and complications. In one study, 47 percent of the patients continued to have symptoms of foot pain

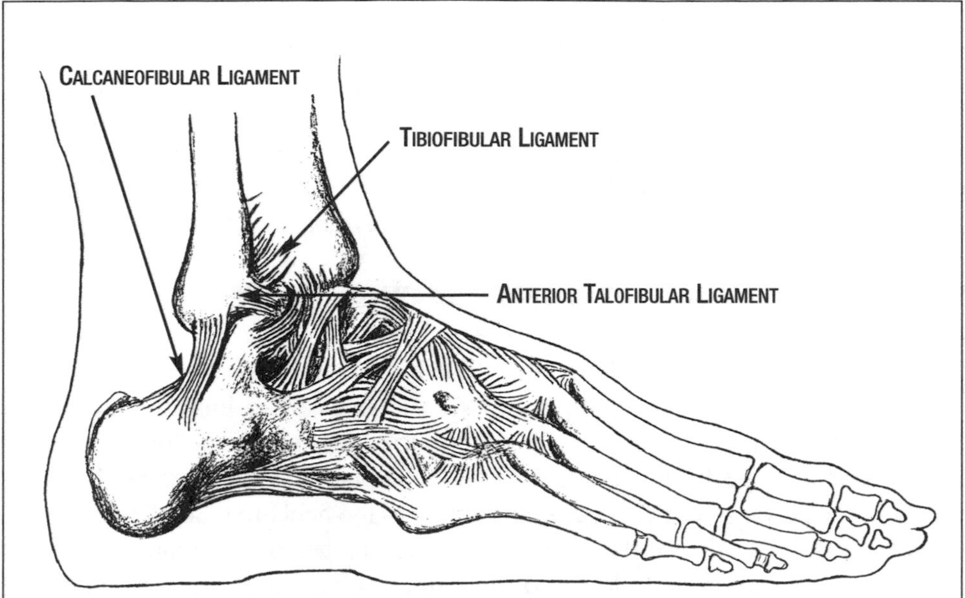

Figure 13-6: Ligament Anatomy of the Foot
Inversion or turning in of the foot causes the most common sprain of any ligament by injuring the anterior talofibular ligament.

after surgery.[7] The reason for continued symptoms after surgery or chemical injections may be that the chronic foot pain or numbness is due to ligament weakness and not a pinched nerve.

Tarsal Tunnel Syndrome

Another diagnosis used for chronic burning foot and/or toe pain is Tarsal Tunnel Syndrome. Tarsal Tunnel Syndrome is very similar to Carpal Tunnel Syndrome of the hand **(see Chapter 13)** except it involves the foot. The tibial nerve runs in a canal on the inside of the foot called the tarsal tunnel. When the tibial nerve gets pinched here, it is called Tarsal Tunnel Syndrome. The symptoms described for this syndrome include pain in the ankle, arch, toes, or heel.[8]

Chronic burning arch, toe, or heel pain is most often due to ligament weakness at the ball of the foot or soft tissue weakness in the arch of the foot, rather than pinching of a nerve as in Tarsal Tunnel Syndrome. The ball of the foot is called the metatarsal joints and supports half the body weight during walking.[9]

Since these structures bear the bulk of the body weight when a person stands, walks, or runs, it is no wonder that these are generally the first structures to weaken. Metatarsal ligament weakness is manifested by pain at the ball of the feet which often radiates into the toes. This is called metatarsalgia. **(See Figure 13-3.)** A weakened arch causes the foot to feel weak and tired especially after a day of standing or walking. It can also radiate pain into the big toe side of the foot.

Chronic metatarsal ligament weakness and arch weakness (also known as plantar fasciitis) can cause numbness in the foot and toes in the same areas of pain. Pain and numbness in the foot can also be caused by ligament and tendon laxity in the knee. The lateral collateral ligament can refer pain and numbness down the lateral side of the leg and foot and the medial collateral ligament down the medial side. **(Refer to Figures 12-5 and 12-6.)** Thus, patients with foot pain or numbness, need to have their knees looked at to see if there is any evidence of ligament weakness.

REFERRAL PAIN PATTERNS OF THE FOOT

As we all know, the foot bone is connected to the leg bone, is connected to the hip bone, is connected to the back bone. The hip and back also need to be poked on if someone suffers from foot pain and/or numbness. Hip joint weakness and ligament laxity can refer symptoms to the big toes. The sacroiliac joint commonly refers pain to the lateral foot area. The sacrospinous and sacrotuberous ligaments in the pelvis refer pain and/or numbness to the heel area. So all these areas must be examined to see if they are contributing to a person's symptoms.

It is quite common for a doctor to limit an examination of a patient with foot pain to just the foot. This is a mistake, as foot pain is often a reflection of a knee or back problem. Treatment directed at the foot in such cases most likely will have unsatisfactory results.

Most chronic foot pain and numbness are not due to a nerve being pinched but due to weakness in the ligaments and soft tissue structures that support the ball of the foot and the arch. Prolotherapy injections start these areas to grow new and stronger tissue. Once this tissue gains normal strength the pain, numbness, and disability stop. If there is evidence for weakness in the ligaments of the knee or back then these are also treated. It was Dr. Hemwall's experience, having treated thousands of patients with chronic foot pain, that nerve entrapment surgery was never required. Generally, after four treatments with Prolotherapy the person experienced total resolution of the pain and/or numbness.

Many people, despite surgery, still have pain in their feet from so-called Morton's Neuroma or Tarsal Tunnel Syndrome. The reason for this is that chronic foot, heel, toe, or arch pain is most often due to ligament weakness in the metatarsal joints, or weakness in the plantar fascia that supports the arch. Ligament weakness around the knee, hip, sacroiliac joint, or pelvis can also cause radiating pains and numbness into the foot area. Prolotherapy injections help strengthen these areas. Once they are strong, the chronic foot, heel, arch, and toe pain subsides.

SUMMARY

In summary, chronic ankle and foot pain is relatively common and almost expected, as the feet bear tons of force every day just from the process of walking. Often, chronic foot pain begins from a collapse of the medial arch. This occurs because the spring ligaments and plantar fascia can no longer support the arch. Treatments, such as arch supports, may provide temporary benefit. Prolotherapy injections to strengthen the arch provide permanent results.

"Heel spurs" are due to weakened ligamentous support of the plantar fascia. Prolotherapy to strengthen the plantar fascia will eliminate chronic heel pain. Bunions, an overgrowth of bone, are due to weakness of the metatarsal ligaments. Prolotherapy eliminates the pain of bunions, but does not correct the deformity.

The most common ligament injury is the ankle sprain. Taping and exercising for this condition often have only temporary results. Prolotherapy can permanently strengthen the ligaments of the ankle, eliminating chronic ankle sprains. Because Prolotherapy helps grow the ligaments that are associated with bunions, "heel spurs," "plantar fasciitis," ankle sprains, fallen arches, and Morton's Neuroma, chronic pain from these conditions is eliminated. It is for this reason that many people are choosing to Prolo their chronic ankle and foot pain away! ■

Chapter 14

Prolo All Your Degenerative Conditions Away!

Case History

Helen called us crying on the phone. Both of her knees had given out, she was in terrible pain, and was unable to get out of the bed. Helen was in bad shape. When we saw her, Helen relayed to us that she recently underwent a knee arthroscopy. The orthopedist told her that her knees were shot. No cartilage or ligaments were left to hold everything together. She was told to just sit and wait until she could afford a knee replacement. Helen was financially strapped because she was unable to perform her job of cleaning houses due to her bad knees. The outlook did not look good for Helen. She was looking at facing the welfare system, unemployment, and trying to find a way to feed her family. All she could do was cry. Upon physical examination, the orthopedist was right, her knees were shot. There was no cartilage and very loose, weak ligaments.

We asked Helen how she got into this condition in the first place, being that she was only 37 years old. She explained that as a youngster she would entertain the other kids by bending her knees backward. She was apparently born with very loose ligaments.

Helen received her first Prolotherapy treatment to her knees that day. She needed more than the typical four or five treatments because of the severity of her case. Prolotherapy was a much better option for a 37-year-old than a knee replacement.

Immediately after the injections, Helen was able to stand up and stated that her knees already felt better. The little bit of anesthetic in the Prolotherapy solution, which was injected directly into the painful areas, provided immediate pain relief. Helen received nine Prolotherapy sessions over the next several months. After the second set of Prolotherapy injections, she experienced enough pain relief to start scrubbing floors. She was instructed to wear kneepads while she worked and to stop entertaining the kids by bending her knees backwards. She has lived a wonderful eight years without pain. Yes, her knees were shot, but she received new knees as evidenced by the amount of cartilage in her post-Prolotherapy x-rays. **(See actual x-rays—before-and-after Prolotherapy, Figure 14-1.)** The best part is that her new knees came without a surgeon's knife, but by the gentle touch of a Prolotherapy syringe!

Degenerative Joint Disease Versus Aging

Getting old has nothing to do with getting pain! Many people come in to our office, doubtful that anything can help them, resigning themselves to living with chronic pain because they are older. Hogwash! There is always a cause for chronic pain. The cause is not old age. This is exemplified when looking at the articular cartilage in the joints of an older person versus the joints of someone

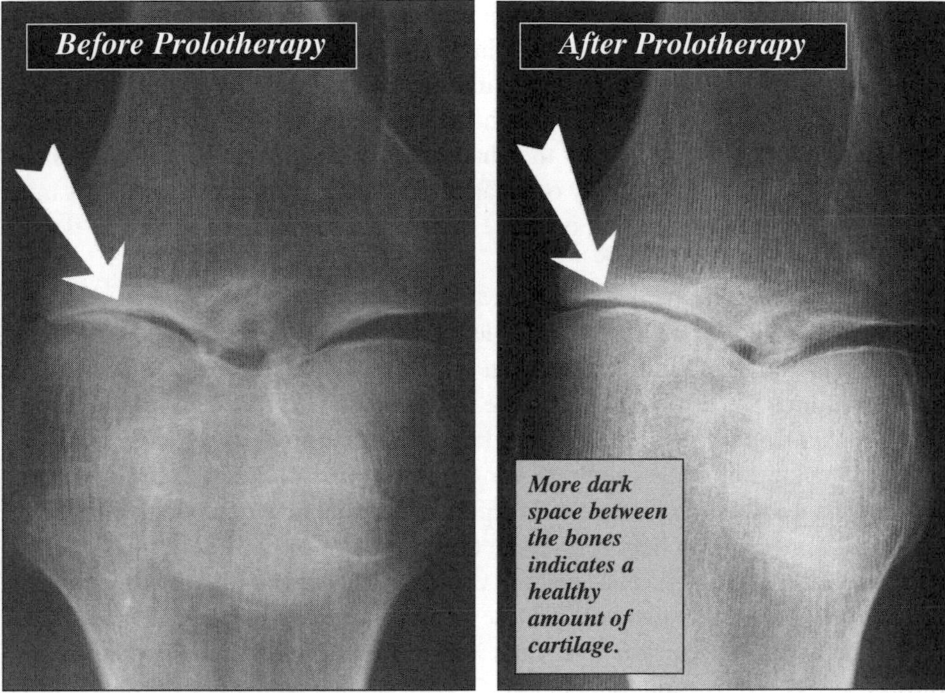

Figure 14-1: Actual Patient X-Rays, Before-and-After Prolotherapy
Prolotherapy stimulates the body to repair the painful area, including cartilage.*

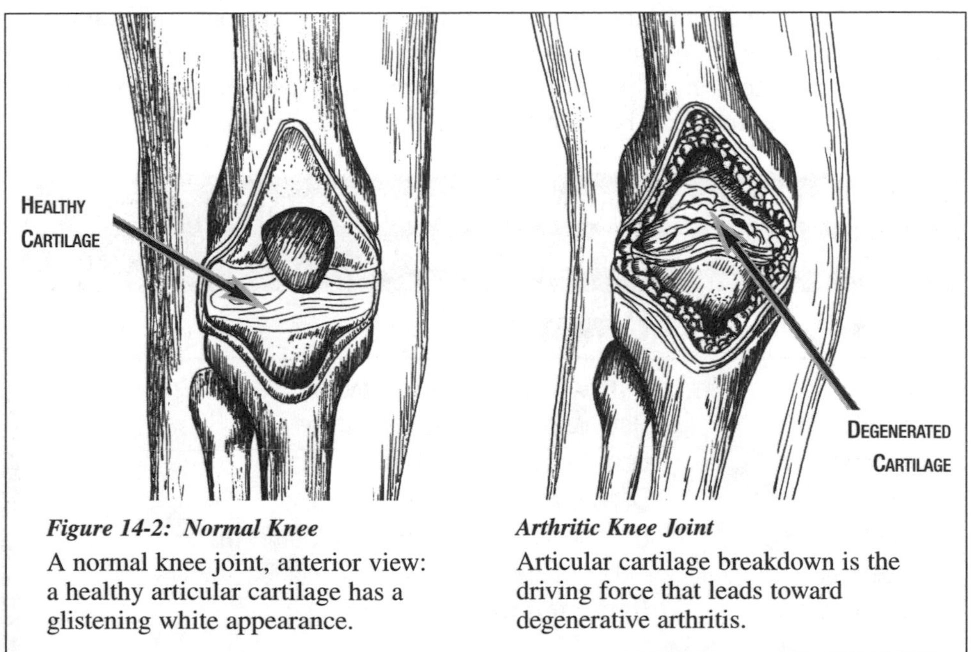

Figure 14-2: Normal Knee
A normal knee joint, anterior view: a healthy articular cartilage has a glistening white appearance.

Arthritic Knee Joint
Articular cartilage breakdown is the driving force that leads toward degenerative arthritis.

****To view more before-and-after Prolotherapy x-rays showing cartilage growth, go to Caring Medical's website at www.caringmedical.com.***

with osteoarthritis (degenerative arthritis) at any age. The joints look totally and completely different! The articular cartilage of an aging person looks nothing like the articular cartilage of a patient with arthritis. **(See Figure 14-2.)**

Pain is the body's signal that something is wrong, weakened, or injured. The most commonly injured tissues in the chronic pain sufferer are the ligaments that stabilize the joints. It is the laxity or weakness in these tissues that produces most degenerative joint disease. This is why Helen, even at age 37, had severe degeneration in her knees.

The bones in a joint such as the knee are no longer held in a stable position following an injury to the ligaments. This leads to instability in the knee with eventual crunching in the joint. Crunching in a joint is a sure sign that the joint-stabilizing structures are in a weakened state. A person who receives Prolotherapy at this point can stop this whole downward spiral. If the joint instability is not treated, the degeneration in the joint will continue. Eventually this will lead to articular cartilage breakdown. Even at this point, Prolotherapy, in conjunction with nutritional remedies can help regenerate the injured tissue. If left untreated, all of the articular cartilage will erode and the person will be left with a joint that is stiff and painful. The orthopedist will call the condition "bone on bone." Prolotherapy can still be tried for "bone on bone," but it is not as successful as when the degenerative process is only mild to moderate. These patients typically experience some pain relief, but not complete relief. To some people, partial pain relief is worth it.

Degenerative joint conditions almost always start because of a soft tissue injury to the joint. Generally, this is an injury to the ligaments, the stabilizing structures of the joint. When the ligaments are stretched and weakened, the other structures in the joint must perform functions that they were not designed to do. Eventually these structures become fatigued and cartilage begins to break down.

COMMON DEGENERATIVE CONDITIONS TREATED SUCCESSFULLY WITH PROLOTHERAPY

AREA	CONDITION
KNEE	OSTEOARTHRITIS, CHONDROMALACIA PATELLA
HIP	OSTEOARTHRITIS, HIP LIGAMENT SPRAIN
LOWER BACK	DEGENERATED DISC, HERNIATED DISC
NECK	DEGENERATED DISC, HERNIATED DISC
SHOULDER	OSTEOARTHRITIS, ROTATOR CUFF TENDONITIS
ANKLE/FEET	ANKLE LIGAMENT SPRAINS, PLANTAR FASCIITIS
HANDS/FINGERS	OSTEOARTHRITIS, LIGAMENT SPRAINS

Figure 14-3

This process is commonly experienced in the hip and knee joints. This is the reason why over 120,000 hip replacements and 95,000 knee replacements are performed each year in the United States alone.[1,2]

WHAT IS OSTEOARTHRITIS?

Osteoarthritis is the most common form of arthritis affecting many of the population over the age of 50. It is also called "degenerative joint disease" because osteoarthritis involves the deterioration of the articular cartilage that lines the joints and includes related changes in adjacent bone and joint margins. This deterioration occurs because the supporting structures of the joints, primarily the ligaments, become injured. The joint then becomes unstable, loose, and moves excessively. The crunching noises in the joints commonly seen with this condition occur because the bones start hitting together. An overgrowth of bone forms at the areas where the bones are hitting (generally at the joint margins). This overgrowth of bone along with the articular cartilage damage is called osteoarthritis, or degenerative joint disease (DJD).

DJD most frequently occurs in the weight-bearing articulations of the spine, hips, and knees, and the distal interphalangeal joints of the hands. Symptoms of DJD usually include brief joint stiffness upon awakening, joint pain or tenderness following usage, and are associated with the typical characteristic findings on x-ray. The most common DJD conditions treated with Prolotherapy are exhibited in **Figure 14-3**.

The common thinking about DJD is that it occurs due to wear and tear on the joints and is inevitable as you age. Nothing could be farther from the truth! Its root cause is almost always **injury** to the soft tissue supporting structures of the joint. The process of developing DJD begins with ligament weakness. More than 12 studies were done that showed that DJD does not occur as a result of wear and tear. The studies included 1,597 individuals, with an average age of 53 years, who ran an average of 33 miles per week for approximately 16 years. There was no evidence of an increased occurrence of DJD in these people.[3] Prolotherapy also confirms this theory because the pain and disability from DJD are resolved when the ligamentous structures around the joint are treated with Prolotherapy. The process of arthritis and DJD formation is **halted** with Prolotherapy by strengthening the joints' supporting structures. The arthritic process is then completely stopped!

Unfortunately, most people continue to perpetuate the arthritic/DJD process by using the **RICE** protocol. Anti-inflammatory medications, cortisone shots, arthroscopy, and the various surgeries offered to people (all part of the **RICE** protocol) with degenerative joint disease all contribute to the downward spiral in the development of arthritis/DJD. All of these treatments help destroy the articular cartilage, which is the very structure that prevents us from getting arthritis and DJD. The choice is yours: choose arthritis for your future—or choose Prolotherapy.

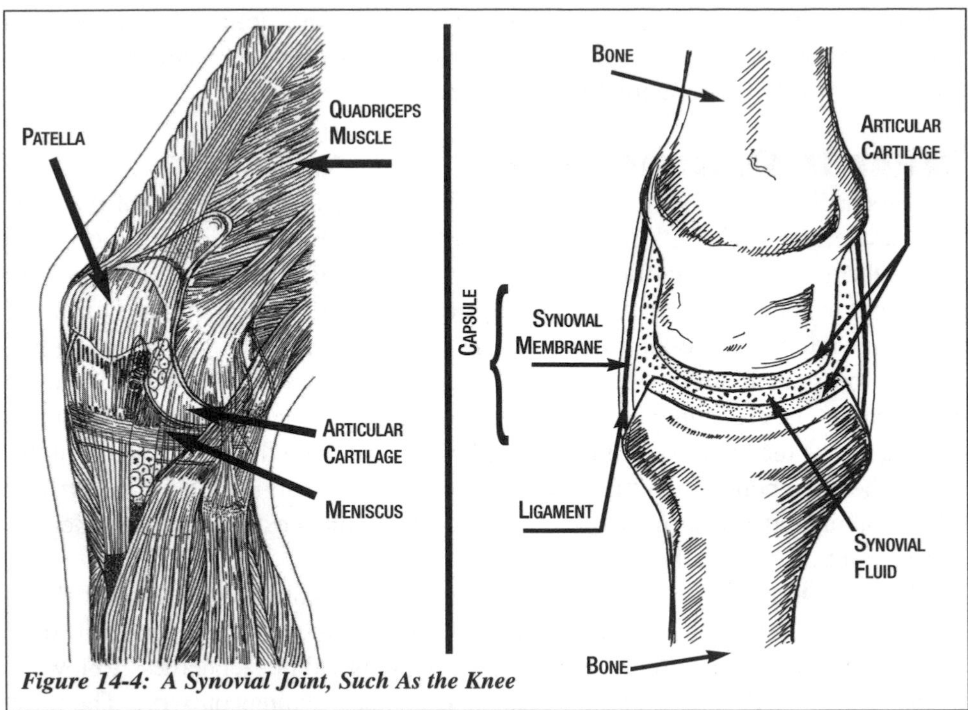

Figure 14-4: A Synovial Joint, Such As the Knee

What Is Articular Cartilage? Is It in Crisis?

Most of the joints in the body are synovial joints. These are movable, highly versatile, lubricated joints. Synovial joints are able to provide normal pain-free movement because of the unique properties of the articular cartilage. The articular cartilage of the synovial joint covers and protects the ends of the bones. Ligaments help provide stability to the joint. A fibrous capsule encloses the structure for protection. Muscles around the joint contract to produce movement. The knee is the largest synovial joint. We will use the knee and hip joints as the primary examples in our discussion on "the cartilage crisis."

Let us examine the knee in more detail. In **Figure 14-4**, at the top of the knee are the massive quadriceps muscles that cause the knee to extend. The hamstring muscles are at the back of the knee and cause it to flex. The knee joint contains a synovial membrane, which is tissue that lines the noncontact surfaces within the joint capsule. This tissue secretes lubricating synovial fluid, which nourishes all the tissues inside the joint capsule. During movement, the stabilizing structures of the knee are the cruciate ligaments (internal joint ligaments) and the collateral ligaments (external joint ligaments). The menisci, which are unique to the knee and the wrist, are pads of fibrous cartilage, which help the weight-bearing bones absorb shock. The ends of the tibia, femur, and patellar bones of the knee joint are covered by articular cartilage, which is the structure that is in crisis.

Articular cartilage plays a vital role in the function of the musculoskeletal system by allowing almost frictionless motion to occur between the surfaces of two bones.[4] Furthermore, articular cartilage distributes the load of the joint articulation over a larger contact area, thereby minimizing the contact stresses, and dissipating the energy force associated with the load.[5] These properties allow the potential for articular cartilage to remain healthy and fully functional throughout decades of life despite the very slow turnover rate of its collagen matrix.

Articular cartilage is normally glassy, white, and very homogeneous in its structure. It is an avascular tissue (no blood vessels), devoid of nerves and lymphatic vessels, and contains just a few cells (chondrocytes) that are embedded in a sea of collagen. Specialized protein structures called proteoglycans, water, and collagen make up the structure. It is the chemical nature and arrangement of these structures that gives articular cartilage its resilience, durability, strength, and efficient weight-bearing and gliding properties.[6]

The average thickness of the articular cartilage in the knee is two to four millimeters. The thickest cartilage of the knee appears on the patella at five millimeters or more.[7] There is no evidence to suggest that the thickness of articular cartilage decreases with age in a healthy individual.[8]

Although the surface of articular cartilage appears smooth on gross examination under electron microscopy, there are depressions and undulations. There are actually about 430 depressions per millimeter of cartilage.[9] These surface irregularities appear to play an important role in joint lubrication and nutritional support by trapping the nutrient-rich, thick synovial fluid.

The cells (chondrocytes) of articular cartilage are responsible for the synthesis of both the collagen and proteoglycans that make up the cartilage. The chondrocytes have the ability to synthesize all the various components of the specialized proteins that make up the proteoglycans.[10]

The ability of these chondrocytes to replicate is really the key question when considering the potential of cartilage to proliferate or repair itself. It has been shown in studies on adult human cartilage that no decrease in cell count occurs with age.[11] This fact only suggests that chondrocytes have the ability to proliferate and repair.

Upon injury, such as mild compression,[12] osteoarthritis,[13] or lacerative injury, the chondrocytes can revert back to a "chondroblastic" state. This is a condition where the chondrocytes are capable of mitotic division, indicative of growth and proliferation.[14] The notion of damaged cartilage having no regenerative properties is responsible for many people being subjected to arthroscopies with subsequent joint replacements. This falsehood occurred because healthy cartilage cells have very little, if any, mitotic activity, thus very little or no ability to proliferate.[15] The fact that healthy cartilage cells (chondrocytes) have no ability to proliferate and repair was discovered in the early 1960s. The first total hip replacement surgery occurred at the same time. A short time later the arthroscope was invented. These occurrences led to the massive proliferation of orthopedic surgery and surgeons throughout the country. Since articular cartilage reportedly had no ability to heal, then removal of any damaged articular cartilage was justified.

CARTILAGE REGENERATION

Much of the research on articular cartilage regeneration was done in the 1980s and 1990s. Not until the early 1980s did Dr. H.J. Mankin discover that the chondrocytes' reaction to injury was to change into a more immature cell called a chondroblast. This type of cell, interestingly enough, is capable of cell proliferation, growth, and healing.[16] His research is so well-accepted that two of his papers on this subject were published in one of the most prestigious medical journals in the world, *The New England Journal of Medicine.*[17, 18] The actual cells that make collagen (chondrocytes) and the other components of articular cartilage gain the ability to replicate, proliferate, and generate new cartilage upon injury. This key fact is vital to understanding the power of Prolotherapy to proliferate cartilage growth.

Prolotherapy involves the injection of various substances, including hypertonic dextrose, sodium morrhuate (an extract of cod liver oil), various minerals, Sarapin (an extract of the pitcher plant), and various other substances. Many of these substances act by causing a mild irritation at the site of the injection. It is believed that this irritation acts in the same mechanism (as documented by Mankin, above) for cartilage formation by inducing the chondrocytes to change to the chondroblastic stage of development. Prolotherapy regenerates cartilage, most likely by inducing mature chondrocytes to a chondroblastic state capable of proliferation and repair. This fact is supported by the numerous patients with "no cartilage" who were set for hip/knee replacements but never needed them after receiving Prolotherapy. It is also supported by the numerous patients, like Helen, who were told that arthroscopy revealed that their cartilage was completely gone, yet chose to try Prolotherapy, only to live long, happy, productive lives. Helen, as you recall, was even able to scrub floors on her knees again (not that we all cherish doing that task). There is only one explanation for the radical transformation of Helen's cartilage from deterioration to a healthy state—Prolotherapy!

Remember, Prolotherapy can help regenerate articular cartilage. This is a good thing. Don't be so quick to opt for the traditional remedies that may actually *worsen* your health.

THE MIGHTY MENISCUS

Articular cartilage has very few friends. Everything is working against him. He has to handle hundreds of pounds with each step and he gets fed scraps from the synovial fluid. Not a job any one of us would want. Its only ally is the mighty meniscus.

The menisci are C-shaped discs of fibrocartilage interposed between the condyles of the femur and tibia. They are composed of about 75 percent collagen, eight to 13 percent protein, and the rest extracellular matrix component.[19] Type I collagen makes up about 90 percent of the total collagen.[20] This is the same type of collagen that makes up ligaments and tendons. **(See Figure 14-5.)**

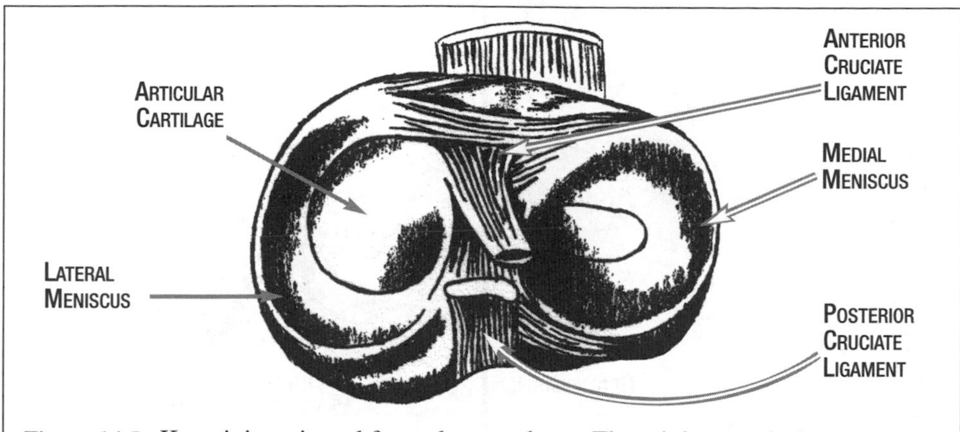

Figure 14-5: Knee joint, viewed from the top, down. The mighty menisci are responsible for shock absorption and lubrication.

The size of the meniscus relative to its corresponding tibial plateau remains remarkably constant throughout development and into adulthood. On the average, the medial meniscus covers about 64 percent of the medial tibial plateau, while the lateral meniscus covers about 84 percent of the lateral tibial plateau.[21] The medial meniscus is larger in diameter than the lateral meniscus. It has an average width of 10 millimeters, and is three to five millimeters thick. The lateral meniscus has a thickness of three to five millimeters, with an average width of 12 to 13 millimeters.[22]

The mighty menisci are responsible for load transmission, shock absorption, lubrication, and improvement of stability of the knees. Most studies indicate that the menisci transmit about 50 percent of the load at the knee, while the remaining 50 percent is borne directly by the articular cartilage and surfaces.[23, 24] The menisci, therefore, protect the articular cartilage from high concentrations of stress by increasing the contact area on the femur and tibia bones. Removing the menisci is probably one of the worse possible scenarios for the articular cartilage because it would decrease the contact area onto the bones and would significantly increase the forces onto the articular cartilage itself. It would only make sense that removing the menisci should be a last resort for the patient, as it will only make the problem worse in the long run.

Essentially every study shows that articular cartilage pressures escalate when the menisci are removed. Ahmed and Burke showed a 40 percent increase in the contact stress while Baratz and associates found a 235 percent increase in articular cartilage contact force following total meniscectomy.[25, 26] If that is not bad enough, other researchers found 450 to 700 percent increases in articular cartilage pressure. A reasonable average estimate taken from the available literature indicates that total meniscectomy results in a two- to three-fold (200 to 300 percent) increase in contact stresses.[27-29]

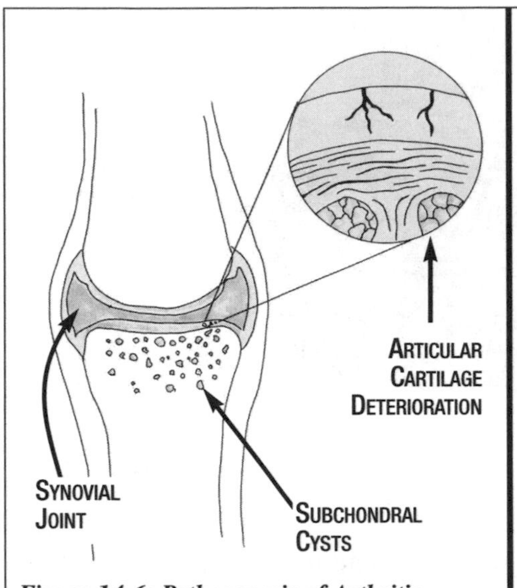

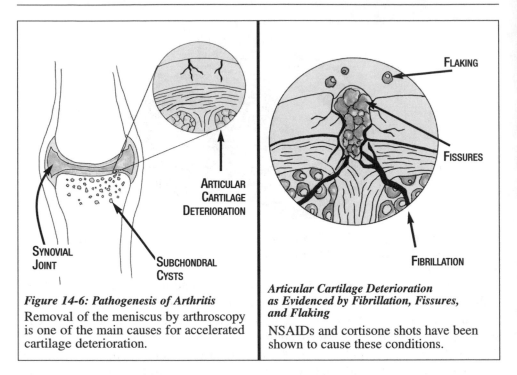

Figure 14-6: Pathogenesis of Arthritis
Removal of the meniscus by arthroscopy is one of the main causes for accelerated cartilage deterioration.

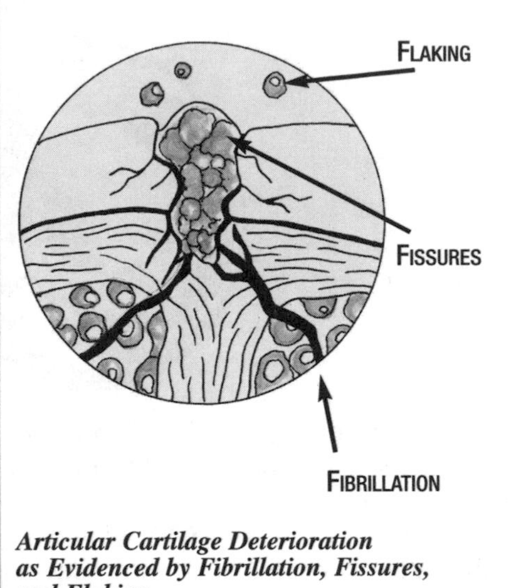

Articular Cartilage Deterioration as Evidenced by Fibrillation, Fissures, and Flaking
NSAIDs and cortisone shots have been shown to cause these conditions.

Removal of the menisci will produce one end result: a degenerated knee sometime in the future. The time is usually sooner rather than later. Following partial or total meniscectomy, articular degenerative changes have been described, including the formation of osteophytic ridges, generalized flattening of the femoral articular surface, and narrowing of the joint space. Roughening and degeneration of the articular cartilage is seen and seems to be proportional to the size of the segment removed. Degenerative changes appear first in the tibiofemoral contact areas, with those areas formerly covered by the meniscus involved later.[30, 31]

Once the menisci are removed, aggressive proliferative arthritis is inevitable. It occurs early in 40 percent of individuals, but is essentially guaranteed long-term.[32-34] This sad fact needs serious consideration when an arthroscopy is proposed. Arthroscopic partial meniscectomy is an extremely common procedure. Besides the proliferative arthritis that results, a concomitant decrease in the ability to function follows. Let no one, especially someone in a white coat with an arthroscope, do anything to your menisci. The health of your articular cartilage depends upon it! The pathogenesis of arthritis following meniscectomy is shown in **Figure 14-6.**

Meniscal removal leads to increased forces on the articular cartilage. This may produce articular cartilage breakdown, which leads to thinning of the articular cartilage. As a result of this, increased pressure on the underlying tibia bone is observed, which leads to more pressure on the ligaments. Ligament tears and

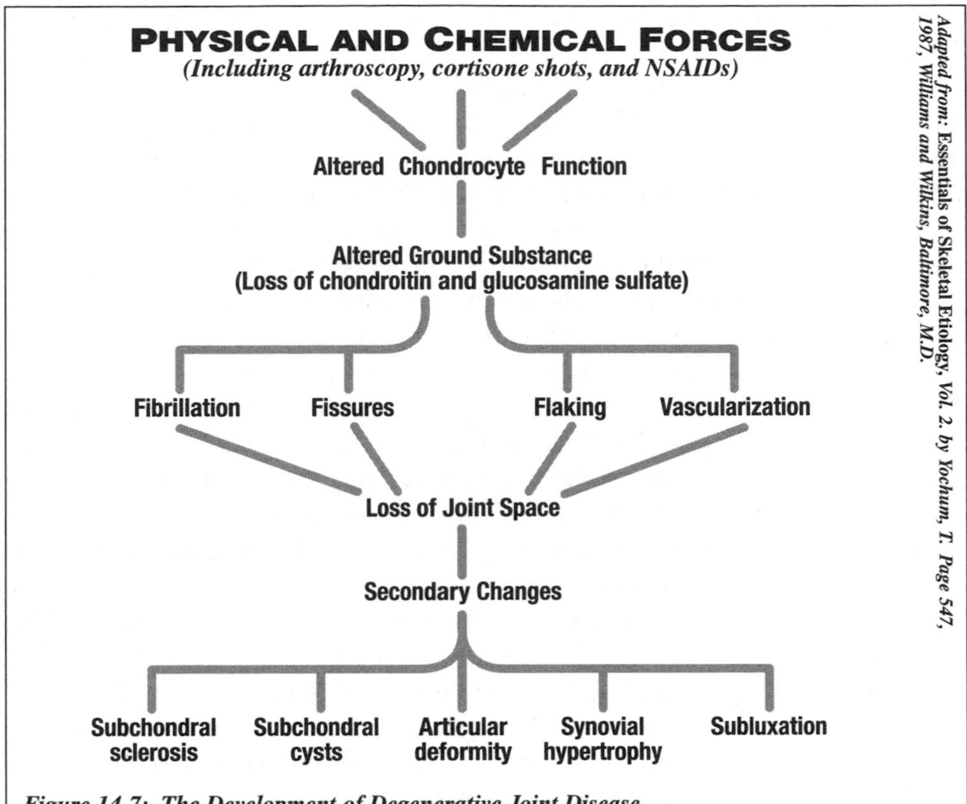

Figure 14-7: The Development of Degenerative Joint Disease
The process can be accelerated by arthroscopy, cortisone shots, and NSAIDs, the primary "tools" of most traditional pain doctors.

chronic pain often result, which further weaken the joint. In response to this weakness, the joint overgrows bone, which is called arthritis.

ARTHROSCOPY: THE QUICKEST WAY TO ARTHRITIS

All patients with knee pain need to remember this fact: There is a high likelihood that you will develop aggressive arthritis in the future if an arthroscope enters your knee joints. **Everyone** should beware! This does not apply to complete ligament tears. These may actually need surgical repair to regain function. For all the other conditions, any tissue removal inside the knee will most likely give you an increased chance of a future filled with arthritis and the accompanying pain and a lessened ability to play sports or perform daily activities. A well-accepted schemata on the development of arthritis is shown in **Figure 14-7.**

Arthritis begins immediately after chondrocyte function is altered. This leads to altered production of ground substance, or proteoglycans. Because the articular cartilage is now in a weakened state, breakdown begins. Orthopedists have fancy terms for this breakdown such as fibrillation, fissures, flaking, and vascularization. When they use these terms it just means your cartilage is going to pot. Thinning articular cartilage shows on x-ray as a loss of joint space. This causes a transmission of pressures that are too high for the bones to handle. The tibial bone in the knee, for example, will attempt to harden by sclerosis, forming cysts. The bone itself will actually overgrow to stabilize the area. This is why arthritic joints are called articular deformities, which is actually bone overgrowth.

Arthritis is not a pleasant thing to have. Anyone with a grandparent in pain from arthritis knows that this is no way to spend retirement. Remember, any physical or chemical force that alters chondrocyte function, and thus proteoglycan formation, will have a tremendous impact on the cartilage crisis.

A patient who receives an arthroscopy receives a direct assault to the surrounding tissues. It is very rare for an orthopedist to just look into a joint. Tissue is shaved and cut because the physician truly believes that this helps the person. Even if the area is fibrillated or has frayed edges, how could removing the tissue possibly help the individual? It does nothing to help repair the area. Clinical experience indicates that arthroscopic shaving or abrasion of fibrillated and irregular cartilage may relieve symptoms temporarily, but long-term it can do nothing but aid in the arthritic process. Many times the argument is made that the cartilage was smoothed by arthroscopy. This now smoother cartilage (because the fibrillations and frayed edges were shaved) will allow a more normal glide of the bones. The research does not support this. Schmid and Schmid reported that shaving did not restore a smooth congruent articular surface and may have caused increased fibrillation and cell necrosis in and adjacent to the original defect.[35]

The best approach to help heal the injured area is Prolotherapy. At minimum, a patient should first try Prolotherapy because arthroscopy can always be done later. In over 12,000 patients treated with Prolotherapy by Drs. Gustav Hemwall and Ross Hauser, only a rare patient has ever needed an arthroscopy referral. Knee conditions respond beautifully to Prolotherapy, because Prolotherapy stimulates the inflammatory process to heal the injured area.

PROLOTHERAPY VERSUS ARTHROSCOPY

Prolotherapy has many advantages over arthroscopy. It is, first of all, a much safer and conservative treatment. It works faster. The procedure does not take long to administer to the patient. The person is in and out of the doctor's office in less than an hour. Prolotherapy stimulates the body to heal the painful area. The new collagen tissue formed is actually stronger. It reduces the chance of long-term arthritis, whereas arthroscopy increases the chances for it. In many ways arthroscopy almost guarantees arthritis. Prolotherapy also increases the chances of athletes being able to play their sports and regular folks staying active for the rest of their lives. Arthroscopy significantly decreases those chances. Most people may return to activity almost immediately after Prolotherapy. They are encouraged to

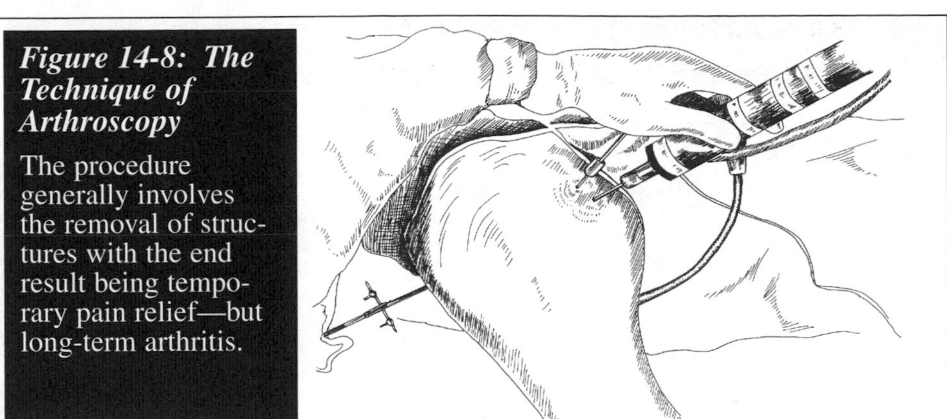

Figure 14-8: The Technique of Arthroscopy

The procedure generally involves the removal of structures with the end result being temporary pain relief—but long-term arthritis.

exercise while getting Prolotherapy, whereas after arthroscopy, patients must often be very cautious and undergo extensive rehabilitation programs. The procedure itself is also much less invasive than putting massive scopes into the knee or shoulder. Arthroscopy requires the joint to be blown up with 100 milliliters of fluid to fit all the scopes into the knee or shoulder. **(See Figure 14-8.)**

Prolotherapy is easier on the pocketbook than surgery. Prolotherapy to the knee usually costs between $200 to 300 per session. Arthroscopy costs several thousand dollars. Including rehabilitation, the costs can be upwards of $10,000.

There are many other advantages to using Prolotherapy over arthroscopy with athletes or chronic pain patients. **(See Figure 14-9.)** The point is, the verdict is in! Say, "Nope to scope!"

Rice Is Not Always Nice!

RICE stands for **R**est, **I**ce, **C**ompression, and **E**levation. It generally involves resting or immobilizing the joint for some time because of an injury. Patients are often taped, braced, casted, or told to rest because their injuries will not heal. Nothing could be worse for the articular cartilage throughout the joints of the body than this. The articular cartilage can only receive nourishment from the synovial fluid when it is pushed into the joint by weight-bearing and loading. The cartilage has no blood supply of its own. Moving, exercising, and loading the joint will allow the nourishment to get into the articular cartilage and the waste products to get out. There is only one effect of **RICE** and immobilization on cartilage—it is not good.

Basic animal research has shown that in as little as six days of immobilizing a joint, pressure necrosis of the articular cartilage can occur with subsequent degenerative arthritis.[36] Another study showed that prolonged immobilization, as occurs with casting, can lead to degeneration of the articular cartilage even in noncontact areas secondary to the adhesion of synovial membrane to the joint surface, which would not happen if the joints were moved. Subsequent use of such immobilized joints also led to degenerative arthritis.[37]

PROLOTHERAPY VERSUS ARTHROSCOPY

	PROLOTHERAPY	ARTHROSCOPY
STIMULATES REPAIR?	YES	NO
INCREASES COLLAGEN STRENGTH?	YES	NO
ARTHRITIS RISK?	DECREASED	INCREASED
RETURN TO NORMAL ACTIVITIES?	QUICK	SLOW
REHABILITATION TIME?	SHORT	LONG
EXERCISE?	ENCOURAGED	CAUTIOUS
COST?	HUNDREDS	THOUSANDS
TIME INVOLVED IN PROCEDURE?	MINUTES	HOURS
INSTRUMENT USED?	THIN NEEDLE	MASSIVE SCOPES

Figure 14-9: Which would you rather have—Prolotherapy OR Arthroscopy?

As expected, immobilization causes a reduction in chondrocyte synthesis.[38] The chondrocytes cannot be nourished without movement, so their ability to make collagen and proteoglycans for the articular cartilage declines with immobility. Studies have confirmed that simple immobilization causes a thinning of articular cartilage and, specifically, a decrease in the glycosaminoglycan and chondroitin sulfate.[39, 40] Exercise, on the other hand, has a dramatic effect of increasing chondrocyte synthesis.[41] This would be expected since exercise enhances the ability of the chondrocytes to receive nutrients and eliminate waste.

Exercise has the following beneficial effects:

- Enhances the nutrition and metabolic activity of articular cartilage.
- Stimulates pluripotential mesenchymal cells to differentiate into articular cartilage.
- Accelerates healing of both articular cartilage and periarticular tissues, such as tendons and ligaments.[42]

The above was all proven by the many studies done by Dr. Robert Salter at the University of Toronto. Dr. Robert Salter is the father of the theory that a limb must be continuously moved after an injury. He found that the healing rate was six times greater comparing movement and exercise with immobility in patients with articular cartilage defects.[43] Articular cartilage injuries which are rested have an over 50 percent chance of causing compromised range of motion of the limb at one year. Cartilage-damaged limbs that are exercised had completely normal motion. Articular cartilage defects in rabbits that were immobilized caused 50 percent of them to develop arthritis at one year. None had visible evidence of arthritis in the exercised group.[44]

Dr. Salter showed that 80 percent of articular cartilage fractures healed with exercise and movement, where none healed in the immobilized group. In an interesting study on infected joints, the researchers showed that continuous passive motion of the joint had a striking and statistically significant protective effect on prevention of progressive degeneration of the articular cartilage, when compared with the effects of immobilization.[45]

Dr. Salter felt the possible explanations for these findings were the following:

- Prevention of adhesions (scar tissue)
- Improvement of nutrition of the cartilage through increased diffusion of synovial fluid
- Enhancement of clearance of lysosomal enzymes and purulent exudate from the infected joints (removal of the bad stuff)
- Stimulation of living chondrocytes to synthesize the various components of the matrix

The mechanism by which exercise improved healing is not particularly clear. However, Dr. Salter did show by x-ray and clinical findings that the animals that received exercise did much better than the ones who were immobilized. This same statement could be said about Prolotherapy. We do not know the exact mechanism of action that Prolotherapy uses to help people heal. The positive results of patients speak for themselves.

Continuous passive motion exercise was also shown to heal or clear a hemarthrosis (blood in the joint) twice as fast as immobilized limbs.[46] This is significant for patients who have massive bruising of a joint. The notion that the area must be iced and compressed to decrease swelling is outdated. Ice and compression will decrease swelling, but will compromise healing. Yes, there is a better way. The best way to resolve swelling is to use the **MEAT** treatment. This involves exercise and proteolytic enzymes, which help clean out the damaged tissue. **(See Chapter 6, Answers to Common Questions About Prolotherapy.)** Exercise or passive motion by a physical therapist is tremendously effective at helping resolve the bleeding and edema but will also aid the healing process.

Dr. Salter summarized his first 18 years of basic research on the biologic concept of continuous passive motion (CPM) exercise with the following conclusions:

- CPM exercise is well tolerated.
- CPM exercise has a significant stimulating effect on the healing of articular tissues, including cartilage, tendons, and ligaments.
- CPM exercise prevents adhesions and joint stiffness.
- CPM exercise does not interfere with the healing of incisions over the moving joint.
- The time-honored principle that healing tissues must be put to rest is incorrect: indeed—it is this principle that must be put to rest rather than the healing soft tissues.

- Regeneration of articular cartilage through neochondrogenesis both with and without periosteal grafts is possible under the influence of CPM exercise.[47]

Dr. Salter wrote those words in the 1980s, yet there are still people with injuries around the world doing the **RICE** protocol today. Putting injured tissues to rest hurts the healing process. Animals continue their activities after an injury, therefore they heal well after an injury. Human beings need to do the same. It is time for a paradigm shift from the **RICE** to **MEAT** protocol to encourage healing of soft tissue and cartilage injuries. Exercise is vital to this process.

ANTI-INFLAME YOUR CARTILAGE INJURY—AND IT WILL STAY!

Again, the reason why arthritis forms in the first place is because an injured area did not heal. The pain of the initial injury may have been relieved, but the injured tissue remains injured, as manifested by decreased strength. Exercise alone does not cause arthritis. Only injury causes arthritis. In a study where dogs were exercised for one year carrying jackets weighing 130 percent of their body weight, all knee joints were inspected for evidence of joint injury and degeneration at the completion of the study. Articular cartilage surfaces from the medial tibial plateau were examined by light microscopy, the cartilage thickness was measured, and intrinsic material properties were determined by mechanical testing. No joints had ligament or meniscal injuries, cartilage erosions, or osteophytes. Light microscopy did not demonstrate fibrillations in the cartilage. Furthermore, the tibial articular cartilage thickness and mechanical properties did not differ between the exercised group and non-exercised group. These results show that a lifetime of regular weight-bearing exercise in dogs with normal joints did not cause alterations in the structure and mechanical properties of articular cartilage that might lead to joint degeneration.[48] Exercise is healthy and does not cause injury if properly performed. If an injury occurs, it is important to treat it until it is completely healed. The worst things for healing an injury are to take anti-inflammatories and receive cortisone injections. These are the main reasons so many people have articular cartilage problems.

Ibuprofen became available over the counter in 1984. People have been reaching over the counter ever since then. Sales of over-the-counter pain relievers were $2.67 billion dollars in 1994. There are numerous studies showing the deleterious effects of anti-inflammatories, such as ibuprofen, on healing. Ibuprofen, the prototype anti-inflammatory medication, has been shown to have an inhibitory effect on bone healing, remodeling, resorption, and metabolism.[49-52] Ibuprofen has also been shown to have a tremendous dose-dependent suppressive effect on articular cartilage healing.[53] As ibuprofen doses increase, healing of the articular cartilage decreases.

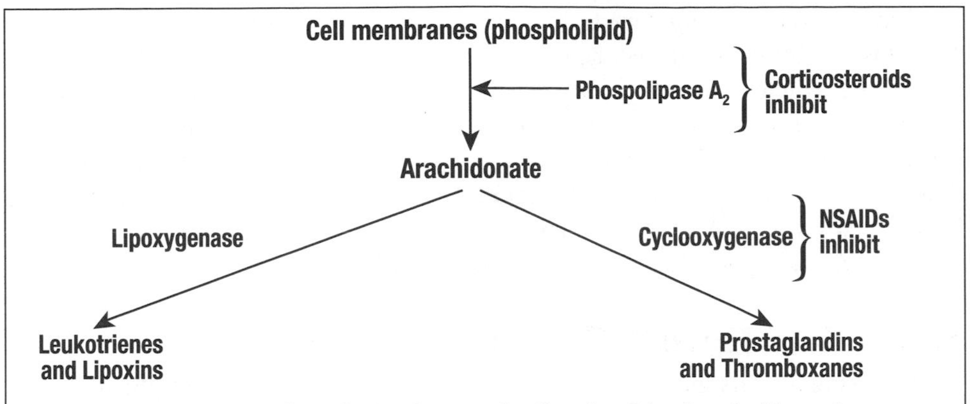

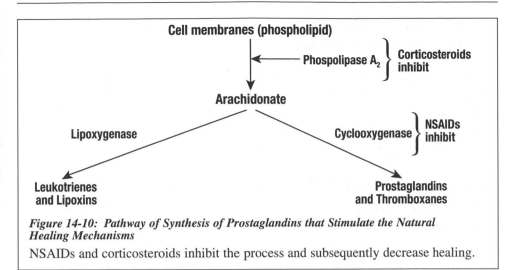

Figure 14-10: Pathway of Synthesis of Prostaglandins that Stimulate the Natural Healing Mechanisms

NSAIDs and corticosteroids inhibit the process and subsequently decrease healing.

Not only is there no evidence that NSAIDs favorably modify the progression of joint breakdown in patients with osteoarthritis or cartilage injury, several NSAIDs, for example, acetylsalicylic acid (aspirin), fenoprofen, tolmetin, and ibuprofen, have been shown to inhibit the synthesis of proteoglycans by normal cartilage.[54-56] Because proteoglycans are essential for the elasticity and compressive stiffness of articular cartilage, suppression of their synthesis as a consequence of NSAID administration must have adverse consequences.

NSAIDs inhibit cyclooxygenase, the enzyme involved in the synthesis of prostaglandins which aid in the inflammatory healing response. NSAIDs have the additional effect of inhibiting the enzymes involved in proteoglycan biosynthesis. **(See Figure 14-10.)** Aspirin and ibuprofen, in concentrations that can be achieved in joint tissues, inhibit glucuronyltransferase, an enzyme responsible for the elongation of chondroitin sulfate chains on the proteoglycan complex.[57, 58] NSAIDs inhibit the synthesis of proteoglycans that are being made by the chondrocytes to heal the articular cartilage damage.[59] The only result that can be obtained from NSAIDs in a patient with articular cartilage damage is a guarantee to produce more damage. This is exactly what is seen.

When animals with anterior cruciate ligament injuries were given NSAIDs the amount of articular cartilage damage that occurred over time was accelerated at a wicked rate. The proteoglycan concentration of the cartilage matrix was also suppressed significantly.[60, 61]

In 1967, Dr. H. Coke was the first medical doctor to suggest that NSAIDs might accelerate bone destruction.[62] More reports confirmed his suspicions shortly thereafter.[63] In a retrospective study of patients with osteoarthritis of the hip, a variety of NSAIDs were considered to have contributed to destruction of the hip joint, as confirmed by x-ray studies.[64] Another study confirmed that the stronger the NSAIDs, the faster the arthritic changes occurred.[65] This is why people who start on the anti-inflammatory train need stronger and stronger medications. The NSAIDs accelerate the degenerative process.

For the athlete or the physically active person, the **RICE** treatment is a scary prospect. It devastates the natural healing response. People are often given NSAIDs along with **RICE**, which further suppresses the local inflammatory reaction that is needed to heal the injured tissues. Instead of recommending Prolotherapy for continued complaints of pain, the usual course of treatment is perhaps the most potent of all anti-healing therapies: the cortisone shot.

WANT NO BONE? TAKE CORTISONE!

Receiving a cortisone shot is one of the quickest ways to lose strength at the ligament-bone junction (fibro-osseous junction). Cortisone and other steroid shots have the same detrimental effects on articular cartilage healing.

Corticosteroids, such as cortisone and prednisone, have adverse effects on bone and soft tissue healing. Corticosteroids inactivate vitamin D, limiting calcium absorption by the gastrointestinal tract and increasing the urinary excretion of calcium. Bone also shows a decrease in calcium uptake, ultimately leading to weakness at the fibro-osseous junction. Corticosteroids also inhibit the release of Growth Hormone, which further decreases soft tissue and bone repair. Ultimately, corticosteroids lead to a decrease in bone, ligament, and tendon strength.[66-71]

Corticosteroids inhibit the synthesis of proteins, collagen, and proteoglycans, particularly cartilage, by inhibiting the production of chondrocytes, which are the cells that comprise the articular cartilage. The net catabolic effect (weakening) of corticosteroids is inhibition of fibroblast production of collagen, ground substance, and angiogenesis (new blood vessel formation). The result is weakened synovial joints, supporting structures, articular cartilage, ligaments, and tendons. This weakness increases the pain, and the increased pain leads to more steroid injections. Cortisone injections should play almost no role in injury care or pain management.

Although anti-inflammatory medications and steroid injections reduce pain, they do so at the cost of destroying tissue. In a study conducted by Siraya Chunekamrai, D.V.M., Ph.D., steroid shots were given to horses with a substance commonly used in humans. The injected tissue was examined under the microscope. The steroid shots induced a tremendous amount of damage including chondrocyte necrosis (cartilage cell damage), hypocellularity (decreased number of cells) in the joint, decreased proteoglycan content and synthesis, and decreased collagen synthesis in the joint. All of these effects were permanent.[72]

Dr. Chunekamrai concluded, "The effects on cartilage of intra-articular injections of methylprednisolone acetate (steroid) were not ameliorated at eight weeks after eight weekly injections, or 16 weeks after a single injection. Cartilage remained biochemically and metabolically impaired."[73] In this study, some of the joints were injected only one time. Even after one steroid injection, cartilage remained biochemically and metabolically impaired. Other studies have con-

PROLOTHERAPY VERSUS CORTISONE	PROLOTHERAPY	CORTISONE
EFFECT ON HEALING	ENHANCED	INHIBITED
EFFECT ON REPAIR	ENHANCED	INHIBITED
EFFECT ON COLLAGEN GROWTH	ENHANCED	INHIBITED
EFFECT ON TENDON STRENGTH	ENHANCED	INHIBITED
EFFECT ON LIGAMENT STRENGTH	ENHANCED	INHIBITED
EFFECT ON CARTILAGE GROWTH	ENHANCED	INHIBITED

Figure 14-11: **To heal an injury, a person needs to receive Prolotherapy.**

firmed similar harmful effects of steroids on joint and cartilage tissue.[74, 75] A cortisone shot can permanently damage joints. Prolotherapy injections have the opposite effect—they permanently strengthen joints. **Figure 14-11** explains the monumental difference between cortisone and Prolotherapy injections.

Unfortunately, many people suffering with chronic pain look for quick relief without thinking about the long-term, potentially harmful side effects that could occur. The problem with cortisone is that immediate pain relief is possible, but in reality it may be permanently reducing the ability to remain active. For example, athletes often receive cortisone shots in order to be able to play. They then go onto the playing field with severe injuries that required cortisone shots to relieve the pain. Because they feel no pain, they play as if the injury does not exist. The injury will, unfortunately, never heal because of the tremendous anti-healing properties of cortisone. The athlete is, therefore, further injuring himself by playing. The same goes for the chronic pain sufferer who is trying to return to normal function.

Cortisone is dangerous because it inhibits just about every aspect of healing. Cortisone inhibits prostaglandin and leukotriene production, as already discussed. It also inhibits chondrocyte production of protein polysaccharides (proteoglycans), which are the major constituents of articular ground substance.[76] Behrens and his colleagues reported a persistent and highly significant reduction in the synthesis of proteins, collagen, and proteoglycans in the articular cartilage of rabbits who received weekly injections of glucocorticoids. They also reported a progressive loss of endoplasmic reticulum, mitochondria, and Golgi apparatus as the number of injections increased.[77]

THE ROLE OF EXERCISE IN INJURY: RESEARCH WITH EXERCISE AND CORTISONE

Exercise has the opposite effect of cortisone. Exercise has been shown to positively affect articular cartilage by increasing its thickness, enhancing the infusion of nutrients, and increasing matrix synthesis.[78-80] However, the effects of both exercise and cortisone in combination were not studied until recently.

An excellent study pointing out the dangers of an athlete exercising after receiving cortisone was conducted by Dr. Prem Gogia and associates at the Washington University School of Medicine in St. Louis. Animals were divided into three groups: **1.** Group One received a cortisone shot only. **2.** Group Two received a cortisone shot and exercised, and **3.** The Control Group received no treatment. This study was done in 1993 and was the first study to look at the effects of exercising after receiving cortisone shots. The authors did this study because it was common practice in sports medicine to give an athlete with an acute or chronic injury a cortisone shot. Athletes were typically returning to full-intensity sports activities within a few hours to one or two days after receiving the shot. The results of the study were amazing.

STUDY RESULTS UNBELIEVABLE

The animals receiving the cortisone shots showed a decrease in chondrocytes. When they exercised in addition to the cortisone shot, the chondrocyte cell count decreased by a full 25 percent. Degenerated cartilage was seen in all the cortisone-injected animals, but severe cartilage damage was seen in 67 percent of the animals that exercised and also received cortisone. The cortisone and exercise group also showed a significant decline in glycosaminoglycan synthesis compared to the

COMPARISON OF CHANGES IN ARTICULAR CARTILAGE IN AGING AND OSTEOARTHRITIS

CRITERION	AGING	OSTEOARTHRITIS
WATER CONTENT	DECREASED	INCREASED
GLYCOSAMINOGLYCANS AND CHONDROITIN SULFATE	NORMAL OR SLIGHTLY LESS	DECREASED
GLUCOSAMINE	INCREASED	DECREASED
KERATAN SULFATE	INCREASED	DECREASED
HYALURONATE	INCREASED	DECREASED
PROTEOGLYCANS AGGREGATION	NORMAL	DIMINISHED
LINK PROTEIN	FRAGMENTED	NORMAL
PROTEASES	NORMAL	INCREASED

Adapted from The Biology of Osteoarthritis. Herman, D. The New England Journal of Medicine. *1989, Vol. 20, pp. 1322-1329, Table 2.*

Figure 14-12 The Joint Composition in Aging and Osteoarthritis Are Opposites: Chondroitin and glucosamine content are lower in osteoarthritis. Thus, these patients often require supplementation.

other groups. The authors concluded, "The results suggest that running exercise in combination with intra-articular injections results in damage to the femoral articular cartilage." [81]

THE CHOICE IS YOURS: OSTEOARTHRITIS OR PROLOTHERAPY?

Osteoarthritis is not the result of aging. **See Figure 14-12**, which dispels the myths about arthritis and aging. The question to then ask is why do most people have arthritis in numerous areas of their body when they are older? Part of the reason for this is that in osteoarthritis, there is a decrease in chondroitin and glucosamine sulfate levels, which is the basis for their supplementation for this condition.

Otherwise, the answer is simple: Arthritis is the result of an injury to a joint that was never allowed to heal. A normal joint does not get arthritis. An aging joint does not get arthritis. An exercised-to-death joint does not get arthritis. Only an injured joint gets arthritis. The best way to prevent formation of arthritis—if you participate even in the most brutal of sports, such as boxing, martial arts fighting, rugby, or football—is to make sure that your injuries heal. Heal the injury and the likelihood of having a long and prosperous pain-free life is excellent. This means doing the MEAT treatment after the injury. MEAT includes movement, exercise, analgesics, and specific treatments such as heat, ultrasound, massage, and Prolotherapy. Do not allow your injuries to be treated with RICE, anti-inflammatories, cortisone shots, and arthroscopy. If you do these things, the prospects for future arthritis are excellent. The choice is yours: osteoarthritis or Prolotherapy. Perhaps it is for this reason that people around the country are saying no to arthritis and yes to Prolotherapy. ■

Chapter 15

Prolo Your Arthritis Pain Away!

It is important to first note what arthritis is not. It is not a consequence of old age. It is not a Tylenol or Motrin deficiency. It is not the most common reason for chronic disabling pain—no matter what a person's age. Arthritis pain is not a "live with it" condition. There is always a reason for the pain. The most common reason for chronic pain—regardless of age—is ligament laxity. Prolotherapy injections help strengthen weakened ligaments and eliminate chronic pain.

Causes of Osteoarthritis

Osteoarthritis almost always begins as ligament weakness. (Refer to **Figure 15-1.**) Joints are composed of two bones covered with articular cartilage, allowing the joint to glide, and ligaments holding the two bones together. Healthy articular cartilage and ligaments enable the two bones to glide evenly over one another when the bones move.

If the ligaments become weak, the bones will glide over one another in an uneven manner. One area of the bone will bear additional weight on the articular cartilage when the joint is stressed. This uneven distribution of joint stress creates an even greater strain on the weakened ligament in order to stabilize this joint. Eventually all of the ligaments of the joint become lax. The more lax the ligaments become, the more unstable the joint. This increases the abnormal weight distribution inside the joint. This continued stress within the joint causes articular cartilage breakdown, which causes the bones to glide roughly over each other producing a crunching noise when the joint is moved. Grinding or crunching is a warning sign that a cortisone shot awaits you at your conventional doctor's office, unless something is done.

At some point in this process, the body realizes the ligaments can no longer stabilize the joint. Muscles and their respective tendons will then tense in an attempt to stabilize the area on the weakened side of the joint, adding to the person's discomfort. As the muscles and their tendons weaken, which will occur over time, they become more painful and unable to stabilize the joint. They will often "knot," producing painful trigger points. When the muscles and ligaments can no longer stabilize the joint, the bony surfaces rub against each other. In a last attempt to stabilize the joint, additional bone begins accumulating where the bones collide. This bony overgrowth is called osteoarthritis. Eventually, if the process is not stopped at some point, a stiff joint will form. **(See Figure 15-2.)**

At any time during this process, the body can quickly stabilize the joint by swelling. Swelling of a joint indicates the presence of some foreign substance inside the joint or that the joint is loose. Microorganisms, such as bacteria, blood, pieces of cartilage, and various bodily breakdown products, can accumulate in the

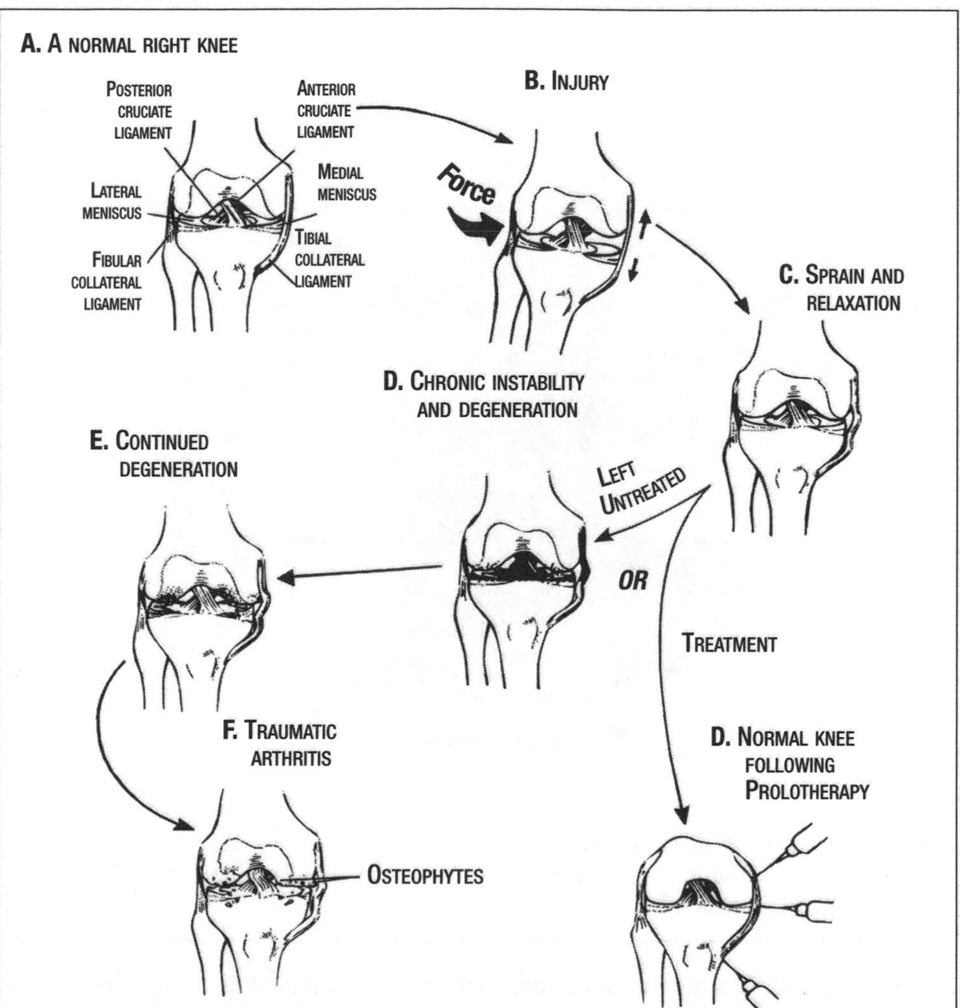

Figure 15-1: How Soft Tissue Injury Leads to Degenerative Arthritis
Following trauma, ligaments become sprained. When healing does not occur, the ligaments become relaxed, resulting in chronic instability and degeneration. When left untreated, post-traumatic "arthritis," or degeneration, follows. This degenerative process can be prevented with appropriate intervention through Prolotherapy.

joints and cause swelling. If a tissue is injured inside and around the joint, typically the joint swells as a protective measure so the body can repair the tissue, which may eventually lead to the development of arthritis.

Treatment of Osteoarthritis

Acute soft tissue injury, if treated improperly, may begin the cascade resulting in arthritis. As discussed in Chapter 7, icing a joint and taking nonsteroidal anti-inflammatory medicines after an acute soft tissue injury, in an attempt to decrease

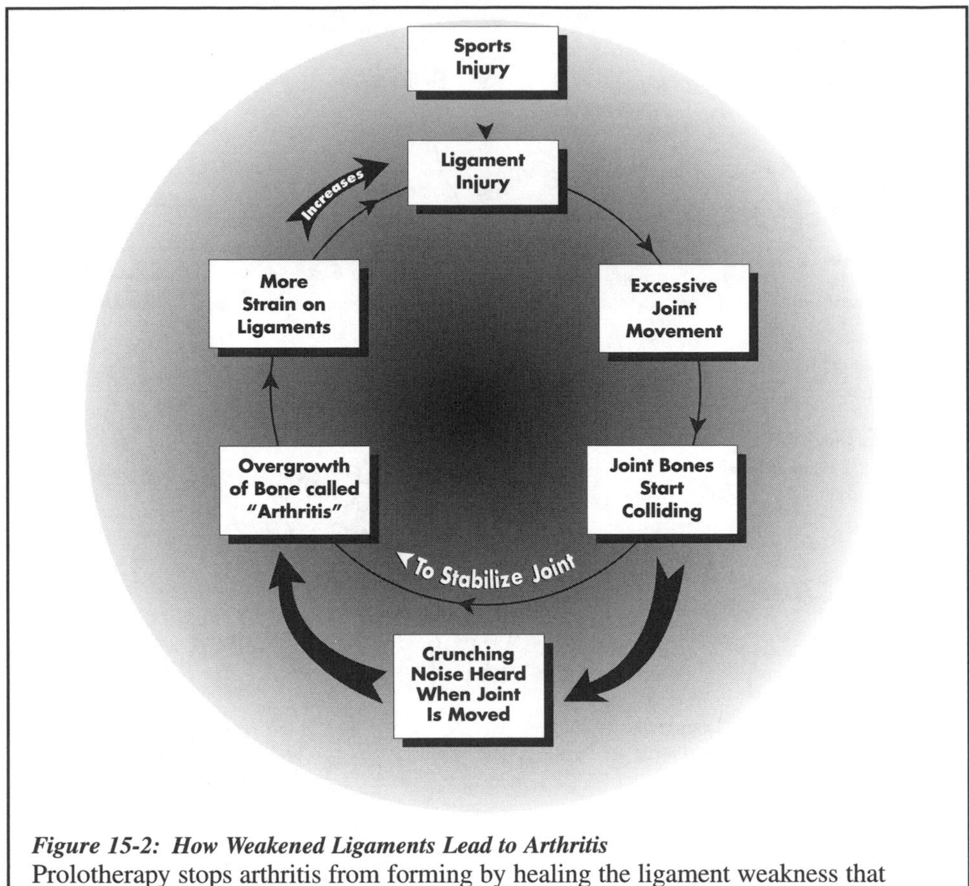

Figure 15-2: How Weakened Ligaments Lead to Arthritis
Prolotherapy stops arthritis from forming by healing the ligament weakness that started and perpetuated the cyle.

the swelling, inhibits the inflammatory mechanisms that heal the body. Treatments such as **R**est, **I**ce, **C**ompression, and **E**levation **(RICE)** almost guarantee that the joint and the injured tissue will not heal. It is important not to interfere with the body's normal healing mechanism—inflammation—when a soft tissue structure such as a ligament or tendon is injured. Treatment that decreases inflammation after an initial injury will slow and prevent healing, resulting in permanently weak tissue, which may eventually lead to the development of arthritis. Treatments that complement the inflammatory process will enhance the healing process.

A better course of action after a soft tissue injury involving a simple sprain of a ligament or strain of a tendon is **M**ovement, **E**xercise, **A**nalgesics (painkillers), and **T**reatment **(MEAT)**. **(Refer to Figure 7-1.)** It is preferable to use natural botanicals such as bromelain or cayenne pepper as analgesics. In the case of severe pain, a narcotic, such as codeine, works wonderfully to decrease the pain without decreasing the inflammation necessary to heal the tissue, if used on a short-term basis. When the body experiences pain, it naturally forms its own narcotic, called endorphins. Completely blocking the pain with narcotics is dangerous because the brain does not recognize that a part of the body is injured. For example, dancing the night away on an injured ankle that feels no pain may cause further damage. Natural botanicals, which do not block all of the pain, are preferred.

Treatment, such as ice, that decreases blood flow to the injured area causes a decrease in the flow of immune cells, which hinders the healing process. Treatment that increases blood flow causes an increase in the flow of immune cells to the injured tissue, which triggers the repair process. Movement, exercise, heat, massage, ultrasound, acupuncture, and physical therapy all improve blood flow and have a positive effect on healing.

Attempting to drastically decrease joint swelling after an acute injury is not advisable. The joint swelling is the body saying, "Hey, buddy, I'm hurt. Don't over do it!" Aggressive treatment to decrease the swelling may entice the injured individual to return to action prematurely. The best course of action is to allow the body to heal itself.

To increase the rate of healing and decrease the length of time the joint is swollen, protease enzymes are very helpful. Papain and chymopapain from papaya fruit, bromelain from pineapple, and pancreatin enzyme preparations will encourage the removal of the damaged tissue, thus reducing the swelling.[1]

An injured ligament not allowed to heal will leave the joint unstable and primed for future arthritis. Prolotherapy blocks the cascade that leads to arthritis by repairing the ligaments that stabilize the joint. The following case study illustrates this scenario.

CASE STUDY

John is a mild-mannered accountant who transforms into "Evil Knievel" on the weekends. One weekend while John was skydiving, a gust of wind caused a rough landing. John severely twisted his knee with resultant swelling. His doctor advised him to follow the **RICE** protocol—**R**est, **I**ce, **C**ompression, and **E**levation. John was also given the latest anti-inflammatory medicine, supposedly even stronger than Motrin, called "Strongton."

John's knee pain, a medial collateral ligament sprain, subsided, but the ligament did not heal completely, thanks to the **RICE** protocol and the anti-inflammatory medicine. Several years later, John noticed occasional grinding in his knee. What John was experiencing was articular cartilage breakdown inside the knee. After several more years, John experienced intermittent pain in the knee. Advertisements persuaded him to take ibuprofen for the pain. Although this relieved the pain, unfortunately for John, the arthritis process was accelerated because his medial collateral ligament injury never healed.

Several years later, John, now in his mid-40s, starts feeling like an old man. In addition to his knee pain, he suffers with a radiating pain down the inside of his lower leg. Not only is skydiving something of the past, but even a simple game of racquetball is a painful experience. John decides to seek medical advice. The doctor x-rays the knee and notices a narrowing of the articular cartilage space. John is told the dreadful news, "John, you have arthritis." At that moment John's mortality flashes before his eyes. The doctor takes out the dreaded prescription pad and writes another prescription for the latest nonsteroidal anti-inflammatory medicine, "Richtin," because it makes the manufacturer rich. What John does not realize is just about everyone who sees that doctor for pain gets exactly the same prescription because that particular drug representative had recently provided the doctor with free samples.

Unfortunately, John does not realize that his pain is not due to a deficiency in any anti-inflammatory medicine. Pain always has a cause, and in most cases the cause can be cured with Prolotherapy. Unfortunately, the physician examined John's knee joint and detected grinding, but did not continue with the necessary palpatory examination. If the physician had been familiar with Prolotherapy and the referral patterns for ligaments, he would have elicited a positive "jump sign" by palpating the medial collateral ligament and pes anserinus tendons. Prolotherapy injections to strengthen the medial collateral ligament and pes anserinus tendons would have stopped the arthritis cascade, as well as eliminate the pain. Once the ligaments and tendons regained normal strength, John would be able to resume his "Evil Knievel" activities, including skydiving, assuming his ticker is okay and his wife lets him.

Because John's doctor is not familiar with Prolotherapy, the only option John is given is taking anti-inflammatory medicine that is leading him on the road to the orthopedist's office. After several more years, a few more anti-inflammatory prescriptions, and some more x-rays, John's family physician sends him to the orthopedic surgeon, his buddy, "the ortho man."

On the initial visit, John explains that he has medial (inside) knee pain that radiates down the inside of his leg. The orthopedist moves John's knee around and orders an x-ray to assist with the diagnosis. John sweats it out as he waits for the orthopedist to return. "The x-ray shows even further narrowing of the articular cartilage," calmly reports the orthopedist, as a smile begins to form at the corners of his mouth. As the orthopedist gives him the bad news, John's heart races and he feels a lump forming in his throat. "John, your arthritis is worse," says the surgeon. However, John is somewhat relieved, when the orthopedist tells him that he can receive a cortisone shot to help the pain. What John does not realize is his radiating medial knee pain is not due to arthritis. He is also not aware that chronic pain is not due to a cortisone deficiency. The orthopedist proceeds to speed up the arthritis process by injecting John with cortisone into his knee.

At this point, John's lax medial collateral ligament and pes anserinus tendon still have not been addressed. Prolotherapy, even at this juncture, would have halted the arthritis cascade and relieved John's pain. **(See Figure 15-3.)**

John's knee feels great for several months after the cortisone shot. He returns as a madman to the racquetball court and resumes running again. What John does

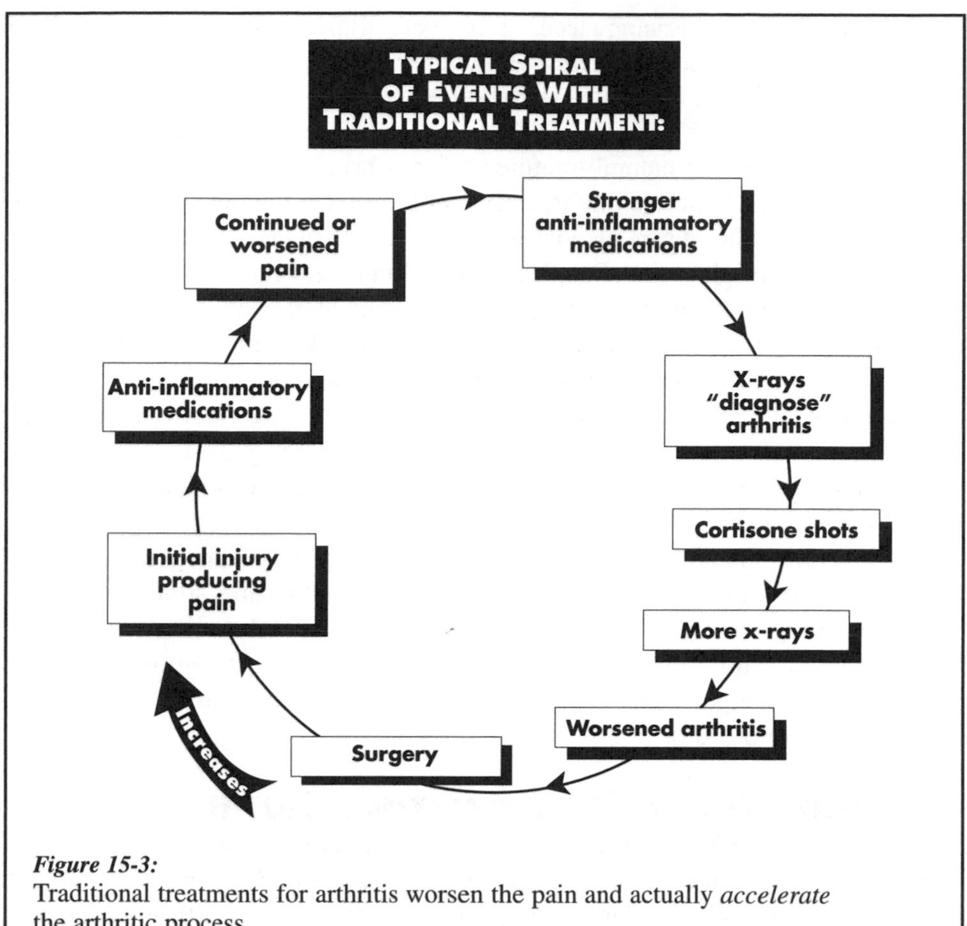

Figure 15-3:
Traditional treatments for arthritis worsen the pain and actually *accelerate* the arthritic process.

not realize is the cortisone was masking the pain. His medial collateral ligaments and tendons that support the inside of the knee were getting weaker. The pain relief which allowed John to return to his activities was actually harmful to his condition. His medial collateral ligaments and pes anserinus tendons were not strong enough to stabilize his knee during the racquetball and running. The knee was crying out for him to stop, but was muzzled by the cortisone. Six months later, the pain has returned and John is back in the orthopedist's office receiving another cortisone shot and a new and improved anti-inflammatory medicine.

This process repeats itself several times. John's knee continues to stiffen until one day he realizes that walking is nothing but a painful experience. He limps, favoring his bad knee. He sees his buddy, the orthopedist. Because they see each other quite often, they have become good friends. The orthopedist recommends another x-ray. Again, John's heart pounds and his hands sweat, as he waits for the report. Soon his stomach feels queasy, like the time he ate that leftover green stuff from the back of the fridge. His heart seems to skip a beat, then his heart leaps into his throat as the verdict is announced. "John, your arthritis has gotten worse." John turns pale, wanting to beg for mercy. His fatal sentence is read, "John, you need a knee replacement." The system claims another victim. Poor John!

John's story is quite common. Perhaps you can relate to it. John's arthritis is severe, but a myriad of natural treatments for arthritis is available. It cannot be overemphasized that chronic disease, whether arthritis, pain, high blood pressure, heart disease, or other disabling conditions, should be managed under the care of a Natural Medicine physician. People generally begin and end with the same treatment system. In the case of chronic pain, if a person starts with traditional medicines, like anti-inflammatories, he or she will end up naked in a strange room with lots of funny-looking people in masks hovering over him or her. This is called the surgical suite. Anyone who has undergone surgery will agree that it is one scary experience. It is not natural for the body to undergo surgery. In John's case, his pain could have been eliminated with Natural Medicine techniques including Prolotherapy.

Prolotherapy should be instituted and will be beneficial at any point along the arthritis cascade. Prolotherapy will strengthen the supporting structures of the joint, decreasing the pressure on the articular cartilage and the bones of the joint. Prolotherapy will not reverse the arthritic bony changes, but strengthens the joint and diminishes the pain. The need for surgical procedures for arthritis can often be eliminated with Prolotherapy.

RHEUMATOID AND INFLAMMATORY ARTHRITIS

Not everyone with arthritis has osteo—or degenerative—arthritis. Rheumatoid arthritis sufferers make up one percent of the population,[2] another one percent have some other kind of inflammatory arthritis. Inflammatory arthritis generally occurs when the body attacks itself by making antibodies against itself. Antibodies are proteins, made by the immune system, that fight microorganisms such as bacteria that invade the body. In general, people with rheumatoid arthritis manufacture rheumatoid factor, and people with systemic lupus erythematosis produce anti-nuclear antibodies that fight against their own system. In these instances, this inflammation is counterproductive because the body is reacting against its own immune system.

The typical treatment for inflammatory arthritis is anti-inflammatory medicines, often stronger than the usual NSAIDs. Corticosteroids, such as prednisone, are typically used. As previously stated, chronic pain, no matter the cause, is not due to a medicine deficiency. Rheumatoid arthritis is not due to a prednisone deficiency. Rheumatoid arthritis does have a cause. Inflammatory arthritis does have a cause. It is for this reason that people suffering from these painful chronic conditions should seek the care of a Natural Medicine physician so the cause of the condition can be treated.

CASE STUDY

Physicians who utilize Natural Medicine techniques in the treatment of rheumatologic diseases have all seen cases resolved. Judy, a 34-year-old woman, came to our office complaining of fatigue, body stiffness, and back pain. She was accompanied by her mother who had the obvious hand deformities of rheumatoid arthritis. **(See Figure 15-4.)** Prolotherapy injections for the loose ligaments in her back and a blood test for the antibodies associated with rheumatologic diseases were recommended. She agreed to both. Oh, if more patients were like Judy. Her blood tests revealed that her body was producing the rheumatoid factor, so she started a Natural Medicine program to alleviate the factor. After six months, her rheumatoid factor was negative. She was pain-free with no signs of rheumatoid arthritis.

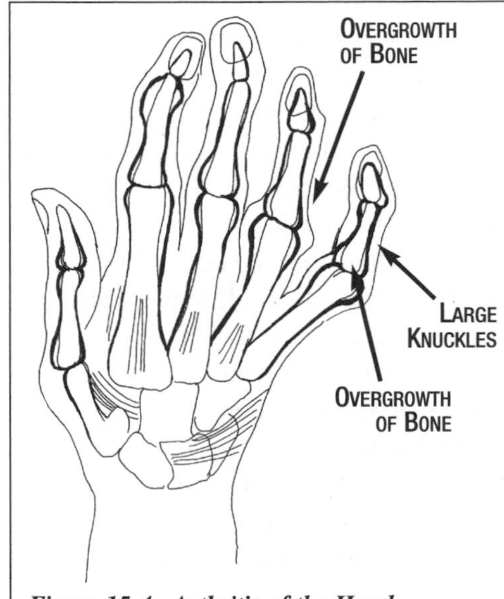

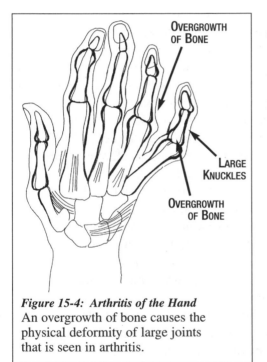

Figure 15-4: Arthritis of the Hand
An overgrowth of bone causes the physical deformity of large joints that is seen in arthritis.

NATURAL MEDICINE TREATMENT

Why would the body produce antibodies against itself? Many Natural Medicine practitioners believe the body is trying to fight a microorganism. When the microorganism, such as bacteria, invades the body, the immune system immediately begins making "torpedoes to kill the enemy." The torpedoes that the white blood cells make are called antibodies. In some individuals, the body forms antibodies against the organism and itself. In this case, antibiotic therapy or another treatment to kill the microorganism should cause a relief in the rheumatoid arthritis symptoms, correct? This is precisely what occurs in many individuals.

Natural Medicine clinicians have long suspected a bacterial etiology for rheumatoid arthritis.[3] A recent double-blind study reported the beneficial effects of antibiotics, such as minocycline, for rheumatoid arthritis.[4] Natural antibiotics, such as garlic, goldenseal, echinacea, and grapeseed extract are used by some to avoid the side effects of synthetic antibiotics. Many Natural Medicine physicians utilize bio-oxidative medicine techniques, including hydrogen peroxide or ozone therapy, and ultraviolet blood irradiation (photoluminescence), as anti-microbial therapies. Dr. Hemwall used a combination of a bacterial vaccine and influenza vaccine to successfully treat inflammatory arthritis. This vaccine protocol was developed by Bernard Bellew, M.D., who successfully treated hundreds of patients with degenerative and rheumatoid arthritis, claiming an 80 to 90 percent success rate.[5] The vaccine helps the body fight and kill the microorganism that is causing the arthritis. He has kept patients' inflammatory arthritis, including rheumatoid arthritis, under control for decades by utilizing this Bellew arthritis vaccine protocol. The combined approach of several of the above methods has allowed many patients to actually get ***cured*** of their rheumatologic diseases, including rheumatoid arthritis.

POSSIBLE CAUSES OF RHEUMATOID AND INFLAMMATORY ARTHRITIS

INTESTINAL PERMEABILITY

Intestinal permeability allows microorganisms and other foreign substances to circulate throughout the body.[6] The "stuff" inside the intestines is actually outside of the body. Contrary to popular belief, you are not what you eat. You are what you absorb. Technically, until something is absorbed it is not inside the body. One of the functions of the lining of the stomach and intestines is to keep out the bad "stuff." Chemicals, heavy metals, and microorganisms are examples of the harmful "stuff." An increase in the intestinal permeability (leaky gut) allows various substances, designed to remain in the intestines, to leak into the body. **(See Figure 15-5.)** Antibodies are then produced as the body attempts to eliminate these toxins. In some individuals these antibodies attack the joints, causing rheumatoid arthritis or other inflammatory arthritides. Various chemical and food sensitivities form due to chemicals and food breakdown products leaking into the body. Repeated exposure to these chemicals and foods causes the body to identify them as foreign invaders, releasing histamine and firing antibodies in response. The histamine and antibody release causes increased intestinal permeability, thereby worsening the arthritis and pain. This vicious cycle will continue until all factors associated with the "leaky gut" are eliminated.

What causes the intestinal permeability in the first place? Heavy metals, medications, infections, allergens, chemicals, tumors, and surgery are often the culprits.[7,8] It is interesting to note the medications prednisone and ibuprofen are well-known irritants and destroyers of the coating of the intestines.[9,10] NSAIDs, commonly prescribed for pain, are some of the worst offenders that cause leaky gut. A bleeding ulcer, the ultimate in increased intestinal permeability, is often the result of taking these medications. This is another reason to avoid these medicines. Rheumatologic diseases are not a prednisone or anti-inflammatory medicine deficiency. These medications, besides not correcting the problem, may exacerbate the condition.

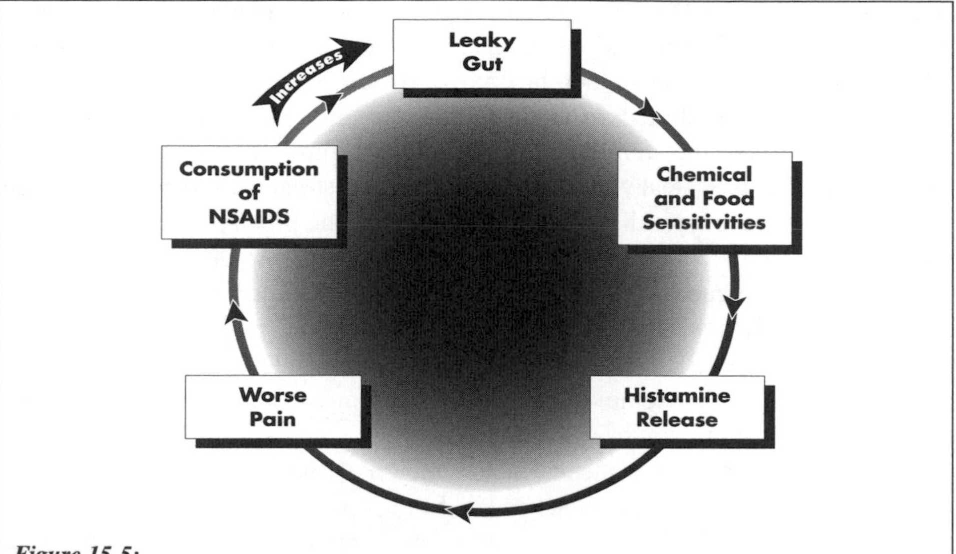

Figure 15-5:
Cycle of Pain Caused by NSAIDs and Leaky Gut
Intensity of pain and complications increase with each repetition of the cycle.

POOR DIET

Most Americans have very poor diets, consisting of large amounts of highly processed fast foods that are very low in nutritional value. Many patients report that they consume ***no*** fruits or vegetables at all. Typical Natural Medicine treatments for rheumatologic conditions include a very healthy diet that is preservative- and chemical free. A diet loaded with organic fruits and vegetables is recommended. An easy way to obtain relief from rheumatoid arthritis is a prolonged juice fast. It is not advisable to attempt any treatment in this book unless under the care of a physician familiar with these techniques. Fasting produces near immediate results because the toxic chemicals and foods are removed and the intestinal lining has an opportunity to repair itself. Every day people subject their bodies to a myriad of chemicals and preservatives from the food they eat. The average American consumes 140 pounds of sugar per year.[11] Is it any wonder that little leaks occur in the system with this kind of assault on the stomach and intestines? A healthy diet free of pesticides, chemicals, and preservatives is necessary for good health. It is, of course, vital to healing the body of rheumatoid arthritis.

HEAVY METALS

As previously mentioned, the intestinal permeability is also increased by heavy-metal exposure. Patients often ask, "How did I get heavy metals?" Open your mouth and take a peek. Amalgam fillings contain a plethora of heavy metals. They are typically comprised of 50 percent mercury, and the rest are various alloys of silver, tin, and nickel.[12] Gold fillings, in actuality, contain very little gold, but are made up of various alloys of silver, tin, and nickel. Since saliva is often acidic, guess what happens when heavy metals are placed in this acid environment? The metals solubilize, meaning the mercury, silver, and tin bond with the saliva that travels to the stomach where they wreak havoc on the digestive tract. One of the results is leaky gut syndrome, or intestinal permeability. Natural Medicine physicians typically check the hair, urine, and blood for heavy metals in people with chronic conditions like rheumatoid arthritis. An amazing amount of waste, such as mercury, silver, and tin accumulates in a person's body over the years. It is highly advisable to remove these as they have a detrimental health effect.[13] A course of chelation therapy is often recommended to remove the heavy metals from the body. Removal of amalgam fillings is sometimes advised for patients with accumulation of heavy metals.

Another result of heavy metals in the mouth is the formation of a battery. Acidic saliva combining with metal in the fillings produces the "battery." We do not know about you, but we do not want a battery only two inches from the base of our brains. Amalgam fillings should be removed by a biological dentist (mercury-free) to prevent these reactions from taking place in the body.

OMEGA-3 FATTY ACID DEFICIENCY

It is difficult to imagine with all the hype to lower the fat in our diets that anyone could be fat or fatty acid deficient. You may find it hard to believe, but some fat is good. Most Americans, unfortunately, have too much fat that hangs over their belt lines due to the over-consumption of total calories. Another type of fat that causes trouble are omega-6 fatty acids. These fatty acids are increased in the body due to the over-consumption of foods fried in hydrogenated vegetable oil as well as consumption of other hydrogenated oils like those found in margarine. Hydrogenated oils are everywhere! Look at the labels the next time you purchase crackers, cookies, and salad dressings. You will be surprised to find that almost all baked goods contain them.

Over-consumption of fried foods, margarine, and other foods with hydrogenated oils will increase the body's inflammatory state and make the symptoms of disease such as rheumatoid arthritis worse. The way to counteract this is to stop porking out on pork fritters and start eating salmon!

Salmon and other fish contain a high amount of omega-3 fatty acids. Omega-3 fatty acids have been shown to reduce the incidence of rheumatologic diseases, as well as their symptomatology.[14] The fatty acids in the fish oil, specifically eicosapentaenoic acid (EPA) and docosahexaenoic acid (DHA), dramatically improve the functional ability and diminish the pain in a myriad of diseases, including psoriasis, psoriatic arthritis, gout, lupus, osteoarthritis, and rheumatoid arthritis.[15]

Apparently for optimum health, a ratio of one-to-one in the diet of omega-6 to omega-3 is the healthiest. Currently, that ratio in the standard American diet is close to 20-to-one.[16] Supplementation with such things as flax seed oil, evening primrose oil, borage oil, and fish oils may help bring the omega-6 to omega-3 ratio into proper proportion and more toward optimal health. This is why part of standard Natural Medicine treatment for inflammatory arthritis, including rheumatoid arthritis, is the high-dose consumption of fish and fish oils. Lipase enzymes are also given so that the fat is digested properly.

IMMUNE DYSFUNCTION

An impairment in the immune system is always associated with chronic disease. This impairment in the immune system will retard soft tissue healing. Someone with a chronic disease, such as rheumatoid arthritis, is more likely to have chronic ligament and tendon laxities due to the deficiency in soft tissue healing. Prolotherapy starts the growth of ligament and tendon tissue, regardless of the etiological cause of the weakness. However, the body actually grows the ligament tissue. The stronger and healthier a person's immune system, the greater the growth of ligament and tendon tissue.

ANTI-INFLAMMATORY AGENTS

Any treatment that decreases the inflammatory response will ultimately slow and potentially stop soft tissue healing and worsen the arthritic condition. Prolotherapy injections cause inflammation that initiates ligament and tendon growth. Avoidance of ice and anti-inflammatory medicines during Prolotherapy treatments is recommended. Ice and anti-inflammatory medicines such as aspirin, Motrin, ibuprofen, and prednisone decrease the healing and growth of tissue that occurs with Prolotherapy. Some patients have needed anti-inflammatory drugs, such as prednisone, because of another chronic disease, like rheumatoid arthritis, and receive Prolotherapy with good results. This is not the ideal situation, however. Weaning the person off the anti-inflammatory medicines prior to starting Prolotherapy is often necessary. Anything that decreases inflammation has the potential to interfere with the healing that occurs with Prolotherapy. Conversely, anything that improves blood flow or strengthens the immune system, has the potential to assist the healing from Prolotherapy. Acupuncture, heat, massage, myofascial release, exercise, electrical stimulation, and physical therapy all improve blood flow and benefit the patient undergoing Prolotherapy.

A person with a chronic disease will often need more than the four sessions of Prolotherapy to heal the ligament and tendon weakness. They often require supplemental therapies to resolve the chronic pain complaint. A patient with chronic pain from inflammatory arthritis, caused by ligament or tendon laxity, will benefit from Prolotherapy injections. If, however, the joint is hot, red, and swollen, then the pain is likely due to the body's production of antibodies against itself. In this case, Prolotherapy injections to that joint would cause additional inflammation and intensify the problem. If the pain is due to a loose joint that is not hot and red, then ligament laxity is the likely culprit. In this case, the physician should take out his strong thumb and elicit a positive "jump sign." If elicited, Prolotherapy injections should begin.

It is not well known that Prolotherapy can stimulate the repair of cartilage—which is often needed for degenerated joints. **Figure 15-6** shows a hip joint before and after ten sessions of Prolotherapy. The more degenerated the joint, the more treatment sessions are typically needed.

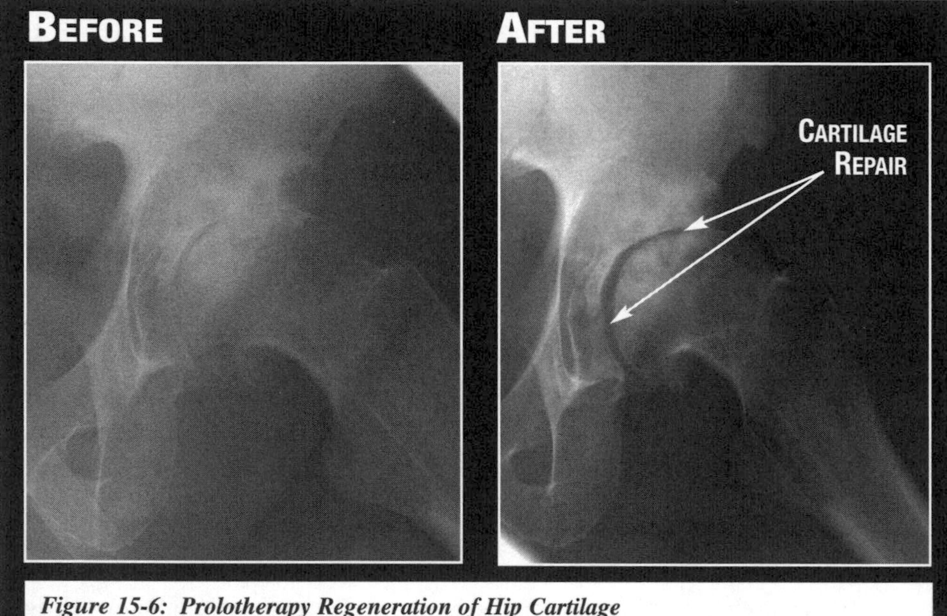

Figure 15-6: Prolotherapy Regeneration of Hip Cartilage
Prolotherapy can bring a significant amount of pain relief and healing in severely degenerated joints.*

Summary

The two main categories of arthritis are degenerative arthritis, also known as osteoarthritis, and inflammatory arthritis, typically rheumatoid arthritis. Ligament laxity is normally the cause of osteo—or degenerative—arthritis. The weak ligament, if not repaired by Prolotherapy, will eventually lead to a loose joint. The muscles and tendons tighten in an attempt to stabilize the joint. When this fails, the articular cartilage deteriorates on one side of the joint. The bones begin rubbing on that side of the joint. This causes an overgrowth of bone, called osteoarthritis. Prolotherapy injections to strengthen the joint stop this arthritis cas-

* ***To view other before and after Prolotherapy x-rays showing cartilage regeneration, see Caring Medical's website at www.caringmedical.com.***

cade. If osteoarthritis has already formed, Prolotherapy will relieve the pain but cannot reverse the bony overgrowth that has already occurred.

Increased intestinal permeability is one etiology for rheumatoid arthritis and inflammatory arthritis. This increased intestinal permeability causes substances such as chemicals, heavy metals, and microorganisms to enter the body. To eliminate the pain from rheumatoid arthritis, a Natural Medicine approach, including a proper diet, avoidance of anti-inflammatory agents, treatment of microorganism invasion, elimination of heavy metals, and a proper balance of omega-6 to omega-3 fatty acids is recommended during Prolotherapy.

Typically, Natural Medicine therapies, in addition to Prolotherapy, are necessary to relieve the chronic pain for the chronic disease patient. Prolotherapy is an excellent adjunct to the management of chronic pain from arthritis. Because of these facts, many people with arthritis are choosing to Prolo their arthritis pain away! ■

CHAPTER 16

Prolo Your RSD, SCI, and Other Neurological Pains Away!

Possibly the worst pain syndrome is Reflex Sympathetic Dystrophy, referred to as RSD. RSD is the granddaddy of pain syndromes. People suffering from RSD experience continual pain that feels like their skin is on fire. To an RSD patient, touching a piece of tissue paper or a bed sheet with the affected limb feels like touching fire.

RSD may appear at any age and is nondiscriminatory, affecting young, old, male, and female. It spreads like wildfire. It may start in the foot, move its way up to the knee, in the back, down the other leg, and up into the arms. People with RSD are panicked, anxious, and searching for anything that will alleviate the pain.

In 1986, the International Association for the Study of Pain Subcommittee on Taxonomy defined Reflex Sympathetic Dystrophy as continuous pain in an extremity with sympathetic hyperactivity. This generally occurs from a trauma such as a bone fracture.[1] The name of the condition was later changed to Sympathetically-Mediated Regional Pain Syndrome. It is a pain syndrome that occurs due to an increase in the activity of the sympathetic nervous system. RSD is very similar to fibromyalgia, in that many people are labeled with both of these conditions when, in fact, they have ligament or tendon laxity. Ligament laxity can cause severe, burning extremity pain. Just as with fibromyalgia, traditional treatments usually provide only temporary benefits.

STAGES OF RSD

RSD is a deteriorating disease, progressing in three stages. In stage I, the acute phase, the pain is described as burning or aching which is exacerbated by touch, emotional upset, or active/passive movement. The pain is often tremendous, much more than is expected with the original injury.[2] For example, two months after a stubbed toe, severe pain may develop far beyond what would normally be expected for such a mild injury. The involved limb becomes edematous (filled with fluid) and may be hot or cold. A bone scan may reveal an increased uptake of the radioactive phosphate compound in the affected area, indicating increased uptake of red blood cells to the area.

In stage II, the dystrophic phase of RSD, the pain is constant and is exacerbated by any sensory input. Excruciating pain is elicited by touching, vibrating, moving, or even blowing on the affected limb. The limb becomes more edematous, cool, and hyperhidrotic (sweaty). The bone scan typically shows a decreased uptake of red blood cells and x-ray films reveal the initial stages of osteoporosis.

Finally, in stage III, the atrophic phase, irreversible damage occurs to the extremity. Because of limited movement of the extremity, the affected limb contracts and the skin becomes cool, thin, and shiny. Because of scar tissue, it is nearly impossible to move the joint, and arthritis and osteoporosis are prevalent, resulting in a permanently frozen or contracted limb. At this time, the pain begins to subside; however, the limb is now essentially useless. The progression from stage I to stage III occurs over several months or years. Unfortunately, this process may repeat itself in other parts of the body.

Causes of RSD

Factors that predispose people to RSD are arthritis, brain injury, spinal cord injury, fracture, herpes, immobilization with a cast or splint, infection, heart attack, soft tissue injury, surgery, nerve injury, sprain, tendonitis or bursitis, vasculitis, and others.[3] RSD experts conclude that trauma is the usual initiating event in the development of RSD.[4-6]

People experiencing chronic pain attempt to decrease inflammation, most often by taking anti-inflammatory medicines, thereby unknowingly diminishing the chance of healing. The majority of people with RSD have also taken anti-inflammatory medicines after their injury, thereby diminishing their chances of healing. In every case of RSD Ross has treated, the patient was previously advised to immobilize the limb, generally the foot or hand, for a prolonged period of time. Immobilizing an injured joint for a prolonged period of time will guarantee inadequate healing of the soft tissue injury.

The traditional treatment for soft tissue or bony injuries, as previously discussed, is **R**est, **I**ce, **C**ompression, and **E**levation **(RICE)**. Rest has the following detrimental effects on the bones and soft tissues of the joints after two weeks of immobilization: fibrosis of periarticular tissue (contracture and weakening of joint capsules and ligaments); cartilage deterioration, producing an overgrowth of bone; atrophy in weight-bearing areas; and regional bony eburnation, sclerosis and resorption (fancy terms for arthritis and osteoporosis). Many of these effects are irreversible.[7]

Periodic short-term immobilization of the joint also has cumulative harmful effects.[8] Periodic immobilization over 30 days or longer leads to progressive osteoarthritis and will decrease range of motion. An immobilization period of as little as four days has a cumulative effect of producing osteoarthritis. An interval of four weeks between immobilization periods does not prevent osteoarthritis from developing.[9] Think about what this is saying. Only four days of joint immobilization will induce changes indicative of osteoarthritis. A cast on an arm or leg for six to eight weeks, or an ankle strap to rest the ankle for a week or two, is a lot longer than four days. Remember, we are talking about cumulative days. It is not uncommon for RSD patients to relay a treatment course of resting the limb for a few days, a doctor wrapping it for a week or two, and another doctor casting it for a month. The patient eventually immobilizes the limb because of the severity of the pain. The immobility triggers the arthritic process and potentially the RSD process as well. Immobility is especially detrimental to the articular cartilage that lines the bones in the joints. The articular cartilage has no blood vessel supply. It depends on the compressive force of the bones to provide joint fluid into the articular cartilage for nourishment. An immobilized joint starves the articular cartilage. Immobility causes a reduction in the cartilage-water content, a decrease in the glycosaminoglycan content, and a loss of hexamines from the periarticular tissue.[10] In other words, the articular cartilage degenerates, beginning a slow death of the cartilage. **(See Figure 16-1.)**

It is common medical knowledge that immobility causes osteoporosis, or weakening of the bones,[11] due to the urinary excretion of calcium from the resorption of bone. This osteoporosis process begins as soon as the limb becomes immobile. The strength of the bones is dependent upon muscle contraction through production of an electrical current with each contraction. The greater the immobility, the greater the osteoporosis.[12] When a tissue is injured, anti-inflammatories and immobility should be avoided. **M**ovement, **E**xercise, **A**nalgesics, and **T**reatment **(MEAT)** as opposed to **RICE** after an injury, in many cases, will prevent the onslaught of RSD.

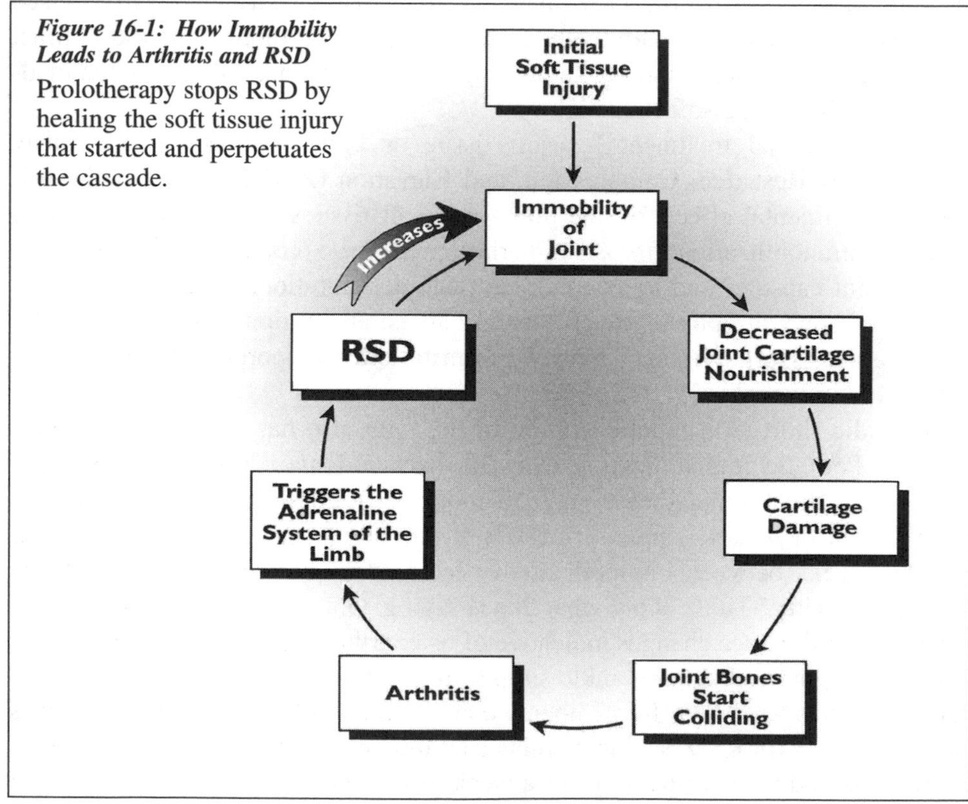

Figure 16-1: How Immobility Leads to Arthritis and RSD

Prolotherapy stops RSD by healing the soft tissue injury that started and perpetuates the cascade.

It is not uncommon after a cast is removed for pain in the limb to remain. The orthopedist interprets this as a normal occurrence caused by stiffness and recommends physical therapy to resolve the problem. Unfortunately for many, therapy does not resolve the problem; consequently, the patient sees another physician. Many do not find relief and, although they may not develop RSD, they have a chronic pain problem. The solution to their problem may be found with a physician familiar with Prolotherapy.

Imagine the magnitude of force required to break a bone. What happens to the ligaments that support the joint around the broken bone? The ligaments are injured. The blood supply to bone is excellent, whereas blood supply to ligament tissue is poor. Small feeder blood vessels, which are sheared during the initial injury, are designed to supply the ligaments with essential nutrients. This worsens the nutritional support that the ligaments receive. Combine this with NSAIDs and immobility, and the ligaments have essentially no hope of healing. This is why patients have chronic pain after their cast is removed despite good physical therapy. Post-casting, post-broken bone pain that does not respond to physical therapy is most likely a ligament injury. Weakened ligaments will not heal with physical therapy. Chronic ligament laxity has only one curative treatment, Prolotherapy.

RSD is often triggered by a traumatic event. This initial injury causes soft tissue damage involving the ligaments. The sympathetic nervous system shuts down to allow increased blood flow to the area in order to heal the injury. This is why initial bone scans clearly reveal RSD. Because the ligaments do not heal, joint deterioration continues. As the joint continues to deteriorate, the sympathetic nervous system's output increases because the ligament injury has not healed.

Physiological Changes Occurring in RSD

What is the source of RSD pain? As the name implies, the sympathetic nervous system becomes hyperactive. Adrenaline activates the sympathetic nervous system when you are nervous. What causes and maintains the hyperactivity of the sympathetic nervous system? The sympathetic nervous system is part of the autonomic nervous system, meaning that it is not under our conscious control. We do not consciously direct our blood vessels to dilate from 1.2 mm in diameter to 1.3 mm because it is a hot day. This happens automatically. For example, it is the bottom of the ninth, your team is down by a run, two outs, and bases are loaded, and it is your turn to bat. You feel your hands get cold and sweaty, your heart pounds, your blood pressure rises, and if you are a Chicago Cub, you strike out. Sorry, Cub fans!

The result of sympathetic stimulation on the blood vessels causes them to constrict, therefore, decreasing the blood supply to the tendons, ligaments, bones, and skin of the limb. Decreased blood supply will also decrease the immune system's ability to heal and will lead to osteoporosis, as the tendons and ligaments become fibrosed or shortened. The skin becomes shiny and pale. Because of impaired joint movement, the articular joint degenerates. The end result of the increased sympathetic activity is a contracted useless limb. It is imperative to properly treat RSD at the onset of its symptomatology.

In 1949, I. Korr, M.D., published the first of a series of papers on sympathetic hyperactivity related to alterations in the sensory input from the musculoskeletal system.[13-16] He described how muscle, joint, or soft tissue injury caused an increase in the activity of the sympathetic nervous system at the injured limb. Biomechanical stress, such as tilting the pelvis or wearing a heel lift, could cause the hyperactivity. Other studies have shown that any type of noxious mechanical deformation or chemical irritation of the soft tissues or joints alters the sensory input to the sympathetic nervous system.[17] This causes the sympathetic nervous system to fire the nerves and the blood vessels to constrict in the limb, triggering the progression of RSD.

Treatment of RSD

The traditional treatment for RSD involves various forms of sympathetic nerve blocks, consisting of injections of anesthetics into the sympathetic ganglion in the neck and back.[18, 19] These sympathetic ganglion blocks cause an immediate increase in temperature to the limb due to the increased blood flow. Often the patient experiences immediate pain relief.

Unfortunately, this treatment is only temporarily effective. RSD patients may receive multiple sympathetic blocks, to the point of having anesthetic pumps placed in their backs, or even have the sympathetic nerves severed in an attempt to find relief from their pain.

Treating the ligament injuries to stabilize the joint during stage I and stage II will eliminate the symptoms of RSD. An evaluation by a physician familiar with Prolotherapy is crucial for proper diagnosis and treatment for anyone who has had a simple injury that has not healed after several months. Prolotherapy injections to repair injured ligaments will keep a simple injury, simple. The further the progression of RSD, the harder it is to treat. If Prolotherapy is performed prior to the stage III changes, the condition is reversible. Prolotherapy can halt the progression of RSD because the initial etiological basis for the disease, ligament injury, is corrected. For example, RSD of the feet is often due to an injury to the anterior talofibular and its accompanying ligaments.

In prolonged cases of RSD, complementary treatments that improve blood flow may be necessary in addition to the Prolotherapy. One such treatment is a topical application of dimethyl sulfoxide, or DMSO. This liquid is applied, typically twice per day, to the skin of the painful limb and has been shown to be very effective in the treatment of RSD pain.[20] Other treatments include chelation therapy, bio-oxidative techniques, heat, exercise, and physical therapy.

Prolotherapy stimulates the body to improve blood flow because it causes inflammation at the fibro-osseous junction. Prolotherapy cannot reverse the

PROLOTHERAPY THROUGH THREE GENERATIONS OF PHYSICIANS

George S. Hackett, M.D., coined the word, "Prolotherapy." He taught Gustav Hemwall, M.D., the technique in 1955. For the next 40 years, Dr. Hemwall taught many physicians Prolotherapy, including his young associate, Ross A. Hauser, M.D.

Minneapolis Morn

MINNEAPOLIS, MINN., WEDNESDAY, SE

MINNEAPOLIS TRIBUNE PHOTO BY POWELL KRUEGER

It Hurts Here Dr. G. A. Hemwall, Chicago (left), got a lesson in back pain Tuesday from Dr. George S. Hackett, Canton, Ohio. The American Academy of Physical Medicine and Rehabilitation ended two days of meetings at the Leamington hotel, and the American Congress of Physical Medicine and Rehabilitation got ready for three days of meetings starting today. Hackett injects what he calls "an irritating solution" into weak backs to strengthen the ligaments—or, as he puts it, "stimulate production of new bone and fibrous tissue cells to strengthen the weld of ligament to bone." The method is not generally accepted, but Hackett claimed good results over 20 years.

Above: George S. Hackett, M.D., who coined the word "Prolotherapy," and Gustav A. Hemwall, M.D., promoting Prolotherapy at a national medical meeting in the early 1960s.

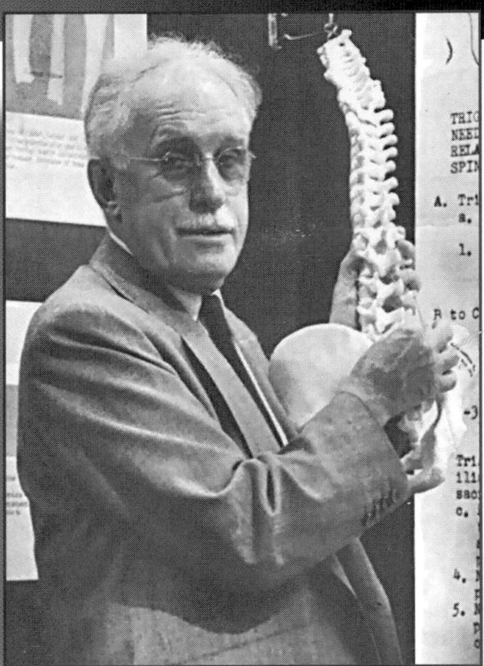

George S. Hackett, M.D. is seen here demonstrating Prolotherapy at the AMA Convention in 1955.

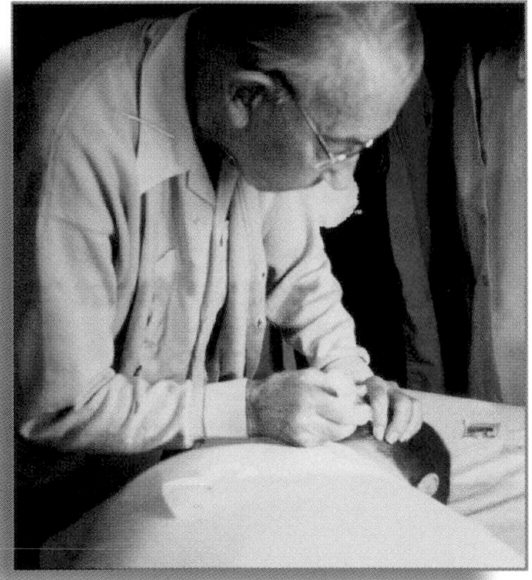

Dr. Hemwall administering Prolotherapy to the neck.

To the right are Dr. Gustav Hemwall and his young associate, Dr. Ross Hauser.

Hackett-Hemwall-Hauser Ligament Referral Patterns

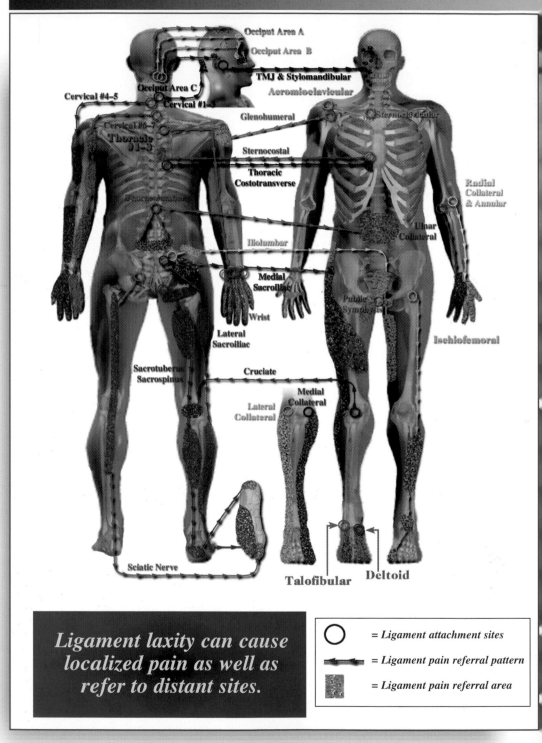

Ligament laxity can cause localized pain as well as refer to distant sites.

 *= Ligament attachment sites*

 *= Ligament pain referral pattern*

 *= Ligament pain referral area*

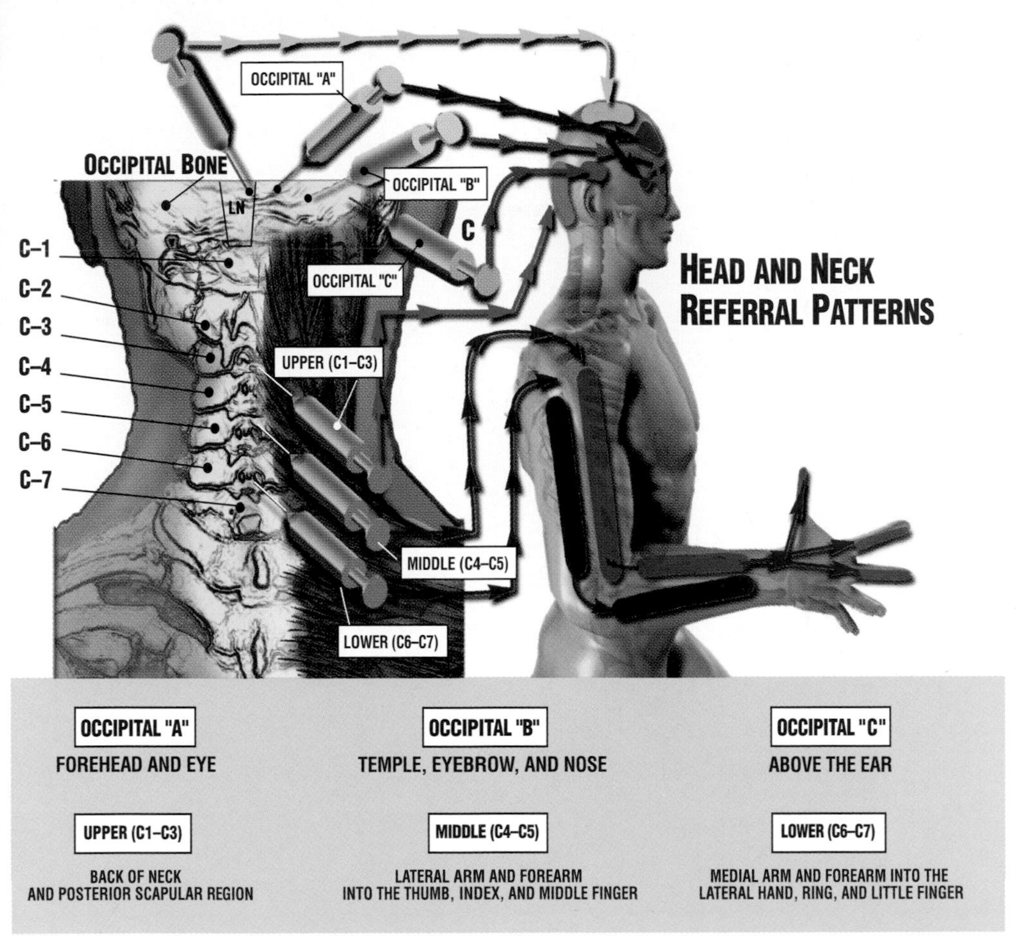

Prolotherapy injections can reproduce localized and referral pain patterns, thus confirming the diagnosis for both the patient and physician. The elimination of pain is, of course, an added bonus!

Prolotherapy: Diagnosis and Treatment All in One!

The Science Behind Prolotherapy...

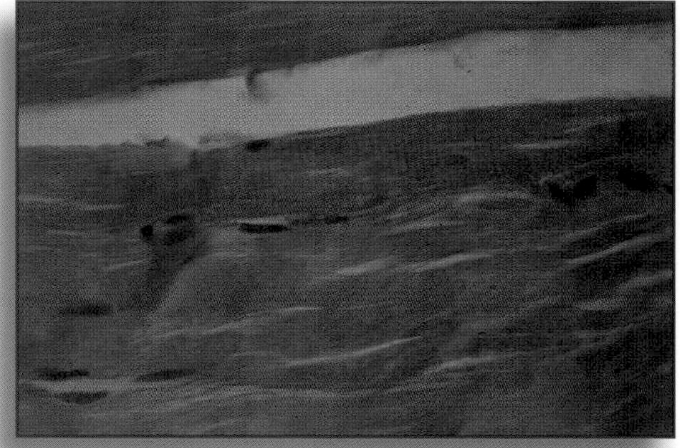

On the left: Normal muscle tissue (prior to Prolotherapy)

In the middle: Muscle tissue 96 hours after an injection with 12.5% dextrose and 0.5% xylocaine.

Note the high concentration of fibroblasts, indicative of a good inflammatory reaction. This is the basic Hackett-Hemwall Prolotherapy solution.

Below left: Muscle tissue 96 hours after an injection with 12.5% dextrose and an equal amount of 1% xylocaine, 2.5% phenol, and 12.5% glycerine. The inflammatory reaction is substantial in comparison with the middle photo. This is the Prolotherapy solution known as P2G.

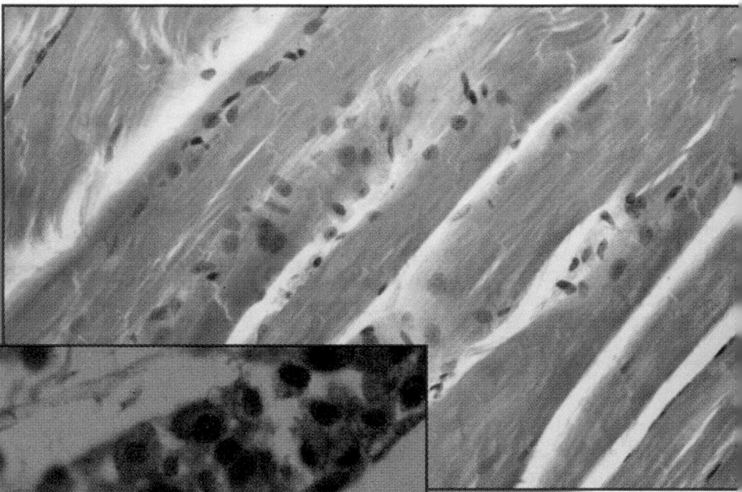

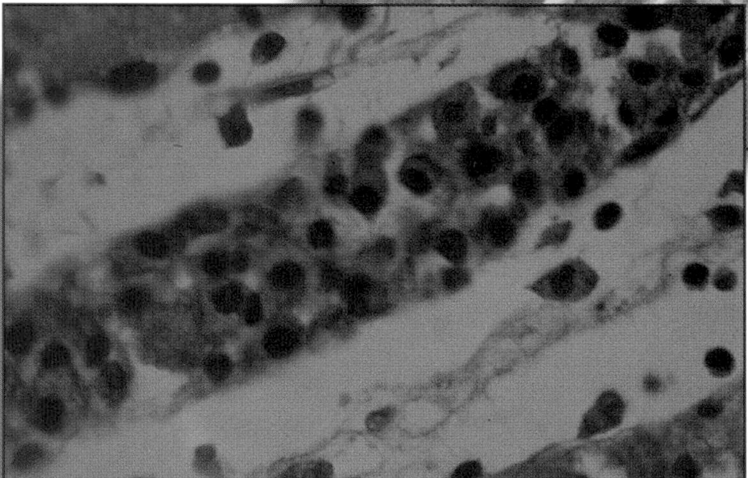

Prolotherapy stimulates the body to repair the painful area. The various solutions, when injected into the injured area, induce the normal inflammatory cascade to help heal such tissues as ligaments, tendons, discs, and cartilage.

Photos compliments of K. Dean Reeves, M.D. Slides made by Gale Bordon, M.D., and given to various members of the Prolotherapy Association in the 1960's. Dr. Bordon's research into the histology of Prolotherapy was presented at the annual Clinical Symposium of the Prolotherapy Association, June 16, 1968, Bellevue Hotel, San Francisco, California. Used with permission from Yvonne Bordon.

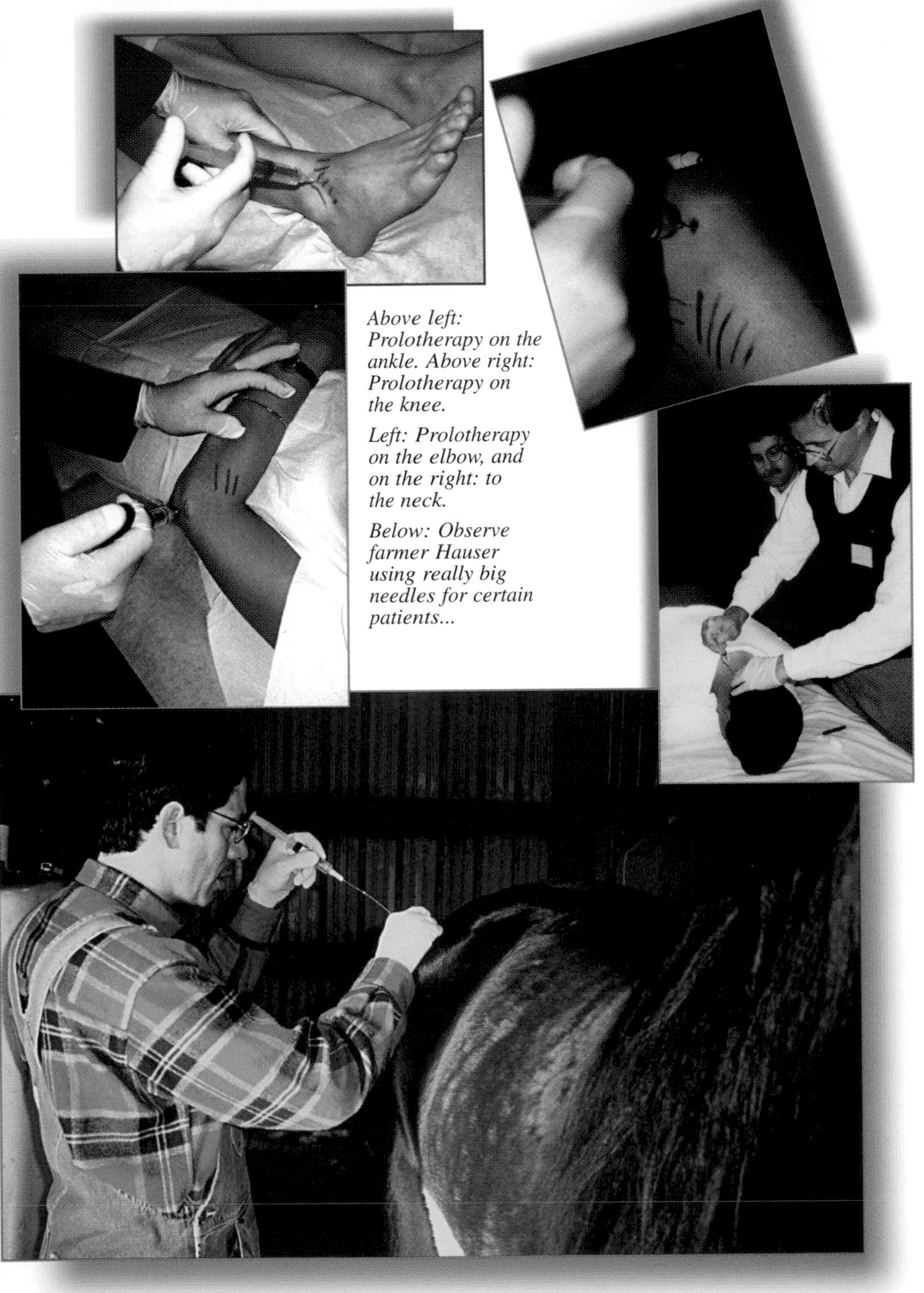

Above left: Prolotherapy on the ankle. Above right: Prolotherapy on the knee.

Left: Prolotherapy on the elbow, and on the right: to the neck.

Below: Observe farmer Hauser using really big needles for certain patients...

Prolotherapy! Repairing the Painful Area

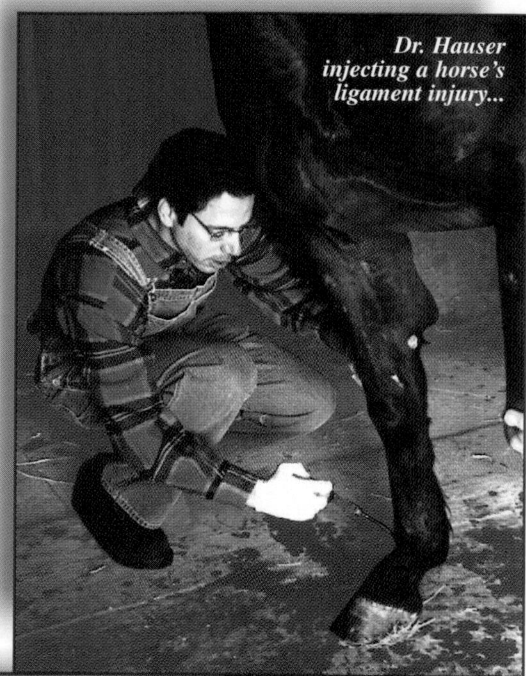

Dr. Hauser injecting a horse's ligament injury...

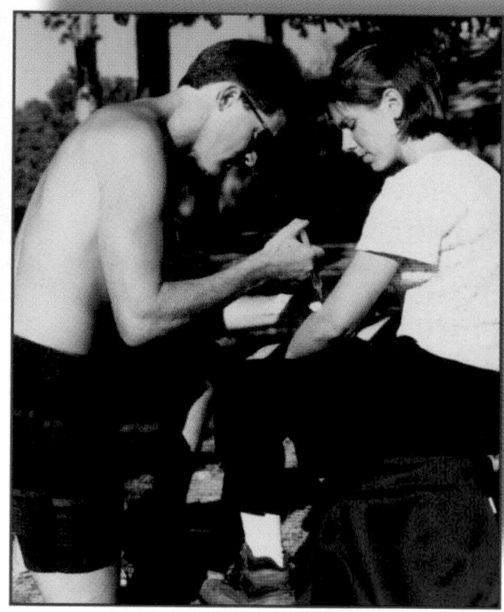

Dr. Mark Wheaton injects Brodie Hackney at a picnic.

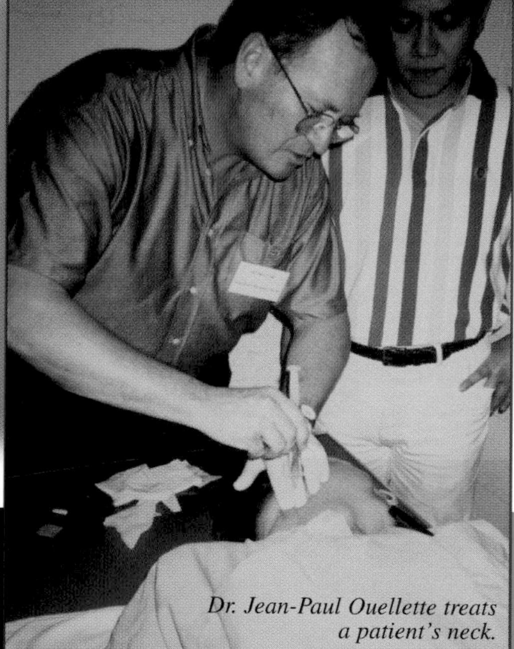

Dr. Jean-Paul Ouellette treats a patient's neck.

Dr. Van Pelt is seen injecting Dr. Mark Wheaton on a kitchen table.

Prolotherapy: It Can Be Done Anywhere!

Prolotherapy is extremely safe. Because of this, it can be done at picnics and on kitchen tables—though it is usually performed in a physician's office. More importantly, however, Prolotherapy helps just about any musculoskeletal problem and thus can be applied to most of the joints of the body.

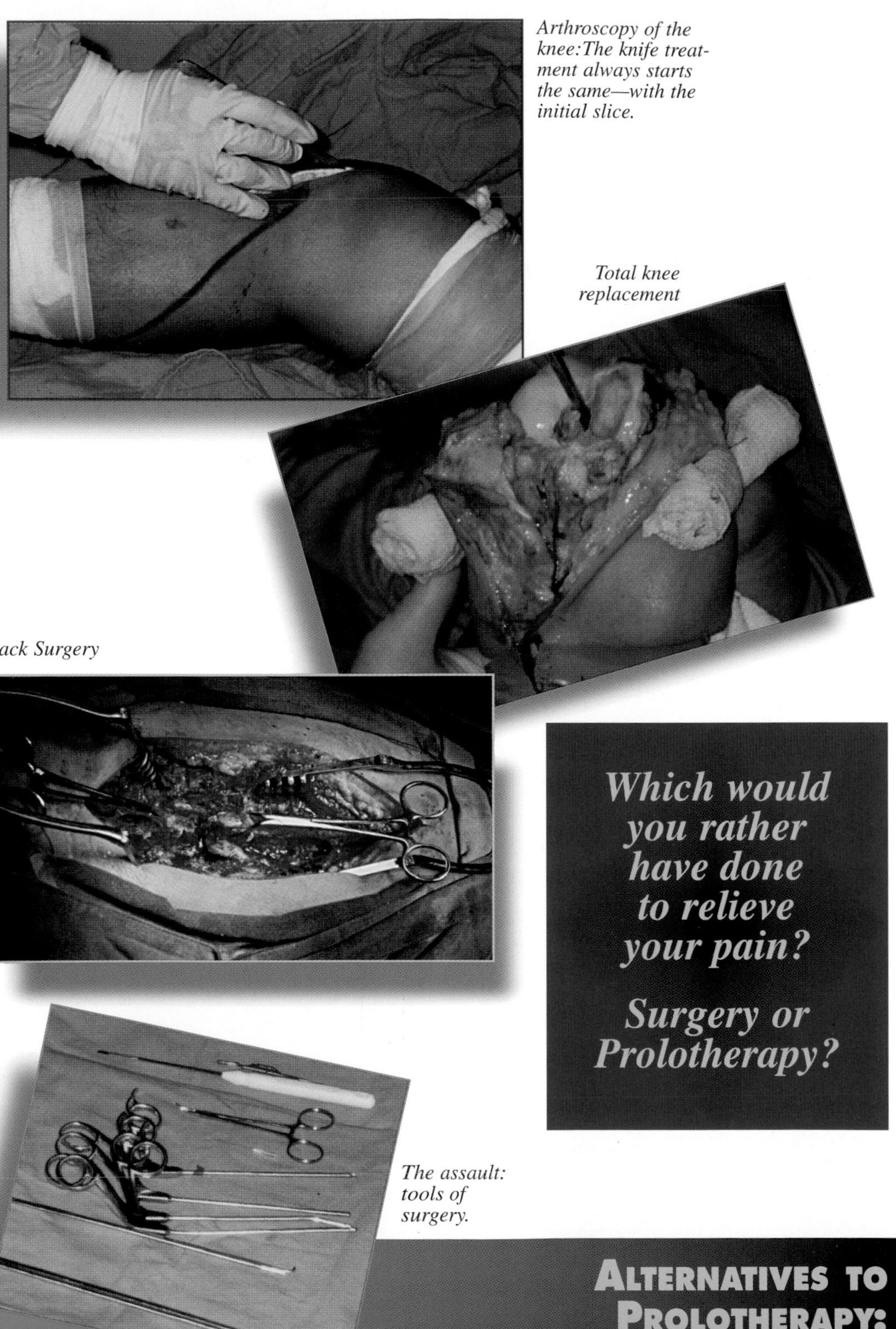

Arthroscopy of the knee: The knife treatment always starts the same—with the initial slice.

Total knee replacement

Back Surgery

The assault: tools of surgery.

Which would you rather have done to relieve your pain?

Surgery or Prolotherapy?

ALTERNATIVES TO PROLOTHERAPY: ARTHROSCOPY AND SURGERY

PROMOTION OF THE BOOKS

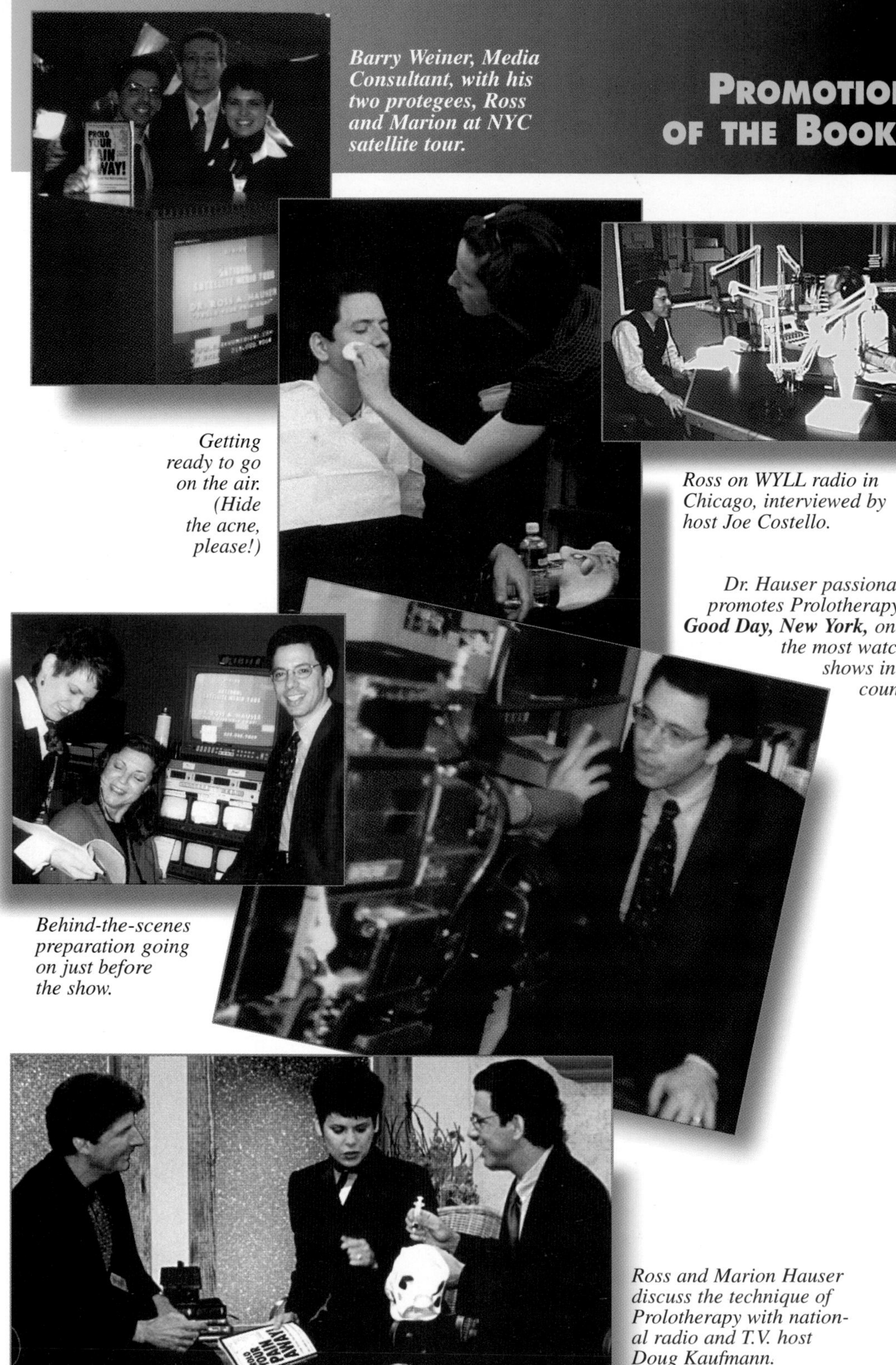

Barry Weiner, Media Consultant, with his two protegees, Ross and Marion at NYC satellite tour.

Getting ready to go on the air. (Hide the acne, please!)

Ross on WYLL radio in Chicago, interviewed by host Joe Costello.

*Dr. Hauser passionatel promotes Prolotherapy o **Good Day, New York,** one c the most watche shows in th countr*

Behind-the-scenes preparation going on just before the show.

Ross and Marion Hauser discuss the technique of Prolotherapy with national radio and T.V. host Doug Kaufmann.

On the far left: One of the Hausers' first dates... waaaay back in 1980.

To the left is a picture at college graduation from the University of Illinois in Champaign-Urbana.

Below are Ross and Marion at Beulah Land in Thebes, Illinois.

Dr. Ross Hauser

The Doctor and the Dietitian™ are grateful to God for "our Christian faith and allowing us to do so much more than we could have ever dreamed..."

Marion Hauser

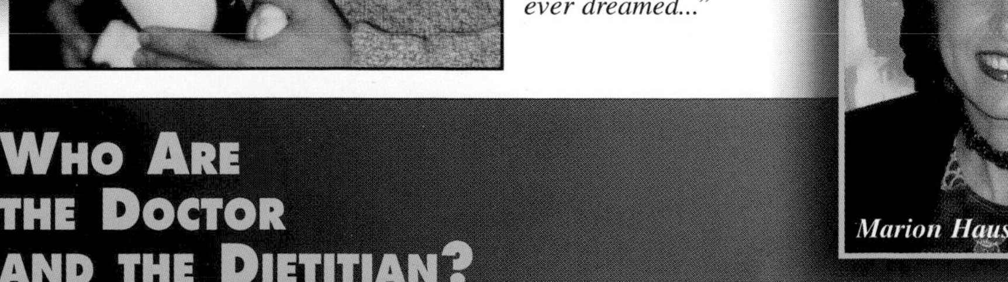

WHO ARE THE DOCTOR AND THE DIETITIAN?

The Life-Changing Procedures of Caring Medical & Rehabilitation Services, S.C.

Above, Patsy Holian, R.N., gets a patient ready for chelation therapy. This begins with proper nutrition, and keeps patients away from the knives of cardiovascular surgeons!

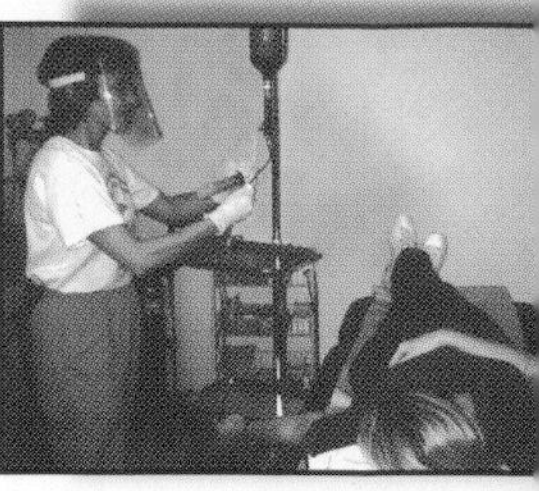

Above, Diane Neuzil, R.N., performs ozone therapy to boost a patient's immune system.

Prolotherapy is a lot of fun, at least for Dr. Hauser and MaryLou Daguio, R.N., (right) as they treat an athlete with shoulder pain...

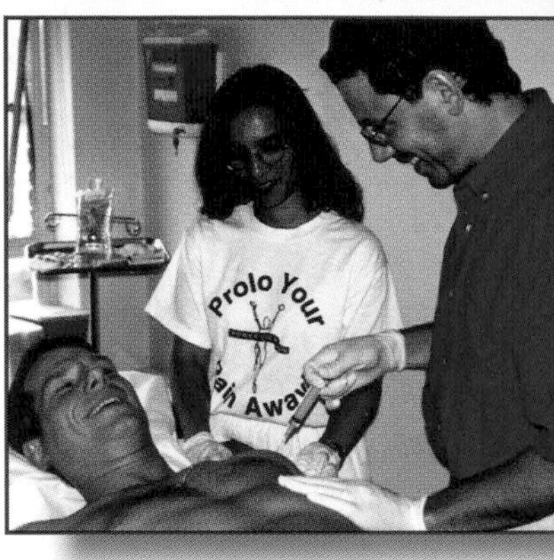

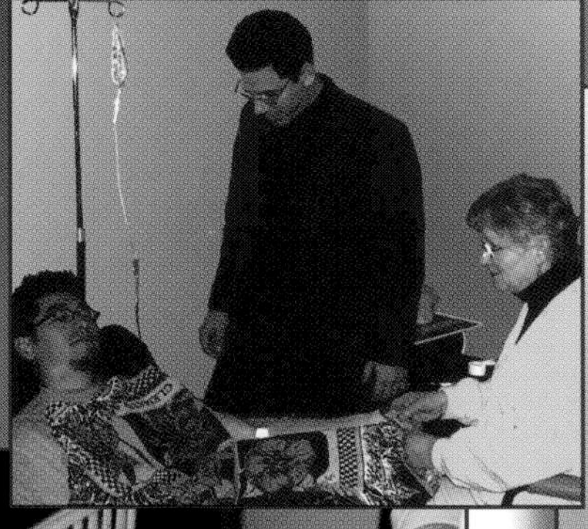

Right, Patsy Holian, R.N., administers IPT (Insulin Potentiation Therapy), a new treatment for cancer.

Neurocranial Restructuring—NCR will take you far!

The process of Photoluminescence detoxifies the blood with ultraviolet light

Caring Medical & Rehabilitation Services in Oak Park, Illinois, is a comprehensive natural medicine clinic utilizing treatment regimes from around the world.

BEULAH LAND MINISTRIES

Artist's rendition of the future site of Beulah Land Natural Medicine Clinic

PROPOSED MEDICAL CENTER
BEULAH LAND NATURAL MEDICINE CLINIC

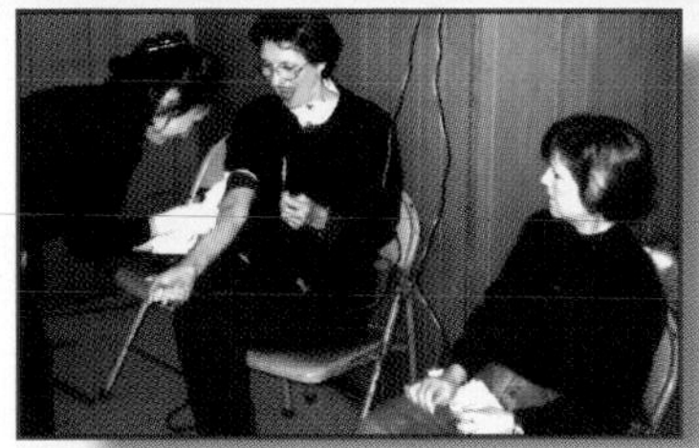

MaryLou Daguio, R.N., starts an IV.

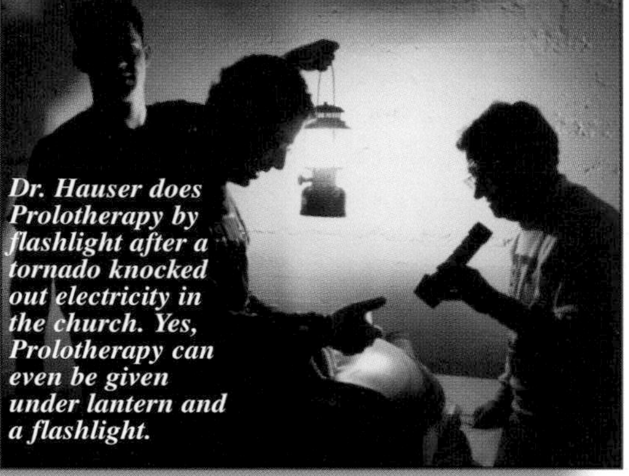

Dr. Hauser does Prolotherapy by flashlight after a tornado knocked out electricity in the church. Yes, Prolotherapy can even be given under lantern and a flashlight.

Left to right: Cathy, Patti, Grace, Diane, MaryLou, Doug, and Nicole mixing Prolo solution, which is a huge project at Beulah Land, since we treat over 500 patients in two days.

Many of the volunteers pose outside the First Baptist Church at Thebes, where the Beulah Land Missionary Clinic is held four times a year.

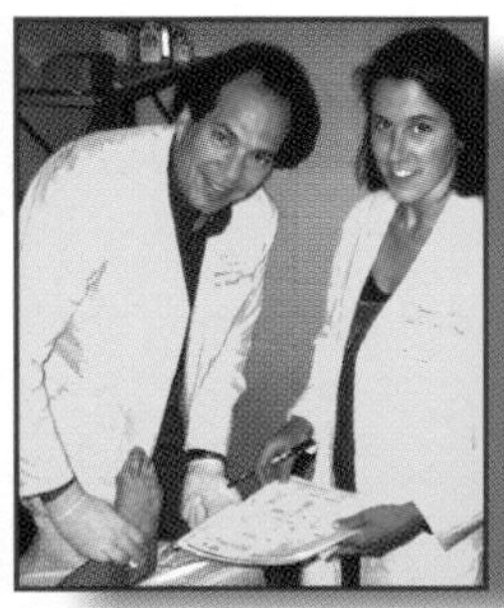

Above: The three "Regulars" of the Clinic: Dr. Mark Wheaton, Dr. Ross Hauser, and Dr. Rodney Van Pelt

Below, Dick Boomer, Marion's dad, running the lab at Beulah Land

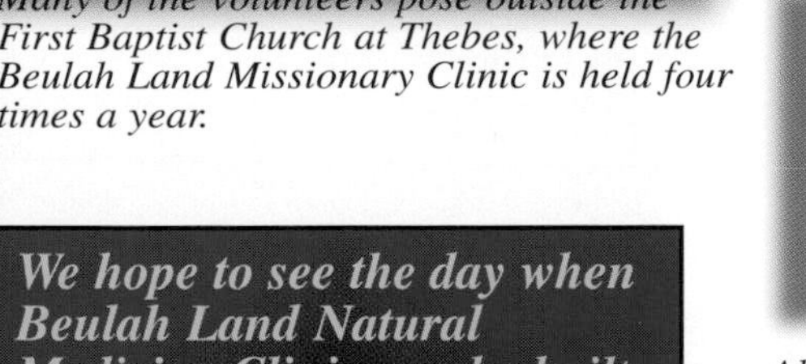

We hope to see the day when Beulah Land Natural Medicine Clinic can be built. Then, we can truly service those in need on a regular basis with such life-changing treatments as Prolotherapy—at no cost.

Above, top: Dr. Rodney Van Pelt and Brodie Hackney at the Beulah Land Natural Medicine Clinic

Directly above, Marion instructs a patient on his diet.

Prolotherapy Will Make You Smile!

Manuel Tuveri is all smiles just prior to his Prolotherapy treatment from Peter Blakemore, medical assistant, and Dr. Hauser.

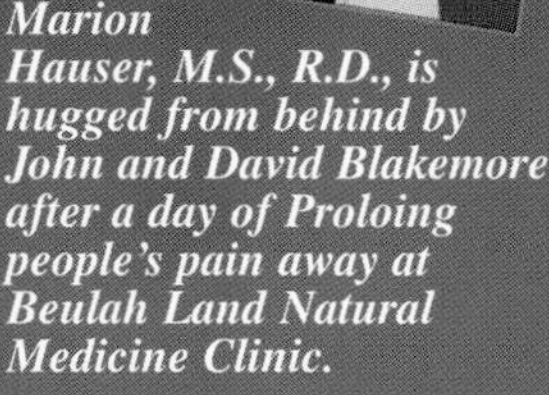

Marion Hauser, M.S., R.D., is hugged from behind by John and David Blakemore after a day of Proloing people's pain away at Beulah Land Natural Medicine Clinic.

Pamela Andrews, Kristin Hoving, and Marion Hauser can't smile enough because of Prolotherapy!

Bonnie McGraw and Ross Hauser are all smiles after another day of Prolo'ing patients' pain away!

Kendall Gill, Chicago Bulls guard, is all smiles after his migraine pain was Prolo'ed away!

destructive changes that have occurred, but can be very helpful in eliminating the pain from RSD.

Case Study of RSD Patient

One patient, Mrs. D., is a typical RSD case. She was in excellent health until she sprained her ankle. After a few days of doctoring it herself, she visited her internist who prescribed NSAIDs. Her pain persisted despite faithful compliance with the prescription. She saw her internist a few more times who prescribed a different NSAID and physical therapy. The next step was a podiatrist who taped the ankle for additional support. Because there was still no pain relief from the ankle sprain, she was fitted for a walking cast to "calm the pain and help the healing." After a month, when the cast was removed, Mrs. D. was left with a stiff sore foot, in addition to her ankle pain. She sought help from several other physicians, and was eventually given the diagnosis of RSD.

When she came to our office, she needed assistance to walk. Pressure readings, taken with a dolimeter, a device that quantitatively measures the amount of pressure necessary to elicit pain, revealed sensitivity to palpation over the entire foot, a hallmark feature of RSD.

Mrs. D. was treated with Prolotherapy to strengthen the ligaments and prescribed topical DMSO to decrease the sensitivity on the foot. She progressed gradually and after four months all pain symptoms were eliminated. She was able to walk, jump, and even skip rope.

Spinal Cord Injury

Another enigma that has eluded modern medicine is the fact that a person, having completely severed his or her spinal cord, still feels terrible pain below the level of the spinal cord injury (SCI). C. Nepomuceno, M.D., documented that 65 percent of people with spinal cord injury experienced pain within six months post-injury, and 90 percent within four years.[21] There have been various names for this phenomenon including Central Dysesthesia Syndrome (*dysesthesia* means burning pain) or Central Pain Syndrome. We call it the "Burning Rectum Syndrome" as the pain most often manifests in or near the rectum.

Traditional Approaches to SCI Pain Management

Whatever the name, many people with spinal cord injury have significant pain below the level of their SCI. The pain is similar to RSD pain and may radiate up or down the leg, but almost always resides in the rectal and pelvic area. Generally, traditional medical therapy provides only limited benefit. Eventually the person becomes addicted to narcotic medicines requiring larger doses to ease the pain. The medical personnel may become discouraged with the patient because of the continual requests for narcotics to control the pain. Soon the patient is labeled a drug addict.

More invasive approaches to control the pain include placement of a pump into the spinal canal, which directly supplies narcotics into the spinal cord. Another approach is placing a spinal cord stimulator next to the spinal cord to "trick" the body so it does not feel the pain. The body, however, is smarter than any computer gizmo and the pain soon returns. Some people have resorted to having their spinal cord severed to relieve the pain. These treatments provide only temporary relief because they do not address the root cause of the problem. Chronic pain is never due to a narcotic deficiency, spinal cord stimulator implant deficiency, or a surgery deficiency. Chronic pain has a definite cause and until that cause is corrected, all other treatments are doomed to provide only temporary relief.

AUTONOMIC NERVOUS SYSTEM

The key to understanding the pain of spinal cord injury (SCI) is the same as for Reflex Sympathetic Dystrophy: the autonomic nervous system. The autonomic nervous system is made up of two branches, the sympathetic nervous system which stimulates, and the parasympathetic nervous system, which calms.

The sympathetic nerves reside in the spinal cord from T1 to L2.[22] This means the ganglia, the main control centers of the sympathetic nerves, travel from thoracic vertebra number one to the lumbar vertebra number two. If a person has a spinal cord lesion at the T6 level or above, when the sympathetic nervous system is stimulated, the body cannot shut it off automatically. For instance, if a person has a complete SCI at T5, and a Foley catheter designed to drain the bladder clogs, the sympathetic nervous system would overactivate, producing muscle spasticity, discrete body sweating (primarily above the lesion), and a significant rise in blood pressure. The brain senses the high blood pressure and sends parasympathetic stimulation through the spinal cord. This causes the heart rate to slow. The parasympathetic stimulation is not able to dilate the blood vessels in the abdomen or lower extremity because the nerve impulse stops at the T4 spinal cord injury. If the situation is not addressed, the result may be stroke or death. This condition is known as autonomic hyperreflexia.[23]

Although bladder distention is the most frequent stimulus in the production of autonomic hyperreflexia, doctors Head and Riddoch noted, "There is scarcely a stimulus—cutaneous, proprioceptive, or visceral—that may not be followed by an outburst of sweating, appropriate to the lesion in each case."[24] In other words, sympathetic stimulation can occur from many different etiologies, including ligament and tendon injury. It has been discussed how sympathetic hyperactivity can lead to burning pain, as in the case of reflex sympathetic dystrophy. Inflammation inside or around a joint can also lead to an increase in sympathetic tone.[25-28] If a joint or ligament is attempting to repair itself, the sympathetic nervous system may fire. If it continues, the condition becomes chronic. Chronic burning rectal or pelvic pain

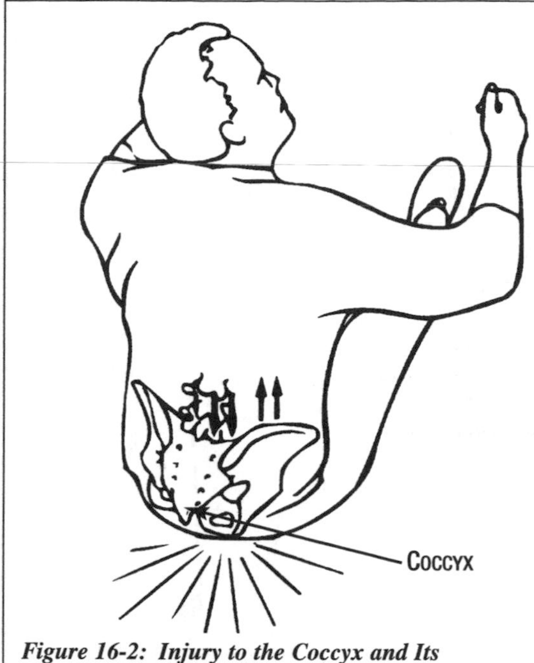

Figure 16-2: Injury to the Coccyx and Its Surrounding Structures from a Fall
Ligament damage in the pelvis is a common cause of coccygodynia (rectal pain).

in an SCI patient is most often from chronic ligament or tendon laxity in the pelvis.

Cause of SCI pain

A weakened ligament naturally tries to repair itself. Joint inflammation from a chronically weak ligament may be a cause for a hyperactive sympathetic nervous system. This may lead to burning pain around the joint inflammation. As with RSD, the burning pain typically starts around the site of the initial injury.

People with complete SCIs cannot move their muscles below the level of the SCI. Because the muscles are paralyzed, the work of the ligaments to stabilize the joints is tremendously increased. The sacroiliac ligaments incur the greatest stress because sitting and sleeping positions necessitate pelvic stabilization. The ligamentous support of the pelvis and sacroiliac joint is at risk for injury during transfer, as in moving from a wheelchair to a bed.

Eventually, the sacroiliac, iliolumbar, sacrotuberous, and sacrospinous ligaments become lax. A well-known cause of coccygodynia (rectal pain) is injury to the sacrococcygeal joint. Coccygodynia is characterized by burning rectal pain. The onset of the pain is sudden, exquisite, and tender to palpation. Pain on movement of the coccyx is characteristic, meaning patients have pain when sitting or changing position.[29]

Coccygodynia (Rectal Pain)

Acute coccygodynia is most often caused by trauma to the coccyx and its surrounding structures, usually due to falling while in the half-seated position. **(See Figure 16-2.)** The coccyx itself is a bony structure attached to the end of the sacrum and is composed of three to five segments. The first and second segments may be separated by an intervertebral disc, but more commonly the segments are fused. The mobility, however, between the first and second segments predisposes this segment of the coccyx to fracture and dislocate.[30]

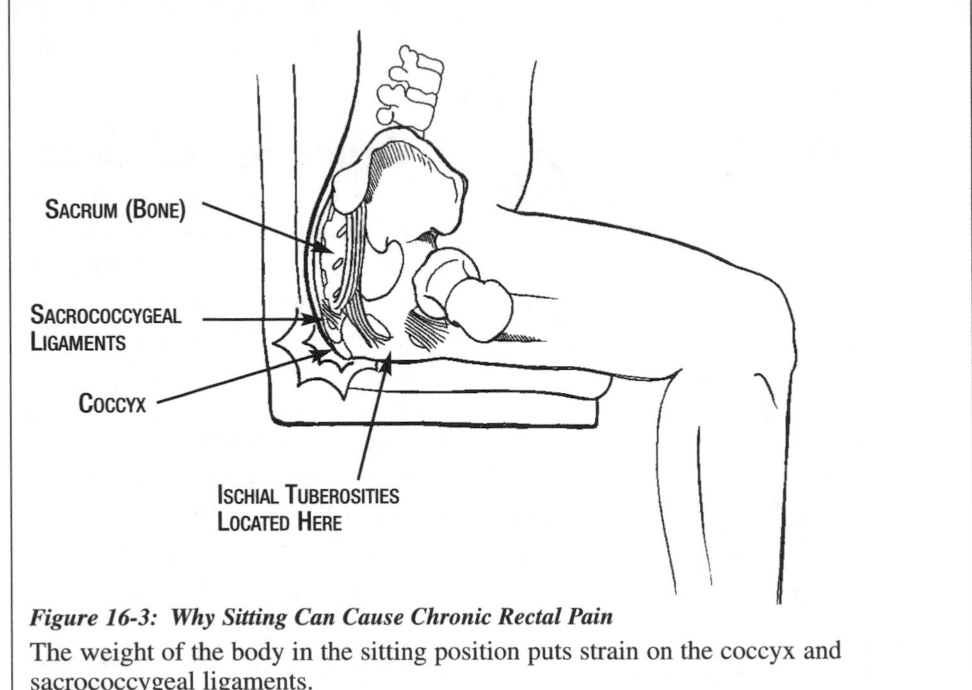

Figure 16-3: Why Sitting Can Cause Chronic Rectal Pain
The weight of the body in the sitting position puts strain on the coccyx and sacrococcygeal ligaments.

On the other hand, chronic coccygodynia is most commonly due to faulty posture while sitting, or trauma to the coccyx during childbirth. Sitting in the slouched position puts stress on the coccyx rather than on the ischial tuberosities. **(See Figure 16-3.)** Other possible causes for coccygeal pain are chronic infection and dysfunction of the musculature of the pelvic floor.

People without SCI, who experience rectal pain, typically elicit a positive "jump sign" when the sacrococcygeal ligament is palpated. Prolotherapy to this ligament is curative in most cases. Some patients may also have laxity in the sacroiliac joint, which requires treatment to resolve the chronic rectal pain.

The presentation of symptoms of coccygodynia in people without spinal cord injury and the dysesthetic syndrome that occurs in people with SCI are almost identical.

Traditional medical treatments for burning rectal pain include various medications, physical therapy, seat cushions, and psychological support. These treatments typically provide only temporary benefits. Prolotherapy injections, which strengthen the supporting structures of the sacrococcygeal joint, eliminate chronic rectal pain because they address the root cause of the problem. Chronic rectal pain from coccygodynia occurs because of a weakness in the sacrococcygeal joint or a weakness between one of the coccygeal segments. Prolotherapy to strengthen the ligamentous support of the weakened area cures chronic rectal pain from coccygodynia.

CASE STUDY

Mike, a complete SCI patient at the fourth thoracic vertebra level, with a stabilizing rod placed in his spine from T2 to T7, suffered a T9 vertebral compression fracture. The surgeons wanted to put another rod down the rest of his vertebrae, but he heard about Prolotherapy and wanted a second opinion before being subjected to the knife. He was a wise man. All wise people with chronic pain obtain a consultation with a physician familiar with Prolotherapy.

He described his most distressing problem as constant burning rectal pain. Because he had no feeling below the level of his spinal cord lesion, it was not possible to elicit a positive "jump sign." Prolotherapy was performed on his thoracic spine and pelvic region.

When he returned for the second Prolotherapy session, he excitedly said, "Look, Doc," and proceeded to bend forward on his wheelchair without the aid of a back brace. He previously required a back brace to support his thoracic spine while sitting. He lifted his hands perpendicular to the floor as he bent forward in his chair—stating he was not able to do this prior to the first Prolotherapy treatment. It was also interesting that prior to the first Prolotherapy treatment, the physicians taking care of him told him he needed surgery to stabilize his spine. Ross even spoke with his primary physician, a fellow Physiatrist, and explained it would be reasonable for Mike to try Prolotherapy to stabilize his spine, and that all conservative treatments should be exhausted prior to any surgical intervention. The Physiatrist had to approve the Prolotherapy for Mike in order to obtain insurance coverage. The Physiatrist would not consent, but Mike decided to have the Prolotherapy and pay for it out of his own pocket. Mike's primary physician was so amazed when Mike returned for a follow-up visit after the first Prolotherapy session, he recommended that the insurance company pay for the Prolotherapy. Not only did they pay for the first Prolotherapy treatment, they agreed to pay for five more treatments.

We did not hear from Mike after his second session of Prolotherapy treatments, so Ross phoned him. Mike exclaimed, "Doc, you know that rectal pain I was having all those years? Well, I don't have that anymore!" This was amazing! After years of medicines, therapies, and cushions, two Prolotherapy treatments and Mike's dysesthetic syndrome was gone. How about his thoracic compression fracture? It has been 18 months since his first visit to our office and Mike's condition has not deteriorated.

Most physicians desire what is best for their patients. Unfortunately, they do not know or understand all the treatment opinions. That is why individuals must take it upon themselves to explore all the treatment options. This is especially true prior to agreeing to the knife treatment.

Vertebral Compression Fractures

Because people with complete SCI have no muscle movements below the level of the injury, severe osteoporosis is common. Osteoporosis is the main cause of vertebral compression fractures. Weakened bones cause a weakness in the fibro-osseous junction, contributing to ligament and tendon laxity.[31] This laxity decreases the stability of the bones, especially around the vertebrae. Eventually, because of the osteoporosis and the weakened ligaments, the vertebrae can no longer support the weight of the body and are compressed. This compressing of the vertebrae is known as a vertebral compression fracture. Prolotherapy helps stabilize the fracture site by causing the growth of ligament tissue at the fibro-osseous junction and strengthens the vertebral ligaments to eliminate the pain.

Neuromas

Burning pains in other parts of the body are believed to be due to nerve injuries or nerve tumors called "neuromas." Conventional treatments include blocking the nerve impulses or removing the "neuromas." Some of these "neuromas" even have names. In the foot, it is called Morton's Neuroma. Dr. Hemwall believed there is no such thing as a "neuroma." When surgically examined, no tumor of the nerve is found. Treatments such as surgery or nerve blocks for these so-called "neuromas" often provide temporary benefit but do not cure the underlying condition because the burning pain does not originate in the nerves. If its origin was in the nerves, then blocking the nerves, burning the nerves, or taking the nerves out would have definitive results.

The most common reason for burning pain anywhere in the body is ligament laxity. Chronic ligament laxity causes the sensory nerve endings within the ligaments to fire, stimulating the sympathetic system to become hyperactive. This leads to the chronic burning pain that people experience. Only Prolotherapy will supply definitive results in eliminating this type of chronic burning pain anywhere in the body.

Post-Stroke Pain

Strokes, medically known as cerebrovascular accident (CVA), are a major cause of long-lasting disability. One of the worst consequences that occurs after a stroke is severe burning pain on the side of the body affected by the stroke. This type of condition is also known as Central Pain Syndrome, Neurogenic Pain, or Thalamic Pain Syndrome.

A person who has lost external sensation in a limb due to a nerve injury or stroke may experience severe burning pain in the area. Why this occurs is still unknown, but is most likely due to a hyperactive autonomic nervous system. This explains why a limb that is completely paralyzed can experience severe pain.

The pain experienced is usually constant, spontaneous, and can, in many cases, be increased by various stimuli such as movements, cold, or warmth. It is usually severe and incapacitating, as it burns, pricks, stings, or aches. Typical treatments include pain medicines, muscle relaxants, physical therapy, and various antidepressant medicines.[32,33] Often the treatments provide minimal relief. A much more effective treatment is Prolotherapy.

An example of this is B.S., a 72-year-old who had a stroke 18 months prior to his first visit with Dr. Hemwall. The stroke left him paralyzed on his left side, where he experienced severe burning pain. He tried all of the above treatments without success. Dr. Hemwall treated him with Prolotherapy to the entire left side of his body and spine. B.S. had dramatic results. B.S. has had some recurrence of his pain, necessitating an occasional Prolotherapy "touch-up."

Prolotherapy injections cause the start of ligament and tendon tissue growth. It must be the stimulation of this growth that is registered in the spinal cord and/or brain that shuts down the pain-provoking stimulus. Since post-stroke or post-nerve injury pain syndromes have no real treatment, Prolotherapy is a wonderful treatment option that could have curative results. It is for this reason that many people with post-stroke pain are choosing to Prolo their pain away!

PHANTOM PAIN

Another fascinating pain syndrome is the so-called "phantom pain." Early in the 1900s the famous French surgeon, Ambroise Pare, wrote, "Truly, it is a thing wondrous, strange, and prodigious, which will scarce be credited, unless by such as have seen with their own eyes and heard with their own ears, the patients who many months after cutting away the leg, grievously complained that they yet felt exceeding great pain of that leg so cut off."[34]

Phantom sensation, phantom pain, or stump pain occurs in people who have had an amputation, suffered a stroke, or incurred paralysis of a section of the body. A weird sensation or pain is felt where the limb no longer exists or where there is no feeling. A typical scenario involves a gangrenous foot requiring amputation. Yes, some surgeries are necessary. After the surgery, some patients still experience the foot pain even though the foot is no longer there. **(See Figure 16-4.)**

Physicians will try anything to relieve the phantom pain. This includes the use of pain medicines, anticonvulsants, antidepressants, nerve injections, prosthesis changes, physical therapy, and various "knife treatments" (surgeries). These treatments provide only temporary relief because they do not address the root cause of the problem.

The current theory on the development of phantom pain is that the absence of the limb or absence of sensation in the limb causes an increase in nerve input from the brain to the limb. The additional nerve input causes the weird sensations and pain, but since the limb is absent, there is no system to deactivate the impulse.[35]

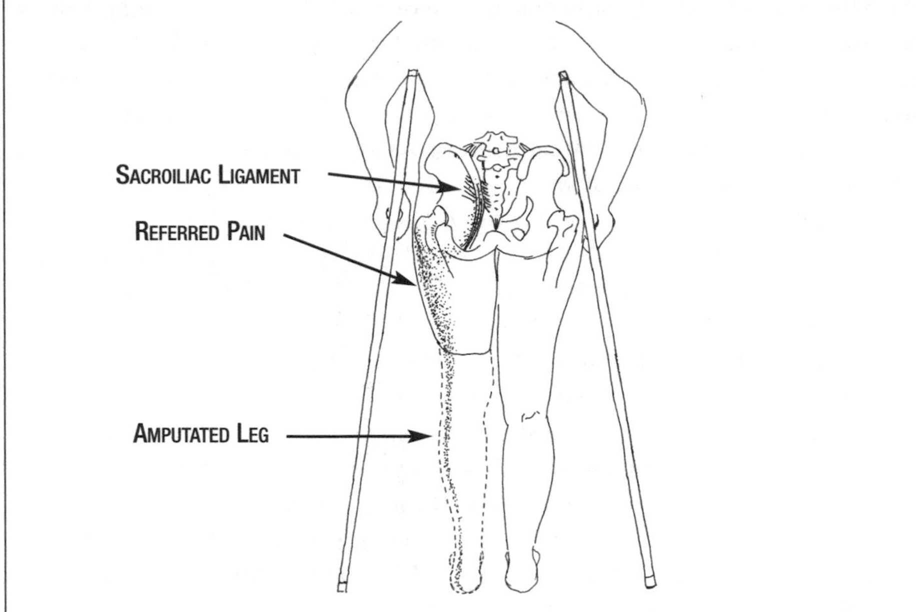

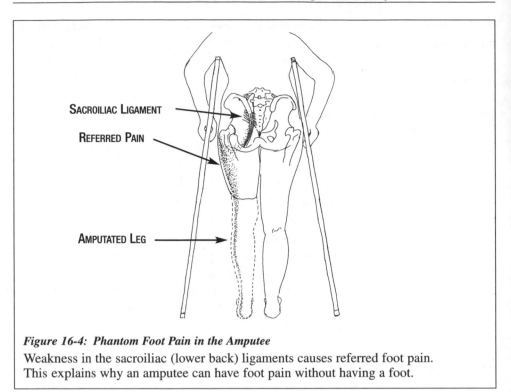

Figure 16-4: Phantom Foot Pain in the Amputee
Weakness in the sacroiliac (lower back) ligaments causes referred foot pain. This explains why an amputee can have foot pain without having a foot.

In the early 1970s, Dr. Hemwall treated a patient with terrible foot pain. Much to his surprise, upon examination, he had no foot! The person had an amputation of the leg years before. Nothing eased the pain he had. Dr. Hemwall knew that a common cause of foot pain was a referral pain from sacroiliac ligament laxity. He used his **MRI** (his thumb) and elicited a positive "jump sign" at the sacroiliac ligament. Dr. Hemwall treated him with Prolotherapy. This patient with the terrible phantom pain became the first person healed of this condition through the use of Prolotherapy. Since that time, many others have had their phantom pains permanently eliminated with Prolotherapy.

Sacroiliac ligament laxity with referral pain to the foot, does not have any origins in the foot. The foot pain is actually from the ligament laxity in the pelvis. Most physicians do not know the referral pain patterns of ligaments, so they fail to check for ligament laxity in the pelvis of phantom pain patients.

Phantom pain occurs in patients with amputations, spinal cord injury, or strokes. These medical conditions put additional strain on the sacroiliac ligaments. The sacroiliac joints play a greater role in stabilizing the pelvis and eventually become lax. The lax sacroiliac or other pelvic ligaments cause a referral pattern down the limb, which is known as phantom pain. **(See Figure 16-4.)** Prolotherapy is very effective in treating this condition.

Summary

Chronic burning pain from reflex sympathetic dystrophy, coccygodynia, neuromas, and spinal cord injury are often not due to a nerve injury. This is why typical treatments, such as nerve blocks, medicines, and surgical procedures aimed at the nerves, provide only temporary relief. Chronic burning pains, anywhere in the body, are usually caused by chronic ligament laxity. Prolotherapy causes a strengthening of the ligaments and has the potential to permanently eliminate dysesthetic syndromes that cause severe burning and other discomfort in the extremities. Because of this fact, many individuals are choosing to Prolo their RSD, SCI, and other neurological pains away! ■

Chapter 17

Prolo Your Unusual Pains Away!

Whether people say their backs hurt, their chests hurt, or their tushies hurt, most of us get tired of hearing them complain. More often than not, a person's back, chest, or tush really does hurt. People often have very unusual pain complaints. The more doctors people see for a pain complaint, the more likely their pain is real.

Unusual pain complaints are also a sign of ligament weakness. Even while at rest, a ligament can tense and cause pain, which explains how a person who is just sitting or lying down can have pain. Don't be too quick to call a spouse, brother, or friend "nutso" because of his or her pain. An evaluation by a physician experienced in Prolotherapy to look for ligament weakness and a positive "jump sign" should first be conducted. If ligament laxity can be found, most unusual pain complaints can be eliminated with Prolotherapy.

Pregnancy back pain, spastic torticollis, osteoporosis, bone pain due to cancer, and other unusual pains can be effectively treated with Prolotherapy.

Back Pain of Pregnancy

Steve, a pilot for a major airline carrier, arranged his schedule to fly into Chicago in order to receive Prolotherapy. Steve had what he termed "you name it, it hurts" syndrome. He had more surgeries on his temporomandibular joint than the Chicago Cubs have had losing seasons. He had benign congenital hypermobility, a condition found in only five percent of the population. With this condition, a person is born with unusually weak or lax ligaments. This makes him or her more prone to chronically loose joints and subsequent chronic pain. Because all of his joints were loose due to lax ligaments, every joint area of his body needed to be strengthened with Prolotherapy injections. Needless to say, Steve's treatments were quite extensive. His body responded wonderfully to the treatment and, after his third treatment, his chiropractor noted that most of his vertebral segments were now stable.

What does this have to do with back pain of pregnancy, you ask? Steve's wife, Angie, accompanied him on his fourth visit. Angie had her own story to tell. She experienced terrible back pain while pregnant with their second child and vowed that she would never have another child. She explained that the back pain started with her pregnancy and continued to plague her after the baby was born.

When talking more with Angie, she told us that she always carried her baby on her left hip. When asked what side of her back hurt, the answer was the left.

During pregnancy, women develop a positive "basketball-belly sign." This type of "basketball-belly sign" is permissible. During pregnancy, a woman's body secretes a hormone called relaxin, which causes ligaments to loosen allowing the baby to pass through the birth canal. Ligament laxity is normal during pregnancy. The baby's position in the pelvic region during pregnancy, the lax ligaments to allow delivery, and the mother carrying her baby on her hip after the baby is born all contribute to a resultant sacroiliac laxity and lower back pain.

In 1942, William Mengert, M.D., wrote, "It is now generally accepted that the overwhelming majority of backaches and sciaticas during pregnancy are due to pelvic girdle relaxation."[1] The average mobility of the joint is increased by 33 percent, leading to lax ligaments in people experiencing back pain from the sacroiliac joint.[2]

Angie, seeing firsthand her husband's positive response to Prolotherapy, decided to try the treatment for her lower back pain. Ross warned her that a possible side effect of relief from her back pain would be a desire to have more children. After her first treatment, 50 percent of her back pain was alleviated.

When Angie came for her second treatment, she asked if the back pain would return with another pregnancy. She was told that Prolotherapy causes permanent strengthening of the ligaments and she could have all the children she wanted without fear of recurrent back pain. If some of her pain did return, however, a "touch-up" treatment would be all that was necessary. It was also suggested that if she did have another baby she should name him Ross. We did not hear from her for some time. Steve then called and announced they had another baby girl. Angie remained pain-free. Joyce Ann is the baby's name, although to us she will always be Ross, or at least Rose.

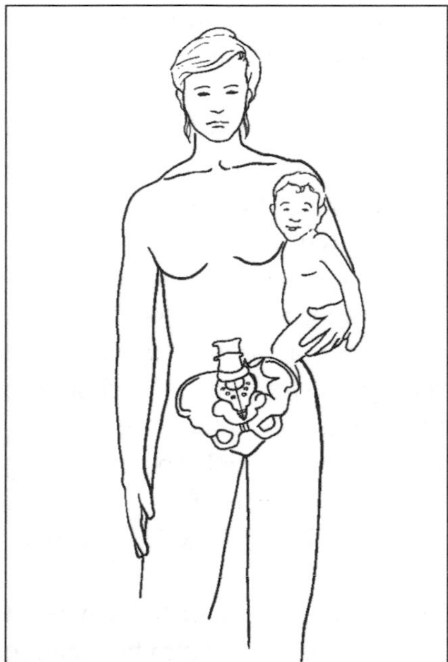

Figure 17-1: Mother Carrying Baby on the Hip

Carrying a weight on the hip, such as a baby, causes stress to the sacroiliac joint, which can lead to lower back pain and sciatica.

Ross also told Angie that her hips are not wide for carrying a baby on them, but are wide to get a baby out! A woman should never carry a baby on her hip. Many months are required after pregnancy for the sacroiliac joints to regain normal strength. It is imperative not to place any undue stress on the hips during this time. In Angie's case, carrying her first baby on her left hip was causing additional stress on the left sacroiliac joint. Her sacroiliac joints were already loose and painful during pregnancy. The addition of carrying a child on the hip after pregnancy did not give the sacroiliac joint a chance to heal. She then developed chronic sacroiliac laxity and its accompanying buddy—back pain. Prolotherapy in her case was curative and another wonderful life entered the world. **(See Figure 17-1.)**

Prolotherapy is an excellent treatment for back pain caused by pregnancy. Prolotherapy strengthens joints to relieve back pain but does not interfere with the birthing process. Prolotherapy has definitive results and can make pregnancy much more bearable. Prolotherapy is the treatment of choice for chronic low back pain that may occur during or linger after pregnancy if all other conservative treatments have proven unsuccessful.

SPASTIC TORTICOLLIS

Joan struggled with spastic torticollis for several years prior to coming to our office. Spastic torticollis is a condition in which the head will twitch or turn uncontrollably and tilt to one side. Joan needed to turn her body to the side in order to see straight ahead. In addition to the social stigma, she experienced debilitating neck pain. Her attempts to relieve her pain with physical therapy, muscle relaxants, and Valium proved unsuccessful. Spastic torticollis is not due to a Valium deficiency. Joan had heard about Prolotherapy and wanted to give it a try.

Like all chronic painful conditions, spastic torticollis has a cause, which is typically ligament laxity. Spastic torticollis causes involuntary muscle spasms in the neck.[3] The muscle spasms cause the neck to continually jerk the head to one side. Eventually, because the muscles continue to tighten, it becomes impossible to turn the head to the side.

Upon examining Joan, a positive "jump sign" was elicited when the cervical vertebral ligaments were palpated. Her twitching neck made the treatment difficult, but with persistence it was successfully completed. After the second treatment, Joan reported that she could sleep facing to the left.

Joan came all the way to Illinois from Tennessee to receive her treatment. When she heard that Ross was going to be in South Carolina for a conference, she and a friend waited at the hotel for him to arrive. The hotel room was quickly converted into an examining room. Ross has given Prolotherapy treatments in churches, schools, homes, and hotels all around the country. He has given them on couches, beds, kitchen tables, the floor, dining room tables, and occasionally on examining room tables. We carry Prolotherapy supplies with us whenever we travel. Occasionally, Prolotherapy treatments are given at our office in Oak Park, Illinois. (Of course, if you call 40 hours a week "occasionally!")

After five treatments, Joan was a new woman. She was fortunate to have heard about Prolotherapy. She had become pain-free, with the ability to turn her head in both directions.

People with spastic torticollis who are not familiar with Prolotherapy subject themselves to a series of painful and noncurative treatments. Surgery to cut tight muscles used to be the standard mode of treatment. The latest treatment involves injecting botulism toxin into the muscles. The toxin paralyzes the tight muscles and allows the head to straighten for a period of time.

Similar to the case of reflex sympathetic dystrophy, spastic torticollis patients will often describe an injury to the neck prior to the onset of the condition. **(See Figure 17-2.)** It is advisable that a person with spastic torticollis receive an evaluation from a physician familiar with Prolotherapy before undergoing surgery or receiving toxin injections.

Once a ligament is loose, as occurs in a neck injury, the overlying muscles must tighten to support the structure. If only one side of the neck ligaments loosen, then the muscles on that side of the neck will become spastic. This is how spastic torticollis may form.

If significant shortening of the neck muscles has already occurred, botulism injections may be helpful in conjunction with Prolotherapy. If shortening of the muscles has not occurred, the person with spastic torticollis has an excellent chance to have complete neck pain relief with Prolotherapy. The ligaments in the neck, when strengthened, will cause muscle spasms to cease and allow the neck to regain full range of motion. Prolotherapy will terminate the chronic neck pain from spastic torticollis because it addresses the root cause of the problem.

OSTEOPOROSIS AND COMPRESSION FRACTURES

The problems associated with osteoporosis keep many doctors in business. Children drinking soda pop, eating candy, and chomping on potato chips make good prospects for future osteoporosis patients; all these contribute to the onset of this disease. This is due to the inadequate amount of calcium, magnesium, and vitamin D in these so-called "foods." (A more appropriate name for these items would be "edible chemicals.") The phosphorus from soda pop actually leaches calcium out of the bone, making eventual osteoporosis very likely.

An estimated 1.2 million osteoporotic fractures occur annually and more than half occur in the vertebrae.[4] The incidence of osteoporosis is directly correlated to testosterone production in men and estrogen and progesterone production in women. Women are especially at risk after menopause because of the drastic cessation of hormone production, whereas men experience a more gradual decline in hormone production as they age.

At Caring Medical and Rehabilitation Services, we recommend that all women take natural hormone replacements at the start of menopause and see a Natural Medicine physician for a natural health maintenance program. **(See Appendix F, Nutriceuticals: Helping the Body to Heal.)** Exercise, calcium, magnesium, a healthy diet, and natural hormones are excellent ways for women to keep their bones strong and maintain a zest for life.

Osteoporosis may cause vertebral compression, a painful and disabling condition. A vertebral compression fracture will normally occur in the thoracic or

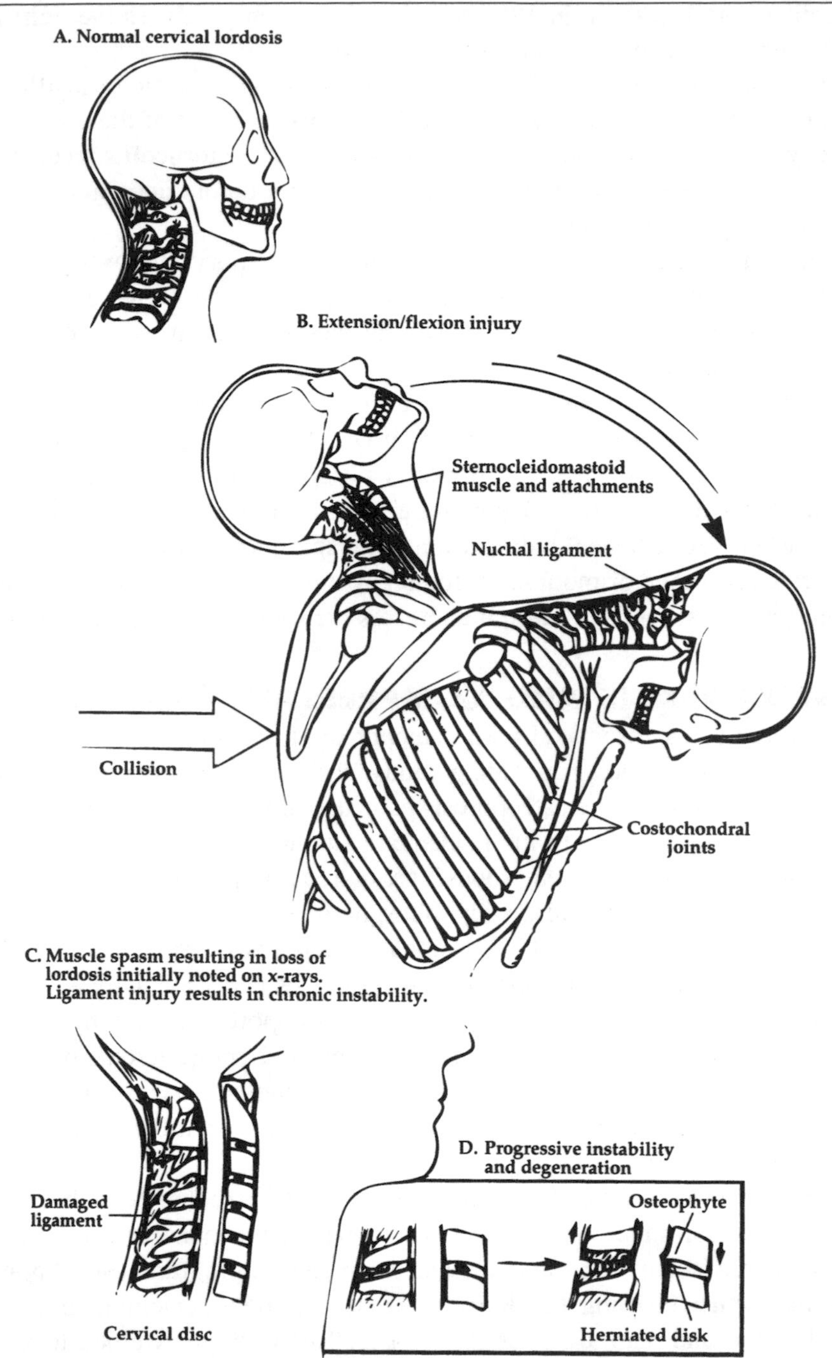

Figure 17-2: How a Whiplash Injury Causes Soft Tissue Injury
Non-healed soft tissue injury can eventually lead to conditions such as arthritis and spastic torticollis.

lumbar region of the back. Untreated compression fractures from osteoporosis in the thoracic region may lead to a humpback deformity.[5]

The mainstay treatment for a vertebral compression fracture is wearing a brace to properly position the back while the fracture heals. The problem with this treatment is that the vertebral fractures from osteoporosis are not a back brace deficiency. Thus, this type of treatment, even if exercise and nonsteroidal anti-inflammatory agents are added for good measure, does not cure the underlying cause of the problem.

Prolotherapy, in strengthening the fibro-osseous junction, the ligament-bony interface, permanently stabilizes the compressed vertebral segment. The strengthening of the ligament and periosteal interface realign the area resulting in improved posture. Prolotherapy, however, is not a complete treatment for osteoporosis compression fractures. The underlying cause must be corrected or the osteoporosis will recur.

Whether the cause is nutritional, hormonal, or a chronic disease, the underlying etiology of the osteoporosis must be addressed to ensure long-term healing. Prolotherapy to strengthen the vertebral supporting ligaments, in conjunction with Natural Medicine treatments, is effective in healing the pain and disability caused by osteoporosis-induced vertebral compression fractures.

BONE PAIN ASSOCIATED WITH CANCER

People with all different kinds of chronic diseases and many different kinds of pain syndromes visit Caring Medical and Rehabilitation Services, the Natural Medicine clinic we operate in Oak Park, Illinois. Some patients at the clinic are trying Natural Medicine techniques in order to stimulate their immune systems and enable their bodies to fight cancer.

Cancer, by definition, is a group of cells that say to the body, "I'm the boss." The cancer cells grow and steal blood, blood vessels, and nutrients from the body, invading any area where they can grow. Many pain syndromes are associated with cancer, but the most severe pain occurs when the cancer invades the bone. Traditional treatments for cancer pain include narcotic medications or some type of radioactivity directed at the cancer site.[6,7]

Cancer does not usually cause bone pain until the outside of the bone, the periosteum, is cracked. The inside of the bone does not contain nerve endings and thus cannot feel pain, but the outside of the bone is loaded with nerve endings.[8] This helps explain why injuries at the fibro-osseous junction are so painful.

Bone pain from cancer is brutal, often requiring high doses of narcotic medications to relieve the pain. Unfortunately, these high doses of medications leave a person dependent on drugs and in an altered mental state. Treatments that allow for a decrease in the amount of narcotic medications would greatly improve the cancer patient's quality of life.

In the early 1960s, Marsha, a four-year post-mastectomy patient, visited Dr. Hemwall because of dull back pain. Dr. Hemwall treated her mid-back region with Prolotherapy. He instructed her to have the area x-rayed and follow up with her primary physician. Several years later, Dr. Hemwall learned that at the time he treated her, Marsha had a recurrence of breast cancer, according to the x-ray. Interestingly, the Prolotherapy treatment had eliminated Marsha's bone pain from the cancer and greatly improved her quality of life. This was the first of five cases where Dr. Hemwall used Prolotherapy to eliminate bone pain associated with cancer.

Prolotherapy is helpful in eliminating or diminishing cancer bone pain because strengthening the area, the fibro-osseous junction, causes the nerve endings in the periosteum to stop firing. Prolotherapy does not affect the underlying cancerous condition. The etiological basis for the cancer must be corrected whether a person decides to use traditional medical treatments or Natural Medicine treatments. Prolotherapy is an effective tool to assist with pain from cancer invading the bone.

BUTTOCK PAIN

Some people experience pain in the posterior, while others are a pain in the posterior. When you sit down, your tush normally rests on the ischial tuberosity. Since many of us have sedentary jobs and buttocks that are a few sizes too big, the soft tissue surrounding the ischial tuberosity bones is compressed. The structures that attach to the ischial tuberosity are the sacrotuberous ligaments and the hamstring muscles. **(See Figure 17-3.)**

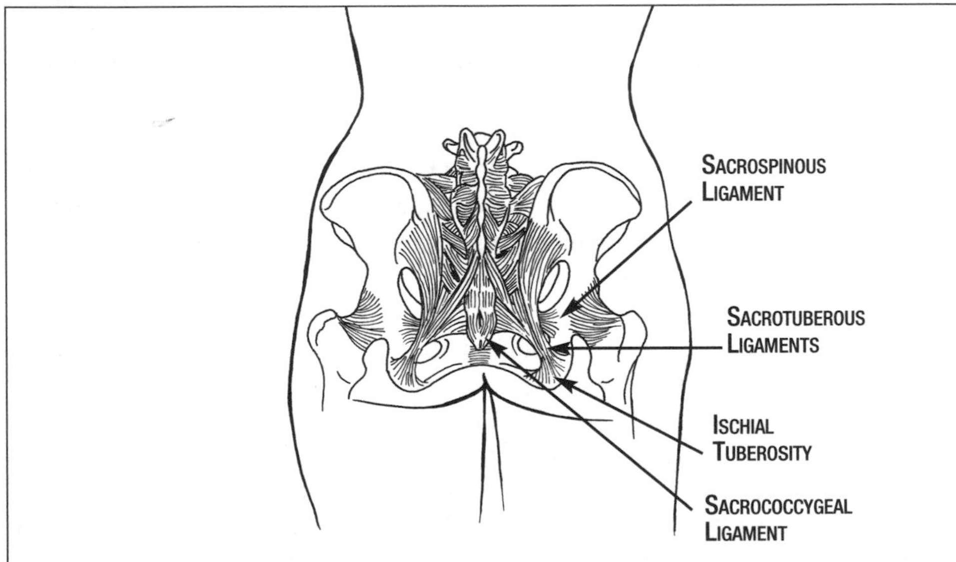

Figure 17-3: Ischial Tuberosity and Its Relationship to the Pelvic Bones and Ligaments
Important structures attach to the ischial tuberosity, including the sacrotuberous ligaments and the hamstring muscles.

The most common cause of pain at the cheek line in the buttock area is weakness in the structures that attach to the ischial tuberosity. The condition that is manifested by buttock pain and tenderness over the ischial tuberosity is known in traditional medical lingo as ischial bursitis. A bursa is a fluid-filled sac that allows tendons and muscles to glide over the bones. Bursitis means inflammation of the bursa. True bursitis pain is so painful that any pressure to the bursa would elicit a positive "hit the ceiling" sign. True bursitis is extremely rare. If a physician diagnoses bursitis and recommends a cortisone shot to relieve the inflammation, a fast exit out the door is strongly suggested. Remember, chronic pain is not due to a cortisone deficiency and is rarely due to bursitis.

Prolotherapy injections for buttock pain are given all along the ischial tuberosity, where the hamstring muscles and sacrotuberous ligaments attach. Prolotherapy will strengthen this area. After four sessions of Prolotherapy, the buttock pain is usually eliminated. Unfortunately, the ischial tuberosity is an area that is rarely examined by traditional physicians.

Rectal, Vaginal, Testicular, and Tailbone Pain

It is amusing to hear the diagnoses people have been given for their conditions. Just recently, a patient said she had vulvodynia. She was very happy that someone had finally given her a diagnosis for her pain. She was crushed when she was told that this meant vaginal pain. Vulva means vaginal and dynia means pain. All the doctor did was tell her something she already knew. She had vaginal pain. Diagnoses like lumbago or lumbalgia (back pain), cervicalgia (neck pain), fibromyalgia (body pain), or proctalgia (rectal pain) are not diagnoses. They are terms for the symptoms.

Roughly 15 percent of the population at one time or another will experience rectal pain, which is commonly diagnosed as proctalgia or proctalgia fugax.[9] It is characterized by episodic sharp pain in the rectal region, lasting for several seconds to several minutes. Traditional treatments include pain medications, steroid injections, counseling, or biofeedback.[10] Since no standard medical treatment is very effective, both the physician and the patient are easily frustrated. Often the patient is labeled as having irritable bowel syndrome, again a fancy diagnosis which just labels the symptoms.

Rectal, vaginal, testicular, or tailbone pain, like pain anywhere else in the body, has a cause. Generally, these pains can be reproduced when the ligaments around the pelvis are palpated. The most commonly affected areas are the ligaments around the sacrococcygeal junction, which includes the sacrococcygeal ligament, sacrotuberous, and sacrospinous ligaments. **(See Figure 17-3.)** Since these ligaments are near the rectum, it makes sense that rectal or groin pains originate from these structures. When Prolotherapy has strengthened these ligaments, chronic rectal pain dissipates.

Another common cause of chronic groin, testicular, or vaginal pain is iliolumbar ligament weakness, because this ligament refers pain from the lower back to

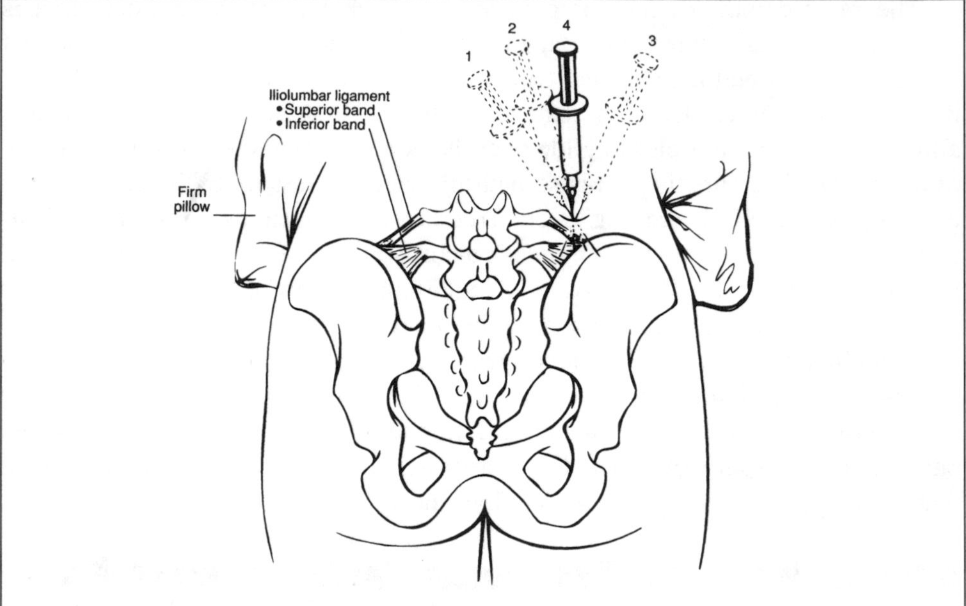

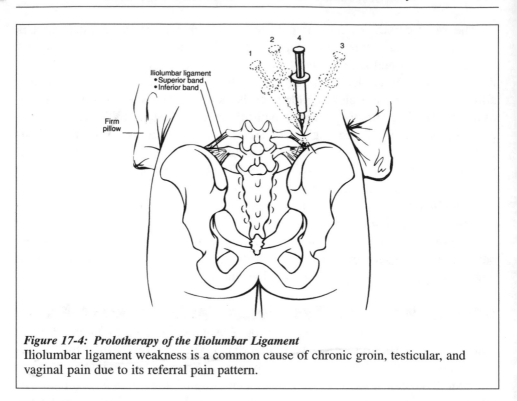

Figure 17-4: Prolotherapy of the Iliolumbar Ligament
Iliolumbar ligament weakness is a common cause of chronic groin, testicular, and vaginal pain due to its referral pain pattern.

these areas. Prolotherapy of the iliolumbar ligament can be curative for chronic groin, testicular, or vaginal pain. **(See Figure 17-4.)**

D.B., a 45-year-old gentleman, went to see Bernadette Kohn, M.D., because of severe burning pain near the rectum. His job entailed extensive traveling and his pain made sitting nearly impossible. After sitting for five minutes, the pain, which he described as a "burning poker up you know where" would hit. He endured two back surgeries with only minor relief of his pain. He even went to a well-known clinic where he was told the "scar tissue" from his previous surgeries was causing his pain. He was advised to live with the pain.

Live with the pain?! Hogwash! Who wants to live with pain?! Fortunately for D.B., he consulted a physician trained in Prolotherapy. His first Prolotherapy treatment enabled D.B. to travel for more than two hours without pain in his tailbone area. Dr. Kohn reported that D.B. was extremely grateful for the Prolotherapy treatment he received.

Chronic rectal or tailbone pain can be horribly disabling as this case illustrates. After extensive testing, patients are often given dubious diagnoses such as proctalgia fugax, anorectal neuralgia, levator ani syndrome, coccygodynia, or spastic pelvic floor syndrome.[11-14] Typical conservative traditional treatments include pain medicines, sitz baths (sitting in a warm tub), local anesthetic creams, massage, muscle relaxants, electrical stimulation gizmos, or the end-all pain treatment, an anti-depressant medication. Such treatments generally have unsatisfactory results because they do not correct the underlying cause of the chronic rectal pain.

As in other parts of the body, the most important evaluation in analyzing chronic rectal pain is palpation of the area. A positive "jump sign" can typically be elicited by palpation of the sacrococcygeal ligaments. If no "jump sign" is elicited, then the other pelvic ligaments are palpated, such as the sacrotuberous, sacrospinous, iliolumbar, and sacroiliac ligaments. When a positive "jump sign" is elicited over the painful ligament, both the patient and the doctor know that the cause of the pain is a weakened ligament.

A weakened sacrococcygeal ligament is stretched even further when a person sits, especially during a bowel movement. **(Refer to Figure 17-3.)** People with chronic rectal or tailbone pain often have an increase in pain at these times. The best treatment for a weakened ligament is Prolotherapy. Prolotherapy treatments to the weakened pelvic ligaments help these areas heal and return to normal strength. Once the sacrococcygeal, iliolumbar, and other weakened pelvic ligaments are strong again, the chronic rectal pain abates. This is why many people with chronic rectal, tailbone, groin, testicular, and vaginal pains are choosing to Prolo their pain away!

Slipping Rib Syndrome

Dawn, a 35-year-old, was rushed to the hospital for the fourth time in less than a year complaining of severe chest pain, fearing a heart attack. After EKGs, blood tests, x-rays, and a stay in the intensive care unit, the cause of her pain was still unknown. Everyone began to wonder if she was a little crazy.

As Ross examined her, Dawn initially explained that she was not currently having severe chest pain but did feel a dull ache in her chest. She needed one more diagnostic test, the trusty **MRI**—**M**y **R**eproducibility **I**nstrument. In a second, the diagnosis was made. Ross pressed on her left fourth thoracic rib attachment onto the sternum and Dawn's severe crushing chest pain immediately returned. Had she ever been examined in this fashion? She said she had not. Dawn's pain was caused by Slipping Rib Syndrome.

An extremely important point illustrated by Dawn's case is that even if an x-ray, blood sample, or EKG do not reveal a cause, they do not eliminate the presence of a physical condition as the source of chest pain. It is much more likely that the chronic chest pain is due to weakened soft tissue, such as a ligament or tendon. If heart and lung tests prove normal, yet the patient claims to still be experiencing pain, the patient is often diagnosed as being crazy. It is imperative for anyone given a psychiatric diagnosis as the basis for the chronic pain to have an evaluation by a physician competent in the treatment of Prolotherapy.

Depression, anxiety, and being a little crazy are not the etiological bases for most chronic pain. They can be associated factors involved in the problem, but they are normally not the cause. If depressed people complain of shoulder pain,

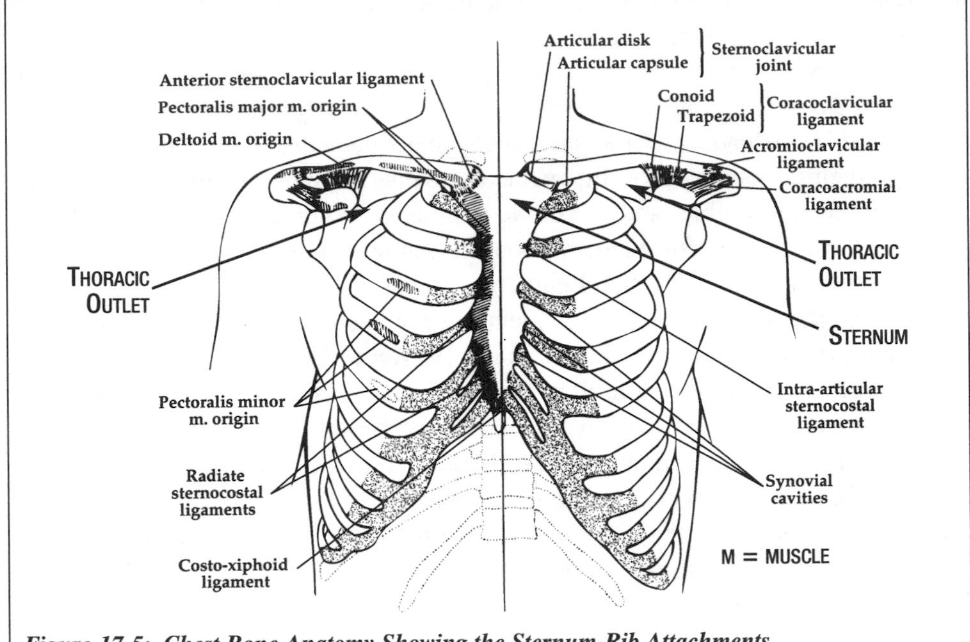

Figure 17-5: Chest Bone Anatomy Showing the Sternum-Rib Attachments
Weakness of the sternocostal ligaments is a common cause of chronic chest pain.

most likely they have shoulder pain. Chronic pain should be assumed to be originating from a weakened soft tissue, such as a ligament or tendon. This condition should be treated with Prolotherapy before the diagnosis of "cuckoo" is made. A weak tendon, like the rotator cuff, or ligament, such as the coracoacromial ligament, may be the cause. If traditional treatments leave the patient with the impression that the pain is all psychological, then an evaluation by a Prolotherapist will save them from a psychological stigma and a life of chronic pain. Dawn's pain was indeed real and it was eliminated by Prolotherapy.

Slipping Rib Syndrome, also known as Tietze's Syndrome, was first described in 1921 by Alexander Tietze, M.D., as chest pain over the sternoclavicular and costochondral junctions.[15] Other names include xiphoidalgia, costochondritis, or anterior chest-wall syndrome. But the most descriptive and accurate name for the actual etiological basis of the condition is Slipping Rib Syndrome.[16] It is interesting to note that just one year after Dr. Tietze's description, Slipping Rib Syndrome was described in medical literature.[17]

In Dawn's case, a rib was slipping out of place because the ligaments that hold the ribs to the sternum, the sternocostal ligaments, were weak. **(See Figure 17-5.)** Without muscles to hold the ribs in place, loose ligaments allow slipping of the rib which causes further stretching of the ligament, manifesting itself by producing severe pain. The loose ribs can also pinch intercostal nerves, sending excruciating pains around the chest into the back. Sternocostal and costochondral ligaments refer pain from the front of the chest to the mid back. Likewise, costovertebral ligament sprains refer pain from the back of the rib segment to the sternum where the rib attaches. **(See Figures 17-6A-D.)**

Traditional medicine believes the condition is caused by inflammation in the costochondral junction, causing costochondritis. The treatment of choice in traditional medical circles is, you guessed it, an NSAID, a nonsteroidal anti-inflammatory drug. Chronic pain, no matter what the cause, is not due to a NSAID deficiency. Slipping Rib Syndrome is caused by weakness of the sternocostal, costochondral, or costovertebral ligaments. Prolotherapy will strengthen these ligament junctions in all the areas where the ribs are hypermobile.

Slipping Rib Syndrome may be caused by hypermobility of the anterior end of the costal cartilage, located at the rib-cartilage interface, called the costochondral junction. Most often, the tenth rib is the source because, unlike ribs one through seven which attach to the sternum, the eighth, ninth, and tenth ribs are attached anteriorly to each other by loose, fibrous tissue.[18] This provides increased mobility, but a greater susceptibility to trauma. Slipping rib cartilage may cause no pain or only intermittent pain.[19]

Slipping Rib Syndrome is also more likely to occur in the lower ribs because of the poor blood supply to the cartilaginous tissue and ligaments. Injury to the cartilage tissue in the lower ribs or the sternocostal ligaments in the upper ribs seldom completely heals naturally. The sternocostal, rib-sternum, and costochondral joints undergo stress when the rib cage expands or contracts abnormally or when excessive pressure is applied on the ribs themselves.

In order for the rib cage to expand and contract with each breath, the costochondral and the sternocostal junctions are naturally loose. Humans breathe 12 times per minute, 720 times per hour, 19,280 times per day, which stresses these ligamentous-rib junctions. Additional stressors include any condition that makes breathing more difficult. A simple coughing attack due to a cold may cause the development of Slipping Rib Syndrome. Conditions such as bronchitis, emphysema, allergies, and asthma cause additional stress to the sternocostal and costochondral junctions. Even sinusitis, with the associated nose blowing, can be the initial event that leads to chronic chest pain from Slipping Rib Syndrome.

Other causes of Slipping Rib Syndrome include the feared "fall asleep in the backseat of a crowded car syndrome." A person falls asleep in a crowded car with the door handle jutting into a rib. The rib slips out of place and the problem begins. Another cause of Slipping Rib Syndrome is the result of surgery to the lungs, chest, heart, or breast, with resection of the lymph nodes, which puts a tremendous stress on the rib attachments because the surgeon must separate the ribs to remove the injured tissue. Unresolved chest or upper back pain following a thoracotomy, chest operation, or CPR is most likely due to ligament laxity in the rib-sternum or the rib-vertebral junction.

The ribs are attached in the front as well as in the back of the body. A loose rib in the front is likely also loose in the back. The rib-vertebral junction is known

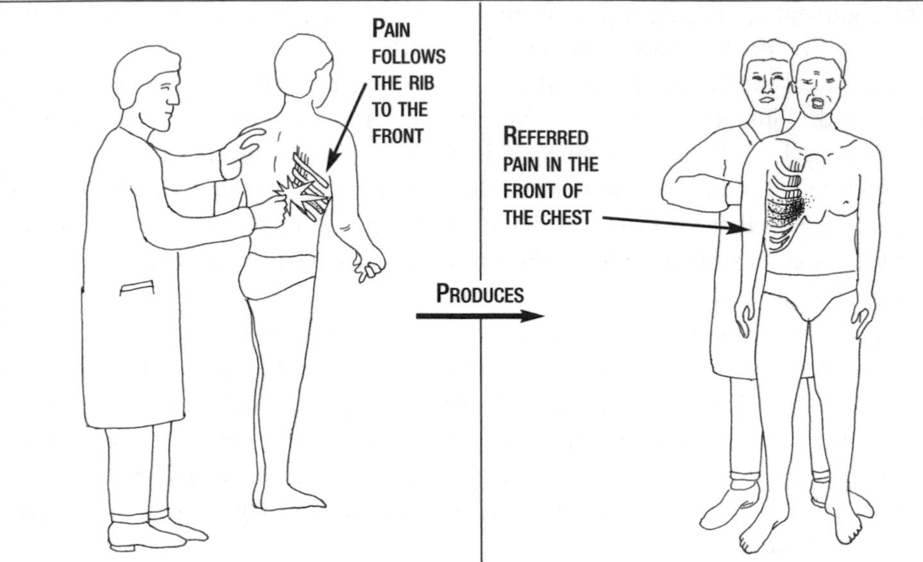

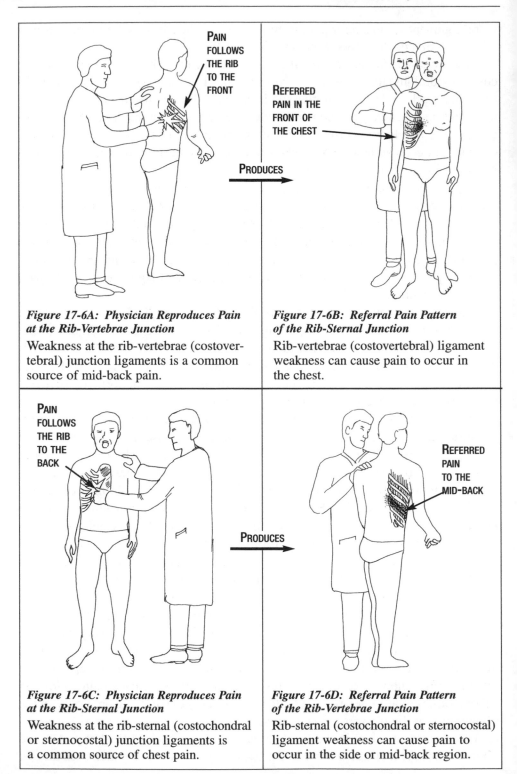

Figure 17-6A: Physician Reproduces Pain at the Rib-Vertebrae Junction

Weakness at the rib-vertebrae (costovertebral) junction ligaments is a common source of mid-back pain.

Figure 17-6B: Referral Pain Pattern of the Rib-Sternal Junction

Rib-vertebrae (costovertebral) ligament weakness can cause pain to occur in the chest.

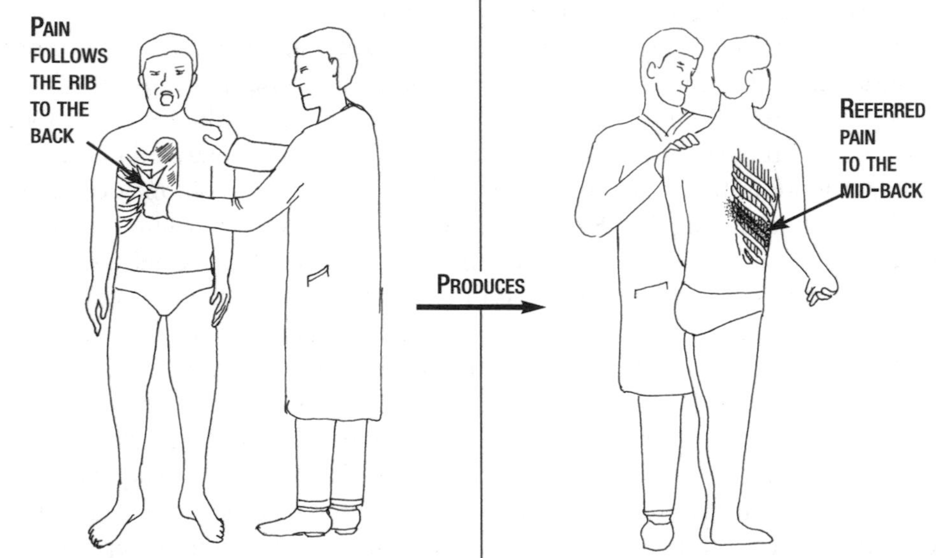

Figure 17-6C: Physician Reproduces Pain at the Rib-Sternal Junction

Weakness at the rib-sternal (costochondral or sternocostal) junction ligaments is a common source of chest pain.

Figure 17-6D: Referral Pain Pattern of the Rib-Vertebrae Junction

Rib-sternal (costochondral or sternocostal) ligament weakness can cause pain to occur in the side or mid-back region.

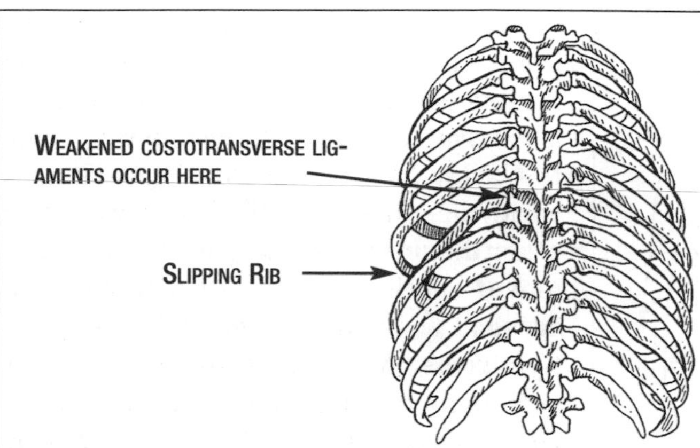

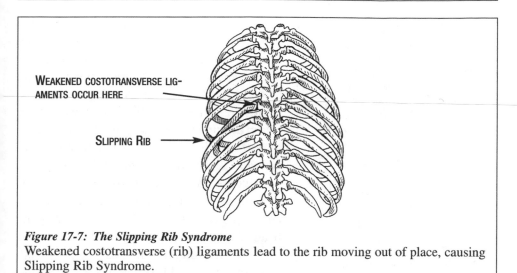

Figure 17-7: The Slipping Rib Syndrome
Weakened costotransverse (rib) ligaments lead to the rib moving out of place, causing Slipping Rib Syndrome.

as the costovertebral junction, and is secured by the costotransverse ligaments. Unexplained upper back pain, between the shoulder blades and costovertebral, (rib-vertebrae pain) is likely due to joint laxity and/or weakness in the costotransverse ligaments. **(See Figure 17-7.)**

Chronic chest pain, especially in young people, is often due to weakness in the sternocostal and costochondral junctions. Chronic mid-upper back pain is due to weakness at the costovertebral junction. Both conditions may lead to Slipping Rib Syndrome, where the rib intermittently slips out of place, causing a stretching of the ligamentous support of the rib in the front and back. The result is periodic episodes of severe pain and underlying chronic chest and/or upper back pain. Prolotherapy, by strengthening these areas, provides definitive results in the relief of the chronic chest pain or chronic upper-back pain from Slipping Rib Syndrome.

THORACIC OUTLET SYNDROME

"I have Thoracic Outlet Syndrome." "No you don't." "Yes, I do!" "No, you don't!" Such is the typical conversations we have with patients when they come in with this diagnosis. Thoracic Outlet Syndrome is another unusual pain syndrome that completely and miraculously is often "cured" by Prolotherapy.

The thoracic outlet consists of the space between the inferior border of the clavicle and the upper border of the first rib. **(See Figure 17-5.)** The subclavian artery, subclavian vein, and brachial plexus nerves (the nerves to the arm) exit the neck region and go into the arm via this space. In Thoracic Outlet Syndrome (TOS), the space is, presumably, narrowed, causing a compression of these structures. The symptoms of TOS include: pain in the neck, shoulder, and arm; coldness in the hand; and numbness in the arm and hand. However, in severe cases of compression of the subclavian vessels, Raynaud's phenomenon, claudication,

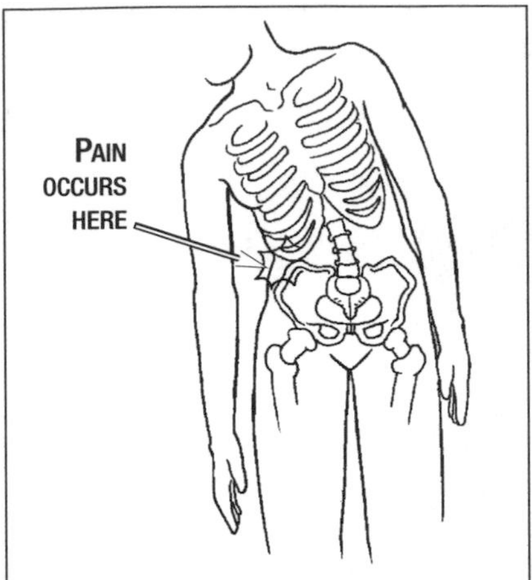

Figure 17-8: Iliocostalis Syndrome
In Iliocostalis Syndrome, the lower ribs contact the iliac crest when bending sideways.

thrombosis, and edema can occur in the involved extremity.[20] TOS is a legitimate condition and does occur but **its prevalence is extremely rare! Most people who come to Caring Medical, in Oak Park, Illinois, with the diagnosis of TOS leave with other diagnoses such as glenohumeral ligament sprain, rotator cuff tendinopathy, cervical ligament sprain, or Slipping Rib Syndrome.** All of the pain and numbness symptoms of TOS can occur from these later four conditions, all of which respond beautifully to Prolotherapy.

The reason it makes sense that Prolotherapy would be a cure for the symptoms of so-called "TOS" is the fact that the condition almost exclusively occurs in women with long necks and low-set droopy shoulders.[21] Activities that involve abduction of the shoulders, such as combing the hair, painting walls, and hanging pictures, cause worsening of the symptoms. Passively abducting the arm (having someone do it for the person) relieves the symptoms. In other words, when the shoulder is actively raised over the head (the person does it themselves) the symptoms of pain and/or numbness down the arms occur, however, when the exact same movement is done passively (by another person) the symptoms do not occur. This type of symptomatology is a perfect description of ligament and tendon weakness (laxity). The injured ligament and tendon give localized and referral pain when doing strenuous movements, but when someone else takes the brunt of the force, no such symptoms occur.

"The doctor said I have Thoracic Outlet Syndrome and I need surgery to give the nerves more room." Sometimes it is difficult to convince someone they need Prolotherapy. The people with so-called TOS almost unanimously have normal reflexes and nerve conduction studies. This gives further indication that a nerve is not getting pinched. Furthermore, surgically slicing structures to give the nerve more room will not eliminate the symptoms the person is having and could, quite possibly, cause more problems. The person with the symptoms of TOS doesn't need a surgical procedure to cut out a rib or slice a muscle to give the brachial plexus more room, he/she needs Prolotherapy to the pain-producing structure(s). Prolotherapy to the neck ligaments, shoulder ligaments and tendons, or to a rib that is slipping is all that is needed to cure the symptoms of so-called TOS.

Iliocostalis Syndrome

Undiagnosed chronic side pain affects many people, occurring most often in people suffering from osteoporosis. Iliocostalis Syndrome, also known as Iliocostal Friction Syndrome, is a condition caused by friction of the lower ribs against the iliac crest, leading to irritation of soft tissues.[22]

The distance between the lower ribs and iliac crest is normally sufficient to prevent contact, even when bending to the side. When the lower ribs of Iliocostalis Syndrome patients come into contact with the iliac crest, especially when side-bending, friction and damage is caused to the tendons and muscles that insert at the iliac crest and the lower rib cage. **(See Figure 17-8.)**

The condition commonly occurs from a vertebral deformity such as scoliosis, disc degeneration, or the most common cause: vertebral compression fractures. This bone-to-bone contact manifests itself as back or side pain. Palpation along the iliac crest is usually painful but rarely elicits the classic positive "jump sign." A more definitive method of diagnosing the problem is feeling the contact of the ribs and the iliac crest upon bending to the side.

Prolotherapy will strengthen the muscles and tendons that insert onto the iliac crest and lower rib margins, as well as the fibro-osseous junction.[23] If the muscles and tendons are pinched when the bones collide during side-bending, they will have strength to tolerate the event after Prolotherapy; though it is recommended not to bend sideways to prevent the rib and pelvic bones from colliding. Prolotherapy is very effective in eliminating the chronic side pains caused by Iliocostalis Syndrome.

Summary

Many chronic pain sufferers have not found relief with traditional medicine. When blood tests and x-rays do not reveal a cause, they are told their pain is psychological. Chronic pain is most often caused by ligament or tendon laxity. Prolotherapy is effective at eliminating chronic pain because it helps ligaments and tendons grow. Prior to agreeing with a psychological diagnosis for pain, or agreeing to surgery, we would advise that an evaluation be performed by a physician familiar with Prolotherapy.

The etiological basis for many unusual pain syndromes, such as spastic torticollis, bone pain associated with cancer, ischial tendonitis, Slipping Rib Syndrome, vulvodynia, proctalgia fugax, coccygodynia, and Iliocostalis Syndrome, is often due to a weakness at the fibro-osseous junction of soft tissue, such as a ligament or tendon. Chronic low back pain in pregnancy may be due to lax ligaments, specifically the sacroiliac ligaments. Prolotherapy injections stimulate the growth of ligament and tendon tissue at the fibro-osseous junction, strengthen the area, and resolve the chronic pain syndrome. It is for this reason that many people are choosing to Prolo their unusual pain syndromes away! ■

CHAPTER 18

Prolo Your Fibromyalgia Pain Away!

When a person first seeks help for pain, a specific diagnosis such as tendonitis is generally given. When the pain continues, an MRI scan or some such study will be ordered. The diagnosis then changes to a "disc problem." After more unsuccessful treatments, the pain sufferer will be sent to a pain center where the diagnosis of depression will be made. After several thousands of dollars of treatment, diagnostic tests, and a lot of frustration and misery, the person will be given that all-inclusive, "so everyone will know I'm not crazy" diagnosis: fibromyalgia. Nearly anyone who has had pain long enough and seeks enough medical opinions will eventually be labeled with this diagnosis.

THE TYPICAL PROGRESSION TO THE DIAGNOSIS OF FIBROMYALGIA

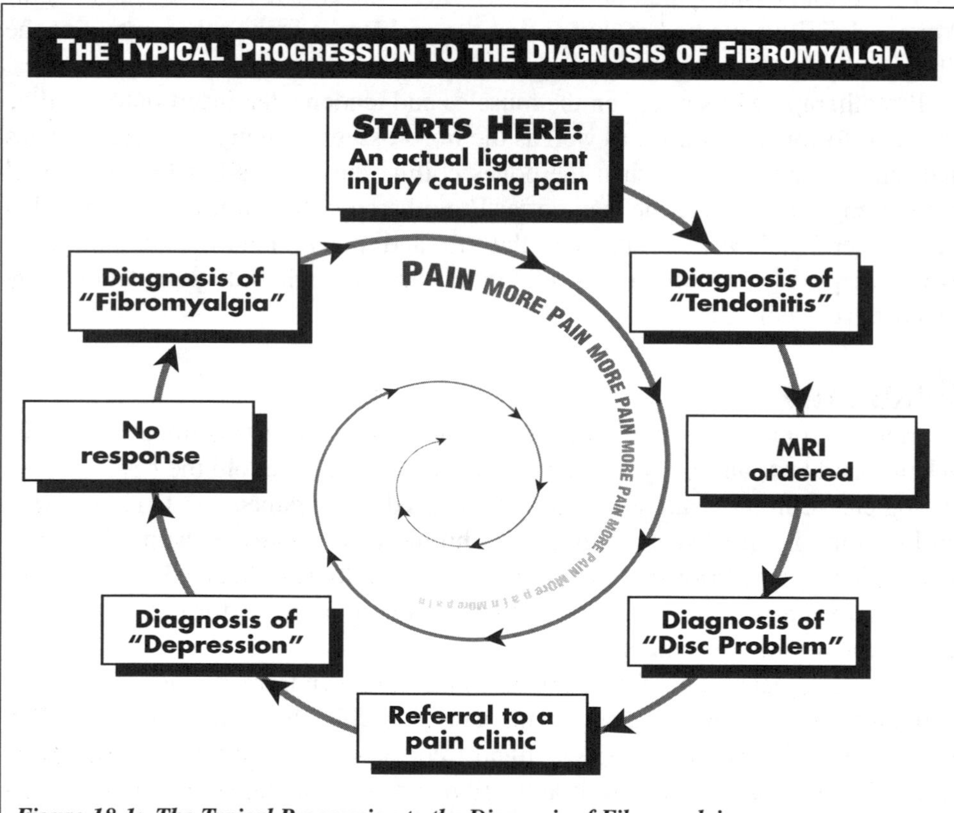

Figure 18-1: The Typical Progression to the Diagnosis of Fibromyalgia
Simple ligament laxity causes trigger points and chronic pain, but because it isn't diagnosed and treated properly, the above scenario is all too frequent.

It is important to remember that nothing of the etiology is revealed when a physician gives a patient a "diagnosis" with the word "syndrome" on the end of it. A "syndrome" is what physicians call a constellation of symptoms for which the actual cause is unknown. A good example of this is what we call the "Couch Potato Syndrome." This syndrome typically describes a balding, middle-aged man with a "basketball-belly," who enjoys watching, talking, and reading about sports, but couldn't walk around the block without getting chest pain. People with this syndrome typically reside in a lounge chair that envelops the body upon contact and a remote channel changer is a must. You see, the physician "diagnosed" "Couch Potato Syndrome," but this says nothing about the etiology of the condition. It is much more important to know the cause of pain than to have a label placed on it. The diagnosis of fibromyalgia, Chronic Pain Syndrome, or Myofascial Pain Syndrome does not determine the etiology and, thus, the cure for the condition. **(See Figure 18-1.)**

Diagnosis of Fibromyalgia

Traditional medicine will label someone with fibromyalgia if they meet certain diagnostic criteria.[1] Unfortunately, the criteria are somewhat vague. The main criterion is the presence of aches or pains at more than four sites, for more than three months, with no underlying condition causing the pain. This is why we believe this "diagnosis" is erroneous because a cause for chronic pain can **almost always** be found. Other symptoms revealed by a patient's medical history that cause them to be labeled with fibromyalgia may include pain in at least 11 of 18 specific tender points, a "hurt all over" feeling, anxiety or tension, poor sleep, general fatigue, and/or irritable bowel syndrome.[2] **(See Figure 18-2.)**

Fibromyalgia Case Study

Pamela came to the office with the diagnosis of "fibromyalgia." She said that about eight years ago, the plague of migraine headaches began. Pamela received several medications, which provided some relief. She had also been taking antibiotics during this time for chronic sinus infections. After several years, she started having trouble sleeping and felt very tired. She tried chiropractic care, physical therapy, and had seen several orthopedists, neurologists, and internists for what she said was an aching of the muscles. Her x-rays and blood tests were normal. Eventually, she consulted a rheumatologist who diagnosed her with fibromyalgia. She was happy that her condition had finally been diagnosed, but she soon became depressed when she learned that there were no treatment options available and that the current recommendation was that she must "learn to live with it."

The advice to anyone with the diagnosis of "fibromyalgia" is to find a Natural Medicine physician immediately. Only a doctor who practices Natural Medicine will offer any advice that has the potential to be curative for the fibromyalgia patient. Doctors who practice Natural Medicine know that the constellation of symptoms known as "fibromyalgia" **can be cured.**

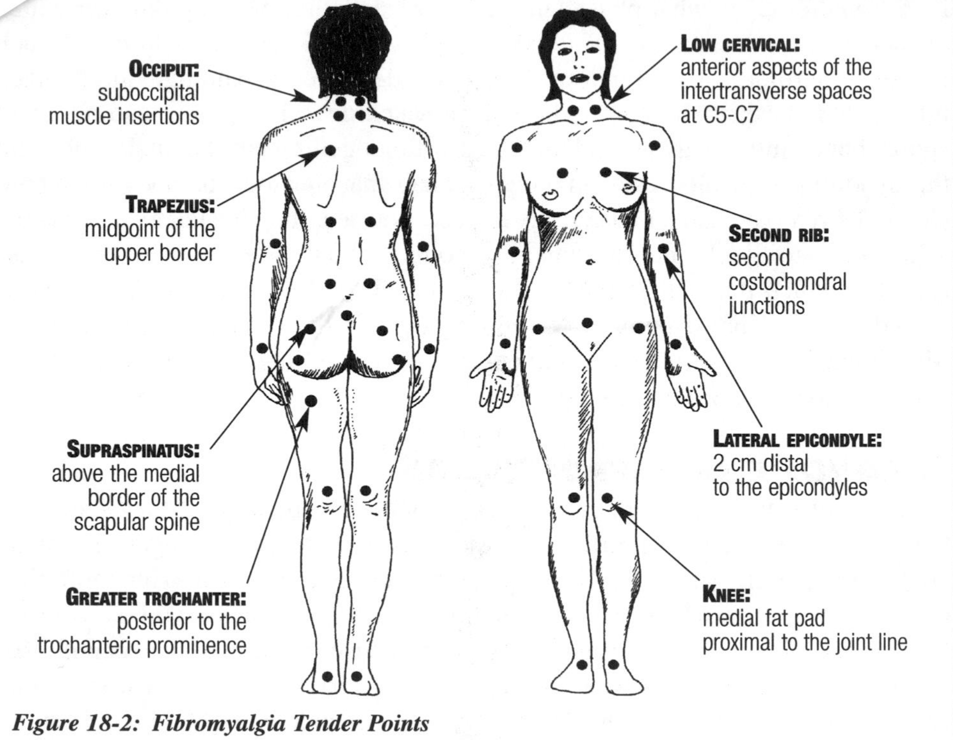

Figure 18-2: Fibromyalgia Tender Points
General locations of the 18 tender points that make up the criteria for identifying fibromyalgia.

Adapted from: **Primer on the Rheumatic Diseases, Tenth Edition, © 1993, *the Arthritis Foundation.***

The key to Pamela's history was that the condition started in her neck. She noted, after further questioning, that her neck was constantly sore. This was indicative of ligament laxity and was found on palpatory examination eliciting a positive "jump sign." Prolotherapy was performed on her neck. The chronic ligament laxity, which led to the neck pain and migraine headaches, also caused her to have chronic insomnia. People with chronic pain typically do not get much deep sleep.[3] That is why they wake up feeling non-rested even after 10 hours of sleep.

The Importance of Sleep

Upon falling asleep, a person enters stage I and stage II sleep, which is a very light sleep. After approximately 90 minutes, the person will enter stages III and IV, or deep sleep. It is during deep sleep that hormones, like Growth Hormone, are secreted. **(See Figure 18-3.)** Growth Hormone, as you will recall, is one of the anabolic hormones that the body needs to repair itself. If a person does not enter the deep stages of sleep, the ability to repair injured tissue is hampered. More than 50 percent of body weight is muscle tissue. It is imperative that the body is able to repair this muscle tissue from its daily use. The body does its repair during the deep

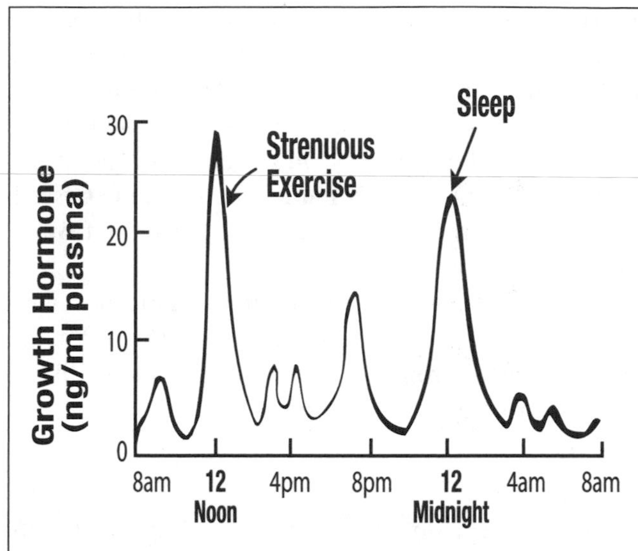

Figure 18-3: Growth Hormone Secreted During Sleep

Adapted from **Textbook of Medical Physiology,** *by A. Guyton and J. Hall, © 1996, W.B. Saunders Co., Philadelphia.*

stages of sleep. If this is not accomplished, the end result is muscle aching. Do you see the cycle? A person has a localized pain, such as neck pain, that does not resolve. Eventually, the chronic pain causes chronic insomnia. The chronic insomnia causes a decrease in the body's ability to repair itself. This causes pain to move to other parts of the body, causing more insomnia. A vicious cycle continues.

In a 1976 study, Harvey Moldofsky, M.D., solicited healthy volunteers and allowed them to sleep only in stages I and II. Dr. Moldofsky put electrodes on their heads and gave them a little zap, not enough to wake them but enough to keep them from achieving stage III or IV sleep, the deep stages of sleep.[4] Guess how long it took before the previously healthy volunteers had diffuse body aches, tender points, and symptomatology exactly mimicking fibromyalgia? **Seven days!** In other words, after seven days of non-restful sleep, these previously healthy people met all the criteria for fibromyalgia, except for the chronicity of the problem.

We all know what this is like. For two days your throat feels scratchy, but you tell yourself, "Nah, I'm not sick." You work another 12-hour day. You mow the lawn, clean out the garage, and do the grocery shopping. The next day you say, "Yeah, I'm sick," as you lay in bed looking for sympathy. After a few days of laying in bed fighting a fever and runny nose, your entire body hurts. It's stiff, sore, and you are exhausted. Do you have fibromyalgia after this? Of course not; you have a cold. Chronic insomnia is the number one reason people have diffuse body aching. To cure diffuse body aching, the cause of the chronic insomnia must be found.

If the chronic insomnia began because of a pain complaint at a particular part of the body, then there is an excellent chance that Prolotherapy can cure the problem. If the chronic insomnia is due to a marital problem, job stress, or other psychological issues, then this is the area that needs to be addressed. Everyone should find a way to reduce their stress level. Let's face it. We all experience stress in our lives.

Realizing that God loves us is our best stress reducer. Our slate is clean before Him because we accepted Jesus Christ as our Savior. Jesus took all of our sins upon Himself at the cross when He died. His perfect life is attributed to us before God because we personally accepted Jesus Christ as our Savior. What we have to look forward to is an eternity with God. The Bible says in Revelation 21:4, referring to heaven, "there will be no more pain... ." It is hard to be sad and stressed knowing that streets paved with gold are awaiting us. Personal prayer and Bible reading are wonderful ways to keep life's priorities in focus.

There are many other ways to reduce the stress of life. Exercise is the most natural way to reduce stress, as well as help your body attain a deep sleep. We all know what it is like to be totally exhausted from physical labor and sleep "like a baby." We achieved the deep sleep our body was craving.

Depression

What about depression? Many people with chronic pain are diagnosed with clinical depression as the cause of their chronic pain. Our response to this is: Follow the person who made that diagnosis and punch him in the back every five minutes. How long do you think it would be before he or she, too, is depressed? It would probably be similar to the study done by Dr. Moldofsky. After seven days of pain, a previously healthy person can show signs of clinical depression. If a previously healthy person develops chronic pain and is diagnosed with depression, it is logical that pain relief will alleviate the depression. This is exactly what occurs. When Prolotherapy is given to the painful area, the chronic pain dissipates and the smile returns to the patient's face. There have been many sour-faced individuals upon first arrival to the office who later began to enjoy life again. It is amazing what pain relief can do to a person's countenance.

Yeast Infections

In regard to Pamela, the other clue to her case was that she had been on several antibiotics. Antibiotics destroy the normal and necessary bacteria in the intestines and cause Candida (yeast) overgrowth. We tested for yeast antibodies in her blood and found high levels present. How did the yeast get into the blood for her immune system to develop antibodies against it? It came through the intestinal wall. Thus, Pamela's intestinal wall was too permeable (leaky). **(See Figure 18-4.)**

Herbs and medicines to kill the yeast were prescribed and she was advised to take acidophilus to replenish the normal bacteria. She was also advised to follow a high-protein, low-carbohydrate diet—necessary for someone with this condition.

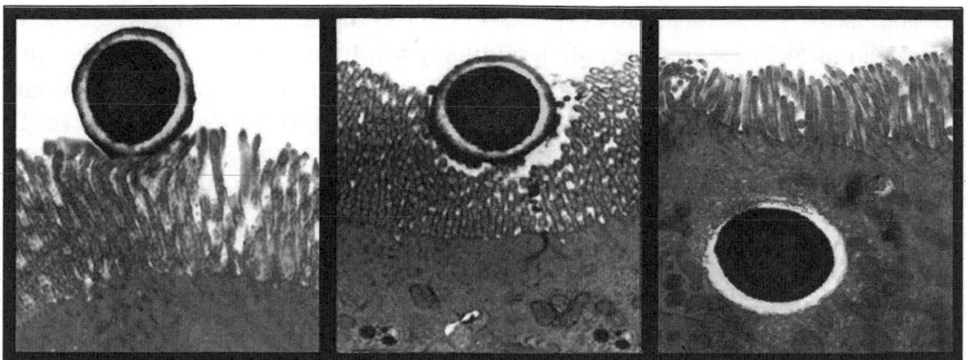

Pictures courtesy of Great Smokies Diagnostic Laboratory, Asheville, North Carolina.

Figure 18-4: Yeast Burrowing Through the Intestinal Wall

Candida fungus infection is one of the causes of "Leaky Gut Syndrome."

Fibromyalgia Has a Cause

Prolotherapy is not an isolated treatment. The physician must investigate all possible factors which may be involved with a person experiencing diffuse body pain.

What happened to Pamela? We don't know. We discharged her from the practice. We assume she's enjoying her life somewhere. Her pain? That got discharged, too.

Most large hospitals have a fibromyalgia support group. How many people must have been diagnosed with fibromyalgia for the hospital to create a support group? People are told they will have recurrent bouts of chronic pain, always feel tired, and are told to live with it. That would drive anyone to a support group! The last line of a fibromyalgia handout from a Chicago hospital reads, "As the wise physician said, 'Once I began to accept that the road was going to be difficult, then it became easier.'" It may be easier for him, but it would be much easier to treat the cause of the chronic pain and alleviate it than attend support groups and live with the pain.

Chronic pain always has a cause. Other etiologies, besides ligament laxity for fibromyalgia-type chronic pain, include multiple chemical sensitivities,[5] hypoadrenocortisolism,[6] hypoglycemia, yeast infection, viral infection,[7] chronic insomnia, increased intestinal permeability, nutrient deficiencies,[8] and poor tissue oxygenation.

To cure the chronic pain, the underlying etiology of the pain must be treated. It is for this reason that people who have the diagnosis of fibromyalgia will be much better served by a physician or health care professional who utilizes natural treatments that address the above conditions.

To make the diagnosis of fibromyalgia, one of the cardinal features is tenderness over specific points on the body. The diagnosis is made when at least 11 of the 18 points are tender. The unilateral sites are the occiput (insertion of the suboccipital muscles), inter-transverse ligaments C5 through C7, trapezius muscle, origin of the supraspinatous muscle, second costochondral junction (ligament), lateral epicondyle (wrist extensor muscle insertions), gluteal area (gluteus maximus muscle), greater trochanter (gluteus medius muscle insertion), and the medial fat pad of the knee (medial collateral ligament). In essence, 14 of the 18 points are located where either a ligament, tendon, or muscle inserts and the remaining four are in the middle of a particular muscle. **(Refer to Figure 18-2.)** Prolotherapy grows ligament, tendon, and muscle tissue where they attach to the bone, thus eliminating trigger points and the pain of fibromyalgia.

Whether a patient has been given the label of fibromyalgia, Myofascial Pain Syndrome, or Post-Surgical Pain Syndrome, the hallmark feature typically is very sensitive trigger point areas. The person often feels a knot in the muscle in that area. These areas are called "trigger points" because they trigger a person's pain if compressed and palpated and cause the positive "jump sign." Trigger points also refer pain to a distal site that becomes painful. In a study published in 1994, K. Dean Reeves, M.D., showed that even in people with severe fibromyalgia, Prolotherapy caused a reduction in pain levels and increased functional abilities in more than 75 percent of patients. In 38 percent of the patients, Prolotherapy was the only effective treatment they ever received. An additional 25 percent said that Prolotherapy was much more effective than any previous treatment. The study showed that overall, 90 percent of the severe fibromyalgia patients benefitted from the Prolotherapy injections.[9]

Benign Congenital Hypermobility

An often overlooked but extremely important reason for chronic body pain is benign congenital hypermobility (BCH). Generalized joint hypermobility (loose joints in the entire body) due to ligamentous laxity occurs in about five percent of the population.[10] This may be a genetic problem. The loose ligaments cause the person to have loose joints. Affected individuals over 40 years of age typically have recurrent joint problems and almost universally suffer from chronic pain. The end result of this condition is often diffuse osteoarthritis.[11]

People with benign congenital hypermobility are prone to bone dislocation. Hypermobile joints are exhibited by bending the elbow or knee past the neutral position, touching the floor with the palm while bending at the waist, and touching the thumb to the forearm. In subtler cases, this condition can only be determined by a physical examination—one of the reasons it is not diagnosed by most physicians. Most physicians are not trained to adequately examine for joint mobility and ligament laxity—another reason why a person with diffuse body pain should be evaluated by a physician familiar with the technique of Prolotherapy.

Prolotherapy is the treatment of choice for benign congenital hypermobility. It is recommended that all hypermobile joints be treated to prevent the formation of arthritis. Patients with chronic pain from diffuse body ligamentous laxity require more than the normal four Prolotherapy sessions. Patients suffering from BCH may also require some Prolotherapy in the future for maintenance purposes.

Ehlers-Danlos Syndrome

J.M. exclaimed, "Without Prolotherapy, I would have died 10 years ago!" J.M. has Ehlers-Danlos Syndrome which causes extreme looseness of the joints. It is an inherited condition in which the connective tissue, made up of ligaments, tendons, and muscles, does not form or heal properly.

Conventional medicine does not have a treatment for regenerating connective tissue and is, therefore, unable to treat Ehlers-Danlos Syndrome. When J.M. finally consulted Gustav A. Hemwall, M.D., the world's most experienced Prolotherapist, she was confined to a wheelchair. Dr. Hemwall treated virtually every joint in her body, since the disease causes all of the joints to become loose. "It was a miracle!" J.M. said during her follow-up visit in April 1997. "I can walk, run, and I'm enjoying life." Because of a genetic defect in connective tissue healing, this particular condition requires periodic Prolotherapy treatments to maintain joint stability.

The usual long-term outcome for people with J.M.'s particular type of Ehlers-Danlos Syndrome is a wheelchair-bound shortened life. Aggressive arthritis forms due to the excessively loose joints, and the joints degenerate beyond repair. Fortunately, she received Prolotherapy before this occurred.

Myofascial Pain Syndrome

Myofascial Pain Syndrome (MPS) is a common painful muscle disorder caused by taut bands or trigger points in the muscles.[12] Myofascial trigger points are tender areas in muscles causing local and referred muscle pain. Trigger points may cause the tight muscles and tight muscles may cause trigger points.

Myofascial Pain Syndrome and fibromyalgia are often diagnosed in the same patient. Fibromyalgia patients typically have myofascial trigger points over numerous areas of the body. Unfortunately, traditional physical therapy and myofascial therapy on the trigger point areas often do not resolve the problem.

Most people with trigger points obtain pain relief with traditional physical therapy modalities such as massage, ultrasound, and stretching; however, the results diminish on their way home from the therapist's office. Traditional medical doctors who treat people with trigger points will give various kinds of injections into these areas.[13] Again, the patient will leave the doctor's office happy, only to be disappointed when the pain returns.

If, after months of therapy and muscle trigger point injections, the pain has not subsided, most likely the etiological source of the trigger point has not been addressed. Myofascial Pain Syndrome trigger points are in the muscle. However, the etiology of the problem is in the ligament, not the muscle.

Muscles chronically contract to stabilize a joint. This chronic contraction causes the muscles to become overworked and spasmodic. Therefore, chronic knotting or muscle spasm is an indication that the underlying joint is loose, due to underlying ligament and/or joint laxity. When a ligament is lax or weakened, the body's t step to stabilize that particular joint is to tighten the muscle. This is why me people have chronic trigger points and are labeled with Myofascial Pain Syndrome. A better diagnosis would be chronic ligament laxity.

Chronic ligament laxity is not affected by muscle trigger point injections, ultrasound, massage, or stretching. Chronic ligament laxity is relieved with Prolotherapy, as Prolotherapy triggers the growth of new ligament tissue. The strengthened ligament holds the joint in place, the muscle relaxes, and the trigger point subsides.

SUMMARY

Myofascial Pain Syndrome and fibromyalgia are often catch-all diagnoses used to put names to chronic pain conditions. They are syndromes which are a constellation of symptoms for which traditional medicine has yet to determine the cause. All chronic pain has an etiology. The most common reason for chronic pain is chronic ligament laxity. The second most common reason is chronic insomnia. Other causes of diffuse chronic body pain are multiple chemical sensitivities, hypoglycemia, hypothyroidism, hypoadrenocortisolism, viral infection, yeast infection, increased gut permeability, nutrient deficiency, and poor tissue oxygenation. To cure fibromyalgic-type complaints, these conditions must be evaluated and treated. For this reason, it is recommended that the person suffering from diffuse body pain see a Natural Medicine physician.

Benign congenital hypermobility is also characterized by diffuse body pain, but the cause is lax ligaments leading to loose joints. All people who have diffuse body pains have tender points on various parts of their bodies. The tender points characteristic of fibromyalgia are primarily the areas where ligaments, tendons, and muscles attach to the bone. Prolotherapy causes the ligaments, tendons, and muscles to grow precisely in these areas where they attach to the bone. Prolotherapy has been shown to be a benefit to more than 90 percent of people suffering from severe fibromyalgia, benign congenital hypermobility, and Myofascial Pain Syndrome. Prolotherapy is an effective treatment for people suffering from diffuse body pain when tenderness is elicited over muscle, ligament, and tendon attachments to the bone. It is for this reason that many people with these conditions are choosing to Prolo their pain away! ■

Chapter 19

Prolo Your Sports Injuries Away!

What do professional swimmers from France, basketball players from New Jersey, hockey players from Chicago, tennis players from Florida, and the thousands of so-called "weekend warriors" all have in common? At some point, while playing their sport of choice, they will each experience a sports injury.

Sports plays a very important role in American society. In addition to the income generated, sports is an outlet for amusement and exercise. Sports also provides an environment for both young and old to develop friendships and, hopefully, character.

Therefore, it is quite a dramatic event when an athlete is sidelined due to injury. Not being able to play sends many into a panic. Fearing they will never again experience the thrill of victory, athletes are willing to do almost anything to get back in the game. The thrill of victory is never forgotten once it has been tasted.

Reasons for Sports Injuries

Most sports injuries are soft tissue injuries involving ligaments, tendons, and muscles.[1] Sports injuries occur when the repetitive strain of the athletic event is too much for a particular ligament, tendon, or muscle to withstand, resulting in a strain—an injured weakened tendon—or a sprain—an injured weakened ligament.

The customary treatment for such injuries, as discussed in Chapters 6 and 7, is **RICE** which refers to treating soft tissue injury with **R**est, **I**ce, **C**ompression, and **E**levation. This treatment regime decreases inflammation when the injured area needs it most, resulting, unfortunately for the athlete, in decreased healing of the injury. Consequently, many sports injuries do not heal completely and are easily re-injured.

A better approach is a treatment known as **MEAT**—**M**ovement, **E**xercise, **A**nalgesics, and specific **T**reatments. Specific treatments that aid in the healing process include ultrasound, heat, and massage, because they increase blood flow. If an injury has not healed after six weeks, more aggressive treatments, including Prolotherapy, should be considered. Prolotherapy can be done immediately after an injury because it has been found to speed recovery.

Stretching, body balancing or body work, chiropractic or osteopathic manipulation, and other physical modalities do help correct problems with posture, tight muscles, and other factors that contribute to sports injuries. Sometimes the patient's technique needs to be improved with coaching or lessons. **(See Figure 19-1.)** The fact remains that sports injuries occur when an area of the body is weak. Sports injuries, whether an ankle sprain or rotator cuff tendonitis, occur because a muscle, ligament, or tendon is not strong enough to perform the task the athlete requires of it. For this reason, the best curative treatment for a sports injury is to strengthen the weakened tissue.

Figure 19-1: The Golfer with Back Pain
Some sports injuries need more help than Prolotherapy can provide…

Many sports injuries are muscle strains. Such injuries cause muscle pain when the injured muscle is contracted. Muscles enjoy a constant blood supply, which brings them necessary healing ingredients. As a result, muscles are usually quick to heal—regardless of the treatment.

As discussed in Chapter 7, ligaments and tendons have poor blood supply and are thus more prone to incomplete healing after an injury. The goal in sports injury therapy should not be pain relief but restoring normal tissue strength, in other words, complete healing of the injured body part. Unfortunately, most athletes are attended to by clinicians who provide pain relief in the form of ibuprofen, aspirin, cortisone shots, and surgery. These therapies can provide pain relief, but they do so at the expense of long-term weakened tissue. We believe most athletes want strong tissue, not weak tissue.

TREATMENT FOR SPORTS INJURIES

Prolotherapy is the best treatment to help cause permanently strong tissue to form where a weakened sports injury exists. Prolotherapy stimulates the healing process and, therefore, decreases the length of time it takes for soft tissue sports injuries to heal. Prolotherapy, because it triggers the growth of normal collagen tissue, causes stronger ligaments and tendons to form. **(See Figure 19-2.)** Consequently, the athlete returns to his or her game stronger. After Prolotherapy treatments, not only is the athlete able to return to the sport, but often the particular area that was injured will be stronger than before the injury and performance will be enhanced.

Frequency of Prolotherapy for Sports Injuries

Because injured athletes often desire to return to their game as soon as possible, Prolotherapy injections may be given weekly instead of every six weeks. This is because athletes do not have the time to wait to grow tissue. They desire tissue growth and they want it now! Sometimes stronger solutions are used to help increase the speed of the healing process. This is not the ideal situation, however. A preferred treatment regime is for athletes to receive Prolotherapy treatments during their off-season so that by the start of the season the injury is healed.

Personal Experience with Prolotherapy

Ross has personally experienced the success of this treatment. Having had habitual ankle sprains during his youth that prevented him from participating in several sports, Prolotherapy treatment to his ankles has enabled Ross to now participate in whatever sport he desires (with his wife's permission, of course). He also enjoy long-distance running and has completed numerous marathons. He was quite frustrated when he once found himself barely able to walk because of debilitating knee pain. Our friend, Rodney Van Pelt, M.D., performed Prolotherapy on the cruciate ligaments in his knee. Only one treatment was necessary to put Ross back into his running shoes. Ross also treated Marion's knee that nearly sidelined her from completing her second marathon this year.

We have had professional as well as amateur athletes come through our office doors and—most importantly—leave and return to playing their sports. It saddens us when we read in the newspaper about a professional athlete undergoing surgery for a sports injury. The knife treatment often is equivalent to a death sentence for the professional athlete. Surgery often ends or severely limits a career.

Role of Surgery in Sports Injuries

Surgery weakens tissue. What do you think the doctor actually does when he or she says, "I'm going to scope the knee"? "Scoping" involves removing a little tissue here, cutting a little tissue there. Frayed tissue is either shaved or cut out. Surgery for sports injuries, even arthroscopic surgery, means the surgeon is going to remove tissue. Realize that removing cartilage, ligament, or any other soft tissues of the body makes that body part weaker.

Rather than weakening their bodies with surgery, athletes should strengthen their bodies with Prolotherapy. Prolotherapy helps frayed, weakened tissue repair itself and makes that particular body part strong again. Surgery often spells death for an athlete. Prolotherapy spells new life!

Prolotherapy: From Tendinosis to Tendonitis

Most athletes are told that they need to do the **RICE** protocol, take NSAIDs, or get a cortisone shot because they have too much inflammation in their injured structure. Too often they find out that these treatments just temporarily stop the pain, only to have it recur with a vengeance. When biopsies are taken of chronically injured structures in athletes, tendinosis, not tendonitis, is found. Tendinosis

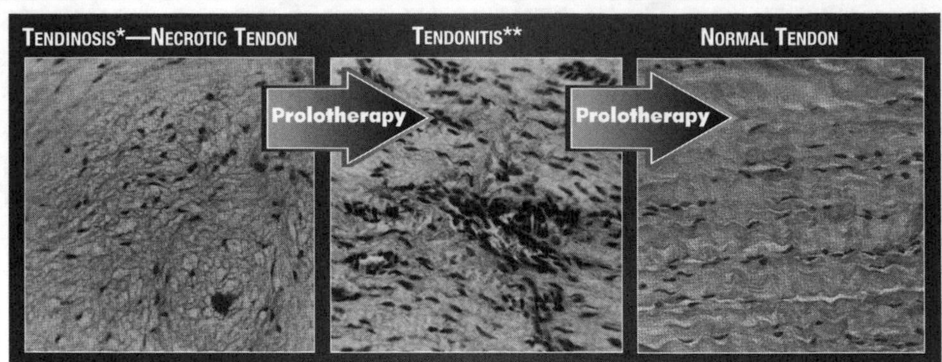

Figure 19-2: The Histology of How Prolotherapy Heals

Athletes with chronic pain do not have inflammatory conditions as evidenced by biopsy. They have tendinosis or degenerated tissue. This is why they need Prolotherapy—not cortisone or NSAIDs.

Used with permission from *Overuse Injuries of the Musculoskeletal System*—Marko M. Peling, CRC Press, 1993, Boca Raton, FL

*Biopsy of tendon of athlete with "overuse injury"

**Biopsy of tendon showing tendonitis. This is what occurs immmediately after Prolotherapy.

refers to degenerated tendon. In other words, the tendon is not actively undergoing regeneration but degeneration, with the obvious absence of inflammatory cells. Prolotherapy stimulates the tendon to repair itself by the process of inflammation. It thus turns a tendinosis into a tendonitis with the objective being a normal strong tendon. **(See Figure 19-2.)** This is why athletes from around the world are realizing that you can cure sports injuries and enhance athletic performance with Prolotherapy.

SUMMARY

In summary, sports injuries are caused because muscle, tendon, or ligament tissue is too weak to perform a particular task. Treatment regimes for soft tissue injury, such as taking ibuprofen and applying ice to the area to reduce inflammation, or undergoing surgery to remove tissue, often provide pain relief but cause incomplete healing, making the athlete prone to re-injury.

A better approach to treatment of sports injuries, more than just pain control, is complete healing of the injured tissue. Prolotherapy, because it stimulates the growth of ligament and tendon tissue, helps sports injuries heal faster. While surgery causes tissue to become weaker, Prolotherapy helps form stronger tissue.

Because athletes want to continue playing their sports without a reduction in ability or fear of reinjury, many are choosing to Prolo their sports injuries away! ■

***NOTE:** For those desiring a more in-depth explanation of Prolotherapy and sports injuries, please read our book,* **Prolo Your Sports Injuries Away!** *available from Beulah Land Press by calling 1-800-RX-PROLO or visiting our website at www.beulahlandpress.com.*

Chapter 20

Prolo Your Animal's Pain Away!

We thought most pet owners were fanatical, until Squeaky came on the scene. Squeaky is the cat we rescued from our farm home in southern Illinois. One weekend she was limping, so we decided to take her home to Oak Park, Illinois, to "rehabilitate" her. Once she was inside our warm home, she dramatically "healed." Whenever we talk about returning her to southern Illinois, her ailment strangely returns. It looks like she has become a permanent part of our family, and that is the understatement of the century!

Duke's Story

It was easy to understand his emotion when a Prolotherapy patient told Ross sadly, "Duke cannot climb the stairs anymore."

He then asked, "Since Prolotherapy was so effective for me, will it work for my dog, Duke?"

Climbing the stairs was painful for Duke, just as it is for humans with joint pain. We asked a veterinarian friend, Shaun Fauley, D.V.M., to assist. Duke, a big, old dog, was favoring his left leg, which led us to believe his hip was the source of his pain. Dr. Fauley anesthetized Duke and we performed Prolotherapy on his left hip and pelvis. One hour later, Duke was up and running. The next day his limp had noticeably decreased. How could Duke have experienced such rapid pain relief?

The answer is the same for Duke as it is for humans. Two-thirds of patients (and animals) feel better immediately after the Prolotherapy treatment. The immediate inflammation caused by the Prolotherapy temporarily stabilizes the painful, loose joints. The new ligament and tendon tissue does not fully form for four to six weeks after the treatment. The time period between the reduction in inflammation and the fully formed tissue is a "window period," between the second and fourth week, during which time the pain may return. **(See Figure 20-1.)** Complete healing occurs when the ligament and tendon tissue regains its normal strength. This normally requires four Prolotherapy sessions for humans. The time frame is less for animals.

In regard to Duke, after two months and one Prolotherapy session his overall function improved 50 percent. Many animals across the country are put to sleep—a gentle way of saying "killed"—because of their painful conditions. Even worse, there are many animals whose owners chase them so they can shove nonsteroidal anti-inflammatory drugs (NSAIDs) or other pain relievers down their throats to alleviate their pain. Animals are smarter than we are. They run *from* NSAIDs. We humans run *to* NSAIDs.

Ross and Dr. Fauley treated Duke again with Prolotherapy injections in his left hip and pelvis. **(See Figure 20-2.)** The last time we saw Duke, he was happily chasing birds.

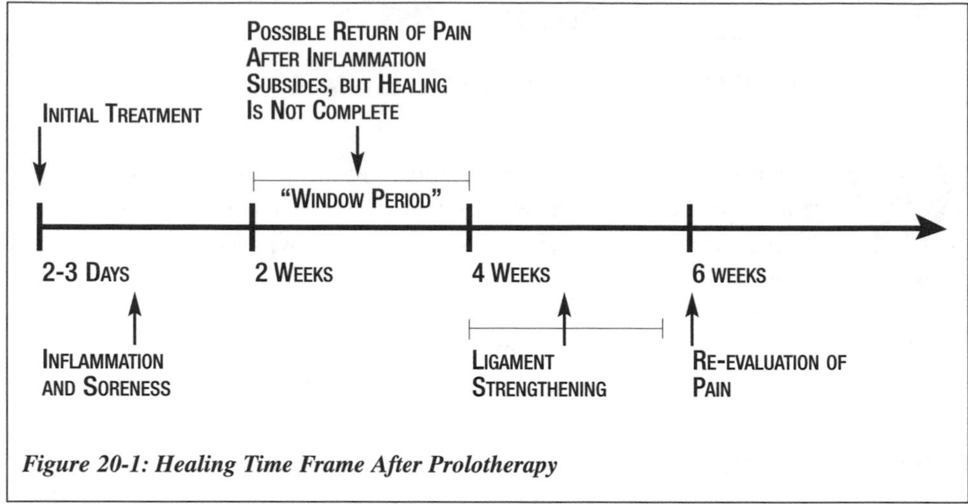

Figure 20-1: Healing Time Frame After Prolotherapy

PROLOTHERAPY IN VETERINARY PRACTICES

As successful as Prolotherapy is for people, it is perhaps even more effective on animals. This may be largely due to the fact that animals eat better than humans do. Your pet rarely treats itself to a triple-hot-fudge-banana-brownie-triple-scoop sundae topped with whipped cream and nuts, or spends more time in the potato chip aisle than the vegetable aisle of the grocery store.

Animals can and do experience pain, just like humans. The only difference is they cannot tell you they are in pain. Animals in pain may become listless, move constantly, groan, and whimper. If the pain is in a weight-bearing joint such as the hip, the animal will limp. The same causes of pain in humans generally apply to animals. As a matter of fact, we have learned most of what we know about pain and pain management in humans from animal studies. Tests on dogs, for example, have shown that hip joint laxity is the most important and reliable factor in determining the likelihood of degenerative joint disease of the hip.[1] A logical conclusion is that ligament laxity causes arthritis in dogs. It is our contension that this situation also occurs in humans. This is the physiological basis of why Prolotherapy stops the progression of the arthritic process. By strengthening the ligaments that surround the joints, Prolotherapy makes the joints stronger. Strong joints do not develop arthritis—only loose or weak ones.

S. Fubini, D.V.M., stated that "lameness related to joint disorders has been reported to be a leading cause of disability among thoroughbred racehorses."[2] Articular cartilage degeneration is the first sign of osteoarthritis in horses, a common and irreversible joint disease. Experiments have clearly indicated that intra-articularly (inside the joint) administered steroids cause depletion of proteoglycan from articular cartilage in normal equine (horse) joints[3, 4] and exacerbate osteoarthritic changes in diseased joints.[5, 6] In other words, steroids cause the

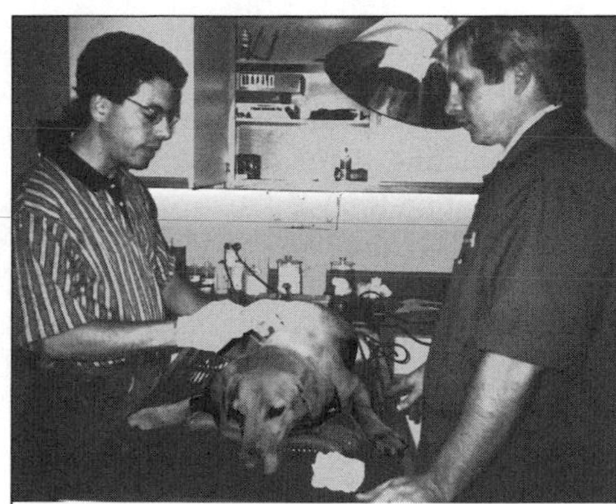

Figure 20-2: Prolo Your Animal's Pain Away!
Here, Ross Hauser, M.D., teaches Shaun Fauley, D.V.M., how to Prolo an animal's pain away. Though initially skeptical, Dr. Fauley is now a strong advocate for Prolotherapy on animals.

degeneration of the cartilage, which leads to osteoarthritis. Steroids cause the same harmful effects in animals as they do in humans. Animals run from steroid injections, but humans will pay big bucks for them.

According to Dr. Fauley, "In traditional veterinary medicine, an animal's pain is typically treated with anti-inflammatory medicine and/or a steroid injection." These treatments do reduce the pain but very seldom cure it. "I believe Prolotherapy is a treatment modality that shows promise of more definitive results on relieving pain in animals." [7]

Although anti-inflammatory medications and steroid injections reduce pain in animals, they do so at the cost of destroying tissue. In a study conducted by Siraya Chunekamrai, D.V.M., Ph.D., horses treated with eight weekly shots of a steroid commonly used in humans exhibited tremendously detrimental effects in the injected tissue. Some of the effects included chondrocyte necrosis (cartilage cell damage), hypocellularity (decreased number of cells) in the joint, decreased proteoglycan content and synthesis, and decreased collagen synthesis in the injected joint. All of these effects were permanent.

Chunekamrai concluded, "The effects on cartilage of intra-articular injections of methylprednisolone acetate (a steroid) were not ameliorated at eight weeks after eight weekly injections, or 16 weeks after a single injection. Cartilage remained biochemically and metabolically impaired." [8] In this study, some of the joints were injected only one time. Even after one steroid injection, cartilage remained biochemically and metabolically impaired. Other studies have confirmed similar harmful effects of steroids on joint and cartilage tissue.[9,10] A cortisone shot can permanently damage joints. Prolotherapy injections have the opposite effect—they permanently strengthen joints.

"Not just a few animals, I've treated hundreds," explains Michael Herron, D.V.M., an orthopedic animal specialist. "Our healing time of muscle, tendon, and ligament injuries has been accelerated by one third, just by using Sclerotherapy." Sclerotherapy is another name for Prolotherapy. "I've treated just about every muscle, ligament, and tendon in greyhound racers and found Sclerotherapy to be extremely effective. Most animals require only one treatment and quickly return to racing." [11]

Dr. Herron has used Sclerotherapy to effectively treat a partial Achilles tear in dogs. The most commonly treated area in a dog, however, is the wrist. Dr. Herron explained that dogs support 60 percent of their weight on the front paw wrist area. Therefore, this becomes the area where the ligaments require strengthening. Sclerotherapy is used anywhere in the animal where the ligaments are injured. Dr. Herron claims an 85-percent success rate in eliminating pain and disability with only one Sclerotherapy treatment in the animals that he treats.[12]

Owners of greyhound racers cannot afford for their dogs not to race, so they turn to Prolotherapy. The question is: Why do athletes turn to cortisone shots and not to Prolotherapy? If NFL, NBA, or PGA players had a Prolotherapist on their medical staffs, the athletes' time on injured-reserve would significantly decrease.

How in the World Did You Get Involved with Prolotherapy on Horses?

The story started about six months ago when Carol had heard Ross on one of the Ohio radio stations talking about our first book, *Prolo Your Pain Away!* Carol struggled with terrible body pain for many years. As soon as she finished listening to that show, she hopped on an airplane and came to see us in Oak Park, Illinois. The first set of Prolotherapy injections—to her back, neck, shoulders, knees, and a few other areas—gave Carol significant relief. She was starting to feel like a new woman. Her husband mentioned that he noticed that she was starting to get her glow and zest for life back.

Sometimes we have the time to add a little country to the office in Oak Park, Illinois, by shooting the breeze with people, even if we are not sitting on the front porch. Unfortunately, we are usually too busy to do this all the time because there are so many people in pain who want to be treated and, hopefully, cured!

One day in late January 1999, Carol came in for her follow-up appointment. During the course of the conversation she asked if Ross had ever treated racehorses. He had never treated racehorses, but told her of his work with veterinarians performing Prolotherapy on dogs and that all of the dogs did very well. Our veterinarian friend, Shaun Fauley, D.V.M., and Ross have helped relieve dogs' hip dysplasia, back pain, and neck pain. Carol thought that because she did so well with Prolotherapy that there was no reason it would not help her friend's horses. Prolotherapy will help an animal's pain. Prolotherapy is nonpartisan—it does not matter the race, color, or breed. That was the end of that conversation and Carol went on her way back to Ohio.

A few weeks later, we received a call from a friend of Carol's, named Gerard. You could tell that he was good country folk. He did not rush while speaking and he had a very friendly tone about his voice. Gerard explained that he was a thoroughbred racehorse trainer. He trained 10 or 11 horses at one time. In 1997, he bred 31 mares—the most in the state of Indiana. In 1998, he bred 22 or 23. It took us a few minutes to figure out why he was calling Caring Medical in Oak Park, Illinois. He then explained that they desperately needed someone to teach him and his staff Prolotherapy, because some of the racehorses were not healing with the usual and customary treatments (similar to humans). Don't ask why, but Ross agreed to do it. We arranged for Ross to examine the horses on February 13, 1999, a day that will go down in history—the day that racehorses' pain was Prolo'd away!

The usual and customary treatment for animals' pain is as bad or worse than the treatment for humans. Animals are not subjected to the massive amounts of surgeries as humans are, due to expense, but they get the same proportional amounts of NSAIDs. Animals are also given a tremendous amount of cortisone shots. The unfortunate thing for animals is that if they do not respond to the cortisone shots, they are "put down" or, in other words, killed. If humans do not respond to the cortisone shots, they get an operation or some other treatment, but a dog or other animal is killed. Every day thousands of dogs and cats are killed because they have hip problems or other chronic pain problems that are easily treated by Prolotherapy. Acceptance of Prolotherapy into modern-day veterinary medicine would be the ultimate in animal activism, as it pertains to cats, dogs, and even racehorses. Many lives could be saved. Remember, you cannot say that something in the chronic pain arena is incurable or chronic until you have tried Prolotherapy and failed. Since animals eat such healthy diets, often only one treatment with Prolotherapy is needed to relieve their musculoskeletal pain problems.

Well, back to the racehorses—because this is a good story. Ross and Gerard met at 9 a.m. at his farm, where Ross saw about 10 horses and met Gerard's son Roy. Then Ross was told to follow them to the track where the injured horses were located. They said it was, "only a short ways away." Having been around enough country folks to know there is not anything in the country that is a short ways away, Ross decided to clock the mileage and fastened both seat belts. He learned quickly that country folks drive fast and these two were no exception. They were not going to wait for some city doctor to catch up! Soon Ross was on a Kojack-like chase trying to catch up to their Ford pick-up! It was not an easy job, that's for sure. After about 25 minutes of driving our little Toyota, covered with mud, they came upon a train, so Ross was given a chance to catch his breath. Like a kid in the backseat of his parents' station wagon, Ross asked Gerard, "How much longer?" "Oh, just a little ways up the road," he quickly replied. Oh no! "A little ways up the road," in country terms, could be another hour! Some 20-plus miles later, they arrived at the track!

It was an awesome site looking into the stalls. We had been to the racetrack before but had never really observed these awesome creatures. Thoroughbred racehorses are gigantic and the muscle structure on these animals is something to behold. A day with those horses provided motivation more than ever to start working out again!

The first horse treated was Broadway Natural. These horse trainers started talking to Ross like he knew horse anatomy. Their conversation went something like this:

"Yeah, Doc, I think her pastern and hock joint are giving her trouble."

Ross thought to himself, "*Pastern and hock joint?* Should I let on that I had no idea what the trainer was talking about?" Instead he replied, "How do you know that?" (You see, Ross learned early in life that if you are clueless about something, just ask a question in return.)

"Well," said the trainer, "she doesn't bring her back leg forward normally, even during walking. Here, I'll show you."

Ross recalls, "I could see the animal's hind leg didn't swing normally." Then he touched the painful area and—you guessed it—the racehorse had a positive "jump sign." Ross remembers thinking, "Thank you, God, you have made the 'jump sign' universal! I know I can do this. I know what the 'jump sign' is—I've written about it! I also know how to relieve the pain—inject it!"

Fortunately, Ross asked what gauge needle they normally used for injections in the horses and found out that they used 20-gauge needles. He had 22-gauge needles, which were a little smaller than the 20-gauge needles, but he grabbed them anyway.

As he hooked the syringe onto the needle, it quickly dawned on Ross that Broadway Natural did not look like an animal who was eager to receive some injections. The conversation between them continued:

Ross asked, "Uh, is this horse going to kick me during the injections?"

"Don't worry, Doc, we'll secure her." The trainer hooked her nose up with some ropes. He put some kind of a noose around the horse's snout, which apparently is used to get horses under control.

Ross' heart started to pound and his palms were starting to sweat. The only thing that flashed through his mind was: how many bones were going to be broken when this horse fell on him? He started questioning himself. "What am I doing here?" "Who am I?" "What is life about?" It is during crisis times that the important matters of life are contemplated.

Figure 20-3: Prolotherapy for the Equine
Thoroughbred racehorses have injuries similar to every other mammalian athlete.

He quickly plunged the needle into Broadway Natural's pastern joint, as quickly as he could, and in rapid succession. About six injections around the joints on both hind legs were given. **(See Figure 20-3.)** After finishing that last injection, Ross took a peek at Broadway Natural. He will never forget that look. It said "If you stick me one more time I am going

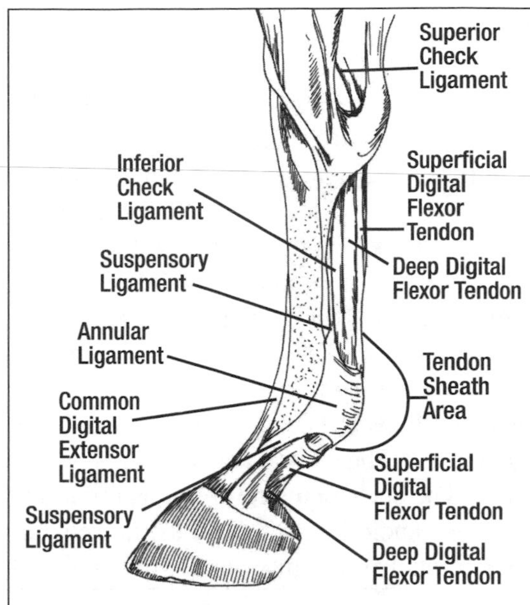

Figure 20-4: The Right Foreleg, Viewed from the Medial (Inside) Side

Racehorses need Prolotherapy desperately, because of all the ligament injuries they suffer. If they don't recover, they become dog meat, literally. A better solution? Prolotherapy.

to ram my stifle (knee) right into your midsection!" The horse did not seem to appreciate the Prolotherapy that she was receiving, or perhaps it was the snout treatment. Within a few minutes the procedure was completed. Hopefully, the treatment of pain in racehorses will never be the same.

That day, Ross treated a number of common horse ailments including back, hip, knee, ankle, stifle, hock, and pastern difficulties. Apparently, suspensory ligament problems are common in racehorses because these ligaments have the job of supporting all the tendons, which are continually worked out during training. **(See Figure 20-4.)**

By the last horse, it was admittedly getting more fun. It is fun injecting humans, but it does not compare at all to the feeling of piercing a seven-inch needle through equine flesh. Wow, what massive muscles. It was a great feeling hitting the lumbar vertebrae and *os coxae*. When the painful area was injected, the animal would buckle, just like in humans. That day was very memorable because the treatments helped those horses and, best of all, some people who "doctor" racehorses learned that there is a cure for racehorses' pains and that cure is Prolotherapy.

FROM DOG MEAT TO CONTENDER— ONLY BECAUSE OF PROLOTHERAPY

About a month after the thoroughbred experience, we were in contact with Gerard. He said that Babe, one of the horses treated, had "gone from dog meat to contender." Upon further clarification of that statement, he said that apparently if racehorses are not racing well, they literally become dog food. Babe, this particular horse, was injured and it was expensive for the owners to keep an injured racehorse alive. She was a few weeks away from becoming dog meat. After the Prolotherapy treatment, Babe came in third in her first race. She had become a contender and made money for the owner in that race. Yes, only Prolotherapy could take an athlete—even a four-legged one—from dog meat to contender.

Racehorse Injuries Due to Ligament and Tendon Injuries

Tendon and ligament injuries represent some of the major problems facing the athletic horse. The most extensively studied and most problematic ligaments and tendons in the horse occur in the lower limbs. The ligaments and tendons of the horse that are most prone to injury are located in the lower legs. They are most obvious below the horse's knee (carpus) and in the hind limb below the horse's hock (tarsus). The tendons and ligaments of the hind limb are injured much less frequently than the corresponding ligaments in the front leg. This is most likely because they are subjected to so much less stress, because the horse normally bears about 70 percent of his or her weight on the front legs.

Injury of the various ligaments of the lower limbs is the major cause of racehorse injuries. The most frequently injured ligaments are the suspensory ligaments, which help support the back of the horse's limb. The six sesamoidean ligaments in the horse's limbs have the job of attaching the sesamoid bones behind the horse's fetlock joints. They help to keep the fetlock joints from falling apart when the joint bends. Injuries to these ligaments heal poorly. Speaking about the fetlock joint, you cannot speak about it enough, because the annular ligament runs over the back of it and converts the space between the sesamoid bones into an actual canal through which the tendons can travel. **Figure 20-5** helps visualize the anatomy and the massive amounts of ligaments and tendons that support these mammoth animals.

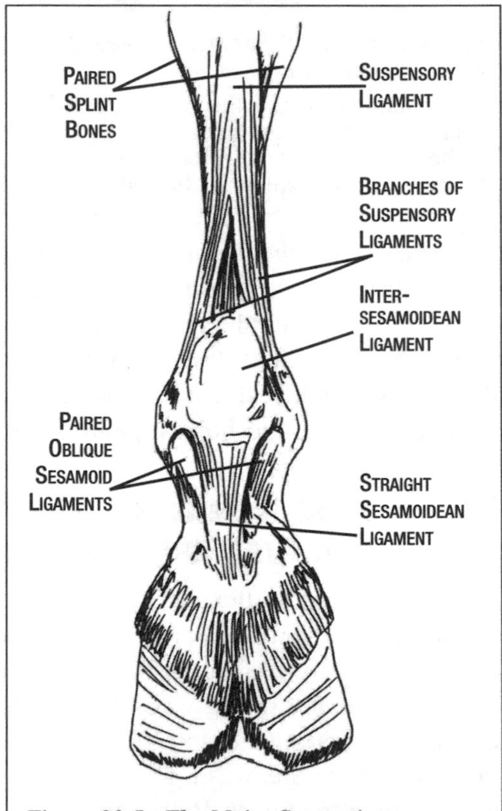

Figure 20-5: The Major Supporting Structures of the Back of a Horse's Leg
This is a Prolotherapist's dream—note all of the ligaments!

Animals can suffer basically all of the same sports injuries that humans experience. Like humans, when horses are working at peak-performance levels, there are actually very small margins of safety for their ligaments and tendons. It has been shown that the horse that is working hard is always right on the edge of exceeding the ability of these tissues to withstand the pressures placed on them. [13] This is true for all elite athletes—they are right on the edge! It is Prolotherapy and nutritional medicine that will give them the edge so that they stay healthy and avoid injury as they push themselves to the limit!

Animal ligament and tendon injuries manifest in ways similar to humans. There is initial swelling, heat, and sensitivity to touch. Animals will typically jerk their legs away or run backwards if the injured ligament or tendon is squeezed. Many horses with injuries to ligaments or tendons feel enough pain to exhibit lameness. It is interesting that veterinarians who treat racehorses generally do not prescribe anti-inflammatories or give cortisone shots to the animals. Dr. David Ramey, in his book *Tendon and Ligament Injuries in the Horse*, explains, "Although they are very effective at controlling swelling and inflammation in the injured tissue, they also have an undesirable side effect of **suppressing the growth of the tissue that forms to repair the injury.** In regards to corticosteroid injections he writes, "…they have a number of undesirable side effects. First, local corticosteroid injections can delay healing of injured tendon and ligament tissue for up to a year. They also reduce the strength of the ultimate repair. Corticosteroid injections directly into the site of the injury have been shown to cause the injured tissue to calcify in some cases." For all you out there who have calcium deposits, how many of you have received a steroid shot in the area? It would be an interesting study, would it not?

Much of what we know about the bad effects of corticosteroids actually comes from animal studies. For instance, S. Fubini, D.V.M., summarized it well by stating that "…lameness related to joint disorders has been reported to be a leading cause of disability among thoroughbred racehorses." [14] Articular cartilage degeneration is the first sign of osteoarthritis in horses, a common irreversible joint disease. Experiments have clearly indicated that intra-articularly (inside the joint) administered steroids cause depletion of proteoglycan from articular cartilage in normal equine (horse) joints [15, 16] and exacerbate osteoarthritic changes in diseased joints. [17, 18] In other words, steroids cause the degeneration of the cartilage, which leads to osteoarthritis. Steroids cause the same harmful effects in animals as they do in humans. Animals run from steroid injections, but humans will pay big bucks for them.

According to veterinarian Dr. Shaun Fauley of Care Animal Clinic in Naperville, Illinois, "In traditional veterinary medicine, an animal's pain is typically treated with anti-inflammatory medicine and/or a steroid injection. These treatments do reduce the pain but very seldom cure it. I believe Prolotherapy is a treatment modality that shows promise to have more definitive results in relieving pain in animals." [19] Dr. Fauley is one of the veterinarians in the country getting excited about doing Prolotherapy.

Although anti-inflammatory medications and steroid injections reduce pain in animals, they do so at the cost of destroying tissue. In a study conducted by Siraya Chunekamrai, D.V.M., Ph.D., horses treated with eight weekly shots of a steroid commonly used in humans exhibited tremendously detrimental effects in the injected tissue. Some of the effects included chondrocyte necrosis (cartilage cell damage), hypocellularity (decreased number of cells) in the joint, decreased proteoglycan content and synthesis, and decreased collagen synthesis in the injected joint. All of these effects were permanent.

Chunekamrai concluded, "The effects on cartilage of intra-articular injections of methylprednisolone acetate (a steroid) were not ameliorated at eight weeks after eight weekly injections, or 16 weeks after a single injection. Cartilage remained biochemically and metabolically impaired." [20] In this study, some of the joints were injected only one time. **Even after one steroid injection, cartilage remained biochemically and metabolically impaired.** Other studies have confirmed similar harmful effects of steroids on joint and cartilage tissue.[21, 22] A cortisone shot can permanently damage joints. Prolotherapy injections have the opposite effect—they permanently strengthen joints.

SUMMARY

Prolotherapy, because it stimulates ligament and tendon growth, can be used anywhere a ligament or tendon is located. It does not matter if it is a dog, cat, horse, bull, parakeet, llama, or Johnny's pet goldfish. In the treatment of both chronic and acutely painful conditions in animals, Prolotherapy has been more than 85-percent successful with only one treatment. If utilized to its full extent, Prolotherapy can end most of the needless suffering of animals (and humans). It is for this reason that many animal owners are choosing to Prolo their animal's pain away! ■

Chapter 21

Prolotherapy: The King of All Injection Techniques

Commonly Asked Questions

Dear Dr. Hauser: *I heard about Prolotherapy. I have a degenerated back. I had epidural injections. Is this the same thing as Prolotherapy? The epidurals did not do anything for my pain. I would appreciate any information you can provide. Sincerely, Pam.*

Dear Dr. Hauser: *I saw your website with the Prolotherapy shots. They appear to just be trigger point injections. I am a runner with a bad Achilles tendon problem. Trigger points helped for a few days—that was it. Are they the same? Thanks for your help. Pete*

Dear Marion Hauser: *I had cortisone shots in my rotator cuff. It helped for a couple of months. I understand Prolotherapy does not use the same ingredients, but is the shot as painful and how long does Prolotherapy pain relief last? My tennis game is suffering—can you help? Sincerely, Roger*

Dear Marion Hauser: *I saw you on TV and you were talking about curing headache pain with Prolotherapy and nutritional things. I have had migraines for years and cannot get rid of them. I have tried tons of medications. Do you think Prolotherapy can help me? These headaches can knock me off my feet for days. Sincerely, Tabitha*

We could easily fill up several pages of the e-mail messages that we receive at drhauser@caringmedical.com. We now have three Prolotherapy-related websites: www.caringmedical.com, www.prolonews.com, and www.sportsprolo.com. People are often amazed at how quickly Dr. Hauser responds to the e-mail and how helpful the information provided has been. Well folks, Ross must confess, he hardly even knows what e-mail is all about.

Ross Digresses

I made a very wise move in 1980. I saw the most beautiful maiden in the land and pursued her until she agreed to date me. Once she did, I made sure I never let her go. Marion and I were married on December 20, 1986. We have a wonderful relationship. Anyone who meets her agrees she is a **B**abe with a capital **B**! People are often amazed at how I landed such a babe, so I will now tell my secret: Poetry.

I believe in love at first sight. I first saw Marion's picture when I was 12; I was hooked. I planned the course just right, so when I met up with her when I was 17 years old, I asked her out on a date. When she started seeing me on a semi-regular basis, I would write her a poem about every week. You see, chicks love poems. Guys today are too busy pumping iron. Chicks would much rather get poems than biceps. Guys still think chicks go for biceps. Biceps went out in the 80s. The Babes of the 21ST century want guys who will listen, who are not afraid to become intimate and share their feelings. For most guys, this is much easier if you just try to put the words into poems. For the guy who is willing to come out of the gym for a couple of hours, there is a wonderful gal waiting to be heard. That is what she wants: to be heard. Did you hear me? That means listen!

The babe I eventually married helps me in so many ways. She is an old-fashioned, yet modern girl. To me she is a sophisticated woman, but looks much younger than her stated age. She can still turn heads! I often tell her that if I wasn't married to her and I saw her on the opposite side of the street, I might just look twice! (I can't say for sure or else she'll get a big head!) Marion cooks, sews, and can make her own clothes, yet she can easily run a clinic servicing 500 patients in a weekend (Beulah Land Natural Medicine Clinic) along with running two companies every day. She commands respect wherever she goes. She has a tremendous talent to lead people, yet follow when needed.

One of the many tasks she does at Caring Medical is answer the e-mail. So the next time you e-mail drhauser@caringmedical.com most likely you will be talking with one of the most brilliant minds in Natural Medicine and Prolotherapy—and that is not me—it's my wife of 17 years, Marion. She probably knows more about Prolotherapy and Natural Medicine than most doctors. Say hello to her for me.

We currently receive about 100 e-mails per day, maybe more. Questions such as those mentioned above have prompted the writing of this chapter. It is important for everyone to realize that not all injection techniques are the same. **There is only one injection technique that is King—Prolotherapy.**

ACCEPT NO IMITATIONS

There is only one type of injection technique that works this way: Prolotherapy. Prolotherapy is an injection technique that stimulates the body to **repair** the painful area. Prolotherapy involves the proliferation of fibroblastic cells. This causes the regeneration of normal connective tissues, such as ligaments and tendons. The solution is injected into the fibro-osseous junction of the bone and connective tissue. The connective tissues are generally either ligaments or tendons. The injection actually causes inflammation that stimulates the natural healing process. This is the gist of what you need to know to figure out if the treatment you are being offered is Prolotherapy. The injections repair the painful area, by proliferating fibroblasts that regenerate normal ligament and tendon tissue at the fibro-osseous junction, by causing inflammation that simulates the natural healing process. Do not be fooled.

WATCH OUT FOR IMITATIONS

By using the above criteria it will be easy to tell that typical trigger point injections, epidural injections, cortisone shots, lidocaine shots, botulism injections, facet blocks, and nerve-root blocks are **not Prolotherapy**. They never were and never will be Prolotherapy. They have almost **nothing** in common with Prolotherapy except that they involve a syringe and a needle.

You may be surprised to know that we do occasionally use cortisone, lidocaine shots, epidural injections, trigger point injections, facet blocks, and a host of other injection techniques. **Ross loves giving injections!** During a typical day at Caring Medical he will give about 1,000-plus injections. During a typical day at Beulah Land Natural Medicine Clinic in Thebes, he will give 2,000-plus injections. Ross wrote to the *Guinness Book of World Records* to try and ask them to allow him to set the record for the most injections given in one hour. He felt with doing finger injections and other parts of the body where the bone is very close to the surface of the skin, that he could do one injection every three seconds which would amount to 1,200 injections in one hour. They wrote a nice letter back saying, "…don't call us, we'll call you." We wish Prolotherapy was just one large shot, but it isn't. **(See Figure 21-1.)**

Typical Case: Allison

Allison, a local high school softball pitching star, came in for her first visit to our office in Oak Park. A key question we always ask, "Do you want to play in college?" This gives an indication of just how serious the athletes are about their sport. She said a definite "yes." Unfortunately, she had not been able to pitch or do much in the last several weeks because of anterior shoulder instability due to injury to her pitching shoulder's glenohumeral ligament. She was eager to start Prolotherapy. Before Ross started injecting she said, "Please be careful and go slow." He said that he could guarantee that he would be careful, but the slow part is a definite no. In a matter of 60 seconds, Prolotherapy to her right shoulder was completely done. "Doctor, thanks for going fast. I now know what you mean. I cannot believe I worried all this time about the pain." Allison did great! She received two more of the "quick" Prolotherapy sessions and is now back to pitching and pitching quite well! We recently heard that she pitched her team to a 14 to 1 victory in the state playoffs!

"It's going to hurt more than the two hundred little ones, but it's much faster."

Figure 21-1: Prolotherapy Cartoon Given to Dr. Hauser by a Patient Who Had Been Successfully "Prolo'ed."

Get It Over Quickly!

Nobody likes shots. Would you rather have a physician slowly inject the needle so that you feel every slow gradual progression of the needle? For shoulder injections, the needle first pierces the skin, then goes through the subcutaneous tissues, and passes through the fat to get to the deltoid muscle, then the fascia, and then down to the fibro-osseous junction of the supraspinatus tendon. The physician could perform this procedure so the patient feels the needle going through each layer, taking a break after every injection, with the paitent still sweating after 10 minutes. Would it not be easier to just say, "Go for it, Doc!" and in 60 seconds the treatment—consisting of 12 injections to the shoulder—will be thoroughly and completely done. Finito! Over! Even people who are completely terrified of needles can handle 60 seconds. The wind sprints that athletes do every day are way more brutal than any Prolotherapy treatment. For those who just cannot stand the thought of needles, anesthesia with Demerol or other anesthetics are available.

Prolotherapy Provides Results: The Research

Prolotherapy repairs the painful area by proliferating fibroblasts, which regenerate normal ligament and tendon tissue at the fibro-osseous junction by causing inflammation that stimulates the natural healing process. In other words, **Prolotherapy stimulates your body to repair the painful areas.** There are two interesting studies to review here: one involving Prolotherapy to ligaments and the other on tendons. Both studies were done in the mid 1980s at the University of Iowa, in the department of orthopedics, and both studies show how Prolotherapy works.

Rabbits' Knees

The first study, by Dr. Y. King Lui, was a double-blind study to assess the influence of a proliferant solution on rabbit medial collateral ligaments (MCL).[1] One rabbit knee was injected five separate times over a six-week period with the proliferant solution sodium morrhuate, an extract of cod liver oil. The other MCL of the knee was injected with saline. The animal was then sacrificed and the ligaments were measured, their strength determined, and the ligaments were examined under the microscope. The results are quite impressive. **(See Figure 21-2.)**

After six weeks, Prolotherapy caused an increase in ligament mass, ligament thickness, and fibro-osseous strength. The authors summarized their findings by stating, "We demonstrated that the strength of the bone-ligament junction (fibro-osseous junction) was **significantly increased** by repeated injections of sodium morrhuate. In addition, **significant increases** in the mass, thickness, and weigh-to-length ratio of injected ligaments were found. Morphological analysis of histological sections collectively showed a statistically significant increase in collagen fibril diameters of the experimental ligament." [1]

In a similar study using sodium morrhuate, J.A. Maynard and associates looked at the results of Prolotherapy in the patellar and Achilles tendons in rabbits. The primary purpose of this investigation was to see if more insight could be gained into the underlying mechanism related to the increased separation force (stronger connective tissue formed) in the Liu study, involving sodium morrhuate injected MCL. This study found that sodium morrhuate alters the morphometric

Effects of Five Prolotherapy Treatments

	Prolotherapy-Injected Ligaments	Saline-Injected Ligaments (Control)	Percent Improvement
Ligament Mass (mg)	132.2	89.7	44
Ligament Thickness (mm)	1.01	0.79	27
Ligament Mass Length (mg/mm)	6.45	4.39	47
Junction Strength (N)	119.1	93.5	28

Figure 21-2: The Effects of Five Prolotherapy Treatments to the Medial Collateral Ligament

Prolotherapy causes a statistically significant increase in ligament mass and strength as well as bone-ligament junction strength.

features of tendons by **increasing** the gross circumference of the collagen fibrils. The researchers found that the increase in circumference appears to be due to an increase in cell population, water content, and ground substance. The researchers further clarified it by stating "the increased cell population is a common characteristic of other studies using sodium morrhuate and apparently is due to the formation of granulation tissue in the injected area. Consequently, not only is there an increase in the number of cells, but also a wider **variety** of cell types, fibroblasts, neutrophils, lymphocytes, plasma cells, and unidentifiable cells in the injected tissues. Interestingly, these findings are similar to dense connective tissues undergoing an injury-repair cycle in which the **proliferation** of cells from surrounding areolar tissue followed by granulation tissue has been well documented. This is followed by **fibroblast proliferation, increased vascular supply, and the deposition of new collagen."** [2] In summary, Prolotherapy stimulates the normal repair process that occurs after a ligament, tendon, or other connective tissue is injured. Studying the tissue under the microscope revealed an increase in the blood circulation, which brings a myriad of immune cells including macrophages, neutrophils, lymphocytes, and fibroblasts. The end result being stronger and thicker connective tissues, such as ligaments and tendons, which are especially stronger at their fibro-osseous junctions.

Injections Now or Later: Every Injured Person Will Need Injections

The skeletal muscles are the largest organ system of the human body and account for nearly 50 percent of the body weight.[3] Not counting heads, bellies, and other divisions of muscles, the *Nomina Anatomica* reported by the International Anatomical Nomenclature Committee, under the Berne Convention, lists 200 paired muscles, or a total of 400 muscles in the human skeletal system.[4] **(See Figure 21-3.)** The majority of these have tendons that allow the muscles to move the joints. All of the joints that are moved contain articular cartilage, so the joint surfaces glide easily over each other. The joints stay in place by the stabilizing effects of the joint capsule and ligaments. For instance, even for the modern

21ST century athlete who desires to excel, over 50 percent of the body weight consists of soft tissue and, most assuredly, will be injured at some time.

Potential injuries await many people, especially athletes. It is not a matter of "Will the athlete be injured?" but "When will the athlete be injured?" **Figure 21-4** lists 62 of the more common injection sites for sports injuries that are lurking every day for athletes and others.

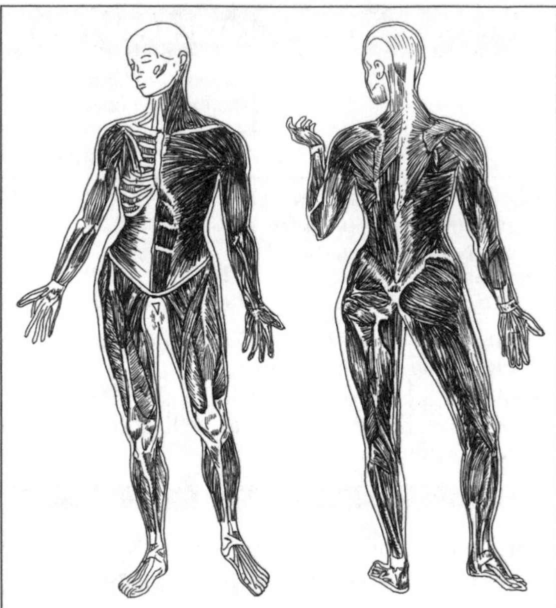

Figure 21-3: Muscles of the Body
There are 400 muscles in the body. Each can have trigger points that cause pain. (Oh, what a scary thought!)

Trigger Points

Almost all of the injuries have one thing in common; they will produce characteristic painful trigger points, indicating that there has been an injury. These trigger points hold the key to curing the injury, but also produce some kind of strong "magnetic force" because they are repeatedly attracted to things like metallic needles filled with cortisone-like substances. There is no logical reason for injuries to be treated with steroids or cortisone shots. There must be some "magnetic force" drawing the needles into the body! Obviously that is a joke, but it does make you wonder. All athletes who are serious about their careers who sustain athletic injuries will be offered a quick fix. At this point, the athletes will make perhaps one of the most important career decisions: "To inject or not to inject—that is the question." The other question is, "What should be injected?" It is best to contemplate these questions while in the privacy of your own home and not while laying on an orthopedist's examining table, after being seen for an injury. **(See Figure 21-5.)** This is not the time to make such an important decision. To help you make the best decision, we will look at why trigger points form and why Prolotherapy is the King of all injection techniques. Long live the King!

What Are Trigger Points and Why Do They Form?

Trigger points explain so much about life, yet they are seldom discussed in medical conversations, let alone in medical school or medical training. Trigger points rule! Once a person starts getting trigger points, they take over—**they literally rule**

POSSIBLE INJECTION SITES GROUPED BY BODY PART

LUMBOSACRAL
Erector spinae
Quadratus lumborum
Sacroiliac joint
Lumbar facet joints
Lumbar and spinous process

HIP
Greater trochanteric bursa
Intra-articular joint
Lateral femoral cutaneous nerve
Piriformis tendon

KNEE
Pre-patellar bursa
Pes anserine bursa
Cruciate ligaments
Collateral ligaments
Bakers' cyst
Intra-articular cartilage
Biceps femoris tendon
Patellar tendon

LEG AND ANKLE
Medial tibial tendo-osseous junction
Tibiotalar joint
Talofibular ligament
Anterior tibialis

LEG AND ANKLE *(Continued)*
Posterior tibialis
Achilles tendon
Pre/post Achilles bursae

FOOT
Tarsal tunnel
Plantar fascia
Interdigital nerve
Metatarsophalangeal joint
Sinus tarsi
Spring ligament

PELVIS
Ischial bursa
Pubic symphysis
Adductor tendon
Hamstring tendon

SHOULDER
Subacromial bursa
Acromioclavicular joint
Longhead biceps sheath
Glenohumeral ligament
Rotator cuff tendon

NECK
Cervico thoracic muscles
Cervical facets
Cervical transverse process
Annular ligament
Collateral ligament
Costovertebral junctions

ELBOW
Cubital tunnel
Medial epicondyle
Lateral epicondyle
Intra-articular joint
Olecranon bursa
Annular ligament
Collateral ligaments

WRIST
Ganglion cyst
Carpal tunnel
De Quervain sheath
Carpometacarpal joint
Radiocarpal joint
Ulno-carpal joint

HAND
Flexor tendon sheath
Flexor tendon cyst
Metacarpal joints
Collateral ligaments

Figure 21-4: Possible Injection Sites Grouped by Body Part

In the case of athletes, it's not a matter of ***if,*** but ***when*** they are going to get injected. A more important question is: Injected with what?

Adapted from Injury Clinic: Injection Techniques and Use in the Treatment of Sports Injuries, *Warren A. Scott © 1996*

your life. Living with trigger points is no fun. They can make you grouchy and edgy. Yes, trigger points rule! It is about time we started taking them seriously.

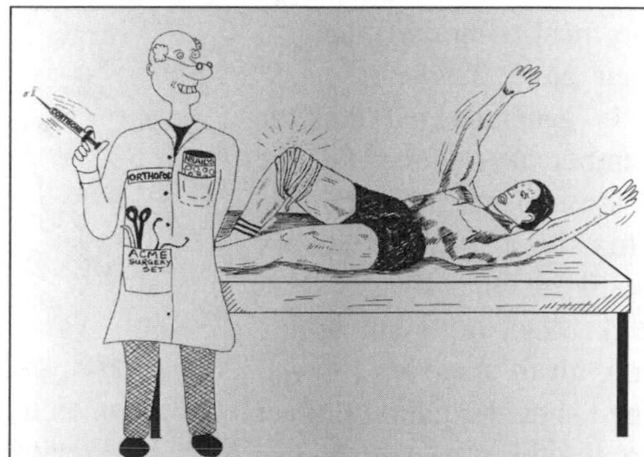

Figure 21-5: The Injured Person's Worst Nightmare

Behold the orthopedist's most "deadly" weapon on cartilage...the cortisone shot.

A trigger point is technically defined as a hyperirritable spot in skeletal muscle that is associated with a hypersensitive palpable nodule in a taut band. The spot is painful on compression and can give rise to characteristic referred pain, referred tenderness, motor dysfunction, and autonomic nervous system phenomena.[5] Trigger points are painful areas in muscles that cause positive "jump signs." They can cause local pain, referred pain down the extremity or at distant sites, muscle weakness, and even autonomic phenomena such as numbness or a severe sensitivity to touch on the skin. Yes, trigger points rule, because people who have them all over the body know that they are present because of the significant pain they are feeling.

Between 85 to 93 percent of musculoskeletal pain sufferers exhibit trigger points.[6, 7] Interestingly enough, about 50 percent of us have latent trigger points just waiting to be activated! That is right! When studies are done on asymptomatic people, about 50 percent of them have these trigger points that refer pain when palpated and are just primed to start causing pain![5, 8, 9] This high percentage of latent trigger points in asymptomatic people explains why some people who sustain small "fender-bender" collisions end up with severe, significant, non-healing pain. This also explains why small "fender-bender" type accidents can lead to unrelenting pain syndromes. The small collisions are not the primary cause for the years of unresolving pain. The underlying trigger points are actually the cause. Remove the trigger points and the pain is completely and permanently cured.

Symptoms from Trigger Points

Trigger points cause pain that is often poorly localized and of aching quality. The pain is often referred to a distant site, along with numbness or paresthesias (prickly feelings). When the trigger point is palpated, the pain may sharpen and the referral pain pattern becomes more distinct. **(See Figure 21-6.)**

Some of the most active people are children, adolescents, and teenagers. Guess what has been found to be the most common source of their pain? Trigger points![10] It is generally felt that the number of trigger points we possess increases with age. This is a typical history heard in our office in Oak Park, "Doctor, I am telling you, all of a sudden I developed shoulder pain. I did not do anything usual. It just appeared all of a sudden." The cause of the pain in such a scenario is a latent trigger point that has become active. Any of us, at any time, may activate a latent trigger point. The key is to get rid of any latent trigger points.

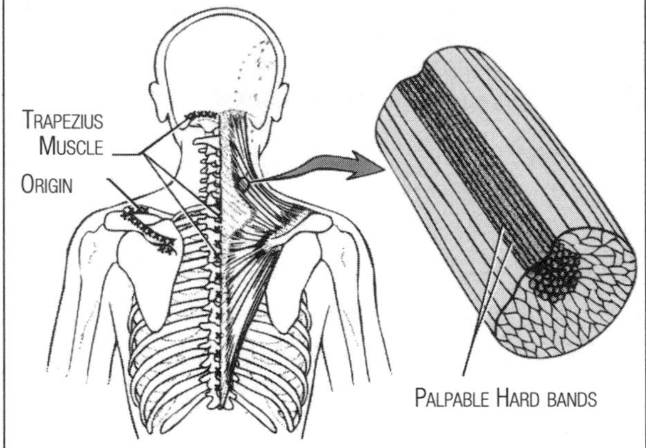

Figure 21-6: Trapezius Muscle Trigger Point
Palpation on the trigger point is not only tender but can refer pain to distant sites. In this case, the trigger point is causing headaches.

Besides causing referred pain, numbness, and paresthesias, trigger points can also cause disturbances in motor and autonomic functions. The disturbances of motor functions include spasm of other muscles, weakness of the involved muscle

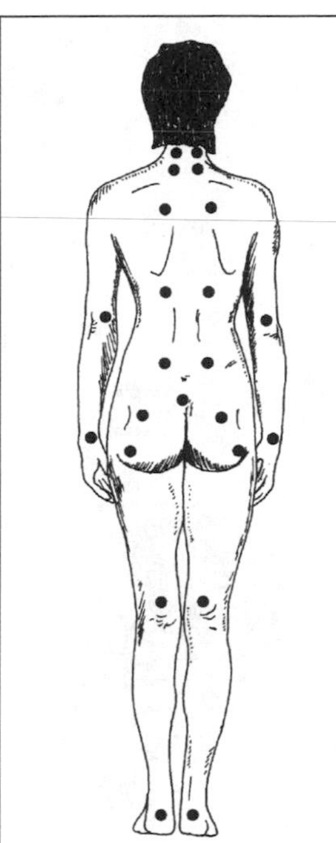

Figure 21-7: Common Trigger Point Sites

The most common areas for trigger points are the shoulders, neck, and lower back. Palpating trigger points gives positive "jump signs."

function, loss of coordination, and decreased work-tolerance of the involved muscle. This is especially devastating for the athlete because muscle control, coordination, and power are the fundamental basics for performing well in sports. Getting rid of the trigger points in these people resolves all the motor problems.

Autonomic problems can also arise from trigger points because of dysfunction of the autonomic nervous system. This is the part of the nervous system that functions automatically, controlling functions such as breathing, balance, circulation, and blood flow. Symptoms of autonomic dysfunction that can occur because of trigger points include abnormal sweating, persistent lacrimation (tearing), persistent coryza (allergic runny nose), excessive salivation, imbalance, dizziness, tinnitus (ringing in the ears), and cold hands and/or feet.[5]

Physical examination generally consists of localized spots of tenderness in the muscles, especially around the regions of the neck, shoulder, lower back, and face. There are trigger points that have been identified in just about every one of the 200 muscle pairs of the body. **(See Figure 21-7.)** Sometimes the trigger points may be felt by palpation as a taut nodule along with a tight muscle around the area. Palpating the trigger point may elicit a muscle contraction, called the local twitch response.

The best test for diagnosing a trigger point is **M**y **R**eproducibility **I**nstrument test (MRI). In this test, the examiner's thumb is pressed into the muscles. **(See Figure 21-8.)** If local and referred pain is elicited, a trigger point has been found. Many times patients will say, "That's it! That is the exact pain that I am feeling." Reproducing the pain will, most likely, give you the source of the pain. The formation and the relief of trigger points have formed much of the basis of pain management, sports medicine and physiotherapy, as we know it today.

Stretching, ultrasound, and ice are the usual and customary methods used to treat trigger points. To understand why Prolotherapy is not yet at the forefront of pain mangement, let's review some of the accepted theories regarding the formation and treatment of trigger points.

THE MYOFASCIAL PAIN THEORY

During a phone conversation with Janet Travell, M.D., about two months before she died, Ross asked her the following question, "Dr. Travell, why do you not believe the major cause of trigger points is injury to the ligaments?" She responded, "Whatever I have written—that is my answer." She had a right to give whatever answer she desired, since she was 95 years old at that time. She and Dr. Hemwall knew each other. She, of course, knew of Dr. Hackett's work in Prolotherapy. Unfortunately, the proposed cause of trigger points in the Travell camp is much different than in the Hackett-Hemwall, and now the Hackett-Hemwall-Hauser camp.

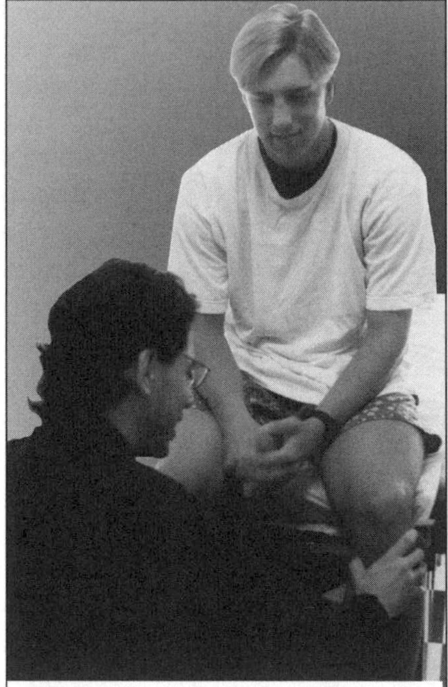

Figure 21-8: A Positive "Jump Sign"
In this photo, Dr. Hauser is eliciting a "positive jump sign" on professional tennis player Gregg Hill.

Janet Travell, M.D., championed the now traditionally accepted Myofascial Pain Theory, describing the pain experienced in the fascia (tissue) surrounding the muscles. Janet Travell published some 40 papers on trigger points between 1942 and 1990 and coined the term Myofascial Pain Syndrome.[11, 12] She published the first volume of *The Trigger Point Manual* in 1983 and the second in 1992.[5] The main tenets for her theory on the muscular origin of pain are from a 1952 report by her and J. Rinzler, in which the pain patterns of trigger points in 32 skeletal muscles were depicted in the medical journal *Postgraduate Medicine*, entitled in one article, "The Myofascial Genesis of Pain."[13]

Myofascial Pain Syndrome refers to the sensory, motor, and autonomic symptoms caused by the myofascial trigger points. Neck pain, headaches, and trigger points in the trapezius muscles that upon palpation reproduced the pain, would indicate a condition called Trapezius Myofascial Pain Syndrome. These names would then become the patients' "diagnoses" so that a name could be given to their pain complaints.

Janet Travell, M.D., and her proteges believe that the main sources of chronic pain are the trigger points, and that the primary pathology causing the trigger points is in the muscle itself or in the small nerves to the muscles. The evidence for this was derived from scientific information where some abnormalities in the excitability of the endplates (nerves) to the trigger points were found, and some biopsy specimens showed evidence of muscle fiber degeneration. The problem with this is that even the text, entitled *Travell & Simons' Myofascial Pain and Dysfunction, The Trigger Point Manual,* published in 1999, states, "In muscles accessible to palpation, a myofascial trigger point is consistently found within a palpable taut band. Theoretically and clinically, the taut band is a basic criterion of a trigger point. However, by itself it is an ambiguous finding. Taut bands are found in asymptomatic subjects with no evidence of tender nodules or trigger points." In regard to taut bands…It is difficult to measure with accuracy, specificity, and reliability. Studies indicate that palpable taut bands can be present in normal muscles without any other indication of abnormality such as tenderness or pain."[5]

The Myofascial Pain Theory is based on the premise that the basic underlying problem is in the muscle or within the electrical activity of the muscle itself. This so-called abnormality causes a taut band in some muscle fibers, which is felt as a taut band or nodule and, thus, a trigger point develops. Treatment is, therefore, directed at correcting this taut nodule through specific treatments to cause trigger point release. The main treatments used are spray and stretch, myofascial release massage, osteopathic techniques such as strain-counterstrain, skin rolling, biofeedback, heat and ice, ultrasound, iontophoresis, electrical stimulation, posture work, and our favorite—injections.

Treating these trigger points and trying to get rid of them is what **drives the chronic pain business in America.** Myofascial trigger points are reportedly aggravated by the following:

- Strenuous use of the muscle
- Passively stretching the muscle
- Pressure on the trigger point
- Placing the involved muscle in the shortened position for a prolonged period of time (this is why people wake up stiff and achy)
- Sustained and repeated contraction of the involved muscle
- Cold damp weather, viral infections, or periods of marked nervous tension

THE TRIGGER POINTS ARE TREATED BY THE FOLLOWING:

- Short periods of rest
- Low, steady passive stretching of the involved muscles
- Moist heat applied to the trigger point
- Short periods of light activity with movement
- Specific physiotherapy modalities for Myofascial Pain Syndrome[14]

Since the condition is caused by a supposed muscle problem, and the trigger points typically involve taut bands or nodules, then it would make sense to stretch those nodules to get them to relax. Those who espouse the Myofascial Pain Syndrome Theory point out, "The key to treating trigger points is to lengthen the muscle fibers that are shortened by the trigger point mechanisms."[14] The main way that myofascial therapists do this is by a spray-and-stretch technique.

Vapocoolant sprays are dispensed in a fine stream onto the skin, and then the muscle is slowly stretched. This technique is generally done by physical therapists. Each muscle is stretched in a particular manner.[5, 14] Other techniques are also utilized to try and stretch the muscle to get rid of the trigger points. This is usually the goal of each session of physiotherapy.

Every physical therapist, chiropractor, osteopath, medical doctor, Rolfer, and other physiotherapists, both in this country and abroad, know about the work of Janet Travell, M.D., and her associates. Anyone doing any kind of pain therapy has a copy of one of her textbooks. Her contribution to pain management and the publicity it brought to the idea of trigger points and the research involved in them has been monumental.

Factors Perpetuating Myofascial Trigger Points

Why do some people get trigger points and others do not? What perpetuates the trigger points? These questions have been intensively studied. The most common factors said to perpetuate myofascial trigger points are mechanical stresses, nutritional inadequacies, metabolic and endocrine deficiencies, psychological factors, chronic medical problems, and impaired sleep. Perhaps the most common of these problems is mechanical stress caused by skeletal asymmetry and disproportions. Asymmetries include lower-limb leg-length inequalities. Inequalities may be seen everywhere, including the feet, where one toe may be longer than another. This is called Morton's foot and is caused by a long second metatarsal bone. Other sources of mechanical stress include muscular stress, misfitting furniture (e.g., poorly positioned computer terminals), poor posture (hunching over the computer), abuse of muscles, and prolonged immobility.

Nutritional, metabolic, and endocrine deficiencies have also been shown to perpetuate trigger points and make some patients unresponsive to therapy. Vitamins B and C deficiencies, as well as iron and other trace mineral deficiencies, are quite common in people with trigger points. Hypometabolism caused by suboptimal thyroid function, hyperuricemia, and hypoglycemia are thought to impair muscle function. Many other factors that perpetuate trigger points have been implicated, including chronic infections, impaired sleep, smoking, stress, and other psychological factors.[15]

Injured Ligaments: The Perpetuating Factor Commonly Overlooked as the Primary Cause of Trigger Point Formation

You do not have to look very far to realize that many of the common treatments for orthopedic injuries do not work very well. Hello! Is anyone listening? These things are not working! It makes us shudder every time we read the newspaper because at any moment there may be a new, invasive, expensive pain treatment described. You cannot even watch TV for one week without seeing that latest, most innovative pain therapy described on one of those news shows such as *Dateline* or *20/20*. One year we were attending a Broadway show in New York City, opened up *Playbill* and in it was an advertisement for percutaneous laser disc decompression advertised to end back pain with "the speed of light." On the flight home from New York, someone was reading *A Consumer's Guide to Total Joint Replacement*. What a great title! It must be from some consumer advocacy group, right? No way! This was an eight-page insert in the February 5, 1999 edition of *USA Today*. It is not enough that 200,000 Americans receive these operations each year. The surgeons want more! At the top of the first page it says, "Sponsored by the American Association of Hip and Knee Surgeons." Do you think they paid for the publications? I doubt it. Guess what was on the back page of the insert? A list of all of the "corporate sponsors." You guessed it—all of the suppliers of those artificial knees, hips, screws, and other things that orthopedists put into people with arthritis and injuries. Imagine the cost to put eight full pages in *USA Today*. For what purpose? The purpose is to assure that more of you receive knee and hip replacements. The sad fact is that a lot of patients will get them because of non-healed injuries.

Other late-breaking news on the pain front is the fact that doctors are now injecting botulism toxin into the myofascial trigger points.[15] Botulism is a condition that kills people. Now doctors are injecting the toxin into people and these people are actually electively receiving it! This fact in and of itself is enough to say, wait! Hold on! Something has to be missing. The current medical therapies cannot even get rid of a simple trigger point. Instead, they actually find the need to inject a poison into people to paralyze their muscles. That is what the botulism toxin does. It paralyzes the muscles. Someone who eats enough botulism bacteria will get massive muscle paralysis, including the breathing muscles, and eventually die of suffocation. Doctors only inject small amounts for trigger points. The fact that there are so many pain treatments, including those for trigger points, gives credence to the theory that trigger points are not a muscle problem, but are due to something else.

Any physiotherapist or masseuse can massage away muscle spasms. A doctor can inject anesthetic into the muscles and immediately eliminate a muscle spasm. Doctors can also give muscle relaxants. The question is: Why do most of the people treated this way experience a **recurrence** of their pain? Most people with trigger points who get spray and stretch, ultrasound, physiotherapy, massage, traditional "trigger point" injections, or chiropractic/osteopathic manipulation have **continual recurrences of their pain *and* their trigger points.**

Pain management is big business. Most of the money spent is not in acute pain but in chronic pain management. Myofascial pain treatments such as massage, trigger point injections, spray and stretch, and ultrasound are effective and produce excellent results **in relieving acute pain**. If the pain persists after a couple of months of receiving these techniques, **the pain will likely never be cured by**

these techniques. Typical scenarios we see are like these: "Bob, how long have you been going to the chiropractor?" Bob replies, "Six years." You question him, "You have been going every couple of weeks for six years? I think I now know why your ligaments are so weak."

"Mary, how many physical therapists, massage therapists, or other physical medicine specialists have you seen?" Mary replies, "I would say 20." You ask her, "Twenty people and they all said it had to do with your posture?" Mary replies, "For the most part." It could go on and on.

Ligament laxity as the cause of trigger points and the main perpetuating factor of trigger point pain is supported by nearly all of the literature to date on trigger points. In all of the data we have researched, most would support that statement. Let's say it again. **Ligament injury is the primary etiological basis for the development of trigger points.** In making the defense we will use Janet Travell, M.D., as our first witness.

In 1946, Drs. Janet and Willard Travell published a paper on the use of sacroiliac manipulation on 400 cases of people with low back pain. The treatment was exceptionally successful in relieving the back pain. In the paper the Travells wrote, "One of the difficulties in the diagnosis of the sacroiliac slip is the uniform failure of the customary roentgenograms to demonstrate any misalignment of the sacrum and ilium." They went on to say that a minor degree of displacement or slipping of the sacroiliac joint is, in fact, one of the manifold causes of the **confused syndrome of low back pain.** The dramatic relief of pain and disability secured by the manipulation described is, in all probability, due to the reduction of such a displacement.

They also noticed that there are often reflex muscle spasms associated with sacroiliac slips. For the relief of pain due to reflex muscular spasm, an important adjunct to sacroiliac manipulation is the infiltration of the spastic muscles with procaine hydrochloride (0.5%) or even with an isotonic solution of sodium chloride.[16] They noticed that shortly after sacroiliac displacement a referred pain may appear in a part or in the whole of the sciatic distribution, giving rise to the clinical syndrome of "sciatica." They attributed this "sciatica" to "trigger zones" in the gluteus minimus muscle. They stated in a previous report that 44 percent of 162 cases of sacroiliac slip had "sciatica complaints."[17] **(See Figure 21-9a through 21-9c.)**

The Travells wrote, "In our experience, trigger zones in the gluteus minimus muscle account to a large extent for radiating pain in the lower extremity in the absence of neurologic signs, not only in cases of sacroiliac displacement but also in many other cases of obscure low back pain. Trigger zones in this muscle apparently bear the same general relation to pain in the hip and leg, as such abnormal foci in the infraspinatus muscle, due to myalgias of the shoulder and arm. The frequency of such trigger mechanisms in the gluteal and lumbosacral regions is indicated by Kellgren's observation that in patients with sciatica, 'ligamentous and muscular lesions form by far the commonest source of pain.'"[17, 18]

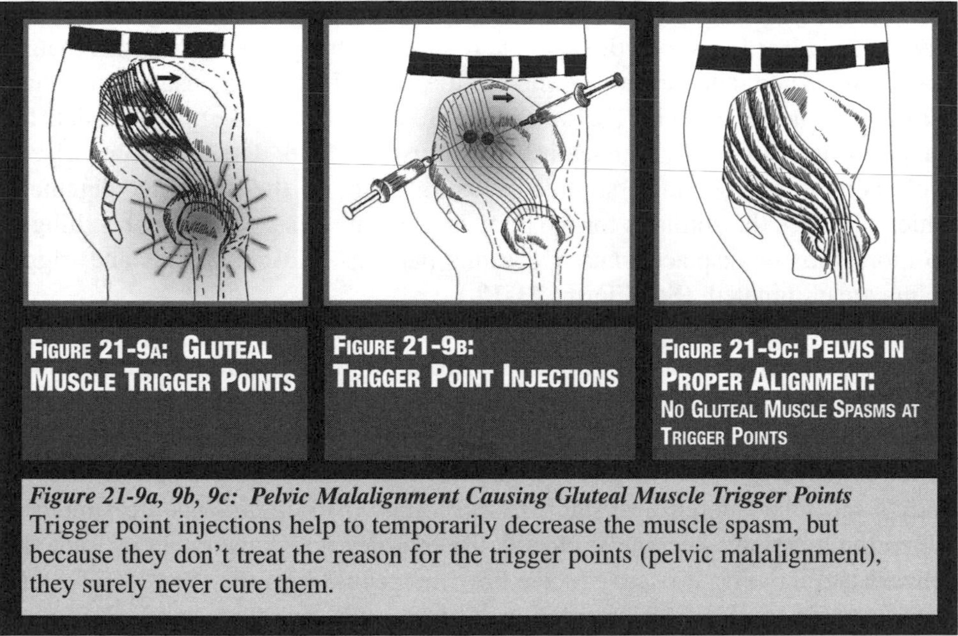

FIGURE 21-9A: GLUTEAL MUSCLE TRIGGER POINTS

FIGURE 21-9B: TRIGGER POINT INJECTIONS

FIGURE 21-9C: PELVIS IN PROPER ALIGNMENT: NO GLUTEAL MUSCLE SPASMS AT TRIGGER POINTS

Figure 21-9a, 9b, 9c: Pelvic Malalignment Causing Gluteal Muscle Trigger Points
Trigger point injections help to temporarily decrease the muscle spasm, but because they don't treat the reason for the trigger points (pelvic malalignment), they surely never cure them.

It is clear from the Travells' paper that trigger points occur with bony "displacements or slips." Bones only move out of alignment if the stabilizing structures themselves have been injured. **The main stabilizing structures in the joints of the body are the ligaments.** It is evident in this paper that manipulation of the sacroiliac joint was helping a lot of people and resulting in many of their sciatic complaints going away. The Travells also wrote something very interesting in this paper. "When reduction of the sacroiliac displacement is not achieved and maintained, by repeated manipulation if necessary, local infiltration and other types of treatment aimed at relaxing spasm of the muscles will commonly **fail** to secure more than transient relief of pain so long as the displacement is allowed to persist."[17] Wow, what a statement! If the manipulation does not hold, you can get rid of that muscle spasm by injecting it to death or use other treatments, but the relief of pain **will be only temporary**. This indicates that the cause of muscle spasm is not a problem in the muscle itself. It must be due to the fact that the sacroiliac joint will not stay in place. Why does this occur? Correct this problem and you will cure the gluteus minimus trigger point problem.

The sacroiliac joint will not stay in place because the sacroiliac ligaments are weakened. When they are weakened, sacroiliac "slips or displacements" occur, which then lead to gluteus minimus muscle spasms. Manipulation of the sacroiliac joint, when it permanently relieves the displacement, allows procaine injections to permanently relieve the muscle spasms in the gluteus minimus when they are needed. However, when the sacroiliac ligament laxity is of such a degree that manipulation alone will not stabilize the joint, the anesthetic injection will not do a thing to help the situation. Only a little bit of pain relief occurs. This is what we have noticed in clinical practice. People in pain are trigger point injected, manipulated, massaged, and physiotherapied to the tune of tens of thousands of dollars for only temporary effects. The treatments do provide temporary pain relief; but for permanent pain relief something else must be done. The something else is Prolotherapy. Prolotherapy stimulates the growth of the sacroiliac ligament, which provides the stimulus for the bony alignments to stay in place, resulting in no more slips or displacements. Once this happens, muscle spasms and trigger points are eliminated. **(See Figure 21-10.)**

Most people do not realize that the body's response to ligamentous injury is muscle spasm. The reason for this is two-fold: to provide joint protection/stabilization and to notify the brain that the body is hurt. Unfortunately, the brains of many people register the pain signal as meaning, "I better take some anti-inflammatories or get a cortisone shot to stop the pain!" The muscle spasms are the body's secondary defense to stabilize the joints, if the ligaments are stretched. When the ligaments become stretched, the muscles now have to act as joint stabilizers and movers. It is easy to see how they could become tense, knotty, and hyperirritable to electrical stimulation. **The muscles are now doing the job of both the ligaments and the muscles, and, therefore, may become increasingly fatigued.** This fatigue is manifested as tightness, trigger points, and, eventually, full-blown Myofascial Pain Syndrome. By focusing on the muscles, the clinicians are missing the central factor in curing the problem. The cure lies in strengthening the ligaments and stopping the reason for the muscle spasms.

If you think about athletics and sports injuries, for example, how many times during rugby, soccer, hockey, basketball, or football matches are the players smashing each other's muscles? The thighs, back, chest, and calves are getting clobbered. A few sessions in the hot tub and a couple of rubdowns, and the muscles feel great. Again, it goes back to the fact that muscle physiology and ligament physiology are **completely different**. Muscles have too big of an aerobic capacity and blood supply not to heal well after injury. Muscles are

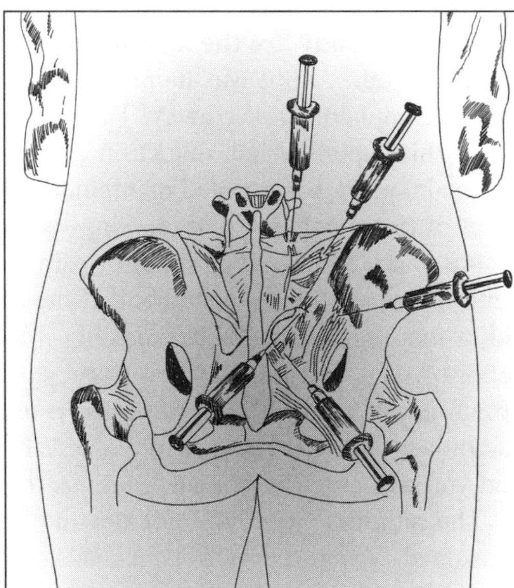

Figure 21-10: Prolotherapy to the Sacroiliac Ligaments
Prolotherapy to the sacroiliac joint treats the cause of the pelvic malalignment and gluteal muscle trigger points, so muscle spasms are **permanently** eliminated.

beefy red and the blood circulation in them can increase 20 times in a matter of minutes during a sprint, for instance. Ligaments, on the other hand, have a horribly slow metabolism, manifested by their white appearance and poor blood supply. You can exercise and obtain physiotherapy day and night, and they will not have any substantial effect on ligament growth and regeneration. There is only one way to stimulate the proliferation of ligaments and that is by Prolotherapy.

LIGAMENT TRIGGER POINTS AND REFERRAL PATTERNS

There is no doubt that muscle trigger points exist and have referral pain patterns. Around the same time that Janet Travell, M.D., was studying muscle trigger points and diagramming the referral pain patterns, George S. Hackett, M.D., of Canton, Ohio, was doing the same thing for ligaments. **(See Figure 21-11.)** He published his work, as Dr. Travell did, in some of the best medical publications of the day, including the *Journal of the American Medical Association,* the *American Journal of Surgery,* and the *AMA Archives of Surgery.*[19-21] In 1956, he published the first edition of his book *Ligament and Tendon Relaxation Treated by Prolotherapy.*[22] So well-accepted was his work, that not only did the American Medical Association allow publication of his research in their journals, but Dr. Hackett himself sold his books and presented his research at AMA conventions in the late 1950s.

DR. GEORGE HACKETT: LIGAMENT REFERRAL PATTERNS

Dr. Hackett was the first one to coin the term Prolotherapy. After doing about 2,000 injections, he diagrammed the referral patterns of the neck and lower back ligaments. **(See Figure 21-11.)** These drawings are very similar to the ones by Dr. Travell. The reason for this is that ligament laxity causes muscle trigger points to develop. The ligament laxity referral patterns and muscle trigger point patterns are very similar because they have the same etiology.

Dr. Hackett is known for some famous lines such as these:

- **"A joint is only as strong as its weakest ligament."**
- **"Most joint pain is ligament pain."**
- **"The evidence appears to be conclusive that relaxed supra- and interspinus ligaments are an etiological factor in the occurrence of ruptured disc."**
- **"The injection of a local anesthetic into the ligaments of an ankle for relief of pain following an injury...if given to enable an athlete to continue activity...is to be deplored."**[22]

The third and fifth editions of Dr. Hackett's books are still available. Anyone serious about further study into the subject of Prolotherapy is encouraged to read one of these. It is best to understand Prolotherapy in the way he put it, "The treatment consists of the injection of a solution within the relaxed ligament and tendon which will stimulate the production of new fibrous tissue and bone cells that will strengthen the '**weld**' of fibrous tissue and bone to stabilize the articulation and permanently eliminate the disability. To the treatment of proliferating new cells, I have applied the name Prolotherapy from the word 'prolix,' Latin meaning offspring: 'proliferate'—to produce new cells in rapid succession (Webster's Dictionary). My definition of Prolotherapy as applied medically in the treatment of skeletal disability is 'the rehabilitation of an incompetent structure by the generation of new cellular tissue."[22]

Dr. Hackett wrote about and published works that proved that ligaments have referral patterns. He did so after giving 20,000 intraligamentous injections in diagnosing and treating ligament and tendon relaxation in 1,816 patients over a 20-year period.[22] He could totally eliminate the ligament trigger point pain as well as the referral pain pattern by doing Prolotherapy, because there was anesthetic in the Prolotherapy solution. This is still done today. Prolotherapy has not only a proliferative effect, but a trigger point abolishing one.

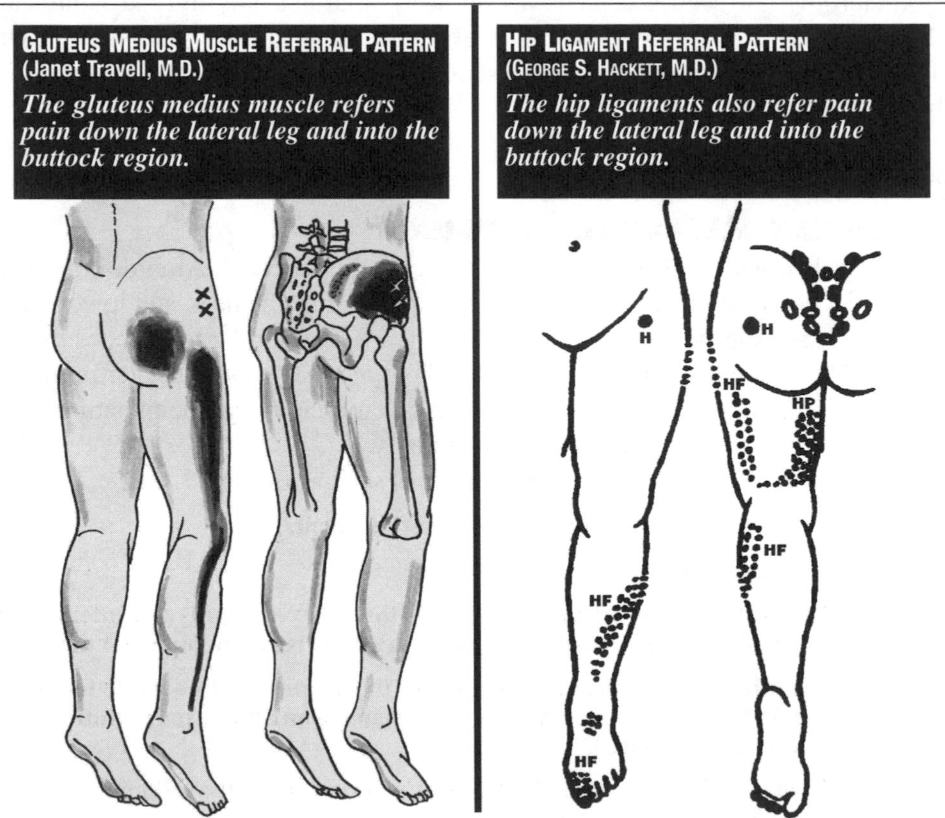

GLUTEUS MEDIUS MUSCLE REFERRAL PATTERN
(Janet Travell, M.D.)
The gluteus medius muscle refers pain down the lateral leg and into the buttock region.
HIP LIGAMENT REFERRAL PATTERN
(GEORGE S. HACKETT, M.D.)
The hip ligaments also refer pain down the lateral leg and into the buttock region.
H
H
HF
HP
HF
HF
HF

Figure 21-11: Components of Travell and Hackett Referral Patterns
Notice the similarities between the referral patterns.

Dr. Hackett was not the only one who identified ligament trigger points and referral pain patterns over the years; we call to the witness stand Janet Travell, M.D., again. She reported on the fact that acute sprains of the ankle were accompanied by multiple trigger points around the ligament and referred pain to the ankle and foot.[23, 24] Others have identified trigger points resulting from acute sprains around the knee, wrist, and metacarpophalangeal joint of the thumb that were eliminated by injection.[25] Leriche, Gorrell, and Kraus also noticed trigger points from ligamentous injury that responded well to injection therapy.[26-29]

Connective Tissue Deficiency Also Fits into the Myofascial Pain Model

There are many reasons given as to why people fail to be cured from traditional myofascial pain treatments to relieve trigger points. People are subjected to numerous trigger point injections with anesthetic and steroids, spray and stretch, manipulation, electrical stimulation, TENS units, massage, and various other kinds of physiotherapy. These treatments provide some temporary relief, but nothing long-lasting or permanent. People with trigger points and various myofascial pain complaints are then given Elavil or some other antidepressant to help them sleep. One of the perpetuating factors for the development of myofascial trigger points, as depicted above, is nutritional, metabolic, and endocrine deficiencies. This obviously fits in perfectly with the localized/systemic connective tissue deficiency model.

As previously mentioned, non-healing of chronic injuries, whether from sports, falls, or other things, is best described as an inability to grow or repair connective tissue. Connective tissue deficiency (or Hauser's Syndrome) is a disorder characterized by deficiency in the amount, function, or strength of the connective tissues, including ligaments and tendons. There are two types of connective tissue deficiency: systemic and localized. The person with aches and pains all over the body most likely has a systemic connective tissue deficiency. A tennis player with a shoulder problem may be described as having a localized connective tissue deficiency problem in his rotator cuff tendon, for example. In the later example, Prolotherapy to the tendon is most likely all that is needed. If no improvement is seen after three treatments, then a systemic connective tissue deficiency is suspected, and diagnostic testing is performed to see why the patient is not healing. The testing may include vitamin and amino acid levels, Metabolic Typing, pH testing, allergy testing, hormone testing, connective tissue breakdown levels, as well as fatty-acid analysis or malabsorption studies. Patients should heal very quickly. The point here is that they will not be cured until their bodies have the ability to be healed by growing and regenerating connective tissue.

It is known that metabolic, nutritional, and endocrine factors play a role in perpetuating trigger points. They do so not because of some underlying muscle pathology, but because the nutrients and hormones necessary to repair and regenerate the tissue that is breaking down each day are not being produced. If the ability to regenerate connective tissues has been lost, then guess what happens with each workout—less and less tissue regeneration. The point will come when the amount of muscle breakdown and other connective tissues outweighs the amount of build-up. Soon pain, weakness, and a decline in physical agility appear. What would be the traditional remedy in such a scenario? Tell someone to work out more frequently and aggressively in order to improve performance. This is the wrong advice. The additional workouts cause an even greater amount of breakdown of connective tissue, so the pain, weakness, and physical condition worsen. Many folks have gone through the above scenario and feel badly because they believe that they are the cause of the injury because they are not working out enough.

Let's take a moment to look at a letter from Jack Nicklaus. **(See Figure 21-12.)** Ross wrote to him in 1993 and he graciously wrote back. In the letter you can see that Jack has been told that the impetus for his perpetuating back pain is related to his not doing certain exercises. In other words, it is **his fault** that he has pain. Well, five years later he had a hip replacement. What would cause his hip to get so deteriorated over the years? Poor exercising ability? No, ligament injury. Ligament injury causes arthritis. Most likely, ligament injury was causing his pain and subsequent muscle spasms and tightness.

For an individual experiencing more and more pain after workouts, and noticing a drop in athletic performance for no apparent reason, an evaluation for connective tissue deficiency is a good idea. It is usually amazing that so many nutrient deficiencies, bowel problems, infections, and hormonal imbalances are easily detected and corrected. Generally within several months, patients not only return to baseline, but **surpass** it running! Their speed increases, their strength increases, and their physical performance starts soaring. They gain unbelievable energy, their muscle tone improves, and their lean body-mass index

Jack Nicklaus

May 4, 1993

Ross A. Hauser, M.D.
715 Lake Street
Oak Park, IL 60301

Dear Dr. Hauser:

Thank you for your recent letter and for your concern about my back.

The media has been paying a lot of attention lately to my back problems, particularly the sciatic nerve problem that plagued me for most of last year. However, I am making steady progress with my trouble spots thanks to the guidance of ________ an anatomical functionalist with whom I began working in November of 1988. ______ put me on an exercise program which tones and strengthens my muscles so that my body provides itself with proper support and alignment from within. I follow this regimen faithfully and, in fact, haven't missed a day since I started.

Of course, it took me a lifetime to develop these problems, and I didn't expect to completely get rid of them overnight. Occasionally I have a flare-up, but _____ has educated me in the ways to work through it.

I appreciate your sending the articles to me; nevertheless, I feel my particular problems will continue to be best addressed by the program I have outlined above. I really do appreciate your concern however, and I wish you continued success.

Sincerely,

/jb

Figure 21-12: Jack Nicklaus' Letter to Ross

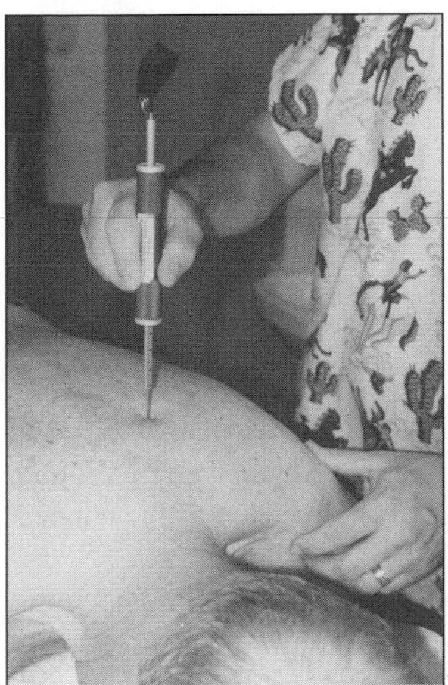

Figure 21-13: The Dolorimeter
This device measures the amount of pressure it takes to elicit pain at the trigger points. It can be used to find latent trigger points or document a person's progress with Prolotherapy.

skyrockets. Especially for athletes who want to excel, all of this analysis and testing should be done **before an injury occurs, preferably in the off-season.**

Patients desiring good preventative medicine should be checked by a Prolotherapy specialist for active and latent trigger points. If these are not treated, they will often appear at an inopportune time.

At Caring Medical in Oak Park, Illinois, sometimes a dolorimeter is used to document the amount of pressure needed to elicit pain over the potential trigger point sites. **(See Figure 21-13.)** Normal values are greater than four pounds of pressure. If less than four pounds of pressure elicit pain over a ligament, tendon, and/or muscle, both the patient and the physician know that this is an area of weakness, and a "latent" trigger point is found (especially if it refers pain to another spot when palpated.) That particular area must be strengthened because it has a localized connective tissue deficiency. If only one or two areas are found, then Prolotherapy or Neural Therapy can be given at those sites. Neural Therapy injections, in this case, are similar to traditional trigger point injections except no steroid is used, only anesthetic. If many trigger points are found, a whole metabolic-nutritional program should be initiated. The painful sites will then be evaluated after the patient has undergone at least from one to three months of aggressive nutritional intervention. Many times, most of the painful areas are eliminated by this intervention alone.

Trigger Point Therapy: Prolotherapy Versus the Rest

Some people are full of trigger points when they are examined. This is often because of the massive amounts of exercising they do, which results in the breakdown of a large amount of connective tissue. If the patient has a good diet and no nutritional, endocrine, or metabolic deficiencies, the regeneration of muscle, ligament, and tendon tissue after exercise occurs, and the indivdual continues to improve performance. However, when the regenerative process slows, for example, due to aging, eating junk food, becoming stressed because of too many pimples or a bad date, then connective tissue deficiency sets in. The development of connective tissue deficiency manifests itself in different ways, depending on the activity.

Figure 21-14: Trigger Point Injections Versus Prolotherapy

	Trigger Point Injections	Prolotherapy
Substance injected	Anesthetic/corticosteroid	Proliferant/anesthetic
Injection site	Muscle belly	Fibro-osseous junction
Mechanism of action	Relax muscles	Regenerate ligaments
Effect on joint stability	None	Enhanced
Immediate pain relief	Yes	Yes
Lasting pain relief	No	Yes
Recurrences	Frequent	Few

A jogger may manifest connective tissue deficiency as an Achilles tendon injury. Prolotherapy to regenerate the tendon is generally all that is needed. If the connective tissue deficiency continues, then various trigger points will form.

As noted above, part of traditional trigger point therapy is injections. Understand that there is a significant difference between traditional trigger point injections and Prolotherapy. These differences are summarized in **Figure 21-14.**

Traditional trigger point injections are done directly into the muscles where the trigger points are located. Some physicians just stick the needle into the trigger point and do not inject any solution; a technique called dry needling. There are various trigger point solutions used, which can include procaine, lidocaine, longer-acting local anesthetics, isotonic saline, corticosteroid, and botulin A toxin, depending on the experience of the physician. Some studies have shown that dry needling is as effective as injecting anesthetics in getting rid of trigger points.[30, 31] The problem is that the most people's trigger points return or are never permanently cured with dry needling or trigger point injections. Traditional trigger point injections do help decrease trigger point pain, and sometimes eliminate it, but rarely do they cure it, regardless of what is injected.

From the beginning it was evident to anyone who read the work of Dr. Hackett, especially for those who actually practiced his Prolotherapy techniques themselves, that every other treatment for chronic pain **pales** in comparison. Dr. Hackett was the consummate researcher. He did the animal studies proving that Prolotherapy did indeed proliferate and regenerate tendon tissue. He went on to human studies, publishing his work in peer-reviewed journals.[19-21] In the third edition of his book *Ligament and Tendon Relaxation Treated by Prolotherapy*, he writes, "I am fully convinced that our present knowledge of ligaments and tendons will result in a reduction of spine operations by 90 percent, similar to that of goiter and mastoid surgery. Every orthopedic surgeon who has visited us to be treated and/or observed our work has enthusiastically adopted the method."[22]

His opinion on steroid injections was "Cortisone preparations allay inflammatory pain in acute conditions but **should not be used in the treatment of chronic ligament and tendon relaxation because it retards and diminishes the normal process of fibro-osteogenetic proliferation that can be stimulated only by**

Prolotherapy. This has been demonstrated in our present series of animal studies in Mercy Hospital. The use of cortisone in acute sprains should be avoided because it interferes with the normal repair of tissues."[22] When cortisone is confronted with Prolotherapy, cortisone bows before the King. **(See Figure 21-15.)**

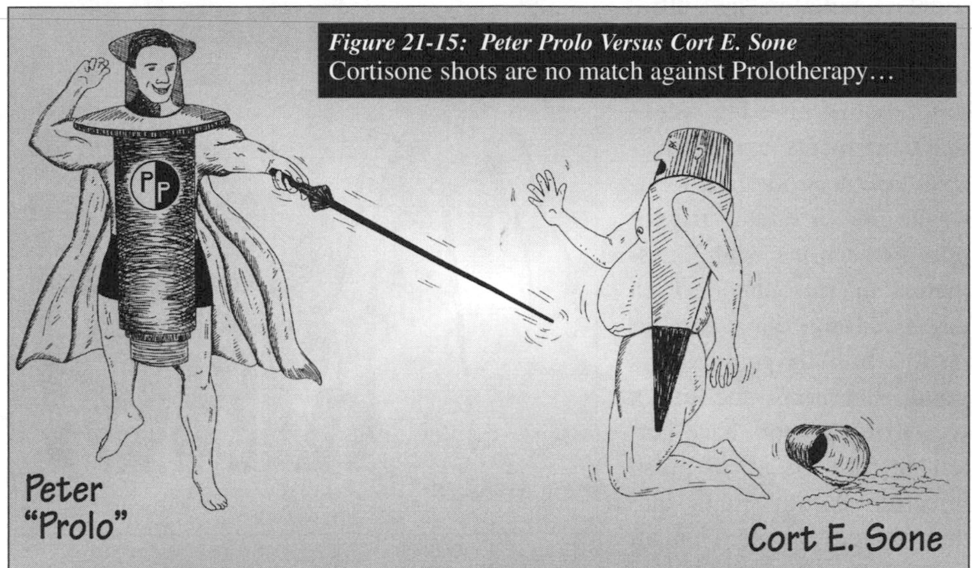

Figure 21-15: Peter Prolo Versus Cort E. Sone
Cortisone shots are no match against Prolotherapy…

Dr. Hackett, for instance, followed 656 of his Prolotherapy patients for 19 years and found that 82 percent of the patients considered themselves cured for an average of 12 years since receiving the initial Prolotherapy.[31] These kinds of statistics would be expected if Prolotherapy does what Dr. Hackett says. "It results in strengthening the 'weld' at the fibro-osseous junction, with restoration of the normal ligament function and permanent elimination of the disability, so that the individual may resume his previous activities."[32]

SUMMARY

There are many other injection techniques used in the treatment of chronic painful conditions and athletic injuries, but it is only Prolotherapy that causes the regeneration of the structures, namely the ligaments, that are responsible for the formation of trigger points. Much of sports medicine and traditional physiotherapy is based on the notion that the muscle is the primary problem as it relates to pain and trigger points. Trigger points are localized knots or taut bands in the muscle that cause local and referred pain. Each year more new, innovative, repackaged medical and surgical treatments are developed to relieve the myriad of pain complaints and athletic injuries. Since most people with pain (85-93 percent) have trigger points, something must be wrong with the treatments available for the chronic pain because not very many of them are being cured of their pain utilizing these techniques.

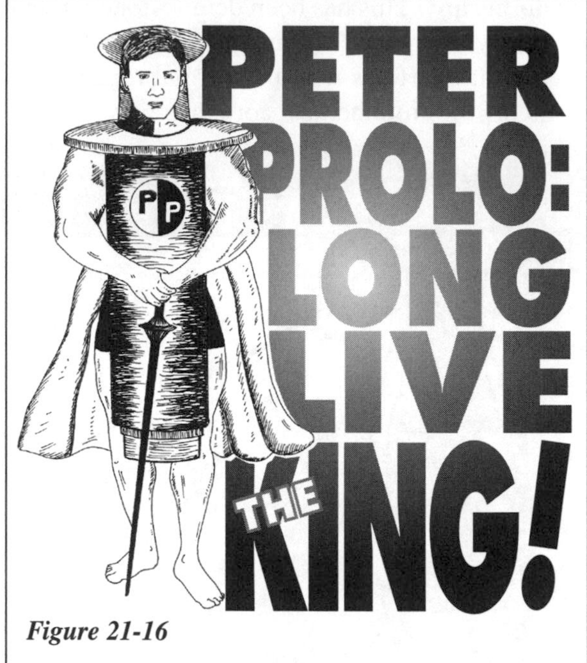

Figure 21-16

Traditional trigger point therapy involves techniques such as spray-and-stretch, massage, posture work, electrical stimulation, and ultrasound. These treatments often provide temporary relief, but within a few weeks the pain recurs and another round of physiotherapy treatments is needed. trigger point injections with anesthetics or steroids, or even dry needling, have similar results. Initially pain relief is good, but soon the effect wears off. Doctors have gotten to the point of even injecting botulin toxin into the trigger points. This all just points to the probability that the whole theory on the etiology of trigger points is wrong. Perhaps it is not primarily a muscle problem.

Muscles have a tremendous blood supply, as evidenced by their red color. Muscles heal very quickly. It is very easy to massage out a knot, yet the knot returns in a few days. Ligaments, on the other hand, are white because they have a very poor blood supply. When ligaments are injured, they often do not heal, causing the muscles to spasm to help stabilize the joint. Trigger points eventually form in and around the injured ligaments, with resultant muscle spasm. Ligament laxity and subsequent joint slippage or displacement are the underlying etiology of most trigger points. Because the underlying ligament laxity is not cured with exercise, traditional trigger point injections, or other trigger point therapies, the underlying etiology of the trigger point development goes unchecked. This explains the lack of curative results with modern orthopedic sports medicine techniques and physiotherapy regimes for the non-healing athlete or chronic pain patient.

Prolotherapy has a tremendous success rate in relieving chronic pain, on the order of an 82-percent cure as demonstrated in Dr. Hackett's studies. Prolotherapy eliminates trigger points and myofascial-type pain syndromes because it gets at the root cause of the trigger point pain, ligament injury. The ligament injury causes joint displacement. The muscles must then tighten to stabilize the joint. They eventually fatigue because, along with the new duty of stabilization, they still have to move the joint. The fatigued muscles form knots as are seen in trigger points.

Prolotherapy stabilizes the joint by stimulating ligamentous hypertrophy, thus eliminating the need for the muscle to be a joint stabilizer. This has the effect of causing muscle relaxation and a permanent resolution of the trigger points. Because of these facts, chronic pain patients from around the country are foregoing temporary pain-relieving treatments and letting the King cure them—the King whose name is Prolotherapy. Long live the King! **(See Figure 21-16.)** ■

CHAPTER 22

The Hauser Corollary

"If nothing changes, nothing changes."
—Ross A. Hauser, M.D.

Simply put, The Hauser Corollary is: "If nothing changes, nothing changes." This seems like a very simple statement, but it is actually quite complicated. As a physician, Ross is faced with the daily task of convincing patients to change their ways in order to improve their overall health. It, therefore, seems appropriate to include The Hauser Corollary in *Curing Chronic Pain with Prolotherapy*. If medical care does not change, then nothing will change. People with injuries will continue to go through the traditional cascade of treatments starting with **RICE**, progressing to NSAIDs, graduating to cortisone shots, and finally getting promoted to arthroscopies, and ending with knee and hip replacements. Yes, "If nothing changes, nothing changes."

Explaining The Hauser Corollary is often the only way to see the light bulb turning on inside a person's head. All too often we hear phrases such as, "I can't eat meat!" "I have to put ice on my knee, otherwise it swells." "I can't take vitamins—they upset my stomach." "My trainer said…" "The orthopedist insists surgery is my only option." "My doctor has never heard of Prolotherapy." "My friend says I need a cortisone shot." "I need my anti-inflammatories!" Yes, there are many applications for The Hauser Corollary.

JENNY: A GOOD EXAMPLE OF THE HAUSER COROLLARY

Jenny is a good example to illustrate this point. Jenny was an avid athlete, playing several sports. She had all the answers before she came in to see us for ankle pain. After evaluating her, it was determined that she was suffering from significant ligament laxity in her ankles, which was the cause of her pain. Perhaps even more important was the fact that she had no specific incident where she could remember injuring her ankles. Jenny also exhibited tenderness on various parts of her body in addition to her ankles. This appeared to be related to nutritional factors. When delving into her history, we discovered that her ankle pain started a couple of years prior to her visit in our office, just after she had started taking the birth control pill because of painful, irregular menstruation. The medication she was taking contained an analogue of estradiol. Her diet consisted of nearly 100 percent carbohydrates, very small amounts of protein, and she was averse to taking vitamins. Yes, she was a good candidate for The Hauser Corollary.

Jenny was, however, open to receiving Prolotherapy on her ankles, but not to correcting the multiple factors that were related to her systemic connective tissue deficiency problem. She had multiple signs and symptoms that confirmed this diagnosis, such as non-healing sports injury with no overt trauma causing the original pain; multiple tender points in other parts of her body, especially about the knees and hips; dry skin; brittle nails and hair; menstrual problems; improper diet for her metabolism; and finally, taking synthetic estradiol. In order for the Prolotherapy to be maximally effective, we needed to address Jenny's inability to heal and convince her that she needed to do something about this in order to make the Prolotherapy worth enduring the shots! Reasoning alone would be insufficient. A visual graphic of The Hauser Corollary would help Jenny understand.

THE HAUSER COROLLARY: A GRAPHIC REPRESENTATION

Prolotherapy is a treatment that stimulates the body to repair painful areas. To put it another way, it is a treatment that causes the body to grow strong connective tissue. This connective tissue is primarily collagen, which makes up ligaments and tendons. Thus, Prolotherapy causes the growth and strengthening of ligaments and tendons. When a person's injury lingers beyond the usual healing time, it typically involves the ligaments and tendons. A weakening of the connective tissue graphically represents this. Prolotherapy injections reverse this by stimulating the connective tissues to heal. As the connective tissue grows and strengthens after Prolotherapy, the person reaches the eventual point where the pain has ceased. For the patient with a strong immune system, no more treatment or additional medical care is needed. Prolotherapy was indeed a cure for this individual. **(See Figure 22-1.)**

The person with systemic connective tissue deficiency, on the other hand, experiences no specific traumatic event to start the pain because the condition itself is weakening the connective tissues. In such an instance, all (or a majority) of the body's connective tissues are weakening. This process occurs normally with age, but with a systemic connective tissue deficiency (perhaps more appropriately called The Hauser Syndrome) a person experiences an accelerated decline in connective tissue strength. This may result in sagging of the skin, thinning of the hair, and a myriad of other symptoms, the most prominent of which is pain. The first area to become painful will typically be the one used the most. For the pitcher it will be the shoulder, for the runner the knee, for the golfer the back, and so on. Just because a golfer gets back pain does not mean that golf is causing the injury. It could be primarily a systemic connective tissue deficiency problem. If the golfer, in such an instance, just receives Prolotherapy, the pain relief from Prolotherapy will only last a certain amount of time. Once the connective tissue strength decreases below the pain-threshold point, the pain will recur. A cure will

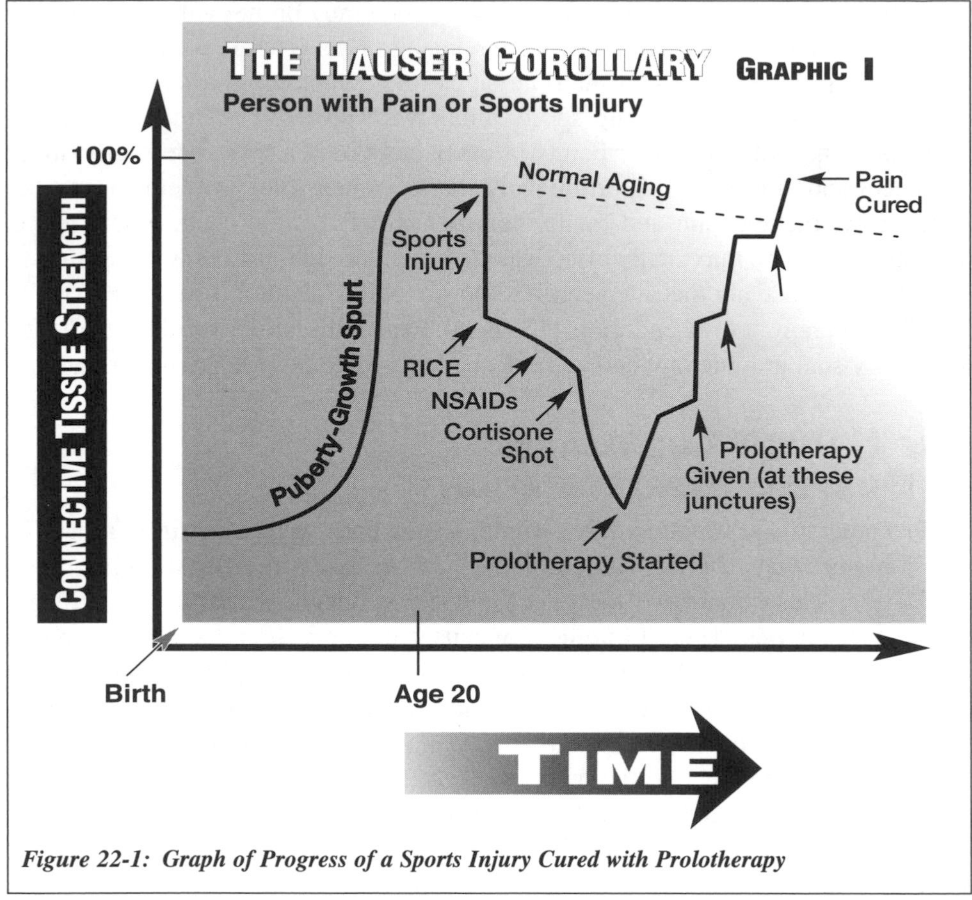

Figure 22-1: Graph of Progress of a Sports Injury Cured with Prolotherapy

only be obtained when the person receives Prolotherapy **along with** additional treatments to correct the connective tissue deficiency problem. **(See Figure 22-2.)**

THERE ARE MANY "JENNYS" OUT THERE!

Seeing connective tissue deficiency as a visual representation really hit home for Jenny. She is still taking her oral contraceptive pills, but has incorporated more protein into her diet and takes some potent nutritional supplements. Even to her amazement, her energy level has improved and the mild aching she experienced in other parts of her body is going away. The Prolotherapy relieved her ankle pain and she is back to playing her various sports. Yes, there are many Jennys out there. People who want to completely heal their injuries also want to remain out of the doctor's office—permanently. In order to accomplish this, they should start eating an appropriate diet and taking supplements to enhance connective tissue regeneration.

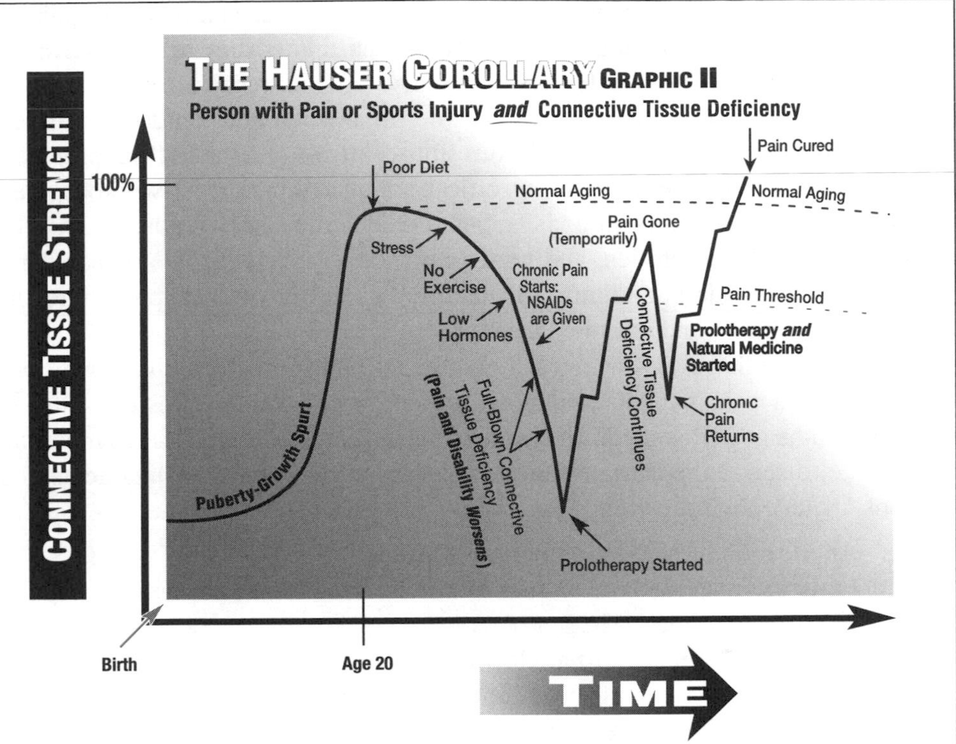

Figure 22-2: Connective Tissue Deficiency Cured with Prolotherapy and Natural Medicine
For people with connective tissue deficiency (Hauser Syndrome), Prolotherapy is utilized along with diet, stress reduction, exercise, nutriticeuticals, anabolic hormones, and other natural remedies to cure the condition.

THE POSITIVE HAUSER COROLLARY

In the positive, The Hauser Corollary states that "If something changes, some thing changes." This sounds just too profound for words, but bear with us! An expanded, more thorough representation of The Hauser Corollary is: **"If nothing changes, nothing definitely changes. If something changes, generally something changes, but eventually something will change with enough changes."** How's that for a lot of words?

For the person with a chronic injury, one can be assured that if the same treat ments continue to be used, then the same result will occur. For example, athletes jump around from athletic trainer to physical therapist, to massage therapist to chiropractor, back to athletic trainer to physical therapist, to acupuncturist to a different massage therapist or chiropractor, and the cycle continues to repeat. Obtaining some symptomatic relief with these types of therapies is fine for the general population, but for the athlete, time is of the essence. Every day an athlete is out with an injury, another two days of rehabilitation and training are necessary to return to the pre-injury level. Thus, it is vital for athletes and others in pain to take it upon themselves to **change the type of treatments they are receiving**.

By applying The Positive Hauser Corollary, patients receive treatments that stimulate connective tissue growth in the ligaments and tendons, namely Prolotherapy, in combination with various nutriceuticals and the **MEAT** protocol. It does not eliminate the need for specific training regimes, post-workout massages, or occasional chiropractic visits, but should abolish such phrases as **RICE**, NSAIDs, anti-inflammatories, and cortisone shots from medicine's vocabulary. The net result of this is a significant decline in the use of such procedures as arthroscopy, surgery, and joint replacement.

It is our hope that everyone, including athletes and sports medicine practitioners, as well as pain patients and practitioners, will take this Positive Hauser Corollary to heart..."If something changes, something changes." The changes we would like to see in the care of chronic injuries, such as those to ligaments and tendons, include the following:

1. Application of heat to injured areas instead of ice
2. Early use of some type of active exercise program as opposed to rest
3. **MEAT** rather than **RICE** protocol
4. Discontinuation of most ankle wraps and braces
5. Women, cease taking estradiol in the form of birth control pills or allopathic hormone replacement
6. Eliminate NSAIDs
7. Use of proteolytic enzymes to reduce swelling
8. Widespread utilization of nutritional supplements to aid healing
9. The removal of cortisone, and its derivatives, in syringes pointed toward athletes and injury victims
10. **M**y **R**eproducibility **I**nstrument (the thumb) to replace mechanical MRI
11. A dramatic decline in the "look and see" arthroscopy
12. Prolotherapy promoted to a **first-line** therapy
13. Surgery only as a measure for emergencies or as a last resort
14. Sports medicine specialist becomes synonymous with Prolotherapist

Only when the principles of this book are applied will people be truly healed. The body has, does, and always will heal by inflammation. This is why we can confidently say, "Cure Your Chronic Pain with Prolotherapy!" There is a cure for injuries and a way to enhance health and strength, and that way is Prolotherapy.

To order products that stimulate connective tissue growth, as developed by Dr. Ross Hauser and the researchers at Ortho Molecular Products, see Appendices H, I, and J. ■

CHAPTER 23

Why Don't You Heal?

Soon after the release of *Prolo Your Pain Away!* we started getting e-mail questions from around the globe, such as these: "Why don't I heal?" "I received Prolotherapy and it didn't work? Why not?" "The doctor treated my lower back and gave me 10 shots—this isn't what you are telling me." "I just can't seem to get off of the Oxycontin the doctor has me on. Will Prolotherapy still help me if I'm on this medication?" "I don't think anything is going to help!" "I have to take my anti-inflammatories. It is the only thing that helps my pain. Can I still get Prolotherapy while on them?"

Believe it or not, at drhauser@caringmedical.com we get some 100-plus e-mails a day from chronic pain patients across the world with similar questions and concerns as the above. It seems prudent to give you the top 10 reasons we find as to WHY YOU DON'T HEAL.

TOP TEN REASONS WHY YOU DON'T HEAL

1. Nutritional Deficiency
2. Hormonal Deficiency
3. Medications: Anti-Inflammatories/Narcotics
4. Ligament/Tendon Laxity
5. Inadequate Prolotherapy
6. Musculoskeletal Asymmetry
7. Allergies
8. Chronic Infection
9. Melancholy Temperament
10. God's Will Not Done Yet

People are initially going to look at this list and say, "None of this applies to me." Well you better read up, Bub, **because it does apply to you!** The reasons why you don't heal are going to be contained in the next few pages. Yes, you don't heal because of one of the above 10 reasons. Find which one and correct it and your pain **will** be cured.

NUTRITIONAL DEFICIENCY

The body has tremendous regenerative capabilities, but one must never forget the fact that many different factors affect connective tissue healing. **(See Figure 23-1.)** Perhaps, the most overlooked factor in healing is nutrition. Generally, by the time someone is seen at Caring Medical in Oak Park, Illinois, they have seen 10 health care clinicians and often none of them have considered any of the 10 causes as to why you don't heal. The first factor that needs to be considered is nutrition.

FACTORS AFFECTING HEALING OF CONNECTIVE TISSUES

- Age
- Gender
- Type of injury
- Severity of injury
- Underlying disease processes
- Hormonal influences
- Dietary intake
- Nutritional status
- Degree of hypoxia (systemic and local)
- Type of tissue(s) affected
- Electrical fields
- Mechanical-load forces
- Temperature
- Pharmacological agents (drugs)
- Mobility (local and whole-body)
- Type of onset (acute or chronic)
- Structural (physical) deformities
- Psychological influences (placebo effects and psychoneuroimmunological links)
- Metabolic and cell turnover rates of connective tissues
- Muscular strength and forces
- Blood supply
- Overall health status
- Timing and return to physical activity
- pH and lactate concentration
- Growth factors, cytokines, eicosanoids

Figure 23-1: Factors Affecting the Healing of Connective Tissues
Reversing Connective Tissue Deficiency Syndrome can involve many factors.
Adapted from *Nutrition Applied to Injury Rehabilitation and Sports Medicine* by L. Bucci, CRC Press, Boca Raton, FL © 1995

By definition, pain means something is weak or injured, assuming a musculoskeletal cause for the pain. Most people can tell the date and time when their pain started. "I was in a car accident on...I fell down the stairs on...I was playing a lot of golf when...My wife kicked me when..." Hopefully, the last incident doesn't pertain to anybody. Most people with pain know what started the pain—they just want to find out how to end it! The first place to start is to look at what you are putting in your mouth to nourish your body.

In just about every nutritional study on Americans, deficiencies are found. To grow ligaments, tendons, or for that matter to heal any bodily structure, it is safe to say that the whole gamut of essential nutrients is needed—this means amino acids, fatty acids, vitamins, minerals, and trace elements that are supposed to be consumed in a healthy diet. Unfortunately, the average person in America gorges on fried fatty foods, in between the nutrient-deficient binges of bread and pasta, which are helped down the old gullet with sugar-laden Pepsis and Coca-Colas. The average American consumes 150 pounds of sugar per year. Did you ever hear the word "ve-ge-ta-ble"?

It would not be a bad idea for the person in chronic pain to receive some nutritional testing to look for nutrient deficiencies. For the person with chronic pain, perhaps the main reason you do not heal is because ***you do not eat correctly!*** Start eating plenty of fruits, vegetables, and proteins. Leave the grains and the sugars to all the overweight people—trust us, they will eat them. Consuming too many carbohydrates is the number one reason people are overweight. The more weight you have, the stronger your joints and ligaments have to be to support the weight.

Weight loss is, therefore, a part of curing chronic pain. What you don't know is that one sugar load hampers immune function for four hours! So the person who has a soda every few hours is suppressing the immune system all day. This is the same immune system that heals your connective tissues. If you want to heal, cut out the sugar and take control of your diet.

	CATABOLIC	ANABOLIC
ESTRADIOL LEVELS	HIGH	LOW
ESTRIOL LEVELS	LOW	HIGH
PROGESTERONE LEVELS	LOW	HIGH
DHEA LEVELS	LOW	HIGH
GROWTH HORMONE LEVELS	LOW	HIGH
TESTOSTERONE LEVELS	LOW	HIGH
AGING EFFECTS	ADVANCED	DIMINISHED
ARTHRITIS RISK	HIGH	LOW
CONNECTIVE TISSUE HEALING	POOR	EXCELLENT
RECOVERY AFTER WORKOUTS	POOR	EXCELLENT
ABILITY TO TRAIN INTENSELY	POOR	EXCELLENT
LIKELIHOOD OF INJURY	HIGH	LOW
HEALING CAPACITY	POOR	EXCELLENT

Figure 23-2: Catabolic Versus Anabolic Profiles

A person whose metabolism is anabolic has a much greater chance to heal an injury than if the metabolism is catabolic.

This is the first step everyone with a chronic condition must take in order to heal. The next step is to begin taking nutritional products that will assist the body in healing the particular disorder. A good place to start is with a high-potency multivitamin. The one that we use is Ortho Molecular's Super-Vites. The nutritional supplements that we use for connective tissue healing have been formulated by us. They are Prolo Max, Pro-Collagen, Pro-Cartilage, and Skin and Nails. For a complete list of natural nutriceutical products that assist healing, please see www.benuts.com.*

HORMONAL DEFICIENCIES

This topic has been covered sufficiently in the connective tissue deficiency chapter, so we won't belabor the point, except to remind you that the engines driving your immune system are your hormones. Everything cannot be blamed on your chronic pain. The person who has thinning hair, loss of sex drive, decreased muscle tone, dry skin, menstrual cramping, irregular menses, chronic fatigue, decreased body temperature, and a feeling of cold has a hormone deficiency until proven otherwise.

To determine why you do not heal, please get at least the following hormones checked: thyroid, Growth Hormone, DHEA, estrogen, progesterone, testosterone, melatonin, and cortisol. For the person in chronic pain, most assuredly, at least one of these will be suboptimal. It must always be kept in mind that certain hormones are anabolic, which means they grow connective tissue, and others are catabolic and promote its breakdown. **(See Figures 23-2 and 23-3.)**

* *To order the products developed and used by the Hausers for connective tissue healing, call 1-877-RX-BEULAH or online at www.beulahlandnutritionals.com or www.benuts.com. Be nuts for your health!*

lementation of a deficiency with natural hormones will generally enhance healing. More important is hormonal **balancing,** making sure that the hormonal milieu is anabolic and not catabolic.

MEDICATIONS: AX THE ANTI-INFLAMMATORIES AND NUKE THE NARCOTICS!

Initially this whole chapter was going to be on nuking the narcotics, but it would not be fair to just single them out! Nothing pains us more than seeing a chronic pain patient addicted to narcotics. Hopefully, after reading this section you will see why. In regard to the anti-inflammatories, they have been covered adequately in this book but, in case you forgot, **nonsteroidal anti-inflammatory drugs (NSAIDs) stop the normal healing inflammatory reaction! In other words, they are anti-healing.** The body heals by inflammation. The person with chronic pain has a choice—anti-inflame your way to terrible arthritis or Prolo your way to freedom from pain!

As detrimental to healing as NSAIDs are, they are no match for narcotics. Why don't we start with the known effects of narcotics and go from there? In case you do not believe us, references will be given.

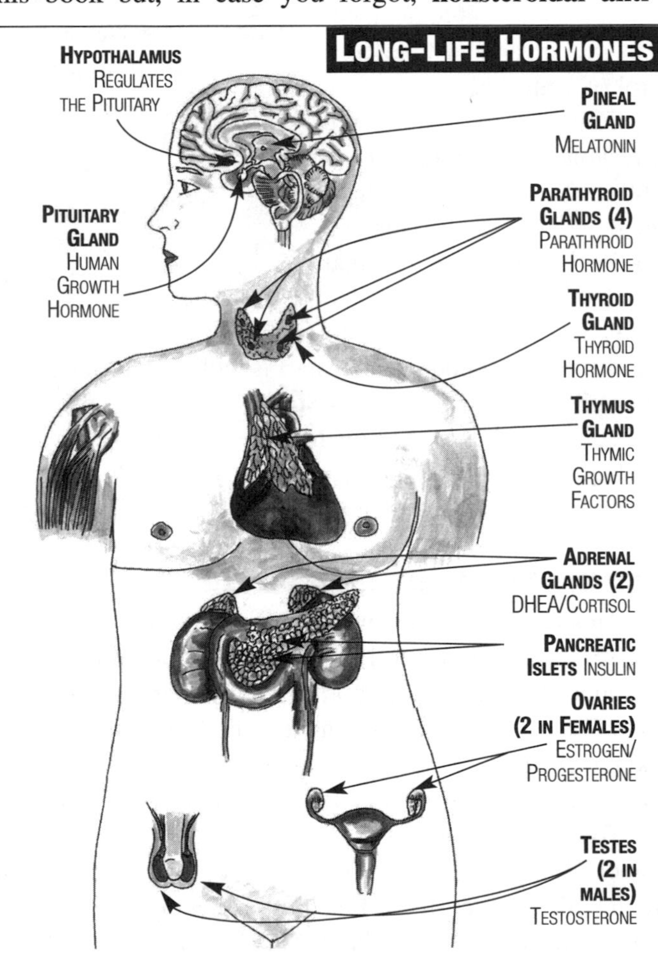

Figure 23-3: The Endocrine System
The endocrine glands secrete the hormones that help the body stay healthy. The hormones DHEA, testosterone, progesterone, and Growth Hormone stimulate the repair of the connective tissues, thus they are anabolic.

The Known Effects of Narcotics on the Immune System

1. Suppression of the cytotoxic activity of natural killer cells[1]
2. Enhanced growth of implanted tumors[1]
3. Depressed T-lymphocyte responsiveness to stimulation[2]
4. Ablate-delayed hypersensitive skin response[3]
5. Spleen atrophy[4]
6. Thymus atrophy[4, 5]
7. Decreased T-lymphocyte numbers[5]
8. Decreased T-cell function[6]
9. Inhibition of antibody production[7]
10. Inhibition of B-cell activity[7]
11. Decreased levels of interferon[8]
12. Increased incidence of infections[9]
13. **Depressed function of all cells of the immune system[10]**

If that last statement is true, is it any wonder when chronic pain patients start narcotics, they never get off? Once patients take regular narcotics for longer than two months, it is doubtful they will ever get off. This is a sad statement—but it is true. If a doctor offered a chronic pain patient chemotherapy, they would most likely decline, even if it gave some pain relief, because everyone knows that chemotherapy can be dangerous. Well, guess what? **Narcotics have the same depressive effects on the immune system as chemotherapy!**

If you do not believe us, then listen to what the premier neuroimmunology journal in the world says. Yes, the *Journal of Neuroimmunology*, in an article from Toby K. Eisenstein and Mary E. Hilburger, from the department of microbiology and immunology at Temple University School of Medicine, stated it plainly.[10] The article is entitled "Opioid Modulation of Immune Responses: Effects on Phagocyte and Lymphoid Cell Populations." It is a review article on the information known to-date as to narcotics effects on the immune system. Their conclusion of the whole matter is, "**In aggregate, the literature supports the existence of *in vivo* neural-immune circuits through which morphine acts to depress the function of *all cells* of the immune system.**" In other words, taking the medical literature as a whole, narcotics suppress ***every*** cell of the immune system.

The body needs an intact immune system to heal. It does not matter if it is after an accident, sports activity, or Prolotherapy, the body heals by inflammation, and inflammation **only** occurs if the body can mount an immune reaction. The person who is on narcotics needs to nuke the narcotics if healing is to take place.

What Are Narcotics?

The term "narcotic" is derived from the Greek word for "stupor" and, at one time, applied to any drug that induced sleep, but most often refer to drugs that have morphine-like, strong analgesic properties.[11] Narcotics are to morphine as NSAIDs are to aspirin. There are numerous NSAIDs because each touts that it is safer and more efficacious than the other. So it is with the various narcotics—each tries to become an even stronger pain reliever with fewer side effects. By definition, narcotics, which act as morphine does, are immunosuppressive. This goes for Vicodin, Darvocet, Duragesic, morphine, Oxycontin, codeine, Percodan, and any other such addictive substance.

At Caring Medical, the above information is explained to the patient on the first visit if they are, unfortunately, narcotic-dependent. It is not necessary to be completely off narcotics to begin Prolotherapy, though this is preferred; but there must be a willingness to begin weaning off of them. For people unable to do so, there is little hope of curing their pain. Typically, a person's dose of narcotics is weaned by 5 to 10 mg per week until he or she is completely off of narcotics. It is always helpful for a person on narcotics to get Metabolic Typing, nutritional testing, and hormonal assessments in order to determine appropriate treatments to enhance their immune function, which is depressed from the narcotics. By taking this approach, we have had success, even with heroin addicts, in not only curing their chronic pain—but also curing their addictions.

Ligament and Tendon Laxity

If you have made it this far reading this book, then you are familiar with why we believe that ligament laxity, tendon laxity, injury, sprain, strain, or whatever you call it, is responsible for most chronic pain. Prolotherapy stimulates the body, via the immune system, to heal these areas. By getting ligaments and tendons back to their normal strength, muscle spasms are relieved, vertebrae stay in place, and, most importantly, chronic pain is relieved. If a person has chronic pain from a weak ligament and/or tendon, as well as an intact immune system, then the odds of Prolotherapy curing the pain are excellent. But there are those patients who appear to have met all of these criteria, yet still have pain after Prolotherapy. These people most likely have received inadequate Prolotherapy.

Inadequate Prolotherapy

People sometimes get upset at us because we can not give out referrals of individual Prolotherapists. The reason for this is simple: Not all prolotherapists are created equal. In the original version of *Prolo Your Pain Away!* we listed the names of some 20 Prolotherapists, yet we would get patient complaints (whether founded or unfounded) about them. The reason that most of these people who wrote were still having pain after their Prolotherapy was that they had inadequate Prolotherapy.*

Prolotherapy's efficaciousness in curing chronic pain is completely dependent on the Prolotherapist's ability to **completely** treat the injured structures. This means that *all* of the injured structures are treated with a strong enough solution

* *We feel that the most informative website for Prolotherapy information is www.prolonews.com, and the best one to find a Prolotherapist in a given area of the country is www.getprolo.com.*

to heal the area in a reasonable period of time. We have heard of peop
30 or 40 sessions of Prolotherapy without good results, or getting three
during a Prolotherapy session for the lower back. As this book discusses, most people are cured of their pain with three to six Prolotherapy sessions. If by the sixth Prolotherapy session, a person has not experienced significant improvement, we search for an additional cause of their pain, such as infection or allergy. People who are receiving 30 or 40 Prolotherapy sessions to cure their chronic pain are paying a lot of unnecessary money—that could have been avoided—if they had gone to a physician who utilized stronger Prolotherapy solutions than they had received and/or did more shots per visit.

A general, good rule of thumb when receiving the Hackett-Hemwall-Hauser technique of Prolotherapy, is to receive 10 to 20 injections for an extremity (knee, ankle, or shoulder) and anywhere from 30 to 60 injections for the neck, back, or thoracic spine. Someone getting three shots to the lower back during a session is probably not getting Prolotherapy, but trigger point injections. Trigger point injections are given into the muscle to decrease muscle spasms. They do **not** stimulate the body to repair the painful area. If you want to know if you are getting Prolotherapy, ask the doctor if the therapy stimulates the immune system to repair the area.

Another reason for suboptimal results with Prolotherapy is due to inadequate inflammation with the Prolotherapy treatment. Remember, **the body heals only by inflammation**. In some people, stronger Prolotherapy solutions are needed to achieve an adequate inflammatory reaction after the treatment. Until the injured structures are completely treated with Prolotherapy—with a strong enough solution—Prolotherapy has not failed. It is important that the patient feel stiff for at least one to two days after a Prolotherapy session. If the stiffness after the treatment lasts only a few hours, then the immune reaction to the treatment, most likely, will not be enough to regenerate the connective tissue needed for healing. In such a situation, there are two options. First, figure out why you have a poor immune response by doing metabolic, nutritional, and hormonal testing, or, second, use a stronger Prolotherapy solution. Physicians who have a lot of experience doing Prolotherapy may have 10 different solutions they use, depending on the individual case.

Musculoskeletal Asymmetry

It is often helpful for patients to receive active physiotherapy, kinesiotherapy, exercise, or rehabilitation while getting Prolotherapy. A good chiropractor, personal trainer, kinesiotherapist, or physical therapist can help a you overcome musculoskeletal asymmetries. These may be as simple as leg-length discrepancies or pelvic torsions, but often, if the pain is chronic, the musculoskeletal asymmetries are numerous. It should be noted that Dr. Hemwall treated people for over 40 years with just Prolotherapy and achieved excellent results. One of the reasons for this is the fact that Prolotherapy often cures musculoskeletal asymmetries, especially those caused by ligament laxities. Most people with chronic pain just need Prolotherapy to elminiate the pain. One person with obvious atrophy of muscles and skeletal malalignments, should also be under the care of a manual therapist, along with a Prolotherapist. One manual therapy that we use at Caring Medical with good success—especially for people with chronic pain—is NeuroCranial Restructing, because NCR will take you far!

SPHENOID BONE MANIPULATION... NCR WILL TAKE YOU FAR!

It has always fascinated us how many people just have pain at one particular spot or just on one side of the body. This makes no sense to many clinicians unless they are familiar with NCR. The technique known as NeuroCranial Restructuring, or NCR, was developed by Dean Howell, N.D., of Bellevue, Washington, in the early 1980s and is extremely effective at opening the nasal cavity. It involves the insufflation of small balloons or finger cots in one or all of the six nasal passages. Just like Prolotherapy, NCR can have wide-ranging effects. **(See Figures 23-4a and 4b.)** Because it manipulates, or moves, the sphenoid bone, not only is breathing improved but posture is also improved, which can usually improve pain and weakness in many different areas of the body. According to Dr. Howell, the sphenoid bone is vital to head balance and posture. Once the sphenoid bone becomes

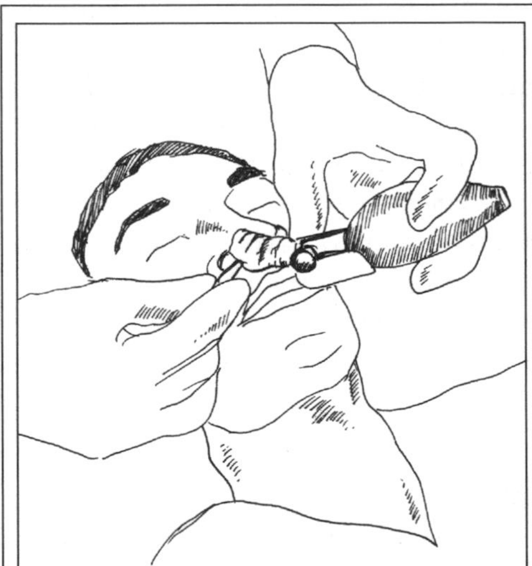

Figure 23-4A: The Technique of NCR
NCR is a type of sphenoid bone manipulation done by insufflating a small balloon in one or all of the six nasal passages.

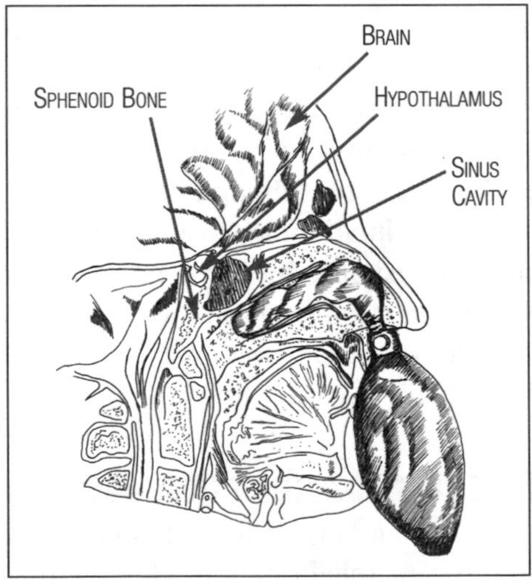

Figure 23-4B: Cross-Section of Face During NCR
NCR has wide-ranging effects because of the sphenoid bone's proximity to such structures as the sinus cavities, hypothalamus, and brain.

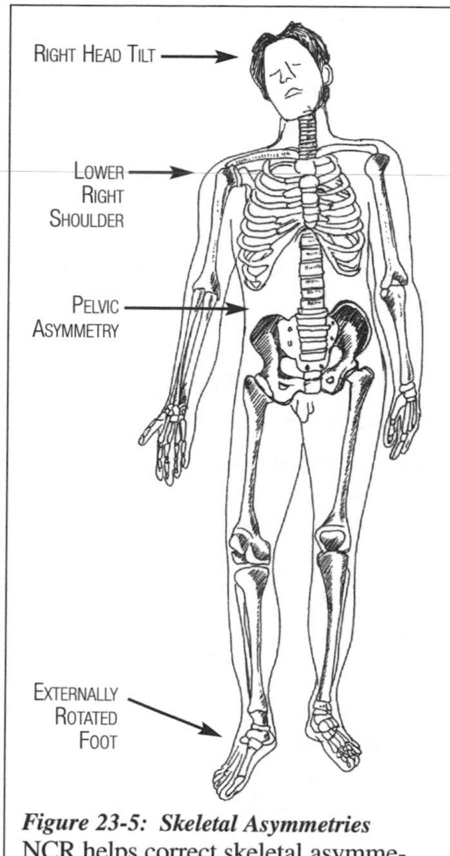

Figure 23-5: Skeletal Asymmetries
NCR helps correct skeletal asymmetries by moving the sphenoid bone.

malaligned, a significant head tilt may result. This puts additional strain on the rest of the body, including the neck, lower back, and pelvis. **(See Figure 23-5.)** This sphenoid bone malalignment is **one cause** for such structural conditions as pelvic imbalances, scoliosis, axis and/or atlas malrotations, leg-length discrepancies, bony subluxations, and facial asymmetries. Dr. Howell coined the term NeuroCranial Restructuring because he was having success in treating conditions such as anxiety, depression, obsessive/compulsive disorder, panic attacks, attention deficit disorder, and other conditions that involve brain and hormone systems just by doing sphenoid bone manipulations. He surmises that NCR increases the blood flow of hormonal levels of certain deficient areas of the brain in the above conditions. It is for this reason that many people around the country can say that NCR has certainly taken them far!

Dr. Hauser Finally Sees the Light: Ross' experience with NCR

It is not natural, nor pleasant, to get a balloon stuck up your nose, nor to have it blown up while it is in there. I learned about NCR from a chiropractor friend of mine, Kurt Ehling. Dr. Ehling and I decided to take one of Dr. Howell's intensive week-long training sessions in Bellevue, Washington. During the week, we observed Dr. Howell treating people with back pain, headaches, fibromyalgia, anxiety, depression, Down's syndrome, and fatigue just utilizing NCR. I can honestly say that by the end of each of their four-day sessions, **all** of the patients felt better. NCR is generally given daily for four days and the person is seen for follow-up one month later.

When learning NCR, Dr. Howell insists that the student treat him (Dr. Howell) and also be treated **by** him. Explaining what it is like to receive NCR is akin to having a baby. Contemplate that for a second. Does that make you want to get NCR? Giving birth to another human being is perhaps the most noble of all endeavors, but how the baby comes out of such a small opening—well, only God knows. It is the same with NCR. For me it felt like a firecracker went off in my head. As I lay there after my first treatment, somewhat dazed with the typical "water up the nose feeling," the only words that I could say were these: "... and I thought sex was good!" It was just the right thing to break the tension, as I was the first student in our group to be treated.

What did NCR do for me? It helped me breathe through my nose for the first time in years, along with helping my own facial tension, TMJ, allergy symptoms, mental clarity, posture, and, best of all, I can now smell again with my nose. My wife is right—my underarms do stink! Since receiving NCR, I have been using deodorant! I can attest that NCR does take you far!

Who Is an NCR Candidate? Yes, That's You!

Many of you right now are saying, "Injections maybe, but balloons up the nose? No way! My sphenoid bone is fine!" Perhaps the reason we utilize NCR at Caring Medical is that, like ligament injury, sphenoid bone rotations do not show up on x-ray. They must be diagnosed by the clinician. The average athlete with chronic pain is the perfect candidate for NCR because athletes get jarred, smashed, and knocked in their heads—or have received such in the past. It is amazing how many athletes and people with chronic pain will say that their pain in the various parts of their body started with a jarring injury to the head. Another common feature is that people with pain will often describe a full feeling in the head. The average physician does not know what to do with a symptom like this. When a person describes nasal stuffiness, headaches, neck pain, numbness around the face or head, mental fogginess, dizziness, vertigo, ringing in the ears, or balance-troubles, Caring Medical thinks "NCR." It may be that you should also be thinking about NCR. You too will learn why athletes and folks around the country are saying, "NCR will take you far!"

Anyone interested in learning more about NCR is encouraged to go to the following website: www.drdeanhowell.com or www.caringmedical.com.

Dr. Dean Howell can be contacted at P.O. Box 448, Tonasket, WA, 98855, toll-free: 888-252-0411 or appointments@drdeanhowell.com.

Allergies

It is hard to explain why Ross' knee hurts when he eats pizza, but it does. It is well-known that allergies can cause localized, as well as systemic, chronic pain. Yes, any allergy to a chemical, inhalant, tree, mold, dust, or food can be the cause of your chronic pain, or the reason why your healing from chronic pain is hampered.

The method utilized at Caring Medical to determine if there is an allergy causing chronic pain is called provocation neutralization. In this type of allergy testing, provoking the **symptom** the person has been having is the goal of the test! A small dose of allergen is given to the patient, and then after 10 minutes the site is examined for a reaction. Even more important is determining if the allergen produces any pain. This is a common type of allergy testing done by Natural

Medicine physicians. Besides a needle and syringe, it is not the type of testing done at conventional allergists' offices. If a person is found to have a reaction to an allergen, then the allergen is neutralized either through injections in the arm or drops in the mouth. When the person is desensitized to that allergen, the symptom is eliminated.

Provocation neutralization is perhaps the best way to find if a particular pain or symptom, such as fatigue, is due to an allergic reaction. The most common allergens that we find causing a person's chronic pain are foods. Food allergies can be tested by the above methods or various blood tests. When a food allergen is found, the person is told to eliminate that food from the diet and see if the particular pain is improved. Often this is the case and, if they so desire, then can undergo desensitization treatment with food drops or food allergen shots, so they can once again eat those particular foods without inducing a symptom. Don't underestimate the power of what you put into your mouth in regard to its pain-provoking or pain-preventing power.

One must always remember that just about anything can be an allergen. This includes chemicals, molds, dust, cat dander, trees, and pollens. Sometimes people have allergic reactions to their own hormones or neurotransmitters. Such reactions must be desensitized. It is for these reasons that any person suffering from chronic pain is best seen by a Natural Medicine physician that utilizes these methods, along with Prolotherapy.

CHRONIC INFECTIONS

"Doctor, I don't have any fevers, so I don't have an infection." So the arguments go. All one has to do is point to the fact that people get cold sores. Most cold sores are a herpes viral infection, yet the people have no fevers. You can have an indolent, low-level, yet raging infection causing your chronic pain without knowing it. The most common ones that we test for in the office are Mycoplasma, Lyme, Babesiosis, and various fungal infections, including *Candida*. Research is mounting that all four of these are much more prevalent than most people think and all of them can cause chronic pain.

MYCOPLASMA INFECTIONS

Many people with chronic pain are also wracked with chronic fatigue. Often the pain is blamed as the cause for the chronic fatigue. Unfortunately, this is not the case in most instances, because Mycoplasma infection is the cause. Mycoplasma is the smallest, simplest known bacterium. These bacteria are invasive and burrow themselves deep within the body tissues, including the brain, central and peripheral nervous systems, muscles and joints, bone marrow, digestive tract, lungs and heart, and the immune system. They can virtually "hide" within the white blood cells of the human body, which makes them undetectable by the immune system and very difficult to treat.

It is now possible to diagnose Mycoplasma by a simple blood test. Researchers are finding that the incidence of Mycoplasma infection in disorders such as Gulf War Syndrome, Chronic Fatigue Syndrome, fibromyalgia, and rheumatoid arthritis is around 65 percent.[12, 13] The most common symptoms found from Mycoplasma infection include fatigue, clouded thinking, depression, memory problems, balance disorders, joint stiffness, and various types of chronic pain.

The main treatment for Mycoplasma infection is long-term antibiotics. Because of the risk of a depletion of the normal flora bacteria in the intestines, Lactobacillus acidophilus is given along with an antifungal regime or medication. For the person desiring to avoid an antibiotic, transfer factors against Mycoplasma are now available. These are special proteins that transfer immunity or increased immune reaction towards the Mycoplasma bacterium.* If the infection is the cause of the person's symptoms, generally a gradual decrease in pain and increase in energy is seen. Remarkable as it sounds, some who have rheumatoid arthritis and other autoimmune diseases, including lupus and scleroderma, have remissions of the disease while on the antibiotics. Anyone with these conditions should get checked for this organism because resolution of your pain or fatigue could depend on it.

Musculoskeletal Manifestations of Lyme Disease

Most people have heard of Lyme Disease but know very little about it. Lyme Disease is caused by the spirochete *Borrelia burgdorferi*, which is carried by infected ticks. This disorder has a variable clinical course and involves multiple systems, affecting the skin, nervous system, heart, and eyes. Early in the illness, many patients experience migratory musculoskeletal pain in joints, bursae, tendons, muscle, or bone, in one or a few locations at a time, frequently lasting only hours or days in a given location. Weeks to months later, untreated patients often have intermittent or chronic arthritis, primarily involving the large joints, especially the knees, over a period of several years.[14, 15] **(See Figure 23-6.)**

Since the clinical course of the disorder is so varied, from mild aches and pains to debilitating memory, neurologic and heart conditions, there is no one symptom that is diagnostic for Lyme Disease. For this reason, it is important for those with chronic pain and/or fatigue to get the various blood and urine tests for the condition. At Caring Medical in Oak Park, we generally go straight to the western blot test, thought to be the most sensitive for the disorder. Another common test we run is the Lyme urine antigen test while the person is taking antibiotics.

The treatment for this condition is similar to Mycoplasma infection, involving long courses of antibiotics. For the person desiring to avoid antibiotics, various nutriceuticals are given, including Lyme transfer factor, immune stimulating herbs, and bovine colostrum. For the chronic musculoskeletal complaints, various connective tissue products are given. **(See Appendix F, Nutriceuticals: Helping the Body to Heal.)**

***** *These are available through Beulah Land Nutritionals by calling 1-877-RX-BEULAH. Or order directly online at www.beulahlandnutritionals.com or www.benuts.com.*

NUMBER OF JOINTS AND PERIARTICULAR SITES OF 28 PATIENTS AFFECTED WITH LYME ARTHRITIS

JOINT	NO. OF PATIENTS AFFECTED	PERIARTICULAR SITE	NO. OF PATIENTS AFFECTED
Knee	27	Back	9
Shoulder	14	Neck	6
Ankle	12	Bicipital	4
Elbow	11	Lateral epicondyle	2
Temporomandibular	11	Lateral collateral	1
Wrist	10	de Quervain's disease	1
Hip	9	Prepatellar	4
Metacarpophalangeal	4	Subacromial	2
Proximal interphalangeal	4	Infraspinatus	2
Distal interphalangeal	4	Olecranon	2
Metatarsophalangeal	4	Sausage digits	2
Sternoclavicular	1	Heel pain	2

Figure 23-6: Joints and Periarticular Sites Affected Out of 28 Patients with Lyme Arthritis

It is important that the western blot test be done before Lyme Disease is ruled out as a diagnosis. We have seen many patients have a positive western blot when other less sensitive tests were negative. Getting the most sensitive test done to make a diagnosis is always prudent when one's body is wracked with pain. It is often the only way to make the correct diagnosis.

BABESIOSIS—I NEVER HEARD OF IT!

Yes, well, a few days ago you probably never heard of Prolotherapy, either! Babesiosis is an infection that may be spread by the same tick that carries borreliosis (Lyme Disease). It is caused by *Babesia microti,* which is a protozoa—not bacteria, virus, fungus, or yeast. Other examples of protozoal infections are malaria and giardia.

Babesia infection can cause all of the same symptoms as Lyme Disease, and in many ways, it masks the disease. Anyone who is suspected of having Lyme Disease should also have Babesiosis testing. Like Lyme Disease, the best test is a blood test. The treatment course of long-term antiobiotics is also similar.

HUMUNGOUS FUNGUS AMONG US!

People are sometimes offended when you tell them they are full of fungus. Because of the indiscriminate use of antibiotics, cortisone shots, prednisone pills, and the like, fungal infections are prevalent. There are various methods to document an internal fungus infection, most commonly a stool culture or blood antibody test. Once a fungal infection, such as *Candida,* is found, antifungal herbal remedies or medications are needed for several months.

MELANCHOLY TEMPERAMENT

"Negative thoughts have a negative effect on the body and positive thoughts have a positive effect on the body."

—Ross A. Hauser, M.D.

"Do not judge, or you too will be judged. For in the same way you judge others, you will be judged, and with the measure you use, it will be measured to you. Why do you look at the speck of sawdust in your brother's eye and pay no attention to the plank in your own eye? How can you say to your brother, 'Let me take the speck out of your eye,' when all the time there is a plank in your own eye? You hypocrite, first take the plank out of your own eye, and then you will see clearly to remove the speck from your brother's eye."

These words were spoken by Jesus Christ, as recorded in the Bible in Matthew 7:1-5. No matter if you are a Christian or not, the principle of "be careful of judging or drawing conclusions" still applies. As it turns out, some people are more apt to judge, be critical, and/or look at the negative side of events. Unfortunately for these people, they are more prone to developing chronic illness and pain. Perhaps the simplest explanation for this is that **negative thoughts have a negative impact on the body and positive thoughts have a positive impact on the body.**

Too often people want to blame the circumstances of their life as the reason why they act a certain way. The fact is, circumstances reveal what is deep down inside of a person. The person who has strong self-esteem and a strong faith can face even the most difficult of situations with grace, peace, and calmness; whereas the person who struggles without these virtues reacts to the same stimulus with bitterness, anger, and resentment. Much of the difference in the way people react to illness and life circumstances, as well as to each other, can be found in the different temperaments people possess.

Temperament is defined as "constitution of a substance, body, or organism with respect to the mixture or balance of its elements, qualities or parts; makeup; characteristic or habitual inclination; or mode of emotional reponse."[16] There are four basic temperaments: choleric, sanguine, phlegmatic, and melancholy; each of which has strengths and weaknesses. Believe it or not, the person to first describe these four temperaments was Hippocrates, who lived from 460 to 370 B.C. The basic characteristics of the four temperaments are found in **Figure 23-7**.

Learning about their own temperament helps people see themselves as others see them. Often these two viewpoints are completely opposite. A complete description of the temperaments, as well as personality profile tests people can take to determine their temperament, are available. We encourage everyone with chronic pain to explore this.[17-20]

After treating many thousands of chronically ill people, it is our contention that a good percentage of them have melancholy temperaments. The strengths of

Characteristics of the Four Temperaments

Temperament	Strengths	Weaknesses
Sanguine	Enjoying	Restless
	Optimistic	Weak-Willed
	Friendly	Egotistical
	Compassionate	Emotionally Unstable
Choleric	Strong Willpower	Hot-Tempered
	Practical	Cruel
	Leader	Impetuous
	Optimistic	Self-Sufficient
Phlegmatic	Witty	Slow and Lazy
	Dependable	Teasing
	Practical	Stubborn
	Efficient	Indecisive
Melancholy	Sensitive	Self-Centered
	Perfectionist	Pessimistic
	Analytical	Moody
	Faithful Friend	Revengeful

Figure 23-7

the melancholic are that they are the richest and most sensitive of all the temperaments. melancholics are the "deepest" of all the temperaments and, thus, are the play-wrights, authors, artists, and those in the creative arts. The melancholic is often thinking, and often thinking too much. "What did he or she mean by that, why did they look at me that way, did the doctor mean such and such?" The melancholy temperament has a strong perfectionist tendency, with standards of excellence that exceed those of others and requirements of acceptability—in any field—that are often higher than anyone can maintain. This is a great set-up for disappointment and, thus, the melancholy tendencies.

The melancholic is very analytical, but in relation to getting ill, this can be a bad thing. "Why did this happen to me?" Because illness doesn't fit into the perfectionist imaginary world in which the melancholic lives, pessimism, bitterness, and self-centeredness results, especially relating to the aches and pains the person experiences.

A good description of the melancholic is as follows. "He is surely more self-centered than any of the other temperaments. He is inclined to that kind of self-examination, that kind of self-contemplation which paralyzes his will and energy. He is always dissecting himself and his own mental conditions, taking off layer after layer as an onion is peeled, until there is nothing direct and artless left in his life; there is only his everlasting self-examination. This self-examination is not only unfortunate, it is harmful. Melancholies usually drift into morbid mental conditions. They are concerned not only about their spiritual state; they are also **unduly concerned about their physical condition**. Everything that touches a melancholic is of prime importance to him, hence no other type can so easily become a hypochondriac." [17]

Good examples of this are people who want to tell you about every single ache or pain, and as soon as one pain goes away, another starts. A melancholic would describe pains in great detail even if they just lasted a few minutes. "My rib started hurting after dinner a few days ago, then it was gone. I wonder what that was?" "Doctor, I got a sharp pain in my foot only upon rising out of bed the other day. What do you think that was?" Most people would ignore a "one-time" pain, but not melancholics. For the melancholics to be truly free of pain, they are going to have to realize they are melancholy and work on minimizing the weaknesses of this personality trait.

Dr. Hauser—Classic Melancholy

I was intrigued by the application of the temperaments when discussing them with a friend of mine, Brodie Hackney. She runs the office of Dr. Mark Wheaton, a close friend and fellow Prolotherapist. By knowing a patient's temperament she is able to communicate with him or her better. I eventually read up on the temperaments and, like most people, I felt I was a sanguine (life of the party) or choleric (the doers of this world), but was shocked to find that my wife and my staff unanimously said I was a melancholic. No ifs, ands, or buts about it. Ross, you are melancholy! The thought horrified me.

For years, my wife had been trying to tell me that I was moody. I could be in a good mood, then all of a sudden become cranky, angry, and have a "woe is me" attitude. I also have struggled with negative thoughts for years. As soon as one of my patients isn't getting better, I am struck with the feeling that "I am a bad doctor," even though the previous 10 patients could have been doing great.

One of the classic melancholy experiences that I recall is when I made dinner and set the table one evening. When Marion came home she said, "Ross, the fork goes on the left side of the plate," as I had put them on the right. Immediately, I became angry and resentful at her for criticizing me. Thoughts immediately came to my mind like "Ross, you are a dummy," "Your wife thinks she is smarter than you," and "Why can't you do anything right?" even though I realized that all my wife said was that the fork goes on the left side of the plate. She was not criticizing me, she was just stating a fact. My melancholy mind pictured my wife coming into the kitchen, giving me a big smooch, and saying something like, "Ross you are the best husband in the world—thanks so much for this." Instead I got, "The fork goes on the left side of the plate."

A person with a melancholy temperament who has difficulties in life, such as marital problems, strained relationships with family or children, a bad job, or money issues, will often **develop physical complaints to cope with these life disappointments.** It is much more difficult for melancholy temperaments to take responsibility for these disappointments and to admit to themselves that life is not all that perky and it is partly their fault. If melancholics do get legitimate musculoskeletal pain, the emotional reaction to it can often be blown out of proportion to the actual structural injury. For such people, Prolotherapy may help them, but they won't admit that they are totally better. They need some of the pain to remain so they have an excuse for not working on the emotional, spiritual, or relational problems they are having.

Once I admitted to myself that I was a melancholy, I had fewer emotional swings. My confidence level is much better, and now when I perceive that people are criticizing me, I can step back and analyze it. More often than not, they are just stating facts. Knowing my temperament has changed my life. I suspect knowing your own temperament will change yours. If it is melancholy, properly thinking about your life in a true and honest sense will help you ***solve*** your problems and your temperament will ***not*** be one of them.

It Is Not God's Will Yet

For the person who does not believe in God, you will not understand or believe this next section. Since Prolotherapy is not politically correct, why not have a section on the spiritual cause of illness? If we are going to be "way out there," why not go all the way to heaven?

For the person who really desires to delve into the subject of the spiritual reasons for illness, besides studying the Bible, we would encourage you to read the book *A More Excellent Way* by Pastor Henry Wright.[21] In the book, he says that the **beginning of all healing of spiritually related diseases begins with:**

1. Your coming back in alignment with God, His Word, His person, His nature, His precepts and what He planned for this planet for you from the beginning. The solution is restoration.
2. Accepting YOURSELF in your relationship with God; getting rid of your self-hatred, getting rid of your self-bitterness, getting rid of your guilt and coming back in line with who you are in the Father through Jesus Christ.
3. Making peace with your brother, your sister, and all others, if at all possible.

There are many causes of pain and illness and one should not overlook the possible "big picture" reason for pain. It could be God's purpose for your life at this particular moment to have pain because He wants you first and foremost to acknowledge Him in your life.

> *"Jesus replied: 'Love the Lord your God with all your heart and with all your soul and with all your mind. This is the first and greatest commandment. And the second is like it: Love your neighbor as yourself. All the Law and the Prophets hang on these two commandments.'"* Matthew 22:37-40

It could be that *your* healing will start the moment you restore the relationship that God desires to have with you by loving the Lord your God with all your heart, soul, mind, and strength. The second relationship that must be restored is loving your neighbor. Notice from the above verses that you cannot love your neighbor if you do not love yourself. It is not possible. For the person who is filled with God's love, it is easy to love themselves and, thus, love their neighbors.

"I pray that out of His glorious riches He may strengthen you with power through His Spirit in your inner being, so that Christ may dwell in your hearts through faith. And I pray that you, being rooted and established in love, may have power, together with all the saints, to grasp how wide and long and high and deep is the love of Christ, and to know this love that surpasses knowledge—that you may be filled to the measure of all the fullness of God." Ephesians 3:16-19

For the person who has experienced the love and forgiveness of God through Jesus Christ, anything is bearable, even horrible, unrelenting pain. For the person who has no belief in God and does not see the higher purpose for everything in life, it is easy to see why depression and hopelessness prevail. God has a purpose for everything and, when one takes an eternal perspective, it is easy to see the many reasons it may not be God's will for your life to free you of the pain.

Chronic pain can help people realize:

1. They need God in their lives.
2. They need forgiveness for their sins through Jesus Christ.
3. They need to start going to church again.
4. They need to work on family and other strained relationships.
5. They need to be more thankful for what they do have in life.
6. They need more humility in their lives.
7. They need to free themselves from all bitterness and anger.
8. They need to love and serve others more than themselves.
9. They need to realize that every day is a gift from God.
10. They need to accept that there are no promises for tomorrow, so live each day to its fullest!

SUMMARY

There are many reasons why a person develops chronic pain. Generally, chronic pain is from inadequate ligament and tendon healing, which stems from a person having nutritional and hormonal deficiencies, along with the taking of anti-inflammatory medications and getting steroid shots. There are additional factors that hamper healing, including musculoskeletal assymmetries, such as leg-length discrepancies, along with chronic infections and allergies. The latter two, in and of themselves, can lead to chronic pain. The most common infections that are found in people with chronic pain are *Borrelia* (Lyme Disease), Mycoplasma, *Babesia,* and fungal infections.

There is a greater tendency for people who suffer from chronic pain to have a melancholy temperament. People with this temperament are very pessimistic because they live in an idealistic world in their minds and, when events or relationships do not develop as they had hoped, melancholy sets in. Sometimes the chronic pain they are suffering from is a direct result of this melancholy attitude.

Pain always has a cause and, for some, the cause is spiritual. There are many reasons why, for some, it is not God's will yet that they be freed from their pain. Pain can help a person realize his or her need for God, change an attitude, or restore a relationship. Yes, chronic pain can be life-changing and, for many, it changes their lives for the better.

RESOURCES

To learn more about Christianity, the Bible, and health we have found the following books very helpful:

The Word on Health
By Dr. Michael D. Jacobson
Moody Press, Chicago, Illinois

What a Christian Believes
By Dr. Ray Pritchard
Crossway Books, Wheaton, Illinois

Anchor for Your Soul
By Dr. Ray Pritchard
Moody Press, Chicago, Illinois

Keep Believing
By Dr. Ray Pritchard
Moody Press, Chicago, Illinois ■

APPENDIX A

Neural Therapy

Some people experience chronic pain that is not due to ligament or tendon weakness. Some chronic pain stems from nerve irritation. This type of pain may be relieved by a treatment known as Neural Therapy.

Neural Therapy is a gentle healing technique developed in Germany that involves the injection of local anesthetics into autonomic ganglia, peripheral nerves, scars, glands, acupuncture points, trigger points, and other tissues.[1] **(See Figure Appendix A-1.)** What are autonomic ganglia? The body contains two nervous systems: the somatic and the autonomic. The somatic nervous system is under a person's voluntary control. The autonomic nervous system functions automatically. The autonomic ganglia is the place where the center of the autonomic nerves are located.

SOMATIC AND AUTONOMIC NERVOUS SYSTEMS

The nerves in the somatic nervous system control skin sensation and muscle movement. Picking up a cup of tea, for example, requires the somatic nervous system to sense the cup with the fingers and contract the muscles to lift the cup. These are the same nerves that are pinched in a herniated disc.

The autonomic nervous system is automatically activated. Life-sustaining functions like breathing, blood flow, pupil dilation, and perspiration are activated by the autonomic nervous system. People do not think about the blood vessels in their hands constricting when they are outside on a cold, winter day. This occurs automatically. The functioning of the autonomic nervous system is crucial, as it controls blood flow throughout the body. Illness often begins when the blood flow to an extremity or an organ is decreased.

A limb with decreased blood flow feels cold and may experience dull burning pain. Even atrophy (breakdown) of the skin and muscles may occur. Decreased blood flow to an organ hinders its ability to function. Decreased blood flow to the thyroid gland may result in hypothyroidism. In this instance, the amount of thyroid hormone the body produces is decreased, resulting in sluggishness, weight gain, and lower body temperature. Does that sound like anyone you know?

Disturbed autonomic nervous system function has been implicated in the following diseases: headaches, migraines, dizziness, confusion, optic neuritis, chronic ear infections, tinnitus, vertigo, hay fever, sinusitis, tonsillitis, asthma, liver disease, gallbladder disease, menstrual pain, eczema, and a host of others. Neural Therapy, because it increases blood flow, may have profoundly positive effects on such conditions.[2]

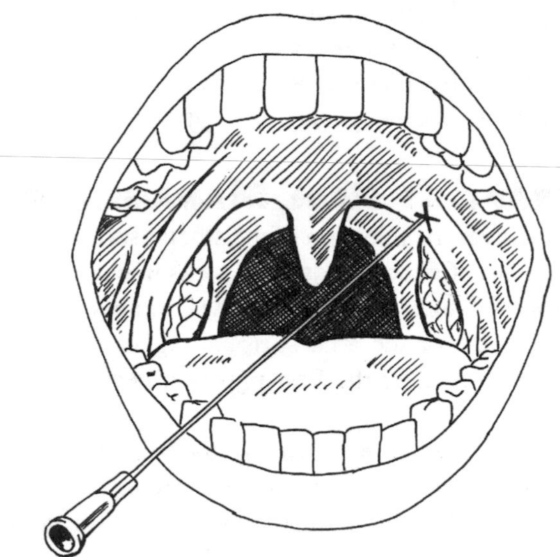

Figure A-1: Neural Therapy on the Tonsils
Any previously traumatized, surgerized, or infected site or tissue can be an interference field for the autonomic nervous system.

INTERFERENCE FIELDS

The founder of Neural Therapy, Ferdinand Huneke, M.D., felt one of its beneficial effects was the elimination of interference fields. An interference field is any pathologically damaged tissue which, on account of an excessively strong or long-standing stimulus or of a summation of stimuli that cannot be abated, is in a state of unphysiological permanent excitation.[3] In layman's terms, any time a tissue is injured it can continually excite the autonomic nervous system. These centers of irritation through the autonomic nervous system may cause disease in other parts of the body.

Most interference fields are found in the head region. According to Dr. Huneke, teeth and tonsils are the two most common—probably because they are close to the brain and nerves. **(See Figure A-1)** An infected tooth can set up an interference field, causing a person to have chronic low back pain or a heart arrhythmia. A patient may have chronic low back pain that is unresponsive to surgical and conservative treatments because an interference field is present.

Scars are the next most common interference fields. Any scar, no matter how small or old, even if it dates back to early childhood, can be the interference field causing therapy-resistant rheumatoid arthritis, hearing loss, sciatica, or other serious disorders.[4]

A good analogy of the interference field is heart arrhythmia, or irregular heartbeats. In a heart arrhythmia an area of the heart sends off an independent, electrical impulse. This impulse is not under the normal control of the heart's electrical system. It acts independently and automatically. During a heart attack, the heart may produce extra beats, called premature ventricular contractions (PVCs). One of the standard treatments for PVCs is an intravenous infusion of lidocaine, an anesthetic. This treatment effectively stops this type of arrhythmia.

NEURAL THERAPY AS PAIN MANAGEMENT

Neural Therapy involves the injection of anesthetic solutions, such as lidocaine or procaine, into these interference fields. The areas injected may include various areas of the teeth, tonsils, autonomic nervous system nerves, or ganglia, somatic or peripheral nerves, scars, or the area surrounding various organs. Immediate pain relief is often observed after the first injection because nerve irritation has been resolved.

Most traditional physicians are not aware of the role of the autonomic nervous system or do not diagnose problems involving it because an autonomic nervous system cannot be tested. The autonomic nervous system does not appear on x-rays; only somatic nervous system nerves can be seen.

To diagnose an autonomic nervous system problem, the clinician must understand interference fields as well as Neural Therapy. An autonomic nervous system disorder should be suspected if any of the following conditions are evident: burning pain, excessively cool or hot extremities, pale or red hands or feet, skin sensitivity to touch, scars, root canals, chronic problems occurring after an infection or accident, chronic pain not responsive to other forms of therapy, shooting burning nerve pain, pinched nerve, or a chronic medical condition that has not responded to other treatments.

While Neural Therapy is used more frequently as a healing modality in European countries than in the United States, nevertheless, Caring Medical offers this treatment, if appropriate, as an option after an initial consultation.

To learn more about Neural Therapy, consult the *Illustrated Atlas of the Techniques of Neural Therapy with Local Anesthetics,* a textbook from Germany.[5]

At our office, Neural Therapy has been a wonderful adjunctive therapy for the treatment of chronic pain and illness. A person with chronic pain often has evidence of both ligament laxity and autonomic nervous system dysfunction. In such a case, both Prolotherapy and Neural Therapy are warranted. Because chronic pain sometimes has an autonomic nervous system component, many are choosing Neural Therapy to get rid of their pain! ■

APPENDIX B

Prolotherapy Referral List

While Prolotherapy is a technique that is still relatively unknown, it is gaining popularity. We have included a list of physicians whom we know personally and who utilize the Hackett-Hemwall technique of Prolotherapy daily in their practices. They also regularly volunteer at Beulah Land Natural Medicine Clinic.

ROSS A. HAUSER, M.D.
CARING MEDICAL & REHABILITATION SERVICES, S.C.
715 LAKE STREET, SUITE 600
OAK PARK, ILLINOIS, 60301
708-848-7789
www.caringmedical.com
drhauser@caringmedical.com

RODNEY VAN PELT, M.D.
776 S. STATE STREET
UKIAH, CALIFORNIA 95482
707-463-1782
(ALSO WITH OFFICES IN AUBURN AND SAN FRANCISCO, CA)

MARK T. WHEATON, M.D.
21920 MINNETONKA BLVD.
EXCELSIOR, MN 55331
952-593-0500
drmark@wheatons.com

INTERNET PROLOTHERAPY REFERRAL LIST

We believe that the best site on the internet for Prolotherapy referrals is www.getprolo.com. On this site, you will find doctors all over the country who do Prolotherapy.

FOR FURTHER INFORMATION, PLEASE SEE:

www.caringmedical.com
www.prolonews.com
www.sportsprolo.com

TEACHING TAPES FOR PHYSICIANS

Teaching tapes that illustrate the technique of Prolotherapy, by David Brewer, M.D., Ross Hauser, M.D., Gustav A. Hemwall, M.D., and Jean-Paul Ouellette, M.D., can be ordered by calling 1-800-RX-PROLO. ■

APPENDIX C

The Prolotherapy Crusade

"You will observe with concern how long a useful truth may be known and exists, before it is generally received and practiced on."
—Benjamin Franklin

"Father, forgive them for they do not know what they are doing."
—Jesus Christ, in Luke 23:34

"...it is now up to you, the injured and hurting, to take up the crusade that the world may know that there is a cure after hurting for sports injuries and chronic pain...and that is Prolotherapy."

This book is just the latest in a long list of writings that have been done to get Prolotherapy accepted into the mainstream treatment of those suffering from chronic pain and sports injury. Enclosed are some of the samplings of other "less known" writings/presentations that have occurred over the years:

1950s...PROLOTHERAPY ENTERS THE RING

It was during the 1950s that modern allopathic medicine first heard the term "Prolotherapy." George S. Hackett, M.D., compiled his research in a book entitled *Ligament and Tendon Relaxation Treated by Prolotherapy* and began making presentations at the American Medical Association Conventions. **(See Figures C-1, C-2, and C-3.)**

American Medical Association, 104th Annual Meeting
Program of the Scientific Assembly
Atlantic City, June 6-10, 1955

Diagnosis and Treatment of Back Disabilities
George S. Hackett, M.D., Canton, Ohio

"Relaxation of the posterior ligaments of the spine and pelvis is the most frequent cause of back pain and disability. Diagnosis is made by trigger point pressure and confirmed by injecting an anaesthetic within the ligament. The local and referred pain are immediately reproduced and disappear within two minutes. The patient's confidence is established. Treatment consists of injection of a proliferant within the ligament which stimulates the production of bone and fibrous tissue, which becomes permanent. New areas of referred pain in the groin, buttocks, and extremities have been identified during the past 16 years while making over 3,000 injections within the ligaments of 563 patients, with 82 percent considering themselves cured. Ages range from 15 to 81 years. Longest duration before treatment was 49 years; the average was four and one-half years. X-rays of animal experiments carried out over two years reveal the proliferation of abundant permanent tissue at the fibro-osseous junction."

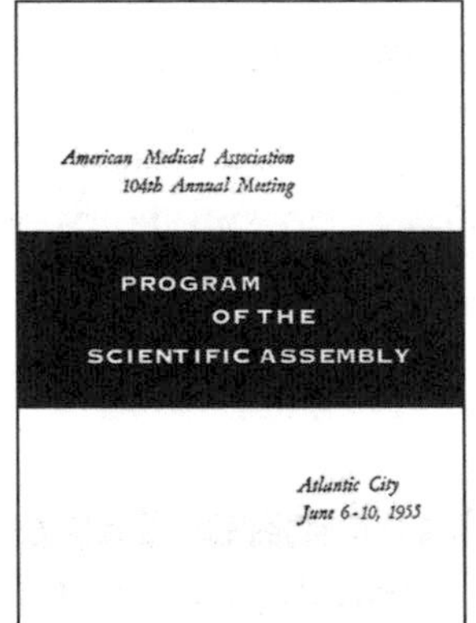
American Medical Association
104th Annual Meeting
PROGRAM
OF THE
SCIENTIFIC ASSEMBLY
Atlantic City
June 6-10, 1955

Figure C-1: During the 1950s, George S. Hackett, M.D., made presentations on Prolotherapy at the AMA national conventions.

Dr. Hackett found a few open-minded physicians at that time, such as Gustav A. Hemwall, M.D., whom he trained and, subsequently, began referring patients to him and a few others as news of this chronic pain cure spread. **(See Figures C-4 and C-5.)**

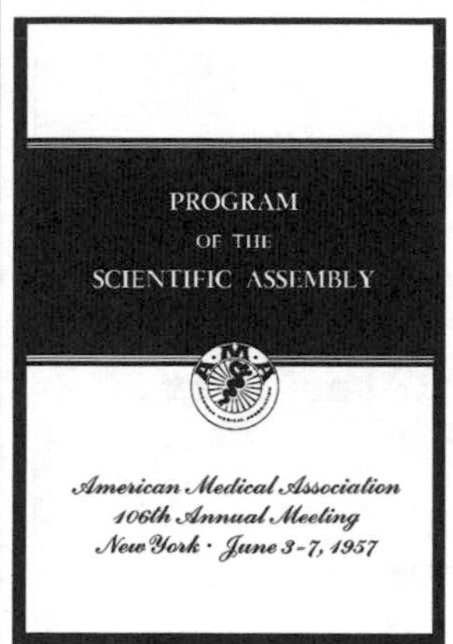

Figure C-2

American Medical Association, 106th Annual Meeting
Program of the Scientific Assembly
New York, June 3-7, 1957

Pain, Referred Pain and Sciatica in Back Diagnosis and Treatment
George S. Hackett, M.D., Mercy Hospital, Canton, Ohio

"Referred pain into the extremities and sciatica results more often from relaxed ligaments of unstable joints than from all other causes combined. Referred pain areas into the groin, lower abdomen, genitalia, buttocks and extremities, to as far as the toes, from articular ligaments that support the lumbar and pelvic joints have been established from observations while making over 10,000 intraligamentous injections in the diagnosis and treatment of 1,207 patients during the past 18 years. Articular ligament relaxation has been found to be the cause of more chronic low back disability than from any other entity. The trigger points of pain of specific disabled ligaments have been established. In diagnosis, knowledge of the referred pain areas directs attention to specific ligaments, and in conjunction with the trigger points of pain, enables the physician to accurately locate the cause of the disability. Ninety percent of the patients with joint instability are cured by the intraligamentous injection of a proliferating solution which stimulates the production of new bone and fibrous tissue cells to permanently strengthen the ligaments."

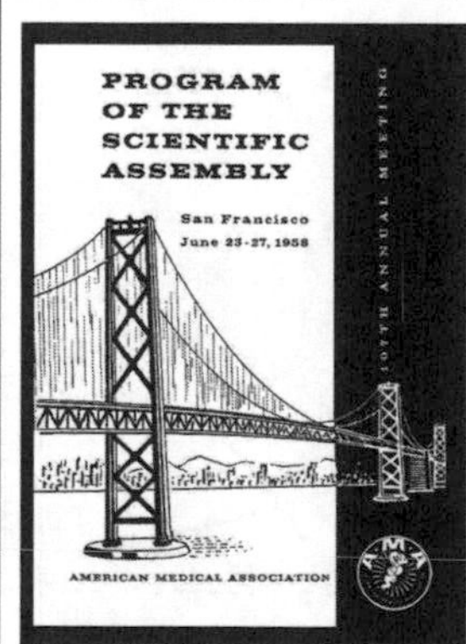

Figure C-3: Information in this appendix is from abstracts of Dr. Hackett's presentations and is used with the permission of the American Medical Association, Chicago, Illinois.

American Medical Association, 107th Annual Meeting
Program of the Scientific Assembly
San Francisco, June 23-27, 1958

Cervical Whiplash Injury
George S. Hackett, M.D., Canton, Ohio

"Chronic whiplash cervical pain has its origin within incompetent occipital tendons and cervical articular ligaments which stretch under normal tension and permit an over-stimulation of the non-stretchable sensory nerve fibrils at the fibro-osseous junction. It results in headache and specific referred pain areas to as far as the eyes, temples, and fingers. The diagnosis is invariably confirmed by intraligamentous needling with an anesthetic solution. Eighty-two percent of 1,656 patients throughout 19 years considered themselves permanently cured by Prolotherapy (rehabilitation of an incompetent structure by the proliferation of new cells—bone and fibrous tissue 'weld')."

GEORGE S. HACKETT, M. D.
616 FIRST NATIONAL BANK BUILDING
CANTON 2. OHIO

Jan. 25, 1957

Mrs. Lloyd D. Anderson
315 South 12th Street
Albia, Iowa

Dear Mrs. Anderson:

In reply to your letter of the 21st, I would suggest that you consult: -

Gustav A. Hemwall, M.D.
839 North Central Avenue
Chicago, Illinois.

Dr. Hemwall is the only man that I know of in your part of the country who is experienced with this technic of treatment. He was out here on several occasions and was instructed in the technic by me, and I can recommend him highly.

As to whether your condition could be benefitted by this procedure, it is impossible to give you any answer without first having examined you to determine your disability.

If I can be of further service, please feel free to call on me.

Sincerely,

Geo S. Hackett

George S. Hackett, M.D.

GSH/mak

Figure C-4: Dr. Hackett taught Dr. Hemwall the technique of Prolotherapy in the mid 1950s and began referring patients to him.

LENN J. SPENCER
R. R. # L
REYNOLDS, INDIANA

February 6, 1957

Gustav A. Hemwall, M.D.
839 N. Central Avenue,
Chicago, Ill.

Dr. Hemwall:

I am a farmer 43 years old and I have been informed by Dr. George S. Hackett that you are carrying out his treatment for back trouble. I have had a bad back for several years and I have tried to run down every lead. I have been through several clinics and seen several Doctors. I have been told everything from a ruptured disc to Arthritis and rheumatism but I still have plenty of trouble.

What would you think about me comming to see you? Have you got any idea how many trips I would have to make and what it would cost me for this treatment, Or would you think it would be possible for my local Doctor to give this treatment if he had the book HACKETT JOINT RELAXATION?

Please write and let me know what you think I should do. Thank you for your kind obligation.

Yours very truly,

Lenn. Spencer.

Lenn J. Spencer

sks

Feb 11, 1957

Dear Mr. Spencer:

I would be very glad to see you and give you my opinion as to whether or not the injections would be helpful to you. The treatment would probably involve three trips to Chicago and the total cost would be about $100.00

If your Doctor would care to make the trip with you we would be very happy to see you with him. I believe that it is helpful to see the treatment demonstrated before attempting to take careof severe cases.

If you decide to come to Chicago we will be glad to arrange an appointment.

Sincerely yours,

GAH

Figure C-5: Dr. Hemwall was known for his kindness and approachability as well as his skill as a Prolotherapist.

1960s... A Time of Relative Peace

While much of the world was in turmoil during the 1960s, it was a time of steady growth in the popularity of Prolotherapy. At this time, various professional societies were formed to teach and promote Prolotherapy. Yes, this was a time of relative peace. Unfortunately by the late 1960s and early 70s, the CT scan was developed and could now show the physicians and the lay public parts of the anatomy that were previously undetectable. The physicians determined from the results of these scans that the discs were causing people's pain, not the ligaments. The only method to treat disc disease was surgical, and thus the surgical age of treating chronic pain began.

Janet Travell's Myofascial Pain Theory was taking hold, along with the above disc theory, as the prevailing method of teaching and training physiotherapists and conservative physicians in how to treat chronic pain. Prolotherapy was now considered a "second-class citizen" and remained that way for quite some time.

MARVIN F. TIESENGA, M.D., s.c.
715 LAKE STREET
OAK PARK, ILL. 60301
386-1078
October 29, 1981

Peter C. Pulos M.D.
Medical Practice Committee
Chicago Medical Society
515 North Dearborn street
Chicago, Illinois 60610

Dear Dr. Pulos:

I am writing to you regarding prolotherapy as practiced by Dr. G. A. Hemwall and the question of insurance compensation for the procedure.

Dr. Hemwall is a physician of excellent reputation in the Oak Park community. For many years he has had an interest in pain problems and the treatment of these problems using prolotherapy. Over the years most of us at West Suburban Hospital have referred numerous patients to Dr. Hemwall with gratifying results. Often these patients were people who had been to many places such as the Mayo Clinic or Lahey Clinic as well as numerous local physicians without finding relief. Of these people the vast majority are helped if not cured of their pain.

From my experience I have no doubt that Dr. Hemwall has saved the insurance companies millions of dollars over the years by his treatment. Without it I am certain that many would have continued to be x-rayed, hospitalized or operated upon at much greater cost. In view of this it would seem to me to be an injustice to Dr. Hemwall and his patients to deny compensation for prolotherapy.

Sincerely,

Marvin Tiesenga M.D.

Figure C-6: Dr. Hemwall recruited friends like Dr. Tiesenga, a prominent surgeon in the Chicago area, to testify for him before the Chicago Medical Society.

1970s and 1980s... Dr. Hemwall Leads the Fight

Gustav A. Hemwall, M.D., never wavered in his fight to see Prolotherapy accepted as a procedure to cure chronic pain. You only have to look at some of his opponents to see that he was tough! Who could be bigger opponents than the Chicago Medical Society and the insurance company, Blue Cross and Blue Shield? Fortunately, Dr. Hemwall had some heavy hitters in his corner, including C. Everett Koop, M.D., the prominent Professor of Pediatric Surgery at the University of Pennsylvania Hospitals. **(See Figures C-6, C-7, C-8, C-9, C-10, C-11.)**

Chicago
Medical Society

The Medical Society of Cook County

810 South Michigan Avenue, Chicago, Illinois 60604. Telephone (312) 922-0417

November 1, 1979

Legal Research Assistant
Life Investors Insurance
Company of America.
814 Commerce Drive
Oak Brook, IL 60521

Re: CMS File

Your File
Policy No.
National Ass'n. Business Owners

Dear

After extensive inquiries by the Medical Practice Committee on the efficacy and the legitimacy of the treatment referred to as 'prolotherapy' we are left with the conclusion that there is no body of scientific data which supports this method of medical treatment. While we are unable to state that the treament is effective and accepted by the medical community, neither can we state that it is rejected by the medical community since we do not have scientific data upon which to base our judgment.

It is the opinion of the Committee that, while the treatment does not enjoy widespread acceptance in medical circles, it is a well recognized procedure in veterinary medicine: animal models of disease and treatment form the basis for a great deal of medical knowledge and progress.

It is significant to this Committee that Dr. Hemwall has performed this procedure on a great many people over an eighteen year period of time and our Society has never received a patient complaint on the procedure. It appears to us that this record speaks for successful treatment. We do not feel that either we, or an insurance carrier, are in a position to declare an uncommon, but apparently successful, procedure as an improper one. Because the method is not widely used does not mean that it is not compensable.

A search of our records reveals that another Committee of our Society was presented with a similar question regarding 'prolotherapy' and they found it an accepted procedure and recommended payment of the physician's fees. We agree.

Sincerely,

Michael Treister, M.D.

Michael Treister, M.D.
Chairman
Medical Practice Committee

MT:WDF/SFO:vvm

xc: Gustav A. Hemwall, M.D.
Edward J. King, Counsel

Figure C-7: Dr. Hemwall battled for the rights of his patients (as seen in ***Figures C-7, C-8, and C-9***) to receive insurance reimbursement for Prolotherapy. Each time the Chicago Medical Society found Prolotherapy an acceptable and compensable procedure.

Chicago
Medical Society

The Medical Society of Cook County

515 NORTH DEARBORN STREET, CHICAGO, ILLINOIS 60610, TELEPHONE (312) 670-2550

November 5, 1987

RE: Prolotherapy
Chubb Life America Insurance Co.
Renate Stollenwerk/patient
Group Policy No.
Claim No.

Dear

We apologize for the length of time this review has taken, however the Medical Practice Committee of the Chicago Medical Society has spent much time reviewing the subject of Prolotherapy. Attached is a copy of an article published in The Western Journal of Medicine, 1982, which is a study that attempts to establish the value of Prolotherapy. In addition, we have enclosed a list of references that address the use of this procedure.

The term Prolotherapy has not found favor with many insurance companies because it does not fit with their various codes. However, upon reviewing a list of procedures that have HCFA assigned codes published by Blue Shield of Illinois (HCSC) 5/15/86, Prolotherapy is coded M0076 on page 84. It is our understanding that two years ago, the Prolotherapy Association was incorporated into a new organization called the American Association of Orthopaedic Medicine. The insurance company may wish to contact this association for additional scientific studies.

We understand that this procedure has been used by many medical and osteopathic physicians both in this country and in Europe. It is significant that Dr. Hemwall has performed this procedure on many people for almost 30 years and our Society has never received a complaint on the use of the procedure. It appears to the committee that this record speaks for successful treatment, and it is long past the stage where it is considered experimental. It is our opinion that an insurance carrier is not in a position to declare a method that is not widely used, but apparently successful, an improper one.

In light of our current review, it is the opinion of the Medical Practice Committee that the procedure of ligament injection, known as Prolotherapy, is a clinically accepted procedure and we recommend payment of the physicians fees by the insurance company.

We thank you for bringing your concerns to our attention and by copy of this letter and attached materials, Chubb LifeAmerica Insurance Company will be informed of our recommendation.

Sincerely,

Peter C. Pulos, M.D.
Chairman
Medical Practice Committee

PCP:lm
cc: Steven Prylak
Assistant Vice President
Group Claims Department
Chubb LifeAmerica

encls.

Figure C-8: Again, the Chicago Medical Society finds Prolotherapy a clinically acceptable procedure.

Chicago Medical Society

The Medical Society of Cook County

310 SOUTH MICHIGAN AVENUE, CHICAGO, ILLINOIS 60604. TELEPHONE (312) 922-0417

April 20, 1976

Gustav Hemwall, M.D.
715 Lake Street
Oak Park, IL 60301

Re:
Carrier: Aetna Life & Casualty
Date of Treatment: August 10, 1975
CMS No.

Dear Doctor Hemwall:

In response to the insurance carrier's request of whether your treatment is an approved and appropriate method, the Subcommittee on Insurance Mediation has made a decision on the above entitled matter.

On the basis of the information presented, it the Committee's opinion that this procedure is an accepted procedure.

By copy of this letter, the insurance carrier will be informed of our recommendation.

Cordially,

Carell Hutchinson Jr. MD

Carell Hutchinson, JR., M.D.
Chairman
Subcommittee on Insurance Mediation

CH:scm
cc: Aetna Life & Casualty

Figure C-9: According to the Chicago Medical Society's multiple reviews, even in the 1970s Prolotherapy met the criterion as a reimbursable medical procedure.

UNIVERSITY of PENNSYLVANIA
PHILADELPHIA, PA. 19104

C. EVERETT KOOP, M.D.
Professor of Pediatric Surgery

Please reply to office of
Surgeon-in-Chief
Children's Hospital
One Children's Center
34th Street and
Civic Center Boulevard
Philadelphia, Pa. 19104

G. A. Hemwall, M.D.
715 Lake Street
Oak Park IL 60302

June 5, 1978

Dear Dr. Hemwall:

I understand you are having difficulty in getting payment for prolotherapy from Blue Cross/Blue Shield. I deplore this activity which exists also in the State of Pennsylvania. I deplore it because the people who make the decision have absolutely no concept about what prolotherapy is and what it can accomplish and I deplore it because many times the people who are most vociferous in denouncing prolotherapy have no compunction whatever in doing extensive spinal surgery which is not only dangerous, and non-rewarding to the patient, but from the point of Blue Cross/Blue Shield is frightfully expensive.

I feel as strongly as I do because I am an extremely active clinical surgeon, teacher, lecturer, etc., and am heavily involved in community affairs. I was at one time almost incapacitated because of pain and eventually was incapacitated because of paralysis of my right arm. I had been diagnosed at the University of Pennsylvania as having intractable pain, a situation I could not accept. Prolotherapy has been responsible, completely and totally, for restoring me to active surgical health and it has been my experience over and over again that I have been able to do the same for other people so diagnosed.

Although I am a pediatric surgeon and have little need to use prolotherapy in my own patients in the pediatric group, I have for many years now been practicing prolotherapy on the parents of my patients and on my friends who were getting what I thought was poor medical and surgical therapy in reference to pain, paresthesia, etc. Prolotheraphy is not a panacea, but it is a rare patient that I select for such treatment who has not been extraordinarily grateful for the relief of pain and the return to productive life.

I have had a go around with Blue Cross/Blue Shield in the State of Pennsylvania on several occasions and I am on the basis of their decisions against prolotherapy boiling mad. In this city and in this state my integrity is unquestioned by the press, and by thousands upon thousands of patients who have been satisfied with what I have done for them. I have told Blue Cross/Blue Shield that their arbitary decision in this matter is something the public should know about and if indeed they do not show more reasonable attitude toward this effective therapy in view of the other things that they tolerate and permit, I will indeed take my concern to the public which I know will not be beneficial for Blue Cross/Blue Shield.

Very sincerely yours,

C. Everett Koop, M.D.

CEK:ei

Figure C-10: Dr. Hemwall brought in the real heavy hitters to challenge Blue Cross and Blue Shield, such as the prominent pediatric surgeon, C. Everett Koop (**Note in this Figure, above, and also Figure C-11.**) Notice Dr. Koop was fighting his own insurance battles regarding Prolotherapy with Blue Cross and Blue Shield at the time.

DEPARTMENT OF HEALTH & HUMAN SERVICES

The Surgeon General of the
Public Health Service
Rockville MD 20857

AUG 22 1986

Everett Nicholas, M.D.
1 Erie Court
Oak Park, Illinois 60302

Dear Dr. Nicholas:

This is in response to your request for a statement concerning prolotherapy. I respond as a patient who has benefited from it and as a practicing surgeon who used it successfully, but certainly not in my official capacity as the Surgeon General of the U.S. Public Health Service.

I think that prolotherapy is an effective method of pain relief, when properly practiced. Prolotherapy frequently works when all other therapy has failed. I say this in spite of the fact that official groups and some insurance companies have taken a contrary point of view. I cannot help but believe these decisions are made in ignorance or because of conflicts of interest.

I was diagnosed as having intractable pain by two neurologic groups in prominent academic institutions, but was totally relieved of my symptoms when treated by Dr. Hemwall at West Suburban Hospital in Illinois. I have benefited from this therapy on a number of occasions since that time.

As a surgeon I found very little use for prolotherapy in my practice, which was confined to children. However, on many occasions I was able to relieve my patients' parents of pain by using the techniques I had learned from Dr. Hemwall.

I trust this information will be helpful to you.

Sincerely yours,

C. Everett Koop, M.D.
Surgeon General

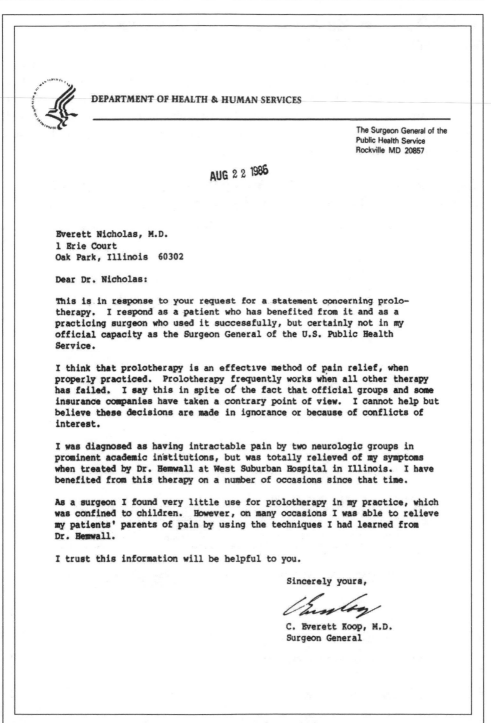

Figure C-11: C. Everett Koop, M.D., crusaded for Prolotherapy—even as Surgeon General of the United States.

1990s AND BEYOND... THE PROLOTHERAPY CRUSADE RAGES ON...

As patients and physicians became bolder in their quest for proper health care and reimbursement, the Prolotherapy crusade raged on. Sometimes the battles were won, other times they were lost. One thing is for certain: the fight will continue! Caring Medical will continue what Dr. Hemwall started! Yes, the battle will wage until Prolotherapy achieves its rightful place in "modern" pain therapies! **(See Figures C-12, C-13, C-14, and C-15.)**

CARING MEDICAL AND REHABILITATION SERVICES JOINED THE FIGHT WITH MANY OF OUR PATIENTS

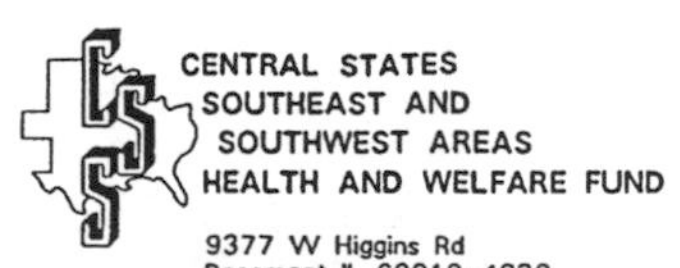

CENTRAL STATES
SOUTHEAST AND
SOUTHWEST AREAS
HEALTH AND WELFARE FUND

9377 W Higgins Rd
Rosemont IL 60018-4938
(800) 323-5000

April 23, 1996

ROSS A HAUSER MD
715 LAKE ST SUITE 600
OAK PARK IL 60301

RE:

Dear Dr. Hauser :

This letter is in reply to your recent inquiry regarding need for prolotherapy treatments.

I am happy to say that the prolotherapy treatments will be payable for four sessions one month apart from each other under the Major Medical portion of Benefit Plan ET1. Under this Plan, there is a $100 per calendar year deductible ($200 for the family). Once that has been met, we will pay 80% of our reasonable and customary allowance for all remaining eligible charges. must be covered on the date(s) on which services are rendered.

If you have any questions, please write the Research and Correspondence Department at P.O. Box 5111, Des Plaines, IL 60017.

Sincerely,

Aileen M. Troia
Analyst
Research & Correspondence Dept.

cc:
cc: Local Union No. 706

Figure C-12: For the patient who is willing to go to battle, victory against insurance companies is possible! **(Note Figures C-12 and C-13.)**

MMA

Mennonite Mutual Aid
1110 North Main Street
Post Office Box 483
Goshen, IN 46527

Toll-free: 1-800-348-7468
Telephone: 219 533-9511
Fax: 219 533-5264

June 17, 1997

Ross A. Hauser, M.D.
Caring Medical & Rehab Services, Inc.
715 Lake Street, Ste 600
Oak Park, IL 60301

Insured:
Patient: Agreement No.: 5090476
Effective Date: February 1, 1990

Thank you for inquiring about 's benefits for Prolotherapy. Our medical review team has reviewed the packet of information you sent.

We will approve coverage for up to three treatments. After the $1,000 is met, we will pay 80 percent of the next $5,000, then 100 percent to the end of the calendar year. The maximum lifetime benefit is $1 million. The deductible and coinsurance are applied each calendar year.

Benefits are limited to the reasonable and customary charges and the medical team will review for proper coding.

A final decision on any claim cannot be made until we receive the actual charges and review them according to the guidelines of the certificate.

Thank you for contacting us to verify the benefits. If you have further questions about coverage we provide, please let me know.

Sincerely,

Polly Kauffman

Polly Kauffman
Managed Care Assistant

cc:

Figure C-13: Some insurance companies do read the studies on Prolotherapy and appropriately reimburse.

THE MEDICARE BATTLE

Medicare still does not cover Prolotherapy. Patients, like Walter R. Donovan, however, are letting those in charge of Medicare know just what they feel about that fact! **(Note Figures C-14 and C-15.)**

MEDICARE

Health Care Service Corporation
233 North Michigan Avenue
Chicago, Illinois 60601-5655

RECEIVED JUN 12 1996

June 10, 1996

Kurt Pottinger
c/o Dr. Ross Hauser
715 Lake Street
Suite 600
Oak Park, Illinois
60301

Dear Kurt:

As you requested, I did check with our Medical Director, Douglas Busby MD, regarding Medicare coverage of Prolo Therapy. Per Dr. Busby, this treatment is still considered investigational and as such is not recognized for payment by Medicare Part B.

I hope you find this information helpful.

Sincerely yours,

Kathie Wood

Kathie Wood
Medicare Part B
Provider Education - Chicago

kw

Figure C-14: Unfortunately for the seniors, Prolotherapy is a non-covered procedure under Medicare and must be paid for by the patient. Hopefully, if people write enough letters, the battle for appropriate reimbursement of Prolotherapy by Medicare and other insurance companies will be won!

379-B Stirling Drive
Cranbury, N.J. 08512
December 14, 1998

Ms. Donna Shalala, Secretary
Dept. of Health & Human Services
200 Independence Ave. S. W.
Washington, D. C. 20201

Dear Ms. Shalala:

I hope your staff will consider my letter worthy of your personal attention.

Perhaps you have heard of Prolotherapy---the injection of substances at the site where ligaments and tendons attach to the bone. When properly administered, Prolotherapy has no side effects and is effective in either eliminating or significantly decreasing chronic pain.

Ross A. Hauser, M.D. has published a book entitled "Prolo Your Pain Away" which C. Everett Koop, M.D. and former U.S. Surgeon General considers a must-read for anyone experiencing chronic musculoskeletal pain. Dr. Koop, in the preface of Dr. Hauser's book, points out that many physicians are not aware of Prolotherapy and even fewer are adept at this form of treatment. As a result, Prolotherapy is not understood nor recommended by traditional physicians. Dr. Koop personally benefitted as a patient and successfully used Prolotherapy on the parents of his pediatric patients.

Prolotherapy offers a win/win opportunity. The patient gets relief from chronic pain without surgery and health insurance plans avoid the high cost of surgery, hospitalization, drugs and rehabilitation.

Alternative therapies should not be rejected when the evidence exists that they work.

At present, Medicare does not pay for Prolotherapy. I respectfully request that your department consider approving reimbursement of Prolotherapy for a trial period. Doctors should be encouraged to refer patients to qualified physiatrist's to avoid surgery (which often makes the problem worse). If after a fair trial period Prolotherapy has not proven its worth coverage can be withdrawn.

Over the past 22 years the Medical Practice Committee of the Chicago Medical Society found Prolotherapy to be an accepted procedure that deserved reimbursement by the insurance carrier.

The courtesy of a reply will be appreciated. Enjoy the Holidays!!

Of course, as a Prolotherapy patient and being retired on a fixed income I would be delighted if I could get retroactive benefits.

Walter R. Donovan

CC: R. A. Hauser, M.D. - Caring Medical & Rehabilititation Services,S.C.
715 Lake St. Suite 600
Oak Park, IL 60301

CC: C. E. Koop, M.D. Sc D - Koop Institute - Dartmouth
Hanover, N.H. 03755-3862

Figure C-15: Patients are the ones who will ultimately be responsible for changing the way pain management is done in this country. May Walter Donovan multiply himself many-fold!

PHYSICIANS DO PROLOTHERAPY AT THEIR OWN RISK!

Physicians around the country are also on the battlefield for Prolotherapy, as Drs. Booneville and Milton can testify. Since Prolotherapy is still not considered the "standard of care" to the medical powers that be, physicians are placed in situations to stand up and defend their rationale for performing Prolotherapy. Saying that it cures chronic pain is often not enough. Sometimes we need help from one another. You can see in Dr. Milton's case—he called on Dr. Koop, the former Surgeon General of the United States of America. (**See Figures C-16, C-17, and C-18.**)

MINNESOTA BOARD OF MEDICAL PRACTICE
2700 University Avenue West, #106 St. Paul, MN 55114-1080 (612) 642-0538

PERSONAL AND CONFIDENTIAL

March 3, 1993

Mark W. Bonneville, M.D.
3790 117th Lane NW
Coon Rapids, MN 55433

RE: Report regarding your brochure on the use of prolotherapy
File No.: PMG0293E10688

Dear Dr. Bonneville:

The Board has received a report regarding the above-captioned brochure. The report alleges that the brochure contains several misrepresentations, including:

1.) The statement that the injection of the proliferant solution will cause new ligament tissue and bone tissue to form is inaccurate (the solution is stated to be Dextrose and lidocaine);

2.) The success rates do not differ from what is usually expected with no treatment;

3.) Listing the CPT codes in the brochure seems very unprofessional.

Please provide a written response to this report within two weeks.

In addition, please explain Dr. Michael Jacobson's background and role in this matter.

In your response, please refer to the file number listed above.

Thank you for your cooperation.

Sincerely,

Pamela M Giefer

Pamela M. Giefer
Medical Regulations Analyst

pmg

Figure C-16: Some medical boards are uninformed about Prolotherapy, and Prolotherapists practice the procedure at their own risk!

Michael G. Milton, M. D.
Family Practice
526 College Drive
Barnesville, GA 30204
770-358-3284

Dr. Ross A. Hauser
715 Lake Street, Suite 600
Oak Park, IL 60301

Dear Dr. Hauser:

It began innocently enough with an invitation to discuss prolotherapy at our weekly physician education meeting. I had been practicing for about 6 months in this area at that time. I had wanted to do a prolotherapy talk anyway so I felt this was a good opportunity. The meeting went well, but I received a letter a couple weeks later saying that I was practicing outside of the "standard of care" and that I had to discuss this with the Medical Services Committee.

Apparently, there was some concern over the way I practice medicine and I was being called upon to justify what I was doing. I met with the Medical Services Committee and again explained why I use prolotherapy. It has now been 2 to 3 months and I have not heard any final word from them about what their plans are. Of particular note, the committee did not know that a local orthopedic surgeon had been referring patients to me for prolotherapy (I informed them of this).

I also sent a letter to C. Everett Koop explaining my situation and he wrote a letter for me that I could present to the Medical Services Committee. His letter was very encouraging for me. I continue to use prolotherapy in my community and am very pleased with the results. The real benefactors though are the patients who have experienced pain relief from this safe and effective treatment.

Sincerely,

Michael G. Milton, M.D.

Figure C-17: The standard of care for curing chronic pain in some areas of the country does not include Prolotherapy. Thank God there are physicians such as Dr. Michael Milton who will take a stand.

C. Everett Koop, M.D.

November 5, 1998

Michael Milton, MD
Family Practice
526 College Drive
Barnesville, GA 30204

Dear Dr. Milton:

You have a tough task ahead of you. Even in my position in academia, I ran into all the same problems you did. I was a pediatric surgeon and there is very little need for prolotherapy in pediatrics. However I did a number of the parents of my juvenile patients but I never charged them and I was therefore not considered to be a potential source of competition to orthopedists, neurosurgeons, etc.

I can attest to the fact that prolotherapy is safe, effective, and in cases such as my own and many patients I treated was effective when nothing else was. There is no question about the fact that it is extraordinarily less expensive than conventional therapy aimed at back pain, especially surgery which does not relieve the patient.

You may use that statement in your presentation.

Unfortunately you will find that a lot of the medical profession has a closed mind to innovation, especially if it's simpler than current therapy and has the potential of elimination high-cost procedures. I found the best way was to demonstrate its efficacy on a patient or family member of one of the detractors. That particular demonstration, if allowed, is a powerful one.

I wish you well as you pioneer with a very necessary therapy which could be a boon to countless patients who suffer at the present time from ligamental relaxation.

Sincerely yours,

C. Everett Koop, M.D.

Figure C-18: C. Everett Koop, M.D., comes to the rescue for Prolotherapy again!

PROLOTHERAPY: THE CHRONIC PAIN TREATMENT FOR THE NEW MILLENNIUM

Because of the Internet and advanced telecommunications, it is now possible for just about everyone, everywhere to learn about various treatments for their particular ailments. Because of this, books such as *Prolo Your Sports Injuries Away!* along with *Prolo Your Pain Away!* are now being read around the world. We receive e-mails every week from physicians in other countries desiring to learn more about Prolotherapy. It is going to be difficult for the powers that be to stop the acceptance of Prolotherapy. When physicians such as Lloyd Saberski, former director of the Yale Pain Clinic, acknowledge the benefits of Prolotherapy, the ammunition is becoming quite powerful. Patients can use these things to show their insurance carriers that they should pay their claims. As long as Prolotherapists have patients like Cathy DiNapoli fighting for Prolotherapy, even if a few fights are lost, in the end, victory is assured! **(See Figures C-19 and C-20.)**

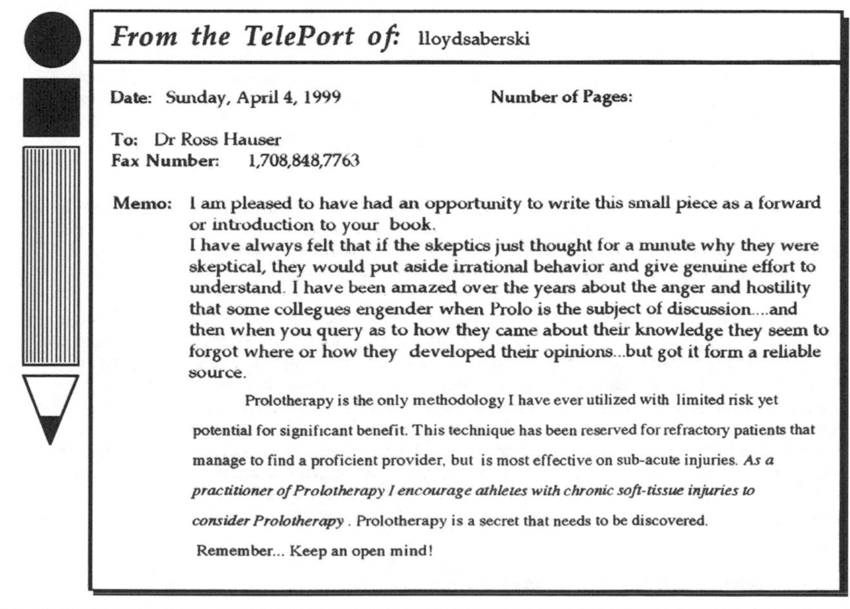
From the TelePort of: lloydsaberski

Date: Sunday, April 4, 1999 **Number of Pages:**

To: Dr Ross Hauser
Fax Number: 1,708,848,7763

Memo: I am pleased to have had an opportunity to write this small piece as a forward or introduction to your book.
I have always felt that if the skeptics just thought for a minute why they were skeptical, they would put aside irrational behavior and give genuine effort to understand. I have been amazed over the years about the anger and hostility that some collegues engender when Prolo is the subject of discussion....and then when you query as to how they came about their knowledge they seem to forgot where or how they developed their opinions...but got it form a reliable source.

Prolotherapy is the only methodology I have ever utilized with limited risk yet potential for significant benefit. This technique has been reserved for refractory patients that manage to find a proficient provider, but is most effective on sub-acute injuries. *As a practitioner of Prolotherapy I encourage athletes with chronic soft-tissue injuries to consider Prolotherapy*. Prolotherapy is a secret that needs to be discovered.

Remember... Keep an open mind!

Figure C-19: Prolotherapy Has Many Supporters
The new breed of Prolotherapists includes Lloyd Saberski, M.D., former director of the Yale Pain Clinic. As professors and other prominent physicians at university medical centers extol the benefits of Prolotherapy, it is bound to have an affect on such important issues as appropriate insurance reimbursement and availability of the technique to the patient.

Yes, it has been decades that the Prolotherapy crusade has been raging, yet the battle continues. Some of the battles are won and others are lost, but there is one fact of which you can be certain: Those who have been cured of their pain and those who treat these patients will continue the battle until Prolotherapy receives its rightful place as the gold standard in the treatment of chronic musculoskeletal pain. ■

1110 Jorie Blvd., Suite 300
Oak Brook, IL 60523
May 3, 2000

Ross A. Hauser, M.D.
715 Lake Street
Oak Park, IL 60301

Dear Dr. Hauser,

I wanted to take this opportunity to thank you! After years of struggling with lower back pain, traditional medicine and physical therapy, it was wonderful to find something that really works.

As you know, I've suffered from on and off lower back problems for almost thirty years. For the past seven or so, though, it seemed to get worse and more frequent, despite exercises and stretches. That's because in addition to the disk problems that I had targeted with exercise, I had also developed loose ligaments leading to joint rotation of the sacroiliac. This was diagnosed by a physical therapist who gave me exercises for it, which I added to my routine.

A few years later, though, the problem returned. I went to see an orthopedist, who prescribed physical therapy and an "SI" belt and an anesthesiologist for "pain management." Well, physical therapy helped, but I was still very limited. The "pain management" was a waste of time. My back still hurt. I could not hike or bike, let alone ride my horse. Then a friend told me about prolotherapy and shortly thereafter, I was in your office, getting needles, lots of needles, into my already sore back.

Well, after seven of these sessions, I was out and about, hiking, biking and riding my horse, with no SI belt, thank you very much! Absolutely pain free. I was able to do the simple things that had been difficult and painful, like getting dressed in the morning, or crouching down to feed my kitties. Although I have since given up horseback riding as tempting fate, I continue to hike and bike.

My HMO turned down my claim for reimbursement because you are not one of their physicians and even if you had been, I would have needed a referral from my primary care physician. I appealed the decision and was treated to a hearing. It was quite an experience. I walked into a room filled with 22 people! They had all been working on my case. I still lost, because they said Prolotherapy was not scientifically proven, that my back would have gotten better by itself and that I had not given the insurance company a chance to offer me alternatives. Actually, I had asked to see a doctor at the Spinal Rehabilitation Center and was turned down. The only doctors they would approve were the orthopedist and the anesthesiologist. So this HMO paid for the orthopedist, the anesthesiologist and the physical therapy. They did not pay for what worked best, the Prolotherapy. Well, my consolation is that they spent a whole lot more money denying my claim then they would have spent paying it!

Doctor, thanks again. I hope you continue to practice for years!

Sincerely,

Cathy DiNapoli

Cathy DiNapoli

Figure C-20: Even when insurance companies deny coverage for Prolotherapy, the patient still wins because his or her pain is gone. The battle, however, will not end until Prolotherapy achieves its rightful place as the cure for chronic pain as Cathy and others can testify!

Appendix D

Beulah Land Natural Medicine Clinic

Beulah Land Natural Medicine Clinic is a free clinic devoted through the grace of God to the prevention and treatment of human disease. This is accomplished through prayer, faithfulness to God through Jesus Christ, rest, nutrition, exercise, and the utilization of natural substances for healing and wellness.

Beulah Land Natural Medicine Clinic is located in very rural southern Illinois, in the town of Thebes. Thebes is located one hour north of Paducah, Kentucky; one hour south of Carbondale, Illinois; and 30 minutes west of Cape Girardeau, Missouri. We started the clinic in 1994.

Why would a Chicago couple choose Thebes, Illinois, to start a charity Natural Medicine clinic? Good question. In 1985, we each dedicated our lives to what we felt and continue to feel is the most important thing in life: faith in God through Jesus Christ. We both realized that where we go after this earthly life is the most important factor in our beliefs. The things of this world are finite; eternity lasts forever.

We both came to realize that what the Bible said was true. The Bible speaks about heaven in Revelation 21:27 saying, "Nothing impure will ever enter into it, nor will anyone who does what is shameful or deceitful, but only those whose names are written in the Lamb's book of life." We wanted to have eternal life with God. We wanted to see our names written in the Lamb's book of life.

We realized that in order to have eternal life with God in heaven, we must accept Jesus Christ as our Savior. Our own works or accomplishments could not cleanse the impurities (sins) in our lives. The only way this could happen was to accept the sacrifice of Jesus Christ for our sins and to believe that He died and rose again. We both did this. For this reason, we believe that our names are written in the Lamb's book of life.

Shortly after this experience, we joined Harrison Street Bible Church in Oak Park, Illinois. The church's senior pastor and his wife, John and Louisa Blakemore, were originally from Olive Branch, a small town in southern Illinois. Pastor John had a special place in his heart for the people of this area, even though he was working in Oak Park.

Pastor John's son, Peter, returned to Oak Park to co-pastor Harrison Street Bible Church after receiving theological training at Bob Jones University. Pastor Peter and his family soon became some of our closest friends and confidants. Pastor Peter was the kindest man we have ever known. Under his encouragement, we started a charity Natural Medicine clinic at Harrison Street Bible Church in 1991. This clinic met in the church basement and was staffed by volunteers.

In early 1994, we decided we needed a weekend away from our usual routine. What could be farther away than Thebes, Illinois, which is a mere 400 miles away from Chicago and located out in the middle of the country? We got much more than we bargained for by the end of the trip. We ended up buying a 120-acre piece of property surrounded by a national forest on three sides. We named the property after Pastor John's favorite song: "Beulah Land." Beulah Land comes from the Bible verse Isaiah 62:4: "No longer will they call you Deserted, or name your land Desolate. But you will be called Hephzibah, and your land Beulah; for the LORD will take delight in you, and your land will be married."

This verse describes the restoration of the relationship between God and His people Israel. We felt that this land would be restored, just as Israel had been restored. There is now a house on the property where all of the volunteers reside during the clinic days.

In late 1994, the first Beulah Land Natural Medicine Clinic was held in the basement of the First Baptist Church in Thebes, Illinois. The clinic offers many state-of the-art Natural Medicine techniques, including nutritional counseling, natural hormone treatments, chiropractic manipulation, physiotherapy, Metabolic Typing, intravenous therapies, and, of course, Prolotherapy. Volunteers from all over the United States staff the Beulah Land Natural Medicine Clinic. The doctors who regularly volunteer with us are Kurt Ehling, D.C., a wonderful chiropractic physician from Morton, Illinois; Rodney Van Pelt, M.D., an expert in Prolotherapy from Ukiah, California; Mark Wheaton, M.D., another expert in Prolotherapy from Minnetonka, Minnesota; and William Hambach, D.C., a very skilled chiropractor from Oak Park, Illinois.

The clinic is an outreach ministry to help people in the same manner as Jesus did. Many people sought help from Jesus for physical illnesses. This is well illustrated in the Bible verse Matthew 4:23: "Jesus went throughout Galilee, teaching in the synagogues, preaching the good news of the kingdom, and healing every disease and sickness among the people." He often gave them encouragement to live justly and uprightly and for people to commit their ways to God. We try to do just that at Beulah Land Natural Medicine Clinic.

We hope that Beulah Land Natural Medicine Clinic will become a renowned medical center like the Mayo Clinic—except that Natural Medicine would be practiced and the people would receive the best treatments free of charge. Due to the devastating effects of chronic illnesses, many people do not have the financial resources to receive Natural Medicine therapies. Beulah Land is a place where treatments are offered free of charge and hope is given.

Since 1994, Beulah Land Ministries has been formed as a not-for-profit, tax-exempt corporation that runs Beulah Land Natural Medicine Clinic. We see more and more patients at each clinic. We are very close to outgrowing our current space at the First Baptist Church. We hope to be able to build a facility in the near future where care can be provided year-round. We look forward to what God has in store for us in the future.

Beulah Land Ministries can always use additional assistance. If you are interested in volunteering to work in the clinic or to help with the building project, please let us know. If you feel led to make a tax-deductible donation, please contact us! ■

TO CONTACT BEULAH LAND NATURAL MEDICINE CLINIC:
Write to:

Beulah Land • RR1 Box 189, Thebes, Illinois 62990 • 618-764-2323
URL: www.beulahlandclinic.com
E-Mail: beulamed@midwest.net

OR CONTACT OUR OAK PARK OFFICE AT:
Caring Medical and Rehabilitation Services
715 Lake Street, Suite 600 • Oak Park, Illinois 60301
URL: www.caringmedical.com
E-Mail: info@caringmedical.com

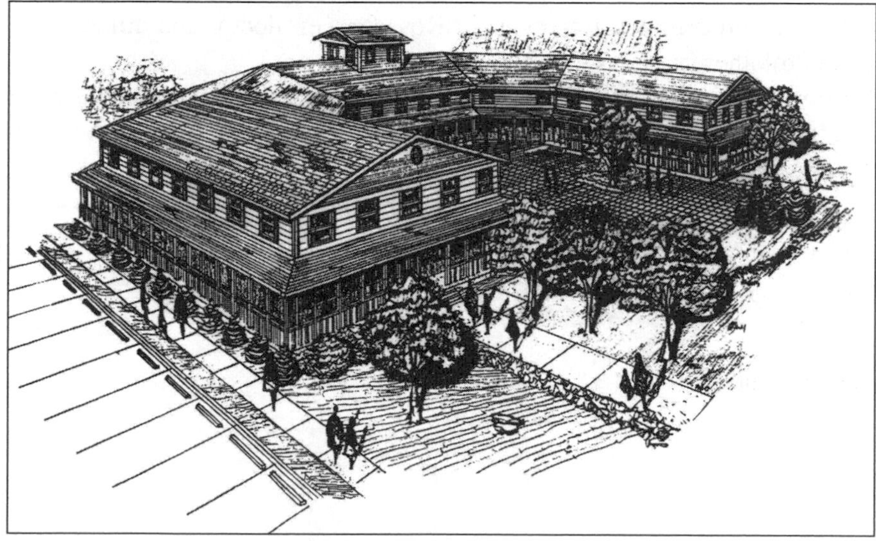

Artist's Rendering of the Proposed Beulah Land Clinic Building

Please consider a tax-deductible donation to Beulah Land Natural Medicine Clinic. Your gift of any amount will help those less fortunate to get the medical attention they need! You can make your donations many ways!

BY CHECK:

Mail to: Beulah Land Ministries
% Caring Medical and Rehabilitation Services
715 Lake Street, Suite 600
Oak Park, Illinois 60301

BY CREDIT CARD:

Call: 708-848-7789

Appendix E

Letters of Appreciation

Because of the success of Prolotherapy in relieving pain, we have quite a collection of "thank you" letters from all over the country and around the world, from patients and doctors who have learned this technique. We enjoy receiving these letters. Believe it or not, seldom do physicians hear the words "thank you." These are words that we all need to say more often.

We would like to take this opportunity to say "thank you" to the patients that have had enough confidence in us to let Ross be their doctor and utilize the technique of Prolotherapy to relieve their pain.

We hope you enjoy these "thank you" letters that have been an encouragement to us. We hope some day to receive a "thank you" letter from you when you Prolo your pain away! ■

Marion A. Hauser, MS, RD
Ross A. Hauser M.D.

Ross and Marion Hauser

June 16, 1997

Dear Dr. Hauser,
First I would like to thank-you for bringing your Clinic to Southern Illinois.

I was diagnosed with Osteoarthritis in both knees and lower back last year. I was in severe pain and almost to the point of not being able to walk or do simple household tasks. The Specialist had told me I would have to have my right knee replaced or I would probably not be able to walk without severe pain. So I was almost willing to try anything. I went to the Beulah Land Clinic in Thebes at the suggestion of a friend and am very glad I did. I had Prolotherapy on both knees and lower back. I have had three treatments so far and am virtually pain free in my left knee and lower back. I still have some pain in my right knee, but not even a quarter of what it used to be. I am back to walking any where from three to five miles a day, so feel very fortunate. I would highly recommend this treatment to any one who has a problem like mine.

Again Thank-You very much and am looking forward to your return Trip to Southern Illinois

Yours Truly,
Sharon Calvert

State: PA
City: State College

Hi Dr. Hauser,
Well, two days ago I was out windsurfing in 25 knots of wind, even getting some freestyle moves in, and having a grand old time. Today I'm ready to go again and it's hard to wipe the smile off my face. Around five months ago I was getting to low end of a long downward spiral with my lower back, all starting with L3-L4 surgery 15 years ago. I'm 42, athletic, and I could probably win a gold medal in my dedication to therapist-prescibed low back exercises. But five months ago my back exercising approach was simply not overcoming the frequent and severe instability flare ups I was having (during a flare up I was OK lying down but could barely support my own torso weight standing up). The doctors said two of my discs were degenerating slightly but that was all they could say. No real explanation for the flareups.

They also mentioned that alot of people have horrible-looking discs on an MRI, yet have no back problems at all. I read every book and checked out every option I could find; fusion, steriod injections, IDET(intra discal electrothermal therapy), and others. I flew to a nationally recognized spine clinic in Florida, and visited the doctor in California who developed the IDET procedure). None of the options seemed to add up. Then amidst my endless search someone handed me your book "Prolo Your Pain Away". I read it three times, then went onto the web and found every article I could on Prolotherapy. It all made sense, and I knew I fit the symptoms.

So here I am after four Prolo treatments, and four months from the day I walked into your office, feeling stronger in my back than I have felt in a long time. The staff at Caring Medical has been absolutely great. My advice to others who qualify for low back Prolo is simple. Go to an experienced prolotherapist (you know who I went to), follow the treatment guideline (diet, moderate exercise, and rest), and be patient (it isn't instant). The injections are a little irritating but I'll take them any day to a life of anguish. Right now I am up to my full regimen of low back exercises, and plan to keep them up to avoid problems in the future.

Many sincere thanks and keep up the great work.

Dave Kurtz

Kenneth Addison, Ph.D.

Organizational Development • Training
Counseling • Psychotherapy

09/20/00

Dr. Ross Hauser, Director
Caring Medical & Rehabilitation Center
715 Lake Street
Oak Park, IL 606301

Dear Dr. Hauser,

This letter is to let you know what an extraordinary difference Prolo Therapy has made in my life. My back problem stems from an injury that I sustained in 1980 when I was involved in a multiple car accident. I was hospitalized in traction for over three weeks. Eventually, I was able to get some relief for my pain from a chiropractor and my condition improved until 1988 when the pain returned and I began to lose mobility. This turn of events was particularly devastating for me since I had been a college athlete and continued to pursue sports as an important part of my physical, and social life. I became, as a result, very depressed and withdrawn.

By the end of 1989 the pain had become so severe that my chiropractor recommended I seek medical assistance. By 1990, my pain could not be controlled by medication and I was reduced to using a cane to walk. In June of 1990 my doctor referred me to a back surgeon who indicated that surgery was necessary or I might lose use of my left leg. So, on the July 13th, I had a partial diskectomy performed at L-4 and L-5. Initially, the procedure went well, but after I arrived in the recovery room I had a cardiac episode and was placed in intensive care for about a week. After two more weeks in the hospital I was allowed to go home under the care of a visiting nurse. As a result of my surgery, I regained almost full use of my left leg, but I still had severe pain.

This pain continued for the next several years and then in 1998 it escalated to an agonizing level. The pain radiating down both leg and I began to lose the use of them. My doctor became worried and referred me to a neurosurgeon who indicated that I needed a laminectomy at L-4. So, on May 1, 1998 I had my second back surgery, which unfortunately was not totally successful. The surgeon indicated that I was experiencing lumbar stencsis and needed additional surgery. So, a month later I was readmitted for my third back surgery during which they performed a lumbar fusion using titanium cages at L-3 and L-4. Unfortunately, I had another cardiac episode and was again placed in intensive care for six days. This was followed by an extensive stay in a rehabilitation hospital and eight months convalescing. Finally, I was able to return to work some nine month later, but I was still in a lot of pain and had to use a cane.

It was about a year later that a patient of yours recommended that I try Prolo Therapy. So, I did and it was like a miracle. After the second treatment I was able to put down my cane and walk with very little pain and after the third treatment I was relatively pain free with only few minor flare-ups. I also start Chelation Therapy, because I had very little stamina and suspected I had clogged arteries. Well, for the first time since I can remember I am able to exercise. In fact, I am able to use my home gym, and amazingly I am walking two to four miles a day. I have been so impressed by Prolo Therapy that I have recommended it to six friends. Unfortunately, only two followed up on my recommendation, but both of them have had success with the Prolo Therapy. So, again thanking for your caring service.

Sincerely, yours

Dr. Kenneth Addison

PFB

Dr. Ross A. Hauser
715 Lake Street
Oak Park, IL. 60301

Sept 13, 2000

Dear Dr. Hauser,

First of all I'd like to thank you for returning the knee that God originally blessed me with fifty years ago (that's a heck of a warranty policy). After injuries in football, skydiving, and a number of other recreational sports, I limped onto the stage at The Natural USA Bodybuilding Championships in New York in 1993 and returned to the plane in a wheelchair! By God's grace I "wheeled" away with the first place trophy in the Master's Division, but my knee was never the same.

I learned to live with pain, discomfort, and instability. Pickup games with my two boys in B-ball or football were no longer a consideration. Every step became a measured one and lateral movements were out of the question. Each morning I would descend our stairway one stair at a time, have breakfast, read God's word, and often pray for a new knee! My prayers were answered.

I received my fourth series of Prolotherapy shots a month ago and I walk pain free! I not only walk pain free, I **run** pain free. I cranked my treadmill up to 7 miles an hour today and the only difficulty I had was sucking in enough O_2 (it's been awhile)! Since my initial visit I have sent twenty people to Caring Medical for Prolotherapy and the success stories keep on coming.

Thank you. Thank you for serving God with the gift that he has blessed you with, and for allowing so many of his children to be recipients of that gift as well.

Gratefully,

Douglas F. Benbow

"YOUR BODY IS A TEMPLE OF THE HOLY SPIRIT, WHO LIVES IN YOU... THEREFORE, HONOR GOD WITH YOUR BODY." **1 Cor 6: 19, 20**

Prolo-therapy has changed my life. It is an answer to much prayer. When I came to the clinic for the first time in January 2000, I had had a surgery on my back to remove a disk in November 1999. The surgeon told me he did the best he could, but I was looking at a lifetime of pain and surgeries, because of my many herniated disks and extensive tissue damage. Unfortunately, my condition would only get worse & worse. After my 1st proto-therapy treatment, I was in less pain than I had been in 4 years. I have now had 4 treatments. It has been a miracle! I can do things and enjoy life more than I have in 4 years. I can work in the yard and pick up my grandchildren again. Shopping & riding in a car are something I enjoy without terrible pain. I thank God every day for the wonderful clinic and the doctors who give so freely of their time and knowledge.

Deborah Patello 10-13-00

Dear Dr. Hauser and Staff,

I wanted to send you this letter and say thank you for clearing up my pain. I was diagnosed with three bulging discs in the lumbar spine and one of them was supposedly herniated. The pain radiated down my left leg, sometimes all the way into my foot. It was difficult walking, sitting, standing, sneezing, and coughing. I walked with a very noticeable limp. I felt like I was about one hundred years old. I couldn't do a lot of my job at the same pace I normally would. After work I would come home, take a shower, and lay in bed with a heating pad on my back. It was a struggle doing my household chores. My wife had to do most of the work around the house because I was in so much pain.

My wife saw one of your specials on WGN one night while flipping through the channels. It caught her attention because everything you said in your report described my situation to the T. She took down your web sight and we visited it the next day. We were excited to see you had a book about the Prolo Therapy procedures. That afternoon we went out and bought the book and as soon as we returned home my wife started reading the book. She was very enthused and encouraged me to try to get to see this doctor. So we called and set an appointment and was surprised you got us in as fast as you did. We were in to see Dr. Hauser only one or two weeks after calling. Once we set the appointment I started reading the book for myself. It was very encouraging until I got to the part that said some people require up to eighty injections and maybe as many as eight visits. Regardless of the fear I had inside I went through with the visit because it sounded too good to be true. My first visit I received sixty injections in my lumbar spine. After about a week I was able to walk much better. I was excited to be able to perform on my job the way I normally did. I have since gone through two more sets of injections and am feeling very little pain. I don't have to take any pain pills anymore, and seldom put the heating pad on my back. Although I still have some minor pain occasionally I am able to do all the things I was doing before I injured my back.

Thank you Dr. Hauser for giving me my life back. The doctor I was seeing at the time wanted to put me through surgery. I, on the other hand, had no intention of going through surgery if I could help it. I am only thirty-one years old and do not want anyone cutting me open and taking out what God gave me. I also want to say thank you to you and your staff for the friendly environment that made going through these injections virtually pain free. Of course, I still felt the needle as it pierced the skin a couple of times. Over all though, it was very bearable and seems to be a success. I will pass your name on to anyone who is having problems with their back.

Neal

Dear Dr. Hauser,

The Lord has His favor upon you. He is working through you onto your patience. He is performing modern day miracles through you.

I came to you with a severly herneated disk. It was out seven MM. I was in excrutiating pain. I couldnt walk, I couldnt do anything, not even the simplest of house chores.

I had consulted other doctors before coming to you. Their end result was spinal fusion.

I chose prolotherapy through you. Now Im 100% healed, no limatations. Best of all, Im completly healed. I feel great!! It also gives me great relief knowing it will never happen again unless I re injure it.

I Thank God for you, and sending me to you. I cant recommend you enough to those in pain. May the Lord keep his favor upon you, so He may give peace to others through you. Thank you, Dr. Hauser

God Speed,

Susan Lowry

APPENDIX F

Nutriceuticals: Helping the Body to Heal

With Doug Skinkis, Former Manager, Beulah Land Nutritionals, Assistant Executive Director of Caring Medical

Perhaps the greatest gift a person can receive is health. Yet, society as a whole tends to take this gift for granted. We spend endless hours trying to invest our money wisely, but we do not take the time to invest in our health. Do not put off making healthy choices until tomorrow, because by then it may be too late! Preventing illness and maintaining health is much easier than correcting an end-stage disease such as cancer or coronary artery disease. All the money in the world is not worth as much as a healthy body. Nutriceuticals can be the key for many to reaching their health goals.

The Hausers have learned that proper diet, nutritional supplementation, and exercise cannot only keep them healthy, but the patients of Caring Medical and Rehabilitation Services as well. Eating fast, fried foods, lazily watching endless hours of television, and not exercising is something we all can understand. With this in mind, the Hausers teamed up with Beulah Land Nutritionals to furnish their patients, as well as the public, with the best that nutriceuticals have to offer. Dr. Hauser functions as a consultant to Beulah Land Nutritionals (BLN). Marion Hauser, a registered dietician with a Master's degree in Nutrition, is the CEO of BLN.

For the past 10 years, they have worked with Ortho Molecular Products to develop nutriceuticals that assist the body's ability to heal connective tissues. This route was taken because most disease starts as a deficiency in the connective tissues, which comprise 30 to 40 percent of the human body. Connective tissues are made of collagen and glycosaminoglycans and are the substrates for such structures as ligaments and tendons, muscles and fascia, as well as the tissues that lie between the organ cells.

Beulah Land Nutritionals understands that each product offered is a vital tool in the treatment of patients and for keeping the general public healthy. That is why we make sure that the products we carry meet certain criteria:

1. **Pharmaceutical Grade Quality:** There are several grades that each and every ingredient can have within a product. This determines the quality of

the product. We make sure that the products carried at BLN are of the highest pharmaceutical grade.

2. **High Concentration:** We understand that people do not like to take pills. We, therefore, look for our products to contain a high level of ingredients within each capsule. This means the consumer takes fewer capsules per day.
3. **Standardized:** Most nutritional products on the market are not standardized for their active components. The products we sell have been tested for the amount of key ingredients. This ensures that the product actually contains the items on the label and in the concentrations reported on the label.
4. **Natural:** The products are made of natural ingredients.
5. **No artificial ingredients**: The products contain only natural ingredients—not artificial ingredients, such as dyes or fillers.

When the Hausers recommend a product from BLN, they know that the person will receive a high-quality product. They also know that, in the long run, that person will end up paying less money than if he or she were to buy "over-the-counter" supplements or vitamins. For example, when compared to other multivitamin products, the multivitamins sold through BLN contain more ingredients per capsule. The product also contains "high-grade" ingredients. Many "over-the-counter" products contain ingredients that are not organically grown and, therefore, contain pesticides and the like. The old adage comes into play here—you get what you pay for. You get more for your money at BLN...more product, more quality, and more results.

We have compiled a short list of some of the more popular products at BLN. We recommend these products to many of their friends, family, and patients. Each product name is followed by its most common uses. Keep in mind, many natural supplements are used for several different conditions. Just because you do not see a certain condition listed, does not mean that the supplement cannot help you stay healthy, and ultimately cure your specific condition. Always consult with your doctor if you need more product information or description of its use.

BEULAH LAND NUTRITIONALS' TOP TWENTY-FIVE

1. PROLO MAX

Specially designed by Dr. Ross Hauser to help with connective tissue repair of ligaments and tendons in order to help relieve chronic pain. It is commonly used to assist with Prolotherapy.

Ingredients: Potassium and Magnesium Ascorbate, Magnesium, Fo Ti Root Powder, MSM, L-Proline, Siberian Ginseng, L-Cysteine, Horsetail Leaf Powder, RNA, Gotu Kola Leaf Extract, Activan, and Glucosamine.

Natural Medicine Uses: Chronic pain, muscle spasms, or arthritis.

2. TRMA

TRMA is an enzyme that is part of the Thera-Zyme Enzyme product line. Thera-Zyme Enzymes are made from only premium ingredients, which meet Good Manufacturing Practice standards. Thera-Zyme Enzyme products do not contain fillers, lubricants, soy, wheat, corn, dairy, egg, sugar, starch, salt, additives, or preservatives. TRMA is used for soft tissue repair. It contains a high dose of protease enzyme and synergistic nutrients, antioxidant enzymes, calcium, and organic minerals to support soft tissue.

Ingredients: Calcium Lactate and Kelp, combined with Protease and Catalase in the pH balancing system.

Natural Medicine Uses: Chronic pain, arthritis, muscle spasms, frequent infections, poor immune system, autoimmune disease, sports injuries, edema, trauma.

3. SMI

SMI is also part of the Thera-Zyme Enzyme product line. SMI (small intestine support formula) is used to provide microorganisms to nutritionally support the small intestine.

Ingredients: Concentrated Cellulase, Carbohydrase, Lactobacillus Acidophilus, Lactobacillus Casei, Bifidobacterium Longum, and Lactobacillus Salivarius.

Natural Medicine Uses: History of chronic yeast infections, foul odor to stool or urine, frequent or prolonged use of antibiotics, constipation, allergies, or Leaky Gut Syndrome.

4. Adrene LN-Support

Adrenal glands play a crucial role in the body's resistance to stress. If an individual is exposed to a great deal of stress, the adrenal gland will become overused and not produce enough hormone. This leaves the individual fatigued or anxious, more susceptible to allergies or infection, and with a decreased ability to handle stress.

Ingredients: Vitamins A, C, E, B_6, and B_{12}, Niacin, Pantothenic Acid, Calcium, Magnesium, Maganese, Sodium, Bovine Adrenal Concentrate, Bovine Whole Pituitary, Pyridoxal 5-Phosphate, and an herbal blend of Wild Yam Root Extract, Chamomile Flowers, Licorice Root, Siberian Ginseng, and Dandelion Root Extract.

Natural Medicine Uses: Anxiety, inability to handle stress, depression, fatigue, inability to hold a chiropractic manipulation, low blood pressure, cold hands and/or feet, or poor healing.

5. BIL

BIL is another product of Thera-Zyme Enzymes. It is used to help support the biliary (liver/gallbladder) system.

Ingredients: Fennel Seed, Turmeric Root, Lecithin, Cinnamon Bark, Ginger Root combined with Protease, L-Taurine, Lipase, Cellulase in the pH balancing system.

Natural Medicine Uses: History of gallbladder stones or gallbladder surgery, loss of appetite, Irritable Bowel Syndrome, abdominal pain after eating, or inability to digest lots of protein.

6. SUPER VITS WITHOUT IRON

Super Vites without Iron is a multiple vitamin-mineral complex that is the essential base for all nutritional protocols.

Ingredients at recommended dosage:

Vitamin A (fish liver oil) 5000IU	Magnesium (as asparate, buffered amino acid chelate, citrate) 500mg
Vitamin A (beta carotene) 20,000IU	Zinc (as chelazome) 30mg
Vitamin C (as ascorbic acid, calcium ascorbate) 800mg	Selenium (as amino acid complex) 200mcg
Vitamin D3 (fish liver oil) 100IU	Copper (as lysinate) 2mg
Vitamin E (d-alpha tocopherol succinate) 200IU	Manganese (as chelazome) 5mg
Thiamine (B1 as Thiamine HCI) 75mg	Chromium (as chromemate) 200mcg
Riboflavin (B2) 75mg	Molybdenum (as amino acid chelate) 50mcg
Niacin 75mg	Potassium (as citrate) 99mg
Vitamin B6 (as Pyrodoxine HCl) 215mg	Choline Bitartrate 150mg
Folic Acid 800mcg	PABA 150mg
Vitamin B12 (as Cyanocobalamin) 150 mcg	Inositol 100mg
Biotin 75mcg	Rutin 100mg
Pantothenic Acid (D Calcium Pantothenate) 100mg	Montmorillonite 50mg
Calcium (as hydroxyapatite, ascorbate) 250mg	N-Acetyl-L-Cysteine 25mg
Iodine (kelp) 225mcg	Vanadyl Sulfate 2mg
	Boron (proteinate) 2mg

Natural Medicine Uses: General health and well-being.

7. COD LIVER OIL (ORANGE FLAVORED)

Cod and other cold water fish contain omega-3 fatty acids. Omega-3 fatty acids are used to help keep blood flowing smoothly, help regulate cholesterol and triglyceride levels, raise HDL ("good" cholesterol), lubricate the joints, and improve utilization of calcium for making bones.

Ingredients: Vitamins A and D, EPA, DHA, Cod Liver Oil, Glycerin, Sorbitol, Lecithin, Cellulose, Orange Flavor, Apple Pectin, Oxyguard (antioxidant mixture), and Beta Carotene.

Natural Medicine Uses: Arthritis, chronic pain, muscle aching, skin rashes, dry skin, autoimmune diseases.

8. PRO-CARTILAGE

Pro-Cartilage is a blend of herbs used to help with many degenerative conditions.

Ingredients: Ascorbic Acid, Glucosamine, Chondroitin Sulfate, and Bromelain.

Natural Medicine Uses: Arthritis, cartilage injuries, meniscal tears, chronic pain, loss of joint mobility, or ligament injuries.

9. L-GLUTATHIONE

L-Glutathione, is used as an antioxidant, sulfur source, and for detoxification.

Ingredients: L-Glutathione 75mg.

Natural Medicine Uses: Emphysema, mercury and heavy metal detoxification, bronchitis, antioxidant support, cataracts, or macular degeneration.

10. BEULAH'S GTF

Beulah's GTF is used for blood sugar disorders such as hyperinsulinemia, diabetes, and hypoglycemia. (Physician must monitor changing insulin needs.)

Ingredients: Biotin, Chromium, Vanadyl Sulfate 50 mg, Lipoic Acid 300mg and Gymnema.

Natural Medicine Uses: Hypoglycemia, hyperinsulinemia, or diabetes.

11. LIPID LOWER

Lipid Lower is used for people with heart disease.

Ingredients: Chromium, Inositol Hexaniacinate, Gugulipids, Artichoke Extract, and Guar Gum.

Natural Medicine Uses: Coronary artery disease, high triglycerides, high cholesterol, or low HDL.

12. MAGNESIUM REACTED

Magnesium Reacted is a very absorbable form of magnesium.

Ingredients: Chelated Magnesium 250 mg.

Natural Medicine Uses: Anxiety, muscle weakness, heart disease, high blood pressure, PMS, asthma, anxiety, tremors, chronic fatigue, fibromyalgia, or muscle cramps.

13. SILYMARIN FORTE

Silymarin Forte is an herbal blend used to help support the liver.

Ingredients: Standardized Milk Thistle Seed Extract.

Natural Medicine Uses: Cirrhosis, hepatitis, toxicity, gallstones, chronic fatigue, or liver congestion.

14. NATURAL E WITH MIXED TOCOPHEROLS

Natural Vitamin E is a completely natural form of Vitamin E that includes mixed tocopherols.

Ingredients: Mixed tocopherols, 400 IU.

Natural Medicine Uses: Blood clotting disorders, coronary artery disease, antioxidant support, stroke, or PMS.

15. MSCLR

MSCLR is another Thera-Zyme product that assists people with: chronic pain, muscle stiffness, and soft-tissue healing.

Ingredients: Burdock Root, Wild Yam Root, combined with Amylase, Catalase, and Cellulase in a pH balancing system.

Natural Medicine Uses: Muscular cramps, muscular fatigue, sports injuries, soft tissue injuries, or chronic pain.

16. Bromelain Max

Bromelain Max is a protease enzyme that helps clean up the "bad" inflammation.

Ingredients: Bromelain, Papain.

Natural Medicine Uses: Chronic pain, swelling, edema, sports injuries, or trauma.

17. Cardio Support

Carditrol is a combination product used for cardiac support.

Ingredients: Hawthorne Extract, L-Taurine, L-Carnitine, and Magnesium.

Natural Medicine Uses: Congestive heart failure, coronary artery disease, angina, or hypertension.

18. Menstrual Support

Menstrual Support is a blend of herbs that is used to help support the female organs.

Ingredients: Ascorbic Acid, Chaste Berry, Dong Quai Root, Yarrow Leaf, Ladies Mantel (whole plant) Powder, and Mother Wort Leaf Powder.

Natural Medicine Uses: Breast cancer risk, uterine cancer risk, PMS, fibroids, menstrual cramps, excessive menstrual bleeding, or irregular menstruation.

19. Stimmune

Stimmune is a combination used to promote a healthy immune system.

Ingredients: Aloe Vera, Olive Leaf S.E. 20%, and Zinc.

Natural Medicine Uses: Immune deficiency, colds, flu, viruses, or dietary infections.

21. Pro-Collagen

Pro-Collagen was specially designed by Dr. Hauser to provide nutritional support for the connective tissues.

Ingredients: Vitamin A, Vitamin D_3, Folic Acid, Vitamin B, Biotin, Selenium, Betaine HCL, Para-Aminobenzoic Acid, MSM, Nettles Leaf Powder, Horsetail Grass Powder, Saw Palmetto Berry Extract, and Fo Ti Root Powder.

Natural Medicine Uses: Brittle hair and nails, thinning hair, connective tissue deficiency, or chronic pain.

22. Beulah's Skin and Nails

Beulah's Skin and Nails was also designed by Dr. Hauser to provide nutritional support for collagen of the body, especially in the skin and nails.

Ingredients: Vitamin A, B Vitamins, L-Proline, Silica, Burdock Root Extract, Nettles Leaf, Gotu Kola, Dandelion Root, and Milk Thistle.

Natural Medicine Uses: Skin irritations, eczema, acne, chronic pain, connective tissue deficiency, aging skin.

23. Vita Vessel

Vita Vessel was designed by Dr. Hauser to provide nutritional support for the connective tissues of the vasculature.

Ingredients: Troxerutin, Butcher's Broom, and Horse Chestnut Extract.

Natural Medicine Uses: Varicose veins, aneurysms, easy bruisability, or circulatory problems.

24. Osteo Care

Ingredients: Osteo Care contains Vitamin D 600 IU, Vitamin K 150 mcg, Folic Acid 800 mcg, Calcium 200 mg, Phosphorus 50 mg, Magnesium 150 mg, Selenium 200 mcg, Copper 2 mg, Manganese 10 mg, Molybdenum 150 mcg, Ipriflavone 600 mg, Boron 5 mg, Strontium 100 mg, and Montimorillonite 150 mg.

Natural Medicine Uses: Osteo Care may be used to help with the prevention of bone loss and to improve bone density.

25. Malic Acid

Ingredients: Malic Acid.

Natural Medicine Uses: Chronic body pain, muscle aches, soft tissue injury.

Beulah Land Nutritionals strongly suggests consulting your doctor before starting on any medications or supplements.

The staff at Beulah Land Nutritionals works hand-in-hand with Ross and Marion Hauser. We use their knowledge as well as that of our suppliers to come up with a collection of the best and most effective supplements and vitamins around. *You can trust Benuts to provide you with valuable products.* ■

Appendix G

Mesotherapy

Mesotherapy is a treatment that stimulates the mesoderm, or middle layer of the skin, which will, in turn, relieve a wide variety of symptoms and ailments. The connective tissue of the body, primarily the collagen, which makes up the skin, bone, ligaments, tendons, and muscle, is derived from the mesoderm. The mesoderm also involves the fat or adipose tissue and connective tissues around organs. **(See Figure G-1)** Dr. M. Pistor originated the technique of Mesotherapy in France in 1952. It is commonly practiced in France, where more than 15,000 practitioners utilize Mesotherapy for the care of their patients. Mesotherapy is also practiced in many other countries around the world, including Belgium, Columbia, Argentina, and throughout Europe.

Embryonic Origin	Adult Derivative
Ectoderm	Skin Brain Breast Sweat glands
Mesoderm	Fibrous Tissue *(Connective)* Cartilage Bone Muscle Fat
Endoderm	Gut Liver Lung Pancreas

Figure G-1: Three Germ Layers and the Tissues Derived from Them

Mesotherapy is an interventional natural medicine technique. Mesotherapy must be performed by a licensed health care clinician who is permitted to do injections. At our office, Caring Medical and Rehabilitation Services, this includes the physicians, physician assistants, and nurses. **(See Figure G-2.)** The technique involves the injection of substances to stimulate the mesoderm for various biological purposes. For instance, if the mesoderm circulation is poor, a vasodilator is used; if excessive inflammation is present, an anti-inflammatory medication is used; or if inflammation/stimulation is needed; a fibroblast proliferating solution is injected. Conditions such as cellulite are due to lymphatic and nervous insufficiency, therefore a stimulator of venous and lymph flow is used. We use natural plant extracts whenever possible; however, traditional pharmacologic agents are sometimes required.

Uses for Mesotherapy

The compounds injected into the mesoderm during Mesotherapy depend upon the pathophysiology of the disease process. In general, the substances fall into the following classes: vasodilators, anti-inflammatories, muscle relaxants, decontractants (reduce contractures), proteolytic enzymes, biologics (including vitamins, minerals, and plant extracts), vaccines, anti-infectants, hormones, hormone blockers, general medicine physiologics, and anesthetics.

Mesotherapy is effective for a multitude of conditions because it helps reverse the physiology of that condition. In rheumatoid arthritis, for example, plant and pharmacologic agents are used to control inflammation; whereas connective tissue stimulators (such as silica, biotin, and proteolytic enzymes) that promote inflammation and healing are given to the athlete with a ligament tear or degenerated tendon. The pathophysiology is multifactorial in many conditions, therefore, multiple agents are used. **(See Figure G-3.)**

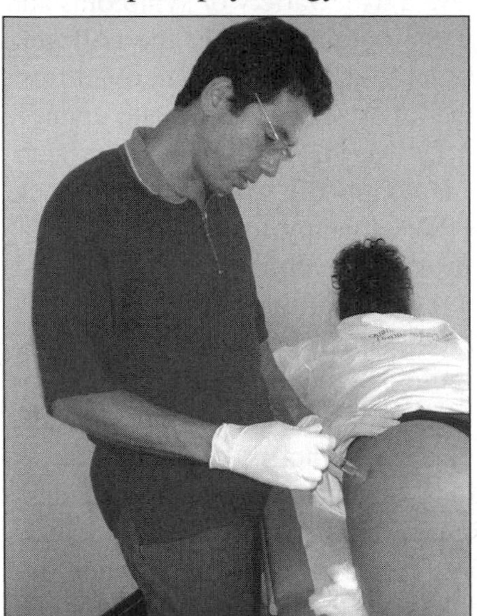

Figure G-2: Here Dr. Hauser is seen performing Mesotherapy on a patient at Caring Medical and Rehabilitation Services.

For example, cellulite is a condition involving the circulation as well as the lymph flow of the adipose tissue; thus a vasodilator (increases blood flow), a stimulator of lymph drainage, and a lipolytic agent (breaks down fat tissue) are used. Another example of using multiple agents is for hair growth. Male and female balding is related to many factors, including excessive androgens (sex hormones), poor scalp blood flow, and nutrient deficiencies. The mesotherapy protocol for hair growth, therefore, involves the use of a combination of nutrients (such as biotin, hyaluronic acid, and silica, for example), vasodilators, and androgen blockers.

Dr. Jacque Le Coz, former president of the French Society of Mesotherapy and Mesotherapist for some of the French

PHARMACOLOGICAL CLASS	POSSIBLE AGENT	PURPOSE
VASODILATOR	PENTOXIFYILLINE	INCREASE CIRCULATION
NSAID	TORADOL	ANTI-INFLAMMATORY
CNS SEDATIVE	NORFLEX	MUSCLE RELAXANT
ENZYMES	HYALURONIDASE	DECREASE SCAR TISSUE
NUTRIENTS	BIOTIN	STIMULATE REPAIR
VACCINES	BACTERIAL PROTEINS	STIMULATE IMMUNE SYSTEM
ANTIBIOTICS	METRONIDAZOLE	ANTI-INFECTION
HORMONES	PROGESTERONE	HORMONE REPLACEMENT
HORMONE BLOCKERS	FINASTERIDE	HAIR GROWTH
GENERAL MEDICINES	COMPAZINE	CORRECT PHYSIOLOGY
ANESTHETICS	PROCAINE	INCREASE CIRCULATION
CALCIUM METABOLISM	CALCITONIN	REMOVE BONE SPURS
BIOLOGICS	INTERFERON	IMMUNE STIMULATION

Figure G-3: Many different pharmacological and natural agents are used during Mesotherapy.

National Sports Teams, has written three books on Mesotherapy, including *Mesotherapie et Medecine Esthetique* (Solal Publishing, France), *Mesotherapie et Traumatologie Sportive* (Masson Publishing, France), and *Mesotherapie en Medecine Generale* (Masson Publishing, France). Dr. Le Coz was privileged to become the pupil of the founder of mesotherapy, Dr. M Pistor, and even became like a son to him. Dr. Pistor wrote the prefaces to each of Dr. Le Coz's books. Dr. Hauser received training in mesotherapy from Dr. Le Coz at his Paris clinic.

As outlined in Dr. Le Coz's books, Mesotherapy has been shown to be effective for the following conditions:

SPORTS INJURIES:

ARTHROPATHY	LIGAMENT SPRAIN	OVERUSE INJURIES	STRESS FRACTURES
BARRÉ-LIEOU SYNDROME	MENSICAL TEAR	PERIOSTITIS	TENDON CALCIFICATIONS
CHRONIC JOINT SWELLING	MUSCULAR BRUISE	PLANTAR FASCIITIS	TENDON DEGENERATION
EPICONDYLITIS	MUSCLE TEAR	SHIN SPLINTS	TENDON STRAIN

SKIN INJURIES:

ACNE	HAIR LOSS	OBESITY STRETCH LINES	TELANGIECTASIAS
ALOPECIA	HERPES INFECTION	PSORIASIS	VENOUS INSUFFICIENCY
CELLULITE	HYPERTROPHIC SCARS	RIDES	VITILIGO
CONTUSIONS	LIPODYSTROPHY	SCAR DISORDERS	WRINKLES
ECZEMA	MALE/FEMALE HAIR LOSS	SUN DAMAGED SKIN	

CHRONIC PAINFUL INJURIES:

BONE SPURS	DEGENERATIVE ARTHRITIS	MIGRAINE HEADACHES	DYSTROPHY
BURSITIS	DEGENERATIVE DISC DISEASE	MUSCLE SPASMS	RHEUMATOID ARTHRITIS
CALCIFIC TENDONITIS	DUPYTREN'S CONTRACTURE	MYOFASCIAL PAIN	SPONDYLOLISTHESIS
CARPAL TUNNEL SYNDROME	FIBROMYALGIA	NEURALGIA	TARSAL TUNNEL SYNDROME
CAUSALGIA	FROZEN SHOULDER	OSTEOCHONDROSIS	TENSION HEADACHE
CERVICOBRACHALGIA	GOUT	POST-FRACTURE PAIN	TMJ SYNDROME
CHONDROMALACIA	HERNIATED DISC PAIN	POST-SURGICAL PAIN	TRIGEMINAL NEURALGIA
CHRONIC LOW BACK PAIN	HERPES ZOSTER PAIN	POST-WHIPLASH PAIN	TRIGGER FINGER
CONTRACTURES	LIGAMENT SPRAIN	PSEUDOGOUT	ULNAR NEUROPATHY
DE QUERVAIN'S TENOSYNOVITIS		RADICULOPATHY	
		REFLEX SYMPATHETIC	

List continues on the next page.

GENERAL MEDICAL CONDITIONS

ALLERGIES	COMPULSIVE BEHAVIOR	HEARING LOSS	PROSTATITIS
ALOPECIA	CONSTIPATION	HEMORRHOIDS	RESTLESS LEGS
ASTHMA	CORONARY INSUFFICIENCY	HEPATITIS	RHEUMATOID ARTHRITIS
AUTOIMMUNE DISASES	DEGENERATIVE ARTHRITIS	INSOMNIA	SLOW METABOLISM
BRONCHITIS	DEPRESSION	IRRITABLE BOWEL SYNDROME	SPASMATIC COLITIS
CHILDHOOD INFECTIONS	DYSMENORRHEA	LYMPHEDEMA	VAGINAL/ANAL ITCHING
CHRONIC FATIGUE	GASTRITIS	MENSTRUAL IRREGULARITY	VASCULAR INSUFFICIENCY
CHRONIC INFECTIONS	GENERALIZED ANXIETY	MIGRAINE HEADACHE	VERTIGO
CHRONIC SINUSITIS	GENITAL HERPES	OBESITY	
CHRONIC UTIs	GLAUCOMA	PRESBYOPIA	
CIGARETTE ADDICTION	GLOSSODYNIA		

MESOTHERAPY FOR CALCIFICATIONS AND BONE SPURS

Traditional medicine currently offers only one method to remove bone spurs: surgery. Bone spurs generally form as the body's response to stabilize a weak structure. Prolotherapy is therefore, successful because it strengthens weakened connective tissues, and relieves the pain of bone spurs. Mesotherapy and Endotherapy (deeper injections with the same solutions) offer **non-surgical alternatives** to decreasing and eliminating the actual bone spurs, not just the pain of the bone spurs. By using compounds that affect calcium metabolism, such as EDTA, a calcium chelator, and Calcitonin, a calcium hormone, these treatments can successfully remove bone spurs over a period of time. **(See Figure G-4.)**

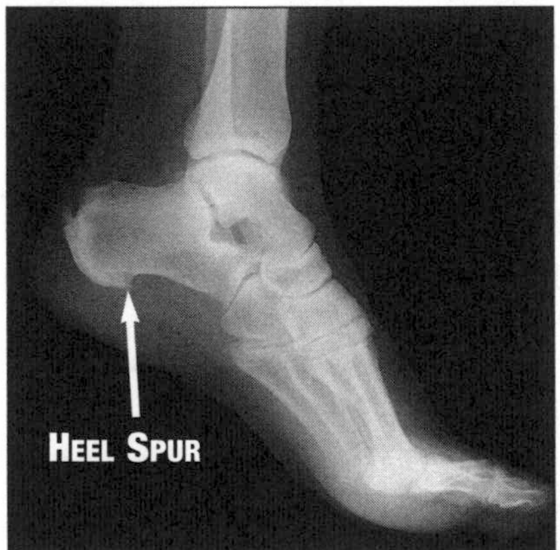

Figure G-4: Bone spurs of the heel can be treated with Mesotherapy; a non-surgical alternative to resolve bone spurs and the associated pain.

Athletes commonly experience calcifications in structures like the biceps and rotator cuff tendons. Mesotherapy and Endotherapy are useful treatments to employ when these structures are painful. These treatments will, over time, help the body rid itself of the abnormal physiology that led to the calcifications, thus, reducing their size and negative effects.

MESOTHERAPY FOR MEDICAL ESTHETICS

Many Mesotherapists practice the specialty of Medical Esthetics because of the beautifying effects Mesotherapy has on the skin. The skin can be treated successfully with Mesotherapy. Wrinkles and cellulite respond well to Mesotherapy. The injections reach not only the different layers of the skin, but the subcutaneous fat as well, helping reverse the physiology that makes cellulite form.

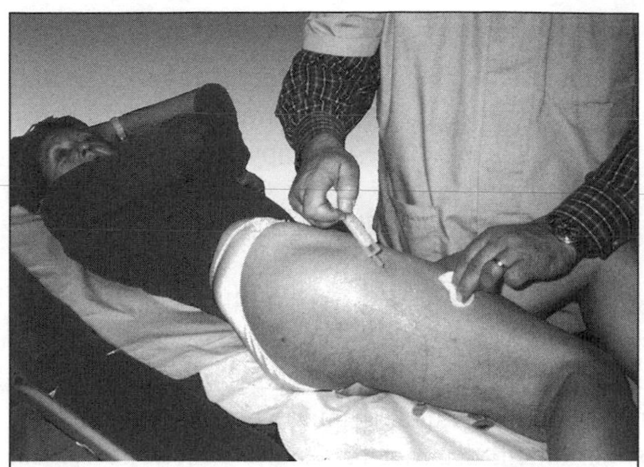

Figure G-5: Mesotherapy Treatment for Cellulite

CELLULITE

Cellulite is a condition in which the person (more often women) experience abnormal "nodules" of fat forming in their midsection and thighs. This gives the appearance of a ruffling of the skin. The condition is caused by abnormal physiology in the skin and subcutaneous fat. It involves a type of insufficiency in the venolymphatic system. Mesotherapy injections are given to not only improve the venous and lymphatic flow, but to break down the fat nodules as well. **(See Figure G-5)** The solutions generally contain a vasodilator, lymph flow stimulator, and anesthetic.

Because cellulite involves an abnormality in fat accumulation, Mesotherapy injections should be done in conjunction with a comprehensive natural medicine program designed to improve overall metabolism. This would have the effect of increasing weight loss and improving overall health. Hormone imbalances are often at the core of the problem and need to be corrected to have maximum benefits. If cellulite recurs because the person stopped their natural medicine program, then the process will need to be repeated.

WRINKLES

Wrinkles, like other conditions involving the skin, have a multifactorial etiology. Excessive skin wrinkles or rides, can be caused by overall dehydration, excessive sun exposure, genetics, facial expressions, muscle atrophy, fatty acid deficiencies, hormone imbalances, nutrient deficiencies, and many other causes. As with cellulite treatment, it is best to utilize Mesotherapy for wrinkles in the context of a comprehensive natural medicine program to correct some of the above causes. For the person with stress and increased muscle contraction in the forehead, Botox injections can be given. Excessive wrinkles can also be a sign of advanced or aggressive aging, which emphasizes the need even more to utilize Mesotherapy, along side of a comprehensive anti-aging regime. This may involve the use of regenerative therapies, natural hormone replacement, nutriceuticals, appropriate metabolic-type diet, and other anti-aging measures. As with cellulite, Mesotherapy for wrinkles may need to be repeated after the initial series.

THE TECHNIQUE OF MESOTHERAPY

For those who have been fortunate enough to have Prolotherapy or Neural Therapy injections, you will be happy to know that the injections of Mesotherapy hurt less than Prolotherapy or Neural Therapy. Mesotherapy injections involve extremely small needles that penetrate the body only a very small depth, which is typically four to six millimeters. Many of the needle sticks are not even felt because often times the skin is pinched by the clinician prior to and during the injections.

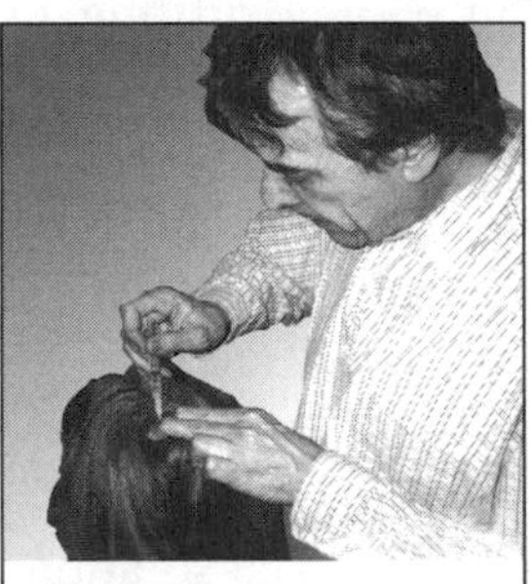

Figure G-6: Dr. J. Le Coz performs mesotherapy to reverse hair loss.

Mesotherapy treatments are typically given once per week. As improvement is seen, the treatments may be given less frequently, such as once every two weeks or once per month. If quicker improvement is necessary, such as an athlete desiring to resume athletic activities, treatments may be given twice per week.

Mesotherapy can involve anywhere between eight and 300 shots, depending on the condition and amount of area covered. When more than 20 shots are given, it is typically because the person is getting multipricking or Mesolift done. Both of these Mesotherapy techniques involve very superficial, quick injections, taking less than a couple of minutes to do all of the injections, thereby maximizing the amount of area stimulated. This is often necessary for conditions such as cellulite, wrinkles, and hair loss, where a maximum area must be stimulated to produce a good result. **(See Figure G-6.)**

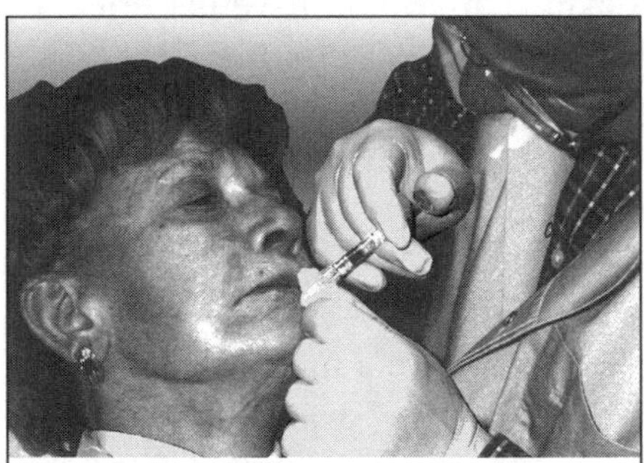

Figure G-7: Mesotherapy for Beauty
Dr. A. Lejunie of France demonstrates using hyaluronic acid injections to remove wrinkles. Dr. Hauser observed Dr. Lejunie in his Paris office using mesotherapy in many ways to help a person become beautifully healthy.

The number of Mesotherapy treatments needed depends upon many variables, including the condition, the abnormal physiology causing the condition, as well as the chronicity of the problem. A minimum of three to five sessions of Mesotherapy are generally done to access response. For long term chronic conditions such as cellulite and wrinkles, at least 15 sessions of mesotherapy will be needed. **(See Figure G-7.)** For more acute conditions, such as sports injuries, only one to three sessions may be needed.

MESOTHERAPY, PROLOTHERAPY, AND NEURAL THERAPY

Caring Medical and Rehabilitation Services, along with Caring Cancer and Interventional Natural Medicine Center do many different types of injection techniques, so it is easy to get them confused. A good condensed summary of the techniques is found below:

PROLOTHERAPY: Prolotherapy is a treatment that stimulates the body to repair painful areas. The injections involve the use of substances that stimulate fibroblastic proliferation primarily at the junction of the bones, ligaments, and tendons. It is thus a periosteal (bone-ligament, bone-tendon junctions) injection. Prolotherapy is also given into joints to stimulate the repair of intraarticular structures, such as menisci and cartilage.

NEURAL THERAPY: Neural Therapy is a treatment used to eliminate interference fields of the autonomic nervous system or the sympathetic nervous system. These are often around the mouth, in areas such as the teeth or tonsils, as well as scars, nerves, and organs. Neural Therapy typically involves the injection of procaine into these areas.

MESOTHERAPY: Mesotherapy is a treatment to stimulate the repair of the mesoderm, including the skin, connective tissues, and adipose tissue. The injections are given into the mesoderm, which is just under the skin. It can be used for painful, as well as general medical conditions.

As most chronic conditions have multiple causes, several different treatment modalities must be utilized to optimize the successful outcome of treatment. Mesotherapy can be used with essentially all traditional and natural medicine treatments. It complements the other treatments, aiding in the healing of the patient. Mesotherapy is often used at Caring Medical, in conjunction with treatments such as Prolotherapy and Neural Therapy. Mesotherapy has another advantage, in that it decreases the pain of these other injection techniques.

At the end of this chapter is a chart explaining some helpful nutritional products that we offer, used in conjunction with the above techniques. **(See Figure G-8.)**

WHERE CAN I GET MESOTHERAPY?

For those people with conditions necessitating a comprehensive natural medicine approach to their problem, we recommend that you see one of the natural medicine specialists at Caring Medical, here in Oak Park, Illinois. Besides being proficient at Mesotherapy, other treatments can be utilized, including appropriate diet, nutritional supplementation, natural hormone replacement, rejuvenation therapies, chelation therapy, ozone therapy, photoluminescence, Prolotherapy, Neural Therapy and many others. To make an appointment, call 708-848-7789 or email scheduling@caringmedical.com.

ITEM	INGREDIENTS	USE
Genista Soy Protein Powder	19 grams of soy protein	Meal Replacement, Soy Protein Supplement
Pro-Cartilage	Ascorbic acid, Glucosamine, Chondroitin Sulfate, and Bromelain	Aids soft tissue healing.
Pro-Collagen	Vitamin A, Vitamin D3, Folic Acid, B-12, Biotin, PABA MSM, Nettles, Horsetail, Saw Palmetto, Fo Ti Root	Support for hair loss; thinning, balding, dull or graying hair; and brittle nails.
Prolo Max	Potassium, Magnesium, Fo Ti Root, MSM, L-Proline, Siberian Ginseng, L-Cysteine, Horsetail, RNA, Gotu-Kola, Activan, and Glucosamine.	Supports connective tissue growth heals sports injuries, musculoskeletal pain, and after Prolotherapy.
Skin & Nails	Multi vitamin/mineral, L-Proline Silica, Burdock Root, Nettles, Gotu Kola, Dandelion Root, Milk Thistle, Grape Seed	Connective tissue healing and promotes healthy skin and stronger nails.
Vita Vessel	Horse Chestnut Butcher's Broom, Gota Kola, and Troxerutin	Treats varicose veins blood clots, hemorrhoids, and overall blood circulation.
Weight-Less	Citrimax	Aids in eliminating carbohydrate cravings and boosts metabolism.

Figure G-8: **Nutritional Products that Assist Connective Tissue Healing***

** These products can be purchased directly by calling 708-848-7789—or via the internet at www.benuts.com.*

THE END...

Yes, after a decade of doing Prolotherapy and years of writing about Prolotherapy, these are the last lines of this book. Let us just say "thank you" for your interest in learning the concepts provided here. We hope that you will apply the principles discussed in this book to your life. If you do, you, like us, will say that no matter what happens in life, no matter how bad the pain, you can always *"Prolo Your Pain Away!"* ■

Sincerely with warm regards… until our next book…

Marion A. Hauser, MS, RD
Ross A. Hauser M.D.

Ross and Marion Hauser
The Doctor and the Dietitian™

NOTES

DEDICATION

1. *The Holy Bible*, New International Version, Matthew 11:4-5.
2. *The Holy Bible*, New International Version, Matthew 25:34-40.

ACKNOWLEDGEMENTS

1. *The Holy Bible*, New International Version, Psalm 71:14-16.

CHAPTER 2

PROLOTHERAPY: THE TECHNIQUE AND ITS HISTORY

1. Schneider, R. Fatality after injection of sclerosing agent to precipitate fibro-osseous proliferation. *Journal of the American Medical Association.* 1959; 170:1768-1772.
2. An abstract of a poster presentation (poster #49) at the 59th Annual Assembly of the American Academy of Physical Medicine and Rehabilitation printed in the *Archives of Physical Medicine and Rehabilitation.*
3. Kim, M. Myofascial trigger point therapy: comparison of dextrose, water, saline, and lidocaine. *Archives of Physical Medicine and Rehabilitation.* 1997; 78:1028.
4. Klein, R. A randomized double-blind trial of dextrose-glycerine-phenol injections for chronic, low back pain. *Journal of Spinal Disorders.* 1993; 6:23-33.
5. Ongley, M. A new approach to the treatment of chronic low back pain. *Lancet.* 1987; 2:143-146.
6. Travell, J. *Myofascial Pain and Dysfunction.* Baltimore, M.D.: Williams and Wilkins, 1983, pp. 103-164.
7. Wiesel, S. A study of computer-related assisted tomography. The incidence of positive CAT scans in an asymptomatic group of patients. *Spine.* 1984; 9:549-551.
8. From a phone conversation with C. Everett Koop, M.D., on May 16, 1997.
9. Boyd, Nathaniel. *Stay Out of the Hospital.* New York, NY: The Two Continents Publishing Group, Ltd., 1976, pp. 125-128.
10. *Ibid.*

CHAPTER 3

THE PROLOTHERAPY PIONEER: GEORGE S. HACKETT, M.D.

1. Hauser, R. and Hauser, M. *Prolo Your Sports Injuries Away!* Oak Park, IL, Beulah Land Press, 2001.
2. Hackett, G. *Ligament and Tendon Relaxation Treated By Prolotherapy.* Third Edition. Springfield, IL: Charles C. Thomas, 1958.
3. Hackett, G. Joint stabilization: An experimental, histologic study with comments on the clinical application in ligament proliferation. *American Journal of Surgery.* 1955; 89:968-973.

4. Hackett, G. Back pain following trauma and disease—Prolotherapy. *Military Medicine*. 1961; July: 517-525.
5. Hackett, G. Prolotherapy in whiplash and low back pain. *Postgraduate Medicine*. 1960; February: 214-219.
6. Hackett, G. Low back pain. *The British Journal of Physical Medicine*. 1956; 19:25-35.
7. Hackett, G. Prolotherapy for headache. *Headache*. 1962; April: 3-11.
8. Kayfetz, D., Blumentahl, L. and Hackett, G. Whiplash injury and other ligamentous headache—its management with Prolotherapy. *Headache*. 1963; 3:1-8.
9. Hackett, G. Referred pain from low back ligament disability. *AMA Archives of Surgery*. 1956; 73:878-883.
10. Hackett, G. Referred pain and sciatica in low back diagnosis. *Journal of the American Medical Association.* 1957; 163:183.
11. Hackett, G. Prolotherapy for sciatica from weak pelvic ligaments and bone dystrophy. *Clinical Medicine*. 1961; Volume 8, Number 12.
12. Hackett, G. Shearing injury to the sacroiliac joint. *Journal of the International College of Surgeons*. 1954; 22:631-642.

CHAPTER 4
WHY PROLOTHERAPY WORKS

1. Hackett, G. *Ligament and Tendon Relaxation Treated by Prolotherapy.* Third Edition. Springfield, IL: Charles C. Thomas, 1958, p. 5.
2. Babcock, P. et al. *Webster's Third New International Dictionary.* Springfield, MA: G. & C. Merriam Co., 1971, p. 1815.
3. Browner, B. *Skeletal Trauma.* Volume 1. Philadelphia, PA: W.B. Saunders, 1992, pp. 87-88.
4. Deese, J. Compressive neuropathies of the lower extremity. *Journal of Musculoskeletal Medicine.* 1988; November: 68-91.
5. Kayfetz, D. Occipital-cervical (whiplash) injuries treated by Prolotherapy. *Medical Trial Technique Quarterly.* 1963; June: 9-29
6. Rhalmi, S. Immunohistochemical study of nerves in lumbar spine ligaments. *Spine.* 1993; 18:264-267.
7. Ahmed, M. Neuropeptide Y, tyrosine hydroxylase and vasoactive intestinal polypeptide-immunoreactive nerve fibers in the vertebral bodies, discs, dura mater, and spinal ligaments of the rat lumbar spine. *Spine.* 1993; 18:268-273.
8. Hackett G., Hemwall, G., and Montgomery, G. *Ligament and Tendon Relaxation Treated by Prolotherapy.* Fifth Edition. Oak Park, IL: Gustav A. Hemwall, Publisher, 1993, p. 20.
9. Rhalmi, S. Immunohistochemical study of nerves in lumbar spine ligaments. *Spine.* 1993; 18:264-267.

10. Ahmed, M. Neuropeptide Y., Tyrosine hydroxylase and vasoactive intestinal polypeptide-immunoreactive nerve fibers in the vertebral bodies, discs, dura mater, and spinal ligaments of the rat lumbar spine. *Spine.* 1993; 18:268-273.
11. Robbins, S. *Pathologic Basis of Disease.* Third Edition. Philadelphia, PA: W.B. Saunders, 1984, p. 40.

Chapter 5

Prolotherapy Provides Results

1. Hackett, G. *Ligament and Tendon Relaxation Treated by Prolotherapy.* Third Edition. Springfield, IL: Charles C. Thomas, 1958, p. 5.
2. Hackett, G. Referred pain and sciatica in diagnosis of low back disability. *Journal of the American Medical Association.* 1957; 163:183-185.
3. Hackett, G. Joint stabilization. *American Journal of Surgery.* 1955; 89:968-973.
4. Hackett, G. Referred pain from low back ligament disability. *AMA Archives of Surgery.* 73:878-883, November 1956.
5. Liu, Y. An *in situ* study of the influence of a sclerosing solution in rabbit medial collateral ligaments and its junction strength. *Connective Tissue Research.* 1983; 2:95-102.
6. Maynard, J. Morphological and biomechanical effects of sodium morrhuate on tendons. *Journal of Orthopaedic Research.* 1985; 3:236-248.
7. *Ibid.*
8. Klein, R. Proliferant injections for low back pain: histologic changes of injected ligaments and objective measures of lumbar spine mobility before and after treatment. *Journal of Neurology, Orthopedic Medicine and Surgery.* 1989; 10:141-144.
9. Interview with Thomas Dorman, M.D. *Nutrition and Healing.* 1994, pp. 5-6.
10. Dorman, T. Treatment for spinal pain arising in ligaments using Prolotherapy: a retrospective study. *Journal of Orthopaedic Medicine.* 1991; 13(1):13-19.
11. Ongley, M. and Dorman T. et al. Ligament instability of knees: a new approach to treatment. *Manual Medicine.* 1988; 3:152-154.
12. Klein R. A randomized double-blind trial of dextrose-glycerine-phenol injections for chronic, low back pain. *Journal of Spinal Disorders.* 1993; 6:23-33.
13. Ongley, M. A new approach to the treatment of chronic low back pain. *Lancet.* 1987; 2:143-146.
14. Reeves, K. Prolotherapy: present and future applications in soft-tissue pain and disability. *Physical Medicine and Rehabilitation Clinics of North America.* 1995; 6:917-925.
15. Reeves, K. Technique of Prolotherapy. *Physiatric Procedures.* Edited by Lennard, T. Philadelphia, PA: Hanley and Belfus, Inc., 1995 pp. 57-70.

16. Reeves, K. Prolotherapy: Basic science, clinical studies, and technique. *Pain Procedures in Clinical Practice.* Second Edition, Edited by Lennard, T. Philadelphia, PA: Hanley and Belfus, Inc., 2000, pp. 172-189.
17. Reeves K. and Hassanein, K. Randomized, prospective double-blind placebo-controlled study of dextrose Prolotherapy for knee osteoarthritis with or without ACL laxity. *Alternative Therapies.* 2000; 6:68-79.
18. Reeves K. and Hassanein, K. Randomized, prospective, placebo-controlled double-blind study of dextrose Prolotherapy for osteoarthritic thumb and finger joints: evidence of clinical efficacy. *Journal of Alternative and Complementary Medicine.* 2000, 6:311-320.
19. Schwartz, R. Prolotherapy: a literature review and retrospective study. *Journal of Neurology, Orthopedic Medicine, and Surgery.* 1991; 12:220-223.
20. Wilkinson, H. Broad-spectrum approach to the failed back. Lecture presentation at the American College of Osteopathic Pain Management and Sclerotherapy meeting on May 3, 1997.

CHAPTER 6

ANSWERS TO COMMON QUESTIONS ABOUT PROLOTHERAPY

1. Meyers, A. Prolotherapy treatment of low back pain and sciatica. Bulletin of the Hospital for Joint Disease. 1961; 22:1.
2. Woo, S. Injury and repair of the musculoskeletal soft tissues. *American Academy of Orthopaedic Surgeons,* 1987.
3. Mankin, H. Localization of tritiated thymidine in articular cartilage of rabbits inhibits growth in immature cartilage. *Journal of Bone and Joint Surgery.* 1962; 44A:682.
4. Butler, D. Biomechanics of ligaments and tendons. *Exercise and Sports Scientific Review.* 1975; 6:125.
5. Bland, J. *Disorders of the Cervical Spine.* Philadelphia, PA: W.B. Saunders, 1987.
6. Letter written April 20, 1976 by Carell Hutchingson, Jr., M.D., as chairman of the Subcommittee on Insurance Mediation for the Chicago Medical Society, CMS No. 76-M-005.
7. Letter written November 1, 1979 by Michael Treister, M.D., as chairman of the Medical Practice Committee for the Chicago Medical Society, CMS File 79-G-069.
8. Letter written November 5, 1987 by Peter C. Pulos, M.D., as chairman of the Medical Practice Committee for the Chicago Medical Society, Claim No. 725514.
9. Reeves, K. Technique of Prolotherapy. From *Physiatric Procedures in Clinical Practice.* Philadelphia, PA: Hanley and Belfus, Inc., 1994, pp. 57-70.
10. Reeves, K. Prolotherapy, present and future applications in soft-tissue pain and disability. *Physical Medicine and Rehabilitation Clinics of North America.* 1995; 6:917-925.

11. Dorman, T. *Diagnosis and Injection Techniques in Orthopedic Medicine.* Baltimore, M.D.: Williams and Wilkins, 1991.

12. Faber, W. and Walker, M. Instant pain relief. Milwaukee, WI: *Biological Publications,* 1991.

13. Faber, W. and Walker, M. *Pain, Pain Go Away.* San Jose, CA: ISHI Press International, 1990.

14. Butler, D. Biomechanics of ligaments and tendons. *Exercise and Sports Scientific Review.* 1975; 6:125.

15. Tipton, C. Influence of immobilization, training, exogenous hormones, and surgical repair of knee ligaments from hypophysectomized rats. *American Journal of Physiology.* 1971; 221:1114.

16. Nachemson, A. Some mechanical properties of the third human lumbar interlaminar ligament. *Journal of Biomechanics.* 1968; 1:211.

17. Akeson, W. The connective tissue response to immobility: an accelerated aging response. *Experimental Gerontology.* 1968; 3:239.

18. Travell, J. *Myofascial Pain and Dysfunction.* Baltimore, M.D.: Williams and Wilkins, 1983, pp. 103-164.

19. Schumacher, H. *Primer on the Rheumatic Diseases.* Tenth Edition. Atlanta, GA: Arthritis Foundation, 1993, pp. 8-11.

20. Ballard, W. Biochemical aspects of aging and degeneration in the invertebral disc.*Contemporary Orthopaedics.* 1992; 24:453-458.

21. Jacobs, R. Pathogenesis of idiopathic scoliosis. Chicago, IL: *Scoliosis Research Society,* 1984, pp. 107-118.

22. Crowninsheild, R. The strength and failure characteristics of rat medial collateral ligaments.*Journal of Trauma.* 1976; 16:99.

23. Travell, J. *Myofascial Pain and Dysfunction.* Baltimore, M.D.: Williams and Wilkins, 1983, pp. 103-164.

24. Tipton, C. Response of adrenalectomized rats to exercise. *Endocrinology.* 1972; 91:573.

25. Tipton, C. Response of thyroidectomized rats to training. *American Journal of Physiology.* 1972; 215:1137.

26. Bucci, L. *Nutrition Applied to Injury Rehabilitation and Sports Medicine.* Boca Raton, FL: CRC Press, 1995, pp. 167-176.

27. Batmanghelidj, F. *Your Body's Many Cries for Water.* Second Edition. Falls Church, VA: Global Health Solutions, Inc., 1996, pp. 8-11.

28. Welbourne, T. Increased plasma bicarbonate and growth hormone after an oral glutamine load. *American Journal of Clinical Nutrition.* 1995, pp. 1058-1061.

29. Hurson, M. Metabolic effects of arginine in a healthy elderly population. *Journal of Parenteral and Enteral Nutrition.* 1995, pp. 227-230.

30. Dominguez, R. and Gajda, R. *Total Body Training.* East Dundee, IL: Moving Force Systems, 1982, pp. 33-37.

31. Laros, G. Influence of physical activity on ligament insertions in the knees of dogs. *Journal of Bone and Joint Surgery.* 1971; 53:275.

32. Hunter, L. *Rehabilitation of the Injured Knee.* St. Louis, MO: C.V. Mosby, 1984.

33. Arnoczky, S. Meniscal degeneration due to knee instability: an experimental study in the dog. *Trans. Orthop. Res. Soc.* 1979; 4:79.

34. Hunter, L. *Rehabilitation of the Injured Knee.* St. Louis, MO: C.V. Mosby, 1984.

35. Arnoczky, S. Meniscal degeneration due to knee instability: an experimental study in the dog. *Trans. Orthop. Res. Soc.* 1979; 4:79.

36. Tipton, C. The influence of physical activity on ligaments and tendons. *Med. Sci. Sports.* 1975; 7:165.

37. Woo, S. Effect of immobilization and exercise on strength characteristics of bone-medial collateral ligament-bone complex. Am. Soc. Mech. Eng. Symp. 1979; 32:62.

38. Hunter, L. *Rehabilitation of the Injured Knee.* St. Louis, MO: C.V. Mosby, 1984.

39. Noyes, F. Biomechanics of anterior cruciate ligament failure: an analysis of strain rate sensitivity and mechanism of failure in primates. *Journal of Bone and Joint Surgery.* 1974; 56A:236.

40. Noyes, F. Biomechanics of ligament failure: an analysis of immobilization, exercise and reconditioning effects in primates. *Journal of Bone and Joint Surgery.* 1974; 56A:1406.

41. Laros, G. Influence of physical activity on ligament insertions in the knees of dogs. *Journal of Bone and Joint Surgery.* 1971; 53A:275.

42. Hunter, L. *Rehabilitation of the Injured Knee.* St. Louis, MO: C.V. Mosby, 1984.

43. Akeson, W. Immobility effects on synovial joints: the pathomechanics of joint contracture. *Biorheology.* 1980; 17:95.

44. Ho, S. Comparison of various icing times in decreasing bone metabolism and blood flow in the knee. *American Journal of Sports Medicine.* 1990; 18:376-378.

45. McGaw, W. The effect of tension on collagen remodeling by fibroblasts: a sterological ultrastructural study. *Connective Tissue Research.* 1986; 14:229-235.

46. Bucci, L. *Nutrition Applied to Injury Rehabilitation and Sports Medicine.* Boca Raton, FL: CRC Press, 1995, pp. 167-176.

47. Hardy, M. The biology of scar formation. *Physical Therapy.* 1989; 69:12.

48. Mishra, D. Anti-inflammatory medication after muscle injury: a treatment resulting in short-term improvement but subsequent loss of muscle function. *Journal of Bone and Joint Surgery.* 1995; 77A:1510-1519.

49. Brandt, K. Should osteoarthritis be treated with nonsteroidal anti-inflammatory drugs? *Rheumatic Disease Clinics of North America.* 1993; 19:697-712.

50. Brandt, K. The effects of salicylates and other nonsteroidal anti-inflammatory drugs on articular cartilage. *American Journal of Medicine.* 1984; 77:65-69.

51. Obeid, G. Effect of ibuprofen on the healing and remodeling of bone and articular cartilage in the rabbit temporomandibular joint. *Journal of Oral and Maxillofacial Surgeons*. 1992, pp. 843-850.

52. Dupont, M. The efficacy of anti-inflammatory medication in the treatment of the acutely sprained ankle. *American Journal of Sports Medicine.* 1987; 15:41-45.

53. Newman, N. Acetabular bone destruction related to nonsteroidal anti-inflammatory drugs. *Lancet.* 1985; July 6:11-13.

54. Serup, J. and Oveson, J. Salicylate arthropathy: accelerated coxarthrosis during long-term treatment with acetylsalicylic acid. *Praxis.* 1981; 70:359.

55. Ronningen, H. and Langeland, N. Indomethacin treatment in osteoarthritis of the hip joint. *Acta Ortho. Scand.* 1979; 50:169-174.

56. Newman, N. Acetabular bone destruction related to nonsteroidal anti-inflammatory drugs. *Lancet.* 1985; July 6:11-13.

57. Serup, J. and Ovesen, J. Salicylate arthropathy: accelerated coxarthrosis during long-term treatment with acetylsalicylic acid. *Praxis.* 1981; 70:359.

58. Ronningen, H. and Langeland, N. Indomethacin treatment in osteoarthritis of the hip joint. *Acta Ortho. Scand.* 1979; 50:169-174.

59. Akil, M., Amos, R.S., and Stewart, P. Infertility may sometimes be associated with NSAID consumption. *British Journal of Rheumatism.* 1996; 35:76-78.

60. Wrenn, R. An experimental study of the effect of cortisone on the healing process and tensile strength of tendons. *Journal of Bone and Joint Surgery.* 1954; 36A:588-601.

61. Truhan, A. Corticosteroids: a review with emphasis on complications of prolonged systemic therapy. *Annals of Allergy.* 1989; 62:375-390.

62. Roenigk, R. *Dermatologic Surgery.* Marcel Dekker, Inc., p. 155.

63. Davis, G. Adverse effects of corticosteroids. *Systemic Clinical Dermatology.* 1986; 4(1):161-169.

64. Gogia, P. Hydrocortisone and exercise effects on articular cartilage in rats. *Archives of Physical Medicine and Rehabilitation.* 1993; 74:463-467.

65. Chandler, G.N. Deleterious effect of intra-articular hydrocortisone. *Lancet.* 1958; 2:661-663.

66. Wiley, R. *Biobalance.* Tacoma, WA: Life Sciences Press, 1989, pp. 7-18.

67. Reams, C. *Choose Life or Death.* Fifth Edition. Tampa, FL: Holistic Laboratories, 1990, pp. 80-85.

68. Wiley, R. *Biobalance.* Tacoma, WA: Life Sciences Press, 1989, pp. 7-18.

69. Sears, B. *The Zone.* New York, NY: Harper Collins Publishers, Inc., 1995.

CHAPTER 7

PROLOTHERAPY, INFLAMMATION, AND HEALING: WHAT'S THE CONNECTION?

1. Robbins, S. *Pathologic Basis of Disease.* Third Edition. Philadelphia, PA: W.B. Saunders, 1984, p. 40.

2. Greenfield, B. *Rehabilitation of the Knee: A Problem-Solving Approach.* Philadelphia, PA: F.A. Davis, 1993.
3. Woo, S. Injury and repair of the musculoskeletal soft tissues. *American Academy of Orthopaedic Surgeons,* 1987.
4. Mankin, H. Localization of tritiated thymidine in articular cartilage of rabbits inhibits growth in immature cartilage. *Journal of Bone and Joint Surgery.* 1962; 44A:682.
5. Robbins, S. *Pathologic Basis of Disease.* Third Edition. Philadelphia, PA: W.B. Saunders, 1984, p. 40.
6. Greenfield, B. *Rehabilitation of the Knee: A Problem-Solving Approach.* Philadelphia, PA: F.A. Davis Co., 1993.
7. Woo, S. Injury and repair of the musculoskeletal soft tissues. *American Academy of Orthopaedic Surgeons.* 1987.
8. Benedetti, R. Clinical results of simultaneous adjacent interdigital neurectomy in the foot. *Foot and Ankle International.* 1996; 17:264-268.

CHAPTER 8

PROLO YOUR BACK PAIN AWAY!

1. Boden, S. Abnormal magnetic-resonance scans of the lumbar spine in asymptomatic subjects. *The Journal of Bone and Joint Surgery*. 1990; 72A:403-408.
2. Jensen, M. Magnetic resonance imaging of the lumbar spine in people without back pain. *New England Journal of Medicine*. 1994; 331:69-73.
3. Boden, S. Abnormal magnetic-resonance scans of the lumbar spine in asymptomatic subjects. *Journal of Bone and Joint Surgery*. 1990; 72A:403-408.
4. Jensen, M. Magnetic resonance imaging of the lumbar spine in people without back pain. *New England Journal of Medicine*. 1994; 331:69-73.
5. Hackett, G. Shearing injury to the sacroiliac joint. *Journal of the International College of Surgeons*. 1954; 22:631-639.
6. Bellamy, N. What do we know about the sacroiliac joint? *Seminars in Arthritis and Rheumatism.* 1983; 12:282-313.
7. Paris, S. Physical signs of instability. *Spine*. 1985; 10:277-279.
8. Hackett, G. Shearing injury to the sacroiliac joint. *Journal of the International College of Surgeons*. 1954; 22:631-639.
9. Mueller, R. Anesthesia in *Current Surgical Diagnosis and Treatment.* Seventh Edition. Los Altos, CA: 1983, pp. 162-169.
10. Burton, C. Conservative management of low back pain. *Postgraduate Medicine.* 5:168-183.
11. Merriman, J. Prolotherapy versus operative fusion in the treatment of joint instability of the spine and pelvis. *Journal of the International College of Surgeons*. 1964; 42:150-159.
12. *Ibid.*
13. Maynard, J. Morphological and biomechanical effects of sodium morrhuate on tendons. *Journal of Orthopaedic Research*. 1985; 3:236-248.

14. Turner, J. et al. Patient outcomes after lumbar spinal fusions. *Journal of the American Medical Association*. 1992; 286:907-910.
15. Schwarzer, A. The sacroiliac joint in chronic low back pain. *Spine*. 1995; 20:31-37.
16. Adams, R. and Victor, M. (eds.), *Principles of Neurology*. Fourth Edition. St. Louis, MO: McGraw Hill, 1989, pp. 737-738.
17. Hoffman, G. Spinal arachnoiditis—what is the clinical spectrum? *Spine*. 1983; 8:538-540.
18. Guyer, D. The long-range prognosis of arachnoiditis. *Spine*. 1989; 14:1332-1341.
19. Jackson, A. Does degenerative disease of the lumbar spine cause arachnoiditis? A magnetic resonance study and review of the literature. *British Journal of Radiology*. 1994; 64:840-847.
20. Guyer, D. The long-range prognosis of arachnoiditis. *Spine*. 1989; 14:1332-1341.
21. U.S. Preventive Services Task Force. Screening for adolescent idiopathic scoliosis. *Journal of the American Medical Association*. 1993; 269:2667-2672.
22. Bradford, D. Adult scoliosis. *Clinical Orthopaedics and Related Research*. 1988; 229:70-86.
23. Gunnoe, B. "Adult idiopathic scoliosis." *Orthopaedic Review*. 1990; 19:35-43.
24. Keim, H. Adult scoliosis and its management. *Orthopaedic Review*. 1981; 10:41-48.
25. Winter, R. Pain patterns in adult scoliosis. *Orthopedic Clinics of North America*. 1988; 19:339-345.

CHAPTER 9

PROLO YOUR HEADACHE, NECK, TMJ, EAR, AND MOUTH PAIN AWAY!

1. Bellamy, N. What do we know about the sacroiliac joint? *Seminars in Arthritis and Rheumatism*. 1983; 12:282-313.
2. Barré, J. *Rev. Neurol*. 1926; 33:1246.
3. Tamura, T. Cranial symptoms after cervical injury—aetiology and treatment of the Barré-Lieou Syndrome. *Journal of Bone and Joint Surgery*, 1989; 71B:283-287.
4. Bland, J. *Disorders of the Cervical Spine*. Philadelphia, PA: W.B. Saunders, 1987.
5. Kayfetz, D. Whiplash injury and other ligamentous headache—its management with Prolotherapy. *Headache*. 1963; 3:1-8.
6. Claussen, C.F. and Claussen E. Neurootological contributions to the diagnostic follow-up after whiplash injuries. *Acta Otolaryngology* (Stockh). 1995; Suppl. 520:53-56.
7. Hackett, G. Prolotherapy for headache. *Headache*. 1962; 1:3-11.
8. Hackett, G. Prolotherapy in whiplash and low back pain. *Postgraduate Medicine*. 1960, pp. 214-219.

9. Kayfetz, D. Whiplash injury and other ligamentous headache—its management with Prolotherapy. *Headache*. 1963; 3:1-8.
10. Merriman, J. Presentation at the Hackett Foundation Prolotherapy Meeting, Indianapolis, IN, October 1995.
11. Caviness, V. Current concepts in headache. *New England Journal of Medicine*. 1980; 302:446-450.
12. Darnell, M. A proposed chronology of events for forward-head posture. *Journal of Craniomandibular Practice*. 1983; 1:49-54.
13. Rocabado, M. Biomechanical relationship of the cranial, cervical and hyoid regions. *Physical Therapy*. 1983; 1:62-66.
14. Schultz, L. A treatment for subluxation of the temporomandibular joint. *Journal of the American Medical Association*. September 25, 1937, pp. 1032-1035.
15. Schultz, L. Twenty years' experience in treating hypermobility of the temporomandibular joints. *American Journal of Surgery*. 1956; 92:925-928.
16. Cheshire, W. Botulin toxin in the treatment of myofascial pain syndrome. *Pain*. 1994; 59:65-69.
17. *Headache Relief Newsletter*, Edition 13, Philadelphia, PA: The Pain Center, 1995.
18. Thigpen, C. The styloid process. *Trans American Laryngological Rhinology Otology Association*. 1932; 28:408-412.
19. Eagle, W. Elongated styloid process. *Archives of Otolaryngology*. 1937; 25:584-587.
20. Shankland, W. Differential diagnosis of headaches. *Journal of Craniomandibular Practice*. 1986; 4:47-53.
21. Ernest, E. Three disorders that frequently cause temporomandibular joint pain: internal derangement, temporal tendonitis, and Ernest syndrome. *Journal of Neurological Orthopedic Surgery*. 1986; 7:189-191.
22. Shankland, W. Ernest syndrome as a consequence of stylomandibular ligament injury: a report of 68 patients. *Journal of Prosthetic Dentistry*. 1987; 57:501-506.
23. Wong, E. Temporal headaches and associated symptoms relating to the styloid process and its attachments. *Annals of Academic Medicine* (Singapore). 1995; 24:124-128.

Chapter 10

Prolo Your Shoulder Pain Away!

1. Matsen, F. Anterior glenohumeral instability. *Clinics in Sports Medicine*. 1983; 2:319-336.
2. Bonafede, R. Shoulder pain. *Postgraduate Medicine*. 1987; 82:185-193.
3. Frieman, B. Rotator cuff disease: a review of diagnosis, pathophysiology, and current trends in treatment. *Archives of Physical Medicine and Rehabilitation*. 1994; 75:604-609.
4. *Ibid.*

5. Andersen, L. Shoulder pain in hemiplegia. *American Journal of Occupational Therapy*. 1985; 39:11-18.
6. Scott, J. Injuries to the acromioclavicular joint. *Injury: The British Journal of Accident Surgery*. 1967; 5:13-18.
7. Butters, K. Office evaluation and management of the shoulder impingement syndrome. *Orthopedic Clinics of North America*. 1988; 19:755-765.
8. Chandnani, V. MRI findings in asymptomatic shoulders: a blind analysis using symptomatic shoulders as controls. *Clinical Imaging*. 1992; 16:25-30.
9. Neumann, C. MR imaging of the shoulder: appearance of the supraspinatus tendon in asymptomatic volunteers. *American Journal of Radiology*. 1992; 158:1281-1287.
10. Sher, J. Abnormal findings on magnetic resonance images of asymptomatic shoulders. *Journal of Bone and Joint Surgery*. 1995; 77A:10-15.
11. Neumann, C. MR imaging of the shoulder: appearance of the supraspinatus tendon in asymptomatic volunteers. *American Journal of Radiology*. 1992; 158:1281-1287.
12. Sher, J. Abnormal findings on magnetic resonance images of asymptomatic shoulders. *Journal of Bone and Joint Surgery*. 1995; 77A:10-15.

CHAPTER 11

PROLO YOUR ELBOW, WRIST, AND HAND PAIN AWAY!

1. Armstrong, T. Upper-extremity pain in the workplace—role of usage in causality in clinical concepts. From *Regional Musculoskeletal Illness*. Grune and Straton, Inc., 1987, pp. 333-354.
2. Dominguez, R. and Gajda, R. *Total Body Training*. East Dundee, IL: Moving Force Systems, 1982, pp. 33-37.
3. Bucci, L. *Nutrition Applied to Injury Rehabilitation and Sports Medicine*. Boca Raton, FL: CRC Press, 1995, pp. 167-176.
4. Cooney, W. Anatomy and mechanics of carpal instability. *Surgical Rounds for Orthopedics*. 1989, pp. 5-24.
5. *Ibid.*
6. Kozin, S. Injuries to the perilunar carpus. *Orthopaedic Review.* 1992; 21:435-448.
7. Waters, P. Unusual arthritic disorders in the hand: part one. *Surgical Rounds for Orthopaedics.* 1990, pp. 15-20.
8. Laseter, G. Management of the stiff hand: a practical approach. *Orthopedic Clinics of North America*. 1983; 14:749-765.

CHAPTER 12

PROLO YOUR GROIN, HIP, AND KNEE PAIN AWAY!

1. Meisenbach, R. Sacroiliac relaxation: with analysis of 84 cases. *Surgery, Gynecology and Obstetrics.* 1911; 12:411-434.
2. *Ibid.*

3. Hirschberg, G. Iliolumbar syndrome as a common cause of low back pain: diagnosis and prognosis. *Archives of Physical Medicine and Rehabilitation*. 1979; 60:415-419.
4. Schwarzer, A. The sacroiliac joint in chronic low back pain. *Spine*. 1995; 20:31-37.
5. Friberg, O. Clinical symptoms and biomechanics of lumbar spine and hip joint in leg-length inequality. *Spine*. 1983; 18:643-651.
6. Cummings, G. The effect of imposed leg-length difference on pelvic bone symmetry. *Spine*. 1993; 18:368-373.
7. Ober, F. The role of the iliotibial band and fascia lata as a factor in the causation of low-back disabilities and sciatica. *Journal of Bone and Joint Surgery*. 1936; p. 18.
8. Swezey, R. Pseudo-radiculopathy in subacute trochanteric bursitis of the subgluteus maximus bursa. *Archives of Physical Medicine and Rehabilitation*. 1976; 57:387-390.
9. Ober, F. The role of the iliotibial band and fascia lata as a factor in the causation of low-back disabilities and sciatica. *Journal of Bone and Joint Surgery*. 1936; p. 18.
10. Schwartz, R. Prolotherapy: a literature review and retrospective study. *Journal of Orthopaedic Medicine and Surgery*. 1991; 12:220-223.
11. Peterson, L. *Sports Injuries, Their Prevention and Treatment*. Chicago, IL: Year Book Medical, 1986, pp. 18-63.
12. Ongley, M. Ligament instability of knees: a new approach to treatment. *Manual Medicine*. 1988; 3:152-154.
13. Graham, G. Early osteoarthritis in young sportsmen with severe anterolateral instability of the knee. *Injury: British Journal of Accident Surgery*. 1988; 19:247-248.
14. Ongley, M. Ligament instability of knees: a new approach to treatment. *Manual Medicine*. 1988; 3:152-154.
15. Hryhorowych, A. Pes anserinus tendonitis: a major component of knee pain in elderly individuals with degenerative joint disease. Abstract presented at the American Academy of Physical Medicine and Rehabilitation Meeting, November, 1993.
16. Kidd, R. Recent developments in the understanding of Osgood-Schlatter disease: a literature review. *Journal of Orthopaedic Medicine*. 1993; 15:59-63.

CHAPTER 13

PROLO YOUR ANKLE AND FOOT PAIN AWAY!

1. Mann, R. Pain in the foot. *Postgraduate Medicine*. 1987; 82:154-174.
2. Mankin, H. Localization of tritiated thymidine in articular cartilage of rabbits inhibits growth in immature cartilage. *Journal of Bone and Joint Surgery*. 1962; 44A:682.
3. Karr, S. Subcalcaneal heel pain. *Orthopedic Clinics of North America*. 1994; 25:161-175.

4. Merriman, J. Presentation at the Hackett Foundation Prolotherapy Meeting, Indianapolis, IN, October 1995.
5. Trevino, S. Management of acute and chronic lateral ligament injuries of the ankle. *Orthopedic Clinics of North America.* 1994; 25:1-16.
6. Kirvela, O. Treatment of painful neuromas with neurolytic blockade. *Pain.* 1990; 41:161-165.
7. Benedetti, R. Clinical results of simultaneous adjacent interdigital neurectomy in the foot. *Foot and Ankle International.* 1996; 17:264-268.
8. Deese, J. Compressive neuropathies of the lower extremity. *Journal of Musculoskeletal Medicine.* 1988; November: 68-91
9. Hollinshead, W. *Functional Anatomy of the Limb and Back.* Fifth Edition. Philadelphia, PA: W.B. Saunders, pp. 316-338.

CHAPTER 14

PROLO ALL YOUR DEGENERATIVE CONDITIONS AWAY!

1. NIH *Consensus Statement on Total Hip Replacement,* 1994; 12:1-31. Published by the NIH, Kensington, M.D..
2. Cohen, N. Composition and dynamics of articular cartilage; structure, function and maintaining healthy state. *JOSPT.* 1998; 28:203-215.
3. Saaf, J. Effects of exercise on articular cartilage. *Acta Ortho. Scand.* 1950; 20:1-83.
4. Buckwalter, J. Articular cartilage. Part one: Tissue design and chondrocyte-matrix interactions. *Journal of Bone and Joint Surgery.* 1997; 79A: 600-611.
5. Mow, V. *Structure-function relationships for articular cartilage and effects of joint instability and trauma on cartilage function.*
6. *Ibid.*
7. Brandt, K. (ed.) Cartilage Changes in Osteoarthritis, pp. 22-42. Indianapolis, IN: *Indiana University School of Medicine Press,* 1990.
8. Mow, V. *Structure-function relationships for articular cartilage and effects of joint instability and trauma on cartilage function.*
9. Mow, V. *Structure-function relationships for articular cartilage and effects of joint instability and trauma on cartilage function.*
10. Mankin, H. The articular cartilages: a review. In *American Academy of Orthopaedic Surgeons: Instructional Course Lectures, Vol. 19.* St. Louis, MO: C.V. Mosby, 1970.
11. Stockwell, R. The cell density of human articular cartilage and costal cartilage. *Journal of Anatomy.* 1967; 101:753.
12. Crelin, E. Changes induced by sustained pressure in the knee joint articular cartilage of adult rabbits. *Anat. Rec.* 1964; 149:113.
13. Mankin, H. Biochemical and metabolic abnormalities in articular cartilage from osteoarthritic human hips. *Journal of Bone and Joint Surgery.* 1970; 52A:424.
14. Mankin, H. The response of articular cartilage to mechanical injury. *Journal of Bone and Joint Surgery.* 1982; 64A:460.

15. Hunter, L. *Rehabilitation of the Injured Knee.* St. Louis, MO: C.V. Mosby, 1984, pp. 149-209.

16. Mankin, H. The response of articular cartilage to mechanical injury. *Journal of Bone and Joint Surgery.* 1982; 64A:460.

17. Mankin, H. The reaction of articular cartilage to injury and osteoarthritis (first of two parts). *New England Journal of Medicine.* 1974; 291:1285.

18. Mankin, H. The reaction of articular cartilage to injury and osteoarthritis (second of two parts). *New England Journal of Medicine.* 1974; 291:1335.

19. Ingman, A. Variations of collagenous and noncollagenous proteins of human knee joint menisci with age and degeneration. *Gerontologia.* 1074; 86:245-252.

20. Arnoczky, S. Meniscus. In *Injury and Repair of the Musculoskeletal Soft Tissues.* Edited by Woo, S. Park Ridge, IL: *American Academy of Orthopaedic Surgeons,* 1987, pp. 487-537.

21. Clark, C. Development of the menisci of the human knee joint. *Journal of Bone and Joint Surgery.* 1983; 65A:538-547.

22. Bessette, G. The meniscus. *Orthopaedics.* 1992; 15:35-42.

23. Shrive, N. Load-bearing in the knee joint. *Clinical Orthopaedics.* 1978; 131:279-287.

24. Radin, E. Role of menisci in the distribution of stress in the knee. *Clinical Orthopaedics.* 1984; 185:290-294.

25. Ahmed, A. *In vitro* measurements of the static pressure distribution in synovial joints. Part one: tibial surface of the knee. *Journal of Biomechanical Engineering.* 1983; 105:216-225.

26. Baratz, M. Meniscal tears: the effect of meniscectomy and of repair on intra-articular contact areas and stress in the human knee. *American Journal of Sports Medicine.* 1986; 14:270-275.

27. Bessette, G. The meniscus. *Orthopaedics.* 1992; 15:35-42.

28. Radin, E. Role of the menisci in the distribution of stress in the knee. *Clinical Orthopaedics.* 1984; 185:290-294.

29. Seedhom, B. Transmission of the load in the knee joint with special reference to the role of the menisci. *Eng. Med.* 1979: 8:220-228.

30. Bessette, G. The meniscus. *Orthopaedics.* 1992; 15:35-42.

31. Dandy, D. The diagnosis of problems after meniscectomy. *Journal of Bone and Joint Surgery.* 1975; 57B:349-352.

32. *Ibid.*

33. Maletius, W. The effect of partial meniscectomy on the long-term prognosis of knees with localized, severe chondral damage. *American Journal of Sports Medicine.* 1996; 24:258-262.

34. Bolano, L. Isolated arthroscopic partial meniscectomy. *American Journal of Sports Medicine.* 1993; 21:432-437.

35. Schmid, A. and Schmid, F. Results after cartilage shaving studied by electron microscopy. *American Journal of Sports Medicine.* 1987; 15:386-387.

36. Salter, R. The effects of continuous compression on living articular cartilage. An experimental investigation. *Journal of Bone and Joint Surgery.* 1960; 42A:31.

37. Salter, R. The pathological changes in articular cartilage associated with persistent joint deformity: an experimental investigation. In Gordon, D. (ed.), *Studies of Rheumatoid Disease: Proceedings of the Third Canadian Conference on Research in the Rheumatic Diseases.* Toronto: University of Toronto Press, 1965, p. 33.

38. *Ibid.*

39. Salter, R. The effects of continuous compression on living articular cartilage. An experimental investigation. *Journal of Bone and Joint Surgery.* 1960; 42A:31.

40. Salter, R. The pathological changes in articular cartilage associated with persistent joint deformity: an experimental investigation. In Gordon, D. (ed.), *Studies of Rheumatoid Disease: Proceedings of the Third Canadian Conference on Research in the Rheumatic Diseases.* Toronto: University of Toronto Press, 1965, p. 33.

41. Kuettner, K. *Articular Cartilage and Osteoarthritis.* New York, NY: Raven Press, 1992.

42. Salter, R. The biological concept of continuous passive motion of synovial joints. *Clinical Orthopaedics and Related Research.* 1989; 242:12-25

43. Salter, R. The effects of continuous compression on living articular cartilage. An experimental investigation. *Journal of Bone and Joint Surgery.* 1960; 42A:31.

44. Salter, R. Continuous passive motion and the repair of full-thickness defects—a one-year follow-up (Abstract). *Orthop. Trans.* 1982; 6:266.

45. Salter, R. The healing of intra-articular fractures with continuous passive motion. In Copper R. (ed.) *American Academy of Orthopaedic Surgeons Instructional Course Lectures.* St. Louis, MO: C.V. Mosby, 1979.

46. Palmoski, M. Effects of some nonsteroidal anti-inflammatory drugs on proteoglycan metabolism and organization in canine articular cartilage. *Arthritis and Rheumatism.* 1980; 23:1010-1020.

47. Salter, R. The biologic concept of continuous passive motion of synovial joints. *Clinical Orthopaedics and Related Research.* 1989; 242:12-25.

48. Newton, P. The effect of lifelong exercise on canine articular cartilage. *American Journal of Sports Medicine.* 1997; 25:282-287.

49. Tornkvist, H. Effect of ibuprofen and indomethacin on bone metabolism reflected in bone strength. *Clinical Orthopedics.* 1984; 187:225.

50. Lindholm, T. Ibuprofen: effect on bone formation and calcification exerted by the anti-inflammatory drug ibuprofen. *Scandinavian Journal of Rheumatology.* 1981; 10:38.

51. Williams, R. Ibuprofen: an inhibitor of alveolar bone resorption in beagles. *J. Periodont. Res.* 1988; 23:225.
52. Tornkvist, H. Effect of ibuprofen and indomethacin on bone metabolism reflected in bone strength. *Clinical Orthopedics.* 1984; 187:225.
53. Obeid, G. Effect of ibuprofen on the healing and remodeling of bone and articular cartilage in the rabbit temporomandibular joint. *Journal of Maxillofacial Surgery.* 1992, pp. 843-849.
54. Brandt, K. The effects of salicylates and other nonsteroidal anti-inflammatory drugs on articular cartilage. *American Journal of Medicine.* 1984; 77:65-69.
55. Palmoski, M. Effects of some nonsteroidal anti-inflammatory drugs on proteoglycan metabolism and organization in canine articular cartilage. *Arthritis and Rheumatism.* 1980; 23:1010-1020.
56. Palmoski, M. Effect of salicylate on proteoglycan metabolism in normal canine articular cartilage *in vitro. Arthritis and Rheumatism.* 1979; 22: 746-754.
57. Palmoski, M. Marked suppression by salicylate of the augmented proteoglycan synthesis in osteoarthritic cartilage. *Arthritis and Rheumatism.* 1980; 23:83-91.
58. Hugenberg, S. Suppression by nonsteroidal anti-inflammatory drugs on proteoglycan synthesis in articular cartilage. *Arthritis and Rheumatism.* 1992; 35:R29.
59. Brandt, K. Should osteoarthritis be treated with nonsteroidal anti-inflammatory drugs? *Rheumatic Disease Clinics of North America.* 1993; 19:697-712.
60. Palmoski, M. *In vitro* effect of aspirin on canine osteoarthritic cartilage. *Arthritis and Rheumatism.* 1983; 26:994-1001.
61. Palmoski, M. Marked suppression by salicylate of the augmented proteoglycan synthesis in osteoarthritic cartilage. *Arthritis and Rheumatism.* 1980; 23:83-91.
62. Coke, H. Long-term indomethacin therapy of coxarthrosis. *Annals of Rheumatic Diseases.* 1967; 26:346-347.
63. Solomon, L. Drug-induced arthropathy and neurosis of the femoral head. *Journal of Bone and Joint Surgery* (Britian). 1973; 55:246-261.
64. Newman, N. Acetabular bone destruction related to nonsteroidal anti-inflammatory drugs. *Lancet.* 1985; 2:11-14.
65. Rashad, S. Effects of nonsteroidal anti-inflammatory drugs on the course of osteoarthritis. *Lancet.* 1989; 2:519-522.
66. Wrenn, R. An experimental study on the effect of cortisone on the healing process and tensile strength of tendons. *Journal of Bone and Joint Surgery.* 1954; 36A:588-601.
67. Truhan, A. Corticosteroids: a review with emphasis on complication of prolonged systemic therapy. *Annals of Allergy.* 1989; 62:375-390.
68. Roenigk, R. *Dermatologic Surgery.* Marcel Dekker, Inc., p. 155.

69. Davis, G. Adverse effects of corticosteroids. *Systemic Clinical Dermatology.* 1986; 4:161-169.
70. Gogia, P. Hydrocortisone and exercise effects on articular cartilage in rats. *Archives of Physical Medicine and Rehabilitation.* 1993; 74:463-467.
71. Chandler, G. Deleterious effect of intra-articular hydrocortisone. *Lancet.* 1958; 2:661-663.
72. Chunekamrai, S. Changes in articular cartilage after intra-articular injections of methylprednisolone acetate in horses. *American Journal of Veterinary Research.* 1989; 50:1733-1741.
73. *Ibid.*
74. Pool, R. Corticosteroid therapy in common joint and tendon injuries of the horse: effect on joints. *Proceedings of the American Association of Equine Practice.* 1980; 26:397-406.
75. From personal correspondence between the authors and Michael Herron, D.V.M.
76. Behrens, F. Alteration of rabbit articular cartilage of intra-articular injections of glucocorticoids. *Journal of Bone and Joint Surgery.* 1975; 57A:70-76.
77. *Ibid.*
78. Eklhom, R. On the relationship between articular changes and function. *Acta Ortho. Scand.* 1951; 21:81-98.
79. Lanier, R. Effects of exercise on the knee joints of inbred mice. *Anat. Rec.* 1946; 94:311-319.
80. Saaf, J. Effects of exercise on articular cartilage. *Acta Ortho. Scand.* 1950; 20:1-83.
81. Gogia, P. Hydrocortisone and exercise effects on articular cartilage in rats. *Archives of Physical Medicine and Rehabilitation.* 1993; 74: 463-467.

CHAPTER 15

PROLO YOUR ARTHRITIS PAIN AWAY!

1. Christie, R. The medical uses of proteolytic enzymes. From *Topics in Enzyme and Fermentation Biotechnology*. Chichester, England: Ellis Horwood Ltd., 1980, p. 25.
2. *Primer on the Rheumatic Diseases*. Ninth Edition. Atlanta, GA: Arthritis Foundation, 1988, p. 83.
3. Svartz, D. The primary cause of rheumatoid arthritis is an infection—the infectious agent exists in milk. *Acta Med. Scand.* 1972; 192:231-239.
4. Kloppenburg, M. Minocycline in active rheumatoid arthritis. *Arthritis and Rheumatism.* 1994; 37:629-636.
5. From personal correspondence between Dr. Bellew and Dr. Hemwall, mid-1970s.

6. Rooney, P. A short review of the relationship between intestinal permeability and inflammatory joint disease. *Clinical and Experimental Rheumatology*. 1990; 8:75-83.
7. Galland, L. Leaky gut syndrome: breaking the vicious cycle. *Townsend Letter for Doctors*. 1995; August/September: pp. 62-68.
8. Crissinger, K. Pathophysiology of gastrointestinal mucosal permeability. *Journal of Internal Medicine* (Suppl.) 1990; 732:145-154.
9. Jenkins, R. Increased intestinal permeability in patients with rheumatoid arthritis: a side effect of oral nonsteroidal anti-inflammatory drug therapy? *British Journal of Rheumatology*. 1987; 26:103-107.
10. Bjarnason, I. Importance of local versus systemic effects of nonsteroidal anti-inflammatory drugs in increasing small intestinal permeability in man. *Gut*. 1991; 32:275-277.
11. Crayhoun, R. *Nutrition Made Simple*. New York, NY: M. Evans and Company, Inc., 1994, pp. 19-25.
12. Lorschider, F. Mercury exposure from "silver tooth" fillings: emerging evidence questions a traditional dental paradigm. *The FASEB Journal*. 1995; 9:504-508.
13. Goyer, R. Nutrition and metal toxicity. *American Journal of Clinical Nutrition*. 1995; 61:646S-650S.
14. McCarthy, G. Dietary fish oil and rheumatic diseases. *Seminars in Arthritis and Rheumatism*. 1992; 21:368-375.
15. *Ibid.*
16. Simopoulos, A. Omega-3 fatty acids in health and disease and in growth and development. *American Journal of Clinical Nutrition*. 1991; 54:438-463.

CHAPTER 16
PROLO YOUR RSD, SCI, AND OTHER NEUROLOGICAL PAINS AWAY!

1. Merskey, H. (ed.), International Association for the Study of Pain (ISAP): subcomittee on taxonomy, classification of chronic pain, description of pain terms. *Pain*. 1986; 3 (Suppl).
2. Mandel, S. Sympathetic dystrophies. *Postgraduate Medicine*. 1990; 87:213-218.
3. *Ibid.*
4. Shumacker, H. A personal overview of causalgia and other reflex dystrophies. *Annals of Surgery*. 1985; 201:278-289.
5. Schutzer, S. The treatment of reflex sympathetic dystrophy syndrome. *Journal of Bone and Joint Surgery*. 1984; 66A:625-628.
6. Shelton, R. Reflex sympathetic dystrophy: a review. *Journal of the American Academy of Dermatology*. 1990; 22:513-519.
7. Langenskiold, A. Osteoarthritis of the knee in the rabbit produced by immobilization: attempts to achieve a reproducible model for studies on pathogenesis and therapy. *Acta. Ortho. Scand*. 1979; 50:1.

8. Videman, T. Connective tissue and immobilization. *Clinical Orthopaedics and Related Research.* 1987; 221:26-32.
9. Videman, T. Experimental osteoarthritis in the rabbit: comparison of different periods of repeated immobilization. *Acta. Ortho. Scand.* 1982; 53:339.
10. Enneking, W. The intra-articular effects of immobilization on the human knee. *Journal of Bone and Joint Surgery.* 1972; 54:973-985.
11. Kottke, F. (ed.), *Krusen's Handbook of Physical Medicine and Rehabilitation.* Fourth Edition. Philadelphia, PA: W.B. Saunders, 1990, pp. 1122-1127.
12. Abramson, A. Influence of weight-bearing and muscle contraction on disuse osteoporosis. *Archives of Physical Medicine and Rehabilitation.* 1961; March: 147-152.
13. Korr, I. Effects of experimental myofascial insults on cutaneous patterns of sympathetic activity in man. *Journal of Neural Transmission.* 1962; 23:330-355.
14. Korr, I. Experimental alterations in segmental sympathetic (sweat gland) activity through myofascial and postural disturbances. *Federal Proceedings.* 1949; 8:88.
15. Korr, I. Patterns of electrical skin resistance in man. *Acta. Neuroveget (Wien)* 1958; 17:77-96.
16. Korr, I. Cutaneous patterns of sympathetic activity in clinical abnormalities of the musculoskeletal system. *J. Neural Transm.* 1964; 25:589-606.
17. Slosberg, M. Effects of altered afferent articular input on sensation, proprioception, muscle tone and sympathetic reflex responses. *Journal of Manipulative and Physiological Therapeutics.* 1988; 11:400-408.
18. Schumaker, H. A personal overview of causalgia and other reflex dystrophies. *Annals of Surgery.* 1985; 201:278-289.
19. Schutzer, S. The treatment of reflex sympathetic dystrophy syndrome. *Journal of Bone and Joint Surgery.* 1984; 66A:625-628.
20. Geertzen, J. Reflex sympathy dystrophy: early treatment and psychological aspects. *Archives of Physical Medicine and Rehabilitation.* 1994; 75:442-446.
21. Nepomuceno, C. Pain in patients with spinal cord injury. *Archives of Physical Medicine and Rehabilitation.* 1979; 60:605-609.
22. McLeod, J. Disorders of the autonomic nervous system: part one, pathophysiology and clinical features. *Annals of Neurology.* 1987; 21:419-426.
23. Erickson, R. Autonomic hyperreflexia: pathophysiology and medical management. *Archives of Physical Medicine and Rehabilitation.* 1980; 61:431-440.
24. Head, H. Autonomic bladder, excessive sweating, and some reflex conditions, in gross injuries of the spinal cord. *Brain.* 1917; 46:188-263.
25. Korr, I. Effects of experimental myofascial insults on cutaneous patterns of sympathetic activity in man. *Journal of Neural Transmission.* 1962; 23:330-355.

26. Korr, I. Experimental alterations in segmental sympathetic (sweat gland) activity through myofascial and postural disturbances. *Federal Procedings*. 1949; 8:88.

27. Korr, I. Patterns of electrical skin resistance in man. *Acta. Neuroveget (Wien)*. 1958; 17:77-96.

28. Korr, I. Cutaneous patterns of sympathetic activity in clinical abnormalities of the musculoskeletal system. *J. Neural Transm*. 1964; 25:589-606.

29. Traycoff, R. Sacrococcygeal pain syndromes: diagnosis and treatment. *Orthopedics*. 1989; 12:1373-1377.

30. *Ibid.*

31. Hackett, G. Prolotherapy for sciatica from weak pelvic ligaments and bone dystrophy. *Clinical Medicine*. 1961; p. 8.

32. Leijon, G. Central post-stroke pain—a controlled trial of amitriptyline and carbamazepine. *Pain*. 1989; 36:27-36.

33. Leijon, G. Central post-stroke pain—neurological symptoms and pain characteristics. *Pain*. 1989; 36:13-15.

34. Kiel, G. So-called initial description of phantom pain by Ambroise Pare. Chose digne d'admiration et quasi incredible: the "douleur es parties mortes et amputees." *Fortschr. Med.* 1990; 108:62-66.

35. Davis, R. Phantom sensation, phantom pain, and stump pain. *Archives of Physical Medicine and Rehabilitation*. 1993; 74:79-91.

CHAPTER 17

PROLO YOUR UNUSUAL PAINS AWAY!

1. Mengert, W. Referred pelvic pain. *Southern Medical Journal*. 1943; 36:256-263.

2. Pitikin, H. Sacrathrogenetic telagia, part two: a study of referred pain. *Journal of Bone and Joint Surgery*. 1936; 18:365-374.

3. DeLisa, J. *Rehabilitation Medicine*. Philadelphia, PA: J.B. Lippincott, 1988.

4. Browner, B. *Skeletal Trauma*. Philadelphia, PA: W.B. Saunders, 1992.

5. Hollinshead, W. *Functional Anatomy of the Limbs and Back*. Philadelphia, PA: W.B. Saunders, 1981.

6. Taddeini, L. Pain syndromes associated with cancer. *Postgraduate Medicine*. 1984; 75:101-108.

7. Laing, A. Strontium—89 chloride for pain palliation in prostatic skeletal malignancy. *British Journal of Radiology*. 1991; 64:816-822.

8. Kirvela, O. Treatment of painful neuromas with neurolytic blockade. *Pain*. 1990; 41:161-165.

9. Nidorf, D. Proctalgia fugax. *American Family Physician*. 1995; 52:2238-2240.

10. Ger, G. Evaluation and treatment of chronic intractable rectal pain—a frustrating endeavor. *Diseases of the Colon and Rectum*. 1993; 36:139-145.

11. Nidorf, D. Proctalgia fugax. *American Family Physician.* 1995; 52: 2238-2240.
12. Ger, G. Evaluation and treatment of chronic intractable rectal pain—a frustrating endeavor. *Diseases of the Colon and Rectum.* 1993; 36:139-145.
13. Babb, R. Proctalgia fugax. *Postgraduate Medicine.* 1996; 99:263-264.
14. Morris, L. Use of high-voltage pulsed galvanic stimulation for patients with levator ani syndrome. *Physical Therapy.* 1987; 67:1522-1525.
15. Tietze, A. Uber eine eigenartige hafung ion fallen mit dystrophie der rippenknorpel. *Berl. Klin. Wchnschr.* 1921: 58:829.
16. Rawlings, M. The "rib syndrome." *Diseases of the Chest.* 1962; 41:432-441.
17. Davies-Colley, R. Slipping rib. *New England Journal of Medicine.* 296:432-433.
18. McBeath, A. The rib-tip syndrome. *Journal of Bone and Joint Surgery.* 1975; 57A:795-797.
19. Holmes, J. A study of the slipping-rib cartilage syndrome. *New England Journal of Medicine.* 1941; 224:928-932.
20. Kelly, TR. Thoracic outlet syndrome: Current concepts of treatment. *Annals of Surgery* 1979; 190(5):657-662.
21. Phull, P. Management of cervical pain. In *Rehabilitation Medicine.* Delisa, J. (ed.), Philadelphia, PA: Lippincott Publisher, 1988, pp. 761-764.
22. Hirschberg, G. Medical management of iliocostal pain. *Geriatrics.* 1992; 47:62-67.
23. *Ibid.*

CHAPTER 18

PROLO YOUR FIBROMYALGIA PAIN AWAY!

1. Yunnus, M. Primary fibromyalgia syndrome and myofascial pain syndrome: clinical features and muscle pathology. *Archives of Physical Medicine and Rehabilitation.* 1988; 69:451-454.
2. Pillemer, S. *The Fibromyalgia Syndrome.* The Harworth Medical Press, Inc., 1994.
3. Bennett, R. Fibrositis. From *The Textbook of Rheumatology,* Third Edition, Philadelphia, PA: W.B. Saunders, 1987, pp. 541-553.
4. Moldofsky, H. Induction of neurasthenic musculoskeletal pain syndrome by selective sleep stage deprivation. *Psychosomatic Medicine.* 1976; 38:35.
5. Buchwald, D. Comparison of patients with chronic fatigue syndrome, fibromyalgia, and multiple chemical sensitivities. *Archives of Internal Medicine.* 1994; 154:2049-2053.
6. Crofford, L. Hypothalamic-pituitary-adrenal axis perturbations in patients with fibromyalgia. *Arthritis and Rheumatism.* 1994; 37:1583-1592.
7. Goldenberg, D. Do infections trigger fibromyalgia? *Arthritis and Rheumatism.* 1993; 36:1489-1492.

8. Travell, J. *Myofascial Pain and Dysfunction.* Baltimore, M.D.: Williams and Wilkins, 1983, pp. 103-164.
9. Reeves, K. Treatment of consecutive severe fibromyalgia patients with Prolotherapy. *Journal of Orthopaedic Medicine.* 1994; 16:84-89.
10. McCarty, D. *Arthritis and Allied Conditions.* Twelfth Edition. Lea and Febiger, 1993.
11. Kowitz, R. *Osteoarthritis.* Second Edition. Philadelphia, PA: W.B. Saunders, 1992.
12. Travell, J. *Myofascial Pain and Dysfunction.* Baltimore, M.D.: Williams and Wilkins, 1983, pp. 103-164.
13. Hong, C. Difference in pain relief after trigger point injections in myofascial pain patients with and without fibromyalgia. *Archives of Physical Medicine and Rehabilitation.* 1996; 77:1161-1166.

Chapter 19

Prolo Your Sports Injuries Away!

1. Peterson, L. *Sports Injuries: Their Prevention and Treatment.* Chicago, IL: Year Book Medical, 1986, pp. 18-63.

Chapter 20

Prolo Your Animal's Pain Away!

1. Smith, G. Coxofemoral joint laxity from distraction radiography and its contemporaneous and prospective correlation with laxity, subjective score and evidence of degenerative joint disease from conventional hip-extended radiography in dogs. *American Journal of Veterinary Research.* 1993; 54:1021-1042.
2. Fubini, S. Effect of intramuscularly administered polysulfated glycosaminoglycan on articular cartilage from equine joints injected with methylprednisolone acetate. *American Journal of Veterinary Research.* 1993; 54:1359-1364.
3. Chunekamrai, S. Changes in articular cartilage after intra-articular injections of methylprednisolone acetate in horses. *American Journal of Veterinary Research.* 1989; 50:1733-1741.
4. Trotter, G. Effects of intra-articular administration of methylprednisolone acetate on normal equine articular cartilage. *American Journal of Veterinary Research.* 1991; 52:83-87.
5. Shoemaker, S. Effects of intra-articular administration of acetate on normal articular cartilage and on healing of experimentally induced osteochondral defects in horses. *American Journal of Veterinary Research.* 1992; 53:1446-1453.
6. Megher, D. The effects of intra-articular corticosteroids and continued training on carpal chip fractures of horses. *Proceedings of the American Association of Equine Practice.* 1970; 16:405-412.
7. From a conversation with Shaun Fauley, D.V.M., in May 1997.

8. Chunekamrai, S. Changes in articular cartilage after intra-articular injections of methylprednisolone acetate in horses. *American Journal of Veterinary Research.* 1989; 50:1733-1741.
9. Pool, R. Corticosteroid therapy in common joint and tendon injuries of the horse: effect on joints. *Proceedings of the American Association of Equine Practice.* 1980; 26:397-406.
10. From personal correspondence between the authors and Michael Herron, D.V.M.
11. *Ibid.*
12. *Ibid.*
13. Ramey, D. *Tendon and Ligament Injuries in the Horse.* New York City, NY: Howel Book House, 1996.
14. Fubini, S. Effect of intramuscularly administered polysulfated glycosaminoglycan on articular cartilage from equine joints injected with methylprednisolone acetate. *American Journal of Veterinary Research.* 1993; 54:1359-1364.
15. Chunekamrai, S. Changes in articular cartilage after intra-articular injections of methylprednisolone acetate in horses. *American Journal of Veterinary Research.* 1989; 50:1733-1741.
16. Trotter, G. Effects of intra-articular administration of methylprednisolone acetate on normal equine articular cartilage. *American Journal of Veterinary Research.* 1991; 52:83-87.
17. Shoemaker, S. Effects of intra-articular administration of acetate on normal articular cartilage and on healing of experimentally induced osteochondral defects in horses. *American Journal of Veterinary Research.* 1992; 53:1446-1453.
18. Megher, D. The effects of intra-articular corticosteroids and continued training on carpal chip fractures of horses. *Proceedings of the American Association of Equine Practice.* 1970; 16:405-412.
19. From a conversation with Shaun Fauley, D.V.M., in May 1997.
20. Chunekamrai, S. Changes in articular cartilage after intra-articular injections of methylprednisolone acetate in horses. *American Journal of Veterinary Research.* 1989; 50:1733-1741.
21. Pool, R. Corticosteroid therapy in common joint and tendon injuries of the horse: effect on joints. *Proceedings of the American Association of Equine Practice.* 1980; 26:397-406.
22. Meagher, D. The effects of intra-articular corticosteroids and continued training on carpal chip fractures of horses. *Proceedings of the American Association of Equine Practice.* 1979; 16:405-412.

Chapter 21
Prolotherapy: The King of All Injection Techniques

1. Liu, Y. An *in situ* study of the influence of a sclerosing solution in rabbits' medial collateral ligaments and its junction strength. *Connective Tissue Research.* 1983; 11:95-102.

2. Maynard, J. Morphological and biochemical effects of sodium morrhuate on tendons. *Journal of Orthopaedic Research.* 1985; 3:236-248.

3. Lockhart, R. *Anatomy of the Human Body.* Second Edition. Philadelphia, PA: J.B. Lippincott, 1969; pp. 144.

4. International Anatomical Nomenclature Committee: *Nomina Anatomica.* Excerpta Medical Foundation, Amersterdam, 1966; pp. 38-43.

5. Simons, D. and Travell, J. *Myofascial Pain and Dysfunction: The Trigger Point Manual.* Volume 1. Baltimore, M.D.: Williams and Wilkins, 1999; pp. 1-94.

6. Fishbain, D. Male and female chronic pain patients categorized by DSM-III psychiatric diagnostic criteria. *Pain.* 1986; 26:181-197.

7. Gerwin, R. A study of 96 subjects examined both for fibromyalgia and myofascial pain (Abstract). *Journal of Musculoskeletal Pain.* 1995; 3:121.

8. Sola, A. Incidence of hypersensitive areas in posterior shoulder muscles. *American Journal of Physical Medicine.* 1955; 34:585-590.

9. Frohlich, D. Piriformissyndrom: eine haufige differentialdiagnose des lumboglutaalen schmerzes (Piriformis syndrome: a frequent item in the differential diagnosis of lumbogluteal pain). *Manuelle Medizin.* 1995; 33:7-10.

10. Bates, T. Myofascial pain in childhood. *Journal of Pediatrics.* 1958; 53:198-209.

11. Travell, J. Pain and disability of the shoulder and arm: treatment by intra-muscular infiltration with procaine hydrochloride. *Journal of the American Medical Association* 1942; 120:417-422.

12. Travell, J. Myofascial pain syndromes: mysteries of the history. In *Advances in Pain Research and Therapy: Myofascial Pain and Fibromyalgia,* Volume 17. Edited by Fricton, J. New York, NY: Raven Press, 1990; pp. 129-137.

13. Travell J. and Rinzler S. The myofascial genesis of pain. *Postgraduate Medicine.* 1952; 11:425-434.

14. Simons, D. and Travell, J. *Myofascial Pain and Dysfunction: The Trigger Point Manual.* Volume 1. Baltimore, M.D.: Williams and Wilkins, 1999; 94-177.

15. Simons, D. and Travell, J. *Myofascial Pain and Dysfunction: The Trigger Point Manual.* Volume 1. Baltimore, M.D.: Williams and Wilkins, 1999; pp. 178-235.

16. Travell, J. and Travell, W. Therapy of low back pain by manipulation and of referred pain in the lower extremity by procaine infiltration. *Archives of Physical Medicine.* 1946; September: 537-547.

17. Kellgren, J. Sciatica. *Lancet.* 1941; 1:561.

18. Hackett, G. Referred pain and sciatica in diagnosis of low back disability. *Journal of the American Medical Association* 1957; 163:183-185.

19. Hackett, G. Joint stabilization. *American Journal of Surgery.* 1955; 89: 968-973.

20. Hackett, G. Referred pain from low back ligament disability. *AMA Archives of Surgery.* 1956; 73:878-883.
21. Hackett, G. *Ligament and Tendon Relaxation Treated by Prolotherapy.* First Edition. Springfield, IL: Charles C. Thomas, 1956.
22. Hackett, G. *Ligament and Tendon Relaxation Treated by Prolotherapy.* Third Edition. Springfield, IL: Charles C. Thomas, 1958.
23. Travell, J. Pain mechanisms in connective tissue. In *Connective Tissues, Transactions of the Second Conference.* 1951, Edited by Ragan, C. Josiah Macy, Jr. Foundation, New York, 1952, pp. 96-102, 105-109, 111.
24. Travell, J. Basis for the multiple uses of local block of somatic trigger areas (procaine infiltration and ethyl chloride spray). *Mississippi Valley Medical Journal.* 1949; 71:13-22.
25. Travell, J. Mechanism of relief of pain in sprains by local injection techniques. *Fed. Proc.* 1947; 6:378.
26. Gorrell, R. Troublesome ankle disorders and what to do about them. *Consultant.* 1976; 16:64-69.
27. Leriche, R. Des effetes de l'anesthesie a la novocaine des ligament et des insertions tendineuses per-articulaires dans certaines maladies articulaires et dans vices de position fonctionnels des articulations. *Gazette des Hopitaux.* 1930; 103:1294.
28. Kraus, H. *Clinical Treatment of Back and Neck Pain.* New York, NY: McGraw-Hill, 1970, pp. 95-107.
29. Hong, C. Lidocaine injection versus dry needling to myofascial trigger point: the importance of the local twitch response. *American Journal of Physical Medicine and Rehabilitation*. 1994; 73:256-263.
30. Jaeger, B. Double-blind controlled study of different myofascial trigger point injection techniques (Abstract). *Pain.* 1987; 4:S292.
31. Hackett, G. Low back pain. *British Journal of Physical Medicine.* 1956; 19:25-35.
32. Hackett, G. Prolotherapy in whiplash and low back pain. *Postgraduate Medicine.* 1960; February: 214-219.

Chapter 23
Why Don't You Heal?

1. Sibinga, N. Opioid peptides and opioid receptors in cells of the immune system. *Annu. Rev. Immunol.*, 1988; 6:219-249.
2. Bryant, H. Role of adrenal cortical activation in the immunosuppressive effects of chronic morphine treatment. *Endocrinology*. 1991; 128:3253-3258.
3. Pellis, N. Suppression of the induction of delayed hypersensitivity in rats by repetitive morphine treatments. *Experimental Neurology*. 1986; 93:92-97.
4. Lopez, M. Spleen and thymus cells subsets modified by long-term morphine administration and murine AIDS. *International Journal of Immunopharmacology*. 1993; 15:909-918.

5. Sei, Y. Morphine-induced thymic hypoplasia is glucocorticoid-dependent. *Journal of Immunology*. 1991; 146:194-198.
6. Bryant, H. Immunosuppressive effects of chronic morphine treatment in mice. *Life Sciences*. 1987; 41:1731-1738.
7. Bussiere, J. Differential effects of morphine and naltrexone on the antibody response in various mouse strains. *Immunotoxicol.* 1992; 14:657-673.
8. Hung, C. *Proc. Soc. Exp. Biol. Med.* 1973; 142:106-111.
9. Nair, M. A decreased natural and antibody-dependent cellular cytotoxic activities in intravenous drug abusers. *Clin. Immunol. Immunopathol.* 1986; 38:68-78.
10. Eisenstein, T. Opioid modulation of immune responses: effects on phagocyte and lymphoid cell populations. *Journal of Neuroimmunology*. 1998; 83:36-44.
11. Gilman, A. *The Pharmacological Basis of Therapeutics*. Elmsford, NY: Pergamon Press, 1990, p. 486.
12. Nicolson, G. Mycoplasma infections in chronic illnesses: fibromyalgia and chronic fatigue syndromes, Gulf War illness, HIV-AIDS and rheumatoid arthritis. *Medical Sentinel*. 1999; 4:172-175.
13. Nicolson, G. Diagnosis and treatment of chronic mycoplasmal infections in fibromyalgia and chronic fatigue syndromes: relationship to Gulf War illness. *Biomedical Therapy*. 1998; 16:266-271.
14. Steere, A. Musculoskeletal manifestations of Lyme disease. *American Journal of Medicine*. 1995; 98:4A-45S.
15. Tortorice, K. Clinical features and treatment of Lyme disease. *Pharmacotherapy*. 1989; 9:363-371.
16. *Merriam Webster's Collegiate Dictionary*, Tenth Edition, Springfield, MA: Merriam-Webster, Inc. 1995.
17. Hallesby, O. *Temperament and the Christian Faith*. Minneapolis, MN, Augsburg Publishing House, 1962.
18. LaHaye, T. *Transformed Temperaments*. Wheaton, IL: Tyndale House Publishers, 1971.
19. LaHaye, T. *Spirit-Controlled Temperament*. Wheaton, IL: Tyndale House Publishers, 1966.
20. Littauer, F. *Personality Plus*. Grand Rapids, MI: Fleming H. Revell, 1992.
21. Wright, H. *A More Excellent Way*. Thomaston, GA: Pleasant Valley Publications, 1999.

Appendix A

Neural Therapy

1. Klinghardt, D. Neural Therapy. *Townsend Letter for Doctors and Patients.* July 1995, pp. 96-98.
2. Dosch, P. *Facts About Neural Therapy.* First English Edition. Heidelberg, Germany: Haug Publishers, 1985, pp. 25-30.

3. Dosch, P. *Manual of Neural Therapy.* First English Edition. Heidelberg, Germany: Haug Publishers, 1984, pp. 74-77.
4. *Ibid.*
5. Dosch, P. *Illustrated Atlas of the Techniques of Neural Therapy with Local Anesthetics.* First English Edition. Heidelberg, Germany: Haug Publishers, 1985.

INDEX

A

B

N

O

P

R

Other Books by Beulah Land Press

Beulah Land Press is pleased to offer these books on Prolotherapy written by Dr. Ross and Marion Hauser.

- ***Prolo Your Pain Away!*** *Curing Chronic Pain with Prolotherapy*
- ***Prolo Your Sports Injuries Away!***
  Curing Sports Injuries and Enhancing Athletic Performance with Prolotherapy
- ***Prolo Your Arthritis Pain Away!***
  Curing Disabling and Disfiguring Arthritis Pain with Prolotherapy
- ***Prolo Your Back Pain Away!***
  Curing Chronic Back Pain with Prolotherapy
- ***Prolo Your Headache and Neck Pain Away!***
  Curing Migraines and Neck Pain with Prolotherapy
- ***Prolo Your Fibromyalgia Pain Away!***
  Curing Disabling Body Pain with Prolotherapy
- ***Ligament and Tendon Relaxation Treated by Prolotherapy***
  By George S. Hackett, M.D., Gustav A. Hemwall, M.D., and Gerald A. Montgomery, M.D.

About these books:

Prolo Your Pain Away!

Read the book that has changed chronic pain management forever. "This is the best book ever written about Prolotherapy," says Robert C. Atkins, M.D., best-selling author of *New Diet Revolution* and medical director of the Atkins Center for Complementary Medicine in New York City, New York. *Prolo Your Pain Away!* details in common lay language the conditions that can be cured with Prolotherapy, including arthritis, back pain, migraines, neck pain, fibromyalgia, spastic torticollis, osteoporosis, fracture pain, cancer pain, whiplash, sports injuries, loose joints, TMJ, tendonitis, sciatica, herniated discs, and more! Find out why C. Everett Koop, M.D., former Surgeon General of the United States, and a former chronic pain sufferer who was cured by Prolotherapy, says "*Prolo Your Pain Away!* is a must-read for anyone experiencing chronic musculoskeletal pain."

Prolo Your Sports Injuries Away!

Just as the original book *Prolo Your Pain Away!* affected the pain management field, *Prolo Your Sports Injuries Away!* has rattled the sports world. Learn the 20 myths of sports medicine, including the myths of anti-inflammatory medications; why cortisone shots actually weaken tissue; how ice, rest, and immobilization may actually hurt the athlete; why the common practice of taping and bracing does not stabilize injured areas; and why the arthroscope is one of the athlete's worst nightmares!

Did you ever wonder why most career runners and athletes end up with arthritis? This book will explain why this happens and how you can prevent it from happening to you! Prolotherapy is an athlete's best friend because it addresses the root cause of most sports injuries: ligament and tendon weakness. By stimulating the body to repair the painful area, Prolotherapy can make an injured area stronger than its original, uninjured counterpart! Athletes around the country are hailing Prolotherapy as the treatment that not only added more years to their careers, but also gave them that additional edge by enhancing their athletic performance. You will learn why Prolotherapy has become the sports medicine treatment of the future and why athletes around the country are curing their sports injuries and enhancing their athletic performance with Prolotherapy.

Prolo Your Arthritis Pain Away!

Studies estimate that 40 million people in the United States suffer from some form of arthritis. By the year 2020 that number will be nearly 60 million. The traditional treatments for arthritis involve anti-inflammatory medication, cortisone shots, and joint replacement surgery. People are often left with the diagnosis of: "There is nothing else we can do for you." Nothing could be further from the truth. What most people do not realize is that arthritis forms because of an underlying ligament and joint weakness problem. The body responds to this weakness by overgrowing bony formations in the unstable areas, hoping to provide some stabilization to the weak joint. Unfortunately, this is not only painful, but often disfiguring.

Prolotherapy is the best technique available to stimulate the body to strengthen the joint and surrounding ligaments. By doing this, the arthritis process stops and the pain can be eliminated. This book details why arthritis sufferers around the country are throwing away the anti-inflammatory medications and returning to the activities that they used to enjoy. Prolotherapy has given life back to many arthritis sufferers. Gone are the days of waking up feeling stiff and sore.

Prolo Your Back Pain Away!

Stan Mikita, former Chicago Blackhawks hockey star and hall-of-famer, was about to cut a magnificent career short because of a back injury. Six weeks prior to the 1971-1972 season opening, Mr. Mikita could not even get out of bed because of severe sciatica and back pain. He found Prolotherapy as a treatment option that got him back on his skates again. Learn why Stan enthusiastically says, "Prolotherapy definitely extended my NHL career eight years and gave me complete relief of my back pain!" Learn why MRI scans may erroneously diagnose "disc problems," forcing people into unnecessary surgeries. Prolotherapy can help the painful conditions such as degenerated disc disease, sciatica, arthritis, spinal stenosis, and even herniated discs. This is why people with chronic back pain are saying "no" to surgery and "yes" to Prolotherapy!

Prolo Your Headache and Neck Pain Away!

Years ago, it was going to be another ruined evening for the Hausers. Marion had another migraine headache. She finally decided to try Prolotherapy to put an end to the suffering. Boy, is she glad that she did! You will also be glad if you suffer from migraines, tension, or cluster headaches. Marion went from being a skeptic to someone who now writes books on the topic! Prolotherapy stimulates the body to repair painful areas. Don't most headaches start out with neck or shoulder pain? Learn about a lesser-known syndrome called Barré-Lieou Syndrome, which is one of the most common causes of headaches. Some of the associated symptoms include ringing in the ears, sinus pressure, dizziness, and neck pain. Ligament injury in the neck is usually the cause of head-forward posture, which leads to chronic neck pain and headaches. Prolotherapy causes the vertebrae in the neck to stay in alignment. Good alignment means good posture. Good posture means fewer headaches. No more headaches mean good-bye to pain pills. Learn why many former headache sufferers found hope with Prolotherapy.

Prolo Your Fibromyalgia Pain Away!

An epidemic number of people in the United States wake up in the morning feeling tired, sore, and achy. Upon physical examination, tender points are found all over the body. Women may be given the concurrent diagnoses of migraine headaches and endometriosis. They are told to exercise and take antidepressant medication. Nothing can be done to cure the problem…until now. Learn why over 90 percent of fibromyalgia sufferers respond well to Prolotherapy. People with Fibromyalgia often suffer from fungal infections, which have a tremendously detrimental effect on soft tissue formation, including the ligaments and tendons. Treatment of this infection, in conjunction with Prolotherapy, has given hope to many suffering from the often-debilitating symptoms of fibromyalgia.

Ligament and Tendon Relaxation Treated by Prolotherapy

After performing Prolotherapy for over 40 years, the world's most experienced Prolotherapist, Gustav A. Hemwall, M.D., died at the age of 90. His legacy and experience are preserved in this fifth edition of the book written by the originator himself, George S. Hackett, M.D. Dr. Hackett wrote many of the words in this book. This book was written to demonstrate the technique of Prolotherapy to physicians. Many case studies are also presented. Much of what is known about Prolotherapy comes from the authors of this book. ■

PURCHASING INFORMATION:
Beulah Land Press • 715 Lake Street • Oak Park, Illinois 60301
1-800-RX-PROLO (1-800-797-7656)
www.benuts.com or www.beulahlandpress.com

FOR FURTHER INFORMATION:
www.caringmedical.com and www.proloinfo.com

For More Information about Our Office

Would you like to become a patient? We have a national referral base and see patients from all over the country. Dr. Ross Hauser and his associates are some of the country's most experienced clinicians in Prolotherapy and other Natural Medicine techniques. Caring Medical is a comprehensive Natural Medicine center only minutes from downtown Chicago in the beautiful suburb of Oak Park, Illinois. The center is only 30 minutes from either O'Hare or Midway airports.

Besides Prolotherapy, the center also offers:

- Metabolic Typing
- Mid-Life Medicine Assessments
- Chelation Therapy
- Insulin Potentiation Therapy (for cancer)
- Natural Hormone Replacement
- Nutritional/Herbal Counseling
- Ozone Therapy
- Neural Therapy
- Mesotherapy
- Photoluminescence
- Other specific regimes to reverse connective tissue deficiency

Caring Medical services clients with every human disease, including chronic pain, rheumatologic diseases, chronic fatigue, cancer, diabetes, high blood pressure, digestive and heart conditions, as well as other chronic disabling diseases.

To learn more about the life-changing Natural Medicine regimes at Caring Medical, you can contact our office in one of the following ways:

Contact Our Oak Park Office at:

Caring Medical and Rehabilitation Services
715 Lake Street, Suite 600
Oak Park, Illinois 60301
Phone: 708-848-7789 • **Fax:** 708-848-7763
URL: www.caringmedical.com
E-Mail: drhauser@caringmedical.com

Caring Medical believes the care of the patient begins with caring.™

The Doctor & the Dietitian™

Talk to us!

"The Doctor"

drhauser@caringmedical.com

Ross Hauser, M.D., is the Medical Director of Caring Medical & Rehabilitation Services. He received his M.D. from the University of Illinois, Chicago; his BS degree from the University of Illinois, Urbana-Champaign; and completed his residency in physical Medicine and Rehabilitation at Loyola-Hines VA-Marianjoy Hospitals.

Marion Hauser, M.S., R.D. is the Executive Director of Caring Medical & Rehabilitation Services and a registered and licensed dietitian. Marion received her MS degree in Nutrition from Eastern Illinois University; completed her Dietetic Internship at Sarah Bush Lincoln Health Center in Charleston, Illinois; and received her B.S. degree from the University of Illinois, Urbana-Champaign in Nutrition.

"The Dietitian

Beulah Land Press

The Doctor: Ross A. Hauser, M.D.
The Dietitian: Marion A. Hauser, M.S., R.D.

READ FOR YOUR HEALTH! ORDER FROM THE PUBLISHER AT A SUBSTANTIAL DISCOUNT!

Prolo Your Sports Injuries Away!

Curing Sports Injuries and Enhancing Athletic Performance with Prolotherapy

Prolo Your Arthritis Pain Away!

Curing Disfiguring and Disabling Arthritis Pain with Prolotherapy

Prolo Your Back Pain Away!

Curing Chronic Back Pain with Prolotherapy

Prolo Your Fibromyalgia Pain Away!

Curing Disabling Body Pain with Prolotherapy

Prolo Your Headache and Neck Pain Away!

Curing Migraines and Chronic Neck Pain with Prolotherapy.

Prolo Your Pain Away!

Curing Chronic Pain with Prolotherapy

Treating Cancer with Insulin Potentiation Therapy

Learn How Insulin Can Help Target Chemotherapy and Be Used as Part of a Comprehensive Natural Medicine Approach to Reverse Cancer and Cancer Physiology

CHECK THE SITE FOR MORE BOOKS! STAY TUNED FOR FUTURE BOOK RELEASES!

PURCHASING INFORMATION

BEULAH LAND PRESS • 715 LAKE ST. • STE. 706 • OAK PARK, IL 60301

1-800-RX-PROLO • 1-877-RX-BEULAH

www.beulahlandpress.com www.caringmedical.com www.benuts.com

For More Information

About Your Health...

Would you like to read about relevant, new topics of importance to your health?

Would you like to know what Caring Medical is doing these days? Subscribe now to the Caring Medical Newsletter and find out!

To subscribe to our weekly e-newsletters, go to this link:

caringmedical.com/media/subscriptions.asp

Or, e-mail us at:

drhauser@caringmedical.com

Timely, pertinent information about *your* health is available.

E-mail us now.*

** All e-newsletters are free-of-charge.*

Convinced?

After reading this book, are you convinced that Caring Medical & Rehabilitation Services can help you?

Here is some helpful information on how to become a patient:

- ★ Call: ***708-848-7789 or 1-800-Rx-Prolo***
- ★ E-mail: ***scheduling@caringmedical.com***
- ★ Go to: ***http://caringmedical.com/about/patientinfo/appointments.asp*** to complete the "make an appointment" page.

Our team of professionals is here to provide you with ***awesome*** *service. Give us a call!*